The SAGE Encyclopedia of
Educational Technology

Editorial Board

The SAGE Encyclopedia of
Educational
Technology

Editor

J. Michael Spector
University of North Texas

2

⑤SAGE reference

Los Angeles | London | New Delhi
Singapore | Washington DC | Boston

Los Angeles | London | New Delhi
Singapore | Washington DC | Boston

FOR INFORMATION:

SAGE Publications, Inc.
2455 Teller Road
Thousand Oaks, California 91320
E-mail: order@sagepub.com

SAGE Publications Ltd.
1 Oliver's Yard
55 City Road
London, EC1Y 1SP
United Kingdom

SAGE Publications India Pvt. Ltd.
B 1/I 1 Mohan Cooperative Industrial Area
Mathura Road, New Delhi 110 044
India

SAGE Publications Asia-Pacific Pte. Ltd.
3 Church Street
#10-04 Samsung Hub
Singapore 049483

Acquisitions Editor: Jim Brace-Thompson
Developmental Editors: Carole Maurer, Shirin Parsavand
Production Editor: Tracy Buyan
Reference Systems Manager: Leticia Gutierrez
Reference Systems Coordinators: Anna Villaseñor
Copy Editors: Diane DiMura, Robin Gold
Typesetter: Hurix Systems (P) Ltd.
Proofreaders: Kristin Bergstad, Lawrence W. Baker
Indexer: Maria Sosnowski
Cover Designer: Candice Harman
Marketing Manager: Carmel Schrire

Printed in the United States of America.

Library of Congress Cataloging-in-Publication Data

The SAGE encyclopedia of educational technology / editor, J. Michael Spector, University of North Texas.

pages cm

Includes bibliographical references and index.

ISBN 978-1-4522-5822-5 (hardcover : alk. paper) 1. Educational technology. I. Spector, J. Michael.

LB1028.3.S235 2015

371.33'03—dc23

2014047587

SFI Certified Sourcing
www.sfiprogram.org
SFI-00453

SFI label applies to text stock

15 16 17 18 19 10 9 8 7 6 5 4 3 2 1

Contents

List of Entries

Reader's Guide

The Reader's Guide is provided to assist readers in locating articles on related topics. It classifies articles into 28 general topical categories. Entries may be listed under more than one topic.

Adaptive Learning Systems

Adaptive and Responsive Websites
Adaptive Learning Software and Platforms
Avatars and Agents in Virtual Systems
Cloud-Based Adaptive Systems
Data Mining and Recommendation Engines
Design and Creation of Adaptive Educational Systems
Dynamic Student Profiles
Intelligent Tutoring Systems
Learners and Instructional Control in Adaptive Systems
Learning Analytics
Learning Analytics for Programming Competencies
Learning Analytics for Writing Competencies
Personalized Learning and Instruction
Student Modeling
System and Learner Control in Adaptive Systems
Technologies That Learn and Adapt to Users

Adult Education and Workforce Development

Diffusion of New Technologies in the Workplace
Distance Learning for Degree Completion for
    Working Adults
Distance Learning for Professional Development
Education in Workplace Settings
Information and Communication Technologies:
    Competencies in the 21st Century Workforce
Information and Communication Technologies:
    Knowledge Management
Information and Communication Technologies:
    Organizational Learning
Learning in the Defense Sector With Simulated
    Systems
Learning in the Health Sector With Simulated Systems
Learning in the Manufacturing Sector With Simulated
    Systems
Learning in the Marketing Sector With Simulated
    Systems
Technology and Information Literacy

Training Using Virtual Worlds
Wearable Learning Environments
Web 2.0/3.0 in the Workplace

Agent Technologies

Agent Technologies for Evaluation
Agents for Handheld Devices
Agents in E-Learning in the Business Sector
Agents in Informal E-Learning
Animated Agents in Learning Systems
Pedagogical Agents
Virtual Tutees

Analysis of Educational Needs and Requirements

Causal Influence Diagrams
Cognitive Task Analysis
Competency Models and Frameworks
Critical Decision Method
Knowledge and Skill Hierarchies
Knowledge Elicitation
Learning Analytics
Learning Analytics for Programming Competencies
Learning Analytics for Writing Competencies
Skill Decomposition
Structural Learning Theory
Think Aloud Protocol Analysis
Workflow Analysis

Communication Technologies

Asynchronous Tools and Technologies
Blogs as a Communication Tool
Collaborative Communication Tools and Technologies
Cybersecurity
Data Streaming
Digital Identity
Message Design for Digital Media
Multimedia and Image Design

Training Using Virtual Worlds
Transmedia in Education
Virtual Worlds

Internet and Information Resources

Cloud Computing
Cloud-Based Adaptive Systems
Creative Commons
Desktop and Virtual Publishing
Digital Archives
Digital Curation
Digital Storytelling
Intellectual Property
Internet: Impact and Potential for Learning and
    Instruction
Internet of Things
Metatagging of Learning Objects and Apps
Online Mentoring
Web Analytics

Journals

British Journal of Educational Technology: http://
    onlinelibrary.wiley.com/journal/10.1111/%28I
    SSN%291467-8535
Computers & Education: http://www.journals.elsevier
    .com/computers-and-education/
Computers in Human Behavior: http://www
    .sciencedirect.com/science/journal/07475632
*Contemporary Issues in Technology and Teacher
    Education:* http://www.citejournal.org/vol14/iss3/
Distance Education: http://www.tandfonline.com/toc/
    cdie20/current
Educational Researcher: http://www.aera.net/
    Publications/Journals/EducationalResearcher/
    tabid/12609/Default.aspx
Educational Technology Magazine: http://www
    .bookstoread.com/etp
Educational Technology Research & Development:
    http://www.aect.org/Intranet/Publications/index.asp
Evaluation and Program Planning: http://www
    .sciencedirect.com/science/journal/01497189
Innovative Higher Education: http://link.springer.com/
    journal/10755
Instructional Science: http://link.springer.com/
    journal/11251
International Journal of Designs for Learning: http://
    aect.site-ym.com/?page=international_journa
*International Journal of Teaching and Learning in
    Higher Education:* http://www.isetl.org/ijtlhe
International Journal on E-Learning: http://www.aace
    .org/pubs/ijel
*Interpersonal Computing and Technology Journal: An
    Electronic Journal for the 21st Century:* http://
    www.helsinki.fi/science/optek

Journal of Applied Instructional Design: http://www
    .jaidpub.org
*Journal of Computers in Mathematics and Science
    Teaching:* http://www.aace.org/pubs/jcmst/default
    .htm
Journal of Computing in Higher Education: http://
    link.springer.com/journal/12528
Journal of Educational Computing Research: http://
    www.baywood.com/Journals/PreviewJournals
    .asp?Id=0735-6331
Journal of Educational Multimedia and Hypermedia:
    http://www.aace.org/pubs/jemh/default.htm
Journal of Educational Technology & Society: http://
    www.ifets.info
Journal of Higher Education: https://ohiostatepress
    .org/index.htm?journals/jhe/jhemain.htm
Journal of Interactive Learning Research: http://www
    .aace.org/pubs/jilr/default.htm
Journal of Research on Technology in Education:
    http://www.iste.org/resources/product?id=25
Journal of the Learning Sciences: http://www.tandfonline
    .com/toc/hlns20/current
*Knowledge Management & E-Learning: An
    International Journal:* http://www.kmel-journal.org/
    ojs/index.php/online-publication
Performance Improvement Quarterly: http://www.ispi
    .org/content.aspx?id=152
Quarterly Review of Distance Education: http://www
    .infoagepub.com/quarterly-review-of-distance-
    education.html
Review of Research in Education: http://rre.sagepub.com
*Simulation & Gaming: An Interdisciplinary Journal of
    Theory, Practice and Research:* http://www.unice.fr/sg
Smart Learning Environments: http://www.springer
    .com/computer/journal/40561
Syllabus: http://syllabusjournal.org
Technology, Instruction, Cognition and Learning: http://
    www.oldcitypublishing.com/journals/ticl-home/
Technology, Knowledge and Learning: http://www
    .springer.com/education+%26+language/
    learning+%26+instruction/journal/10758
TechTrends: http://link.springer.com/journal/11528
THE Journal (Technological Horizons in Education):
    http://thejournal.com/Home.aspx
Turkish Online Journal of Educational Technology:
    http://www.tojet.net/

Mobile Technologies

Apps for Use at the Elementary Level
Apps for Use at the Secondary Level
Apps for Use in Higher Education
Integrated and Networked Mobile Devices for
    Learning and Instruction
Learning and Instructional Apps

Technology Diffusion and Integration

LEADERSHIP IN E-LEARNING

Leadership in e-learning refers to the role played by dominant individuals and groups in enabling maximal achievement of collective electronic learning (e-learning) goals by students in education. Leaders in e-learning accomplish this by integrating the use of educational technology into mainstream learning and teaching practices in ways that focus on pedagogic benefits for students rather than on using technology for its own sake. Leadership in e-learning differs from prior understandings of leadership in education in placing emphasis on technology-mediated collaborative learning environments that require flexible, responsive distributed leadership approaches combined with advanced group communication skills. Such approaches often require sophisticated problem-solving tactics that can handle the complexity, speed, and fluidity of new technologies and virtual teams in education, placing more emphasis on trusting interconnected relationships than on fixed hierarchical directive organizational management structures.

Although leadership in e-learning is a second-order function that supports the primary role of educational technology in learning and teaching, it is nevertheless relevant because effective leadership has a crucial impact on increasing the organizational success of pedagogical developments and outcomes supported by educational technology, particularly in an era dominated by rapid Web-enabled communications. By contrast, ineffective e-learning leadership tends to hinder and block the take-up of teaching and learning innovations using technology. This entry first defines leadership in e-learning and discusses the roles of e-learning leaders. The entry then discusses how e-learning leadership developed and gives examples of e-learning leadership.

Leadership in e-learning operates both inside and outside educational institutions, in face-to-face and virtual classrooms using electronic devices as well as online learning environments. E-learning leadership functions through formal and informal policy making, strategic planning, and implementation processes at every hierarchical level, from national policy making and institutional senior management, to local teaching, business, and community leadership.

Roles of E-Learning Leaders

Successful leaders of e-learning use their relational powers effectively in both overt and subtle ways to communicate vision, values, meaning making, and strategic goals for e-learning, encouraging ongoing improvements in educational experience and quality. Advanced e-learning leaders in organizations often influence the development of a formal e-learning strategy, drawing on expert curricular and technological teams with the skills, pedagogic knowledge, and social capital to connect with others meaningfully, modeling and transforming the ways in which electronic technologies, virtual learning environments, and multimedia resources can best be developed and implemented in their organizations. Such influential individuals and groups mobilize relationships to implement e-learning objectives, recognizing and articulating the considerable advantages of educational technology for its e-learning potential for student achievements.

Leaders who invest in advanced new technologies and staff development to develop expertise in e-learning can enable communities of teachers to align their existing understandings of learning theory and teaching practice with access to advanced computing facilities, using blended approaches that combine face-to-face classroom teaching with supplementary online e-learning resources.

Using systems such as virtual learning environments, learning management systems, video conferencing systems, podcasting, and social media networks, teachers can offer low-cost asynchronous "anywhere anytime" global Internet connectivity and auxiliary resources for students, providing rapid information retrieval combined with flexible, interactive, and motivating collaborative learning opportunities.

E-learning leaders also act as mentors in pointing out and helping others avoid potential pitfalls in e-learning such as barriers to access, physical and online hardware and software security risks, legal and ethical issues, student isolation and confusion, cyberbullying, reputational damage from the impetuous use of social media, and numerous other possible problematic outcomes connected with the use of electronic technology in education. Effective e-learning leaders accurately assess the pedagogic, technological, and financial resources and services available within educational environments, proposing sustainable, low-cost, well-designed solutions for the delivery, support, assessment, and enhancement of quality in teaching and learning.

Examples of effective leadership in e-learning include intelligent monitoring and guidance from e-learning leaders regarding the use of social media such as Twitter, Facebook, blogs, and wikis by teachers in education. Such media can be highly productive for mobile e-learning and student engagement but may also cause reputational damage when incautiously used. However, command and control leadership approaches forbidding the use of social media by teachers may diminish staff enthusiasm for e-learning innovations. Hence, balanced, flexible, and responsive leadership approaches are needed in which teachers are spontaneously encouraged, supported, and provided resources to engage in e-learning innovations in ways that are trustworthy, reliable, careful, and accountable.

Development of E-Learning Leadership

Leadership research emerged originally from the scientific study of management in the 19th century as leadership is closely linked to management practice. However, research into leadership has also been separable from management studies since the early 20th century, having a long, complex history of at least 100 years that has affected all fields of human endeavor, with many thousands of books and journal articles offering competing definitions and guides on leadership theory and practice. Educational leadership refers to visionary, motivational, and meaning-making social processes whereby a powerful individual or group emerges with the positional or reputational authority to unify others in maximizing the achievement of shared goals in education. When applied to e-learning, educational leadership focuses on the

inspirational vision, mission, values, and group communication of learning goals and the transformational potentials of using educational technology. E-learning management closely complements leadership, being concerned with controlling and monitoring the administration of routine operations in the implementation of day-to-day educational technology tasks and duties.

E-learning is a relatively recent phenomenon that describes the use and application of electronic information and communications technology to achieve learning. The historical origins of e-learning derive from the use of intelligent machines for teaching and assessment by Sidney Pressey in the early 20th century. E-learning developed notably within the fields of computer-assisted instruction and instructional design in the later 20th century, informed by behavioral, cognitivist, and latterly constructivist and social learning theories deriving from educational psychology. E-learning leaders in education are those who inspire and motivate others to achieve the goals of enabling effective learning and teaching from the use of learning technologies such as computers, software, smartphones, tablets, other digital media devices, Web-based resources, social media networks, electronic communications, and virtual learning tools and environments. Leadership in e-learning has existed for as long as e-learning itself, deriving from the relational capabilities and social processes through which the active learning of others has been effected by influential people with expertise in educational technology, operating at various functional levels.

Examples of E-Learning Leadership

Although leaders in e-learning are individuals and groups who effectively communicate an appropriate vision, values, meaning making, and strategic goals in ways that inspire others to achieve, leadership in e-learning is a background function that has not always been recognized as a distinctive field within educational technology research. Leadership has therefore influenced e-learning development in ways that have sometimes been assumed rather than explicitly identified and named. Notable examples of leaders in e-learning include prominent individuals whose work has strongly affected developments in educational technology globally, such as Seymour Papert, David Jonassen, and Gavriel Salomon. The ability of such e-learning thought leaders to take the lead in demonstrating effective uses of educational technologies for learning has inspired generations of teachers and students to engage productively in knowledge creation through mindful engagement with computers.

Jill Jameson

See also Collaborative Learning With Technology; Information and Communication Technologies: Knowledge Management; Information and Communication Technologies: Organizational Learning; Innovators and Risk Takers in Education; Internet: Impact and Potential for Learning and Instruction; Organizational Learning and Performance; Planning for Technology Upgrades and Improvements; Systemic Change and Educational Technology

Further Readings

Avolio, B. J., & Kahai, S. S. (2003). Adding the "E" to e-leadership: How it may impact your leadership. *Organizational Dynamics, 31*(4), 325–338. doi:10.1016/S0090-2616(02)00133-X

Bass, B. M., & Bass, R. (2009). *The Bass handbook of leadership: Theory, research, and managerial applications.* New York, NY: Free Press.

Bostrom, C. (2012). Educational leadership and the e-learning paradigm. *Global Partners in Education Journal, 2*(1), 42. Retrieved from http://www.gpejournal.org/index.php/GPEJ/article/view/39

Gurr, D. (2004). ICT, leadership in education and e-leadership. *Discourse: Studies in the Cultural Politics of Education, 25*(1), 113–124. Retrieved from http://www.editlib.org/p/53118

Jameson, J. (2013). E-leadership in higher education: The fifth "age" of educational technology research. *British Journal of Educational Technology, 44,* 889–915. doi:10.1111/bjet.12103

Jameson, J., Ferrell, G., Kelly, J., Walker, S., & Ryan, M. (2006). Building trust and shared knowledge in communities of e-learning practice: Collaborative leadership in the JISC eLISA and CAMEL lifelong learning projects. *British Journal of Educational Technology, 37,* 949–967. doi:10.1111/j.1467-8535.2006.00669.x

Joint Information Systems Committee. (2004). *Effective practice with e-learning: A good practice guide in designing for learning.* Retrieved from http://www.jisc.ac.uk/media/documents/publications/effectivepracticeelearning.pdf

Jonassen, D. H. (1999). Designing constructivist learning environments. In C. M. Reigeluth (Ed.), *Instructional design theories and models: Vol. 2. A new paradigm of instructional theories* (pp. 215–239). Hillsdale, NJ: Lawrence Erlbaum.

Papert, S. (1980). *Mindstorms: Children, computers, and powerful ideas.* New York, NY: Basic Books.

Salomon, G., Perkins, D. N., & Globerson, T. (1991). Partners in cognition: Extending human intelligence with intelligent technologies. *Educational Researcher, 20*(3), 2–9. doi:10.3102/0013189X020003002

LEARNERS AND INSTRUCTIONAL CONTROL IN ADAPTIVE SYSTEMS

An adaptive system is a means for delivering instruction that attempts to recognize, reconcile, and leverage individual learner differences. Instructional researchers once focused their efforts on finding a universal, best method, for delivering instruction. However, the futility of that quest soon became apparent. Instructional goals and their associated contexts diverge from one another to such an extent that logic does not support the notion that a particular method would consistently be superior. Evidence does not support that a decontextualized instructional tactic has merit on its own accord. Instructional practice has long supported the determination that different learning outcomes require particular instructional interventions; different instructional objectives require different instructional tactics.

Adaptive instruction is a natural outgrowth of this principle. If content requires differential instruction, so might the learners themselves. The interest in adaptive systems begins with the assumptions that what works for one will not work for all and what works for most may not work for one. Many scholars and practitioners have inferred that instructional conditions directly influence outcomes and may be tailored to a learner's aptitude, preferences, and experience for additional effect. The urge to individualize and personalize instruction in response to the unique attributes of the learner resonates in a society that places individualism at the center of its national ethos. Customizing instruction is a logistically challenging activity. Advances in digital technology hold the promise of implanting individualized instruction efficiently. This entry discusses how adaptive instruction works, the broad classifications of adaptive learning systems, and questions to ask before designing an adaptive learning system.

One way of differentiating instructional interventions is to have the learner control significant portions of instructional delivery (pacing, sequence, and content). Ceding control of instructional delivery to a learner assumes that the learner is capable of making productive adaptive choices. Evidence supporting learner control as a method for improving learning outcomes has been largely inconclusive. Although many learners report enhanced satisfaction when given opportunities to exert control, these benefits must be weighed against the learner's potential lack of metacognitive awareness required by the instructional event. Learners may miss important information, or may not persist in practice opportunities sufficiently, when allowed to make their own choices.

When ceding control to the learner is insufficient to foster useful instructional adaptation, the designer may attempt to implement a formal adaptive learning system (ALS). Adaptive learning is an educational structure designed to accommodate individual learner differences by adjusting presentation and practice interventions. The goal of an ALS is to create a personalized learning experience. Learners differ from one another on a number of fronts, including experience, education, background, personality, and interests, among others. Different ALSs will select and emphasize some of these attributes while excluding others.

Classifications of Adaptive Learning Systems

Adaptive learning systems are usefully categorized into three broad classifications: macro-adaption, aptitude treatment interaction, and micro-adaption.

Macro-Adaption

Macro-adaption instruction is differentiated by manipulating primary instructional and curricular components such as objectives, goals, and media. Tracking learners by age, majors, and ability are examples of macro-adaption. Researchers have used pacing and learner control in a number of ALSs such as the Keller Plan, which allowed learners to assess themselves when they felt they were ready. If learners passed an exam, they could advance in the course; if they failed, they would meet with a tutor, restudy, and take another equivalent exam when they were ready. Macro-adaptation strategies can be implemented without a personal individuated interaction with the learner, which is required in the following ALS classifications.

Aptitude-Treatment Interactions

The second ALS classification is aptitude-treatment interactions, in which researchers seek to determine stable learner attributes and match them to particular instructional interventions. Successful aptitude-treatment interactions require a correlation between a learner's attributes and success mediated by a particular method or style of instruction. Strong evidence exists in favor of aptitudes such as prior knowledge as a consideration to individualize instruction. A popular approach to aptitude-treatment interactions is the meshing of learning styles and instructional interventions. *Learning styles* refers to the concept that an individual has an inherent form of acquiring and working with information that places the individual at an advantage, or disadvantage, regarding particular learning strategies. Although a fashionable conception, aptitude-treatment interactions, particularly adaptations based on learning styles and personality traits, have little empirical support. Some evidence indicates that learners reliably report their own traits; however, there is little to support the notion that designers can leverage these traits to improve achievement by matching and selecting them to instructional interventions. It appears that the most successful instructional interventions tend to work equally well for all learners, casting doubt on the extent to which instruction based on unique learner attributes can be effective. Many recommend that all learners be prepared to learn in ways that are effective for particular types of content and that designers of adaptive systems use prior knowledge and experience to tailor the instructional experience.

Micro-Adaptive Instruction

Finally, micro-adaptive instruction focuses on learning gaps and attempts to diagnose and remedy specific problems of comprehension based on knowledge or skill deficiencies. On-task measures can be used in addition to pre-task measures. Response errors, response speed, and emotional and physiological states all can be used in micro-adaptive instruction to control content selection, presentation, and instructional sequence.

Questions to Ask Before Designing an Adaptive Learning System

Any adaptive system must facilitate the interaction with the learner and the instructional content. What the learner does, thinks, or has experienced may be used to control the display of content and instructional activities. The facilitation can be based on a number of theories and models of how these elements interact. Two questions arise when one is evaluating the plausibility of an adaptive learning system. The first question is this: Is there an actual relationship between a learner attribute, characteristic, or set of attributes to specific learning interventions? For example, does one's learning style or preference have a relationship to an instructional intervention? Does a self-characterized visual learner require visual-centric instructional interventions? In this case, evidence would not support that assertion. The second question is this: Does the structure of a particular adaptive learning system facilitate the match between the learner's characteristics and an instructional intervention? For example, one may enjoy philosophy and be likely to purchase philosophy books when encountered. However, an adaptive bookseller may not be capable of facilitating the transaction; the bookseller may misdiagnose an interest in Søren Kierkegaard as an interest in Plato, which will not encourage a purchase.

Assuming a connection between a learner's attributes and an instructional intervention, the form, structure, and quality of an adaptive system will determine whether that relationship can be exploited. Research may inform us as to which aptitude-treatment interactions are viable, but designers will have to augment that information with an appropriately engineered ALS to produce useful, productive knowledge. Early attempts at implementing ALS systems have demonstrated limited advances in effectiveness and efficiency. However, advances in digital technology and artificial intelligence may open opportunities to implement adaptive systems to a broader audience. ALSs with these capabilities are called intelligent tutoring systems and seek to recreate a one-on-one tutoring experience based on selective adaptation.

David R. Moore

See also Adaptive and Responsive Websites; Adaptive Learning Software and Platforms; Adaptive Testing; Learners and Instructional Control in Adaptive Systems; Personal Learning Environments

Further Readings

Ausubel, D. P. (1980). Schemata, cognitive structure, and advance organizers: A reply to Anderson, Spiro, and Anderson. *Journal of American Educational Research, 17*(3), 400–404.

Cronbach, L. J. (1966). The logic of experiments on discovery. In L. S. Shulman & E. R. Keisler (Eds.), *Learning by discovery: A critical appraisal* (pp. 76–92). Chicago, IL: Rand McNally.

Cronbach, L. J., & Snow, R. E. (1977). *Aptitudes and instructional methods: A handbook for research on instructional methods*. New York, NY: Irvington.

Gagné, R. M. (1985). *The conditions of learning and theory of instruction* (4th ed.). New York, NY: Holt, Rinehart & Winston.

Glaser, R. (1972). Individuals and learning: The new aptitudes. *Educational Researcher, 6*, 5–13.

Hopkins, K. D. (1998). *Educational and psychological measurement and evaluation*. Boston, MA: Allyn & Bacon.

Lalley, J. P., & Gentile, J. R. (2009). Adapting instruction to individuals: Based on the evidence, what should it mean? *International Journal of Teaching and Learning in Higher Education, 20*(3), 462–475.

Merrill, M. D. (2002). First principles of instruction. *Educational Technology Research and Development, 5*(3), 43–59.

Milheim, W. D., & Martin, B. L. (1991). Theoretical bases for the use of learner control: Three different perspectives. *Journal of Computer-Based Instruction, 18*(3), 99–105.

Park, O., & Lee, J. (2004). Adaptive instructional systems. In D. H. Jonassen (Ed.), *Handbook of research on educational communications and technology* (pp. 651–684). Mahwah, NJ: Lawrence Erlbaum.

Pashler, H., McDaniel, M., Rohrer, D., & Bjork, R. (2008, December). Learning styles: Concepts and evidence. *Psychological Science in the Public Interest, 9*(3), 105–119.

Vandewaetere, M., Desmet, P., & Clarebout, G. (2011). The contribution of learner characteristics in the development of computer-based adaptive learning environments. *Computers in Human Behavior, 27*, 118–130.

Willingham, D. T. (2005). Do visual, auditory, and kinesthetic learners need visual, auditory, and kinesthetic instruction? *American Educator.* Retrieved from http://www.aft.org/newspubs/periodicals/ae/summer2005/willingham.cfm

LEARNING ANALYTICS

Learning analytics uses dynamic information about learners and learning environments, assessing, eliciting, and analyzing it, for real-time modeling, prediction, and optimization of learning processes, learning environments, and educational decision making. This entry details what is involved in a holistic learning analytics framework and discusses the benefits, concerns, and challenges of learning analytics. The entry concludes by suggesting future directions of learning analytics.

Learning Analytics Framework

The result of the increased availability of vast administrative systems with a great deal of academic and personal information is that educational data management, analysis, and interpretation are becoming complex. Several concepts closely linked to processing such educational information are educational data mining, academic analytics, and learning analytics. However, these concepts are often confused and lack universally agreed upon and applied definitions. Educational data mining (EDM) refers to the process of extracting useful information out of a large collection of complex educational data sets. Academic analytics (AA) is the identification of meaningful patterns in educational data to inform academic issues (e.g., retention, success rates) and produce actionable strategies (e.g., budgeting, human resources). Learning analytics (LA) emphasizes insights and responses to real-time learning processes based on educational information from digital learning environments, administrative systems, and social platforms. Such dynamic educational information is used for real-time interpretation, modeling, prediction, and optimization of learning processes, learning environments, and educational decision making.

Figure 1 illustrates a holistic LA framework, linking various types of educational information in a meaningful way.

Information about the learners' individual characteristics (shown as 1 in Figure 1) includes sociodemographic information, personal preferences and interests, responses to standardized inventories (e.g., learning strategies, achievement motivation, personality), skills and competencies (e.g., computer literacy), prior knowledge and academic performance, and institutional transcript data

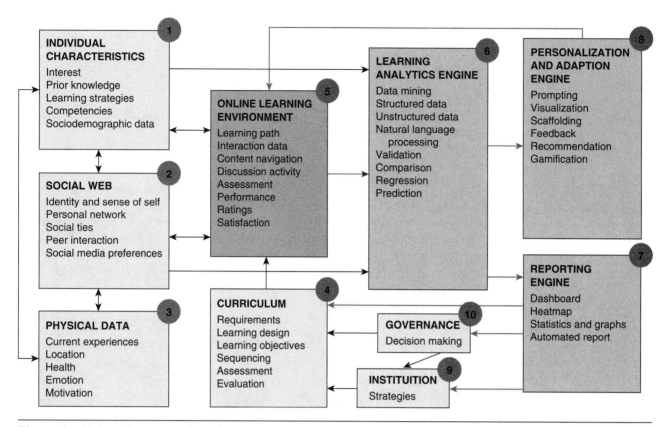

Figure I   Holistic learning analytics framework

(e.g., pass rates, enrollments, dropouts status, special needs). Information from the social Web (2) includes preferences of social media tools (e.g., Twitter, Facebook, LinkedIn) and social network activities (e.g., linked resources, friendships, peer groups, Web identity). Physical data (3) include information about the learner's location, sensor data (e.g., movement), affective states (e.g., motivation, emotion), and current conditions (e.g., health, stress, commitments).

Rich information is available from learners' activities in the online learning environment (4) (i.e., learning management system, personal learning environment, learning blog). These mostly numeric data refer to logging on and off, viewing or posting discussions, navigation patterns, learning paths, content retrieval (i.e., learner-produced data trails), results on assessment tasks, responses to ratings and surveys. More importantly, rich semantic and context-specific information is available from discussion forums as well as from complex learning tasks (e.g., written essays, wikis, blogs). Additionally, interactions of facilitators with students and the online learning environment (OLE) are tracked.

Closely linked to the information available from the OLE is the curriculum information (5), which includes metadata of the OLE. These data reflect the learning design (e.g., sequencing of materials, tasks,

and assessments), and learning objectives as well as expected learning outcomes. Formative and summative evaluation data are directly linked to specific curricula, facilitators, or student cohorts.

The LA engine (6) is based on pedagogical theories and methodological and mathematical approaches. Rich information from various sources (i.e., structured and unstructured data) is processed using specific algorithms (e.g., Bayesian networks, neural networks, natural language processing, survival analysis, hierarchical linear modeling) that are closely linked to the underpinnings of applied pedagogical theories. The results of the data mining process are validated before further analysis is computed for real-time comparisons and identification of patterns, as well as for predictive modeling. The reporting engine (7) uses the results of the LA engine and automatically produces useful information in the form of interactive dashboards, heatmaps, statistics, graphs, and automated reports. These automated reports are used for specific stakeholders such as the governance level (10; e.g., for cross-institutional comparisons), single institutions (9; e.g., for internal comparisons, optimization of sequence of operations), and the curriculum level (4), including insights and reports for learning designers and facilitators for analyzing instructional processes and students' pathways.

The personalization and adaption engine (8) feeds back the results of the learning analytics engine to the OLE. Interactive elements include simple learning prompts and recommendations (e.g., reminder of deadlines, links to further study, social interaction), rich visualizations (e.g., learning paths) as well as informative scaffolds for specific learning activities and assessment tasks. An optimal implementation of such a holistic learning analytics framework uses a real-time data collection, processing, and feedback mechanism. This framework also allows all stakeholders to personalize the LA process to meet their individual requirements.

Benefits of Learning Analytics

The benefits of LA can be associated with four levels of stakeholders (see Figure 2): megalevel (governance), macrolevel (institution), mesolevel (curriculum, teacher/tutor), and microlevel (learner, OLE). An essential prerequisite for LA benefits, however, is the real-time access, analysis, and modeling of relevant educational information. The megalevel facilitates cross-institutional analytics by incorporating data from all levels of the LA framework. Such rich data sets enable the identification and validation of patterns within and across institutions and therefore provide valuable insights for informing educational policy making. The macrolevel enables institution-wide analytics for better understanding learner cohorts to optimize associated processes and allocate critical resources for reducing dropout and increasing retention as well as success rates. The mesolevel supports the curriculum and learning design as well as providing detailed insights about learning processes for course facilitators (i.e., teachers, tutors).

This information can be used for improving the overall quality of courses (e.g., sequencing of learning processes, alignment with higher level outcomes) and for enhancing learning materials (e.g., their alignment to anticipated learning outcomes and associated assessments). The microlevel analytics support the learner through recommendations and help functions implemented in the OLE. Learners benefit from such personalized and adaptive scaffolds and are expected to be more successful in reaching the learning outcomes. Another critical component for improving the benefits of LA is information from the physical environment (e.g., learner's current emotional state), which is not directly linked with the educational data. Accordingly, data may be collected within the OLE through reactive prompts and linked with the available educational information.

Table 1 provides a matrix outlining the benefits of LA for stakeholders including three perspectives: (1) summative, (2) real-time, and (3) predictive. The summative perspective provides detailed insights after completion of a learning phase (e.g., study period, semester, final degree), often compared against previously defined reference points or benchmarks. The real-time perspective uses ongoing information for improving

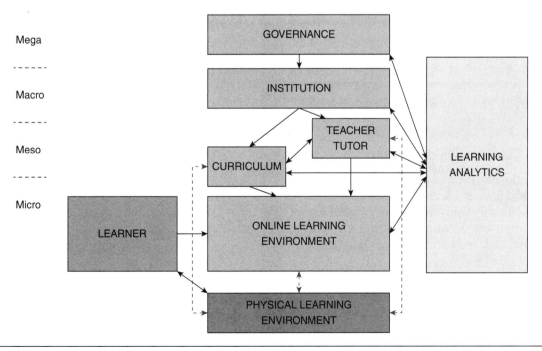

Figure 2 Learning analytics associated with stakeholder levels

Table 1 Matrix of learning analytics benefits

Stakeholder	Perspective		
	Summative	*Real-time*	*Predictive*
Governance	Apply cross-institutional comparisons Develop benchmarks Inform policy making Inform quality assurance processes	Increase productivity Apply rapid response to critical incidents Analyze performance	Model impact of organizational decision making Plan for change management
Institution	Analyze processes Optimize resource allocation Meet institutional standards Compare units across programs and faculties	Monitor processes Evaluate resources Track enrollments Analyze churn	Forecast processes Project attrition Model retention rates Identify gaps
Learning design	Analyze pedagogical models Measure impact of interventions Increase quality of curriculum	Compare learning designs Evaluate learning materials Adjust difficulty levels Provide resources required by learners	Identify learning preferences Plan for future interventions Model difficulty levels Model pathways
Facilitator	Compare learners, cohorts, and courses Analyze teaching practices Increase quality of teaching	Monitor learning progression Create meaningful interventions Increase interaction Modify content to meet cohorts' needs	Identify learners at risk Forecast learning progression Plan interventions Model success rates
Learner	Understand learning habits Compare learning paths Analyze learning outcomes Track progress toward goals	Receive automated interventions and scaffolds Take assessments including just-in-time feedback	Optimize learning paths Adapt to recommendations Increase engagement Increase success rates

processes through direct interventions. The predictive perspective is applied for forecasting the probability of outcomes so users can plan for future strategies and actions.

Concerns and Challenges

More educational data do not always make better educational data. Hence, LA has its obvious limitations, and data collected from various educational sources can have multiple meanings. Therefore, serious concerns and challenges are associated with the application of LA.

• Not all educational data are relevant and equivalent. Therefore, the validity of data and their analyses is critical for generating useful summative, real-time, and predictive insights. This generates a new interdisciplinary research area for cognitive psychology, educational technology, learning design, psychometrics, data management,

artificial intelligence, Web development, and statistics. The challenges are to investigate the complex processes within LA frameworks and to understand their immediate and long-term effects on learning and teaching processes.

• Ethical issues are associated with the use of educational data for LA. These include how personal data are collected and stored as well as how they are analyzed and presented to different stakeholders. Hence, procedures regulating access and usage of educational data need to come into operation before LA frameworks are implemented. This will also include transparency of applied algorithms and weighting of educational data for predictive modeling. Storing and processing anonymized personal data is only a small step toward a more comprehensive educational data governance structure for LA.

• Limited access to educational data generates disadvantages for involved stakeholders. For example, invalid forecasts may lead to inefficient decisions and unforeseen problems. A misalignment of prior knowledge, learning pathways, and learning outcomes could increase churn, and the late identification of learners at risk may create dropouts. A definition of threshold standards for LA could prevent vast gaps between educational institutions and provide equal opportunities for all stakeholders.

• The preparation of stakeholders for applying insights from LA in a meaningful way is vital. Professional development for stakeholders ensures that issues are identified and benefits are transformed into meaningful action. Hence, the increased application of LA requires a new generation of experts with unique interdisciplinary competences. This will also require new infrastructures for administration and research to accelerate the understanding of LA.

• Information from distributed networks and unstructured data cannot be directly linked to educational data collected within an institution's environment. An aggregation of such data and uncontrolled relations to existing educational data increases the chance of critical biases as well as invalid analyses, predictions, and decisions. The challenge is to develop mechanisms to filter biased information and warn stakeholders accordingly.

• An optimal sequence of data collection and economic response times (seconds, minutes, hours, days, weeks) of LA have yet to be determined. This includes the minimum requirements for making valid predictions and creating meaningful interventions. Missing data are a critical challenge for future LA algorithms.

• Besides the analysis of numerical data (e.g., click-streams), a qualitative analysis of semantic rich data (e.g., content of discussion forums, responses to open-ended assessments) enables a better understanding of learners' knowledge and needs. An obvious requirement is the development of automated natural language processing (NLP) capabilities. The major challenge besides the development of real-time NLP is the validation of such algorithms and the link to quantitative educational data.

Future Directions

The major lesson to be learned from 50 years of research in the area of educational technology is that what happens in learning environments is quite complex and multifaceted. Learners' needs and their predispositions are multidimensional and quickly change over time. Numerous approaches for understanding these complex patterns of learning and predicting their future developments for automating instruction have been challenged repeatedly in the past. However, all such attempts to adequately understand learners' needs and choices have failed.

Future applications of LA presuppose a seamless and system-inherent analysis of learners' progression to continuously adapt the learning environment. LA provides the pedagogical and technological background for producing real-time interventions at all times during the learning process. It is expected that the availability of such personalized, dynamic, and timely feedback supports learners' self-regulated learning as well as increases their motivation and success. However, such automated systems may also hinder the development of competences such as critical thinking and autonomous learning. It is expected that a holistic LA framework will provide evidence for increasing the overall quality of learning environments and facilitate the reform of learning and teaching in the 21st century.

Dirk Ifenthaler

See also Adaptive Learning Software and Platforms; Automated Scoring of Essays; Cloud-Based Adaptive Systems; Data Mining and Recommendation Engines; Educational Data Mining; Natural Language Processing in Learning Environments; Personal Learning Environments; Personalized Learning and Instruction; Recommendation Engines; Social Network Analysis; Stealth Assessment; Technologies Supporting Self-Regulated Learning

Further Readings

Greller, W., & Drachsler, H. (2012). Translating learning into numbers: A generic framework for learning analytics. *Journal of Educational Technology & Society, 15*(3), 42–57.

Ifenthaler, D., Pirnay-Dummer, P., & Seel, N. M. (Eds.). (2010). *Computer-based diagnostics and systematic analysis of knowledge.* New York, NY: Springer.

Macfadyen, L., & Dawson, S. (2012). Numbers are not enough: Why e-learning analytics failed to inform an institutional strategic plan. *Journal of Educational Technology & Society, 15*(3), 149–163.

Romero, C., Ventura, S., Pechenizkiy, M., & Baker, R. S. J. d. (Eds.). (2011). *Handbook of educational data mining.* Boca Raton, FL: CRC Press.

LEARNING ANALYTICS FOR PROGRAMMING COMPETENCIES

Programming is a unique activity that uses software development tools, algorithms, software practices, and software design to create software. Competency in programming implies the ability to produce software efficiently and effectively. Learning analytics offers a means to derive programming competency using big data as the underlying premise. This entry provides an overview of the sorts of data generated by learners in a programming environment and examines how these semi-structured data are used by analytical tools to help those learners strengthen their coding skills.

Learners and Learning Traces

Students taking an introductory computer programming class in an online environment, or in any course with a significant digital component, have access to learning activities associated with an array of media, including slideshows, reading material, audio and video lectures, interactive tutors, and automated tests. As they work through the course material in this digital environment, students leave behind digital records, or traces, of their learning activity that track their interaction with the course material, much like a Web analytics system tracks visitors to a website. Similarly, as students complete the associated computer programming assignments, software development traces are generated that can be used to track the student success and coding competency. The same traces can then be used to assess the effectiveness of instruction.

Learning analytics is the science of analysis, discovery, and utilization of learning traces in emergent and related levels of granularity. *Learning trace data* refers to observable raw data of study activities such as reading, writing, conceptualizing, critically thinking, solving problems, storytelling, and visualizing, where a network of study activities leads to a measurable chunk of learning. For instance, the types of sentence openers used by a learner, the range of errors that the student can confidently correct, the level of trust exhibited by the student in sharing information in a forum, and the depth of understanding in a set of concepts are examples of learning traces where one could measure learning over time. In learning analytics, these data are expected to arrive continuously, typically in an interleaved fashion, subject to interpretation at various levels of granularity.

In general, learning traces translate raw data into incoming data for learning analytics, where incoming data are typically big, unstructured, unrelated, and fit multiple models and possibly multiple theories. Importantly, learning traces capture highly personalized study experiences. Although each learning trace is measurable, there is no standard scale of measurement that applies across different types of traces. A learning trace is the least common denominator for a measure of learning.

Analysis using learning analytics may include techniques ranging from data mining to machine learning to big data analysis. This may uncover correlations in highly unconventional data, for example, inherent economic drivers influenced by a curriculum, or functional magnetic resonance imaging/electroencephalogram (fMRI/EEG) indicators for learning capacity, or rate of changes in motivation levels of students with respect to weather. Relations of interest to learning analytics include the emotions, beliefs, and goals among learners across collaborating groups; inter-institutional credit transfer policies among institutions; and mutual respect among instructors.

Learning analytics aims to operate on large volumes of data as well as on large volumes of models produced from the data. These data are not confined to formal and informal data sets, but also include ad hoc data sets with little relationship to learning. Ad hoc data sets include browsing patterns, reading habits, writing style (including freehand writing), coding, posture analyses, collaboration drivers, thinking protocols, chats, domain-specific tool traces, brain-activity traces, recording of cognitive and metacognitive traces, and knowledge traces.

The raw data can be processed for use in data mining, program evaluation, real-time classroom feedback, prediction, visualization, modeling, and other activities. These interpretations can shed light on instructional processes that indicate learner familiarity, comprehension, deliberation, assimilation, evaluation, application, conceptual insight, or skill to various degrees by different types of learners. However, learning analytics makes it possible to go beyond this information to a holistic view of the rates of changes in adaptations, repetitions, and refinements of instructional processes and instructional resources, as well as of the rates of changes in learning processes and learner capabilities.

Learning Analytics for Coding Competency

Novice coders write numerous blocks of code and submit them to the compiler—the computer program that translates source code into a computer program. The compiler verifies the code and provides coders with a summary of the correctness of their code based on a set of accepted syntactical style guides. It is possible to track the coding competency of individual programmers and to make them aware of their current competency levels and what they need to do to improve.

Coding can be observed continuously, from the time a design is introduced until the programming project is completed. For instance, learner interactions during a programming lecture can be recorded and analyzed in real time to estimate the level of effectiveness of the lecture. The online interaction of professional coders in a discussion forum can be analyzed in real time to estimate their coding capacity and sentiments. These observations, along with other traditional data, can supply the "raw data" for learning analytics in coding.

A suite of software tools and sensors can collect data generated by students while they program. The quantity and diversity of data collected using these additional software tools is much larger than the data that are traditionally collected, approaching the realms of big data learning analytics. These data include interactions of learners within the learning management system, classroom videos, formal assessments, informal assessments, questionnaires, observations within the programming environment, observations within language-specific tutors, coding dashboard interactions, and metacognitive tools.

Software development traces are generated by students as they solve computer programming problems, such as the number of compiles; warnings and errors encountered during these compiles; abilities and behaviors of the student in tackling these warnings and errors; the ensuing design changes; the pace of writing code; competency changes during programming; and other interactions captured from the programming environment. One can also go further to look at each student's submissions across multiple coding sessions.

Analysis includes relationship discovery across data sets. For instance, is there a reduction in coding errors over time when students first study a lesson for a significant time before attempting to solve the problem? What are the predominant types of errors, and how well are they addressed in the content? Is there a significant improvement in coding submissions as the student becomes more proficient, or when instructors are informed about potentially demotivated students? Is the level of student documentation an indication of their coding competency? Are there clusters of students who require special attention from the instructor, or who progress faster through the course compared with other students? Does learner competency growth align well with the curricular goals of the institution or the industry? Are students who take part in group study better at self-regulation than are those who study only individually?

Competency growth in coding can be observed within a specific language (e.g., Java) across multiple courses, and across multiple languages (e.g., Java and C++). Competency growth in coding can be observed at the individual student level, the course level, the departmental level, or even the institutional level.

Contemporary technologies enable a sensor-based big data platform that is open, inclusive, adaptable, and precise. Such a platform shows tremendous potential toward improving student accountability and performance with respect to their study tasks. Equally, the accountability and performance of instructors are also continually analyzed. Matching of these two accountabilities would yield optimal learning opportunities.

Vivekanandan Suresh Kumar

See also Assessment of Problem Solving and Higher Order Thinking; Competency Models and Frameworks; Data Mining and Recommendation Engines; Educational Data Mining; Learning Analytics; Measuring and Assessing TPACK (Technological Pedagogical Content Knowledge); Tools for Modeling and Simulation

Further Readings

Ferguson, R. (2012). Learning analytics: Drivers, developments and challenges. *International Journal of Technology Enhanced Learning, 4*(5/6), 304–317.

Gray, J., Boyle, T., & Smith, C. (1998). A constructivist learning environment implemented in Java. In *Proceedings of the 6th Annual Conference on the Teaching of Computing and the 3rd Annual Conference on Integrating Technology Into Computer Science Education: Changing the delivery of computer science education* (pp. 94–97). New York, NY: ACM.

Kim, M., & Lee, E. (2013). A multidimensional analysis tool for visualizing online interactions. *Journal of Educational Technology & Society, 15*(3), 89–102.

Romero, C., Ventura S., & Garcia, E. (2008). Data mining in course management systems: Moodle cases study and tutorial. *Computers & Education, 51*(1), 368–384.

Rountree, J., Rountree, N., Robins, A., & Hannah, R. (2005). Observations of student competency in a CS1 course. In A. Young & D. Tolhurst (Eds.), *Proceedings of the 7th Australasian Conference on Computing Education: Vol. 42* (pp. 145–149). Darlinghurst, Australia: Australian Computer Society.

Shum, S. B., & Ferguson, R. (2012). Social learning analytics. *Journal of Educational Technology & Society, 15*(3), 3–26.

Watson, C., Li, F. W. B., & Godwin, J. L. (2013). Predicting performance in an introductory programming course by logging and analyzing student programming behavior. In *Proceedings of the International Conference on Advanced Learning Technologies* (pp. 319–323). Beijing, China: IEEE.

LEARNING ANALYTICS FOR WRITING COMPETENCIES

Students are expected to be able to write effectively across a wide range of topics, yet seem to have difficulty achieving such a level of mastery. Despite this, effective writing skills continue to be important in school, in the workplace, and in social contexts. To address this gap, many schools and universities have developed specialized techniques to help improve writing skills. These range from providing writing support from peers, professional tutors, or reviewers, to providing explicit strategy instruction, to requiring all students to take a single course focused on the basics of writing, to integrating writing-intensive courses into the disciplines. In this way, students have multiple exposures to writing techniques. However, given the volume of data generated, it can be difficult to assess the impact of such techniques. Advances in technology may provide new techniques for improving writing skills and allow collection and analysis of data collected through those techniques. This entry provides an overview of the data generated by learners in a digital writing environment, describes the writing process, and examines the ways in which learning analytics can be used to strengthen writing skills.

Writing is a goal-oriented activity that involves a range of related processes, such as planning, translating, and reviewing. Planning involves setting goals, generating ideas, and organizing those ideas to fit the goals. Whether writers use pen and paper, laptop computers, or mobile devices, translating converts plans into formal text. A number of technology solutions, such as automatic spelling and grammar checkers, are already widely available to help students produce higher quality writing. The importance of review processes is often underestimated by students, who see it as involving either the correction of minor errors, such as typos, or as evidence that the writer's work is poor. Yet, most reviewing activities fall somewhere between these two extremes. Skilled writers often switch back and forth across all three major processes—planning, translating, and reviewing—as they build and refine their texts. This natural switching complicates attempts to study writing by making it difficult to isolate individual processes.

In addition to drawing on a range of processes and resources, writing activities also take place within a context. The typical in-school writing assignment requires learners to work independently and submit their text to a one-person audience—the teacher. With the introduction of technology in the classroom, the social context of academic writing is changing rapidly. Now, students frequently work with peers across all writing processes, and written work may be published to the whole class or even to more public audiences through the use of social media. As learners become more used to writing collaboratively, there is great potential to use technologies designed to facilitate collaboration and the sharing of information as tools to help students improve their writing.

Mixed initiatives is a technique that allows the gathering of data on a learner's interaction with the writing system, creation of statistical and rule-based assessments, and use of these assessments to automatically and proactively offer feedback to the learner in real time. In addition to traditional academic performance data, mixed-initiative systems collect a range of learning-process data that are not easily observed or recorded by the instructor. For example, such learning-process data may include information on the context in which learners correct grammar, where the context includes the learner's cognitive capacity (e.g., working memory capacity and self-regulatory capacity) to make the correction, the emotional states of the learner before and after the correction was made (e.g., confused state or stressed state), the social and personal study obligations of the learner (e.g., role undertaken in a study group), and instructional constraints placed on the learner (e.g., submission deadline and assessment rubrics).

Technology now makes it possible to track students' writing in real time to provide feedback and assessment. Feedback can be offered at the word level, the phrase level, the sentence level, or at the paragraph level. Technology allows immediate capture of data as students write and processes these data to give real-time feedback to students. Alternatively, teachers can create pattern matchers that identify specific patterns in students' writing using computer tools. The pattern matchers can be embedded within the writing software used by students. Teachers can also attach generic feedback with the pattern matchers. When a pattern of writing (e.g., frequent observation of a particular type of grammatical error) is matched, the corresponding feedback can be presented to students in real time. The pattern matchers could also be associated with grading schemes that enable automatic and continuous assessment of students' writing.

Writing analytics is the science of analysis, discovery, and utilization of writing traces. *Writing trace data* refers to observable raw data of writing-related activities such as goal setting, conceptualizing, critical thinking, writing, reviewing, and annotating, where a network of writing-related activities leads to a measurable chunk of writing capacity. For instance, the following could be observed as a student engages in a writing assignment: (a) the types of sentence openers created by the learner, (b) the range of errors corrected by the learner in creating these sentence openers, and (c) the level of trust exhibited by the student in sharing information about the sentence openers in a forum. These activities are typically intermixed with each other over time. Subjecting this set of observed network of activities to an assessment process would yield a measure of the student's writing capacity on sentence openers, which is termed a *writing trace*.

Writing data are expected to arrive continuously and at different levels of detail. Writing traces translate raw data into incoming data for analytics, where incoming data are typically big, unstructured, unrelated, and fit into multiple models and theories. These traces capture highly personalized study experiences. Although each trace is measurable, there is no standard scale of measurement that applies across different types of traces.

Proven technologies exist to integrate writing traces with learning outcomes. Students can learn to write as and when the situation presents itself, indoors or outdoors, anywhere, rather than being confined to classroom situations. Students do not have to wait for typical feedback from the instructor. Students can receive automated, real-time, context-specific feedback from the mixed-initiative writing analytics system. Such an ever-present feedback mechanism has the potential to not only reduce the instructors' workload but also to improve students' learning efficiency.

One can perceive a mixed initiative as similar to having someone watch over the shoulders of students as they engage in a writing task, and at a pace of their choice. Such a writing platform could measure individual competencies in writing and identify writing competency gaps that can be addressed proactively.

Writing analytics solutions allow learners to plan, to translate, to review, to read, to evaluate, and to revise. Learners can plan outlines using the solution's interface and translate these outlines into parts of the essay. For example, learners can review their writing process for grammar and style, they can read summaries of their own progress and those of their peers, they can evaluate each other's work using a peer review mechanism, and finally, they can revise content using system-generated feedback and peer feedback.

Writing analytics offers open-ended solutions. Teachers can trace the amount of time it took for a student to complete a particular type of sentence. Teachers can visualize changes in key phrases of a paragraph and the associated cognitive triggers that potentially caused these changes. Teachers can situate writing in a number of scenarios such as museum visits, virtual vacations, gaming, classroom collaboration, and social networks.

Tracing the evolution of individual writing skills leads to assessment of writing competency. Writing competency could use simple statistics such as number of specialized words used by students or the average number of words in a sentence. Writing competency could target idea generation by comparing a student's essay, for instance, with that of the teacher's reference essay. Writing competency could estimate the students' capacity for references management, content change management, and content outlining. Writing competency could elaborate on students' ability to organize their writing using opening and concluding sections, a coherent flow of ideas, variation in sentence openers, and continuity between paragraphs. Writing competency could tackle the writing style adopted by students, for instance, transactional writing. Writing competency can also be demonstrated in a student's ability to recover from grammatical errors, style errors, punctuation errors, and semantic errors.

Vivekanandan Suresh Kumar

See also Assessment of Problem Solving and Higher Order Thinking; Competency Models and Frameworks; Data Mining and Recommendation Engines; Educational Data Mining; Learning Analytics; Measuring and Assessing TPACK (Technological Pedagogical Content Knowledge)

Further Readings

Ferguson, R. (2012). Learning analytics: Drivers, developments and challenges. *International Journal of Technology Enhanced Learning, 4*(5/6), 304–317.

Gray, J., Boyle, T., & Smith, C. (1998). A constructivist learning environment implemented in Java. In *Proceedings of the 6th Annual Conference on the Teaching of Computing and the 3rd Annual Conference on Integrating Technology Into Computer Science Education: Changing the delivery of computer science eucation* (pp. 94–97). New York, NY: ACM.

Kim, M., & Lee, E. (2013). A multidimensional analysis tool for visualizing online interactions. *Journal of Educational Technology & Society, 15*(3), 89–102.

Romero, C., Ventura, S., & Garcia, E. (2008). Data mining in course management systems: Moodle cases study and tutorial. *Computers & Education, 51*(1), 368–384.

Rountree, J., Rountree, N., Robins, A., & Hannah, R. (2005) Observations of student competency in a CS1 course. In A. Young & D. Tolhurst (Eds.), *Proceedings of the 7th Australasian Conference on Computing Education: Vol. 42* (pp. 145–149). Darlinghurst, Australia: Australian Computer Society.

Shum, S. B., & Ferguson, R. (2012). Social learning analytics. *Journal of Educational Technology & Society, 15*(3), 3–26.

Watson, C., Li, F. W. B., & Godwin, J. L. (2013). Predicting performance in an introductory programming course by logging and analyzing student programming behavior. In *Proceedings of the International Conference on Advanced Learning Technologies* (pp. 319–323). Beijing, China: IEEE.

LEARNING AND INSTRUCTIONAL APPS

Education is experiencing transformation at all levels through the emergence and use of mobile technologies and mobile applications. At the heart of this transformation are learning and instructional applications for mobile devices, otherwise known as *apps*. Although many software and hardware technologies are used to create apps and multiple devices deliver learning and instructional apps, the term has been most commonly used to represent small, specialized programs or software applications designed to run on various types of mobile devices. This entry first discusses the prevalence and use of apps; the use of apps for learning and instruction; the potential of apps to disrupt traditional educational practices; and instructional strategies and educational theory. The entry then explains the design and development of learning apps, gives some examples of learning apps, and discusses research on learning apps. The entry concludes with current perspectives.

The viability of mobile learning (m-learning) with instructional apps has become a prominent topic because of the dramatic increase of availability and use of smartphone and tablet technologies. Grunwald Associates reported in 2013 that more than half of all U.S. high school students (51%) possess a smartphone in school and more than one in four middle school students (28%) carries a smartphone with installed apps to school every day; similar increases are occurring in many countries. Other portable devices, such as iPads and other tablet computers, have also adopted the app format. The report also indicated that in 2012, learning and instructional apps represented a much smaller portion of the market than did productivity apps. Mobile app use most often was for entertainment, not education, according to the report. Parents of pre-K children perceive the most value from mobile apps and almost three quarters (72%) of the top-selling learning apps targeted this age group, according to the report from Grunwald Associates and other current reports on this topic.

Learning Apps and the Educational System

Seamless, personalized, and bring your own device (BYOD) approaches related to the use of learning apps are engaging students, teachers, and parents in formal as well as informal learning contexts. Although some educational systems have adopted mobile learning technologies and apps, other schools continue to debate how to deal with the challenges of integrating mobile technology applications in classrooms. Advocates cite the unique educational affordances of mobile learning apps such as geolocation, data access, quick response (QR) code readers, and maps. However, only 17% of U.S. schools require the use of mobile or portable devices in the classroom and only 16% allow the use of family-owned mobile devices in the classroom, according to a 2013 Grunwald Associates survey of more than 2,300 parents in the United States. Schools that have adopted a BYOD policy have to deal with safety and security challenges while promoting appropriate use and educating students and parents about portable learning devices. Setting boundaries and teaching digital citizenship behaviors with the use of mobile technology and apps are key drivers for success in school usage, considering the proliferation of these devices in daily life.

Tablet devices from various manufacturers have provided choice in screen size display, and tablet ownership dramatically increased to one in three adults in the United States by 2013. Revenue from apps designed for tablets reached $8.8 billion in the United States in 2013. The emergence of the iPad Mini provided yet another screen size option to the tablet menu of choices. Based on the dramatic personal use statistics, these types of devices are quickly diffusing through the education system as well, promoting the adoption and use of learning apps in the home and across formal and informal learning contexts in the United States and abroad.

In addition to mobile-based technologies, Web-based programs that run in a Web browser may also be referred to as learning and educational productivity apps. Cloud-based services storing files and content centrally allow software application functionality on the Web as well as on mobile devices. For example, the use of the Google Apps ecosystem with its communication tools (such as Gmail, Google Talk, Google Calendar, and Google Hangouts) and productivity tools (e.g., Google Docs, text files, spreadsheets, and presentations) is changing education, permitting collaboration and sharing of centrally stored files in real time. More than 20 million students use Google Apps for education, including those at 72 of the top 100 universities, according to *EdTech* magazine.

Learning Apps and Disruption

Although U.S. schools are lagging behind other parts of the world in the adoption of mobile devices, parents embrace the educational opportunities that learning and instructional apps offer their children in the home. Parents report that mobile apps provide a learning technology with benefits such as promoting curiosity and fostering creativity, as well as teaching problem solving and the content areas of reading, math, science, and language, according to the 2013 report by Grunwald Associates. School policies have not kept pace with the consumer desire, use, and market for learning apps.

In contrast, in other parts of the world, such as in Europe, Africa, and Asia, communities seem to have more fully embraced portable devices for educational experiences because of increasing access and the ability to leverage mobile technology as a way to bypass some countries' education challenges, rural settings, limited electricity, and a lack of educational resources, according to a United Nations Educational, Scientific and Cultural Organization (UNESCO) 2013 report on the future of mobile learning. Mobile devices and apps have the capacity to cross geographic and socioeconomic boundaries, providing improved access to the Internet and learning resources to those who cannot afford stand-alone computer technologies yet who can easily access learning apps on their smartphones. Researchers such as Norbert Pachler, Ben Bachmair, and John Cook of the London Mobile Group have discussed the sociocultural implications of mobile learning apps, including concerns about education systems' ability to keep pace with social developments and with the way young people use mobile applications and technologies in everyday life. The use of mobile learning apps and devices outside the school environment is prompting disruption and reconsideration of traditional educational approaches, theories, and applications across the world.

Learning Apps, Instructional Strategies, and Educational Theory

Ideally, the use of learning and instructional apps for educational purposes would require the identification, selection, delivery, and assessment of high-quality mobile learning activities that align with student learning objectives and competencies. Mobile apps can support instructional strategies such as discovery learning, situated learning, and problem-based learning opportunities as well as self-directed and team-based learning experiences. Mobile apps have been integrated in teaching and learning in support of scientific inquiry, mathematical problem solving, historical tours, literacy learning, language learning, and authentic learning in addressing real-world events and problems. Most apps do not include assessment mechanisms, so evaluation of learning often falls to other types of data collection, observation, or student performance. With the advent of learning analytics, the collection of detailed data related to the use of learning and instructional apps may begin to be leveraged to improve and enhance learning with mobile technologies. Tracking the who, what, and where of instructional content accessing and how it is integrated or leveraged for formal and informal educational purposes will provide another layer of information about learning both inside and outside the classroom. This type of information holds much potential for student feedback and assessment as learning apps become more sophisticated, incorporating these tracking features at the individual level and aggregating data across mass usage by connecting to cloud services and databases of information that can inform teaching and learning. However, privacy and data security when using cloud-based technologies supported by private companies in the classroom are important considerations that universities and schools are only beginning to address.

Theoretical perspectives on learning are also progressing and evolving in relation to the use of learning and instructional apps across informal and formal educational contexts. For example, researchers in the fields of computer science, software engineering, and educational technology have been discussing the theory of ubiquitous computing for several decades. The recent trends toward ubiquitous computing involve small, inexpensive, robust devices integrated into handheld, wearable, and interactive displays. These wearable devices are continuously available and facilitate the use of specific apps for different informational as well as educational purposes, often involving small processors and Global Positioning System (GPS) location and sensor technologies. Another theoretical perspective is pervasive computing, which involves collaborative, networked, multiple, interconnected devices. Pervasive computing promotes a shift from decentralized, stand-alone computers and mainframes to a more pervasive, cloud-based system with software apps that may prompt changes in organizational structures based on continually available interconnected collaborative networks. Seamless learning is a recent theoretical construct that describes learning spaces without boundaries defined by a consistency of learning experiences or use of apps and various applications across different learning environments (e.g., informal and formal contexts, individual, collaborative, and social learning) evolving from the use of multiple devices and applications that are continuously available.

A group of prominent European mobile learning researchers have significantly contributed to applicable theoretical constructs related to mobile learning applications. Constructs discussed in the mobile research and literature address learning from a global perspective including (a) contingent learning and teaching based on location and real-time data collection, (b) situated learning, (c) authentic learning, (d) context-aware learning, (e) augmented reality mobile learning, and (f) personalized learning, among others. Researchers such as Michael Sharples, John Traxler, and Agnes Kukulska-Hulme have contributed much to the evolution of mobile learning research by deploying and studying instructional apps in European, Asian, and African communities.

These existing and emergent theoretical perspectives, along with others related to the ease of use and mobility of learning and instructional apps, contribute to realizing the potential for the world to become the student's classroom, providing improved access to computing power and learning applications in a portable form for use inside and outside the classroom as well as at home. This movement somewhat shifts the traditional role of educational technology to consider cross-context usage and potentially connect formal and informal learning goals and experiences for learners. Tracking the trends of usage of small mobile devices with specific learning apps as well as leveraging the potential for personalized, customizable, context-sensitive data collection through and across these devices holds significant potential for enhancing applied learning experiences. Recent discussions have begun to address the merging of digital and physical artifacts, such as wearable vests with GPS apps, reading real-time scientific data or body conditions with sensor applications, or connection to augmented reality eyewear apps with digital layering of information on the real world. These new interfaces with increased computing power may promote new possibilities in education. Advancing toward the idea of pervasive connectedness to real-time data collection across many of our multiple, everyday devices using targeted apps has the potential to significantly affect teaching and learning as well as integrating this information into our daily lives. The analysis of this continuous data from the world around us can provoke unforeseen associated educational opportunities and learning strategies resulting from the synthesis and use of these data in improved perception, awareness, and metacognition for learning.

Design and Development of Learning and Instructional Apps

There are generally three types of mobile applications: Web, native, and hybrid. These application types vary according to the technologies used for development, how they are viewed, and what is possible with each. Web applications provide a Web page with traditional Web-based components viewed on a mobile device. Native applications supported by iOS and Android operating systems typically are designed for mobile devices and demonstrate improved performance over Web applications running on mobile Web browsers. Hybrid applications typically contain Web browser components that customize the look and feel of the application for efficient mobile display to help optimize update and connection limitations. With the advent of HyperText Markup Language (HTML)5 and Windows-based apps (in addition to iOS and Android applications), more emphasis has been placed on the convergence of these design formats across devices with multiple types of displays or to strive to more efficiently design simultaneously for mobile as well as Web deployment of content.

For example, many current learning apps are now distributed across devices including smartphones, tablets, and various types of handheld technologies using *responsive design*, a term used to describe a design and development strategy to allow efficient ease of use and navigation design across different adjusted, standardized screen sizes and devices. Currently incorporated most prominently in Windows 8 applications, this strategy allows apps to be deployed across many devices and may result in the proliferation of additional learning app development. Many current m-learning apps are designed for short, concise, and efficient interactions with the learner, including video or content review, status checks, just-in-time information, or facilitating students' responses. Additional types of learning and instructional apps have begun to emerge, such as augmented reality mobile apps providing digital layering of information over the real world using the camera as a lens triggered by GPS location or digital markers on mobile devices for entertainment, information, as well as education. These new affordances, along with the gamification of instruction, are providing new ways of interacting with instructional content with mobile devices both inside and outside the classroom. This progression of more sophisticated applications that allow interaction with the real world is expanding the availability of features and functionality. When combined with the power of mobility, these applications provide unprecedented opportunities for innovative educational experiences across contexts.

Examples of Learning Applications

Thousands of learning apps exist today that address multiple categories of use such as promoting creativity and discovery, addressing literacy from a multimodal perspective, learning languages, facilitating scientific inquiry, and promoting collaboration for educational purposes, among other categories of usage. Creativity and discovery tools for young children are abundant and include examples such as Eye Paint Animals, which encourages kids to play, create, and invent employing the mobile camera and movement in the world around them as discovery and artistic creation intersect. Other examples of learning apps include experiences that address specific educational goals such as promoting particular mathematical skills, learning a language or geographical awareness, learning historical facts, or introducing astronomy. Informal educational apps targeted for specific goals might include applications such as Numerosity, which encourages kids to creatively play with numbers and math concepts and provides e-mailed reports to parents related to which mathematical concepts their kids have been exploring and giving suggested activities to extend these skills. Language learning apps include examples such as Byki, which uses a basic flashcard interface and quizzes to help users learn common phrases in multiple languages. Geographical learning apps such as Geography Drive U.S.A. target current and historical facts related to questions-answers for each of the U.S. states. Popular astronomy apps that demonstrate informal learning goals include Pocket Universe, which allows users to learn about and view the night sky or a rendered visualization of the constellations and planets and their locations by looking through the iPhone or iPad camera.

More complex learning experiences in formal education depend on the teacher or instructor's design of a structured lesson that integrates learning apps. Teaching literacy with learning apps may involve multiple learning goals, objectives, and multimodal presentation of information. For example, using different apps for interpretation, communication, and collaboration about identified content to facilitate a student's literacy learning goals is another method for integration of learning apps into instruction. Screencasting apps such as ShowMe or VoiceThread provide voice-over annotations of selected images, photos, graphs, figures, or text for representation and sharing of specific instructional content with other students. Allowing for collaborative visualization and annotation through voice, graphic overlay, or text encourages multimodal representation of ideas and fosters transfer between collaborative visual, verbal, or written content for students individually or in groups. These apps and their specific affordances may be incorporated into a learning design that promotes an active and collaborative learning experience for students to generatively express their own interpretation of educational content.

In science, learning apps are leveraged for inquiry-based learning in the real world, bringing together scientific inquiry skills such as questioning, data collection, analysis, and reporting about real-world phenomena. For example, the EcoMobile project at Harvard University employed a custom-produced augmented reality app that allowed students to investigate water quality in their environment using scientific probes in the classroom and in the field. Facilitating a rich investigative inquiry experience in science, this project was designed to incorporate digital geo-located hot spots to allow groups of students to closely observe a particular ecosystem, integrating information about water quality and the environment for the students to track, analyze, and report. These examples illustrate complex educational experiences facilitated by the affordances of existing and customized learning apps integrated with rich learning objectives structured by educators and learning designers.

Research on Mobile Learning and Apps

Current research on the use of mobile devices with corresponding learning apps in education is beginning to emerge in academic journals. Researchers are examining the type of studies published in mobile learning, the type of mobile technology employed, and the design of mobile learning experiences, with less information available on the effectiveness of particular learning applications or apps. Some major findings indicate that mobile learning technologies and apps are being used or studied most in higher education contexts, followed by elementary school contexts and in professional and applied sciences and humanities subject areas. Many of these meta-analytic studies do not take into account current technologies and emergent learning application affordances. Other researchers are examining the need to embrace and identify the unique characteristics of mobile learning applications, which may distinguish this type of learning experience from other learning experiences, beyond simply the fact that the learner is not in a predetermined location. Researchers involved in redefining ubiquitous learning in the mobile app age describe characteristics such as the on-demand learning need, providing just-in-time information in a timely manner, situating the learning activity in everyday settings, awareness and interaction in context, and self-regulation. Learning challenges also exist with mobile learning apps, according to work by Melody M. Terras and Judith Ramsay, including some concerns about the context-dependent nature of memory given the frequent switches and inconsistency of learning context and scenarios involved in the use of apps. Other concerns have to do with limits on cognitive load and with the meta-cognitive skills needed to learn the right thing at the right time in the right place.

Current Applied Perspectives on Mobile Learning and Apps

Despite these complex examples, perspectives, and concerns, some researchers and theorists involved in studying mobile learning app usage and integration into schools think we may primarily be using new software and technology to implement traditional pedagogical approaches. Many believe we need to do more to exploit the affordances of mobile learning apps to provide children with rich experiences that connect their activities inside and outside the classroom or across their sociocultural lifeworlds of use of mobile learning apps and technologies. Mobile learning apps can integrate location information, promote real-time connection with others, and sense relevant information in context, as well as provide personalized, collaborative, rich learning opportunities and feedback to parents, teachers, employers, and other stakeholders. Capitalizing on these capacities could provide new opportunities in education. Research results from these burgeoning efforts are also supporting this integration of learning app technologies into the classroom as well as informal learning contexts, demonstrating increased student engagement, motivation, and learning gains across projects like those described earlier.

Prominent researchers such as Chris Dede and Elliot Soloway have written that we need also to address some of the concerns about using mobile learning apps and technology in education. Directly addressing the important issues related to technological infrastructure and device management and policies as well as safety and privacy have become paramount, particularly in school-based settings. Understanding the specific affordances and instructional strategies that learning apps and mobile technologies promote is crucial to employing this unique form of educational technology in the most optimal manner for learning. Providing educators with models of use and learning design may allow them to embrace the potential of learning and instructional apps to provide mobile, connected, and seamless learning experiences.

Brenda Bannan

See also Apps for Use at the Elementary Level; Apps for Use at the Secondary Level; Apps for Use in Higher Education; Badges and Skill Certification

Further Readings

Daly, J. (2013). *Google apps for education is leading the way to a cloud-based campus.* Retrieved from http://www.edtech magazine.com/higher/article/2013/05/google-apps-education leading-way-cloud-based-campus

Drinkwater, D. (2013). *U.S. tablet adoption skyrockets to one in three adults.* Retrieved from http://tabtimes.com/news/ ittech-stats-research/2013/06/10/us-tablet-adoption-sky rockets-one-three-adults

EDUCAUSE. (2008). *The seven things you should know about Google apps.* Retrieved from http://net.educause.edu/ir/ library/pdf/ELI7035.pdf

Grunwald Associates. (2013). *Living and learning with mobile devices: What parents think about mobile devices for early childhood and K–12 learning.* Retrieved from http://www .grunwald.com/reports

Pachler, N., Bachmair, B., & Cook, J. (2010). *Mobile learning: Structures, agency, practices.* New York, NY: Springer.

Shuler, C., Winters, N., & West, M. (2013). *The future of mobile learning: Implications for policy makers and planners.* Retrieved from http://unesdoc.unesco.org/images/0021/002196/ 219637e.pdf

Terras, M. M., & Ramsay, J. (2012). The five central psychological challenges facing effective mobile learning. *British Journal of Educational Technology, 43*(5), 820–832.

Traxler, J. (2013). Mobile learning: Shaping the frontiers of learning technologies in the global context. In R. Huang, Kinshuk, & J. M. Spector (Eds.), *Reshaping learning: Frontiers of learning technology in a global context.* New York, NY: Springer.

Wong, L.- H. (2012). A learner-centric view of mobile seamless learning. *British Journal of Educational Technology, 43*(1), 19–23.

Wu, H.- W., Wu, J. Y.- C., Chen, C.- Y., Kao, H.- Y., Lin, C.- H., & Hang, S.- H. (2012). Review of trends from mobile learning studies: A meta-analysis. *Computers & Education, 59,* 817–827.

LEARNING BY MODELING

Modeling is an instructional strategy in which the students learn by observing the teacher. Through modeling, students imitate particular behaviors that facilitate learning. As psychologist Albert Bandura has noted, modeling allows people to learn new behaviors without relying strictly on the effects of their own actions. This entry discusses how modeling is used in instruction, with a particular focus on the use of computer-based simulation.

Modeling can be used across disciplines and in all grade and ability levels. Types of modeling include but are not limited to (1) disposition modeling, (2) task and performance modeling, (3) metacognitive modeling, and (4) student-centered modeling. In dispositional modeling, teachers demonstrate values and ways of thinking to help develop character and communities. In task and performance modeling, teachers demonstrate tasks for students to later carry out on their own. In metacognitive modeling, teachers demonstrate how to think so students can construe data and information, examine statements, and draw conclusions and inferences from the material learned. Finally, from a less "teacher-centered" perspective, in student-centered modeling, students who have mastered concepts and learning outcomes model tasks for their peers. Creating learning models refines students' higher thinking skills. Creating computer-supported simulation models is common practice within inquiry-based learning settings. These help hone newly acquired knowledge and identify remaining learning gaps. By interacting and experimenting with a simulator, students can examine and model phenomena and extrapolate important information.

To be an integral part of the learning process, computer-supported simulators should incorporate information presented concurrently with the simulation. Online tutorials with images and corresponding instructions are mainstream examples of computer-based simulations for learning basic skills.

Computer-Based Modeling and Simulation

Simulation programs are preeminent forms of technology-based modeling. Simulations can allow students to learn from an expert model, role-play to practice new skills, or test learning. Overall, simulations can be characterized as asynchronous media-based activities to ease learners' application of gained knowledge to "real-life" or work situations. Observation of an expert model by means of simulation increases learners' understanding of the expert's thought processes and decision-making strategies. Subsequently, learners can create mental representations and produce the expected behaviors based on recall. Within simulated contexts, the prospect that modeled behaviors will be needed for achieving future events heightens the attention directed to the model. In most simulations for mastery, learners practice behaviors in a safe environment before transferring them into the real work environment.

Educational research has credited simulation with enabling discovery, experimentation, practice, and active construction of knowledge based on concrete models and examples within a risk-free learning environment. Relative to traditional approaches, modeling through simulations and scenarios is highly focused on the learner's behavior rather than on the subject to be mastered. Further diverging from traditional approaches, which may support relatively simple and well-structured materials, simulations can accommodate the learning of complex topics with high interaction or practice demands.

Simulations are diverse and may range from simple scenarios to complex interactive games with rules and measurable outcomes. Initially adopted for military training, simulations are now used in many fields, including marketing, finance, management, clinical education, and foreign languages. The Massachusetts Institute of Technology, for instance, has used simulation games to teach its MBA students the principles of systems dynamics and operations. The American Association of Colleges of Nursing has recognized simulation as a tool to provide students with a range of experiences that they might not otherwise encounter within everyday clinical practice settings.

Effectiveness

Although technology-based learning is not unequivocally shown to be more effective than traditional learning, research suggests that simulations can be particularly effective at increasing comprehension and retention as well as facilitating successful transfer of skills and knowledge in real life. From a workplace training perspective, however, not all the evaluations of the technology have been favorable. Some accounts have argued that simulations have more entertainment than educational value and they have not met their goals of delivering authentic and long-term change for businesses. Challenges to research on simulation, including inconsistent methodology, small sample size, and an overall lack of long-term effectiveness research, hinder the generalizability of the findings and warrant further investigation of the topic.

More of a consensus has been reached, however, on the notion that it is ultimately the responsibility of the facilitator of a simulation to maximize the benefit of a particular program. Ensuring the students' mastery of the learning material remains critical in making a simulator useful. It is therefore essential to help students realize that the simulation is not a game but rather a modeling tool for important learning topics. Researchers have also proposed that real comprehension of the material occurs when students reflect on the experience of running through the simulation. As a result, at least ideally, most classroom simulation runs should lead to a concluding discussion of the observations and lessons learned.

In addition to the facilitator's efforts, students' interest also has a major impact on the effectiveness of a simulation. As with any learning environment, overall interest level in simulation technologies varies among the students. To that end, it was proposed that the students can be broadly categorized in two groups. One group of students will be highly excited and engaged in the simulation, but another group will not want to engage themselves in this new type of technology-based learning.

To best facilitate learning and mastery through simulation, a six-step debriefing model was put forward. The first step, "decompression," involves taking time to relax after running the simulation. The second step, "facts," involves reviewing the factual information inherent in the learning material. The third step, "inferences," includes extending focus questions on the topic. The fourth step, "transfer," involves students applying the concepts learned in the simulation to a real-world example. The fifth step, "generalizations," requires students to draw generalizations and rules based on the simulations completed. Finally, the last step, "applications," involves students applying inferred rules and generalizations to the real world.

Selen Razon and Umit Tokac

See also Instructional Design Models; Learning With Models; Model-Based Approaches; Student Modeling; System Dynamics; Tools for Modeling and Simulation

Further Readings

Bandura, A. (1977). *Social learning theory.* Englewood Cliffs, NJ: Prentice Hall.

Coffey, H. (2014). *Modeling.* Retrieved from http://www.learnnc.org/lp/pages/4697

Eysink, T. H., de Jong, T., Berthold, K., Kolloffel, B., Opfermann, M., & Wouters, P. (2009). Learner performance in multimedia learning arrangements: An analysis across instructional approaches. *American Educational Research Journal, 46,* 1107–1149. doi:10.3102/0002831209340235

Joris, D., & Daniel, R. (2007). *The use of simulation technology in sport finance courses: The case of the Oakland A's baseball business simulator.* MPRA Paper 25802, University Library of Munich, Germany.

Koller, V., Harvey, S., & Magnotta, M. (2006). *Technology-based learning strategies.* Retrieved from http://www.doleta.gov/reports/papers/TBL_Paper_FINAL.pdf

Lasater, K., Johnson, E. A., Ravert, P., & Rink, D. (2014). Role modeling clinical judgment for an unfolding older adult simulation. *Journal of Nursing Education, 53,* 257–264. doi:10.3928/01484834-20140414-01

LEARNING IN MUSEUMS

Museums are increasingly interested in serving their visitor audiences as places of learning. The American Association of Museums in the 1990s delineated guidelines for museum education. Recent research has added greatly to our knowledge about how to enhance learning in museums, based on the very different nature of museums as learning spaces. Museums are designed for public audiences. People visit museums for many reasons, sometimes in school visits, but more often as a leisure-time activity. Some contend that museum learning may be a category of informal learning; others prefer to term this *free-choice learning*, indicating the nature of the informal learning activities, regardless of setting. Museum learning is also lifelong learning.

It has become clear that how people learn in museums involves their active engagement in developing personal and social meaning from the experience. Museum learning is voluntary, self-directed, complex, contextual, experiential, active, multidimensional, fluid, and dynamic. It is often social, especially involving families, with children and family members learning together. What people learn is personal and grounded in their prior knowledge and experience, as well as in their interests and motivation. Museum visitors actively engage in developing personal meaning, by assimilating and accommodating aspects of their experience that are relevant to them. What they experience in the museum also is grounded in the physical context of the museum. Their experience is also related to time: the time they have to spend in the museum, as well as the timing of the visit, along with the activities in which visitors participate before and after their museum visit. This entry first discusses research on learning in museums and how learning is measured. The entry then details museum technologies for learning and discusses models, designs, and strategies for supporting learning in museums.

Research on, and Measurement of, Learning in Museums

Museums are increasingly focusing on the visitor's view, voice, and perspectives. Learning research in museums is aimed at examining what, how, and why people, individually and in groups, learn in museums, and what they consider important about their museum experience, both during their visits and often long after their museum visits.

Types of Studies

Research on learning in museums has ranged widely in terms of theoretical perspectives, purposes, and research questions. Many studies have been conducted on science learning, especially informal science, often conducted collaboratively across many types of educational organizations, schools, universities, and museums. Others have involved cultural practices or been based on sociocultural theories. Many studies have been conducted as evaluations, including needs assessments and formative or summative evaluations, often as part of grant-funded projects.

Museum learning studies focus on things such as (a) conceptual gains, especially relative to scientific knowledge; (b) social interactions; (c) cultural perspectives; (d) the effects of media, programs, and school trips on learning; and (e) perspectives of the meaning of museum institutions themselves.

Measuring Learning in Museums

Learning measures often include instruments and methods designed to measure behaviors, social interactions, conversational discourse, and attitudes, all of which may be changing dynamically. In addition, recent research has demonstrated changes as a result of the museum experience in attitudes, emotions, interests, and knowledge long after the museum visit.

Research Designs and Methodologies

Research designs may be experimental or quasi-experimental, and may rely heavily on more traditional learning measures, such as quizzes or tests, although they may be called something else and delivered orally instead of in writing. More recently, however, museum learning researchers have tended to rely on mixed-methods studies, typically with multiple outcome measures, and triangulation of analyses and findings, to better examine the complexities and nuances of visitors' experiences and learning.

Museum learning specialists rely on a broad array of methodologies, including questionnaires, interviews, focus groups, behavioral observations, time-motion studies, and conversational discourse analysis. Data may often be collected from both individuals and groups. Newer technologies, such as wearable cameras, have also been used to collect data related to the visitors' perspectives on their museum experience. Data may also be collected long after the museum visit, though this is not always easy to do.

Museum Technologies for Learning

Museums have been at the forefront in the use of innovative interactive technologies, both digital and mobile, to support their visitors' experience. Museum tours often are offered using digital audio technologies, delivered via stand-alone devices or, increasingly, cell phones. Many museums have built exhibits that include kiosks or other types of interactive computer displays that allow visitors to explore topics in depth. Games and other types of virtual reality experiences and simulations are also increasingly being developed to enhance the museum visitors' enjoyment and learning from their visits, or to make the museum's offerings available to those at a distance. Mobile apps for tablets and smartphones are also being developed by many museums. These apps may include crowdsourcing to allow the public to engage in research with the museum, or augmented reality to enable users to, again, experience more fully the offerings of the museum.

Some museums are developing increasingly sophisticated databases of their collections available via the Web, some in 2D, but also some in 3D, so that the public as well as researchers can explore more of the museums' holdings than there would be room to exhibit. Museum offerings are also able, via technology, to be shared in several languages. Another aspect of the power of museum technology is that museums often use social media to support ongoing conversations between visitors, educators, and the museum staff. Thus, museums continue to employ technologies in support of learning.

Models, Designs, and Strategies for Supporting Learning in Museums

Contextual Model of Learning

John Falk and Lynn Dierking have developed their *contextual model of learning* based on their work in museums. Their earlier model was called the *interactive experience model*. This model integrates three learning contexts: personal, sociocultural, and physical. Falk and Dierking contend that these contexts are overlapping and integrated, and interact with each other dynamically. Those who develop museum exhibits, programs, and materials may draw on the research into the factors and variables related to these contexts of museum learning.

Designs and Strategies to Enhance Learning in Museums

Earlier, museum education may arguably have been focused to a great extent on developing and evaluating formal educational programs or exhibits, such as teacher training, school tours and programs, classes, workshops, and lectures. However, with the broadened view of museums as learning organizations, museum educators now develop interpretation to go along with exhibits, newsletters, marketing plans, and volunteer and docent training and are increasingly involved in the strategic planning and evaluation related to the museum's new roles and missions.

Museum learning specialists argue that developing the museum experience to enhance learning involves an understanding that museums compete with many other types of leisure-time activities and that the experience includes much more than particular exhibits or programs. The experience includes the marketing and information that drew the visitor, the initial admission and welcome, the visitor's comfort and enjoyment, communication of key information, appealing to the visitor's senses, and having the visit conclude in a satisfying manner.

Families make up a large percentage of museum visitors, and visitors often also come with friends, so supporting the social aspect of the museum visit is critical. For instance, exhibits that are designed for families need to be accessible by people small and tall, old and young. Text and visuals need to be designed for this varied audience as well. Families talk about and share what they are learning; often, family exhibits are highly interactive, multimodal, relevant, and support multiple learning and attitude outcomes.

Museums are becoming more interested in learning about the cultural concerns and interests of their public community audiences. As a consequence, museums are looking for designers and evaluators to help improve displays and activities.

Regardless of approach, museums increasingly rely on formative evaluations to test their programs, exhibits, and offerings with real visitors, even if these evaluations must, at times, of necessity, be done informally. It can be expected that in the future museums will continue to employ and enjoy innovative approaches to development, and research on, learning.

Wilhelmina C. Savenye

See also Design of Engaging Informal Learning Places and Spaces; Informal Learning Strategies; Integrating Informal Learning With Programs at the College/University Level; Integrating Informal Learning With School Programs at the Secondary Level; Learning in Outdoor Settings; Measuring Learning in Informal Contexts

Further Readings

Borun, M., Dritsas, J., Johnson, J. I., Peter, N. E., Wagner, K. F., Fadigan, K., . . . & Wenger, A. (1998). *Family learning in museums: The PISEC perspective.* Philadelphia, PA: Philadelphia/Camden Informal Science Education Collaborative (PISEC), The Franklin Institute.

Diamond, J., Luke, J. J., & Uttal, D. H. (2009). *Practical evaluation guide: Tools for museums and other informal educational settings.* Lanham, MD: AltaMira Press.

Falk, J. H., & Dierking, L. D. (2000). *Learning from museums: Visitor experiences and the making of meaning.* Walnut Creek, CA: AltaMira Press.

Falk, J. H., & Dierking, L. D. (2002). *Lessons without limit: How free-choice learning is transforming education.* Walnut Creek, CA: AltaMira Press.

Falk, J. H., & Dierking, L. D. (2012). *The museum experience revisited* (2nd ed.). Walnut Creek, CA: Left Coast Press.

Hooper-Greenhill, E. (Ed.). (1999). *The educational role of the museum.* London, UK: Routledge.

Johnson, A., Huber, K. A., Cutler, N., Bingmann, M., & Grove, T. (2009). *The museum educator's manual: Educators share successful techniques.* Lanham, MD: AltaMira Press.

Martin, L. M. W. (2007). An emerging research framework for studying free-choice learning and schools. In J. H. Falk, L. D. Dierking, & S. Foutz (Eds.), *In principle, in practice: Museums as learning institutions* (pp. 247–259). Lanham, MD: AltaMira Press.

National Research Council. (2009). *Learning science in informal environments: People, places, and pursuits.* Washington, DC: The National Academies Press. Retrieved from http://www.nap.edu/catalog.php?record_id=12190

Rennie, L. J., & Johnston, D. J. (2007). Research on learning from museums. In J. H. Falk, L. D. Dierking, & S. Foutz (Eds.), *In principle, in practice: Museums as learning institutions* (pp. 57–73). Lanham, MD: AltaMira Press.

Sherman, A. (2014). *How tech is changing the museum experience.* Retrieved June 10, 2014, from http://mashable.com/2011/09/14/high-tech-museums

Weaver, S. (2007). *Creating great visitor experiences: A guide for museums, parks, zoos, gardens, & libraries.* Walnut Creek, CA: Left Coast Press.

Websites

American Association of Museums: http://www.aam-us.org

Center for Advancement of Informal Science Education: http://informalscience.org

MCN Museum Computer Network: http://www.mcn.edu

Museums and the Web: http://www.museumsandtheweb.com

Visitor Studies Association: http://visitorstudies.org

LEARNING IN OUTDOOR SETTINGS

Humans have been learning in the outdoors for all of recorded history. In the past, activities such as horsemanship, hunting, and farming were more likely learned for sustaining life and productivity. Throughout the Industrial Revolution and into the information age, learning in the outdoors has taken on a more specific connotation. In general, the types of learning that occur in outdoor settings fall into these major areas: outdoor education, outdoor recreation, experiential learning, environmental education, and adventure education/therapy. Often theories that support one area of focus such as outdoor education are also espoused in another area of focus such as adventure therapy.

The idea that children are experiencing a "nature deficit disorder," which was popularized by the book *Last Child in the Woods: Saving Our Children From Nature-Deficit Disorder*, by Richard Louv, has spurred interest in the role that nature plays in childhood development. Intentionally ensuring that the young learner is exposed to unique experiences with nature is postulated to help learners with attention deficit disorder, obesity, and academic achievement. Examples of programs that help address nature deficit disorder are interpretive programs that are offered by state and national parks. This entry describes the types of education programs that take place in outdoor settings and what individuals can learn from them. Most of the examples described herein are based in the United States, but analogous examples can be found in many other countries.

Outdoor Education

Outdoor education in the United States is usually broken into two categories—residential and expedition (journey) learning. Residential outdoor schools deliver environmental and natural science education where students spend multiple nights at one site such as a school or base camp; these programs typically last four or five days and comprise short day trips. Often these programs serve fifth- and sixth-grade students, but many programs serve other grades and adults. The Teton Science School (TSS) has been operating in the Yellowstone area in Wyoming since 1967. TSS offers wildlife expeditions, field education, graduate programs, science teacher education, the Journeys School, and a conservation center. TSS is also involved in the local schools in the Teton Valley. For example, the TSS Wolf & Bear Expedition exposes learners to the natural habitat of the gray wolf and grizzly bear to teach learners about hunting patterns, family structure, and safety. The YMCA of the Rockies operates a residential outdoor school where students can participate in day camps or longer events that include a challenge course, archery, fishing, and a zip line. Hundreds of residential outdoor schools expose learners to a full spectrum of outdoor activities and learning.

Expedition- or journey-based outdoor education schools have been developing in the United States since the early 1960s. These schools take learners to the desert, mountains, rivers, and oceans in the United States and around the world. Each school has a specific mission and focus and the expeditions last anywhere from a few days to a semester, with the average duration being just over two weeks. Often participants will explore leadership, character development, and personal change by participating in hiking, climbing, skiing, mountaineering, whitewater rafting, boating, and canyoneering. Outward Bound (OB) is an outdoor education school with 40 schools around the world and more than 200,000 participants a year. OB came to the United States from England in 1961 and set up camp in Marble, Colorado; OB currently engages learners in outdoor activities to promote character development, leadership, and service. The National Outdoor Leadership School (NOLS) is a wilderness education school that has been serving students for 46 years. The values of NOLS are wilderness, education, leadership, safety, community, and excellence. Each of these expedition-based outdoor education schools engages learners in outdoor activities in the wilderness to help them develop their cognitive, affective, and psychomotor domains.

Outdoor Recreation

The difference between outdoor education and outdoor recreation programs is that often learning is secondary to other goals of outdoor recreation, such as physical exertion, relaxation, and community building. The learning that happens in outdoor recreation is an indirect result of participating in the activity. The two main types of outdoor recreation are human-powered and mechanized.

Human-powered outdoor recreation, where the enthusiast is providing the power to participate in the activity, includes hiking, trail running, hunting, biking, rafting and kayaking, skiing, and backpacking. Types of learning that occur in these activities include physical fitness training, map and compass skills, nature interpretation, Leave No Trace skills, and camp craft. Learners can engage in this type of learning through an organized program or activity or they can work toward mastery through a self-guided learning process.

Mechanized outdoor recreation includes off-road vehicles, motorcycles, power boating, snowmobiling, and recreation vehicles where the enthusiast uses a motorized vehicle to engage in the activity. Types of learning that can occur in these activities include mechanics, route finding, and nature interpretation. Often the learner will self-educate in these activities and learn through trial and error.

Environmental Education

Environmental education is a form of education in the outdoors that has a focus on nature and creating a connection between the learner and the natural environment. Activities such as bird watching, nature hikes, and ecotourism can be self-guided learning situations, or they can be led by facilitators. The Sierra Club advertises itself as the oldest outfitter of environmentally friendly travel, offering more than 300 trips each year for all ages and abilities, with the intent of helping humans explore the natural word to learn about conservation, natural history, and wildlife. The Audubon Society Nature Centers also engage learners via nature hikes, conservation, research, and discovery of the natural world. Similar and affiliated environmental programs can be found in other countries. For example, Norway has national programs to involve children and youth in outdoor environmentally oriented activities throughout primary and secondary education.

Experiential, Transformative, and Service Learning

Experiential, transformative, and service learning are closely related and share many of the same or similar theoretical foundations. Experiential learning and transformative learning are often used in outdoor education and outdoor education programs. In experiential learning, the focus is on providing an opportunity for the learner to engage in problem-based activities that challenge a group to use good communication and mutual respect to accomplish tasks.

Team-building and challenge courses are activities often conducted in the outdoors that provide a unique experience (often a problem the learners have never seen) and challenge the learners to come up with unique solutions that require teamwork, communication, and a community effort. A challenge course is a fixed set of initiatives and activities that engage the group in some form of physical or mental challenge that requires creative group problem solving to complete. Project Adventure has been operating since 1971 and delivers training and learning experiences such as adventure programming for K–12 physical education programs, challenge courses, and bullying prevention.

Transformative learning focuses on providing an opportunity for learners to create meaning by engaging new knowledge through an authentic context and exploring through reflective discourse. The role of the outdoor setting serves as a catalyst, often with a goal of some form of interpersonal change. Meditation and tai chi are activities often associated with transformative learning. Often, the intended outcome is to use the outdoors as a medium to explore personal and interpersonal growth.

Service learning can happen in outdoor settings where the learners are engaged in service to others or the environment. An example of service learning would be building hiking trails for the Colorado Fourteeners Initiative. The learners may have little to no experience in building trails, so the facilitators teach them about aspect, gradient, building materials, and construction techniques, and learners immediately put that learning into action by building hiking trails. The learners are providing a service to other users who will have a solid and safe trail to use to climb the 14,000-foot peaks in Colorado, as well as providing service to the environment by helping deter erosion.

School-based field trips can include all three forms of learning (experiential, transformational, and service), depending on the setting and the environment. These trips are often a few hours or a day in length with a small portion being multiday where the goal is for the learners to directly interact with the phenomena being studied instead of just exploring through inference within the classroom. For example, instead of just reading about animal habitats in the classroom, the learners take a trip to a local nature conservancy or open space and explores land and water to discover and describe different habitats.

Adventure and Learning

The term *adventure* often precedes the words *education*, *programming*, and *recreation* when describing learning in the outdoors. These topics have been covered in the sections that address outdoor education and outdoor recreation. Adventure therapy is unique in that the medium for self-exploration and therapeutic change is having an adventure in an outdoor setting. Activities such as team-building and challenge courses that are used in experiential learning are also used in adventure therapy but with a different intent and focus. The learning that is catalyzed in the outdoor setting is primarily intended to help the learner come to some new form of understanding or new behavior that is related to an emotional challenge that the learner is having.

Use of Technology in Learning Outdoors

Outdoor learners have adapted and integrated technology into many aspects of learning and exploring in the outdoors. The increased availability of accessing the Global Positioning System (GPS) has changed how many navigate in the backcountry and over the water. Now individual adventurers can carry a satellite phone and a personal locator beacon into the depths of some of the most remote areas in the world and have connectivity as if they were in a major city. Many environmental education learners carry tablets into the backcountry to assist in wildlife and fauna identification, and there are even mobile apps that record bird calls and then provide the learner with information on the bird making the call. The integration of technology with learning in the outdoors has many more possibilities as devices become smaller, lighter, and more weather resistant.

Conclusion

Although the types of education that can be offered outdoors differ in many ways, they share in common that the outdoor setting is the learning environment and the instruction is designed to maximize the learner's interaction with nature and with other community members to create a unique form of learning that often results in personal change.

Jeffrey M. Foley

See also Constructivist Theory; Experiential Learning; Games for Adult Learners; Informal Learning Strategies; Personal Learning Environments

Further Readings

Drury, J., Bonney, B., Berman, D., & Wagstaff, M. (2005). *The backcountry classroom: Lessons, tools, and activities for teaching outdoor leaders* (2nd ed.). Guilford, CT: Falcon.

Louv, R. (2008). *Last child in the woods*. New York: Workman.

Priest, S., & Gass, M. (2005). *Effective leadership in adventure programming* (2nd ed.). Champaign, IL: Human Kinetics.

Prouty, D., Panicucci, J., & Collinson, R. (Eds.). (2007). *Adventure education: Theory and applications.* Champaign, IL: Human Kinetics.

Warren, K., Sakoffs, M., & Hunt, J. (Eds.). (1995). *The theory of experiential education.* Boulder, CO: Association for Experiential Education.

LEARNING IN THE DEFENSE SECTOR WITH SIMULATED SYSTEMS

Simulation generally refers to the live or virtual representation or enactment of a set of events designed to produce a learning environment similar to real-world experiences. *Simulation* is defined as representing the characteristics and functioning of a system or a process through the use of another system. Simulation training is the technological alternative to conducting conventional training with actual equipment. Proficiency in the military's effective response to threats requires development and maintenance of optimal competence and performance.

The ever-increasing military task complexities imposed by the use of advanced electronic and technological equipment demand that military members process and communicate immense amounts of complex information quickly. Thus, training becomes a vital, albeit expensive, element in maintaining military readiness. The amount of resources required for conventional training methods with actual equipment makes simulated training attractive either as an alternative or as an augmentation, especially considering the lower risks involved for the trainees and the training staff.

In training scenarios, learners participate and enact a situation or actually operate a system to practice their communication, decision-making, and motor skills. In some situations, they do not directly operate a system but provide input and manipulate a simulated scenario. However, simulation training can help develop a shared mental model among teams of learners whose jobs require coordinated action and communication in response to a commonly understood situation. This entry discusses the development of simulated systems for use in the military, their feasibility and cost-effectiveness, and the military classification and use of various types of simulations.

Development

Development of simulations for learning purposes can be traced back throughout human history. One can view tribal games such as wrestling or stone or javelin throwing aiming at moving or fixed targets as simulated learning exercises. The use of war games such as Kriegsspiel dates back to early 19th century when it was circulated to the Prussian army for regular playing. The game was developed using scenarios governed by the rules and regulations governing historical battles. Now war-fighting skills are practiced in shooting ranges and with computer simulations.

With the advent of electronic technology, simulated learning made great progress. Firefighters, police officers, and military personnel train and sharpen their skills in learning environments simulating real situations as closely as possible. Today, simulation technologies used in military learning and instruction range from simple to complex and cover the training spectrum from operating a tank to flying an airplane to training teams for a variety of defense tasks. Perhaps the main reason for this widespread use of simulated training is that simulations offer a real-life learning experience at a lower cost and without jeopardizing the trainee's life or the training equipment. Military simulated training has become an effective way to generate sound practical solutions to training problems because it helps the armed forces enhance their skills and competencies, practice their assigned tasks, and return safely at the completion of their missions.

Feasibility and Cost-Effectiveness

The available advanced technology has also immensely expanded the opportunities for designing and delivering efficient and cost-effective training. Nowadays, one can train individually and collectively right at the station or the home office by using relevant scenarios to enhance individual, group, and organizational performance. Moreover, this can be done more flexibly and customized for individuals and units. The training scenarios can also be created so realistically that trainees have no difficulty in reacting to simulations as if they were in the real environment. In today's simulated training courses, the training materials have the capability of repeated use and low maintenance, which enables training events to become a regular and frequent part of military life. These characteristics, which the U.S. Army calls the integrated training environment, enable commanders to train in different scenarios under various conditions at an affordable cost.

In military training, the application of simulation ranges from realistic operational environments to more abstract game-based scenarios. Between the two ends of this spectrum lie the possibilities of mixing and matching realistic and abstract ideas to create a blended simulated training environment for any specific expertise. For example, training the infantry to clear a building complex during combat represents an example of a field exercise that involves more realistic elements.

Whereas in training high-level cognitive processes on the abstract side of the spectrum, one may task an officer to observe a game-based situation and use the observed information, relate the elements, and synthesize a conclusion through application of an analytical model. A blended simulated environment would be used to train an Air Force pilot to fly a sophisticated fighter jet, which requires skill-based simulated learning in physical simulators, concept-based learning in computer-based simulations, and flying actual planes in different scenarios.

Classification of Simulations

The U.S. Department of Defense classifies military training simulations into three categories: *virtual, live,* and *constructive* simulations. The following is a description and an example of each type.

Virtual Simulation

Virtual simulations are the result of blending the software and hardware components to create a virtual environment for human interaction with the simulation system. In a virtual training, the learners can play a role and provide inputs so that they have the opportunity to practice their motor and decision-making skills to attain expected outcomes.

Some portions of training pilots to fly aircraft are an example of this type of training. The military uses virtual, computer-based systems for the functions and controls of an aircraft located in a physical training simulation. Trainees use this virtual system to practice operating an aircraft in a variety of circumstances without leaving the training facility. The virtual system is built to integrate the operational functions of the aircraft and create a learning environment for trainees' in which they get the opportunity to interact with the system, play the role of a pilot, use the available data, and input the required information to achieve the expected outcome. In this case, the virtual system responds just as an actual aircraft would so that skills developed in the simulator transfer directly to the actual aircraft.

Live Simulation

In live simulation environments, real people operate real equipment to engage in an operational training scenario. A law enforcement drill of a hostage rescue training scenario is an example of live simulation. Both the Navy and Air Force use live simulated training environments to train their pilots. The pilots use real aircraft to participate in a simulated battle with enemy pilots

trained in using adversary tactics. Throughout the practice of a simulated battle, the pilots' performance and decisions are monitored to provide feedback after the completion of the mission. The purpose of this training is to improve the pilots' skills and chances of survival in a real battle.

Constructive Simulation

Constructive simulation refers to a simulated system in which trainees have no roles in manipulating the players and forming the outcomes. The trainees' role in this case is to observe the simulation, identify the interacting elements of the scenario, and collect and analyze the information, based on which they construct their own prediction of the outcome. This type of simulation is aimed at trainees' analytical skills and their prediction of the simulated player or system behavior.

An example of this type of training simulation could be training the security personnel of a shipyard for military vessels. In this situation, the trainees have no role in executing the simulation of shipyard operations. According to the training scenarios relevant to the environment for this training, the actors involved in the scenario play their assigned roles and interact with the live and virtual systems in the environment. The trainee's task is to observe the situation and to identify and neutralize a terrorist threat through a constructive simulation. Trainees in this case have no input in the scenario and no control over what happens in the simulation. They only observe, identify the suspicious elements and their interactions, synthesize the information, and report their findings and their appropriate responses.

Aubteen Darabi

See also Adaptive Learning Software and Platforms; Games to Promote Inquiry Learning; Learning by Modeling; Simulation-Based Learning

Further Readings

CSIAC (2013). *Simulation highlights: A quarterly compilation of simulation articles from leading defense and industry publications.* Retrieved from https://www.thecsiac.com/sites/default/files/Sim%20Highlights%20Winter%202013_0.pdf

Kennedy, H. (1999). *Simulation reshaping military training.* Retrieved from http://www.nationaldefensemagazine.org/archive/1999/November/Pages/Simulation4398.aspx

Page, H. E., & Smith, R. (1998). Introduction to military training simulation: A guide for discrete event simulationists. In D. J. Medeiros, E. Watson, J. Carson, & M. Manivannan (Eds.), *Proceedings of the 1998 Winter Simulation*

Conference (pp. 53–60). Washington, DC: Winter Simulation Conference.

Schatz, S., Folsom-Kovarik, J. T., Bartlett, K., Wray, R. E., & Solina, D. (2012). *Archetypal patterns of life for military training simulations.* Paper presented at Interservice/Industry Training, Simulation, and Education Conference (I/ITSEC). Retrieved from http://www.iitsec.org/about/Publications Proceedings/Documents/BP_Paper_TRNG_12193.pdf

Sennersten, C. (2010). *Model-based simulation training supporting military operational processes* (Doctoral dissertation, Blekinge Institute of Technology, Karlskrona, Sweden). Retrieved from http://www.fysiskplanering.se/fou/forskinfo.nsf/all/2bc8a3a8d1 914b25c125777a0032cc50/$file/Diss_Charlotte%20 Sennersten.pdf

U.S. Army PEO STRI. (n.d.). *Program executive office for simulation, training and instrumentation.* Retrieved from http://www.peostri.army.mil

U.S. Department of Defense. (1997). *DoD modeling and simulation (M&S) glossary* (DoD 5000.59-M). Washington, DC: Author.

LEARNING IN THE HEALTH SECTOR WITH SIMULATED SYSTEMS

Simulation-based medical education involves replicating part or substantial aspects of a clinical work environment for education, assessment, research, and institutional health care training. Medical simulation covers a range of experiences from simple simulation devices that are used as partial-task trainers for simple procedures to comprehensive simulations for whole-task training (e.g., a virtual entire operating room with computerized mannequins).

Advances in science and technology contribute to changes in medicine and medical education. Patient interventions and recovery time have become more efficient because of the development of new devices, new drugs, and less invasive medical procedures. However, such innovations require rapid changes in medical education. At the same time, new policies for patient safety have restricted residents' hours in the hospital. Hence, teachers and young doctors have diminished teaching and training opportunities. Students may have less exposure to a wide range of diseases, and their interaction with patients may occur after a diagnosis has been made. There is a need for uniform safe clinical practice opportunities for students, such as simulations. The use of simulations can optimize the chances that novices learn the skills needed in clinical settings and that experts can refine their skills. This entry discusses the reasons for using simulation in the health sector, the need for fidelity of

the simulation to actual situations in the field, and examples of simulations used in medicine.

Medical-based simulation provides trainees with standardized and safe learning opportunities through repeated specific skills training with guided practice. A prominent advantage of medical simulation is that curriculum goals can be created based on learners' needs rather than patients' needs. Learners need an effective learning environment where they can practice their skills in a safe environment without risk to patients. Simulation training can lead to a reduction in medical errors and increase patient safety. For example, virtual reality simulators are promising tools for training residents in laparoscopic and endoscopy procedures. Unlike errors in the real world, errors in a simulated setting provide opportunities for learners to identify their limitations and practice skills with corrective feedback. Teachers can create and customize learning environments that model and scaffold individual or team competencies. Medical simulations can help learners by tracking their performance over time, providing comparisons with experts' performance, adjusting difficulty level based on their performance, and providing cognitive props or scaffolds to enhance their problem-solving strategies and metacognition.

Aspects of Fidelity in Simulation

Criticism of medical simulation is often influenced by skepticism regarding the transferability of the skills learned in the simulation environment to the clinical setting. Some evidence from other high-risk domains such as aviation and combat situations have shown that the fidelity, or degree to which the characteristics of the simulation match those of the real situation, accounts for transfer of the skills. Albert J. Rehmann and colleagues propose two classes of simulator fidelity depending on the nature of the cues they provide: (a) equipment fidelity, which refers to the degree of duplication of the appearance and feel of the real system; and (b) environmental or psychological fidelity, which concerns the duplication of visual and sensory cues. Simulators can include one or both types of cues, in which case they are called *high-fidelity simulators*. Fidelity dimensions can serve as a blueprint for designing training objectives in medical simulations according to trainees' needs and levels of proficiency. High fidelity is not required for all skills or by all trainees.

Team training simulations, specifically those involving multidisciplinary teams, support whole task trainers, often through the use of high-fidelity simulators such as human patient simulation (HPS) mannequins. HPS are mannequins that are fully integrated with computer software that supports the development of preplanned scenarios. HPS can be programmed to produce vital signs, to respond to medical interventions, and to interact with clinicians like a regular patient does. Team-based simulations are performed in environments that account for high levels of equipment fidelity and, most importantly, for psychological fidelity, which allows modeling the environmental cues and the stressful conditions of the actual work setting. Team-based simulations are mainly used in emergency medicine and trauma teams, anesthesiology crews, and neonatal care.

Team-based simulations are suitable for training and assessing the coordination skills required for effective team performance. For instance, teams can be exposed to scenarios that emphasize the implementation of cognitive strategies needed for team effectiveness. Skills such as decision-making processes, communication strategies, leadership behaviors, and the development of shared representations of the general task and their own individual tasks (referred to as shared mental models) are all supported within team-based simulations.

In addition, team-based simulation provides an excellent platform for looking at the development of teamwork skills during a training program. More recently, Ilian Cruz-Panesso, Kevin Lachapelle, and Susanne P. Lajoie found that team performance can evolve effectively in a relatively short time, within three simulations. However, learning is not linear; it can increase and dip. These learning dips can be explained as periods where learners are having difficulty sorting relevant from irrelevant information. Time and practice are needed before learning translates into competence.

Examples of Simulation Used in Medicine

A particular example of medical-based simulation is BioWorld, which supports clinical reasoning. Clinical reasoning is a process that physicians and health professionals use to make decisions about diagnoses and treatment of patients. The development of effective clinical reasoning requires sustained practice. BioWorld presents learners with a hospital simulation in which they are asked to diagnose a simulated patient by interpreting symptoms, conducting diagnostic tests, prioritizing evidence, and collecting appropriate information. As learners advance, they are prompted to post case evidence to a virtual notepad, which remains visible throughout the case. After solving the case on their own, students are presented with a comparison of their solution with an expert solution. Several features of BioWorld, such as the virtual notepad and the expert solution, help students increase self-assessment skills as well as improve metacognitive awareness.

Although computer-based simulations have been mainstream in medical simulation since the 1980s, other low-tech simulation techniques have been used to provide training in a variety of professional skills, including patient-centered skills and interview skills. For instance, human role-playing between the medical student and standardized patient is one low-tech simulation of the clinical setting. The standardized patient (SP) technique consists of actors who have been trained to portray real patients and who provide medical students with feedback after the performance. SPs are useful for firsthand training and assessing clinical skills, such as medical history taking, performing physical examinations, and educating and advising the patient.

The use of two or more simulation techniques can help to foster emotional regulation and communication skills in cross-cultural medical students. More recently, the team at the Advanced Technologies for Learning in Authentic Settings (ATLAS) Lab at McGill University integrated low-tech simulation techniques, such as SPs and video-based simulations (e.g., video vignettes) into an online problem-based learning (PBL) environment to provide young clinicians in multicultural contexts with real-time facilitation in learning to communicate bad news to patients. Asian and North American students individually delivered bad news to an SP, playing the role of a Middle Eastern patient, who was accompanied by a formal translator. SPs were instructed to show emotional reactions including questioning behavior, crying, and concern of death. Video vignettes of expert physicians from Asia and North America helped model effective communication skills, and PBL sessions, with facilitators from both continents, supported collaborative knowledge construction.

Susanne P. Lajoie, Ilian Cruz-Panesso,
Kevin Lachapelle

See also Simulation-Based Learning; Situated Learning; Virtual Learning Environments

Further Readings

Allen, J., Buffardi, L., & Hays, R. (1991). *The relationship of simulator fidelity to task and performance variables* (Technical Report No. ARI-91-58). Alexandria, VA: Army Research Institute.

Baker, D., Gustafson, S., Beaubien, J., Salas, E., & Barach, P. (2005). Medical teamwork and patient safety: The evidence-based relation. *Literature Review. AHRQ Publication No. 05-0053, April 2005. Agency for Healthcare Research & Quality.* Rockville, MD: AHRQ.

Cruz-Panesso, I. (2011). *Medical team effectiveness in a simulated-based learning environment.* (Unpublished master's thesis). McGill University, Montreal, Canada.

Cruz-Panesso, I., Lachapelle, K., & Lajoie, S. (2010, September). *Practice makes perfect: The learning curve on a simulation-based trauma team course*. Poster presented at The Royal College's International Conference on Residency Education, September 23–25, Ottawa, Canada.

Ericsson, K. A. (2004). Deliberate practice and the acquisition and maintenance of expert performance in medicine and related domains. *Academic Medicine, 79*(10), 70–81.

Gaba, D. M. (2004). The future vision of simulation in health care. *Quality & Safety in Health Care, 13*(Supplement 1), 2–10.

Issenberg, S. B., McGaghie, W. C., Petrusa, E. R., Lee, D., & Scalese, R. J. (2005). Features and uses of high-fidelity medical simulations that lead to effective learning: A BEME systematic review. *Medical Teaching, 27*(1), 10–28.

Lajoie, S. P. (2009). Developing professional expertise with a cognitive apprenticeship model: Examples from avionics and medicine. In K. A. Ericsson (Ed.), *Development of professional expertise: Toward measurement of expert performance and design of optimal learning environments* (pp. 61–83). Cambridge, UK: Cambridge University Press.

Lajoie, S. P., Naismith, L., Hong, Y. J., Poitras, E., Cruz-Panesso, I., Ranellucci, . . . & Wiseman, J. (2013). Technology rich tools to support self-regulated learning and performance in medicine. In R. Azevedo & V. Aleven (Eds.), *International handbook of metacognition and learning technologies* (pp. 229–242). New York, NY: Springer.

Lane, J. L., Slavin, S., & Ziv, A. (2001). Simulation in medical education: A review. *Simulation Gaming, 32*(3), 297–314.

Websites

ATLAS Lab: http://www.mcgill.ca/atlas-lab

BioWorld: http://www.mcgill.ca/atlas-lab/projects/bioworld

Learning Environments Across Disciplines: http://www.leads partnership.ca

LEARNING IN THE MANUFACTURING SECTOR WITH SIMULATED SYSTEMS

Before technology and machinery, manufacturing came in the form of items produced by hand. The apprentice would work with the master, learning the production process, and the craft would be passed down through generations. Although this apprenticeship model may still remain in some forms, it has been ousted by mass manufacturing, which has automated, simplified, and expedited the production of goods. By the beginning of the 19th century, the Industrial Revolution changed production (through automation of processes that would normally be done by hand) and forced manufacturing companies to train their employees to adapt to these changes and use new technologies as well.

Along these lines, the emergence of the assembly line required workers to learn one small task as part of a larger production line (i.e., placing a tire on a car, then passing it to another worker to secure the bolts). Henry Ford notably perfected and automated this process in 1913; workers were then evaluated on their speed and quality, not necessarily their ability to master an entire craft. As long as they could do their jobs quickly and accurately, workers were considered productive. Yet, as production continued to move toward automation, speed, and accuracy, companies sought ways to train employees with these principles in mind.

Many of the same values remain today with respect to training employees in the manufacturing sector as they were in Ford's days. Companies need employees to accurately produce quality goods safely and quickly. Just as the manufacturing process continues to be influenced by newer, enhanced technologies, so is the training of workers. Companies employ simulated systems as part of the training process to teach workers how to do their jobs with competence and proficiency. This entry discusses how simulated systems work, how they are used to train employees in manufacturing, and the potential for their use to expand in training workers for manufacturing jobs.

Simulated Systems

Hands-on learning is one of the most effective ways to teach someone a task. The process is often informal where one worker watches another and eventually transitions into actually doing the job. In other situations, it is a more formalized training process, where the worker is shown how to do a task, and then is tested on that task until he or she successfully meets certain goals. However, as companies continue to expand and technology continues to change, it is often difficult for management to keep up with training demands. Simulated systems are a potential solution to fill this training need.

Simulated systems can automate a training process via a virtual environment or a computer-based simulation of a real-world setting. Simulated systems allow for individualized training of workers en masse, and they can be adapted and changed quickly when needed. For example, consider a mass retailer who has adopted a new cash register system across all of its many stores. The retailer must train as many as 10,000 cashiers and management staff on how to use the new system. Without a simulated systems approach, the operations staff would most likely designate several individuals to train the management team, who would then arrange times to train the cashiering staff, and so forth in a broad train-the-trainer approach. This approach would most likely be time consuming, and take months to roll out to necessary staff.

Consider the same scenario using a simulated system. A simulated cashier environment led by a computer-based program and virtual instructor guides the retailer's employees through the new changes to the system. The training can be done when not working on the actual system and results are reported immediately and directly to management. This simulated system has eliminated the need for inconvenient scheduling, while saving time and money.

Simulated systems include any type of computer-based or virtual training that simulates the worker's real-world environment. As described in the previous scenario, simulated systems offer a hands-on, practical application and demonstration of skills in a computer-based learning environment and allow testing, assessment, practice, and repeated training. The use of simulated systems training has expanded to include nearly every sector, including prominent use in the retail, health care, manufacturing, military, and hospitality industries. In the medical field in particular, simulated systems allow surgeons to learn how to use new equipment and the latest technologies before working on real patients. In the military sector, simulated systems can help train pilots to fly new aircraft before they even set foot on the actual plane. Simulated systems continue to expand as a cutting-edge, technology-based approach to enhancing, or even replacing, former training methods. This holds true for the manufacturing sector as well.

Simulated Systems in Manufacturing

Going back to the example of Ford and the assembly line, imagine if simulated systems were available in the early 20th century. In Ford's time, workers had to be shown how to do certain tasks in the production of cars. One master worker would show newer workers, the newer workers would practice, and so on. If production changes were implemented or a new model was introduced, those workers would need to be retrained, making it fairly difficult to train thousands of workers across three different time shifts. Ford would have benefitted greatly from a simulated system. Today, a virtual model of the production line with specific, practical application and testing showing how to assemble a new part could be seamlessly rolled out to workers, saving time, money, and disruption to the production floor.

Because of the efficiencies offered by simulated systems, these learning tools are becoming an integrated part of manufacturing training programs in the present day. Workers are introduced to new processes, procedures, and technologies in computer-based environments where they practice, learn, and demonstrate tasks before moving to a live situation. In addition to training, these systems allow companies to test new procedures to learn how to remedy potential issues or problems as well and to identify competencies useful for promotion.

Complex tasks that require multiple steps can be streamlined via a simulation before they are implemented. For example, a complex series of stages for manufacturing a product can be tested, revised, and changed via this type of system, making the process more simplified and efficient. As workers learn new ways to approach processes, the company, in turn, saves money and resources in both the training and manufacturing processes.

Implications and Future Directions for Simulated Systems

Although organizations continue to embrace simulated systems training within manufacturing environments, it is still not yet as prevalent in manufacturing as it is in other areas (e.g., medicine or the military sector). However, this approach with respect to training workers shows promise, particularly as a means to streamline processes. Learning through simulated systems also allows large numbers of workers to learn tasks in an efficient, cost-effective manner. As technology continues to change, the way organizations train workers must shift as well. Simulated systems are an effective way to make this type of change and will continue to affect the way workers in the manufacturing sector learn their jobs.

Karen L. Milheim and William D. Milheim

See also Learning With Simulations; Simulation Applications in Engineering Education; Simulation-Based Learning; Training Using Virtual Worlds; Virtual Learning Environments

Further Readings

Carman, M. (2013). The power of simulation-based learning. *Training & Development, 40*(4), 18, 18–20.

Jahangirian, M., Eldabi, T., Naseer, A., Stergioulas, L. K., & Young, T. (2010). Simulation in manufacturing and business: A review. *European Journal of Operational Research, 203*(1), 1–13.

Lu, X., Qi, Y., Zhou, T., & Yao, X. (2012). Constraint-based virtual assembly training system for aircraft engine. In G. Lee (Ed.), *Advances in computational environment science* (pp. 105–112). Heidelberg, Germany: Springer-Verlag.

Sun, S. H., & Tsai, L. Z. (2012). Development of virtual training platform of injection molding machine based on VR technology. *The International Journal of Advanced Manufacturing Technology, 63*(5–8), 609–620.

LEARNING IN THE MARKETING SECTOR WITH SIMULATED SYSTEMS

The American Marketing Association (AMA) defines *marketing* as activities, institutions, and processes involved in creating, communicating, delivering, and exchanging offerings of value for customers, clients, partners, and society. The United Kingdom's Chartered Institute of Marketing defines *marketing* as management processes responsible for identifying, anticipating, and satisfying customer requirements for a profit. These two related definitions define the scope and positioning of marketing.

Peter Drucker sees marketing as a pervasive discipline that is the distinguishing and unique function of a business as a social and managerial process. The scope, pervasive nature, and social and management processes mean that simulated systems are especially appropriate tools for learning about marketing. Further, arguably, marketing people need to take pragmatic and proactive actions and have analytical abilities—all characteristics developed by simulated systems. This entry defines the socio-technical learning system, discusses the components of software simulations used for learning about marketing, and gives some examples of simulated systems used for learning about marketing.

The Socio-Technical Learning System

The learning system (see Figure 1) consists of the socio-technical system of individual learners, teams of learners, a tutor, and the simulation software. This is a feedback system in which learners repeatedly make the decisions that lead to simulated outcomes. Using simulated systems to provide learning is a dynamic process like a servomechanism. Jeremy Hall and Benita Cox discuss this in the context of the cognitive and affective dynamics that parallel the servomechanism's response and stability.

System Components

The socio-technical system's individual learners, learning teams, simulation software system, and a tutor each have different characteristics and needs.

Individual learners define learning needs and prior learning. For academic learners, without real-world experience, learning needs and prior learning are likely to be tightly focused around the same areas. But for experienced business people with extensive experience, learning needs and prior learning are likely to be diverse. Learning teams are necessary as the scope of a marketing learning means that an individual is not

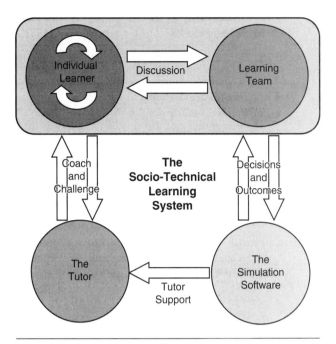

Figure 1   The socio-technical learning system

likely to have all of the necessary knowledge and skills. The diverse knowledge and experience of adult business learners is a key resource. The simulation software system consists of computer software. The tutor provides an expert resource that manages learning and drives it forward and in doing so enhances learning and helps transfer to the real world.

System Interactions

Each learning system component interacts with its neighbors, and these interactions affect and drive learning in a dynamic and changing way as the simulation progresses.

Individual learners will be building on their prior learning, reflecting on actions and outcomes, and through this, reforming and extending mental schema. The active and competitive nature of simulations means that they are likely to lead to deep cognition and engagement.

The interaction between an individual learner and the team builds on an individual's knowledge and skill and enriches learning as the team discusses its actions and as individuals promote and argue their viewpoints; discussion and argument are likely to ensure deep cognition. Learners teach each other and this enhances memorability.

Interaction between the team and the simulation software involves teams submitting or entering their decisions into the simulation software, which then determines outcomes that serve as feedback to the teams for analysis and reflection before they make the next set of decisions. This decision-submission-outcome-analysis process is commonly repeated six or more times as the teams manage the progress of their businesses in the simulated marketplace. As discussed by Hall and Cox, this dynamic response (the *natural* response of the simulation) has implications for the design and use of simulations because it affects the effectiveness and efficiency of learning.

The interactions between the simulation software, the tutor, individuals, and the team provide a regulation loop with the tutor proactively managing or overseeing the learning process. The simulation provides the tutor with information to support question answering and identifying learning opportunities and problems. This allows the tutor to answer learner-initiated questions. The simulation-provided data, coupled with an observation of learner behavior and actions, allow the tutor to coach and challenge the learners, where the coaching drives cognitive learning and the challenging deals with affective issues. The dynamic response of this and the design and use implications are discussed by Hall and Cox as the *managed* response of the simulation.

The Simulation Software System

The marketing simulation software system consists of five components: (1) marketing decisions, (2) marketing models, (3) marketing outcomes, (4) external parameters that influence the system, and (5) internal parameters that influence the system.

Marketing Decisions

Marketing decisions drive the simulated system. A simple but elegant model of marketing decisions is the 4Ps marketing mix model—product, place, price, and promotion—developed by E. Jerome McCarthy in 1960.

Product defines what is offered (as a product or service) to the customer, including tangible and intangible features and services. For example, tangible features might include product *power* and intangible features might include *trust* and *brand image*. *Place* defines who is being sold to (customers) and how the offering is distributed. *Price* defines the financial aspects of the deal with the client; besides setting prices, this may include discounts for volume, payment terms, and so on. *Promotion* decisions define communication with the customer—making the customer aware of what is offered, providing information about the product, creating emotional desire, and so forth.

Other decisions, such as market research or production, may be necessary to connect the marketplace to the business. Market research links to the marketplace to *anticipate* customer needs and production to ensure timely *delivery*.

Marketing Models

The simulation model consists of two major sub-models—the black box models where the marketing decisions and external market drivers are used to determine demand and the white box models where demand is turned into sales, revenue, and so forth, considering operational constraints (such as inventory and capacity).

Marketing Outcomes

The outputs from the marketing models are quantitative measures of marketing activity (volume, revenue, market share, penetration, etc.), operational results (costs, capacity use, inventory, etc.), measures of success (profits, profitability, liquidity, etc.), and qualitative comments that provide clues about subjective, emotional perceptions (such as "some customers feel the price is high").

External Market Drivers

External market drivers are customers, competition, technology, economic, and, perhaps, political, environmental, legal, and sociological drivers and change. Customer drivers are multifaceted, covering needs and wants (tangible, intangible, and emotional), potential demand, and communication aspects. Typically, they drive the black box models rather than the white box models.

Internal Operational Drivers

Internal operational drivers drive the internal operation of the business and comprise aspects such as capacity, resources, inventories, costs, and so on.

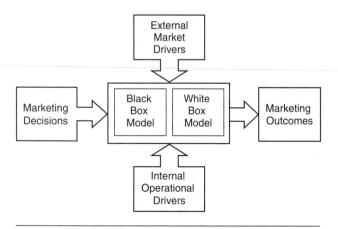

Figure 2   Marketing simulation software system

Typically, they drive the white box models rather than the black box models.

Examples of Marketing Learning Systems

Commonly, simulated systems are used to cover a range of information about marketing concepts, tactical marketing operations, and the impact of marketing on an entire business and its success. Four simulations developed by Hall—the Service Launch Simulation, the Sales Management Interactive Training Experience (SMITE), the Professionals Challenge, and the Global Operations simulation—are examples of how this can work.

Concept learning involves exploring basic marketing ideas, such as the product life cycle. The Service Launch Simulation explores the product life cycle from launch through growth to maturity and decline, as well as the impact of price and promotion on profit generation and cash flow.

Tactical operations learning involves exploring how a particular aspect of marketing, such as sales management, operates and impacts the business. SMITE explores the recruitment, development, and deployment of sales people and how this affects revenue, profits, and profitability of individual customers, individual sales people, regions, and the company as a whole.

Marketing appreciation learning is concerned with understanding the relationship between marketing and the rest of the business. Typically, the marketing learning system is embedded in a total enterprise simulation that is used to develop business acumen. The Professionals Challenge simulation was designed to build the business acumen of professional services company leaders and owners. From the marketing system viewpoint the learners must maintain and build the relationship with existing clients, get new clients, and develop business image and market presence for a portfolio of client groups.

Business strategy learning recognizes that a business's driving force is marketing, and the marketing learning system focuses on positioning a company relative to the external environment and building the internal operation to support this. The Global Operations simulation explores the strategic development of a company around the world with the company deciding all elements of the marketing mix (price, promotion, markets to serve, and new product development) and being constrained by competition, client needs and wants, production capacity and cash.

Jeremy J. S. B. Hall

See also Learning With Simulations; Simulation-Based Learning

Further Readings

Drucker, P. F. (1954). *The practice of management*. New York, NY: Harper.

Hall, J., & Cox, B. (1993). Computerised management games: The feedback process and servomechanism analogy. In *The simulation & gaming yearbook* (pp. 150–159). London, UK: Kogan Page.

Kotler, P. (1991). *Marketing management*. Englewood Cliffs, NJ: Prentice Hall.

McCarthy, J. E. (1960). *Basic marketing: A managerial approach*. Homewood, IL: Richard D. Irwin.

Websites

American Marketing Association definition of marketing: http://www.marketingpower.com/aboutama/pages/definitionofmarketing.aspx

Global Operations simulation: http://www.simulations.co.uk/Globeval.htm

Professionals Challenge simulation: http://www.simulations.co.uk/Professionals%20Challenge.htm

Service Launch simulation: http://www.simulations.co.uk/Seval.htm

SMITE (Sales Management Interactive Training Experience) simulation: http://www.simulations.co.uk/FUNCTN.HTM#SMITE

United Kingdom's Chartered Institute of Marketing: http://www.cim.co.uk/files/7ps.pdf

LEARNING OBJECTS

Learning objects are reusable components of instruction that can be combined into larger instructional structures and reused in other instructional contexts. The main idea of learning objects is to break educational content down into small (relative to the size of an entire course) or discrete instructional components that can be reused in various learning environments, especially in academia and industry. Such environments include computer-based training systems, interactive learning environments, intelligent computer-assisted instruction systems, distance learning systems, and collaborative learning environments. Examples of small learning objects include digital images or photos, live or prerecorded video or audio snippets, bits of text, and animations. Examples of larger learning objects that are also reusable include entire Web pages that combine text, images, and other media, and a complete instructional event, such as an online lecture. Learning objects are typically smaller, shorter, and more easily reconfigured than are traditional instructional media. Learning objects are especially important to the institutional technology of online learning and are part of a major change in the way that educational materials are designed, developed, and delivered to learners.

Learning objects go by a number of different names, including content objects, learning chunks, educational objects, information objects, intelligent objects, knowledge bits, knowledge objects, learning components, media objects, reusable curriculum components, nuggets, reusable information objects, reusable learning objects, testable reusable units of cognition, training components, and (reusable or reconfigurable) units of learning.

Learning objects are self-contained and discrete, and they can be used independently of other objects. Learning objects may be used in multiple contexts for multiple purposes, and they may be grouped together with a small set of related learning objects. They may also be used in traditional structures, such as regular courses.

Ideally, learning objects are modular, freestanding, transportable among applications and environments, and nonsequential (i.e., constituting a single sequence of instruction). They can be used to support a single learning objective. In principle, they should be accessible to broad audiences (i.e., adaptable to and usable by audiences beyond the original target audience). Indeed, in principle they should be accessible by any number of people along with different learning objects chosen by different learners and instructors. For example, as described by Susan Metros, an animated video that simulated the eruption of a volcano could be used in a geology course to explain volcanic eruptions, while having multiple other uses. It could also be used by a history class studying the eruption of Mount Vesuvius in 79 AD that destroyed the Roman cities of Pompeii and Herculaneum. The video might also be used in an animation course as an example of animation design. It might be used in a lecture or be included in online course materials, or watching the video might be a homework assignment for a course or be the basis for a homework writing assignment. A student might also use the video as part of a multimedia presentation to a class about research on volcanoes.

Learning objects are always identifiable by their metadata—each learning object has information about itself that allows it to be found by search engines. These data descriptors are known as *metadata tags*. The metadata associated with a learning object include the educational objective, the knowledge and skills required for successful use (i.e., prerequisites), the topic, the forms of interaction involved (text, voice, etc.), and technology requirements. Metadata should be coherent and unitary, so that a limited number of metatags can capture the main idea of the content. Also, to make it easy to reconfigure and repurpose

them within a different context without losing the essential value or meaning of the text, data, or images, learning objects should not be embedded in or formatted using proprietary software.

To be effective, learning objects should have consistent language and terminology. The information should be easily accessible and comprehensible. For example, technical or detailed information should be presented in tables, bullets, or columns rather than in sentences and paragraphs. The information should be organized for on-screen consumption (dense text should be broken down into smaller bits of text). There should not be backward-forward referencing across learning objects because each learning object is intended to stand on its own and be independent of other objects. However, there should be a uniform writing tone and visual style across related learning objects likely to be used together. The language and content should be appropriate for a broad audience (e.g., no regional terminology or audience-specific humor). Colorful writing should be avoided. Information in one object that requires additional support can reference other learning objects but should do so without violating modularity and without making the learning experience confusing or difficult to use.

Without context, learning objects can be confusing, misleading, or meaningless. After selection of appropriate learning objects based on the needs of learners, the next task is to provide the appropriate context. The context should provide a brief but broad perspective that puts a learner in the position of being able to decide which learning objects to explore in more detail. Learning objects should empower learners by enabling them to participate more actively in the use and contextualization of information. When it comes to learning objects, context has two functions: to orient learning objects to their most likely contexts, and to provide cues for learners to apply their own contexts.

Learning objects will typically include identifiers such as the language of the content (English, French, Chinese, etc.), the subject area (mathematics, sociology, physics, etc.), descriptive text and descriptive keywords, its version number, its status (how recent or old it is, because learning objects have a "life cycle"), the nature of the content (text, webpages, images, sound, video), a glossary of terms (including terms, definitions, and acronyms), quizzes and assessments (including questions and answers), cost, copyrights and other restrictions on use, its relationships to other courses, and its educational level (which grade, which age, the typical learning time, and the difficulty level).

Learning objects have been compared to LEGO pieces and Lincoln Logs because learning objects are typically small pieces of instruction that can be assembled into some larger instructional structure and reused in a variety of situations. This comparison may be misleading, however, because it implies that any learning object may be combined with any other learning object, may be assembled in any way, and is simple to use—these implications are all false. A more apt analogy for learning objects may be the atom, although it is something that naturally exists, rather than being an artifact like a learning object. Not every atom is combinable with every other atom, atoms can be assembled only in ways that are consistent with their structure, and assembling atoms is something that requires knowledge and skill. Learning objects will not be instructionally useful if they are believed to be combinable with every other learning object. The idea that learning objects can be put together in any way is what is known as *theory neutrality*. However, without any instructional theory behind combining learning objects, the combinations of learning objects will more than likely fail to be instructionally useful. Finally, the idea that anyone may combine learning objects without any training and still produce instructionally useful combinations has no evidence to support such a claim.

Learning objects are an improvement over traditional instructional media insofar as learning objects are more flexible. Because they are designed to be used in multiple contexts, they can be reused much more easily. They can increase the speed and efficiency of instructional development because they save teachers and instructional designers the time of breaking instructional materials down into constituent parts. Learning objects can also be updated more easily, and their metadata tags allow them to be searched for much more easily. It is also possible to customize learning objects according to individual and organizational needs. The modularity of learning objects allows the maximization of software that customizes content by permitting the recombination and delivery of content at the level of granularity that is desired. Learning objects also allow organizations to set their own specifications regarding the design, development, and presentation of learning objects based on their needs, while retaining interoperability with other learning systems. Learning objects also are ideally suited to competency-based learning, which has gained a great deal of interest among educators and employers. Learning objects allow the adaptive competency-based approach, by matching learning object metadata with individual competency. Finally, from the standpoint of business, the value of any content is increased every time it is reused. This is because costs are reduced when new design is avoided and because it is possible to sell the learning objects to others, or to provide them to partners in more than one context.

James Edwin Mahon

See also Accelerated Learning; Collaborative Learning With Technology; Cultural Considerations in Technology-Enhanced Learning and Instruction; Distance Learning for Professional Development; History of Educational Technology; Internet: Impact and Potential for Learning and Instruction; Massive Open Online Courses; Metatagging of Learning Objects and Apps

Further Readings

Churchill, D. (2007). Towards a useful classification of learning objects. *Educational Technology Research & Development*, 55, 479–497.

Longmire, W. (2000). *A primer on learning objects*. Retrieved from http://vcampus.uom.ac.mu/cmcp/ILT6011/Res270704/LOR-RLO/Longmire-RLO-primer.doc

McGee, P., & Katz, H. (2005). A learning object life cycle. In G. Richards (Ed.), *Proceedings of World Conference on E-Learning in Corporate, Government, Healthcare, and Higher Education 2005* (pp. 1405–1410). Chesapeake, VA: AACE.

Metros, S. (2004). *Learning objects*. In A. Distefano, K. Rudestam, & R. Silverman (Eds.), *Encyclopedia of distributed learning* (pp. 294–298). Thousand Oaks, CA: Sage. doi:10.4135/9781412950596.n100

Wiley, D. (1999). *The post-LEGO learning object*. Retrieved from http://opencontent.org//docs/post-lego.pdf

Wiley, D. (2000). *The instructional use of learning objects: Online version*. Retrieved from http://reusability.org/read

LEARNING WITH MODELS

Learning with models constitutes a class of experience-based learning processes that uses a constructed model of the world (or a world of thought) to support a learning experience. A model is a representation of something in the world—a kind of abstraction that may range from a set of assumptions to the basis for a complex and realistic simulation. The learning experience is abstract because the model is not the world but an idealized, focused, or reduced version of an understanding about something in the world, such as a representation of expert understanding or a process. The reasons for using models vary from safe or risk-free initial experiences (e.g., in flight simulation) to carefully guiding the learners to a more complex understanding of a complex problem-solving situation. The goal is to create an experience that contradicts a learner's current understanding or change a belief about the topic. But the use of a model to support learning should also allow learners to make use of current understanding and prior knowledge. This entry first discusses the use of models in support of learning, how experts approach models, and the importance of feedback in the learning environment. The entry then discusses the principles of effective learning with models.

If a learning model involves expert knowledge, that knowledge represents an analytic model of the world, as shown in Figure 1. An expert model is less complex and less complete than the real world, as is any model. It subsumes the understanding of the expert on a specific subject matter with a specific focus on the experts' domain.

Models have many uses in support of learning, and one model may be used for multiple purposes. For instance, a model of a medical operation may be used by a counselor to teach about a healing process or by a surgeon to teach about the actual operation. In any case, a second model is created to direct the learning experience, as shown in Figure 1. The learner will interact with this synthetic model of the operation in a simulated learning environment. It is synthetic because the experts design it from their analytic understanding for the purpose of facilitating learning. The learners interact and experience within the context of the synthetic model (the model of the learning environment: the LE model). They use their understanding (the learners' model: the L model) to try to explain to themselves what they experience—a reflection process that may be conscious or unconscious. Even if learners feel like they are learning something completely new, this is almost never the case because new learning builds on prior knowledge and learning. Figure 1 shows the importance of the experts' analytic model in the design and development of a learning environment and its role in didactics as well as guidance and feedback. Although the expert

model is important, gaining access to the learners' models is especially important and quite challenging because it needs to occur during a learning experience or very soon thereafter.

Experts Approach Models Differently

An expert may see the important aspects of the LE model by recognizing the available parts of his or her knowledge, but a learner may draw all kinds of conclusions and have a variety of misconceptions. He or she may focus on circumstantial parts of the experience, misjudge the simplifications, or overgeneralize case aspects. When investigating an LE model, experts might not even recognize all the different (erroneous or unintended) impacts such a model may have on a learner: Expert knowledge involves a kind of bias that may lead experts to overestimate the didactic range of the LE model and underestimate the unintended effects of the learning experience.

The Importance of Feedback

To focus on the correct aspects, the learners need ongoing feedback throughout the learning experience. This feedback should relate to the learners' understanding. A completely self-guided search for feedback by the learner is—even with explicit generic prompting—not likely to succeed. Before a learner can generate his or her own feedback, the learner needs to know that something has gone wrong and have at least a vague understanding of where the misconception is located. A learning environment that includes an expert model and

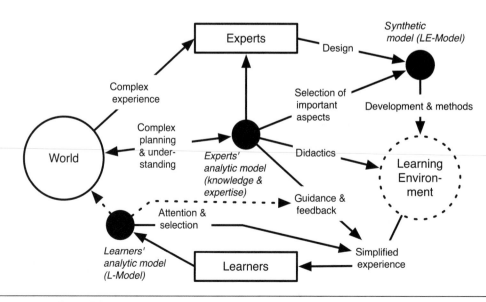

Figure 1   Learning with models

that creates a dynamic learner model is in principle capable of helping a learner interpret progress of learning and generate relevant and timely feedback to support appropriate knowledge development.

Principles

There are generic principles for reducing the chance of unintended knowledge construction. When an LE model is designed, it is important to have *analytic access* to an expert model of the world that resembles the same scope of the task (or any other interaction with the model) that accompanies the learning experience within the learning environment. This includes understanding before the task in the domain, reflection on the processes during the task, and expert's reflection after the task as well as retrospectively when confronted with the expert's performance on the task.

The *epistemic access* is the learner-oriented counterpart. Only if the learners can use their prior experience and are allowed and encouraged to contradict and build on it in sufficiently small steps along the way will they carefully adjust their understanding. This, however, requires an opportunity and time for real *puzzlement* induced and maintained by the learning environment and feedback. During the process of *puzzlement* or cognitive conflict, learners need opportunities to distinguish key aspects from circumstantial information. If they are puzzled, they will use every available resource to reconcile the information—as long as they do not quit and get frustrated. Good cover stories will, however, come with enriched circumstantial information, be it just to make them realistic. The cover story is provided by the learning environment to make the task more plausible to the learner and to give the task a realistic background. For a cover story to make sense, it also needs circumstantial information that does not convey any important parts of the model—for instance, a location or a gender of an individual within the cover story. Even if the gender does not matter in the particular context of the model, the learner could still use this information and try to construct sense out of it, especially when puzzlement is involved. Thus, the *puzzlement* needs to be carefully guided during the work with embedded stories.

The learning experiences need to be embedded in a *diversity of surfaces* to prevent repetitions of the same experience from strengthening the intended expertise and the misconceptions alike. A learning environment thus needs to come with many scenarios for the same goal—for instance, landing a plane in many different cities under many different circumstances in a flight simulator. Should the learner create or modify an L model that is not specific to a very limited task—in other words, when any kind of transfer is desired—the learning environment needs to *decontextualize* the experience from the context of the learning experience. If the learning experience with the model aims at world-like complexity, the environment needs a *multiplicity of goals and of the performance evaluation*. The output criteria for the learners need to be diverse; otherwise, a single solution procedure will develop.

Of course, in some cases a strict sequence of events may be desired. The difference lies in the reason why a sequence is carried out in a specific way. While learning with models, the learner should base his or her reasoning on the change within the L model, as shown in Figure 1. Single-goal learning environments can be prone to a simplified output behavior: If there is another way to create performance—for example, by applying a trick or fast trial-and-error strategies—the intended knowledge may not be constructed within the learner but rather a behavior that circumvents the path to the output. The same holds true for performance evaluation. There should be more than one performance indicator for the evaluation. Most of the time, a verbal reflection will help to uncover misconceptions. To describe learning within the learning environment, it is necessary to have a diagnostic access to learning in addition to simple performance output, which means measuring change at multiple points during the learning process. Having an insight into the current L model at each point in time may help but requires substantial resources not every learning environment may have.

Conclusion

Fulfilling these learning-with-models principles is a complex task in itself that requires expertise on learning with models. If the principles are applied with care and with sufficient knowledge about the individual learners, the learners will make rich world-like experiences on their own and carefully change their beliefs about a topic, a task, or a reasoning process. The learning environment translates the model into something that can be experienced. The environments may take the form of simulations, analogies, problems of all sorts, tasks, reflections, or even simple dialogues or discourses, and many more: basically anything that can be affected systematically by a modeled understanding of the world. For learners, such environments are complex and demanding as well. Instructors need expertise on how to monitor and support such processes.

Pablo N. Pirnay-Dummer

See also Assessing Learning in Simulation-Based Environments; Formative Assessment; Learning by Modeling; Learning With Simulations; Management Flight Simulators; Model-Based Approaches; System Dynamics

Further Readings

Aïmeuer, E. (1998). Application and assessment of cognitive-dissonance in the learning process. *Journal of Universal Computer Science, 4*(3), 216–247.

Ifenthaler, D. (2009). Model-based feedback for improving expertise and expert performance. *Technology, Instruction, Cognition and Learning, 7*(2), 83–101.

Pirnay-Dummer, P., Ifenthaler, D., & Seel, N. M. (2012). Designing model-based learning environments to support mental models for learning. In D. H. Jonassen & S. M. Land (Eds.), *Theoretical foundations of learning environments* (pp. 55–90). New York, NY: Routledge.

Seel, N. M. (1995). Mental models, knowledge transfer and teaching strategies. *Journal of Structural Learning, 12*(3), 197–213.

Seel, N. M. (2003). Model-centered learning and instruction. *Technology, Instruction, Cognition and Learning, 1*(1), 59–85.

LEARNING WITH SIMULATIONS

An instructional simulation consists of a representation of an entity or process and is designed to model real-world objects or phenomena. People learn through simulations by interaction with the modeled system, the process, and the outcome. Two key features of simulations are that they implement a model or models of an observable system, and that they enable manipulation or interaction with the model.

The use of simulation in educational practice may date back to the 16th century. Simulations and their use in education have increased with the advent of computing technology that supports the representation of complex systems during the past 60 years. Instructional simulations have been applied in such diverse fields as health education, military strategies, lean processing, and business marketing.

Simulations and games are two concepts commonly used interchangeably. The primary reason for this confusion is the prominent usage of simulations within games. There are many examples of enormously popular simulation-based games such as the *Sim* series and *Tycoon* role-playing activities in which gamers use models of virtual, microcosmic worlds. Players of these simulations manipulate the success of these worlds through their interactions with them. Although these games employ the characteristics of instructional simulations, games contain elements of competition that have goals, constraints, and rules, with emphases on motivation and entertainment. Conversely, a simulation's primary function is the modeling of a real activity or situation based on fidelity.

The advantages of using simulations in education are apparent. Among these advantages are the compression of time and space, the reduction of safety risks, and the enhanced representation of complex systems. Simulations provide an environment in which learners can engage and test hypotheses by making mistakes without undesirable consequences. Learners receive feedback in response to their actions in a safe, controlled environment. Moreover, simulations help learners explore the effects of changes in real-life situations that take place too quickly or too slowly for normal observation. Further, simulation-based training is often less costly than live training. This entry describes the process of learning with simulations, paradigms of modeling in instructional simulations, and the challenges of designing and using instructional simulations.

Processes of Learning With Simulations

Developing instructional simulations requires an emphasis on educational factors rather than only on technological components. As pictured in Figure 1, the learning cycle can be conceptualized as a simulation intervention in an educational setting. The *instructional simulation* is the representation of the target system that is neither as complex nor realistic as it truly exists. The *modeling* process is the understanding of the structure or behavior of the target system, which is a simplification of the real, complex system. *Simulation* is a simplified system representation where learners can observe the consequences of their actions such as changes occurring as a result of variables, activities, and actions. Instructional simulations require an emphasis on educational factors such as learning goals, learning strategies, and learning activities. They are implemented as components of the process necessary for accomplishing the learning goals. The learning goals can be of different types: the process, the outcome of the process, or both. Simulations involve a wide range of strategic implementations, including microworlds, scientific discovery learning, experiential learning, virtual reality, role-playing, and simulation games. Learners manipulate the simulation by setting and controlling variables, making decisions and choices, or collecting data to observe the consequences of their actions. Instructional simulations also provide feedback to learners to help them achieve the learning goal.

Instructional simulations have been categorized in many ways based on paradigms of functionality, interactivity, and constructed knowledge. Researchers Ton de Jong and Wouter van Joolingen divided simulations in two main categories: operational and practical. Operational (procedural) simulations facilitate the learning of practical knowledge. Students perform a sequence of

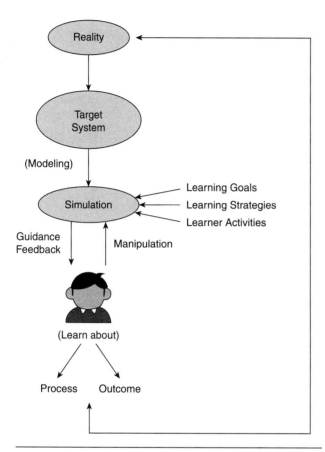

Figure 1   A simulation intervention in an educational setting

actions to reach a performance-based goal. For example, in a surgery simulation, the student can learn how to perform a surgery on a virtual model. Meanwhile, conceptual simulations, which focus on principles, concepts, and facts, facilitate the learning of conceptual knowledge. They provide an opportunity to learn relationships between variables by controlling and manipulating them. For example, in a simulation of a galactic system, the student can change the distance among planets and examine the consequences of gravity shifts. In short, instructional simulations facilitate learning of conceptual knowledge, practical knowledge, or both.

Paradigms of Modeling in Instructional Simulations

The process of designing and building a simulation is described as the modeling process. Many modeling paradigms have emerged, each with a unique modeling strategy. Popular paradigms can be identified as system dynamics models (SDM), agent-based models (ABM) and multiparadigm models. SDMs focus on conceptual knowledge, aiming to provide an environment in which

students learn about the system and its rules by manipulating and observing changes. SDMs are deductive models whose elements change dynamically based on the model that defines the relationships within the system. ABMs focus on individuals who interact on the basis of rules. ABMs are inductive models in which entities interact with each other and the environment according to these rules. Agents are the objects that control the models' behaviors. Learners can explore relationships through manipulation of the agents. An example of an agent-based simulation is *Small-World Trade Network Demo* developed by Mark McBride. This simulation examines the market efficiency of trades made between buyers and sellers of goods. Learners can change factors such as the number of buyers and sellers, seller costs, market efficiency, and other outcomes. System behavior emerges as the result of interaction among agents. In some cases, building a multiparadigm model based on various perspectives can be more appropriate than selecting a single paradigm. In this context, a dynamic learning environment is created for the agents. Students learn about the system and observe consequences by manipulating the variables. Students also behave as agents by interacting with each other and the environment.

Challenges in Designing and Using Instructional Simulations

Effective simulations involve both technological and instructional aspects that require seamless integration. The development of an instructional simulation is commonly a difficult and expensive process that requires the collaboration of expertise from different disciplines. It is a challenging and multidirectional process to develop a realistic and high-fidelity simulation by considering learning goals, strategies, guidance, and feedback. Development costs sometimes exist as one of the most crucial challenges to overcome. In some cases, training in real environments can be more cost-effective and feasible than implementing simulations.

A simulation is a controlled environment and only represents key elements of the real world. One of the critical educational goals is the transferring of learning from simulations back into the real world. This transfer depends on many factors—for example, the representation of reality. Although a simulation needs to represent the real world in the best possible way, it should have a simple, realistic, and perceivable design that results in high learner confidence and manageable cognitive load.

An additional issue is associated with novice learners. Several researchers claim that simulation-based learning is not appropriate unless learners already have a basic understanding of the modeled system. To address this issue, the recommended simulation design is to offer simple simulations at the beginning of instructional activities, and increase in complexity as learners become more knowledgeable with the materials and concepts being presented. Finally, designers and teachers need to have a definitive understanding and awareness of the learners to ensure effective instruction through simulations.

Brett E. Shelton and Cigdem Uz

See also Alignment of Games and Learning Goals; Games in Business and Industry Settings; Games in Medical Training; Games in Military Training; Mobile Tools and Technologies for Learning and Instruction; Simulation-Based Learning; Training Using Virtual Worlds

Further Readings

Alessi, S. M. (2000). Designing educational support in system-dynamics-based interactive learning environments. *Simulation & Gaming, 31*(2), 178–196.

Brant, G., Hooper, E., & Sugrue, B. (1991). Which comes first the simulation or the lecture? *Journal of Educational Computing Research, 7,* 469–481.

Cooper, J. B., & Taqueti, V. R. (2004). A brief history of the development of mannequin simulators for clinical education and training. *Quality & Safety in Health Care, 13*(1), 8–11.

De Jong, T., & van Joolingen, W. R. (1998). Scientific discovery learning with computer simulations of conceptual domains. *Review of Educational Research, 68,* 179–202.

Gibbons, A. S., & Fairweather, G. B. (1998). *Computer-based instruction: Design and development.* Englewood Cliffs, NJ: Educational Technology Publications.

Gibson, D., Prensky, M., & Aldrich Hershey, C. (2006). *Games and simulations in online learning: Research and development frameworks.* Hershey, PA: Idea Group.

Landriscina, F. (2013). *Simulation and learning. A model-centered approach.* New York, NY: Springer.

Ruben, B. D. (1977). Toward a theory of experience-based instruction. *Simulation & Gaming, 8*(2), 211–232.

Ruben, B. D. (1999). *Simulations, games, and experience-based learning: The quest for a new paradigm for teaching and learning.* Thousand Oaks, CA: Sage.

MANAGEMENT FLIGHT SIMULATORS

In general, simulators are designed to imitate aspects of events, situations, or operations to forecast future effects, outcomes, or the cause of a past event. Simulators are useful tools because they provide an environment that is safe, cost effective, flexible, and realistic. Because of improvements in technology, simulators are able to closely resemble the look and feel of real-world operations and processes. This entry discusses the history of management flight simulators, how they are used in the modern business environment, their use as instructional tools, their impact on learning, and examples of management flight simulators.

Although simulators are used in a variety of disciplines, one of the earliest adopters of these tools was aviation. Beginning in 1929 with the development of the first ground-based flight simulator, the Link Trainer, aviation has continuously incorporated various types of flight simulators into education and training. Because the flight environment is very complex, ill defined, and consists of many uncontrollable variables, simulators have proven extremely beneficial in that they can replicate the complexities and uniqueness of the flight environment in a compressed period, allowing for reflection and experimentation with various strategies. During actual flight scenarios, there can be a lack of closeness between the actual decision and subsequent analysis and feedback. Because the feedback time can be greatly reduced in a simulation, the impact of assumptions, decision making, and problem resolution can be determined quickly and safely. This type of experiential learning environment can greatly enhance the learning opportunity for participants and expansion of their mental models.

Business Management Environment

Similarly, the business management environment has become increasingly more dynamic and complex. Management decision making was once developed through one's steady progression via layers of management positions, but organizational structures are now becoming flatter, leading to the subsequent de-layering of management levels. These structural modifications greatly reduce the opportunities for managers to learn while progressing up the corporate ladder, thrusting them into decision-making roles much sooner. Knowledge and skills that were once acquired through years of experience now need to be obtained through other means.

Business management decision making is multifaceted. Technological advances and increasing interconnectivity have emphasized the need for managers to consider the dynamics of global events. Often, managers are facing novel situations and are forced to consider factors that are uncontrollable and unexpected, causing managerial choices to be far from trivial. Many decisions are made without the luxury of knowing the projected impact. Because of this, managers often bias their choices using past knowledge and experiences because of insufficient time to investigate new information and to avoid the risk of trying something unique.

Sound pilot decision making is essential to the safe completion of every flight. Every day pilots are responsible for operating aircraft in a highly unpredictable environment. Airlines would never consider placing a pilot into an operational environment without providing practical experience in a variety of complicated scenarios in flight simulators. These simulators enable pilots to evaluate available information regarding the flight environment and experience the effects of their decisions on the outcome of the flight. The use of simulation allows pilots to learn from their mistakes and determine better strategies for handling a multitude of situations. This type of experiential learning enables pilots to enhance their understanding and better predict the potential outcomes of their decisions.

Business managers exist in similar situations in that they are often operating in highly unpredictable environments. Though there may not be a risk to safety, there may be tremendous risk to the organization. Similar to aviation, management flight simulators provide virtual operating environments in which assumptions and strategies can be employed and results assessed in a shortened cycle time. Individuals can experiment with various strategies and learn from making a series of simulated decisions. Because management flight simulators compress time, these simulators can allow managers to experiment in a "safe" environment with multiple opportunities for action and reflection.

The ability to learn from experience in business can be nonexistent because a decision may be made but the effect may not become apparent until years later, or even after an individual has moved on to another job. Cause and effect are separated in time, so managers might not see the consequences of their actions. If results and feedback are not available, it is difficult to learn and improve.

Management Flight Simulators as Instructional Tools

Advocates of management flight simulators have proposed that these systems are extremely beneficial in disseminating content, whether it is terminology, principles, or procedures. Individuals are then provided opportunities to apply this content in experimental environments and be able to evaluate the results of their actions. Because there are low penalties for miscalculations, both financial and physical, participants can test a wide range of strategies to determine the best possible outcomes. The intent is that the lessons learned during the simulation will be transferrable and applicable in real-world situations, allowing for improved performance in actual operational situations.

Management flight simulators are being used to a greater extent in industry to assist individuals in understanding the impact of their decisions on corporate initiatives. The dynamics of the business environment do not allow managers to experiment with implementation of various strategies or decisions, leaving them to construct plausible outcomes because the real environment lacks the closeness between when decisions are made and when meaningful feedback may be available. The use of

simulation, however, can provide a quicker response time because many simulators can project the impact of a decision as it would appear in several months or several years. Feedback regarding the result of a decision can only be effective if cause and effect are closely related in time.

The use of management flight simulators can also provide ancillary benefits to an organization. During simulated activities, participants are able to experiment with strategies that may affect various organizational departments. Discovering the consequences of these dynamic interactions allows a better understanding of strategic effectiveness across the organization. With thorough feedback and debriefing, management participants can expand the depths of their procedural and conditional knowledge. In addition, these experiences can be motivational and enhance the participants' self-efficacy as decision makers.

For many of these same reasons, management flight simulators are being used regularly in collegiate business programs as well. For individuals who are relatively unfamiliar with the nuances and intricacies of business, the use of management flight simulators can provide an expansive learning environment where students can learn terminology, processes, and procedures and recognize the interrelationships among various business functions, such as accounting, marketing, and operations, among others. The execution of business decisions and strategies may seem relatively simple during class discussions or case-study analyses, but simulation can demonstrate the difficulty of implementing these in a real-world setting. This type of active learning allows the student to be more engaged, which could enhance the retention of knowledge.

Before a management flight simulator can be used as an effective tool, it is critical that it be incorporated into instruction appropriately. To begin with, it is imperative to determine whether the use of a management flight simulator is the best methodology. Simulation may not always be the best instructional strategy to use; other means of instruction may be more effective, depending on the knowledge and experience of the participants relative to the desired outcomes. If simulation is used, it is important to inform the participants of the learning objectives. Often, simulation may involve many elements, making it difficult for participants to extract necessary knowledge from the experience.

Impact of Management Flight Simulators on Learning

Although management flight simulators are used extensively, there is little conclusive research of their impact on learning. Much of the research that has reported increases in learning has relied on the self-reports of students and instructors. Those studies that did focus on valid assessments of learning found improvements in the lower levels of cognition, such as the remember, understand, and apply domains of the revised Bloom's taxonomy. Efforts to measure higher levels of cognition, such as the analyze, evaluate, and create domains, have been limited to participant self-reports of their perceived improved abilities—that is, students tend to believe they have learned. Because of this, the ability to specify the impact of management flight simulators on learning is limited.

Examples of Management Flight Simulators

John Sterman is the Jay W. Forrester Professor of Management in the Massachusetts Institute of Technology Sloan School of Management and is considered the forerunner in the use of management flight simulators to teach the dynamics of corporate operations. Sterman developed the beergame to teach the dynamics of supply chains, distribution, and the fundamental principles of effective management. A taxonomy of other management flight simulators can be found at the Association for Business Simulation and Experiential Learning website.

Mary Niemczyk

See also Learning With Simulations; Professional Development Tools and Technologies; Simulation-Based Learning

Further Readings

Anderson, P., & Lawton, L. (2008). Business simulations and cognitive learning: Developments, desires and future directions. *Simulation & Gaming, 40,* 193–216.

Bakken, B., Gould, J., & Kim, D. (1992). Experimentation in learning organizations: A management flight simulator approach. *European Journal of Operational Research, 59,* 167–182.

Lane, D. (1995). On a resurgence of management simulations and games. *Journal of the Operational Research Society, 46*(5), 604–625.

Websites

Association for Business Simulation and Experiential Learning list of gaming/simulation packages and books: http://absel.org/gaming-packages-by-abselites

Massive Open Online Courses

A massive open online course (MOOC) is a kind of online (Internet-based) course that typically involves a large number of students completing a particular course of study. A MOOC has some dimension of openness in that it may use open educational resources (OERs, which are openly licensed) and students can often enroll and participate free of charge. MOOCs arose to prominence in the late 2000s and have experienced rapid growth in North America and across the world. Recently MOOCs have been widely hyped as representing a fundamental shift in both the practice and business of education. The hype may be decreasing now as the realities of designing, managing, and paying for free large-scale courses present obstacles that institutions must be prepared to overcome. This entry first describes MOOCs, lists some of the entities developing them, and discusses how the courses first developed. The entry then discusses some of the benefits and drawbacks of MOOCs.

Defining a MOOC

MOOCs can be defined by examining the four words that make up the acronym MOOC. The first word is *massive*. MOOCs can be distinguished from other courses in that a MOOC is structured so that hundreds or even thousands of students can be a part of the course, and this large enrollment is expected. The MOOC is designed to accommodate massive enrollment and participation. This may mean that students must self-organize to support themselves during the course. MOOCs are *open* in that they typically feature open enrollment for anyone who wants to participate in a particular course. The openness factor of MOOCs is currently a point of contention, in that some MOOCs are more open than others in the licensing of the content used in such courses. The use of OERs that are free for repurposing and reuse varies among MOOCs to the point that special terms have emerged such as *cMOOC*, denoting more openly licensed courses, and *xMOOC*, denoting courses that may be more closed and designed to scale without as much interaction.

MOOCs are by definition *online*—they are Web-based and usually asynchronous. This is because they are designed to serve a large number of students from many different geographic time zones. And they are *courses*, meaning they have beginning and ending points, learning objectives, assessments, and an instructor. This distinguishes MOOCs from other more informal learning opportunities that exist online such as learning via self-study or via one's personal learning network.

Entities Offering MOOCs

Several key entities are currently offering, supporting, or aggregating MOOCs or experiences that are similar to a MOOC. These include (among others) Coursera, Udacity, Udemy, edX, iversity, Peer 2 Peer University, Saylor.org, Academic Earth, FutureLearn, the Canvas

Network, and ALISON. Of course, many universities around the world are not part of the previously listed organizations or consortia and are offering MOOCs both as a service to learners and as a marketing and promotional tool for their traditional offerings. Universities may see MOOCs as an opportunity to, as economists and entrepreneurs say, "extend the brand" of the institution.

Key MOOC Developments

The term *MOOC* was coined in 2008 by Dave Cormier of the University of Prince Edward Island and senior research fellow Bryan Alexander of the National Institute for Technology in Liberal Education. The term emerged in the context of a course offered by Stephen Downes and George Seimens on connectivism, which enrolled more than 2,000 students, online, at no charge. This type of course was open-ended and was designed for peer interaction and creation and sharing of resources, in the spirit of the OER movement.

Another prominent early MOOC was at Stanford University, where in 2011 Sebastian Thrun and Peter Norvig offered Introduction to Artificial Intelligence, and more than 160,000 students enrolled. This early success motivated Thrun to found the commercial MOOC company Udacity. Soon after, Stanford professors Andrew Ng and Daphne Koller launched the commercial MOOC company Coursera. In the following year, the Massachusetts Institute for Technology (MIT) founded the not-for-profit MITx, and when Harvard University and the University of California at Berkeley joined the initiative, it was renamed edX.

Another key milestone for MOOCs came in 2013 when the Georgia Institute of Technology announced it would offer its master's degree in computer science in a MOOC format. The tuition would be $7,000, which was less than one fourth of the normal tuition for such a degree. In 2013, edX announced a partnership with Google to develop Open edX, an open source platform that would allow individuals or institutions to create and host MOOCs.

Benefits and Drawbacks of MOOCs

MOOCs have many attractive features, and institutions offer them and people participate in them for many reasons. From the student's point of view, MOOCs represent the opportunity to gain access to instruction from faculty and institutions that were previously inaccessible. Taking a course from a prestigious school such as Harvard, MIT, or Stanford would be out of reach for most of the world, but the MOOC offers that opportunity at the cost of only a reliable Internet connection. Although the MOOC is not the residential college course experience, it is much better than not having an opportunity to learn. A student can also usually participate in a MOOC at whatever level he or she desires, and even drop out (as many do), or come back to the archived course materials later. The course resources are typically always available, albeit minus the interaction with the instructor and classmates. MOOCs are relatively easy to offer in multiple languages and in any time zone because they are usually asynchronous.

From an institution's standpoint, offering a MOOC creates the opportunity to reach many more students than would be possible with in-person offerings. This can be viewed as part of the altruistic mission of a university to spread and create knowledge, or as a method to increase market share or at least "mindshare" for the institution and its reputation. Motivations for pursuing a MOOC initiative are likely mixed. More institutions are offering online courses and complete online degree programs even as enrollment at many higher education institutions is flat or declining, partly because of rising education costs. The competition for students is now a nationwide and international contest because of these online programs that make geography (a student's location or home state) irrelevant.

There are drawbacks for students in MOOCs. One primary issue is the lack of interaction with the instructor or with fellow students. Various MOOC designs attempt to address this, with opportunities such as discussion forums, polls, and peer grading. By virtue of its massive nature, however, such a course will not involve a close connection with the instructor. A student in a MOOC must be self-motivated and have the ability to self-regulate and be aware of his or her learning processes (metacognition), and set and meet goals. A MOOC will require significant student time and effort and a relatively high level of digital literacy. Often a MOOC requires the student to produce learning content and take a highly active role in the learning process. A related issue is that MOOCs have low completion rates, at least in percentages, compared with traditional courses. One might question if this is truly a concern because even with a high dropout rate, more students might complete a MOOC in one term than would be conceivable using traditional teaching methods. Still there are reasons why so many students drop out, whether it be the lack of interaction, the open-ended nature of a course, or the lack of "skin in the game"—that is, the course was free so the commitment to work hard and finish is low.

For the institution, there are drawbacks as well. A MOOC can attract significant publicity to accompany massive enrollment, and an instructional or technical failure would be much more publicized than would be the case with a typical university course. MOOCs can also require significant development resources in personnel, equipment, and time, each of which is a real cost. And the business model for MOOCs is currently an open question. Start-up companies such as Coursera and Udacity have received significant funding from venture capitalists, but it is still unclear how these companies will generate revenue. Perhaps advertising, or selling student data to potential employers, will offset development, delivery, and promotional costs. Another institutional issue is credentialing. If free MOOCs are recognized as credit-bearing courses, then why would a student pay to attend on-campus courses? And if MOOCs are not credit-bearing, then the attraction to them would decrease. Or participants would demand recognition of successful learning through some form, certificate, badge, or other recognized "credit" system. This issue of credit for MOOCs will be a key determinant for the future adoption of MOOCs.

Trey Martindale

See also Asynchronous Tools and Technologies; Badges and Skill Certification; Distance Learning for Degree Completion for Working Adults; Open Content Licensing; OpenCourseWare Movement

Further Readings

Chronicle of Higher Education. (2014). *What you need to know about MOOCs.* Retrieved from http://chronicle.com/article/What-You-Need-to-Know-About/133475

Daniel, J. (2012). Making sense of MOOCs: Musings in a maze of myth, paradox and possibility. *Journal of Interactive Media in Education, 2012*(3). Retrieved from http://jime.open.ac.uk/article/2012-18/html

Fini, A. (2009). The technological dimension of a massive open online course: The case of the CCK08 course tools. *The International Review of Research in Open and Distance Learning, 10*(5). Retrieved from http://www.irrodl.org/index.php/irrodl/article/view/643/1402

Glance, D. G., Forsey, M., & Riley, M. (2013, May 6). The pedagogical foundations of massive open online courses. *First Monday, 18*(5). Retrieved from http://firstmonday.org/ojs/index.php/fm/article/view/4350/3673

Guàrdia, L., Maina, M., & Sangrà, A. (2013). MOOC design principles: A pedagogical approach from the learner's perspective. *eLearning Papers, 33.* Retrieved from http://www.openeducationeuropa.eu/en/ download/file/fid/27126

Kop, R., Fournier, H., & Mak, J. S. F. (2011). A pedagogy of abundance or a pedagogy to support human beings? Participant support on massive open online courses. *The International Review of Research in Open and Distance Learning, 12*(7), 74–93.

Liyanagunawardena, T., Adams, A., & Williams, S. (2013). MOOCs: A systematic study of the published literature 2008–2012. *The International Review of Research in Open and Distance Learning, 14*(3), 202–227. Retrieved from http://www.irrodl.org/index.php/irrodl/article/view/1455/2531

McAuley, A., Stewart, B., Siemens, G., & Cormier, D. (2010). *The MOOC model for digital practice.* Charlottetown, Canada: University of Prince Edward Island. Retrieved from http://www.elearnspace.org/Articles/MOOC_Final.pdf

Rodriguez, C. O. (2012). MOOCs and the AI-Stanford like courses: Two successful and distinct course formats for massive open online courses. *European Journal of Open, Distance and E-Learning, 2012*(2). Retrieved from http://www.eurodl.org/?p=current&article&article=516

UBC Wiki (2014). MOOC resources. Retrieved from http://wiki.ubc.ca/Documentation:MOOC/Resources

Yuan, L., & Powell, S. (2013). *MOOCs and open education: Implications for higher education* [White paper]. Bolton, UK: Joint Information Systems Committee, Centre for Educational Technology and Interoperability Standards. Retrieved from http://publications.cetis.ac.uk/2013/667

MEASURING AND ASSESSING LITERACY SKILLS

Academic and workforce literacy skills are fundamental elements of competitive and global labor markets. Assessment and measurement programs are used to determine if appropriate levels of literacy are being achieved. Essential literacy skills include reading, document use, numeracy, writing, oral communication, interpersonal communication, thinking, and computer use. Because of the impact of computer technology and the Internet, literacy skills are now largely construed to include specific digital and information proficiency skills. Information-intensive skills require an increasingly sophisticated appreciation of the quality and reliability of information. Essential skills are foundational prerequisites for developing the ability to find needed information and critically evaluate information sources and content. This entry focuses on information and digital skills as literacy skills and discusses how assessment and measurement of such literacy skills function in education practices.

The Integration of Digital Competence

Information-driven economies and academic and business environments require more complex skills to enable the synthesis and analysis of information. The proliferation of information sources and rapidly changing information access and retrieval technologies necessitate information and digitally focused skills to enable problem solving, collaboration, and teamwork. Tasks that formerly had many manual and low-tech steps (e.g., job-hunting, employee testing, and employee onboarding) now involve complex interactions with employers, governments, and service providers of all types, and depend on digital knowledge. However, information and digital skills do not replace essential skills—they complement, enhance, and interact with them in a number of diverse ways.

In 2010, Renee Hobbs reported on the findings of the Knight Commission on the Information Needs of Communities in a Democracy. One of the commission's recommendations is to place a major focus on preparing teachers to integrate traditional and digital skills and overcome the organizational and knowledge obstacles that impede synergy. There is agreement that teaching literacy requires specialized skills. Another recommendation concerns the need to explore and define measures of digital literacy. Both of these recommendations relate to assessment and measurement of literacy skills.

Assessment of Literacy Skills

Assessment of literacy skills includes gathering and analyzing evidence to make informed and consistent judgments regarding learning effectiveness. Assessment of literacy skills is aligned with related practices such as curriculum development and the establishment of outcomes and measures.

There are multiple ways to classify assessment types. The classifications, including universal screening, progress monitoring, diagnostic or targeted, and outcome effectiveness, match well with identified discrete skills, although more work has to be done to handle overlapping and interacting skill groups.

Valid and useful assessments depend on the expression of clear, explicitly stated purposes, goals, and learning outcomes. Assessment strategies must ensure that sufficient evidence is collected to make a sound judgment of competency. In many cases, workforce assessments rather than educational assessments can be used because evidence is available to demonstrate competence. Criteria that might be used include use and referencing of a wide range of sources and perspectives, clarity, facts, logic and persuasiveness of argument, and presentation of data for different audiences.

Assessment of literacy skills assists organizations in setting and revising goals and determining successful completion and areas of improvement. Literacy skills are known to be essential to successful outcomes, yet much of the knowledge about these skills has not been discovered and communicated in a systematic way. Determining how skills, especially information and digitally focused skills, will be tested is the next task. Programs for simulating scenarios where students are given opportunities to demonstrate the ability to manage and use information, especially in digital environments, are used for this purpose.

Measurement of Literacy Skills

In practice, a comprehensive framework is needed to serve as a foundation to enable standards to be created over time within a knowledge domain to support assessments. Large quantities of data and differing stakeholder objectives are examples of the many factors to be considered. A great deal of analysis is needed to ensure that detailed and accurate descriptions of skills, knowledge, and behavior are developed for each target literacy skill, indicator, and outcome.

Tasks are typically described in evaluation plans detailing standards, indicators, and outcomes; defining data requirements and stores; selecting tools; and implementing the plan to allow assessment of performance data.

Literacy standards are defined and linked to performance indicators—quantitative measures that students must meet to achieve desired outcomes. For example, the Association of College & Research Libraries' Information Literacy Standards for Higher Education (2000) consists of five standards with associated performance indicators and performance outcomes. But measures need to also be locally developed and satisfy the need for faster assessment-measurement-evaluation cycles, faster and personalized feedback, virtual realities, simulations, and access to progress information.

Fast assessments need support from suitable measurement instruments, the entire process of collecting data in a research investigation. Criteria for instruments include validity (i.e., measuring what it is intended) and reliability (i.e., consistency with which an instrument measures a given variable).

Victoria Hill

See also Assessing Literacy Skills in the 21st Century; Assessment of Problem Solving and Higher Order Thinking; Badges and Skill Certification; Cognition and Human Learning; Collaborative Learning and 21st-Century Skills; Competency Models and Frameworks; Knowledge and Skill Hierarchies

Further Readings

Abet.org. (2010). *Student outcomes and performance indicators.* Retrieved from http://www.abet.org/uploadedFiles/Program_Evaluators/Training_Process/program-outcomes-and-performance-indicators.pdf

Association of Colleges & Research Libraries. (2000). *Information literacy competency standards for higher education.* Retrieved from http://www.ala.org/acrl/standards/informationliteracycompetency

Association of College & Research Libraries. (2013, June 4). Rethinking ACRL's information literacy standards: The process begins. *About ACRL, information literacy, standards and guidelines.* Retrieved from http://www.acrl.ala.org/acrlinsider/archives/7329

Cartelli, A. (2010). Frameworks for digital competence assessment: Proposals, instruments, and evaluation. In *Proceedings of Informing Science & IT Education Conference (InSITE).* Retrieved from http://proceedings.informingscience.org/InSITE2010

Hobbs, R. (2010). *A plan of action.* Retrieved from http://www.knightcomm.org/wp-content/uploads/2010/12/Digital_and_Media_Literacy_A_Plan_of_Action.pdf

Kirinić, V. (2011). *Information literacy: Definitions, standards and assessment, related concepts.* Retrieved from http://www.uni-graz.at/iwiwww/archiv/Information_literacy.pdf

Lupton, M., Glanville, C., McDonald, P., & Selzer, D. (2004). *Griffith graduate attributes information literacy toolkit.* Retrieved from http://www.griffith.edu.au/__data/assets/pdf_file/0006/290769/Information-literacy.pdf

Marymount University. (2008, Summer). *Learning outcomes assessment handbook.* Retrieved from http://www.marymount.edu/Media/Website%20Resources/documents/offices/ie/LearnAssessHandbook.pdf

New Brunswick Department of Post-Secondary Education, Training and Labour (PETL). (2011). *Workplace essential skills program strategic plan 2011–2014.* Retrieved from http://bibliotheque.copian.ca/ajout/10452

Organisation for Economic Co-operation and Development. (2001). *Competencies for the knowledge economy, summary* (Chapter 4). Retrieved from http://www.oecd.org

Measuring and Assessing TPACK (Technological Pedagogical Content Knowledge)

In 2005, the term *Technological Pedagogical Content Knowledge* (TPCK) was introduced as a conceptual framework to describe the knowledge base for the effective integration of technology in teaching. Matt Koehler and Punya Mishra built their ideas based on Lee Shulman's notion of Pedagogical Content Knowledge (PCK) and indicated that TPCK consists of Technological Knowledge (TK), Pedagogical Knowledge (PK), Content Knowledge (CK) and the overlapping domains Pedagogical Content Knowledge (PCK), Technological Pedagogical Knowledge (TPK), Technological Content Knowledge (TCK), and Technological Pedagogical Content Knowledge (TPCK).

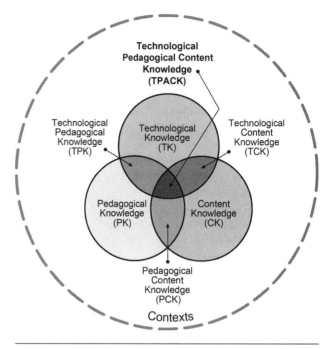

Figure 1   The TPACK model

Source: Reproduced by permission of the publisher, © 2012 by tpack.org.

In 2007, TPCK was changed to TPACK to better reflect the interdependence of the three contributing knowledge domains, and in 2008 "context" was added to the framework because it was argued that teaching with technology does not take place in isolation but is each time situated in a specific educational context.

Since then, the TPACK framework and the accompanying Venn diagram (Figure 1) have been adopted by many researchers and practitioners for describing the knowledge and skills that are needed for the effective integration of information and communication technologies (ICT) in teaching. This also led to the desire to measure whether teachers have sufficient TPACK and whether growth in TPACK can be measured. This entry first discusses researchers' and teacher educators' views on TPACK, then describes the instruments used to measure it. The entry then discusses how these instruments are used and the potential development of a common understanding of TPACK.

Views on TPACK

In many studies, both prospective teachers' and practicing teachers' TPACK is measured through a combination of several instruments (self-assessment surveys, classroom observations, assessment of products or artifacts, etc.). The decision on which instrument to use depends on how the TPACK framework is perceived by the researchers or teacher educators. In some studies,

TPACK is seen as a technology enhancement of PCK, or, in other words, as the integration of the knowledge of subject matter and the knowledge of teaching and learning with knowledge of technology. Other studies present TPACK as the development of understanding of the three main knowledge domains (content, pedagogy, and technology) and their intersections (PCK, TCK, TPK, and TPCK) separately. In this case, a growth in the three basic knowledge domains implies a growth in TPACK. A third view on the framework is to see TPACK as a unique, integrated body of knowledge that can be developed and assessed as a whole.

These different views on TPACK are also reflected in the way a teacher's TPACK can be measured. For instance, most self-assessment surveys that have been used divide TPACK into its seven knowledge domains. Other, more performance-based studies use instruments in which TPACK is considered as a unique body of knowledge.

Instruments to Measure TPACK

Looking at the research literature, two main categories of instruments can be distinguished: self-assessment surveys, and performance-based assessments with a focus on lesson planning, teachers' classroom performance, and performance on specific tasks.

A well-known instrument to measure teachers' self-perception of their TPACK is the TPACK Survey, developed by Denise Schmidt and colleagues, in which prospective teachers and practicing teachers report their perceptions of confidence in TPACK on a 5-point Likert scale with items that reflect all seven domains of the TPACK framework. For example, items in the TPACK Survey that can be used in the context of mathematics are "I keep up with important new technologies" (TK), "I can adapt my teaching style to different learners" (PK), "I have sufficient knowledge about mathematics" (CK), "I can select effective teaching approaches to guide student thinking and learning in mathematics" (PCK), "I know about technologies that I can use for understanding and doing mathematics" (TCK), "I can choose technologies that enhance students' learning for a lesson" (TPK), and "I can teach lessons that appropriately combine mathematics, technologies, and teaching approaches" (TPCK).

Many researchers have adopted the TPACK Survey because most studies show reliable outcomes when this survey is used. By adapting the survey, one can focus, for instance, on a specific technology or pedagogy, or on the T-related knowledge domains only. There has been some discussion about whether it is possible to measure the seven distinct knowledge domains from the TPACK framework with a self-assessment survey. Some studies

report a very good reproduction of the knowledge domains with factor analysis, while other studies indicate that the knowledge domains of the TPACK framework could not be reproduced. To illustrate, some recent studies by the authors of this entry indicate that a factor analysis shows a high interdependence between the T-related domains TK, TPK, TCK, and TPCK. This might suggest that the integration of the knowledge domains goes beyond the three basic knowledge domains and the overlapping areas.

The second category of instruments to assess TPACK is more performance-based. An example of such a performance-based assessment is lesson-planning assessment. This type of instrument is usually used for preservice teachers who have to prepare technology-enhanced lessons. In general, their lesson plan documents are assessed on TPK, TCK, and TPACK, and on "fit." The lesson plan assessment instrument that was developed by Judi Harris, Neal Grandgenett, and Mark Hofer, for instance, measures this fit by asking if the content, the proposed instructional strategies, and selected technology fit together within the overall instructional plan. Most of these instruments are in the form of a rubric: The criteria TPK, TCK, TPCK, and fit can be scored on a 3- to 5-point scale. Next to lesson plan documents, these rubrics are also used to assess other preservice teachers' planning artifacts (such as learning materials) as part of their planned instruction.

Several studies use performance-based assessment instruments to measure tasks and classroom practice. Examples of tasks that can be assessed are design-tasks (design a technology-enhanced lesson for a specific topic and a specific pedagogical approach), comprehension tasks (explain the concept of TPACK), and discussions (discuss the concept of TPACK in a group, discuss how you are going to demonstrate technology integration in your lesson). Classroom practice can be assessed by observing how and to what extent the teacher is integrating technology in his or her lessons. The tasks and classroom practices are assessed by identifying key components and setting criteria and scoring these criteria based on the task at hand. Key components usually are the topics addressed, the instructional strategies and learning activities that are used, and the technologies that are used by the teacher. Similar to the lesson planning assessment, most of these instruments are in the form of a rubric with criteria related to TPK, TCK, TPCK, and the "fit" that can be scored on a 3- to 5-point scale.

Using Instruments in Combination

Instruments are often used in combination, preferably over a longer period, to triangulate findings. The self-assessment surveys and the performance-based assessments make it possible to measure self-assessed, planned, and observed TPACK. This is increasingly important, primarily to be able to measure teachers' TPACK on the several aspects. A study could, for instance, start with measuring teachers' TPACK before they engage in professional development by using a self-assessment survey. After this, teachers engage in professional development and design a technology-enhanced lesson and their design decisions and their planned technology-related activities are assessed by using lesson-planning assessment. After this, their observed TPACK can be measured by observing their actual classroom practices. In the end, the self-assessment survey can be used again to measure teachers' TPACK to see whether their self-assessment changed after the activities in relation to planning and carrying out the technology-enhanced lesson.

Measuring Teachers' TPACK

The question remains whether the self-assessment surveys, lesson-planning assessments, and performance-based assessments are sufficient to measure a teacher's technology integration skills. From studies that are related to technology integration in education, we know that knowledge and skills are important factors and that teachers' attitude toward technology and their pedagogical beliefs play a major role in the success of technology integration. For instance, teachers can have what is called espoused-TPACK, which implies that preservice teachers can talk about pedagogically sound technology integration in a specific topic, but that does not necessarily mean that this will lead to what is called in-use TPACK. Teachers have in-use TPACK when they are able to translate their ideas into the design and implementation of a pedagogically sound technology-enhanced lesson for their content within a specific context.

This requires a combination of knowledge, skills, and attitudes, and the ability to reason professionally. This implies that a professional development program should attend to this, but also that not only knowledge and skills but also beliefs, attitudes, and the ability to reason professionally should be considered when measuring teachers' technology integration activities. A self-assessment survey could therefore be elaborated with scales from other existing instruments to measure teachers' attitudes toward (educational) technology and their pedagogical beliefs. Similarly, rubrics and other assessments forms could be expanded with categories that are related to beliefs and attitudes, but because these are often difficult to observe, these could be replaced by the observation of professional reasoning. Examples of this are only available scarcely at this moment.

Measuring to Come to a Common Understanding of TPACK

Next to using the instruments to measure TPACK and the development of TPACK, further analysis of the data that result from the measurements can help to come to a more common view on TPACK. As indicated, there are different views on the TPACK framework and these differences are also reflected in the way TPACK is measured. There is no consensus in the discourse about TPACK and there is no explicit proof that TPACK is either a subset of the seven knowledge domains or a more integrated unique body of knowledge. What we do know is that the different existing instruments measure different aspects of the framework, and it is probably true that the different existing instruments measure different perspectives on the framework.

Self-assessment surveys usually measure someone's perception of their confidence in TPACK, but because the survey is usually broken down into items on the different knowledge domains of TPACK, it often measures the perception on all the different domains. And because the items are usually formulated very broadly to allow the same instrument to be used in different settings, it could even be argued that these kinds of surveys do not measure someone's self-perceived TPACK and the affordances of technology to support student learning on a specific topic in a specific context, but that it actually measures perceived broad general knowledge about how to use technology in the classroom.

Looking closer, for instance, at the items in the TPACK Survey, one can see that TPACK is addressed in a general and abstract way (e.g., I know how to solve my own technical problems, or I can choose technologies that enhance the content for a lesson). The context circle that surrounds the TPACK model (see Figure 1), however, implies that assessing TPACK means to assess teachers' TPACK in a specific and concrete way and therefore the instrument should contain questions about the specific content, pedagogical approaches, and technology. A similar remark can be made about the rubrics used to assess lesson plans and observable outcomes; they too should reflect the concrete educational practice of the person who is being assessed. If this is not reflected, the validity of the instruments is questionable.

As a contribution to the discourse about understanding TPACK, more research is needed that looks at both teachers' TPACK and their attitudes toward technology. This would allow researchers and teacher educators to get a broader view of knowledge, skills, attitudes, beliefs, and professional reasoning of teachers toward technology integration, which in turn will give more information about the extent to which the technology integration will be successful.

Conclusion

TPACK is a conceptual framework for describing the knowledge base needed for the effective integration of technology in a specific educational context. The TPACK framework is very appealing to both researchers and teacher educators because of the intuitive understanding that the combination of the basic knowledge domains of technological knowledge, pedagogical knowledge, and content knowledge lead to PCK, TPK, TCK, and TPCK. The way to look at TPACK and how the framework is understood differs between researchers, and this has implications for the kind of instruments that are used to measure TPACK.

Two main categories of instruments can be distinguished: self-assessment surveys and performance-based assessments. For both categories, instruments have been developed, tested, and used in a variety of contexts. Using the same instrument in similar studies makes it possible to compare results between different samples, nationally and internationally. The drawback of instruments that can be used throughout the world is that they are often very general in nature. No specific context can be considered because of the diversity of contexts in which the instrument is deployed. Another drawback of the TPACK-specific instruments is that they often do not account for other factors that play a major role in effective technology integration in education, such as teachers' attitude toward technology and teachers' beliefs. However, the existing TPACK instruments can be used to measure the self-assessed, planned, and observed TPACK. When used in combination, especially over a longer period in time, these instruments give a good indication of someone's TPACK development. This means that the instruments that are derived from the TPACK framework can be used to measure TPACK and to give feedback on a teacher's development when it comes to effective technology integration.

Petra Fisser, Joke Voogt, Johan van Braak, and Jo Tondeur

See also Professional Development Tools and Technologies; Technology Integration; Twenty-First-Century Technology Skills

Further Readings

Ertmer, P. A., & Ottenbreit-Leftwich, A. T. (2010). Teacher technology change: How knowledge, confidence, beliefs, and culture intersect. *Journal of Research on Technology in Education, 42*(3), 255–285.

Harris, J., Grandgenett, N., & Hofer, M. (2010). Testing a TPACK-based technology integration assessment rubric. In D. Gibson & B. Dodge (Eds.), *Proceedings of Society for Information Technology & Teacher Education International Conference 2010* (pp. 3833–3840). Chesapeake, VA: Association for the Advancement of Computing in Education.

Knezek, G., & Christensen, R. (2008). The importance of information technology attitudes and competencies in primary and secondary education. In J. Voogt & G. Knezek (Eds.), *International handbook of information technology in primary and secondary education* (pp. 321–332). New York, NY: Springer.

Koehler, M. J., & Mishra, P. (2008). Introducing TPCK. In AACTE (Ed.), *Handbook of technological pedagogical content knowledge (TPCK) for educators* (pp. 3–29). New York, NY: Routledge.

Koehler, M. J., & Mishra, P. (2009). What is technological pedagogical content knowledge? *Contemporary Issues in Technology and Teacher Education, 9*(1), 60–70.

Mishra, P., & Koehler, M. (2006). Technological Pedagogical Content Knowledge: A new framework for teacher knowledge. *Teachers College Record 108*(6), 1017–1054.

Schmidt, D., Baran, E., Thompson, A., Koehler, M., Shin, T., & Mishra, P. (2010). Technological Pedagogical Content Knowledge (TPACK): The development and validation of an assessment instrument for preservice teachers. *Journal of Research on Technology in Education, 42*(2), 123–149.

Voogt, J., Fisser, P., Pareja Roblin, N., Tondeur, J., & Van Braak, J. (2013). Technological Pedagogical Content Knowledge (TPACK)—A review of the literature. *Journal of Computer Assisted Learning, 29*(2), 109–121.

MEASURING CONTACTS AND INTERACTIONS IN SOCIAL NETWORKS

Social networks are platforms for interaction, communication, and collaboration. Online social networking sites such as Facebook, LinkedIn, YouTube, Twitter, and Flickr are among the most popular sites on the Internet. Users of these sites, social actors, establish a social network. Social network platforms allow users to find, share, and organize content, to communicate, and to find contacts. Measuring contacts and interactions in social networks provides an opportunity to study the characteristics of online social network graphs at large scale, to analyze the structure of multiple online social networks, and to understand the complex dynamics of the interactions in social networks. Also, measuring contacts and interactions in social networks is important to improve current technologies of the systems and to develop new applications of online social networks. This entry explains what is examined by social network analysis, discusses research on how information spreads through online social networks, and details social network analysis techniques. The entry then details how relations in social networks are measured and lists the features of some currently available social network analysis software products.

Social Network Analysis (SNA)

Social network analysis (SNA) is a multidisciplinary method and is mostly used by diverse disciplines such as information science, organization studies, complexity, chaos theory, psychology, sociology, anthropology, economics, and management. SNA can be used to examine a diverse range of social networks including health services, emergency services, business links, teenagers' popular preferences, and academic collaborations. SNA maps out how actors interact with each other in organizations, groups, or society. The diverse disciplines study many of the properties of social networks, such as finding the average path length between two actors, analyzing the small-world effect, identifying strong ties that are tightly clustered, and identifying weak ties. SNA exposes the structure of interactions, the flow of communication, and main actors who are important transmitters of information. SNA can identify structural holes in the network that prevent the flow of communication.

Diffusion of Information

Meeyoung Cha, Alan Mislove, and Krishna P. Gummadi conducted research on how information spreads over current online social networks by collecting and analyzing large-scale traces of information dissemination in Flickr by means of a data set including links, users, photos, and photos that are marked as favorites. This study examined the correlation between the locations of favorite marking and the social structure of users, based on the topology that existed on the last day of the crawl. This study's findings indicated that information did not spread widely and quickly in a viral fashion across the social network. According to Cha, Mislove, and Gummadi, the slow pace of information propagation can be related to the process issues in the theory of information diffusion and the challenges in finding relevant information from an overwhelming volume of information to which individuals are exposed.

Diffusion of information theory illustrates how SNA is used to understand organizational behaviors. Fundamentals about the use of SNA are presented in books such as *Diffusion of Innovations* by Everett M. Rogers, *Communication Networks: Toward a New Paradigm for Research* by Rogers and D. Lawrence Kincaid, and *The Hidden Power of Social Networks: Understanding How Work Really Gets Done in Organizations* by Rob Cross and Andrew Parker. The use of SNA allows figuring out how to build bridges to subgroups in the organization to obtain more efficient and maintainable organizations. In addition, John Scott's book *Social Networks Analysis: A Handbook* provides an introduction to the theory and practice of network analysis in the social sciences and mentions that the theory basis of the SNA includes Gestalt theory, field theory, and graph theory.

Social Network Analysis Techniques

Stanley Wasserman and Katherine Faust provide an overview of SNA techniques in their book *Social Networks Analysis: Methods and Applications* and define terms that are used in SNA (see Table 1).

SNA mostly uses survey research, ethnographic research, and documentary research. Network data collection methods include cross-sectional, longitudinal, and combined multiple designs. Network data collection tools include self-administered questionnaires, personal and telephone interviews, observations made at physical sites, archival records, cognitive social structures, small-group experiments, ego-centered surveys, and diaries. The most common type of data includes attribute data, ideational data, and relational data. The corresponding data analysis techniques are variable analysis, typological analysis, and network analysis. Variable analysis measures attributes that are related to attitudes, opinions, and behaviors of actors. Typological analysis measures ideational data that describes meanings, motives, and definitions. Network analysis measures relational data that includes contacts, ties, and connections.

The book *Social Network Analysis* by David Knoke and Song Yang describes network fundamentals, actors, relations, networks, research design elements, and data collection procedures in detail. The book introduces basic methods for analyzing networks via graphs, matrices, relationship measures, centrality and prestige, cliques, structural equivalence, visual displays, and block models. As advanced methods for analyzing networks, it is suggested to use network position measures, logic models, affiliation networks, and lattices. The book covers topics in basic network concepts, data collection, network analytical methodology, the concepts and methods related to social network research problems, and real-world examples.

Table I   Selected definitions that are used in social network analysis

Terms	Definitions
Social network	A set or sets of actors and the relations between actors.
Actor (node)	Discrete individual, corporate, or collective social units.
Relation (tie, line)	The collection of links among members of a group.
Dyadic relationship	A link between two actors.
Direction	The way of the relations that actor sends or receives.
Strength	The emotional intensity or frequency of interaction.
Relational content	A specific substantive connection among actors.
Social network data	Data consists of at least one structural variable measured on a set of actors.
Structural variables	Variables that measure dimensions of dyadic relations.
Composition variables	Actor attributes or characteristics.
Network mode	A distinct set of entities on which structural variables are measured.
One-mode data	Identical send-receive actors.
Two-mode data	Different send-receive actors.
Affiliation network	Links between actors and events.
Bounded network	A set of actors to be sampled or completely enumerated.
Nominalist	Analyst's theoretical interests determine which actors possess the relevant attributes.
Realist	Members themselves recognize and accept a shared identity that defines the group's boundary.
Network sampling	Random selection from a population, both conceptually and empirically.
Egocentric networks	One focal actor (ego) and its direct contacts.
The complete network	An entire population of actors.
Centrality	Measures the distribution of information within the group.
Sociometric coefficients	Measure the level of communication of a specific actor.
Distance-related coefficients	Measure the geodesic distance of the given two nodes of a network.

Source: Aytac Gogus, using terms, explanations, and definitions from Wasserman, S., & Faust, K. (1994). *Social networks analysis: Methods and applications.* Cambridge: UK: Cambridge University Press.

Measurement Studies

The study of interactions in social networks is intended to bring about understanding of the dynamics of the relations of social actors such as individuals, groups, companies, associations, and their behavior.

The relations (ties) between actors (nodes) can be measured in three different levels of measurement: nominal, ordinal, and interval levels.

1. Nominal measurement comprises binary measures and multicategory measures. Binary measures of relations distinguish between the relations being absent or being present and score the relations as 0 for absent and 1 for present. Multicategory measures of relations score actors on the list as having a relationship category.

2. Ordinal measurements can be full-rank ordinal measures or grouped ordinal measures. Full-rank ordinal measures of relations use a rank-order scale. Grouped ordinal measures of relations use the scale −1, 0, and +1 to reflect negative, neutral, and positive coded relations.

3. Interval levels of measurement of relations use scales that show the frequency or intensity of relations.

Table 2 Type of networks

Type of networks	Descriptions of the networks
Random networks	Graphs that are constructed by randomly adding links to a static set of nodes and intend to have short paths between any two nodes.
Power-law networks	Networks that have power-law coefficient-degree nodes such as Internet topologies, the Web, social networks, and neural networks.
Scale-free networks	A class of power-law networks where the high-degree nodes tend to be connected to other high-degree nodes.
Small-world networks	Networks that have a small diameter and exhibit high clustering, such as the Web, scientific collaboration on research papers, film actors, and general social networks.

Source: Aytac Gogus, using terms, explanations, and definitions from Mislove, A., Marcon, M., Gummadi, K. P., Druschel, P., & Bhattacharjee, B. (2007). Measurement and analysis of online social networks. *Proceedings of the 7th ACM SIGCOMM Conference on Internet Measurement* (pp. 29–42, 1495). New York, NY: ACM.

Analysis of complex interaction patterns between multiple social actors and their behavior cannot be simple. Analysis of interactions between social actors guides feedback patterns such as development of lifestyle behavior, peer relations, interrelation between peer network, cooperation of academicians, competition between staff, attitudes of individuals related to their political group, and so forth. The feedback patterns can show attitudes or behaviors that can influence group opinions or polarizations.

Alan Mislove, Massimiliano Marcon, Krishna Gummadi, Peter Druschel, and Bobby Bhattacharjee conducted a large-scale measurement study and analysis of the structure of multiple online social networks such as Flickr, YouTube, LiveJournal, and Orkut. The results of this study emphasize the power-law, small-world, and scale-free properties of online social networks and state that (a) the in-degree of user nodes go with the out-degree; (b) the networks hold a tightly connected core of high-degree nodes; and (c) the core links small groups of strongly clustered, low-degree nodes at the border of the network. This study mentions that complex network theory refers to theoretical work on the properties of various classes of complex graphs. This study also gives summaries of four types of networks (random networks, power-law networks, scale-free networks, and small-world networks) that are studied by many researchers (see Table 2).

Random networks refer to graphs that are constructed by randomly adding links. Power-law networks have power-law coefficient-degree nodes. Scale-free networks have the high-degree nodes that are connected to other high-degree nodes. Small-world networks have a small diameter and exhibit high clustering.

Researchers in psychology and sociology express doubt about the practice of inferring meaningful relationships from social network connections alone.

Christo Wilson, Bryce Boe, Alessandra Sala, Krishna P. N. Puttaswamy, and Ben Y. Zhao from the University of California at Santa Barbara conducted a study on the question: Are social links valid indicators of real user interaction? This study proposed the use of interaction graphs to impart meaning to online social links by quantifying user interactions and analyzing interaction graphs derived from Facebook user traces and presented high-level measurement and analysis results on the Facebook data set. The study analyzed (a) general properties of the Facebook population, including user connectivity in the social graph and growth characteristics over time; (b) the different types of user interactions on Facebook, including how interactions vary across time, applications, and different segments of the user population; and (c) detailed user activities through crawls of user Mini-Feed by paying special attention to social network growth and interactions over fine-grained time scales. This study's results show that the interaction graphs have fewer *supernodes* with extremely high degrees, and the overall network diameter increases significantly. To quantify the impact of the study observations, two well-known social-based applications, Reliable Email (RE:) and SybilGuard, are used. This study's results indicate that studies of social applications should use real indicators of user interactions instead of social graphs.

Social Network Analysis Software

To facilitate network analysis, there are widely available SNA software products such as Cytoscape, NetMiner, UCINET, Pajek, StOCNET (for stochastic networks), GUESS: The Graph Exploration System, MultiNet, and Organization Risk Analyzer (ORA). SNA software facilitates quantitative or qualitative analysis of social networks. The methodology of SNA in terms of data collection, measurement of variables, and data analysis focus on ties between actors. SNA software plays a central and multifaceted role such as allowing data collection, simulation-based analysis methods of social networks. Table 3 summarizes main futures of some network analysis and visualization software.

As online social networks continue to gain popularity, psychologists, sociologists, economists, computer scientists, and scientists from diverse domains continue to investigate the properties of social networks and their impacts on the society and individuals.

Aytac Gogus

See also Model-Based Approaches; Social Media, Identity in; Social Media and Networking; Social Network Analysis; Web 2.0 and Beyond

Further Readings

Cha, M., Mislove, A., & Gummadi, K. P. (2009, April 24–29). A measurement-driven analysis of information propagation in the Flickr social network. Paper presented at *WWW 2009*, Madrid, Spain.

Cross, R. L., & Parker, A. (2004). *The hidden power of social networks: Understanding how work really gets done in organizations.* New York, NY: Harvard Business Review.

Huisman, M., & Van Duijn, M. A. J. (2011). A reader's guide to SNA software. In J. Scott & P. J. Carrington (Eds.), *The SAGE handbook of social network analysis* (pp. 578–600). London, UK: Sage.

Knoke, D., & Yang, S. (2008). *Social network analysis.* Thousand Oaks, CA: Sage.

Marsden, P. V. (2005). Recent developments in network measurement. In P. J. Carrington, J. Scott, & S. Wasserman (Eds.), *Models and methods in social network analysis* (pp. 8–30). Cambridge, UK: Cambridge University Press.

Mislove, A., Marcon, M., Gummadi, K. P., Druschel, P., & Bhattacharjee, B. (2007). Measurement and analysis of online social networks. In *Proceedings of the 7th ACM SIGCOMM Conference on Internet Measurement* (pp. 29–42, 1495). New York, NY: ACM.

Rogers, E. M. (2003). *Diffusion of innovations.* New York, NY: Free Press.

Rogers, E. M., & Kincaid, D. L. (1981). *Communication networks: Toward a new paradigm for research.* New York, NY: Free Press.

Scott, J. (2005). *Social network analysis: A handbook.* London, UK: Sage.

Valente, T. W. (1995). *Network models of the diffusion of innovations.* Cresskill, NJ: Hampton Press.

Wasserman, S., & Faust, K. (1994). *Social networks analysis: Methods and applications.* Cambridge: UK: Cambridge University Press.

Wilson, C., Boe, B., Sala, A., Puttaswamy, K. P. N., & Zhao, B. Y. (2009, April 1–3). User interactions in social networks and their implications. Paper presented at *EuroSys'09*, Nuremberg, Germany.

Table 3 Main features of some network analysis and visualization software

Software	Main Features
NetMiner 4	Analysis of comprehensive network measures, exploratory and confirmatory analysis, interactive visual analytics, what-if network analysis, and built-in statistical procedures and charts.
Netlytic	Automatically summarize large volumes of text and discover social networks from conversations on social media such as Twitter, YouTube, blogs, online forums, and chats.
EgoNet	Collection and analysis of egocentric network data, facilities to assist in creating the questionnaire, collecting the data, and providing general global network measures and data matrixes.
Wolfram Alpha	Computational knowledge engine answering queries on analysis of the social network data.
NodeXL	Network Overview Discovery Exploration for Excel, supports extracting e-mail, Twitter, YouTube, Facebook, WWW, Wiki, and Flickr social networks.
NetworkX	Graph creation, manipulation, analysis, and visualization.
Tulip	Information visualization framework dedicated to the analysis and visualization of relational data.
R	An integrated package of software of data manipulation, calculation, and graphical display.
visone	Analysis and visualization of social networks.

Source: Aytac Gogus, using terms, explanations, and definitions from Huisman, M., & Van Duijn, M. A. J. (2011). A reader's guide to SNA software. In J. Scott & P. J. Carrington (Eds.), *The SAGE handbook of social network analysis* (pp. 578–600). London, UK: Sage.

MEASURING LEARNING IN INFORMAL CONTEXTS

Learning is a process in which individuals use resources from their environment to build on their prior knowledge. The interaction with his or her environment results in a permanent change in a learner's knowledge and behavior. Learning has traditionally taken place within formal learning environments such as the classroom. Informal learning encompasses all learning that occurs outside the confines of the classroom. Informal learning can occur at home, museums, after-school recreation programs, sporting events, historical parks, and trips to local community organizations. Learning activities of an informal nature can also be incorporated as complementary activities within a traditional learning environment such as a high school or university classroom. Informal learning activities differ from traditional learning activities in that participation is typically voluntary and not associated with an accredited program or standardized curriculum. Informal learning has also been synonymously referred to as *free-choice learning* and *life-wide learning*. *Free-choice learning* implies the connotation that learning is nonsequential and self-paced.

Before we can determine how or when learning is occurring in informal learning environments, measurable outcomes must be developed. Methods of assessment must consider the unique features of informal learning environments such as when learning experiences occur, the pacing of instruction, and the location. Assessments typically involve situated feedback from the learner and are associated with low consequences compared with methods of assessments used in traditional classroom environments such as high-stakes exams. This entry discusses the components of informal learning and the various ways informal learning can be measured. The entry then details some of the implications of informal learning for educational technology.

Components of Informal Learning

According to Allison Rossett and Bob Hoffman, six factors distinguish informal from formal learning: the nature of the outcomes, nature of the experience, origin, role of the learner, role of the instructor, and role of the instructional designer. Informal learning typically tends to be exciting and engaging and imposes few restrictions on learners. Because of the lack of structure, learners have the ability to spend as much time as they want on a particular topic or activity and can change to a different activity should they lose excitement. The increased flexibility is often a result of limited-to-no learning objectives. Although a lack of learning objectives may offer more freedom regarding the timing, pacing, and regulations associated with informal learning, objectivists express concerns regarding measuring outcomes.

Learners have more autonomy in informal learning environments and embrace a more participatory role. With limited structure and few extrinsic motivations tied to grades and class rankings, learners are more often intrinsically motivated to participate in informal learning activities. Learners typically self-select activities that reflect their interest in a particular topic. One example is the young man whose car needs new brakes and watches YouTube videos and explores the Internet to learn how to replace them himself. A second example is the woman who is interested in changing her exercise routine and joins an online group to learn about different exercises that she can incorporate into her fitness regimen.

The role of the instructor is very different in an informal learning environment compared with a formal learning environment. The instructor takes on more of a facilitator role to help connect learners with additional resources to further leverage their interest in the particular topic they are learning. Rather than a traditional instructor who is responsible for teaching learners and then evaluating them to measure their gain in knowledge, the instructor in informal learning is a coach who provides guidance and scaffolded support on an as-needed basis.

Measuring Informal Learning

Keeping in mind that learning is a permanent change in behavior caused by one's level of interaction with one's environment, evaluative methods must be used that can identify such a change. Assessment entails the process of measuring and documenting changes in behavior related to learning activities. Depending on the methods used to collect data, these documented changes are then interpreted to determine how much learning has occurred. Strategies used to assess learning must align with learning objectives and goals set forth before the activity. Traditional learning goals used in formalized curricula are often associated with competencies set forth by a guiding institution or accrediting body. Formal assessments of learning may include exams, tests, and quizzes to determine if a learner is able to recall knowledge and apply it to a variety of different contexts. Informal learning can essentially take place anywhere outside of the classroom environment and does not involve examinations or grades to determine the extent of one's increase in knowledge, so broad learning goals must be provided. The National Research Council suggest that informal learning goals encompass learners' abilities to experience excitement and interest within their environment, use concepts to explain and argue phenomena in their world, reflect on their own process of learning, actively participate in activities, and enable self-reflection on what they have learned and how it can be applied to other areas and fields.

Regardless of whether learning is occurring in a formal or informal environment, assessment requires evidence that learning outcomes have been achieved. Many challenges are associated with measuring learning that occurs within informal contexts. One difficulty that poses great challenges for educators and practitioners who are interested in measuring informal learning is that it tends to occur spontaneously. The timing of when informal learning will occur cannot always be planned. Although certain activities such as field trips to a local museum, zoo, or science center may be planned, other types of learning can occur when individuals least expect it (e.g., searching the Internet, watching videos on YouTube, and communicating with others via social media platforms such as Facebook, LinkedIn, and Twitter).

Because of the diversity of informal learning activities, it is difficult to set guidelines for pacing the learning process. Educators and researchers have to look beyond the methods of assessment typically used in traditional classroom learning environments and embrace more qualitative methods of assessment. These methods include self-assessment, blogs, embedded assessment, games, discussions, and learner-created artifacts.

Self-Assessment and Goal Setting

Informal learning activities such as field trips to museums, historical parks, and after-school programs provide learners with the freedom to select activities and topics based on their personal interests. This learning freedom can impose challenges on the educator if he or she is trying to evaluate a group of learners who have chosen different learning paths within their learning environment. Having learners self-assess levels of comfort and familiarity with the material, perceptions of how much they have learned, and any challenges they encountered can help the educator measure any changes in behavior related to the learning activity.

Goal setting can also be used as a way to structure learning activities and align them with methods of assessment. Informal learning activities are often not directly linked to a traditional learning environment, so criterion-based learning goals tend to be nonexistent. Furthermore, the lack of standardized learning activities can make it difficult for educators to construct learning objectives and goals that address the learning needs of the masses. By employing goal setting with the learner as part of the informal learning experience, learners can be guided toward particular activities that will assist them in meeting set goals.

Embedded Assessment

Although informal learning activities tend to be more open-ended and learner-led, formative assessments can be embedded throughout the learning experience. Checkpoints can be placed to determine how much a learner has retained after participating in a particular activity. An example of this occurs frequently at various exhibits in museums. As learners walk through a specific exhibit, they may find videos, questions-and-answer displays, and displays where they can participate in a simulation of what they just read. These types of formative assessments are less intrusive compared with traditional methods of assessment with fewer consequences. Many exhibits at museums, science centers, or amusement parks provide opportunities for learners to test their knowledge by completing games and quizzes as they progress through the venue. These games are often embedded within the exhibit and provide an engaging experience that allows the learner to interact with the environment.

Discussions

Discussion boards are used frequently for many blended and online classes; however, they also serve as a method of assessment for informal learning. Many online groups provide a community of practice where members are able to share information, resources, and opinions with each other. The rate of participation and the discussion content can provide insight as to how much an individual is learning based on his or her level of interactions. Even though a formal grade may not be assigned to a learner's discussion activity, similar rubrics that analyze the thoroughness of his or her posts could be used to determine the extent of learning that has occurred.

Learner-Created Artifacts

One assessment to determine if learning has occurred in an informal learning environment is to examine artifacts produced by the learner as a result of the learning experience. Individuals who visit online groups or communities of practice may decide to create their own videos to share with the group. Learners may decide to develop their own website to provide additional resources for individuals with similar interests. Blogs and wikis provide a forum for learners to engage in reflective writing and share their thoughts and opinions on a particular subject matter.

These forums where individuals can write their thoughts and share opinions provide written evidence of how individuals interpret the information they acquired. The types of information (e.g., photos, links to other websites, topics, and sequencing of topics) that individuals may include within websites they create provides educators and researchers with insight about how they are synthesizing and prioritizing information.

Learner-created artifacts can be qualitatively evaluated to determine whether learners are simply repeating or regurgitating what they learned from another website or learning experience or whether they're able to make inferences and apply the information to a variety of different contexts. A learner-created website that provides examples of how one may choose to design a fitness program will demonstrate that the learner is able to adapt what was learned and make adjustments to suit the constraints imposed by the environment. If the learner is able to go into further detail and provide the rationale for the incorporation of particular stretches and exercises and the implications they will have on the body, evaluators can then make the claim that the learner had demonstrated higher order thinking skills. Individuals tend to create the previously mentioned artifacts for fun and of their own accord. If educators were interested in applying traditional and formalized methods of assessment, they could assess learning using criterion-referenced rubrics that align with learning goals.

Implications of Informal Learning for Educational Technology

Informal learning provides a wide array of activities that can be used independently or in conjunction with formal learning settings to provide learners with authentic experiences within their real world. The continued exploration for methods to assess informal learning activities will affect the ways in which instructional technology is applied to develop learning experiences in a variety of different settings. By identifying assessment activities that help answer questions pertaining to informal learning environments, educational technologists will be better able to design customized learning experiences that are contextually relevant for their intended learning audience. (For example, some of these questions might be: How do informal learning activities influence learners' perceptions about the subject matter? How might informal activities be integrated into a traditional classroom environment? What do learners find appealing about learning in an informal environment? Aligning methods of assessment with informal learning goals leverages the types of instructional strategies that are used to enhance the learning experience. With more rigor placed on assessing the quality and level of learning, it can be expected that the sweeping contrasts between formal and informal learning contexts will diminish and instead become a more integrated learning environment.

Jill Erin Stefaniak

See also Engaged Learning; Evaluation Research; Informal Learning Strategies; Integrating Informal Learning With Programs at the College/University Level; Integrating Informal Learning With School Programs at the Secondary Level; Learning in Museums

Further Readings

Anderson, D., & Nashon, S. (2007). Predators of knowledge construction: Interpreting students' metacognition in an amusement park physics program. *Science Education, 91*(2), 298–320.

Borssard, D., Lewinstein, B., & Booney, R. (2005). Scientific knowledge and attitude change: The impact of a citizen science program. *International Journal of Science Education, 27*(9), 1099–1121.

Brown, J. S., & Duguid, P. (2000, May/June). Balancing act: How to capture knowledge without killing it. *Harvard Business Review, 75*(3), 73–80.

Cross, J. (2007). *Informal learning: Rediscovering natural pathways that inspire innovation and performance.* San Francisco, CA: Wiley.

Delandshere, G. (2002). Assessment as inquiry. *Teachers College Record, 104*(7), 1461–1484.

Falk, J. H., & Dierking, L. D. (2002). *Lessons without limits: How free-choice learning is transforming education.* Walnut Creek, CA: Alta Mira.

National Research Council. (2009). *Learning sciences in informal environments: People, places, pursuits.* Washington, DC: The National Academies Press.

National Research Council, Pellegrino, J. W., Chudowsky, N., & Glaser, R. (Eds.). (2001). *Knowing what students know: The science and design of educational assessment.* Washington, DC: The National Academies Press.

Rossett, A., & Hoffman, B. (2012). Informal learning. In R. A. Reiser & J. V. Dempsey (Eds.), *Trends and issues in instructional design and technology* (3rd ed., pp. 169–177). New York, NY: Pearson.

Savenye, W. C. (2014). Perspectives on assessment of educational technologies for informal learning. In J. M. Spector, M. D. Merrill, J. Elen, & M. J. Bishop (Eds.), *Handbook of research on educational communications and technology* (4th ed., pp. 257–267). New York, NY: Springer.

MEDIA LITERACIES

Literacy in general refers to knowledge and ability with regard to a particular subject or skill. The skill often associated with literacy involves language—specifically, the ability to read and write in a particular language. The subject area sometimes associated with literacy involves the humanities, or, more broadly, a liberal arts education. In earlier times, a literate person was someone who could read and write and who was familiar with great works of literature and prominent scientific theories. The concept has evolved to include multiple literacies, but the underlying notions of knowledge and ability remain as key indicators of a particular literacy. This entry first defines media literacy and discusses its relationship to other literacies. The entry then discusses the implications of media literacy for the development of critical thinking and for learning and instruction.

Media literacy refers to knowledge about a variety of media types (e.g., print, broadcast, Internet, etc.) and their associated representation forms (e.g., newspapers, radio, television, blogs, social networks, animations, movies, etc.), along with the abilities to interpret, modify, create, analyze, and otherwise use media effectively. Because so much information is now available in so many forms accessible through the Internet and other sources, it is necessary to be media literate to be considered a literate or well-educated person in the 21st century.

Because there are many media types and forms of representation, it is often meaningful to consider media literacies in the plural to convey the notion that a person may be media literate with a particular type and representation form but not necessarily literate with another media type and representation form. To be considered media literate implies that an individual has knowledge and associated abilities (the abilities to interpret, modify, create, analyze, and use) with multiple media types and forms of representations.

The National Association for Media Literacy Education (NAMLE) refers to the relevant abilities as *communication competences* and lists them as the ability to *access, analyze, evaluate,* and *communicate* in a variety of forms. The Charter for Media Literacy was created in 2004 to support the establishment of media literacy across Europe. The United Nations Educational, Scientific and Cultural Organization (UNESCO) links media literacy to the proliferation of mass media and new technologies, emphasizing empowerment by (a) understanding media roles and functions, (b) evaluating media content, (c) using media for self-expression, and (d) producing media content. These and other organizations believe that media literacy is critical for individual as well as national success in the 21st century.

Relationship to Other Literacies

Media literacy is now closely associated with information and communications technologies and the related literacies of digital, information, technology, and visual literacies. Because information takes many forms and is conveyed using multiple media types and representations, these related literacies are difficult to separate and treat as distinct literacies. Indeed, if one visits any of the websites cited in the listed at the end of this entry, one

will find text, pictures, graphs, and links to other websites that contain a similar mix of representation forms. To make sense of, and effective use of, any of these sites, one must be able to read the text, so language literacy remains a critical part of the new forms of literacies. However, effective use goes beyond simply understanding the words. There are links to videos, graphs, pictures, and more on these sites. The ability to integrate interpretations of the various types of content into a meaningful whole is important. That ability requires the competencies associated with all of the related literacies discussed in this entry.

Although one can develop competency in any of the related literacies through focused instructional activities and learning resources, the everyday application of these literacies involves the interrelationships of multiple types of literacy.

There are educational analogues to this need for an integrative and holistic approach. Regarding instructional design, theorists have distinguished the types of things to be learned (e.g., facts, concepts, rules, principles, problem-solving strategies, motor skills, attitudes, and more), and then argued that each of these types was best supported with particular kinds of learning activities and instructional approaches. However, outside a school context, one rarely encounters any of these types in isolation. Everyday experience presents facts along with concepts, principles, and problems to be solved all at once, which means that practical experience demands an integrative and holistic approach to instructional design. This conclusion is reinforced by a recent emphasis on integrating technological, pedagogical, and content knowledge into learning and instruction. Likewise, an integrative and holistic approach to multiple literacies, including media literacy, is likely to be productive in supporting many educational goals, including the development of critical thinkers, effective problem solvers, responsible citizens, and lifelong learners.

Implications for the Development of Critical Thinking

NAMLE and UNESCO both stress the relationship of media literacy and skills associated with critical thinking in general. Indeed, in terms of the underlying literacy abilities (e.g., accessing, evaluating, analyzing, communicating, creating, etc.), it is easy to apply those same abilities to each of the various related literacies (e.g., accessing information, analyzing digital representations, communicating via media, etc.). It is also easy to conceptualize those same abilities in terms of critical reasoning skills. For example, a person adept at critical reasoning can find and locate relevant information, analyze an argument in terms of the assumptions made, evaluate the implications of accepting the argument's conclusion, engage in a dialogue with proponents and those opposed to a perspective, create one's own position, and so on. In short, higher order reasoning and critical thinking require the same kinds of underlying abilities associated with all the various literacies.

A likely conclusion is that the development of the various types of literacies, including media literacy, is directly related to the development of critical thinking skills. Such a conclusion is advocated by the United Nations Alliance of Civilizations (UNAOC) Media & Information Literacy Clearinghouse and the Media Literacy Clearinghouse created by Frank W. Baker.

Implications for Learning and Instruction

What, then, are the implications of the critical importance of media literacy and related literacy skills for instructional programs and learning environments? One possible implication for primary education is that traditional emphasis on reading, writing, and arithmetic needs to be infused with and informed by the information and communication technologies that children already encounter in their daily lives. It is not simply the ability to read and write that is important to teach. As part of their primary education, children should develop the ability to interpret and create multiple types and forms of representation. Likewise, adolescents need to be able to use those technologies to access, analyze, evaluate, communicate, and create media artifacts to become effective problem solvers, productive workers, responsible citizens, and critical thinkers. That is what an educational system aims to achieve, and given that children and adolescents already have familiarity with and enthusiasm for various media types, achieving those educational goals should not be so difficult.

Concluding Remarks

Developing media literacy and related literacy skills should be emphasized throughout educational programs at every level. Marshall McLuhan's famous phrase "the medium is the message" is more appropriate now than when he introduced the notion in 1964. There is an undeniable relationship between the content of a message and the form of representation and type of media used for that content. The representational form and media type influence how the message is perceived and interpreted. As Edward Tufte has argued, a message can be embedded in an artifact that can either hinder or facilitate a desired interpretation. All too often, the design of a message is not well integrated with the representational form and type of media used for the message. Media literacy and its close relatives (digital literacy, information literacy, and technology literacy) are critical components of becoming an educated individual in the digital age of the 21st century.

J. Michael Spector

See also Digital Literacy: Overview and Definition; Digital Literacy in Higher Education; Information, Technology, and Media Literacies; Information and Communications Technologies for Formal Learning; Information Visualization; Message Design for Digital Media; Visual Literacy Skills in Science, Technology, Engineering, and Mathematics Education

Further Readings

Alvermann, D. E., & Hagood, M. C. (2000). Critical media literacy: Research, theory and practice in "New Times." *The Journal of Education Research, 93*(3), 193–205.

Buckingham, D. (2003). *Media education: Literacy, learning and contemporary culture.* Cambridge, UK: Polity Press.

De Abreu, B. S., & Mihailidis, P. (Ed.). (2014). *Media literacy education in action: Theoretical and pedagogical perspectives.* New York, NY: Routledge.

Hobbs, R., & Jensen, A. (2009). The past, present and future of media literacy education. *Journal of Media Literacy Education, 1*(1), 1–11.

Livingstone, S. (2004). Media literacy and the challenge of new information and communication technologies. *Communication Review, 1*(7), 3–14.

Scheibe, C., & Rogow, F. (2012). *The teacher's guide to media literacy: Critical thinking in a digital world.* Thousand Oaks, CA: Corwin.

Spector, J. M., & Anderson, T. M. (Eds.). (2000). *Integrated and holistic perspectives on learning, instruction and technology: Understanding complexity.* Dordrecht, Netherlands: Kluwer Academic.

Websites

European Charter for Media Literacy: http://www.euromedia literacy.eu

Media Literacy Clearinghouse: http://www.frankwbaker.com/default1.htm

National Association for Media Literacy Education (NAMLE) media literacy definitions: http://namle.net/publications/media-literacy-definitions/comment-page-1/

United Nations Alliance of Civilizations (UNAOC) Media & Information Literacy Clearinghouse: http://milunesco.unaoc.org

United Nations Educational, Scientific and Cultural Organization (UNESCO) media literacy page: http://www.unesco.org/new/en/communication-and-information/media-development/media-literacy

MESSAGE DESIGN FOR DIGITAL MEDIA

In its broadest sense, message design explores the optimal arrangement of words, images, sounds, and motion to communicate meaning most effectively to a particular audience within a given context. Instructional message design, therefore, seeks to create learning materials that are optimally effective in communicating educational content. Within the context of instruction, message design has historically existed at the intersection of communication and learning theories. Whereas communication models explore how best to construct and send messages, learning models focus on how messages are received, decoded, and committed to memory. The idea has been to find ways to design optimally effective instructional messages that will most effectively mediate learners' cognitive processing.

In addition to myriad nondigital media, the instructional message designer's *palette* of available digital media includes audio, video, text, graphics, animation, and interactivity—or some combination of these, often referred to as *multimedia*. Thus, within the context of educational technology, the instructional message designer's task is to translate the methods identified during the instructional design process into the actual digital materials that will be used to bring about the desired change in student knowledge. This entry discusses the theoretical and historical foundations of message design for instruction, some of the major research work done on message design for digital media, and the future of message design research.

Theoretical and Historical Foundations

The study of message design for instruction began in the first half of the 20th century and was, at the time, firmly rooted in a transmission-based, behaviorist orientation. From this perspective, knowledge is *transmitted* from an educator to a learner through a series of carefully designed strategies aimed at creating the conditions necessary for learning. Instructional message design from a behaviorist perspective, therefore, focused on discovering how the nature of the message stimulus affected learner response.

After World War I (1918–1950), media research studies focused largely on the use of educational film and radio, which compared the effects on learning outcomes of instruction delivered with an existing film or radio production with instruction delivered without the medium (often called media comparison studies in the research literature). Although teachers reported these programs were often enjoyable, in many cases the productions' lack of pedagogical design and inattentiveness to the realities of classroom conditions made the content difficult for particular audiences of learners to understand. During this period, researchers made little effort to identify and explore how design variables within the production of these media might affect learning from them.

After World War II, several major postwar military film research studies began manipulating specifically defined variables within the media production to explore their effects on appropriate audiences under controlled conditions. Studies sponsored by the U.S. Navy and Army at the Pennsylvania State University and the Air Force training sites between 1947 and 1957 were among the first to provide specific design guidelines for media producers aimed specifically at improving the way their instructional messages affected learning. Nonetheless, there were few significant forays into exploring the nature of communication within the educational technology field until after the launch of *Audio-Visual Communication Review* in 1953, which first introduced the term *educational communication* and was aimed at exploring the design of instructional materials from a combined communication and learning theory perspective. At roughly the same time, realism theorists such as Edgar Dale, C. R. Carpenter, James J. Gibson, and Charles W. Morris began exploring the fundamental components of instructional media and the psychology behind them to understand their pedagogical capabilities more clearly.

These and other instructional message design theorists were also influenced during this period by a shift that was occurring away from behaviorist models of learning that were aimed at observable learner responses toward new cognitivist models of learning that emphasized mental processes. In the cognitivist view, learning is an active process of acquiring, organizing, and constructing new understandings from incoming stimuli; therefore, designers should work to manipulate the attributes of an instructional message to delineate salient features, organize presentations, and connect to learners' existing knowledge structures. The study of instructional message design from roughly 1980 to 1995 was thus guided largely by emerging information-processing theories related to attention, perception, information decoding, long-term memory storage, and processing limitations.

In this way, research on instructional message design has evolved over the years from inconclusive "media-against-media" studies to theory-based research that has helped the field interpret findings from a cognitive processing perspective. The design principles derived from these later studies are still largely in use.

Major Contributions

Malcolm L. Fleming and W. Howard Levie's 1978 edition of *Instructional Message Design: Principles From the Behavioral Sciences* was among the first major works to derive applied instructional message design principles from the basic research that was being done at the time. This first edition of the book took a very broad—albeit rather behavioristically oriented—view of instructional message design as the bridge between learning theory research and instructional practice. Fifteen years later, the second, 1993, edition was updated to reflect the influence of cognitive theory on the field. Fleming and Levie organized their texts generally around the functions of instructional messages within the instructional communications system (like motivation, concept learning, and attitude change), but other authors were more specifically focused on some media attribute (such as text, sound, color, or images) to identify optimally effective ways to facilitate cognitive processes. Contributions taking this media attributes approach included David H. Jonassen's *Technology of Text* (1982, 1985), James Hartley's *Designing Instructional Text* (1986), and Harvey A. Houghton and Dale M. Willows's *The Psychology of Illustration* (1987).

Interest at the time in media attributes likely emerged from—and contributed to—the media debates of the 1980s and early 1990s regarding whether media (television, film, radio) could influence learning in and of themselves. On one side of the debate, Richard Clark and others argued the research evidence demonstrated that many different types of media could accomplish the same instructional goals and that, therefore, specific media attributes were not having any unique cognitive effect on learning outcomes; instead, other intervening variables must be involved in learning gains. On the other side, Robert Kozma and colleagues suggested that the question should not be whether media influence learning, but should rather be reframed to explore the complexity of *how* media influence learning. Kozma and other critics of the position that media do not influence learning suggested that each medium does carry with it a set of attributes or *affordances* that support particular kinds of message representations and varyingly support learners' decoding of those messages. Understanding how those attributes affect learners' cognitive processes, these authors argued, will allow us to design more effective instructional messages.

From this perspective, Richard Mayer and his colleagues have more recently been exploring how the brain processes multimedia messages based on three major principles of cognitive theory: the dual channel principle, the limited capacity (cognitive load) principle, and the active processing principle. Working under the umbrella term *multimedia learning*, Mayer has argued that the three goals of multimedia instruction design should be to minimize extraneous cognitive processing, manage essential processing, and foster generative processing during learning. From the findings of the systematic research being done in this area, instructional message designers have an empirically tested set of guidelines for understanding how presentations that contain multiple media—particularly combinations of words and pictures—are likely to affect learners' cognitive processing.

Future Directions

Instructional message design's early roots in transmission-oriented communication models dovetailed nicely with the objectivist conceptions of knowledge that were foundational to both behaviorist and cognitivist learning theories. From the objectivist perspective, educators were responsible for producing prepackaged or prescripted instructional messages that were didactically designed to be optimally effective for producing learning in the given audience within the particular context. This view also meshed well with the limited digital technologies available at the time: The idea was to automate the process of teaching by setting up, in advance, the conditions under which learning will inevitably occur and delivering those messages via a mechanical device. However, given the considerable changes in communications and learning theory as well as the available interactive technologies, some have recently begun suggesting that it may be time to reconsider many of the foundational instructional message design concepts that have remained essentially the same since 1995.

From this perspective, some have argued that the most appropriate metaphor for instruction is conversation, and that our thinking about instructional communications should move from earlier transmission-based models to a transaction-oriented view instead. Further, proponents of this view suggest we should adopt the position that these conversations cannot be designed; rather, we should concern ourselves with understanding and creating the conditions within which conversations occur and can be leveraged for learning. Designing adaptive systems that respond appropriately within a conversation model of message design will require becoming more mindful of the noncognitive factors that contribute to human meaning making and redefining the field more broadly to seek affordances for all in the conversation to actively participate. Brent Wilson has offered four pillars of practice that he suggested should underlie a broader view of instructional design practices in the future: (a) individual cognition and behavior, (b) social and cultural learning, (c) values, and (d) aesthetics. He argued that although cognition and behavior have been well studied by instructional message design researchers over the years, little consideration has been given to the other three pillars in the literature.

For example, Deepak Subramony and other concerned authors have documented the lack of attention that important issues of multiculturalism have received in the field and the extent to which that neglect has alienated many learning groups. These authors have suggested that designing more culturally aware learning materials based on *relevant* cultural attributes of learners will not be easy given the current lack of research in this area. However, to avoid producing products that are ineffective, underused, or culturally insensitive, instructional message design can and should play a role in exploring issues of multiculturalism. Similarly, Patrick Parrish has been advocating for the importance of aesthetics in learning experiences and has come up with a set of principles and guidelines for thinking differently about message design. According to Parrish, aesthetic considerations of the learning experience go beyond the traditional instructional system components of subject matter, instructional method, learner, instructor, and context to include also the way the learner feels about the instructional situation. The idea is to provide much more than just an attractive interface but rather to create more holistic experiences aimed at helping learners construct meaning.

According to these and other authors, the future of message design research should be refocused on the design of interactive learning environments rather than continuing to explore the design of pre-specified instructional routines to be passively received by the learner. In response, new fields of inquiry, such as computer-supported collaborative learning (CSCL), have begun to emerge that explore how online multimedia environments can be designed to support collaborative learning activities. A great deal of the research that is currently being done in this area regarding the nature of collaborative technologies, group composition, task, tutors, community building, assessment, scaffolding collaboration, and knowledge construction can be said to fall under the aegis of message design. However, further research is needed on which technologies provide the affordances for meaningful communication and collaboration, how to integrate multimedia resources into collaborative workspaces and communication media, and how to use multimedia resources to foster social presence.

Thus, the research in instructional message design has varied rather markedly over the years in its focus and perspectives on the scope of the field. Barbara Grabowski characterized the variation in the instructional message design literature by distinguishing between message design research focused on the physical form of messages versus that focused on the inductive composition of messages. According to Grabowski, design decisions about messages' *form* involve manipulating the physical organization of a message to accommodate fundamental information processing capabilities that tend to be relatively similar across learners. Calling this category of guidelines *message design for instruction*, these are the techniques dealing with external factors out of the learner's control that affect attention, perception, and—to some degree—comprehension as well. Decisions about *inductive composition*, however, involve incorporating *message design for learning* strategies that activate (or induce) the cognitive processes needed for learning actually to occur and meaningfully relate the message content to the learners' existing knowledge structures. Grabowski suggested that, though necessary, message design for instruction is not sufficient for learning. Therefore, attending both to the form and to the inductive structure of messages appears to be equally important.

M. J. Bishop

See also Cognition and Human Learning; History of Educational Technology; Instructional Design Models

Further Readings

Bishop, M. J. (2013). Instructional design: Past, present, and future relevance. In J. M. Spector, M. D. Merrill, J. Elen, & M. J. Bishop (Eds.), *Handbook for research in educational communications and technology* (4th ed.). New York, NY: Springer.

Clark, R. E. (Ed.). (2001). *Learning from media: Arguments, analysis, and evidence.* Greenwich, CT: Information Age Publishing.

Fleming, M., & Levie, W. H. (Eds.). (1993). *Instructional message design: Principles From the behavioral and cognitive sciences* (2nd ed.). Englewood Cliffs, NJ: Educational Technology Publications.

Gibbons, A. S. (2014). *An architectural approach to instructional design.* New York, NY: Routledge.

Mayer, R. E. (2013). Multimedia learning. In J. M. Spector, M. D. Merrill, J. Elen, & M. J. Bishop (Eds.), *Handbook of research on educational communications and technology* (4th ed.). New York, NY: Springer.

Richey, R. C., Klein, J. D., & Tracey, M. W. (2011). *The instructional design knowledge base: Theory, research, and practice.* New York, NY: Routledge.

Saettler, L. P. (1990). *The evolution of American educational technology.* Englewood, CO: Libraries Unlimited.

Salomon, G. (1979/1994). *Interaction of media, cognition and learning: An exploration of how symbolic forms cultivate mental skills and affect knowledge acquisition.* Hillsdale, NJ: Lawrence Erlbaum.

Smith, K. M., & Boling, E. (2009). What do we make of design? Design as a concept in educational technology. *Educational Technology, 49*(4), 3–17.

Wilson, B. G. (2005). Broadening our foundation for instructional design: Four pillars of practice. *Educational Technology, 45*(2), 10–15.

METATAGGING OF LEARNING OBJECTS AND APPS

Metatagging is the process of adding metadata to an information resource to enable search and retrieval of this resource on the web. *Metadata* are data about an information resource or simply data about data. More specifically, metadata describe the different characteristics and attributes of an information resource—for example, the title, the author, the date of creation, and the subject. They consist of data items that are associated with the information resources, which are called metadata elements or tags. In the field of technology-enhanced learning (TEL), metadata are used for characterizing learning objects (LOs) and apps toward facilitating their search and retrieval from learning object repositories and app markets or app stores correspondingly. An *LO* is any type of digital resource that can be reused to support learning, whereas a *learning app* is a software program or group of software programs that can be used to perform tasks that support learning, as defined by Guillermo Vega-Gorgojo and colleagues.

A popular way of metatagging LOs and learning apps is by using formal and globally agreed-on classification systems. This implies that either the authors of the LOs or the developer of the learning app or metadata experts will describe them with the use of appropriate metadata authoring tools or that automatic mechanisms (such as metadata harvesting, content extraction, automatic indexing, classification, or text and data mining) will be used to generate the metadata elements' values. With the emergence of Web 2.0 applications, other means of metatagging LOs and learning apps have been investigated and proposed, such as social tagging. This means that metadata are not only created by metadata experts or the authors and developers of the LOs/learning apps. Instead, the generation of metadata is also done by the actual end-users of the LOs or learning apps, who can describe them with tags that are meaningful to them. This entry first discusses the existing standards for formal metatagging of learning objects and apps. Then, the entry discusses social metatagging of learning objects and apps by end users.

Formal Metatagging of Learning Objects and Apps

Formal metatagging of LOs and apps is achieved by using globally agreed-on metadata models. According to the National Information Standards Organization, metadata models are structured sets of metadata elements designed and agreed to describe a particular type of information resource. Metadata specifications are well-defined and widely accepted metadata models, usually developed and promoted by individual organizations or consortia of partners from industry or academia. When a specification is widely recognized and adopted by a standardization organization, it then becomes a metadata standard. Existing metadata standards for LOs include the following:

• *The Dublin Core Metadata Element Set (DCMES),* which has been developed by the Dublin Core Metadata Initiative (DCMI) and is a standard for describing general information resources available online. Nevertheless, DCMES has also been used for describing LOs with metadata.

• *The IEEE Learning Object Metadata (IEEE LOM),* which has been developed by the IEEE (Institute of Electrical and Electronics Engineers) Learning Technologies Standards Committee working group, titled "WG12—Learning Object Metadata." IEEE LOM has been based on early versions of the metadata models of the Alliance of Remote Instructional Authoring and Distribution Network for Europe (ARIADNE) and IMS Global Learning Consortium Learning Resource Metadata. IEEE LOM has been the dominant metadata standard for describing LOs in a wide range of existing learning object repositories.

• *The ISO/IEC 19788 Metadata Learning Resource (MLR),* which is under development by a subcommittee of the Joint Technical Committee 1 of the International Organization for Standardization (ISO) and the International Electrotechnical Commission (IEC). The subcommittee working on MLR is the ISO/IEC JTC 1/SC 36 Information Technology for Learning, Education and Training. MLR is based primarily on DCMES and IEEE LOM and supports two key principles: (a) *modularity*—the standard is structured in several parts, which allows users to group different metadata elements according to their nature, facilitating further growth of the standard with new parts; and (b) *compatibility*—this means that it opts for compatibility with DCMES and IEEE LOM.

Regarding learning apps, existing metadata specifications define metadata for apps that are developed in the form of widgets. According to the World Wide Web Consortium (W3C), a widget denotes a small portable Web-enabled application, often geared toward performing a single task. Metadata specifications of widgets include (a) the *W3C Widget Configuration and Packaging Specification* developed by W3C, (b) the *OpenAjax Metadata 1.0 Specification* developed by the OpenAjax Alliance, and (c) the *OpenSocial Metadata Specification* developed by the OpenSocial Foundation.

Despite the existence of widely accepted metadata specifications and standards, it is not possible for generic standards to fully meet specific requirements and thoroughly accommodate the particular needs of different educational communities requiring local extensions or modifications to these standards. As a result, a common practice of generating metadata application profiles has emerged as a means of addressing this problem. According to the Workshop on Learning Technologies (WS-LT) of the European Committee for Standardization (CEN/ISSS), a metadata application profile is an assemblage of metadata elements selected from one or more metadata models and combined in a compound model. Metadata application profiles provide the means to implement the principles of modularity and extensibility. The purpose of a metadata application profile is to adapt or combine existing metadata models into a package that is tailored to the functional requirements of a particular application, while retaining interoperability with the original base metadata models. Within this context, some software tools have been developed to facilitate the process of developing metadata application profiles, as discussed by Demetrios Sampson and colleagues.

Social Metatagging of Learning Objects and Apps

Social metatagging of LOs and apps is achieved by enabling the actual end-users of these LOs and apps to add freely chosen tags to them. This means that social metatagging produces an unstructured set of tags that is typically referred to as "folksonomy," which can constitute an alternative (superset or subset) of the corresponding taxonomy used in formal metatagging.

Different types of tags used for social metatagging of LOs and apps can be summarized as follows:

Content-based tags: These tags are used to describe the actual content of an LO or app. Indicative examples of such tags could be physics, mathematics, chemistry, and so on.

Context-based tags: These tags are used to describe the educational context where an LO or app will be used. Indicative examples of such tags could be primary, secondary, higher education (for formal education) or in a science center or museum (for nonformal education).

Purpose tags: These tags focus on capturing aspects of intent rather than content-related information. For LOs and apps, these tags could denote the educational objectives that an LO or app intends to target.

Subjective tags: These tags are used to express user's opinion or emotions. Indicative examples of such tags could be *funny, cool, amusing,* and so forth.

In conclusion, metatagging of LOs and apps has attracted the attention of both researchers and practitioners. The anticipated benefits are that search and retrieval of LOs and apps on the web can be facilitated. The current trend is to move from the expert-based descriptions following formal metatagging standards and specifications to a less formal user-based tagging, namely social metatagging. This is expected to offer additional benefits such as a personalized way of searching based on end-users' tags, as well as a mechanism to capture end-users' contextual value of LOs and apps.

Panagiotis Zervas and Demetrios G. Sampson

See also Learning and Instructional Apps; Learning Objects; Repositories for Learning and Instructional Apps

Further Readings

Dublin Core Metadata Element Set, Version 1.1 (2004). Reference description. Retrieved November 29, 2013, from http://dublincore.org/documents/2004/12/20/dces

IEEE Learning Technology Standards Committee (LTSC) (2005). Final standard for learning object metadata. Retrieved November 29, 2013, from http://ltsc.ieee.org/wg12/files/IEEE_1484_12_03_d8_submitted.pdf

ISO/IEC 19788–1 (2011). *Information technology—Learning, education and training—Metadata for learning resources.*

Part 1: Framework. International Organization for Standardization. Retrieved from http://www.iso.org/iso/catalogue_detail.htm?csnumber=50772

OpenAjax Alliance (2010). OpenAjax metadata 1.0 specification. Retrieved November 29, 2013, from http://www.openajax.org/member/wiki/OpenAjax_Metadata_Specification

OpenSocial Foundation (2013). OpenSocial metadata specification. Retrieved November 29, 2013, from https://opensocial.atlassian.net/wiki/display/OSD/Specs

Sampson, D., Zervas P., & Chloros, G. (2012). Supporting the process of developing and managing LOM application profiles: The ASK-LOM-AP tool. *IEEE Transactions on Learning Technologies (TLT), 5*(3), 238–250.

Sampson, D., Zervas P., & Kalamatianos, A. (2011). ASK-LOST 2.0: A Web-based tool for social tagging digital educational resources in learning environments. In B. White, I. King, & P. Tsang (Eds.), *Social media tools and platforms in learning environments* (pp. 387–435). New York, NY: Springer.

Smith, N., Van Coillie, M., & Duval, E. (2006). Guidelines and support for building application profiles in e-learning. In N. Smith, M. Van Coillie, & E. Duval (Eds.), *CEN/ISSS WS/LT learning technologies workshop CWA* (pp. 1–26). Brussels, Belgium: CEN Workshop Agreements.

Vega-Gorgojo, G., Bote-Lorenzo, M. L., Gómez-Sánchez, E., Dimitriadis, Y. A., & Asensio-Pérez, J. I. (2006). A semantic approach to discovering learning services in grid-based collaborative systems. *Future Generation Computer Systems, 22*(6), 709–719.

World Wide Web Consortium (W3C). (2012). W3C widget configuration and packaging specification. Retrieved November 29, 2013, from http://www.w3.org/TR/widgets

METHODS FOR TEACHING DIGITAL LITERACY SKILLS

Digital literacy skills relate to the use of digital technology tools in activities that locate, create, communicate, and evaluate information within a networked (online) environment, mediated by digital computing technologies. *Digital information* is a symbolic representation of data in media whereas *digital literacy*, in this context, is the ability to create, share, understand, and think critically about the messages conveyed using the signs and symbols that have been defined within the media system.

An interesting transposition in digital technology usage in and out of the classroom has occurred during the past 25 years, corresponding to the growth of the World Wide Web. During the 1980s and 1990s, learners typically encountered these educational technologies first in the classroom given their limited availability and high cost. This is no longer the case because learners now possess knowledge and experience with digital media gained outside of school, including high-speed Internet and mobile applications that are not supported in the classroom, thus creating a new digital divide. Learners may be less motivated to learn because of the perceptions that their culture and values are not reflected in the curriculum and that school-based learning has limited value and relevance to their future educational and professional aspirations.

Teaching digital literacy skills in primary, secondary, and postsecondary education for adult learners is critical to closing the digital divide to adequately address issues of exclusion and marginalization that confront 21st-century learners. An aim of school curricula, particularly at the primary and secondary education level, is to provide learners with knowledge, skills, and understanding so they can make sense of the world. This requires a change in teaching practice and curriculum to foster digital literacy and to provide learners with the skills needed to become discerning participants in their own learning. This entry discusses digital literacy skills that are important for K–12 students to learn, the theory behind digital literacy, and methods for teaching digital literacy skills.

Epistemological Framework

Teaching digital literacy skills requires a different epistemological framework than teaching other forms of literacy. This includes pedagogical, cognitive, and evaluation skills to demonstrate how digital media might support pedagogical goals and simultaneously foster understanding of how the message is transformed by the media. This is not the same as teaching how to use technology. Groups of learners typically characterized as *digital natives*, the *net generation*, or *millennials* may be quite comfortable using technology, whether it is a game console, computer, tablet, website, search engine, smartphone, or increasingly, wearable technology. Indeed, information and communications technologies (ICT) have become ubiquitous, permeating every aspect of modern society: education, work, public services, entertainment, and culture. The skills needed for separating good information from bad are lacking among all groups. To overcome this knowledge and skills deficiency requires creating digital fluency by combining critical thinking, net savviness, and diversity of sources in media evaluation and usage, according to Carl Miller and Jamie Bartlett.

Critical Thinking

Critical thinking, in the form of evaluative techniques, refers to the way users rate the reliability and accuracy of content via the Internet. Research suggests that the perceived veracity of information retrieved from the Internet is judged higher than that of television, radio, or newspaper media among digital natives, although most recognize that possible biases and inaccuracies exist.

Net Savviness

Net savviness is the quality of critical decision making that comes from understanding how websites are built and the way that search engines work. Many K–12 students aren't aware, for instance, that different search engines employ different mechanisms to search different indexes, thus delivering different results with varying degrees of credibility. There is an overwhelming tendency to accept whatever appears at the top of a set of search results.

Diversity of Sources

Diversity and a preponderance of the evidence is the third epistemological principle identified by Miller and Bartlett. In essence, an underlying tenet of scientific inquiry is that we always begin with a hypothesis or rule that we must try to prove is false. Only through this level of scientific inquiry are we able to arrive at the truth. It is human nature to search for evidence to prove one's own theory, rather than to try to falsify one's beliefs—that is, to prove ourselves right rather than wrong.

Theory to Practice

The concept of digital literacy as an activity, mediated by digital technology tools to locate, create, communicate, and evaluate information, is clearly established in activity theory, which states that all activity is directed toward a performance outcome or object. Through the application of activity theory, it can be argued that digital media, accessed via the Internet, acts as a mediator of learning practices and values in ways that are distinctly different from that of print-based media. When a new tool is introduced into a learning activity system, the learners' sense of its affordances and constraints evolves over time whereas actions, aligned with goals in the context of the tool, provide new interpretations of content. The components of a learning activity system organically influence and transform one another as the system moves toward homeostasis, thus providing context for the tool. The system in turn provides guidance for the use of the tool to promote and establish digital literacy, through the mediating effect of rules and role-based interactions within the learning community.

When one works within this systems view of mediated learning activity, there are identifiable best practices for incorporating digital literacy in the classroom, as suggested by Melissa Mallon and Donald Gilstrap:

- Digital literacy should be pedagogically led and integrated soundly into the curriculum.
- Educators should use social software and collaborative technologies to encourage learners to work together.
- Educators should focus on skills that facilitate lifelong learning and transferable skills.
- Learners should use technology tools to create assessable deliverables.

In essence, educators must model the behaviors and skills of digital literacy in their own practice and in the way that they interact with their learners through digital media in and out of the classroom to be perceived as credible.

Teaching Methods

Methods for teaching digital literacy skills begin by providing learners with access to digital technologies in the classroom when it is appropriate and useful. Educators must also model creative and critical ways to locate, create, communicate, and evaluate information within a networked environment to further the learners' subject knowledge, regardless of subject area. A guide for putting digital literacy into practice, for primary and secondary education, is suggested by Sarah Hague and Cassie Payton within a pedagogical framework that includes the following components:

Functional skills: Hands-on, experiential learning to develop competency in basic ICT skills may apply to learners in all age ranges depending on whether the technology is provided or in accordance with bring your own device (BYOD) policies.

Creativity: This is how learners think, construct knowledge objects, and apply methods for sharing and distribution of knowledge. Suggested projects to build creativity in digital literacy can involve websites, videos, podcasts, blogs, wikis, digital portfolios, and e-books.

Collaboration: Meaningful learning requires dialogue, discussion, and exchange of ideas with and in relation to others for socially constructed meaning-making to occur.

Communication: Digital literacy requires additional higher order communication skills in a world where much communication is mediated by digital technology.

Ability to find and select information: These are fundamental skills that are essential for knowledge development as learners learn how to learn; related pedagogy is inquiry-based learning. Novice searchers may require additional guidance and scaffolding to include discussion of copyright, intellectual property, and plagiarism.

Critical thinking and evaluation: Critical thinking is at the core of digital literacy; it includes analysis and transformation of information to create new knowledge; it requires reflection to evaluate and consider different interpretations.

Cultural and social understanding: These provide learners with a language and context for digital literacy to promote broader understanding and interaction in the creation of meaning.

E-safety: In teaching digital literacy, educators have an obligation to support learners in development of skills, knowledge, and understanding that will enable them to make informed decisions to protect themselves on an ongoing basis.

Timothy Boileau

See also Activity Theory; Assessing Literacy Skills in the 21st Century; Digital Curation; Digital Divide; Digital Literacy: Overview and Definition

Further Readings

Hague, C., & Payton, S. (2010). Digital literacy across the curriculum. Retrieved from http://www.futurelab.org.uk/resources/digital-literacy-across-curriculum-handbook

Hobbs, R. (2010). Digital and media literacy: A plan of action. Washington, DC: Aspen Institute. Retrieved from http://www.knightcomm.org/digital-and-media-literacy-a-plan-of-action

Jimoyiannis, A., & Gravani, M. (2011). Exploring adult digital literacy using learners' and educators' perceptions and experiences: The case of the second chance schools in Greece. *Journal of Educational Technology & Society, 14*(1), 217–227.

Mallon, M., & Gilstrap, D. (2014). Digital literacy and the emergence of technology-based curriculum theories. In D. Loveless, B. Griffith, M. Bérci, E. Ortlieb, & P. Sullivan (Eds.), *Academic knowledge construction and multimodal curriculum development* (pp. 15–29). Hershey, PA: IGI Global.

Miller, C., & Bartlett, J. (2012). Digital fluency: Towards young people's critical use of the Internet. *Journal of Information Literacy, 6*(2), 35–55.

MINDTOOLS

When a learner uses a computer application as a *mindtool*, it means that the learner is using that software program to engage in constructive, higher order, critical thinking. The concept was developed by David Jonassen, who was a professor of learning technologies and educational psychology at the University of Missouri until his death in 2012. The focus of his professional life was on problem solving, and his mindtools concept was particularly influential. His first book on the concept was *Computers in the Classroom: Mindtools for Critical Thinking*, published in 1995. This entry details the concept of mindtools and discusses its impact.

Mindtools Elaborated

Jonassen distinguished mindtools, or cognitive tools, from traditional computer learning applications. Using mindtools means that learners work *with* the technology to represent their knowledge, rather than learning *from* the technology, as is the case with traditional tutorial or drill and practice applications. Jonassen characterizes mindtools as tools and environments developed to function as problem-solving and reasoning companions, designed especially to support and facilitate critical thinking and higher order learning. Examples include databases, expert systems, microworlds, and spreadsheets.

Since Jonassen's first book on mindtools was published, the concept has been widely propagated and adopted in both K–12 and higher education settings. The book itself is now in its third edition and has been translated into several languages including Mandarin Chinese and Korean.

Mindtools can be used by learners of all ages. Its use to create computer-based concept maps is one mindtool application that is particularly flexible in this respect as both young children and adult learners are able to represent what they know in these interconnected systems of nodes with labeled links between nodes. Although some commonly used mindtools such as spreadsheets or systems modeling software may be more applicable for older learners, mindtools have a wide reach in terms of learning applications.

Mindtools Characterized

Even though the mindtools concept is relatively dated by technology standards, it continues to have an enduring impact on the field. The following characteristics of mindtools are crucial to their continued influence:

Mindtools are ubiquitous. They are not quite everywhere, but they are readily available and easy to find. Mindtools such as spreadsheets, concept maps, or semantic networks are available from many different sources and in many different forms (e.g., resident on your own computer, installed on a school district network, or in the Internet cloud). With the growth of the Internet and suites of online tools such as those offered by Apple, Google, Microsoft, and others, this is even truer today than it was when Jonassen first introduced the mindtools concept. However, although mindtools are widely available, learners must know how to use them effectively. For example, a concept-mapping tool becomes a mindtool when it is used in a student-focused way in which students create their own concept maps, rather than simply using those provided by a teacher.

Mindtools are discipline-free. Because the learner provides the content for the mindtool, that content could be biology, art history, mathematics, or practically anything. At the root of the mindtools concept is the notion that students are in effect *teaching* the technology what they know. Thus, by their very nature, mindtools can be applied in almost any discipline. Both students studying English literature and those studying earth science can effectively construct linked concept maps that represent their growing knowledge of a field of study.

Mindtools are cheap. Mindtools are widely available and often inexpensive, and many are free or available as shareware. Although this may not be the most esoteric point about these tools, from a practical point of view, it is an important one—especially for K–12 teachers who often end up paying for teaching supplies out of their own pockets. Having a technology tool that is both effective and free or inexpensive is a powerful combination.

Mindtools are cognitively accessible. This concept applies both to individual tools and to the concept of a mindtool itself. Jonassen claimed that he could teach a class to get started using any of the mindtools in a matter of minutes. This was initially true in face-to-face settings; the advent of easily produced videos and screen captures allows instructors to teach and students to learn mindtools relatively easily in online settings as well. Ultimately, concept maps, spreadsheets, and other mindtools are not difficult tools to use; some students may come into a classroom already knowing the mechanics of such tools.

Mindtools are durable. Technologies come and go. One of the reasons that Jonassen's mindtool concept has had a lasting impact is that many *new* technologies can act as mindtools. Online versions of spreadsheets (e.g., Google Sheets) and presentation software (e.g., Prezi) exist, and online concept mapping tools allow learners new ways of representing what they know. In addition to expanding the suite of tools available to act as mindtools, this also allows instructors or designers who implement the mindtools concept to keep their instruction fresh by maintaining the mindtools pedagogy of learning *with* technology rather than *from* it, as well as using new, cloud-based applications as mindtools.

The Impact of Mindtools

The lasting impact of mindtools in education is rooted in the characteristics just described: (a) they are easy to learn to use, (b) they can be used by many types of learners in any domain, (c) they are cheap, and (d) they are passing the test of time. Their impact can be further described in terms of the uniqueness of the mindtools concept itself.

When Jonassen coined the term *mindtools*, he turned many researchers and educators' view of technology upside down. Although the field was excited about the promise of educational technologies ("look what these computers can do!"), and focused on how the computer was going to drive education, Jonassen made us stop and focus on how those technologies could be used to promote problem solving and critical thinking, rather than simply marveling at the technology itself.

His concept of mindtools shifted the focal point from the technology to the learner and to learning. Jonassen's mindtools concept tells us that the computer is only a *tool* for helping the learner learn. But the human—not the technology—has to do the learning. The mindtools concept places the burden of synthesizing and analyzing knowledge structures on the human and the job of externally representing the structures, remembering them, and manipulating them on the computer. The computer is better than the human at remembering, but the human is better at analysis. As Jonassen emphasized, accounting for this difference in distributing the work enables the technology and the learner to become intellectual partners. This distribution of labor is why the mindtools concept continues and is likely to continue to have an impact on education (learning, performance, and instruction). In the future, new mindtools may emerge in online settings and flipped classrooms, as well as face-to-face ones for learners of all ages.

Rose Marra

See also Cognition and Human Learning; Constructivist Theory; Learning by Modeling; Learning With Models; Learning With Simulations; Simulation-Based Learning

Further Readings

Hoeffner, K., Kendall, M., Stellenwerf, C., Thames, P., & Williams, P. (1993, November). Problem solving with a spreadsheet. *Arithmetic Teacher*, 52–56.

Hung, W., & Strobel, J. (2011). Definition, conceptualization, and utilization: A review of research on concept mapping as a pedagogical mindtool. In T. Bastiaens & M. Ebner (Eds.), *Proceedings of World Conference on Educational Multimedia, Hypermedia and Telecommunications 2011* (pp. 3004–3011). Chesapeake, VA: AACE.

Jonassen, D. H. (1995). *Mindtools for engaging critical thinking in the classroom*. Columbus, OH: Prentice Hall.

Jonassen, D. H. (2005). *Modeling with technology: Mindtools for conceptual change,* (3rd ed.). Columbus, OH: Prentice Hall.

Jonassen, D. H., & Carr, C. S. (2000). Mindtools: Affording multiple knowledge representations for learning. In S. P. Lajoie (Ed.), *Computers as cognitive tools: Vol. 2. No more walls: Theory change, paradigm shifts, and their influence on the use of computers for instructional purposes* (pp. 165–196). Mahwah, NJ: Lawrence Erlbaum.

Jonassen, D. H., Carr, C., & Yueh, H-P. (1998). Computers as mindtools for engaging learners in critical thinking. *TechTrends, 43*(2), 24–32.

Marra, R. (2013). Mindtools in online education: Enabling meaningful learning. In J. M. Spector, B. B. Lockee, S. E. Smaldino, & M. C. Herring (Eds.), *Learning, problem solving, and mindtools: Essays in honor of David H. Jonassen* (pp. 265–286). New York, NY: Routledge.

Nersessian, N. J. (1999). Model-based reasoning in conceptual change. In L. Magnani, N. J. Nersessian, & P. Thagard (Eds.), *Models are used to represent reality* (pp. 5–22). New York, NY: Kluwer Academic.

Sundheim, B. R. (1992). Column operations: A spreadsheet model. *Journal of Chemical Education, 69*(8), 650–654.

MOBILE ASSISTIVE TECHNOLOGIES

Mobile assistive technology includes portable mobile technology devices (e.g., e-readers, smartphones, tablets, personal media players) and associated software applications (apps) used to support the learning and functional needs of persons with disabilities (e.g., sensory, communication, physical, cognitive). These mobile technologies compensate for or improve someone's ability to do something he or she otherwise would have accomplished with great difficulty, ineffectively—or not at all. This entry discusses how mobile assistive technologies can help students with disabilities, the statutory foundations of mobile assistive technologies, and features and uses of mobile assistive technologies.

To understand how mobile technology can help a student with disabilities, consider a high school student with dyslexia who must read a science chapter for her biology class, outline key ideas, and post questions to classmates on the class Moodle site (virtual learning platform). She uses a mobile tablet with a text-to-speech app (e.g., Voice Dream Reader) that converts the electronic files from the digital copy of the book chapter on bioethics into simulated speech. To efficiently follow along, she adjusts the speaking rate in the app so that as the content is read aloud she can follow along comfortably while the words are highlighted on the screen. This multimodal input helps her attend to and remember the vocabulary and ideas in the chapter. She is able to pause the app (and return to an earlier section of the chapter) while she writes down key ideas from the chapter. Without these supports, her reading is labored and taxing, with gaps in comprehension.

Mobile assistive technology is one class of assistive technology (AT), the broader umbrella term for a range of devices and tools that address functional skill needs because of a disability. When mobile devices are considered a kind of assistive technology, decisions about the best fit of a particular tool are made at an individual level. Services needed to evaluate, acquire, train, maintain, or repair assistive mobile technologies are also covered by the term *mobile assistive technology.*

Technology use in education for students with disabilities is broader. The U.S. Department of Education reports that most students with disabilities in K–12 education are educated for most of their school day in a general education setting with other students. Technology-oriented pedagogies used in schools are especially important for students with disabilities. Some of these include one-to-one technology programs (provision of one digital or computing device per student for learning) and mobile learning (access to educational tools, resources, and information using mobile devices). Mobile technology use also supports universal design for learning, or UDL (a framework for proactive design of flexible curriculum and instruction addressing wide learner variability). David Rose and colleagues discuss the complementary and unique aspects of AT and UDL, which together improve education and success for students with disabilities.

Mainstream mobile technologies (mobile technologies readily available for general use and not designed solely for individuals with disabilities), such as tablets and smartphones, now include many accessibility features. Some of these include word prediction (software or device-generated word choices based on the first or second letter(s) typed by the user), text to speech (conversion of digital text to audible speech), and screen magnification (customized enlargement of screen display). This class of technologies is referred to as *accessible technology*. Distinctions between technologies currently designated as assistive and technologies with accessibility features that are used more generally are likely to become more blurred as technologies evolve.

Statutory Foundations of Mobile Assistive Technology

Statutory requirements for AT included in federal legislation have shaped current availability and use of mobile assistive technology in education and the community. The 1988 Technology-Related Assistance for Individuals with Disabilities Act (PL 100-407) in the United States provided a definition of an *AT device* as any device used to increase, maintain, or improve the capabilities of those with disabilities; and *AT service* was defined as any service that directly assists someone with a disability in the selection, acquisition, and use of an AT device. These definitions were applied in subsequent federal statutes in the United States, including the Individuals with Disabilities Education Improvement Act (PL 108–446) that is intended to ensure equity and quality in education for pre-K–12 students with disabilities. Specific mobile technology devices may be classified as assistive if they fit the guidelines in federal legislation. Section 508 of the American Rehabilitation Act (PL 105–220) requires federal agencies to ensure that the electronic and information technologies they develop, acquire, and use (websites, telephones, computers, software) are accessible to people with disabilities. The intent of that law is to remove roadblocks to information technology use and encourage development of new accessible technologies.

The 21st Century Communications and Video Accessibility Act of 2010 (PL 111–260) updated protections and accessibility in current digital and mobile telecommunications for people with disabilities. Smartphones and mobile devices with Web browsers must be usable by people with visual impairments, blindness, and those using hearing aids. Captioned television programs must also include captions when they are broadcast on the Internet. Similar laws exist in other countries in support of those with disabilities

Features of Mobile Devices and Assistive Technologies

Mobile technology used as assistive technology is characterized by its portable nature, size, and freedom of use across learning, home, employment, and community settings. This is especially important for students with disabilities who require these assistive technologies for success in different contexts. Mobile technologies include options for personalization based on individual learning, and physical, cognitive, and perceptual needs (e.g., varying choices of alert tones, vibrations, or visual signals to indicate different communications or program feedback). Further customization through apps selected according to an individual's needs and ongoing learning is possible. Customary mobile technologies include cell phones and smartphones, tablets, e-book readers, MP3 players, digital recorders, multifunction devices, smartpens (digital pens pairing written notes to recorded lectures or events), personal digital assistants (handheld personal organization devices often with calendar, note, reminders, and e-mail), and Global Positioning System (GPS) devices. Many mobile devices use touchscreen interfaces requiring touch (or stylus) input between the user and device (swipes and taps). Sensory feedback (auditory, visual, tactile, or haptic) provides a multimodal tool for learning and interaction.

Standard accessibility features included in mobile operating systems (e.g., iOS, Windows, and Android) are important features of device consideration for people with and without disabilities. Common accessibility features on many mobile devices include screen readers (identifies and reads aloud what is displayed on the screen), speech recognition (records spoken word and converts to digital text), magnification, and on-screen keyboard (visual keyboard display with control capability through mouth, eye, voice, or other physical movement). Mobile device considerations include screen or device size, input options (touch, voice, vision, motion sensing, muscle movement), output options (audio, haptic), accessibility features, device memory, battery life (duration needed for untethered use), connectivity (Internet access or reliability in different environments), student preference, curation of apps (categorizing, cataloging of available apps), and cost.

Mobile Assistive Technology Uses

Research on mobile technology use for students with disabilities is emerging and should not be considered disability specific. Any particular device or app may have functions for different users and purposes. Vision needs may be addressed through magnification and contrast setting adjustments, screen and text readers, and voice activated GPS used for navigation assistance. Some mobile devices have capabilities to integrate with Braille display devices. Mobile devices with integrated cameras can be used with apps that perform a range of functions. For example, apps using optical character recognition (OCR) technologies take pictures of objects with text and then read the text aloud. Students can take pictures of food labels, mail, and other printed instructional text and have it read aloud.

To address hearing needs, mobile devices with video capability allow communication options such as video calls in which callers can use sign language. Subtitles and movies/programs with closed captions can be accessed for learning and enjoyment. The development of augmentative and alternative communication (AAC) apps (the use of other methods or tools to support or replace verbal communication) have increased options for communication and interaction for students with disabilities. These apps are often less costly and stigmatizing than is a dedicated device. David McNaughton and Janet Light provide a comprehensive analysis of the benefits and challenges of mobile technologies and AAC.

Mobile technology use for individuals with autism spectrum disorder and intellectual disability has gained increased attention and use. Varied mobile devices have been used to assist these students in learning social skills, remembering steps in a learning or life skill, recreational enjoyment, communication, personal organization, and self-monitoring. In particular, use of video modeling (an intervention using a video model of someone completing a particular academic, social, or employment skill that can be imitated) provided on mobile devices has increased because of portability and use across natural contexts.

For students with learning disabilities, mobile devices provide a portable and personalized tool providing access to many AT programs previously deployed to stationary computers. AT software established as effective technologies for persons with learning disabilities (e.g., word processors, spell checkers, word prediction, speech recognition, etc.) are now available on many mobile technologies. Marshall Raskind provides a summary of assistive and mobile technologies that compensate for the reading, writing, language, math, organization, studying, and remembering needs of these individuals. Mobile app versions of integrated AT literacy software supporting a range of reading, writing, research and studying needs are often available. The apps may have slightly different features than their software counterparts.

Mobile AT tools are immediately available, personalized, and less stigmatizing. They support a range of learning needs through the growing app market and ongoing technology innovations. Enhanced student self-confidence, independence, achievement, communication, and motivation may be evidenced through mobile AT use. Continued expansion of mobile technology use for people with disabilities is expected to occur.

Christina M. Curran

See also Assistive Technology; Assistive Technology for Persons With Autism Spectrum Disorder; Mobile Devices: Impact on Learning and Instruction; Mobile Tools and Technologies for Learning and Instruction; Universal Design; Universal Design for Learning

Further Readings

McNaughton, D., & Light, J. (2013). The iPad and mobile technology revolution: Benefits and challenges for individuals who required augmentative and alternative communication. *Augmentative and Alternative Communication, 29*(2), 107–116.

Mechling, L. C. (2011). Review of twenty-first century portable electronic devices for persons with moderate intellectual disabilities and autism spectrum disorders. *Education and Training in Autism and Developmental Disabilities, 46*(4), 479–498.

Raskind, M. (2013, April). Assistive technology. Info sheet. Council for Learning Disabilities. Retrieved from http://www.cldinternational.org/Infosheets/assistive.asp

Rose, D. H., Hasselbring, T. S., Stahl, S., & Zabala, J. (2009). Assistive technology, NIMAS, and UDL: From some students to all students. In T. Gordon, J. W. Gravel, & L. A. Schifer (Eds.), *A policy reader in universal design for learning* (pp. 507–518). Cambridge, MA: Harvard Education Press.

Stachowiak, J. R. (2014). The changing face of assistive technology: From PC to mobile to cloud computing. In B. DaCosata & S. Seok (Eds.), *Assistive technology research, practice and theory* (pp. 90–98). Hershey, PA: IGI Global.

MOBILE DEVICES: IMPACT ON LEARNING AND INSTRUCTION

Technology has been touted as being the one thing that has the ability to change education. Educators have long been searching for a "magic bullet" to fix all that ails a less than 21st-century educational system. Even though computers have been used in education since the 1980s, when about 75% of high schools and 30% of elementary schools were said to be using computers for educational purposes, students are still not using computers regularly in every school. Nonetheless, almost every study that has been conducted relating to the use of computers in schools reports an increased level of engagement by the students that is attributed to the students' use of the computers. But sadly, increases in student achievement—read: test scores—are elusive.

Why hasn't the use of computers in schools had the hoped-for impact on student achievement? Briefly, K–12 education is a complex system, with many interacting pieces. Technology by itself is only one small piece in that complex system. That said, mobile devices may well be better suited to affect K–12 education in general, and student achievement in particular, when compared with desktop and laptop computers.

Indeed, psychological principles form the basis for why mobile learning devices may well be the key technology that enables learning. In 1906, John Dewey argued that learning comes about when individuals engage in activities and reflect on those activities. The popular version of Dewey's theory is called "learn by doing." Moreover, Dewey argued that the job of a teacher is not to tell students information, but rather to give students carefully designed tasks because in the doing of those tasks and in the reflecting on those tasks, learning will take place. Still further, for Dewey, learning was about building connections between and among the ideas in an individual's mind. Mobile devices, then, because of their small size and light weight, are suited to learning by doing because they can support students in doing tasks inside and, most importantly, outside the classroom. This entry discusses the advantages mobile devices offer over other types of technology used in learning and instruction, the types of pedagogy they support, and how sensors that are either part of mobile devices or available as apps running on mobile devices can be used in learning and instruction.

The best device for any particular student depends on many factors including grade level, subject matter, and the nature of the tasks needing to be accomplished. Luckily, a wide range of devices is currently being used and this range will only increase in the future. For many educators, tablet computers may have a more positive connotation than smartphones. This may be because students were using cell phones for communication and entertainment before tablets came into widespread use. The remainder of this entry uses the term *mobile learning devices*, or MLDs, to discuss smartphones and tablets when used in education. The term as used here does not include laptops. Although laptops are sometimes referred to as mobile devices, they cannot comfortably be used in transit and are not as likely to be at hand as is a smartphone.

MLDs' Ease of Use in the Classroom

Certain benefits of using MLDs for learning and instruction simply result from the core design of these devices, as described in this section.

- *Instant-on/instant-off*: When the on button is touched on an MLD, typically the device springs to life and is usable virtually immediately. Similarly, turning off an MLD results in its functionality becoming unavailable at the press of that button. Teachers routinely decry

the amount of time wasted waiting for computers to boot up and to shut down. With MLDs, the students need only touch the on button and the device is ready for the students to begin work. The same is true when students are ready to stop working—they simply turn the device off.
- *School-day long battery*: The battery life on most MLDs is much longer than that of a laptop computer. So, assuming that students come to school with their MLDs fully charged, students can, more often than not, use their MLDs for all classes or activities without having to plug in and charge up during the day.
- *Palm-sized*: Because mobile learning devices are smaller and easier to manage than larger laptop computers, it is very easy for students to pass their MLDs around a table or to hold them up to show their classmates what they have found or the artifacts they have created using their MLDs.
- *Low cost*: When compared with a laptop or desktop computer, MLDs tend to be less inexpensive. Indeed, full functionality tablets can be purchased for $100—less than the cost of many athletic shoes. Because of their low cost, going 1:1—each child has his or her own MLD for use 24/7—is rapidly moving within reach of schools.

In 1:1 situations, a computing device can be used as an essential tool for learning—that is, as a tool used for virtually all learning activities in the class and outside the class. When computing devices (e.g., MLDs, laptops) are used as essential tools, increases in student achievement have been observed. In contrast, there is no empirical evidence that using a computing device as a supplemental tool leads to increased student achievement. Supplemental use is the norm in schools because, until the arrival of MLDs, the cost of a computing device was significant and 1:1 classrooms were the exception, not the norm.

All-the-Time, Everywhere Learning Enables Learning in Context

Mobile learning devices enable all-the-time, everywhere learning. Although some learning activities require an Internet connection, many of the tasks that students do on MLDs can be done using the native apps on the devices and thus can be done anywhere. There are apps that enable students to do activities such as concept mapping or mind mapping, KWL charting (showing what they know, want to know, and have learned), drawing and animating, writing, and so forth, and there is no shortage of single-purpose, content-specific drill and practice applications for mobile learning devices.

There are media of all sorts—from straight text to multimedia "books."

Indeed, children spend more time outside the classroom than they do inside the classroom, and learning is not limited to the time students are in classrooms. MLDs can support learners as they live in their everyday worlds—for example, having dinner with their families, going to a museum, being on vacation with their families. And, supporting all-the-time, everywhere learning, many MLDs have two methods of providing access to the Internet: (a) Wi-Fi, when it is available, and (b) via the MLDs' cellular radio that can provide a connection to the Internet beyond Wi-Fi hotspots. Increasingly youths own smartphones, with these two types of Internet connections, rather than just feature phones, which tend not to provide access to the Internet. Indeed, as the cost of smartphones continues to plummet, youth ownership will correspondingly increase. With the right mind-set, mobile devices can be tools for learning, as well as tools for social networking and entertainment. Some examples of activities in which learning is ongoing, 24/7, outside of school, are the following:

• In thriving fan fiction communities, youths and adults meet online and post stories that they have written that expand on popular fiction. For instance, a vibrant community of fans writes stories based on the Harry Potter book series. With an Internet-connected mobile device, young people can easily participate in fan fiction communities.

• "Fantasy sports" leagues are also highly active. Fantasy baseball is a game in which participants pick major league baseball players to play on their "teams," and they score points by using their players' real life statistics. Participants in fantasy sports leagues, while focused on sport, must acquire an understanding of statistics to be successful. A mobile device makes participation in a fantasy sports league much easier and much more fluid.

• Snapchat, the app that enables individuals to send photos to their friends that can be viewed for only a short time (e.g., 10 seconds), introduced a new feature in 2013: "snapchat stories," which link together snaps to create a narrative. Learning how to tell a good story is important and not necessarily an easy skill to develop. Today's youths do not necessarily write a great deal of text. But now, Snapchat supports these same youths in telling a story with pictures, where short pieces of text provide the glue to hold the narrative together. A mobile device is virtually the only way to participate in this expanding informal learning activity.

Fan fiction communities and fantasy sports leagues can be seen as "affinity communities," or communities where individuals with common interests get together and communicate and learn together. This form of informal learning—outside the classroom learning—can be every bit as compelling and important as formal, classroom learning.

An MLD that goes with students from the classroom into the world can enable students to connect what they do in school with what they see and do in their daily activities. The MLD then can build connections for learners between the abstract ideas discussed in the classroom and the concrete, real-world activities they experience outside the classroom. For example:

• Students are studying the plant cycle in school. The students can then use their MLDs to photograph examples of plant types and features that they have studied while they are outside the classroom.
• Students studying about the Vietnam War can use the voice recorder capability on their mobile devices to record interviews with people in their communities who fought in that war.
• For math classes, students can find and photograph examples of geometric shapes or angles as evidence of the theories or ideas they have been working with in class.
• Students can use a quick response (QR) code reader app such as QR Code Reader or QR Droid at some zoos, museums, and botanical gardens to gain more information about exhibits relating to their in-school activities. In addition to still photos, students can also capture video examples of animal behavior while at the zoo or demonstrations of plant grafting at the botanical gardens, or do video interviews for other classes.

MLDs Afford a Range of Pedagogies

In classrooms where direct instruction is employed, the teacher mediates the connection of the learner to various forms of information. That is, children must wait to hear it from a teacher, or see it on a video that the teacher shares, or read it in an assignment that a teacher assigns. However, when each child has his or her own mobile learning device, the need for mediation is eliminated. An MLD connected to the Internet, via Wi-Fi or cellular, enables learners to have direct and immediate access to information, events, locations, data, and so forth via the Web. Students can delve as deeply as they want into a subject that particularly interests them. There are documented examples where students, even students as young as 8 years old, working in their free time have researched topics that were of interest to their parents so they could share their knowledge. Mobile learning devices give students the power to explore the world at will and yet, by using proper filtering, they can still be protected.

Another pedagogical strategy that is facilitated by MLDs is that of the flipped classroom, which was popularized by the online learning site Khan Academy. Khan Academy began when founder Salman Khan began tutoring a cousin in math online, then began posting a series of short videos to YouTube to explain mathematical concepts. The Khan Academy website now contains thousands of video tutorials on various subjects, which some schools are incorporating into their classes using the flipped classroom model. The model requires students to watch videos at home for homework and then use class time to discuss the ideas presented in the videos and to work on assignments based on what they saw in the videos. Using a mobile learning device, every student has a means of watching the required videos at home in preparation for class the following day. Students can do this homework any place they happen to be if they have an Internet connection.

With software on mobile devices such as WeCollabrify, collaboration is enabled within apps when students are sitting around a table in a group at school or when they are at home after school. As long as students have mobile learning devices, the appropriate software, and an Internet connection, they are able to connect with another student or group of students regardless of where each is located and share the app—that is, whatever a child writes on one screen appears on all other screens of the group members in real time. In addition, the students are able to talk to each other while they are working together using Voice over Internet Protocol (VoIP) on their MLDs.

MLDs support learners in building connections while they are engaged in a broad range of activities. In particular, in creating artifacts using media construction tools such as concept mapping, writing, and drawing that reflect their immediate experiences, students are necessarily building connections between the ideas in their artifacts and their experiences in the everyday world.

Further, because an MLD is truly a personal computer, available 24/7, curriculum could be developed that takes advantage of the MLD's broad range of capabilities, so that the MLD is used as an essential tool for learning. In contrast, because computers have been expensive and thus classrooms have had precious little access to computers, their use is more supplemental—as an add-on to the existing curriculum. Research has shown that when computers are used as a supplement to the existing curriculum—which was designed, initially, for pencil-and-paper technology—no increases in student achievement,

attributable to students' use of computers, have been observed.

However, there are 1:1 elementary school classrooms—where every child has a smartphone, 24/7—in Singapore where the curriculum in science and English has been designed from the ground up to take advantage of the affordances of the smartphones. In those classrooms, the youngsters are using smartphones as essential tools for learning. And, in those classrooms where the computing device is used as an essential tool, increases in student achievement have been observed.

Using Sensors in MLDs for Learning

MLDs, in addition to having the capability of taking a photo or a video that records a conversation or sound, have a number of other capabilities that are not found in laptops or desktop computers. For example, smartphones have Global Positioning System (GPS) capability. One way students can use this capability is for geocaching, a type of treasure hunt that involves students using GPS coordinates to navigate to a location where they attempt to locate a hidden geocache. Students can participate in activities affiliated with the geocaching website, and teachers often organize class geocaching exercises related to specific local educational goals.

Another capability that mobile learning devices have that most computers don't have is the accelerometer. (Newer laptop computers are now coming with accelerometers built in to detect a drop and stop the hard drive, but it isn't clear that software developers can gain access to that accelerometer to create interesting pedagogical applications.) Besides enabling the device to detect screen orientation and thus rotate the screen appropriately, creative app developers have designed apps that take advantage of the built-in accelerometer. For example, an "air painting" app causes the phone to display something like a neon vapor trail like the one left behind a jet as it moves through the air. Or, using the accelerometer, a smartphone can be turned into a pedometer to measure steps taken.

Apps on MLDs that employ sensors such as the accelerometer and the GPS can be particularly useful in science classes. In the past, one of the few successes of technology that has empirical evidence of its positive impact on gains in learning is microcomputer-based labs (MBL). A microcomputer-based lab enabled students to collect, store, process, and analyze data with sensors connected to a microcomputer or personal computer. Initially, the sensors were tied to the desktop computers because personal computers were desktops. For example, a learner would walk back and forth in front of a motion detector and see a graph of that motion. The motion detector made visible the underlying mathematical characterization of motion.

Once laptop computers came available, sensors—now called probeware—allowed students to go into the field, to the local stream, to the manufacturing plant, or any number of locations where real-world data could be collected for scientific investigation. Typical sensors are those that measure factors such as dissolved oxygen, pH, UVA and UVB rays, electric current and voltage, pressure, temperature, force, and light intensity.

Unfortunately, the cost of an MBL setup is significant and thus schools typically purchase a small number of them. In no way has MBL been 1:1. But now, with the emergence of MLDs and their pervasive presence, it is conceivable that MBL can go 1:1. Sensor technology must also go down in cost—but that will happen when the volume of sensors produced dramatically increases to support 1:1 MBL on MLDs.

In fact, medical device companies are already producing low-cost sensors that can be attached to smartphones. For example:

- For $99, one can buy a sensor that works with a smartphone to produce an electroencephalogram that detects and displays the quality of one's sleep by monitoring brain waves.
- For $199, one can buy a case into which one places a smartphone that will allow individuals to record their own echocardiograms simply by placing their fingers on the back of the case. The recorded echocardiogram can then be sent via the Internet to a doctor for interpretation.
- Using a sensor attached to one's abdomen, one can monitor blood glucose level via one's smartphone and watch the level fluctuate based on foods one has eaten recently.
- It is now possible to turn a smartphone into a "lab on a chip" so that physiological fluids such as sweat, saliva, and urine can be monitored.
- Still further, researchers are studying the medical use of nanosensors, microscopic sensory points that can be used to measure physical and chemical changes. One research project involves using nanosensors in the bloodstream to detect cells that have been shed from the lining of the arteries, a precursor to a heart attack. The nanosensors could then send a signal to a smartphone to trigger an alert that the user is likely to have a heart attack within a week or two.

Such medically oriented sensors could enable students to engage in data collection on an unprecedented level and may also cut down on the number of doctor visits required since they allow people to perform medical tests that formerly had to be done in an office.

The data that students collect with MLDs could affect their own learning of science and science itself. By collecting data on an ongoing basis and over a wide geographic area, citizen scientists may well change how science proceeds.

Putting the Pieces Together: A Hypothetical Scenario

The following hypothetical scenario illustrates how K–12 students could make use of the advantages and affordances of MLDs discussed earlier:

With the goal of surveying CO_2 emissions in parking lots on "football Saturday," 12 middle school students divided into four teams have been placed in four parking lots ringing the University of Michigan's "Big House"—its fabled and exceptionally large football stadium. Another group of students—two students coleading the survey, and four more students, each managing a team at a parking lot—is stationed in their science room at a school in Ann Arbor.

Each student in the three-person parking lot teams has a CO_2 sensor attached to his or her MLD, while also running a version of the MLD-based data collection and analysis tool Zydeco that has been "collabrified"—made to enable two or more students to simultaneously use Zydeco while each student is using his or her own device; that is, the tool now supports synchronous collaboration. Using what is called here Zydeco Collaborate, each team in a particular parking lot is "in" a collaborative session, which means that the team members can talk verbally with each other through Zydeco Collaborate, and they can all interact with Zydeco Collaborate at the same time (e.g., see the comments made by each student, add a comment to what another student said, add data).

The parking lot coordinator back at the school is also a member of the team's collaborative session and can thus also participate in real time in his or her team's collaboration session—that is, talk to the team in the parking lot, add input through Zydeco Collaborate, and see others adding input.

The team at the school is directing students in the parking lots to get a good sample of vehicles; based on what vehicles have already arrived, and based on the CO_2 profile of a particular vehicle, the parking lot coordinator directs students to monitor specific vehicles—always taking care to position the students safely.

At the end of their study, the students will have participated in an authentic scientific study, using sophisticated—but low-cost—tools. Their data could be used by scientists studying human-made CO_2 discharge. Perhaps the students could even present their findings during the halftime break of the football game.

Conclusion

There are challenges facing the use of MLDs in schools. Curricula need to be developed and provided to teachers that exploit the affordances of MLDs, professional development needs to be developed to help teachers understand how to effectively employ the new MLD-based curricular materials, security needs to be addressed, and the privacy of children's data needs to be guaranteed. Finally, there are concerns about cost, even if low-cost devices come onto the market. Despite these challenges, mobile devices have the potential to have a greater impact in K–12 education than desktop computers or even laptop computers have.

Mobile devices can become indispensable to the learner when used for everything from reading content materials, to writing a blog collaboratively, to gathering and analyzing pollution data, to watching engaging videos.

Indeed, the empirical evidence is clear: Only when computers are used as essential devices in the K–12 classroom do students experience increases in achievement. Supplemental use—the overwhelming dominant usage pattern in K–12 schools over the past 50 plus years—does not lead to increased student achievement. Mobile devices can become essential tools for learning in K–12 classrooms when used to support virtually all the learning tasks that a student undertakes.

Elliot Soloway and Cathleen Norris

See also Apps for Use at the Elementary Level; Apps for Use at the Secondary Level; Mobile Tools and Technologies for Learning and Instruction

Further Readings

Blumenfeld, P. C., Soloway, E., Marx, R. W., Krajcik, J. S., Guzdial, M., & Palincsar, A. (1991). Motivating project-based learning: Sustaining the doing, supporting the learning. *Educational psychologist, 26*(3–4), 369–398.

Bransford, J. D., Brown, A., & Cocking, R. (2000). *How people learn: Mind, brain, experience and school* (expanded ed.). Washington, DC: The National Academies Press.

Krajcik, J. S. (1991). Developing students' understanding of chemical concepts. In S. M. Glynn, R. H. Yeany, & B. K. Britton (Eds.), *The psychology of learning science* (pp. 117–147). New York, NY: Routledge.

Norris, C., & Soloway, E. (2011). Learning and schooling in the age of mobilism. *Educational Technology, 51*(6), 3–10.

Norris, C., & Soloway, E. (2011, November–December). The 10 barriers to technology adoption: Technology will absolutely change K–12 learning. *District Administration Magazine.* Retrieved from http://www.districtadministration .com/article/10-barriers-technology-adoption

Norris, C., & Soloway, E. (2013, June 5). Is a laptop a mobile computer? And why is that even an important question? *THE Journal, Being Mobile Blog.* Retrieved from http:// thejournal.com/articles/2013/06/05/is-a-laptop.aspx

Schuler, C. (2012). iLearn II: An analysis of the education category of Apple's App Store. Retrieved from http://www .joanganzcooneycenter.org/wp-content/uploads/2012/01/ ilearnii.pdf

Whyley, D. (2010). *Embedding 1:1 computer provision: Main findings from device comparison case studies, 2008–2009: A look into sustaining mobile learning in a changing environment.* Retrieved from http://tinyurl.com/oomugfv

Websites

Whytek Consulting blog: http://www.whytekconsulting.co.uk/ blog

Mobile Tools and Technologies for Learning and Instruction

The fast and widespread adoption of mobile devices has enabled major changes in the way individuals, groups of individuals, businesses, and governments go about their daily activities. With mobile technologies as the catalyzing agent, education too is experiencing its biggest change in more than 150 years. This entry first discusses the development of mobile devices and how they are used in the classroom. The entry then discusses more recent innovations in mobile technology and the challenges teachers face in using these tools.

In 1991, Jeff Hawkins, inventor of the Palm computing device, commented on the inevitability of computing being incorporated into mobile devices. This was quite prescient, inasmuch as 1991 was 4 years before Microsoft's Windows 95 Operating System helped transform the Internet from an early-adopter technology to a mass-market consumer technology. It was also an accurate prediction:

- In 2013, the number of tablet computing devices shipped surpassed the number of desktop and laptop PCs shipped.
- In the fourth quarter of 2013, sales of smartphones surpassed sales of feature phones for the first time.
- Companies were expected to ship more than a billion smartphones in 2014.

Complementing Hawkins's comment is a comment in 2013 by Eric Schmidt, chairman of the board at Google and its first CEO, that, indeed, mobile is no longer just a trend, but an established reality.

What's a Mobile Computer?

There is no consensus on the definition of *mobile computers*; some use this term to mean laptops as well as smartphones and tablets. However, from a K–12 learner's perspective, a mobile computer is one that is ready-at-hand—very lightweight, palm-sized and able to be turned on instantly—so that it can be used outside the classroom as well as in the classroom. This can enable, for example, a student to take a picture, for inclusion in his or her school project, of the impressive root system of a Banyan tree spotted while walking home from school. Given that definition, laptops, although they are transportable, are not mobile computers and are not discussed in this entry. A mobile computer enables a student to make connections between what are often abstract ideas (e.g., roots of trees) explored in a classroom with his or her concrete, daily experiences (e.g., seeing the exposed roots of a Banyan tree) outside the classroom.

Early Mobile Devices

The introduction of the Palm handheld computing device was initially hailed as "the educational computer" because of its relatively low cost. Although there were major projects in the United Kingdom, United States, and Singapore that used Palm devices and Windows PocketPCs as essential tools for activities such as reading, writing, and drawing to support instruction, rather than just supplemental tools (e.g., drill-and-practice games) to support pieces of instruction, the reality is that the generation of mobile devices (e.g., Palm devices, PocketPCs) that appeared before Apple's introduction of its iPhone had little practical impact on elementary and secondary education. The cost of those devices was still relatively high ($300 to $600), and it was a challenge to link them reliably and consistently to

the Internet. The promise, then, of mobile computing for education, during the period from 2000 to 2007, remained just that—a promise.

Mobile Revolution

Apple's introduction of the iPhone in 2007 was the beginning of the mobile revolution. The device was easy to use, and it was constantly connected to the Internet—Apple required that the iPhone be purchased with cellular connectivity to the Internet. The iPhone revolutionized culture in developed nations of the world, but educators in elementary and secondary schools were still not convinced. Mobile phones had been banned in virtually every classroom in the world and smart mobile phones weren't any more acceptable. Although a small handful of classrooms worldwide explored the use of iPods and then iPod Touches for language learning, the iPhone, continuing the tradition of Palm and PocketPC devices, had essentially no impact on elementary and secondary education.

The iPad Tidal Wave

With the introduction of the Apple iPad in 2010, worldwide, elementary and secondary schools have awakened to mobile. By mid-2013, the iPad had a 94% share of the market for U.S. K–12 schools. Why the iPad? The iPad does not need cellular connectivity, which from a school's perspective is relatively high cost when compared with using the school's existing Wi-Fi network. And, the iPad's 10-inch screen addressed educators' concerns that a smartphone's screen was too small for instruction. The iPad mini, too, with its 7-inch screen—but with the same resolution as its larger-screened cousin—has seen adoption in elementary and secondary education. With Apple's iPad being first-to-market, along with Apple's already favored position in K–12 schools and its aggressive school marketing focus, the lower cost Android tablets ($50 to $200 for 7-inch screen devices and $250 to $350 for 10-inch screen devices), which have essentially the same functionality as the more expensive iPads, have seen virtually no adoption in U.S. schools.

Tools: It's All About the Apps!

What are schools doing with the iPads? An answer to that question must reference the apps being used. Here is a short summary of popular types of tools and apps:

- *Writing*: Images of students using iPads for writing—essentially as stand-ins for laptops—abound. There is some question, however, whether writing is an effective use of an iPad, given the amount of space taken up on the screen by the on-screen keyboard or need to purchase a separate keyboard attachment.

- *Multimedia content creation apps*: There are a small, but very popular, set of multimedia creation tools—for example, iMovie, that students use to create stories, presentations, and so on. Kathy Shrock's iPads for Teaching website is a comprehensive source of reviews of media creation apps for the iPad.
- *Early learning apps*: The lion's share of the apps on the iPad target early learners, which means they support a drill-and-practice pedagogy. In general, it appears that from math drills to word drills, these sorts of apps dominate those that are purchased in elementary schools.

The Curricular Challenge Remains

iPads present the same challenge to teachers that teachers have faced since the introduction of computing: Who is helping the everyday classroom teacher understand how to use various apps to supplement their existing curriculum? As has been the case since the introduction of desktops and then laptops, the responsibility for figuring out how to use these technologies is placed largely on the classroom teachers. Given the responsibilities and demands already on these teachers, it is no wonder that classrooms don't see much innovative use of the technology.

Breaking with tradition, then, schools—and districts—need to work collaboratively to develop, test, and disseminate curricular materials that exploit the unique opportunities afforded by mobile technologies. Typically, such teamwork won't happen unless school administrators provide the teams with additional resources (e.g., release time, technology-support personnel)—a challenge given the realities of school budgets.

The Next Generation: The Internet of Things and Wearable Computing Devices

As we move headlong into what the authors of this entry call the age of mobilism, pundits are predicting that the Internet of Things, with the potential of connecting trillions of physical objects that can be equipped with sensors (e.g., temperature, motion) or effectors (e.g., connection to the controller of a home furnace, refrigerator, light switches) will be the next big thing and may well be more disruptive than mobile technologies have been. And some percentage of those connected things will be computing devices that are being worn by individuals (or one's pets)—for example, watches that sense temperature and heart rate and can serve as an electrocardiogram (EKG). Indeed, wearable computing, itself, is predicted to be bigger than mobile.

Schools may well be able to take advantage of the Internet of Things to fundamentally and irrevocably change how science is taught, for example. Using the next generation of microcomputer-based lab (MBL), students will be able to use scientific instruments that they are wearing (e.g., pedometers to capture movement) or that are stationed in the environment (e.g., instruments that measure emissions of greenhouse gases by automobiles) that are connected via cellular or Wi-Fi to cloud-based computing and storage to explore science questions and topics.

Conclusion

Today, mobile tools and technologies in schools often mean iPads and drill-and-practice apps. They are generally used as supplements to the existing curricula—curricula that were designed before mobile technologies—or even digital technologies—were invented. Research by Cathleen Norris and Elliot Soloway suggests that such supplemental use will have no significant impact on increasing student achievement.

Before mobile tools and technologies will have an impact on elementary and secondary education, a major change needs to occur: Curricula need to be developed that leverage the unique affordances of the devices, and teachers must be prepared to use those new curricula. As well, if mobile tools and technologies are to have an impact, schools must address all the other barriers that have blocked the adoption and scaling of computing technologies.

Indeed, based on documented classroom experiences, these mobile devices, when coupled with appropriate curricula in the hands of properly prepared teachers, can move learners beyond the direct-instruction pedagogy of yesterday's classrooms to support the new demands for teaching and learning 21st-century skills such as the 4C's—critical thinking, communication, collaboration, and creativity—that are promoted by the Partnership for 21st Century Skills. Using mobile devices as part of a project-based pedagogy can help children develop into imaginative and entrepreneurial thinkers.

Cathleen Norris and Elliot Soloway

See also Apps for Use at the Elementary Level; Apps for Use at the Secondary Level; Mobile Devices: Impact on Learning and Instruction

Further Readings

Norris, C., & Soloway, E. (2011). Learning and schooling in the age of mobilism, *Educational Technology, 51*(6), 3–10.

Norris, C., & Soloway, E. (2011, November–December). The 10 barriers to technology adoption: Technology will absolutely change K–12 learning. *District Administration Magazine.* Retrieved from http://www.districtadministration.com/article/10-barriers-technology-adoption

Norris, C., & Soloway, E. (2013, June 5). Is a laptop a mobile computer? And why is that even an important question? *THE Journal, Being Mobile Blog.* Retrieved from http://thejournal.com/articles/2013/06/05/is-a-laptop.aspx

Schaffhauser, D. (2013). IDC on tablet market share in education: Dominance can be fleeting. *THE Journal.* Retrieved from http://thejournal.com/articles/2013/10/31/idc-on-tablet-market-share-in-education-dominance-can-be-fleeting.aspx#OJ11ITYVuRSI6G21.99

Schuler, C. (2012). iLearn II: An analysis of the education category of Apple's App Store. Retrieved from http://www.joanganzcooneycenter.org/wp-content/uploads/2012/01/ilearnii.pdf

Whyley, D. (2010). Embedding 1:1 computer provision: Main findings from device comparison case studies, 2008–2009: A look into sustaining mobile learning in a changing environment. Retrieved from http://tinyurl.com/oomugfv

Websites

Kathy Schrock's iPads in the classroom website: http://www.ipads4teaching.net/ipads-in-the-classroom.html

MODEL-BASED APPROACHES

Model-based approaches describe the underlying phenomena of human thinking and learning. Central to model-based approaches is the construct of mental models, which are characterized as internal representations for understanding objects and actions of the world as well as predicting future events. Given that mental models are multimodal and multidimensional internal constructs, a direct assessment of mental models is impossible. Nevertheless, computer-based tools for the assessment of externalized mental models have been developed that provide rich opportunities for applications in research and practice. This entry first discusses the theory of mental models and how mental models are created in the learning process. The entry then discusses tools for the assessment of mental models and future directions for model-based assessment and analysis.

Mental Models

The theory of mental models is based on the assumption that cognitive processing takes place through mental representations in which individuals organize symbolic representations of experience or thought that constitute a systematic representation of an experience or thought as a means of understanding it. To create plausibility, the individual constructs an internal model that both integrates the relevant semantic knowledge and meets the perceived requirements of the situation. This internal model is referred to as *mental model.*

Individuals construct mental models on the basis of retrievable knowledge to understand a given situation, task, or problem. These models work well when they fit with both the individual's knowledge and the explanatory need regarding given phenomena to be mastered cognitively. By means of a mental model, an individual is also able to simulate real actions in imagination. Mental models allow one to judge the consequences of actions, interpret them, and draw appropriate conclusions.

Since the concept of mental models was introduced in the 1980s, proponents of schema theories have criticized it. They consider mental models as mere instantiations of local schemas but not as a discrete theoretical construct. Still, cognitive scientists agree on the point that schemas and mental models serve different cognitive functions. Schemas represent the generic and abstract knowledge acquired on the basis of manifold individual experiences with objects, persons, situations, and behaviors. As soon as a schema is fully developed, it can be applied immediately to assimilate information about new experiences. Mental models are constructed by individuals in the case of novel problems for which no schema can be retrieved from memory. In accordance with this argumentation, a theoretical model has been introduced that integrates the theoretical concepts of schemas and mental models into a more comprehensive architecture of cognition with the aim of explaining their mutually compensating cognitive functions (see Figure 1).

This architecture corresponds with Jean Piaget's epistemology and the basic cognitive functions of assimilation and accommodation. Assimilation depends on the availability and activation of cognitive schemas, which allow new information to be integrated into already existing cognitive structures. If a schema does not fit immediately with the requirements of a new task, it can be adjusted to meet the new requirements by means of accretion, tuning, or reorganization. However, if such an adjustment is not successful, accommodation must take place before an individual's knowledge concerning the construction of a mental model can be reorganized and structured. When no schema is available, a construction of a mental model occurs. Accordingly, an individual constructs a mental model that integrates relevant bits of knowledge into a coherent structure step by step to meet the requirements of a task or a problem.

According to this architecture, mental models are constructed to meet the specific requirements of situations, tasks, or problems the individual is facing and for which a schema is not available. A sufficient assimilation resistance is a necessary precondition for mental model construction. A schema is a slot-filler structure,

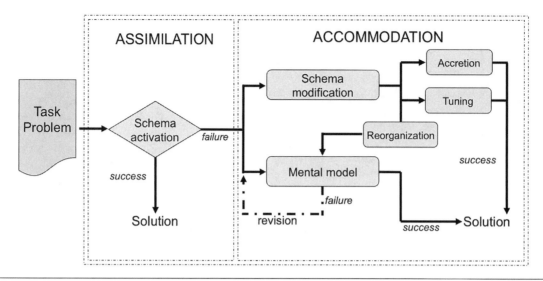

Figure 1   Cognitive architecture of mental models and schemas

Source: Ifenthaler, D., & Seel, N. M. (2011). A longitudinal perspective on inductive reasoning tasks. Illuminating the probability of change. *Learning and Instruction, 21*(4), 538–549. doi:10.1016/j.learninstruc.2010.08.004.

whereas a mental model contains assumptions that must be justified by observations.

Given the dynamic and iterative definition of mental models, commonly used unidimensional descriptors of mental models (e.g., structural maps of components) are not sufficient. The complexity of mental models includes declarative, procedural, causal, strategic, and metacognitive components. Additionally, mental models possess multiple forms of representation.

Model-Based Learning

Model-based learning describes the construction and learning-dependent progression of mental models by an individual. The construction of a mental model integrates prior knowledge and information about the phenomenon in question into an initial mental model. Compared with that of a novice, an expert's initial mental model is considered more elaborate and complex. Therefore, mental models mediate between an initial state and a desired final state in the learning process. The novice will create, through an iterative process, various types of mental models to successfully (with success judged under subjective plausibility) solve a specific situation or problem. In contrast, an expert will recognize the type of problem and map an existing schema onto the specific situation or problem to solve it. The long-term perspective on the learning-dependent changes in mental models and schemas are particularly interesting. Specifically, approaches of model-based learning aim to identify transition points within a learning progression at which the shift from mental models

(fluctuation in probability of change) to schemas (decrease in probability of change) occurs (see Figure 2).

Accordingly, educators have immense interest in assessing and analyzing initial mental models and comparing them with more expert-like mental models to identify the most appropriate ways to bridge the gap through interventions.

Model-Based Tools for Assessment

Mental models are multimodal and multidimensional internal representations and therefore cannot be assessed directly. The essential question concerning the assessment of mental models is which elicitation strategy for externalization can be used. Externalizations are the only available artifacts for the assessment of mental models. An externalization always involves interpretation; the externalization needs interpretation for its creation as well as for its analysis. This interpretation can be done by the individual who externalizes the mental models, by other individuals (e.g., educator, scientist), or by technology. Despite a long research tradition, the relationship between mental models and their externalizations is not well understood. Still, cognitive scientists agree that there is a reciprocal relationship between mental models and their externalizations. Mental models guide the externalization process and the externalization regulates the construction of mental models.

Numerous approaches for externalizing mental models have been discussed, tested, and analyzed. A variety of computer-based mindtools, or cognitive tools, have been suggested for externalizing domain knowledge,

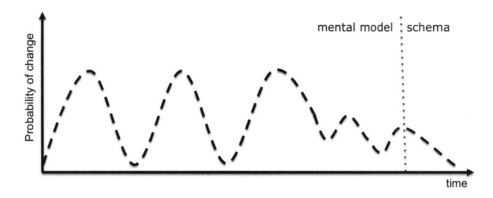

Figure 2   Learning-dependent progression of mental models

Source: Ifenthaler, D., & Seel, N. M. (2013). Model-based reasoning. *Computers & Education, 64,* 131–142. doi:10.1016/j .compedu.2012.11.014.

systems, problems, experiences, and thinking processes. Computer-based knowledge mapping techniques, for example, are considered to be highly suitable for externalizing structural components of mental models. System dynamics tools (e.g., Systems Thinking for Education and Research [STELLA], Powersim, Model-It) are regarded to be suitable for externalizing the procedural components of mental models. Conversely, there are strong arguments that written natural language is closely related to the internal representation of mental models, and therefore think-aloud protocols as well as written essays contain several components of mental models (e.g., domain-specific, procedural, structural components).

Recently, promising tools for the assessment of mental models have been developed that provide rich opportunities for applications in research and practice. Such model-based assessment tools include Pathfinder Networks, ALA-Reader and ALA-Mapper (with ALA standing for analysis of lexical aggregates), jMAP Dynamic Evaluation of Enhanced Problem-solving (DEEP), highly integrated model assessment technology and tools (HIMATT), and automated knowledge visualization and assessment (AKOVIA).

Pathfinder Networks are a well-established system for deriving and representing the organization of mental models. Its analysis includes three steps: First, individuals rate the relatedness between a set of concepts on a scale from low (e.g., one) to high (e.g., five). The total of pairwise comparisons is calculated as $(n^2–n)/2$ (where n is equal to the total number of concepts). The first step results in a proximity data set. Second, the proximity data is transformed into a Pathfinder Network. Such a network representation consists of a least-weighted path that links all included concepts. Third, comparisons between different Pathfinder Networks are calculated. Since the 1990s, numerous empirical research

studies in several domains have been conducted and proven the utility of Pathfinder Networks. They have been applied to study conceptual structures of experts and similarities between expert representations. They were used for the assessment of knowledge structures in training programs as well as knowledge and problem elicitation.

ALA-Reader and ALA-Mapper are text analysis tools for analyzing network representations. They convert the links between terms (propositions) and the distance between terms (associations) in network representations into proximity array files that can then be analyzed by Pathfinder Network analysis. To convert written text into proximity arrays, ALA-Reader-Mapper finds and associates preselected key terms. The analysis of written text is realized sentence by sentence, or linearly within and across sentences. ALA-Reader and ALA-Mapper have been applied as tools for scoring written essays and for measuring individual knowledge structure.

jMAP is implemented as a Microsoft Excel application that enables individuals to elicit causal understanding of a phenomenon in question, visualize changes of individuals' representations, and determine the degree of match between novices and experts. The strength of the causal relations (links) between two concepts is designated by varying the densities of the relations as well as using evidentiary support. jMAP codes the causal representation into a transitional frequency matrix based on the causal strength and the evidentiary support. If multiple causal representations are available, they can be aggregated. Applications of jMAP include the assessment of solving complex ill-structured problems.

HIMATT is a combined tool set that was developed to convey the benefits of various methodological approaches to one environment. HIMATT integrates the features of DEEP, Model Inspection Trace of

Concepts and Relations (MITOCAR), Text-MITOCAR (T-MITOCAR), and structure, matching, deep structure (SMD) technology. The architecture consists of two major platforms: HIMATT Research Engine and HIMATT Subject Environment. Functions for conducting and analyzing experiments are implemented within the HIMATT Research Engine. These functions include experiment management, researcher management, subject management, visualization function, and analysis and compare function. The HIMATT Subject Environment provides assigned experiments to individual subjects dynamically.

The core unit in HIMATT is the experiment, which can be laid out flexibly by the researcher. The subject management function includes multiple options for adding and organizing a pool of subjects. Once an experiment has been laid out completely and subjects have been added to the database, researchers can assign subjects to experiments. The visualization function presents the externalized mental model as a picture to the user. This function allows the user to choose from specific experiments and knowledge graphs, which are then available images for download. The analysis function consists of descriptive measures to account for specific features of the externalized mental model, such as interconnectedness and ruggedness. Using the compare function, users may compare any kind of externalization with standardized similarity measures. These measures range from surface-oriented structural comparisons to integrated semantic similarity measures. The similarity measures range from 0 to 1 for better in-between comparability. Matrices of multiple models can be compared simultaneously. HIMATT and its tools have been successfully applied within classical experimental settings and fields of applications within the domains of instructional planning, medical diagnosis, and geology. Further, empirical studies showed that HIMATT measures helped distinguish inexperienced from highly experienced problem solvers in all domains examined so far.

AKOVIA is based on the HIMATT framework; however, it concentrates on the model-based assessment methods. Instead of limiting the framework to a narrow set of externalization procedures, AKOVIA was developed to integrate a large number of interfaces to different methods, which accounts for the multimodal and multidimensional components of mental models. The main applications of AKOVIA are clearly in analysis and comparison, whereas the assessment step itself is left to the tools and experimental setups of the researchers. AKOVIA is designed to complement various kinds of technologies because it uses interfaces that allow many forms of data to be analyzed. The visualizations of the externalized mental models have been shown to

have an especially positive effect on learning within tasks that involve writing. Thus, the possible applications reach beyond the structural and semantic analysis and comparison of externalized mental models.

Future Directions

It is worthwhile to compare the model-based assessment and analysis approaches described earlier to illustrate their advantages, disadvantages, strengths, and limitations. Given the complexity of mental models and their various forms of externalizations, no ideal solution is available so far. However, within the last 5 years, strong progress has been made in the development of model-based assessment and analysis tools.

Model-based approaches require multiple perspectives on the same construct. Making decisions about the kind of representation of mental models as well as the type of tool to be used may be made on the strengths and weaknesses of available model-based tools. It is worth the effort to evaluate at least a representative selection of the available model-based tools. As long as mental models are not observable directly, there will be a need for different perspectives on the states and changes of these internal constructs. Every model-based tool at our current disposal is only a heuristic to narrow the gap of the unknown functions between what is considered to be a mental model (internal) and its externalization.

Dirk Ifenthaler

See also Assessing Learning in Simulation-Based Environments; Knowledge Elicitation; Learning by Modeling; Learning With Models; Learning With Simulations; Mindtools; Simulation-Based Learning; System Dynamics; Tools for Modeling and Simulation

Further Readings

Buckley, B. C. (2012). Model-based learning. In N. M. Seel (Ed.), *Encyclopedia of the sciences of learning* (pp. 2300–2303). New York, NY: Springer.

Craik, K. J. W. (1943). *The nature of explanation.* Cambridge, UK: Cambridge University Press.

Gentner, D., & Stevens, A. L. (Eds.). (1983). *Mental models.* Hillsdale, NJ: Lawrence Erlbaum.

Ifenthaler, D., & Pirnay-Dummer, P. (2014). Model-based tools for knowledge assessment. In J. M. Spector, M. D. Merrill, J. Elen, & M. J. Bishop (Eds.), *Handbook of research on educational communications and technology* (4th ed., pp. 289–301). New York, NY: Springer.

Ifenthaler, D., Pirnay-Dummer, P., & Seel, N. M. (Eds.). (2010). *Computer-based diagnostics and systematic analysis of knowledge.* New York, NY: Springer.

Ifenthaler, D., & Seel, N. M. (2011). A longitudinal perspective on inductive reasoning tasks. Illuminating the probability of change. *Learning and Instruction, 21*(4), 538–549. doi:10.1016/j.learninstruc.2010.08.004

Ifenthaler, D., & Seel, N. M. (2013). Model-based reasoning. *Computers & Education, 64*, 131–142. doi:10.1016/j.compedu.2012.11.014

Johnson-Laird, P. N. (1983). *Mental models. Towards a cognitive science of language, inference, and consciousness.* Cambridge, UK: Cambridge University Press.

Jonassen, D. H., & Cho, Y. H. (2008). Externalizing mental models with mindtools. In D. Ifenthaler, P. Pirnay-Dummer, & J. M. Spector (Eds.), *Understanding models for learning and instruction: Essays in honor of Norbert M. Seel* (pp. 145–160). New York, NY: Springer.

Seel, N. M. (2014). Model-based learning and performance. In J. M. Spector, M. D. Merrill, J. Elen, & M. J. Bishop (Eds.), *Handbook of research on educational communications and technology* (4th ed., pp. 465–484). New York, NY: Springer.

Spector, J. M. (2010). Mental representations and their analysis: An epistemological perspective. In D. Ifenthaler, P. Pirnay-Dummer, & N. M. Seel (Eds.), *Computer-based diagnostics and systematic analysis of knowledge* (pp. 27–40). New York, NY: Springer.

MOOCs

See Massive Open Online Courses

Motivation, Emotion Control, and Volition

Motivation refers to a person's desire to attain a goal. *Volition* refers to his or her control to exert follow-through efforts to attain the goal. Motivation initiates the goal attainment process, and the process does not proceed without motivation. Without volition, the goal cannot be attained. For example, people who want to lose weight begin to pursue the goal of weight loss. The process toward weight loss begins from their desire and when they do not want to lose weight any longer, the process stops. However, motivation alone does not lead to weight loss. Volition to control oneself (e.g., avoid thinking of sweets) and one's surroundings (e.g., remove sweets from his or her reach) is necessary to overcome obstacles (e.g., binge sweet eating) and attain the goal of weight loss. *Emotion control* is part of volition that involves the process of maximizing positive emotions and minimizing negative emotions. For example, people

who try to avoid sweets can often experience the emotion of frustration; distracting oneself by envisioning a healthier, better-looking body can reduce negative emotions such as frustration and invite positive emotions such as anticipated joy. Emotion control affects motivation. Frustration can weaken motivation, and joy can prolong motivation.

Motivation, emotion control, and volition work *together* to help a person attain a goal, including goals in learning contexts. This entry (a) introduces the integrative role of motivation, emotion control, and volition in the process of learning and (b) discusses implications of understanding such a role for teaching and learning as well as the use of educational technology.

Integrative Role of Motivation, Emotion Control, and Volition in Learning

Motivation plays a critical role in learning. When students lack motivation, they do not engage in learning tasks. Many researchers and practitioners have long recognized the importance of motivation in learning and have made much effort in improving student motivation. In more recent years, the role of emotions in learning has received much attention. Research on anxiety has a long history; other kinds of emotions experienced in academic settings such as frustration, shame, anger, enjoyment, and pride have been studied relatively less.

As other academic emotions, including both negative and positive emotions, are acknowledged as a critical factor in learning, educators have begun to investigate how to improve student emotional experiences. The concept of emotional scaffolding has emerged to highlight the teacher's role in tailoring learning activities to students' emotional experiences. Many educational technologies are also used with the purpose of improving motivation and emotions. For example, educational game users often aim to transfer the joy of playing games into learning. Pedagogical agents include affect-aware tutors and relational agents whose purpose is to promote positive emotions in learners.

Even when efforts are made to provide students with positive emotional experiences, neither teachers nor technologies can ensure the efforts work for all students. Thus, some scholars believe that student learning about emotion control is more practical than attempting to accommodate learning environments to all students. Emotion control involves cognitive appraisal and reappraisal of the contexts in which students are experiencing emotions. The emotion regulation model of James J. Gross is often used in the context of learning about and performing emotion control. The model depicts the following five strategies—situation selection (i.e., choosing an environment), situation modification (i.e., altering the environment in which the person already finds himself or herself), attentional deployment (i.e., turning attention to something else), cognitive change (i.e., reevaluating the environment), and response modulation (i.e., repressing emotions that are occurring).

Emotion control needs to be practiced alongside motivational support. As briefly discussed earlier, motivation and emotions are interrelated. For example, anger can diminish motivation but enjoyment can boost motivation. Considering such a reciprocal influence between motivation and emotions, both motivation and emotions need to be optimized. John Keller's motivational design model called ARCS (for attention, relevance, confidence, and satisfaction) can be used to enhance motivation. The concept of motivation regulation can be also used.

Optimized motivation and emotions are necessary for student engagement and learning but not always sufficient. When difficulties and distractions are encountered, volition, which helps students control emotions and motivation as well as actions, is required. Students with volition follow through with their goals, plans, and actions by optimizing themselves and their environments. Several scholars, including Paul R. Pintrich, argue that volition needs to be taught because not all students are volitional. Most recently, a model to teach volition, called the volition support (VoS) model, was developed by ChanMin Kim. The model highlights an integrative view of motivation, emotion control, and volition and comprises the following four stages: (1) goal initiation ("Want it"), (2) goal formation ("Plan for it"), (3) action control ("Do it"), and (4) emotion control ("Finish it"). The first stage is to increase students' perception of task value and desire to pursue a goal. The second stage is to help them set their goals and make plans. The third stage is to help them control actions to follow through with their goals and plans. The last stage is to help them control emotions.

Implications for Teaching, Learning, and the Use of Educational Technology

There has been a call for more attention to the integrative view of motivation, emotion control, and volition in recent years because of advances in educational technology. Especially, the development of online learning environments has transformed formal and informal education. To succeed in online learning, students need to be more in control of their own learning because of a lack of social support compared with what is found in face-to-face settings. However, many students struggle in online courses. Empirical studies show that in online learning environments, motivation withers away more easily, emotions play a more critical role than motivation, and volition is needed more.

As more difficulties are present, there is a greater need for motivation, emotion control, and volition. For example, in online remediation courses, negative emotions such as anxiety and anger are prevalent, which worsens motivation to study. However, students in remedial courses tend to lack volition. They would have been more likely to have succeeded in their previous courses had they been equipped with volition. When students are not capable of controlling their own learning, self-paced online courses lower the possibility of engagement and learning even further. Such courses limit the quantity and quality of communications between the student and the instructor as well as among students; this in turn negatively affects motivation, emotion control, and volition.

Implications for Teaching: Improving Teacher Education

To improve teacher education, there needs to be an understanding of the integrative role of motivation, emotion control, and volition in the process of learning. Teachers need to (a) be aware of challenges that their students encounter with emotions, motivation, and volition and (b) know when and how to help their students. For example, the strategies described in the VoS model can be tools teachers can use to diagnose challenges and teach students to be volitional.

Implications for Learning: Becoming a Lifelong Learner

When students learn to be volitional in one setting, it is important that the learned volition skills are applied in other contexts. The transfer of volition skills is also important because no learning context can accommodate every student's needs; students need to be trained to cope with contexts that are not aligned with their preferences. In this way, they can become successful lifelong learners. However, transfer is rarely discussed in the volition literature. Pintrich noted that volition can be more transferable than self-regulated learning skills that are context-specific. Although a few researchers recognize the need to understand how volition transfers, it has not been empirically studied. Models to teach volition open the door to advanced research on the transfer of volition that leads to more lifelong learners.

Implications for the Use of Educational Technology: Embedding Volition Support in Technologies

Understanding the integrative role of motivation, emotion control, and volition in the process of learning should help educations design and develop instructional interventions that teach volition skills. Many scholars note that students with volition perform at higher levels. However, there are not many studies on such interventions. Recent research shows how the VoS model can be applied to developing a three-dimensional environment in which students can learn to be motivated and volitional as well as experience positive emotions. This also shows the potential use of various technologies, such as videos and social networking media, in which strategies teaching volition can be embedded.

ChanMin Kim

See also ARCS Model; Games: Impact on Interest and Motivation

Further Readings

Gollwitzer, P. M. (1999). Implementation intentions: Strong effects of simple plans. *American Psychologist, 54,* 493–503.

Gollwitzer, P. M., & Brandstätter, V. (1997). Implementation intentions and effective goal pursuit. *Journal of Personality and Social Psychology, 73,* 186–199.

Gross, J. J. (2008). Emotion regulation. In M. Lewis, J. M. Haviland-Jones, & L. F. Barrett (Eds.), *Handbook of emotions* (3rd ed., pp. 497–512). New York, NY: Guilford.

Heckhausen, H., & Strang, H. (1988). Efficiency under record performance demands: Exertion control—An individual difference variable? *Journal of Personality and Social Psychology, 55*(3), 489–498.

Heckhausen, J. (2007). The motivation-volition divide and its resolution in action-phase models of developmental regulation. *Research in Human Development, 4*(3–4), 163–180.

Keller, J. M. (2008). An integrative theory of motivation, volition, and performance. *Technology, Instruction, Cognition and Learning, 6,* 79–104.

Keller, J. M. (2010). *Motivational design for learning and performance: The ARCS model approach.* New York, NY: Springer.

Kim, C., & Bennekin, K. N. (2013). Design and implementation of volitional control support in mathematics courses. *Educational Technology Research & Development, 61*(5), 793–817. doi:10.1007/s11423-013-9309-2

Kuhl, J. (1987). Action control: The maintenance of motivational states. In F. Halisch & J. Kuhl (Eds.), *Motivation, intention and volition* (pp. 279–291). Berlin, Germany: Springer-Verlag.

Pintrich, P. R. (1999). Taking control of research on volitional control: Challenges for future theory and research. *Learning and Individual Differences, 11*(3), 335.

MULTIMEDIA AND IMAGE DESIGN

Multimedia is defined as the use of more than one media and refers to a variety of media combinations, including, but not limited to, static images combined with text, animated and narrated images, interactive graphics, information graphics, narrated images, images accompanied by music, and so on. *Multimedia and image design for learning* refers to the effectiveness, efficiency, and appeal of combined image-driven media for instructional goals. Given the number of potential media combinations, heuristics to guide an instructional designer in working with multimedia are evolving. An abundance of instructional design models provide a foundation for instructional design practice, but none that are suitable for all applications or specific to the variety of media combinations possible.

Research by Ruth Clark, Richard Mayer, and others provides a focus for design regarding the composition of effective instructional images used in combination with other media. This entry examines multimedia image design in the context of the larger learning environment using a design framework consisting of four learning architectures intersected by digital literacy and interaction control variables.

Clark identifies four architectures for learning (see Table 1) that provide a foundation for considering multimedia image design. A *receptive architecture* is a learning environment that is minimally interactive and provides image-based support in the form of one-way communication between an instructional artifact and a learner. In general, receptive architecture images are accessible to the learner in a number of forms, some of which are static, animated, narrated, or filmed. Learners view these images, but instructional designers lack specific data, or learner feedback, about how the images are actually interpreted by the learner.

An exploratory architecture is a learning environment that reflects and uses real-world tools, problems, and images. Learners in exploratory environments are also encouraged to generate unique images or imagery, including but not limited to knowledge and data visualizations. The instructor or facilitator has limited control of learner access to images in these environments. Take, for example, the image filters in Web-based search engines. These filters provide access to an unlimited number of images. Designers have limited control over which images learners will select and use to accomplish instructional goals.

A directive architecture is a learning environment that is deliberately interactive. Images in directive environments have greater potential to support learner understanding. Feedback in the form of quiz-based prompts, hypertext rollovers, links, and the like provide opportunities for the learner to interact with the images to check their understanding. Interactive graphics such as the *Wall Street Journal* website's Make Your Own Deficit-Reduction Plan graphic from December 2012 allow readers to see consequences of hypothetical decision making as they increase and decrease the dollar amounts of a variety of budget items.

Table 1   Multimedia image design framework

	Learner accesses "reads" images	Learner constructs "writes" images

Design emphasis on the visual interface and embedded cues	**Receptive architecture** (Clark, 2000)
	
	Instruction focuses on absorbing information.
	
	Involves access to a visual artifact (a job-aid, book, slide-based lecture, movie, demonstration).
	
	Uses the instructional strategy structure:
	ACCESS → INTERPRET
	
	Employs other visual strategies such as
	
	Access → Read
	Access → Observe
	Access → Watch
	Access → Locate
		Exploratory architecture (Clark, 2000)
		
		Involves self-directed exploration for learning. Learners generate or construct visual outcomes. Reality TV's *Project Runway, Iron Chef,* and *Trading Spaces* exemplify learning in this architecture. Constructivist learning theory supports this architecture.
		
		Uses the instructional strategy structure: RESPOND TO A CHALLENGE → EXPLORE → GENERATE
		
		Employs other visual strategies such as RESPOND TO A CHALLENGE → EXPLORE →:
		    Create digital story, cartoon, comic strip
		    Create unique visualization/poster/ advertisement
		    Create a website
		    Create an information graphic
		    Produce a film or YouTube video
		    Create a map showing parts-to-whole relationships
		    Create a visual product (clothing, building, tool)

Design emphasis on strong instructional support (feedback and interaction)	**Directive architecture** (Clark, 2000) Instruction focuses on acquisition of knowledge, attitudes, and skills. Instructional content tends to have a hierarchical and sequential nature. Behaviorist learning theory supports directive strategies. Involves access to a visual artifact (a job-aid, book, slide-based lecture, movie, demonstration). Uses the instructional strategy structure: **ACCESS → PRACTICE → CHECK UNDERSTANDING** Employs other visual strategies such as Access → Identify visual examples/non-examples → Check understanding Access → Draft/sketch examples → Check understanding Access → Organize information visually (mind map, flowchart, outline, list, chart) → Check understanding	**Guided-discovery architecture** (Clark, 2000) Instruction focuses on activating prior knowledge and challenging a learner or group of learners to solve a problem or think critically. A facilitator supports learners with feedback and direction when needed. Learners visualize and create images (see exploratory architecture examples above) using technology and check their understanding using rubrics, tools, and facilitator feedback. Cognitive learning theory supports this architecture. Uses the instructional strategy structure (Merrill, 2002): **ACTIVATE → DEMONSTRATE → APPLY → INTEGRATE** Employs other visual strategies such as Activate → Identify problem → Access data → Generate information (learner organizes/calculates data to create information) → Produce visualization (knowledge). This is also known as a *Data → Information → Knowledge strategy.*

A guided-discovery architecture is a learning environment that promotes a higher level of intentional learner interaction. Images in guided discovery environments are likely to be learner-generated. Learners are more likely to be required to compose images that represent what they are learning, such as electronic slide presentations, electronically generated comic strips, digital stories, concept maps, Wordles, YouTube videos, and so on.

Read and Write Levels of Learner Digital Literacy

Figure 1 categorizes learner interaction with images using two types of new media literacy gleaned from the literature. Definitions of visual and digital literacies are similar. *Visual literacy* is defined by Roberts Braden and others as the ability to understand and use images, including the ability to think, learn, and express oneself using images. *Digital literacy* describes the ability to act effectively in a digital environment; a digital environment involves information represented in numeric form and primarily for computer; literacy includes the ability to read and interpret a variety of media to reproduce information and images, and to evaluate and use new knowledge gained from a range of digital environments. The Braden definition includes reference to mostly higher order learning skills, whereas other definitions of visual literacy include both lower order and higher order literacy skills. *Lower order literacy skills* refer to learner location of or access to an image. The learner to some degree interprets (reads) an image. *Higher order literacy skills* refer to learner interaction with images that require composition skills. The learner critically thinks about and composes visual messages.

Image-Focused Instructional Strategies

Instructional strategies are catalysts for learning that create a path between Point A (where a learner begins,

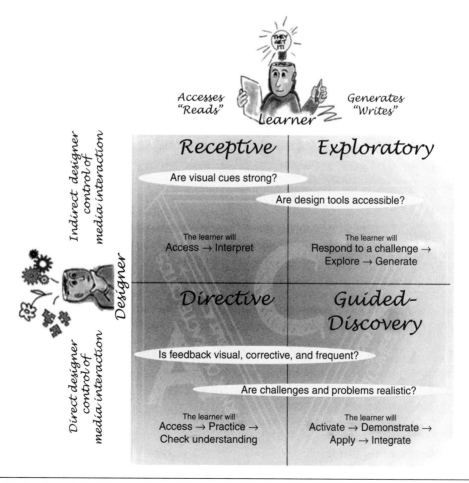

Figure I   Clark's four learning architectures and designer control of interaction

determined partly by prior knowledge and experiences) and Point B (the intended outcome, or learner achievement of a learning goal). The following section uses Clark's four architectures to describe basic instructional strategies for visually rich learning experiences.

Multimedia Image Design Strategies for a Receptive Learning Architecture

Clark describes a receptive learning architecture as one that assumes learners will absorb information, and thus learn. Images in receptive architectures are likely to be located, accessed, watched, and observed.

Given a lack of goal-specific, instructional interaction, such as checks for understanding and feedback, a potential risk of learner misunderstanding exists, making multimedia image design critically important at this level. Designed images may support germane cognitive load or may pose an extraneous load. The image designer may create an image that is worth 1,000 words or create an image that creates 1,000 points of confusion.

Despite the risk, however, Mayer's research supports the use of images in instruction. His research found a multimedia effect; pictures and text together are more effective than all text and no pictures. Dual coding theory explains why: Images are processed and stored in separate visual and verbal channels, creating two memory sources for later recall, a verbal memory and a visual one, as well as the potential to integrate both channels in a way that creates greater understanding.

Receptive architectures are considered a *low*-order architecture, but it may be more fruitful to consider visually rich receptive learning environments as *essential*-order for knowledge, skill, and attitude-related learning.

Multimedia Image Design for an Exploratory Learning Architecture

The exploratory architecture defines learning through a constructivist lens as an environment that requires the learner to create and generate meaning, often of a unique and personal nature. Exploratory multimedia learning environments involve learner-set goals. Learners create visualizations to help them explore, learn, understand, and solve problems or to acquire new skills. Learners design and create multimedia presentations, digital stories, transformational visuals (unconventional images based on learner-generated metaphors), knowledge visualizations, interactive graphics, and potentially new forms of images that are, as yet, undiscovered and unimagined.

Writing, with words alone, tends to be a cognitively challenging task, involving higher order skills in analysis, evaluation, and creation. Multimedia "writing," or composition, requires significant skill, involving an ability to combine words and images effectively, with the potential to create a depth of meaning that neither could achieve alone.

Learners who compose visual images employ many of the same skills that instructional designers employ when they create or select visuals for learning. Most learners, however, have limited experience, training, and skill in visual composition. Principles of visual composition focus on facilitating the viewer's selection, organization, and integration of cognitive processes. Learners are more likely to create images that are perceived as intended if they help their audience pay attention to the most important content, follow the reading order of an image, and integrate elements within the image so that it conveys a "big picture." A learner who is able to effectively employ contrast, alignment, repetition, and proximity using color, type, shape, depth, and space is more likely to achieve visual communication goals.

Multimedia Image Design in a Directive Learning Architecture

The directive learning architecture defines learning through a behaviorist lens as an environment focused on the acquisition and strengthening of knowledge, skills, and attitudes. This environment is characterized by mastery of sequenced and hierarchically arranged visual and verbal content, often presented step-by-step and accompanied with frequent feedback. Directive learning strategies mitigate the risk of misunderstanding present in receptive architectures because they provide many interaction opportunities for learners. For example, rather than viewing a static image showing the impact of supply and demand on pricing, a directive strategy might model how economic charts are read, building in learner activities and checks for understanding.

Where receptive and exploratory architectures provide information, the designer of directive architecture sequences the information and employs many opportunities for learner rehearsal with corrective feedback. Where receptive and exploratory environments focus on the design of, and access to, information, directive (and guided) environments focus on designing interaction that directs and guides the learning process.

Multimedia and Image Design in a Guided-Discovery Learning Architecture

The guided-discovery learning architecture defines learning through a cognitive learning theory lens. Guided-discovery learning architectures are described as environments focused on helping learners discover information and build or construct unique (and frequently visual) representations of knowledge. This architecture focuses on scaffolding the learning experience. Case studies, instructional simulations and games, cognitive apprenticeships, and other strategies that require problem solving and realistic tasks, characterize this architecture. Discovery learning, inquiry learning, and other titles are assigned to guided-learning architectures. Twenty-first-century skills with learning goals that include creativity, collaboration, communication, and critical thinking call for guided learning architectures and introduce the need for art and design skills in students. A fourth "r," art, joins reading, writing, and arithmetic as an important skill.

M. David Merrill's first principles of instruction involve promoting a guided learning architecture using an activation-demonstration-application-integration strategy. In the context of a real task or problem-solving situation, learners review relevant experiences to *activate* memory, they experience new information as tasks and skills are *demonstrated,* and they demonstrate their understanding by *applying* and *integrating* what they have learned to create knowledge, often personalized and thus memorable. In strategies such as these, many opportunities arise requiring the learner to compose visual solutions and requiring the learner to employ the same visual design principles that designers employ in receptive learning architectures.

A data-information-knowledge-visual strategy falls within the guided learning architecture. This strategy requires learners to gather data, organize it to create meaning, and visualize it to generate knowledge. For example, a human resources case study might require students to gather a number of facts about elderly customers (the *data* phase of the data-information-knowledge-visual strategy). Students would then be asked to create a table or chart showing how elderly customers' needs are similar to, as well as different from, those of young customers (the information phase of the data-information-knowledge-visual strategy). After creating this chart, students are required to construct a visual to represent their new and unique understanding of the elderly customer (the knowledge phase of the data-information-knowledge-visual strategy). Students might create a map for the elderly customer, create a digital story about an elderly customer, create advertising to attract the elderly customer, create interactive support tools to help the elderly customer make decisions, or construct some other form of visual expression (such as a detailed plan or blueprint for an event created specifically to improve the elderly customer experience).

Future Research

Many questions drive our discovery of effective multimedia image design heuristics. Specific multimedia design guidelines are needed by instructional designers, and they are needed for learners as well as learners who construct visual representations of ideas, understanding, and questions. Will art become the fourth "r"? What form will art take in the context of science, technology, engineering, and mathematics? How do people interpret information graphics? How are knowledge visualization skills taught? These questions and many more will be asked in the years ahead to form new lines of research focusing on learner, as well as designer, construction of images.

Linda L. Lohr

See also Digital Literacy: Overview and Definition; Media Literacies; Visual Search Engines

Further Readings

Beauchamp, D. G., Braden, R. A., & Baca, J. C. (Eds.). (1993). *Visual literacy in the digital age.* Blacksburg, VA: International Visual Literacy Association.

Clark, R. C. (2000). Four architectures of learning. *Performance Improvement, 39*(10), 31–37.

Clark, R. C., & Mayer, R. E. (2011). *E-learning and the science of instruction: Proven guidelines for consumers and designers of multimedia learning.* San Francisco, CA: Pfeiffer.

Deubel, P. (2003). An investigation of behaviorist and cognitive approaches to instructional multimedia design. *Journal of Educational Multimedia and Hypermedia, 12*(1), 63–90.

Jones-Kavalier, B. R., & Flannagin, S. L. (2006). Connecting the digital dots: Literacy of the 21st century. *EDUCAUSE Quarterly, 6*(2), 8–10.

Krathwohl, D. R. (2002). A revision of Bloom's taxonomy: An overview. *Theory Into Practice, 41*(4), 212–218.

Lambert, J., & Cuper, P. (2008). Multimedia technologies and familiar spaces: 21st-century teaching for 21st-century learners. *Contemporary Issues in Technology and Teacher Education, 8*(3). Retrieved from http://www.citejournal.org/vol8/iss3/currentpractice/article1.cfm

Levin, J. R. (1981). On the functions of pictures in prose. In F. J. Pirozzolo & M. C. Wittrock (Eds.), *Neuropsychological and cognitive processes in reading* (pp. 203–228). San Diego, CA: Academic Press.

Lohr, L. L. (2007). *Creating graphics for learning and performance: Lessons in visual literacy.* Cleveland, OH: Prentice Hall.

Mayer, R. E. (2001). *Multimedia learning.* New York, NY: Cambridge University Press.

Merrill, M. D. (2002). First principles of instruction. *Educational technology research and development, 50*(3), 43–59.

Partnership for 21st Century Skills. (2006). *Results that matter: 21st century skills and high school reform.* Retrieved from http://www.21stcenturyskills.org/documents/RTM2006.pdf

Pavio, A. (1986). *Mental representations: A dual coding approach.* Oxford, UK: Oxford University Press.

NATURAL LANGUAGE PROCESSING IN LEARNING ENVIRONMENTS

Natural language processing (NLP) is a field of artificial intelligence concerned with the interaction between computer science and natural languages. It has grown rapidly in recent years and has found direct applicability in a number of different domains. One such domain is that of education, where NLP has been successfully used to build automatic systems for assessment, instruction, and educational data mining.

Assessment

Several NLP techniques have been developed to address various aspects of assessment, such as the detection of reading level, the identification of errors in written text, or the automatic grading of essays, short answers, or multiple-choice questions.

Reading Level Assessment

Reading level assessment is used to determine language competency by finding the appropriate reading level for English students or for second language learners. Reading assessment is particularly relevant in a climate where as many as 25% of the students in many U.S. states have limited English proficiency. To meet the needs of these students, teachers often have to identify educational materials that have a low reading difficulty, while covering content that is relevant for the students' level.

NLP can be used to determine the reading level of a text automatically, by using a statistical learning approach to assign a text automatically to one of several known reading levels for which training corpora exist. Each text is transformed into a feature vector, using several features such as readability metrics (e.g., Dale-Chall, Flesch-Kincaid), N-grams collected from the text, syntactic information, sentence length, number of words from a given vocabulary of "easy" words, discourse structure, measures of text coherence, and so on. Next, a machine learning algorithm is applied to categorize the text with the unknown reading level into one of the existing training levels. Several machine learning algorithms can be used, with the best results to date being obtained by support vector machines.

Grading

Computer grading has started to be used on a large scale in student evaluations such as the Test of English as a Foreign Language (TOEFL), the SAT, and the Graduate Management Admission Test (GMAT). Computer grading is often used to replace one of the human graders in settings where multiple graders are requested. Discrepancies between the automatic and human grader are adjudicated by another human.

Systems designed for essay grading rely on features based on writing characteristics and are based on the guidelines provided to human graders. These features typically cover rhetorical structure (e.g., relations and arguments); syntactic structure, meant to identify variety (e.g., number of different clauses) and correctness; and topical content, to determine if the vocabulary used is relevant to the essay's topic. The essay scoring features can be combined using automatic methods such as linear regression of existing data sets of human-scored essays.

Automatic grading can also be used for short answers, where the aim is to determine the extent to which a student answer contains the information included in a correct instructor answer. Most of the approaches for short answer grading rely on measures of text similarity, which often results in scores that can then be translated into grades. Optimized combinations between different measures can be learned by training on existing sets of human-graded answers. Automatic feedback on errors can also be provided, but that usually requires additional manual annotations of the expected components of a correct answer.

Error Detection

Another research area that has received significant attention is that of error detection, mainly targeted at the writing of non-native English speakers. Errors that are commonly detected are vocabulary use and syntactic structures, with the latter covering mistakes in the use of verb arguments, particles, prepositions, and so on. As with many other NLP systems, the approaches that work best for error detection are based on statistical learning, where several syntactic and topical features are extracted from the text and then combined by learning from manually annotated writing errors.

Instruction

Although NLP is more commonly used in assessment, its use in supporting instruction is growing. NLP helps manage dialogue, interpret student responses, and generate system dialogue moves in intelligent tutoring systems (ITS). NLP is also used to identify and replace challenging words in text adaptation and is now entering use to support teachers in the classroom.

Intelligent Tutoring Systems (ITS)

Most ITSs use NLP to provide natural conversational interaction with students. These conversational agents often use NLP in the process of understanding students' interactions, managing dialogue, and sometimes generating the tutor's response.

ITS student response understanding has been handled in ways paralleling the use of NLP for assessment. The most common methods include using latent semantic analysis (LSA), pattern matching, and lexical similarity. However, in an ITS, it is also much more common for systems to develop a user model and to interpret a student's response based on the preceding series of related student contributions. Furthermore, an ITS should base dialogue on the specific facets of a response that need to be addressed and on the specific way in which the student's response differs from the desired answer, whereas assessment generally is designed only to assign the appropriate grade.

Dialogue management is a key NLP component in an ITS. The dialogue manager decides how to respond to a student given the learning objectives, subject domain model, user model, dialogue history, understanding of student interactions, and other context information such as the student's emotions. The user model is created in large part by applying NLP to extract meaning from user interactions. Emotion recognition and analysis can also be supported through NLP tools.

Common ITS dialogue moves take the form of assertions, feedback, hints, prompts, and follow-up questions. Current NLP research is focusing on generating these moves dynamically, particularly questions.

Question Generation

Automatic question generation is a relatively new NLP research area. Given domain-specific text and a dialogue context, question generation systems must perform concept selection, question type selection, and question realization. Concept selection consists of determining the most appropriate question-worthy information. The NLP system must determine the key concepts, the relations between them (e.g., temporal, causal, evidence), and based on that, which concepts must be understood before students learn another key concept. Question type selection decides whether to ask, for example, a causal consequence question, a compare-and-contrast question, and so on. Key to making this decision is a classification of other questions in the prior discourse, requiring NLP analysis. Then question realization actually produces a grammatical surface form of the question.

One common means of constructed-response question realization uses NLP to extract keywords for a Web query, performs information retrieval to find existing questions on the Web, and classifies those questions by type and quality. A second strategy starts with a question template, which is completed by filling its slots with the key concept(s) (e.g., What is the relationship between _____ and _____?). A third common means of question realization relies on a syntactic parse of the sentence(s) identified in concept selection, followed by restructuring the sentences into a question form.

Multiple-choice question realization follows similar methods but also requires NLP to create good distractor items. This is accomplished using lexical resources such as thesauri or by linguistic analysis of the text to find other concepts with similar characteristics such as part-of-speech, frequency, relations, concept co-occurrence, and so on.

Concept Maps

NLP is being used to identify the key concepts in text and the relations between those concepts. These are converted into a concept map, with nodes corresponding to the concepts and edges corresponding to relations between concepts.

Digital Library Curation

NLP is being applied to evaluate the quality of educational material submitted to digital libraries. Such evaluations involve sentiment analysis to verify that the material is not strongly opinionated. Similar techniques are used to ensure the material was not authored by, for example, companies desiring to sell their services or beliefs. Grammatical analysis factors into the quality evaluation. Reading level analysis determines whether an article is appropriate for the given audience.

Educational Data Mining (EDM)

NLP provides tools to help cluster and analyze student answers for EDM. This allows researchers to identify differences in patterns in the language of high-performing versus lower-performing students. Using the question classification, NLP could be used to identify the types of questions and teacher interactions that result in deeper learning by students.

EDM can also be used to find educational materials online, by using specialized information retrieval systems that find materials that are relevant for a given topic and determine their educational value. To this end, text classification has been successfully used to automatically assign an educational value to online materials.

Conclusion

NLP is an active field of research, and current and future work in this area promises to lead to new, exciting systems for use in learning environments. The recent development of massive open online courses (MOOC) is likely to bring new perspectives on the use of NLP in learning, as they can be both a source of very large data sets for use in NLP systems, as well as test beds for the direct application of such systems. Future work in this area is also likely to include the development of domain-specific applications, as well as enhanced performance for existing assessment and instruction systems.

Rada Mihalcea and Rodney Nielsen

See also Assistive Technology; Automated Scoring of Essays; Data Mining and Recommendation Engines; Educational Data Mining; Emerging Educational Technologies; Human-Computer Interaction; Intelligent Tutoring Systems

Further Readings

Attali, Y., & Burstein, J. (2006). Automated essay scoring with e-rater V.2.0. *Journal of Technology, Learning, and Assessment*, 4(3). Retrieved from http://ejournals.bc.edu/ojs/index.php/jtla/article/view/1650/1492

Baker, R. S. J. d., Yacef, K. (2009). The state of educational data mining in 2009: A review and future visions. *Journal of Educational Data Mining*, 1(1), 3–17.

Foster, J., Sultan, M. A., Devaul, H., Okoye, I., & Sumner, T. (2012). Identifying core concepts in educational resources. In *Proceedings of the 12th ACM/IEEE-CS Joint Conference on Digital Libraries* (pp. 35–42). New York, NY: ACM.

Hassan, S., & Mihalcea, R. (2011). Learning to identify educational materials. *ACM Transactions on Speech and Language Processing (TSLP)*, 8(2).

Hoehl, J., & Lewis, C. (2011). Mobile web on the desktop: Simpler web browsing. In *Proceedings of the 13th International ACM SIGACCESS Conference on Computers and Accessibility* (pp. 263–264). New York, NY: ACM.

Mohler, M., & Mihalcea, R. (2009). Text-to-text semantic similarity for automatic short answer grading. In *Proceedings of the European Chapter of the Association for Computational Linguistics* (Athens, Greece, pp. 567–575). Stroudsburg, PA: Association for Computational Linguistics.

Nielsen, R. (2008). Question generation: Proposed challenge tasks and their evaluation. Retrieved from http://rodneynielsen.com/papers/nielsenr_QG08_QG_proposed_chlng_tasks_n_their_eval.pdf

Nielsen, R., Ward, W., & Martin, J. (2009). Recognizing entailment in intelligent tutoring systems [Special issue 4]. *Natural Language Engineering*, 15, 479–501.

Petersen, S. E., Ostendorf, M. (2006). Assessing the reading level of web pages. In *Proceedings of the International Conference on Spoken Language Processing* (pp. 833–836). Pittsburgh, PA.

Rus, V., & Graesser, A. C. (Eds.). (2009). *The question generation shared task and evaluation challenge*. Retrieved from http://www.questiongeneration.org/

Wetzler, P., Bethard, S., Butcher, K. R., Martin, J. H., & Sumner, T. (2009). Automatically assessing resource quality for educational digital libraries. In *Proceedings of the 3rd Workshop on Information Credibility on the Web* (Madrid, Spain) (pp. 3–10). New York, NY: ACM.

NEUROLOGICALLY BASED LEARNING AND INSTRUCTION

The mind-body problem has been discussed for many years. This problem has emerged with the idea that the central nervous system in humans anatomically and physiologically affects the human mind and is impressed by it in return. Although numerous approaches exist to clarify this issue, the currently accepted approach is psychophysical interactionism. This approach asserts that the body and mind are two separate entities, but that they interact with each other (modifying and transforming the other). According to this approach, the mind is systematically carrying out complex processes that reveal behaviors. All biological and physical activities are associated with mental activity. This entry first discusses historical thinking on the mind and behavior, then describes the structure of the brain and explains individual differences in neurological functions. Finally, the entry discusses the implications of neurological research for curriculum and instruction.

The body-mind problem has created a wide variety of disciplines in academic medicine, including psychiatry, neurology, neuropsychiatry, neurosurgery, and psychology. Vast knowledge has led to these divisions. Reducing humans to subunits reveals the risk of alienation from a human in its entirety. For example, although psychologists usually talk about the *mind*, medical doctors may almost ignore the mind.

In behaviorism, which was popular in the 20th century, the stimulus-response configuration was highlighted. In Gestalt psychology, perception was highlighted within the framework of the whole and its parts. The theory of behaviorism has been inadequate to explain the complexity and diversity of human behaviors. The advances in schema theory and memory theories have moved cognitive psychology to the forefront of the agenda again. Usage of computers has accelerated artificial intelligence studies. Learning is modeled by using information processing theory.

Studies in cognitive psychology and neuroscience have revealed a new field called cognitive neuroscience. In this field, body-brain and mind-cognition are matched. Research areas within cognitive neuroscience include cognition, motor functions, language processing, problem solving, perception, sensation, and memory.

The brain itself is a structure divided into several regions. Those in the brain geography field usually give names to these regions and reveal their functions to create a brain map. For example, motor skills occur in the cerebellum, perceptual learning occurs in the neocortex, and habits, addiction, and procedural knowledge learning take place in the depths of the brain called the basal ganglia.

Inside the Brain

Everything that enters our perception through our sense organs is converted into electrical signals that move in nerve cells of our body and brain. Despite the deep processing that occurs in the background, we react to these stimuli instantaneously. The human brain consists of networks of neurons. The Milky Way metaphor is well known; it can be used to explain the quantity of neurons in the brain as being similar to such a quantity of stars.

The structure of a neuron is a nerve cell that looks much like a tree. However, unlike in a tree's structure, two neurons are connected together by clinging to one's branches through the other's roots. A simple search yields a description of the technical parts of a neuron in detail. The highlighted parts we need to know are the chemical signals called *neurotransmitters*. There are two different types of neurotransmitters. The first is called *excitatory* because this type increases the electric potential on the point where the neurons get connected. The second type is called *inhibitory* because this one decreases the electric potential. More than 50 chemicals are known as neurotransmitters. For example, acetylcholine is a transmitter known to be related to learning and memory. Dopamine, serotonin, and noradrenaline are commonly known in our daily lives; they are also neurotransmitters.

These chemicals cause the neurons to fire because all neurons are electrically excitable. After firing, the electrochemical signals are transmitted between connected neurons. When a stimulus activates in our perception the firing starts. This firing can be seen with electroencephalography (EEG) technology. In response to sensory input, our cognition reacts by uncovering the experiences, feelings, and thoughts related to the stimulus. New learning occurs during this process. New learning is converted into neurochemical language and stored in encrypted form. these processes are carried out at the level of milliseconds.

The nodes where the two neurons become connected are called synapses. The synapses are restructured with new learning patterns. If relationships with existing learning increase, then the synapses grow stronger. Not using learning weakens the synapses. Thus, the networked structure of synapses varies continuously, even while sleeping. During sleep, electrochemical activities of the brain continue as well. Human cognition consists overall of a pattern of billions of neurons that are scattered throughout the brain. With today's technology, the brain is no longer a closed box. Others can watch brain activity live and analyze thoughts and emotions with brain imaging technologies such as functional magnetic resonance imaging (fMRI), computerized tomography (CT), positron emission tomography (PET), EEG, magnetoencephalography (MEG), and transcranial magnetic stimulation (TMS). Even though these systems easily watch the activities of the brain, human cognition is only watched by the owner.

Chemicals, hormones, proteins, and ions take an active role in changing our cognitive situation. There is a very complex and an extraordinary perfection in the brain. For example, GAP43 protein is known to be associated with learning. Each of these types of components affects the plasticity of the brain according to its own roles. Recent research claims that the plasticity of the brain has the power to change the mind and personal characteristics even in adulthood. Lifelong learning is extremely important at this point. If we want to adapt ourselves to changing conditions and to make our brains gain more plasticity, we should support adult education.

Determining Individual Differences

As discussed earlier, we can surely say that learning processes occur in the brain. So here is the question: why are the brain functions differentiated in healthy individuals? This situation is called *individual differences*. We can divide them into two types—that is, cognitive and noncognitive differences. Cognitive differences, such as perception, attention, memory, speed of motor functions, and so forth, are measured using neuropsychological tests. Noncognitive differences, such as interests, locus of control, self-efficacy, and so on, are measured using psychological tests.

Damage and diseases in the brain can be determined with the help of neuropsychological tests without requiring any brain imaging technologies. Standardized, reliable, and valid tests should only be conducted by competent individuals. Practitioners hold licenses enabling them to use the tests after they are trained on the tests. Neuropsychological tests are being used in cognitive disorders for diagnosis, monitoring, and rehabilitation. Reaction time is very important in these tests, so they have paper-and-pencil and computerized forms. Computerized forms are more reliable; they can calculate the score in real time and the test management process is standard for each participant, with no error. Unlike general psychological tests, neuropsychological tests are administered in a one-on-one format, and they are administered by individuals who hold appropriate certificates.

An enhanced-cued recall test is used for detecting problems in some cognitive processes, such as encoding, storage, retrieval, and using the cues while recalling the stored information. The Line Orientation Test (LOT) was developed for measuring visuospatial perception and orientation. LOT is sensitive to some deficits in complex visual perception. To measure attention, which is one of the cognitive differences, the digit span test, trail making test, and Stroop test are used. Memory issues in themselves are so varied that many different memory types have been identified so far. Different types of memory are associated with different areas of the brain. For example, working memory (WM) holds the information for a short time and

processes and transforms that information. WM capacity develops over time as long as we use it. Following a text or a speech, note taking while listening, planning, calculating, and decision making are some skills for which WM has an active role. The anatomical position of working memory is at the dorsolateral prefrontal cortex of the brain. The n-back tests, parallel tasks, complex span test, and so on are used to measure WM levels and capacity. Conversely, procedural memory is known to be associated with skills such as cycling, driving, using a keyboard, and so on. These skills are so automatic that no one thinks about the steps involved. The more one has procedural automatic pre-knowledge levels, the less the individual perceives the task as complex. Then he or she becomes successful and quick, while creating a strategy according to the task.

The brain manages the organism. The brain is the center of consciousness, perception, cognitive processes (decision making, critical thinking, scientific thinking, etc.)—in total, "learning." Sometimes genetic or environmental factors can cause various learning disorders and individual differences. For example, attention deficit disorder, dyslexia, dysgraphia, dyscalculia, synesthesia, and stress and anxiety disorders also affect individuals' learning performance and methods. Students should be evaluated for these disorders in the framework of individual differences. If they have any of these disorders, the learning materials and activities should be designed according to their levels, and the evaluation methods should be different from those of their peers.

Taking the Next Step

Humans are the only creatures who can form representations about the outside world, who can bring meaning, value, and emotion to the outside world, and who are affected by their own meaning, value, and emotions in return. To increase the intrinsic motivation and self-confidence of learners, they should be aided in becoming aware of their brainpower. We should teach about this wonderful and mysterious structure. If learners know about how the brain works, what the brain needs, and how learning occurs, this knowledge will lead to more efficient use of their brain capacity.

Curricula should not be built for teaching theoretical content aimed at simply storing information. Curricula should be built for supporting cognitive activities such as real-life problem solving and creative problem solving. Students should be taught about strategies, methods, and techniques to make their learning effective. In this context, to answer the question of which criteria instructional designers should consider according to individual differences, the following suggestions may be made:

- Individuals with low working memory capacity should be guided about the learning environment, the task, and the content. The areas where attention needs to be focused should be spelled out. Content should be delivered in lessons of short duration and at frequent intervals and the guidance in exercises should be reduced gradually.
- For increasing the persistence of learning, activities and exercises to provide semantic encoding, which is the deep level of processing, should be designed.
- To manage their cognitive resources, individuals can be equipped with self-regulation skills. Strategies such as chunking, encoding, imaging, and mnemonics should be taught to increase their capacity.
- In addition, metacognitive awareness should be enhanced by teaching metacognitive strategies.
- Learning environments should give opportunities to go back and take notes while learning with audiovisual tools.
- Learning environments should track users' log data and formulate their working memory level or learning abilities based on cognitive profiling methodologies, and then, they should apply adaptive systems per individual.

Interdisciplinary studies are very important in learning. Data collection tools may be varied and enriched by applying support and resources from different fields. Using learning analytics can enable richer analysis. Cognitive theory and cognitive neuroscience are moving forward by interacting each other. The data collected via research based on these theories can be tested by using latent growth models. Biology and developmental psychology offer important information as well. Physiological activities such as sleep, getting proper nutrition, and physical exercise, even meditation, are important for the mind and thinking. How may we blend all this information under the umbrella of pedagogy? When we consider the society in which an individual lives, and the effect of the society on him or her, we may find ourselves waiting in front of the doors of sociology and environmental psychology.

Individuals show variations, called cognitive growth, in the process of growing from childhood to adolescence and then to adulthood. The same process is valid for societies as well. From ancient times to the present space age, humankind has grown cognitively. In brief, while people evolve, they restructure the environment, and the new structured environment improves people in a cyclic way. When we look back at the pages of history, the path we now are walking is very exciting. Advances in genetic science are producing very important outputs.

Cognitive computing is also very hot topic, taking the form of machine learning with semantic networks.

The findings derived from neuroscience should be applied to education policy and curriculum development. We can easily put into practice Benjamin Bloom's mastery learning theory that given enough time, attention, and help, any student can learn anything with today's technology. Learning environments that consider individual differences can be presented by employing adaptive learning in learning management systems. The aim of new instructional design theories should be to determine individual differences, to design the learning environment according to a learner's needs, and then to present the content in the necessary order.

Vildan Cevik

See also Cognition and Human Learning; Four-Component Instructional Design (4C/ID); Informal Learning Strategies; Knowledge and Skill Hierarchies; Neuroscience and Learning; Personalized Learning and Instruction; Technologies for Persons With Dyslexia; Technologies for Students With Attention Deficit Disorder

Further Readings

Boleyn-Fitzgerald, M. (2010). *Pictures of the mind: What the new neuroscience tells us about who we are.* Upper Saddle River, NJ: Pearson Education.

Chang, T. W., El-Bishouty, M. M., Graf, S., & Kinshuk (2013). An approach for detecting students' working memory capacity from their behavior in learning systems. *Proceedings of the International Conference on Advanced Learning Technologies (ICALT 2013)* (July 2013, Beijing, China, pp. 82–86). Los Alamitos, CA: IEEE Computer Society.

Eagleman, D. (2011). *Incognito: The secret lives of the brain.* New York, NY: Pantheon.

Solso, R., Maclin, O. H., & Maclin, M. K. (2007). *Cognitive psychology* (8th ed.). Boston, MA: Pearson Education.

Sousa, D. A. (2006). *How the brain learns* (3rd ed.). Thousand Oaks, CA: Corwin.

Sousa, D. A. (Ed.). (2011). *Educational neuroscience.* Thousand Oaks, CA: Corwin.

Terry, S. (2008). *Learning and memory: Basic principles, processes and procedures* (4th ed.). Boston, MA: Pearson.

Neuroscience and Learning

Understanding the complex functions of the brain (e.g., sensation, emotion, consciousness, cognition, and action) is a core concern in neuroscience. With its 200 billion neurons and trillions of synapses (neuronal connectors), the brain is one of the most complex structures known. Each neuron has the processing capability of a small computer, and a considerable number of neurons are active simultaneously. This means that a human brain has computational power roughly equal to billions of interacting computers and a more advanced network of nodes than the Internet has. This entry discusses how our very limited understanding of the brain informs what we know about how people learn, including how they learn to read and learn mathematics. This entry also discusses popular myths about the brain, caveats about neuroscience research findings, and promising future directions for research.

Neuroscience and Learning to Read

Learning to read is a process that requires the learner to acquire a number of complex skills, including morphology (formation of words), orthography (spelling), phonetics (mapping words to sounds), syntax (word order), and semantics (extraction of meaning from words and sentences). Fluent readers have automated these skills to the extent that the entire process from seeing to understanding occurs very rapidly—within about 600 milliseconds.

Though certain brain structures are biologically primed for language (e.g., Broca's area and Wernicke's area), language acquisition requires experience. Language circuits are known to be most receptive to experience-dependent changes at certain stages of the individual's development. For example, sound discrimination is best developed in the first 10 months of age and accents are acquired most effectively before 12 years of age. If the initial exposure to a foreign language occurs between 1 and 3 years of age, grammar is processed by the left hemisphere, but when second language exposure occurs later, there is typically an aberrant activation pattern consistent with significant difficulties with second-language grammar.

Reading of alphabetic scripts is also lateralized to the left hemisphere. The occipital-temporal areas of the brain are most active when processing letter shapes and orthography. Activation in these areas increases with reading skills and is diminished in children with developmental dyslexia.

One of the major debates in literacy education and research has been whether the whole language text immersion approach is more effective than is the development of phonetic skills. Neuroscience research aimed at delineating the brain areas that support reading provides useful insights regarding this issue. The so-called dual-route theory provides a framework for describing reading in the brain at the level of the word. Supported by dozens of neuroimaging studies, this theory proposes that words are first processed by the primary visual cortex and then pre-lexical processing occurs at the left occipito-temporal junction. After that, processing follows one of two complementary pathways. The assembled pathway involves an intermediate step of converting letters and words into sounds, which occurs in certain left temporal and frontal areas, including Broca's area. The discovery of this pathway suggests the importance of the phonic approach to reading instruction. In case of the second route, the addressed pathway, information is transferred directly from pre-lexical processing to semantic processing (meaning extraction), which implies the significance of using the whole language approach to teach reading. Both pathways terminate in Wernicke's area, which is known to be involved in the understanding of written and spoken language. These results confirm the assumptions of the dual-route framework, which helps explain different patterns of activation observed in participants during a reading task. This neuroscience finding is also consistent with the conclusions of the 2000 U.S. National Reading Panel that highlight the educational benefits of a balanced approach to reading instruction, which combines whole language and phonics approaches.

Neuroscience and Learning Mathematics

The mere representation of numbers in the brain involves a complex circuit that brings together the sense of magnitude with visual and verbal representations. As is the case with literacy, development of quantitative skills requires a synergy of physiology and experience. Some brain structures are believed to be genetically assigned to the numerical sense, additional neural circuits are shaped to fit this function by experience through neural recycling. The number sense system is supported bilaterally by the intraparietal areas—these regions are activated during tasks that involve number comparison regardless of the representation format used (e.g., Arabic numerals, dots, number words).

An interesting series of experiments was conducted to explore the cognitive and neural activity underlying learning exact arithmetic and approximate arithmetic. Language-specific exact arithmetic was shown to use networks involved in word-association processes and transfer poorly to a different language or to novel facts. Usha Goswami reported that many mathematical problems are rehearsed to such an extent in elementary school that they are stored as declarative knowledge. This also explains word-association processing behind drill-and-practice counting exercises and rote learning as with learning the multiplication tables. In contrast, approximate arithmetic was found to be language independent, relying on a sense of numerical magnitudes and using bilateral areas of the parietal lobes involved in visuospatial processing. Laure Zago and colleagues found that a region associated with the representation of fingers (left parieto-premotor circuit) was activated during adults' arithmetic performance, which may explain the importance of using finger counting as a strategy for the acquisition of calculation skills in children.

Research on the processing of quantitative information provides insight as to why some children have good mathematical skills but have trouble reading and processing symbolic notations. For example, patients with parietal damage know that there are two hours between nine and eleven but fail to subtract nine from eleven in symbolic notation. Similarly, they are not able to answer which number falls between three and five but have no difficulty identifying which month falls between June and August. These findings indicate that mathematics is dissociated from other domains such as reading, and even within the domain of mathematics, different abilities can be dissociated from one another. This conclusion highlights the importance of providing multiple forms of representation and assessment.

Neuroscience and Mathematical Problem Solving

Neural activity in the prefrontal and parietal areas of the brain was explored in a study on mathematical problem solving. This study examined whether activity in these regions tracked with subsequent errors in solving algebraic equations. Unlike previous studies that used recognition paradigms (e.g., decide whether $2 + 2 = 5$ is correct) to assess the relationship of neural functioning with performance, participants in this study were asked to generate an answer themselves. The prefrontal region, which in previous studies exhibited activity modulated by retrieval demands, showed activation that was greater when equations were solved correctly, with no errors. More intense activity in this region was observed for successful problem solvers. However, the parietal cortex that has been associated with representing the number of transformations to the equation showed no significant differences in activation between poor and effective problem solvers. This finding suggests that successful mathematical problem solving is related to retrieval abilities rather than to difficulty in representing or updating changes in the equation.

A previous study of error detection in mathematical processing reported effects of accuracy in the prefrontal cortex, whereas parietal regions were not affected by the accuracy of the equation. Instead, the parietal cortex was modulated by the number of operands in the equation, consistent with previous work showing activation increases with increases in the number of mathematical steps that are required to solve the equation. Taken together, these results imply that students may be better served practicing equations with varying levels of retrieval demands rather than working with large quantities of equation operands.

Neuromyths

The term *neuromyths* refers to the growing number of misconceptions about the brain, its functions, and the implications for other domains such as parenting, early childhood education, marketing, and others. Many of these myths were developed in an attempt to explain and predict human learning. Neuromyths are difficult to debunk because they are typically rooted in valid neuroscience and psychology literature while reflecting extreme extrapolations beyond the data.

The most persistent neuromyth in education, perhaps, is the myth of the first 3 years. The assumption behind this myth is that most synapses (and hence most of the critical brain functions) are developed from birth to the age of 3, and if missed (e.g., because of injury or limited experience), brain functions may never develop. The neuroscientific origins of this myth are numerous. From the neuroscience perspective, learning can be defined as the creation of new connections between neurons (synapses), or the strengthening of existing synapses. After two months of growth, the synaptic density of the brain increases exponentially and exceeds that of an adult, peaking at 10 months of age. There is then a steady decline until age 10, when the adult number of synapses is reached. There have also been studies demonstrating that rats living in enriched environments (i.e., cage with other rodents and objects) had increased synaptic density and were thus better able to perform the maze learning test than were rats living in poor or isolated environments. The seemingly important implications for educational practice stemming from these findings have led teachers and parents to generalize, exaggerate, and extrapolate far beyond the actual scientific evidence, resulting in new approaches to parenting and early childhood education that involve brain stimulating music, videos, and gymnastics for newborns.

Conversely, empirical research in education suggests that learning cannot be reduced to the creation of new brain synapses in highly artificial contexts characteristic of laboratory experiments. For example, a number of studies in education show that children growing up in what could be defined as an impoverished environment may over time come to excel in school and go on to higher education. There are too many social, environmental, affective, and experience-dependent factors to consider when defining what an enriched environment should be for students. Although grammar is indeed learned faster and easier at a young age, the capacity to enrich vocabulary actually improves throughout the life span because it depends heavily on experience. Also, contrary to the common belief that the brain loses neurons with age, the number of neurons in the cerebral cortex is not age-dependent, and parts of the brain such as the hippocampus can actually generate new neurons. *Understanding the Brain: The Birth of a Learning Science*, a 2007 report from the Organisation for Economic Co-operation and Development, provides a systematic discussion of the origins, common exaggerations, oversimplifications, and extrapolations of popular neuromyths, as well as evidence that helps refute them.

Conclusions, Caveats, and Promising Research Directions

Each of the areas discussed in this entry lies at the intersection of neuroscience and education; however, caution must be exercised in drawing conclusions for learning and instruction. Neuroscientists examine cognitive functions in such highly controlled, artificial laboratory environments and at such a fine level of detail that their findings are frequently deemed unusable. Most current neuroscience methods limit access to such important educational considerations as context, and localizing cognitive functions to different brain areas does little to inform actual educational practice.

Although educators are often disappointed that neuroscience findings do not lead to direct and straightforward applications, no such direct application exists in other fields. In the case of education, a growing number of scholars discuss educational applications of neuroscience with optimism. Ton De Jong and colleagues report new and exciting developments in cognitive, affective, and social neuroscience relative to the neural activity underlying metacognition and self-regulation, multimodal processing, and social cognition. Use of functional magnetic resonance imaging (fMRI) to develop cognitive models to explain and predict complex problem solving is explored by John R. Anderson and associates. Goswami argues for the integration of educational, cognitive, and neuroscience research paradigms and illustrates the application of this integrative framework using the concept of biomarkers, or cognitive signatures, that can potentially help identify children with learning difficulties very early in their development.

Interaction of neuroscience and education can be facilitated in many ways. Most reviews discussing the implications of neuroscience for education conduct post-hoc interpretations of neuroscience findings, trying to identify results most relevant to education. This process consumes time and resources, and it does not always result in usable knowledge for educators. Instead, real interdisciplinary research should be fostered by developing laboratories including neuroscientists, psychologists, and educators, who can collaborate and conduct experimental work on educational neuroscience from the early stages of study conceptualization to the final interpretations. Innovative designs produced as part of such interdisciplinary efforts can allow researchers to study the effects of context and other variables of interest to update and develop new instructional theories and principles. Incorporation of educational neuroscience discoveries into educational policy and practice may shape 21st-century teaching and learning in ways that are analogous to the contributions of educational psychologists such as John Dewey, B. F. Skinner, and Jean Piaget in 20th-century education. The collective work of neuroscientists and educational researchers should continue.

Pavlo D. Antonenko

See also Cognition and Human Learning; Human-Computer Interaction; Neurologically Based Learning and Instruction; Personalized Learning and Instruction

Further Readings

Alivisatos, A. P., Chun, M., Church, G. M., Deisseroth, K., Donoghue, J. P., Greenspan, R. J., . . . Yuste, R. (2013). The brain activity map. *Science, 339,* 1284–1285.

Bruer, J. T. (1999). *The myth of the first three years: A new understanding of early brain development and lifelong learning.* New York, NY: Free Press.

De Jong, T., van Gog, T., Jenks, K., Manlove, S., Van Hell, J. G., Jolles, J., . . . Boschloo, A. (2009). *Explorations in learning and the brain: On the potential of cognitive neuroscience for educational science.* Berlin, Germany: Springer-Verlag.

Dehaene, S. (1997). *The number sense: How the mind creates mathematics.* New York, NY: Oxford University Press.

Gopnik, A., Meltzoff, A. N., & Kuhl, P. K. (1999). *The scientist in the crib: Minds, brains and how children learn.* New York, NY: HarperCollins.

Goswami, U. (2004). Neuroscience and education. *British Journal of Educational Psychology, 74,* 1–14.

Jobard, G., Crivello, F., & Tzourio-Mazoyer, N. (2003). Evaluation of the dual route theory or reading: A meta-analysis of 35 neuroimaging studies. *Neuroimage, 20,* 693–712.

Organisation for Economic Co-operation and Development. (2007). *Understanding the brain: The birth of a learning science.* Paris, France: OECD.

Varma, S., McCandliss, B. D., & Schwartz, D. L. (2008). Scientific and pragmatic challenges for bridging education and neuroscience. *Educational Researcher, 37*(3), 140–152.

New Visual World and Future Competencies

The *new visual world* refers to the ubiquitous presence of digital images that are presented and represented as objects for human use and understanding. It is a world created through digital technologies. The term *new visual world* is used to differentiate visual phenomena appearing in the digital age from those in the old visual world where real or analogue objects are presented and processed by the human eye. This entry first discusses the visual world and historical concepts of it. The entry then discusses the concept of the new visual world and how new technologies allow enhanced perception and increased choices. Finally, the entry lists future competencies that are essential to successfully live in the new visual world.

The Visual World

Human eyes can detect light stimuli ranging from about 400 nanometer (nm) to 700 nm wavelength. They identify colors, shapes, and depth of the physical environment. With this vision, human beings are able to navigate through the physically visible world consisting of three-dimensional spaces. Human vision has been used as a tool for searching for affordances in the given physical visual environment for more than a million years.

Some scholars argue that the visual world is quite incomplete because it is the world perceived via imperfect human vision. For example, Hermann von Helmholtz argued that human vision, because it is optically poor, gathers poor quality information, and thus makes it difficult to assemble clear images of objects. As Helmholtz said, the human visual world could only be the result of some form of unconscious conclusions we make from incomplete data collected via our vision. As Susan Blackmore and her colleagues posited, it could be a mere illusion constructed out of a vague image of real objects around us.

As James J. Gibson argued, the visual world, with imagination and experience, "is extended in depth; it is upright, stable, and without boundaries; it is colored, shadowed, illuminated, and textured; it is composed of surfaces, edges, shapes, and interspaces; finally, and most important of all, it is filled with things which have meanings" (Gibson, 1950, p. 3). The meanings of our visual world are created from our mental images of what we perceive, visualize, and think. Albert Einstein, for example, is known for creating more or less clear images of some ideas or matters first, and then reproducing and combining those images in his mind before expressing them in words.

Internal visual representations of ideas can be retained in human long-term memory, which is often divided into two types: declarative memory and procedural memory. Declarative memory, conscious memory of facts and events, consists of semantic and episodic memories. Semantic memory holds general factual knowledge that is independent of personal experience and context, whereas episodic memory depicts our personal experiences and specific events and is often encoded and retrieved using visual, olfactory, and auditory areas of the brain because it includes contextual elements of a certain experience or event. This suggests that the visual world is not only a visual entity observed through human vision, but also a world operated, imagined, and created in the human mind and memory. This point is supported by a study conducted by Ilju Rha, which revealed the existence of three dimensions in the visual world created in the human mind: interpretation, operation, and creation. The interpretation dimension involves the use of human vision in understanding and developing a clear perception of certain physical objects or a physical environment human beings face. The operation dimension entails visual operations of those physical objects or environment in human mind. The creation dimension engages the process of meaning making, in which the creation of further visualization, visual fantasies, and dreams is taking place.

The New Visual World

The Expanded Human Vision

With the advancement of science and technology, human vision has been drastically improved, and this functionally expanded human vision has contributed to the development of the new visual world. Unaided human vision, a major tool for processing visual information, is quite limited and thus produces incomplete information.

In recent years, various digital technologies have supplemented imperfect human vision. The expanded visible light spectrum has enabled the human eye to see infrared and ultraviolet light, as well as some of the special wavelength lights, such as X-ray or electronic waves. As a result, human beings are now able to identify objects in near or complete darkness, which was impossible with the unaided eye. Moreover, the ranges of visible size and distance have also been expanded. Extremely small objects, such as cells and molecules, can be seen using magnifiers. Distant objects such as galaxies can be observed with telescopes. Also, imperceptible information can be transformed into visible data. For instance, thermal imaging detects heat, which is invisible to our eyes, and shows it with visible colors.

Electrocardiograms depict heartbeats and present them in a visual format. All these developments have contributed to the expansion of human vision capacity and helped people develop much clearer visual perceptions of physical objects and interpret their surrounding visual world more accurately.

Further development of digital technologies has made it possible for human beings to see hidden objects and make certain choices about how to use them. People began to perceive a new visual world. A car navigation system featuring a digital map that offers the same geographical information as the old printed map did, but in a drastically different way, can help show the difference between the old and new visual worlds. Connected with satellites, today's car navigation system offers the latest road information. Users can choose the visual format of the information (e.g., 2D, 3D, or virtual reality), route preference (e.g., highway, freeway, local street, etc.), icon information on places (e.g., parking lots, convenience stores, gas stations, etc.), and other supplementary information, as well as manipulate the viewing scale. The digital road map is not just a road map; it is a tool to see beyond what we can see with the human eye and make choices and decisions regarding circumstances and goals.

Visual Operations Beyond The Physical World

The old visual world is firmly based on the visible physical world, but the new visual world is an extension of what can be seen and it can be produced without direct reference to the external world. That is, the new visual world may or may not exactly resemble the physically existing visual world. Virtual creations that do not resemble the physical world can be made and reproduced (for example, using digital fabricators or 3D printers). Various visual operations and creations then become the basis of human experience in the new visual world.

New Types of Visuals

The new visual world adds several new types of visuals to traditional types of visuals frequently found in the old visual world. The five types listed here are some of the dominant visual types in the new visual world.

Overlay type. This type represents digital visions of physical objects alongside each other—that is, a digital view of reality is created by digital technologies. Examples include street views shown in a car navigation system and in Google Maps and Google Earth, augmented reality visuals, and distance and subject information provided by digital range finders.

Immersive type. This type represents a virtually created visual object that requires total participation of a viewer. A clear example can be found in an avatar of a participant engaging in an immersive visual environment such as Second Life. This avatar is created as a virtual figure representing the participant himself or herself.

Invitational type. This type represents a virtually created visual object that requires only partial or invited participation of a user. Examples of this type are visuals created and posted in social networking sites such as Facebook and KakaoStory or privately set video sharing sites that can be viewed and shared only with invited friends.

Public type. This type refers to visual objects openly shared among people. Visuals uploaded on Flickr, YouTube, TED, SlideShare, and blogs and made available to the public are some examples of this type.

Self-creation type. This type includes the visuals created by individual users by using a wide range of digital tools such as digital cameras, smartphones, 2D and 3D graphic tools, animation tools, mindtools, and so on. The visuals created in this manner will be the ingredients for the previously mentioned types of visuals.

Unlike in the old visual world where experts create most visuals, individual users are the major creators of various types of visuals in the new visual world. We observe that the wide accessibility of digital technologies and graphic tools is facilitating the proliferation of visual images by making it easy for ordinary people to create a wide range of visual-rich resources. The creation dimension in the visual world has become more important than ever, which requires the development of visual communication and creation skills.

Future Competencies

Visual communication and creation skills are needed for the new visual world. These skills are built around key functional areas of human visual intelligence identified by Rha, Sohwa Park, Hyoseon Choi, and Sookkyung Choi: (a) generative visualization (GV), the productive, logical, and intuitive function of human visual intelligence; (b) space-motor visualization (SMV), the spatial and movement function of human visual intelligence; (c) instrumental visualization (IV), the methodological and tactical function of human visual intelligence; (d) proactive visualization (PV), the private, futuristic, and playful function of human visual intelligence; and (e) representational visualization (RV), the responsive and retroactive function of the human visual intelligence.

Ilju Rha

See also Virtual Worlds; Visual Literacy Skills in Science, Technology, Engineering, and Mathematics Education; Visual Search Engines

Further Readings

Gibson, J. J. (1950). *The perception of the visual world.* Boston, MA: Houghton Mifflin.

Hassabis, D., & Maguire, E. A. (2007). Deconstructing episodic memory with construction. *Trends in Cognitive Sciences, 11*(7), 299–306.

Helmholtz, H. (1876). On the limits of the optical capacity of the microscope. *The Monthly Microscopical Journal, 16*(1), 15–39.

Rha, I. (2007). Human visual intelligence and the new territory of educational technology research. *Educational Technology International, 8*(1), 1–16.

Rha, I., Park, S., Choi, H., & Choi, S. (2009). Development and validation of a visualization tendency test. In T. Bastiaens, J. Dron, & C. Xin (Eds.), *Proceedings of World Conference on E-Learning in Corporate, Government, Healthcare, and Higher Education 2009* (pp. 3665–3670). Chesapeake, VA: AACE. Retrieved from http://www.editlib.org/p/33010

Schacter, D. L., Gilbert, D. T., & Wegner, D. M. (2011). Semantic and episodic memory. In D. L. Schacter, D. T. Gilbert, & D. M. Wegner (Eds.), *Psychology* (2nd ed., pp. 240–241). New York, NY: Worth.

Sims, E., O'Leary, R., Cook, J., & Butland, G. (2002). Visual literacy: What is it and do we need it to use learning technologies effectively? *Proceedings of ASCILITE* 2002. Retrieved from http://www.ascilite.org.au/conferences/auckland02/proceedings/papers/ellen_sims_et_al.pdf

Walker, C. M., Winner, E., Hetland, L., Simmons, S., & Goldsmith, L. (2011). Visual thinking: Art students have an advantage in geometric reasoning. *Creative Education, 2*(1), 22–26.

Nine Events of Instruction

See Conditions of Learning: Gagné's Nine Events of Instruction

Norm-Based Assessments

The interaction of technology and norm-based, or norm-referenced, assessment provides opportunities for the collection of interesting information related to student learning and development as well as introducing several issues and concerns. Reviewing the purpose of assessment is critical to the use and interpretation of assessments. Categorizing assessments can clarify purposes and help educators and policy makers address issues. This entry first discusses the benefits and disadvantages of norm-based assessment and its use in computer-based and computer adaptive testing. It then discusses some of the uses and potential uses of norm-based assessments.

A common type of assessment involves the comparison of scores to a standard—*criterion-referenced*—or to those from a group of similar individuals—*norm-referenced*. Royal Van Horn argued for the use of *improvement-referenced* assessment (criterion-referenced measures taken multiple times), but Peter Behuniak proposed that assessment should be *consumer-referenced*. When analyzing the efficacy of norm-referenced assessment, two critical questions become (1) what are the disadvantages and benefits of norm-referenced assessment that cannot be addressed with other approaches, and (2) if norm-referenced assessment is warranted, how can technology be used to make the process efficient and effective?

Dylan Wiliam stated that scores derived from norm-referenced testing are relatively insensitive to instruction; this is the primary challenge for their use in assessment of academic knowledge and skills. As a result, a shift of classroom- and state-based standardized assessments in the United States has occurred toward the emphasis of criterion-referenced. Nevertheless, there are several areas where an effort to use norm-referenced assessment might be justified: (1) increasing the efficiency of norm-referenced assessments when comparisons are made on academic content or skills where there is a lack of coherence of expected standards or taught content, (2) providing learners and other stakeholders information about how students compare with large groups of similar individuals, (3) providing important information for program evaluation if learner input characteristics among the comparison groups are matched, and (4) collecting data on important domains of human development and behavior that do not as yet have established standards and benchmarks.

Computer-Based Testing and Computer Adaptive Testing

Two technological contributions to norm-referenced assessment are computer-based testing and computer adaptive testing. The major advantage of computer-based testing is that results can be provided quickly. An additional advantage is that the testing may be more secure. However, many schools do not have the computer resources for all students to take the exam at the same time. Therefore, paper and pencil tests are available where an adequate number of computers or computer access is not available. A second advantage of computer-based testing is the opportunity for more interactivity. For example, the test developers can provide simulations, have students view video clips, or have students engage in activities.

Computer adaptive testing (CAT) provides a different procedure for presenting the tested content to the test taker. In this process, not all items are given to any specific test taker; rather, the computer adapts to the correct and incorrect answers provided by the test taker and presents items accordingly. Advocates suggest that CAT delivers more valid results if most of the items answered by the test taker match his or her level of knowledge. Wim van der Linden and Peter Pashley showed that a major advantage to test developers is that the processes of item selection and the estimation of item difficulty can be made efficient using the Rasch measurement model. A second advantage is that the testing procedure can be more efficient because each examinee does not answer all possible questions. Rather, the items are organized into what are called *testlets*, which van der Linden described as sets of content-related items. Examinees are systematically provided with testlets until it is determined that they can or cannot answer most of the questions reliably. The test thereby converges on the knowledge and skill of the examinee.

Uses of Norm-Referenced Assessment

In the United States, norm-referenced assessments are widely used for screening high school graduates for admittance to colleges or programs. The ACT and SAT tests are the two primary instruments used. A justification for using norm-referenced assessments for this purpose is twofold: (1) there is a lack of coherence between content taught in high school and college, and (2) there are a limited number of openings that can be allocated in any college admission process—colleges want to select those most likely to succeed.

Why are high stakes norm-referenced assessments used rather than measures of past academic performance such as high school cumulative grade point averages (HSCGPA)? Elchanan Cohn and his colleagues demonstrated that SAT scores predict college success beyond HSCGPA, and Justine Radunzel and Julie Noble provided the same support for the ACT. The rationale for the use of norm-referenced assessment appears to have empirical support.

The Graduate Record Examination (GRE), Graduate Management Admission Test (GMAT), the Law School Admission Test (LSAT), and the Medical College Admission Test (MCAT) are among the tests required

for admittance to graduate or professional studies. A similar question can be raised about the use of these exams: Do they provide predictive power beyond undergraduate cumulative grade point average? In a meta-analytic study, Nathan Kuncel and colleagues demonstrated that the GRE was a valid predictor of success in graduate school beyond what might be expected from undergraduate grades, although the subject-level tests were better predictors than were the more general verbal, quantitative, and analytic scores. Likewise, In-Sue Oh and colleagues demonstrated that the GMAT provided increased predictive power for admittance to business programs.

Internationally, the Programme for International Student Assessment (PISA) and the Trends in International Mathematics and Science Study (TIMSS) are somewhat useful for comparisons of academic content and skills among countries. These tests are seen as an audit of a country's educational system, assessing only a relatively small number of learners in a limited number of schools, districts, and states. The results can be used to make statements about the effectiveness of the combination of nonformal, informal, and formal learning experiences of groups of learners.

Because norm-referenced tests address content and skills beyond what is taught in schools, increasing the efficiency and effectiveness of administering these tests can provide some information about the sociocultural context as a whole. However, this provides less information about how teaching and instruction might be improved. The fact that scores on norm-referenced assessments of learners' academic content knowledge and skills add predictive validity beyond grades in formal learning environments suggests that informal learning experiences are important for predicting success in undergraduate and graduate schooling.

Potential Uses of Norm-Referenced Assessments

The collection of data on domains of human development offers advantages for norm-referenced assessment even though criterion-referenced assessment would be more appropriate if domains had established standards and benchmarks. Several research and theoretical orientations are worthy of consideration. Howard Gardner, Daniel Goleman, and Robert Sternberg and his associates concluded that cognitive intelligence, and by implication norm-referenced assessments of academic knowledge, at best predict one third of the variance in adult success. As much as two thirds of that variance is related to development of other factors such as emotional and social factors and self-regulation. Ed Diener and colleagues developed measures related to an individual's well-being: positive and negative experiences, positive thinking, and psychological well-being. Martin Seligman worked with colleagues to develop measures of the five components of PERMA theory: positive emotion, engagement, positive relationships, meaning and purpose, and accomplishment. The Collaborative for Academic, Social, and Emotional Learning (CASEL) developed a number of instruments to measure five components that provide a foundation for personal development: self-awareness, social awareness, self-management, relationship skills, and responsible decision making. The lack of inclusion of these assessments into the overall assessment process of children, youth, and young adults omits factors that account for most of the variance related to adult success. This is certainly an area where technology-based norm-referenced assessment can add value to the teaching and learning process.

Conclusion

Norm-referenced testing has an important role to play in developing a deeper understanding of teaching and learning. What is most important about efforts to expand the focus of schooling beyond the traditional academic knowledge and skills assessed by most norm-reference tests is that they address nonacademic competencies that the Partnership for 21st Century Skills and others advocate as important for adult success in the 21st century.

William G. Huitt and David M. Monetti

See also Adaptive Testing; Criterion-Referenced Assessments; Dynamic Student Profiles; E-Portfolio Technologies; Formative Assessment; Measuring Learning in Informal Contexts; Objectives-Based Assessments; Performance Assessment; Program Evaluation; Summative Assessment

Further Readings

Behuniak, P. (2002). Consumer-referenced testing. *Phi Delta Kappan, 84*(3), 199–207.

Cohn, E., Cohn, S., Balch, D., & Bradley, J., Jr. (2001). The effect of SAT scores, high-school GPA and other student characteristics on success in college. In *Proceedings of the Annual Meeting of the American Statistical Association* (August 5–9). Retrieved from http://www.amstat.org/sections/SRMS/Proceedings/y2001/Proceed/00187.pdf

Huitt, W. (2011, May). *A holistic view of education and schooling: Guiding students to develop capacities, acquire virtues, and provide service.* Revision of paper presented at the 12th Annual International Conference sponsored by the Athens Institute for Education and Research (ATINER), May 24–27, 2011, Athens, Greece. Retrieved from http://www.edpsycinteractive.org/papers/holistic-view-of-schooling-rev.pdf

Kuncel, N., Hezlett, S., & Ones, D. (2001). A comprehensive meta-analysis of the predictive validity of the Graduate Record Examinations: Implications for graduate student selection and performance. *Psychological Bulletin, 127*(1), 162–181.

Oh, I.-S., Schmidt, F., Shaffer, J., & Huy, L. (2008). The Graduate Management Admission Test (GMAT) is even more valid than we thought: A new development in meta-analysis and its implications for the validity of the GMAT. *Academy of Management Learning & Education, 7*(4), 563–570.

Radunzel, J., & Noble, J. (2012). *Predicting long-term college success through degree completion using ACT® composite score, ACT benchmarks, and high school grade point average.* ACT Research Report Series (5). Iowa City, IA: ACT. Retrieved from http://www.eric.ed.gov/PDFS/ED542027.pdf

van der Linden, W. (2000). Constrained adaptive testing with shadow tests. In W. van der Linden & C. Glas (Eds.), *Computerized adaptive testing: Theory and practice* (pp. 27–52). Dordrecht, Netherlands: Kluwer Academic.

van der Linden, W., & Pashley, P. (2000). Item selection and ability estimation in adaptive testing. In W. van der Linden & C. Glas (Eds.), *Computerized adaptive testing: Theory and practice* (pp. 1–25). Dordrecht, Netherlands: Kluwer Academic.

Van Horn, R. (2003). Computer adaptive tests and computer-based tests. *Phi Delta Kappan, 84*(8), 567, 630–631.

Wiliam, D. (2008). International comparisons and sensitivity to instruction. *Assessment in Education: Principles, Policy & Practice, 15*(3), 253–257.

OBJECTIVES-BASED ASSESSMENTS

Objectives-based assessments refers to measuring how well students have learned with reference to three elements in predetermined instructional goals or objectives: (1) the performance (what the student must be able to do at the end of the instruction), (2) the conditions or circumstances under which this performance is to take place, and (3) the criteria for judging the quality of what the student does. The example in Table 1 illustrates the structure of an objectives-based assessment and its relationship to the instructional objective, providing a foundation for the more detailed explanation that follows. This entry first discusses the background of objectives-based assessment and how technology enables this older assessment approach to retain its relevance in more modern contexts, before detailing the structure of objectives-based assessments.

Background of Objectives-Based Assessments

Objectives-based assessments have their roots in behaviorism, popular in the early- to mid-20th century, where observable and measurable behavior was considered to be the key to determining the amount and quality of learning. With this mind-set, Robert Mager outlined ways of preparing objectives to clearly define what was meant by *learning* in any particular area and to promote objective measurement of that learning—that is, objectives-based assessment. In the same time frame, a committee of educational psychologists developed Bloom's taxonomy, a framework that categorizes educational objectives into progressively higher learning levels and was named after committee chairman Dr. Benjamin Bloom.

Although ideas about learning have changed, Bloom's taxonomy, Mager's work, and objectives-based assessments are still used in formal instructional systems design (ISD), particularly for *training*, where specific learning outcomes are important (e.g., multiplication tables, landing a plane). One reason for their continuing popularity stems directly from the objective and measurable *evidence of learning* that they provide, especially in adult training where certification and liability protection are issues. As a point of interest, this emphasis on objective and measurable behavior is also responsible for several limitations. One is the inability of objectives-based assessments to measure learning beyond the criteria used. A second is the difficulty of creating objectives for subjective learning specific to individuals (e.g., metacognitive knowledge or thinking about thinking). David Krathwohl begins to address this second limitation with his revision to Bloom's taxonomy to include metacognitive knowledge as objective material.

Yet another reason for continued use is the expanding role of technology in design, delivery, data collection, and feedback within the approach. For example, virtual reality and simulation immerse students in authentic but cost- and time-effective assessment environments. Also, technology-enhanced tools (e.g., movie making, photography) present students and instructors with a wider range of performance options to creatively demonstrate competence. These are just two of many examples.

Structure of an Objective-Based Assessment

The example in Table 1 reflects performance, conditions, and criteria for a basic skill required by surgeons learning robotic surgery for a particular system.

Table I   Example of an objective and its related objective-based assessment

Objective	Objective-Based Assessment
Performance: Complete a surgically related task that requires coordinated manipulation of the two robotic arms	**Performance:** Suture a 3-inch (7.62-cm) cut in a surgical glove
Conditions: —Given the simulator for the robot —Given the appropriate tool(s) for the task already mounted on the arm(s) —Given a constrained operating space —Given a starting configuration / "shape" for each arm close to joint limits —Given pre-set motion speeds that will require adjustments for each arm	**Conditions:** —Given the simulator for the robot —Given both the needle holder tools and one threaded needle mounted —Given a visible boundary (radius of 3 inches (7.62 cm) from the cut center —Given a specific set of starting joint angles for arm 1 and a different set of starting joint angles for arm 2 —Given the maximum motion speed for each arm that will require adjustment
Criteria: —Within acceptable tolerances of the robotic arms' joint limits —Without collision between the two arms —Without collision between any arm and held objects —Without collision between an arm (or what it holds) and the operating space —Within specified time limits —Without exceeding pressure limits	**Criteria:** —Having each joint not moving any closer than $10°$ toward any joint limit —Without collision between the two arms —Without collision between any arm and the needle holders and needle —Without collision between an arm, the needle holders/needle, and the boundary —Task completed within 10 minutes —Suture completed without tearing the surgical glove

Objectives-Based Assessments and Performance

As in the example in Table 1, performance always specifies an action that defines what the student is supposed to do to provide objective evidence of learning. The objectives-based assessment requires the learner to actually do or perform the action, task, or activity using some assessment instrument or approach (e.g., multiple-choice tests, cases, immersion in real-life or simulated situations). Objectives-based assessments can be implemented using any testing instrument or approach; however, it is critical that the assessment activity matches the performance defined in the objective. This rule helps determine (and constrain) the types of assessment instruments or approaches that are appropriate. For example, in the assessment in Table 1, a learner must complete a surgical task. Therefore, a multiple-choice test is inappropriate because it does not allow the learner to provide evidence of learning as the performance defines.

Objectives-Based Assessments and Conditions

Objective-based assessments use the conditions outlined in the objective to provide the appropriate environment for the testing exercise or situation. *Givens* indicate what the environment needs to include or limit. These might include conditions that help the instructor administer the test (e.g., given instructor guidance or given Internet access) and conditions related to the subject matter (e.g., given a limited amount of space for tool manipulation).

Conditions contribute to the difficulty and complexity of performance, making the objectives-based assessment harder or easier, more or less stressful, and so forth. For example, time limits tend to increase performance difficulty. In the early stages of learning, conditions may be designed to simplify the performance to match the learner's current skill or knowledge level. In the surgical assessment, for example, performance involves fewer considerations because suturing involves a simulator with a rubber glove rather than a real patient and wound. As learning progresses, conditions can be changed or new conditions added to create an environment that is closer to the complexity and authenticity of real-life situations.

Technology can be instrumental in allowing trainers to control and manipulate contextual conditions; for example, many simulators allow the simulation controller to turn off elements of situational reality for assessment of early learning. Technology also provides opportunities for authentic assessment when realistic conditions are unavailable, too dangerous, or too expensive to access or reproduce during training (e.g., training for operations in space, handling collapsed landing gear).

Objectives-Based Assessments and Criteria

Objectives-based assessments are *criterion-referenced*, meaning that the learner's performance is measured against a set of criteria. The comparison indicates how well the learner performed against the expected "standard" with observable or measurable evidence. Criterion-referenced also means that all criteria used for judging the quality of learning are set with reference to the knowledge and skills of the subject matter.

The criterion-referenced nature of objectives-based assessments lends itself to technological implementation because (a) the knowledge and skills to be learned are known, (b) the criteria are bounded (i.e., measurement does not look at any learning outside of the criteria listed), and (c) the criteria are measurable. Computers, simulators, tablets, and so on are often able to measure performance and respond with meaningful feedback about the learner's performance. In turn, the results and feedback from the assessment can lead back to meaningful and targeted instruction, even without an instructor in the loop.

Criteria can also help set the desired focus of the assessment. In the surgical example, note that neither the objective nor the assessment specifies criteria for judging the quality of the surgery (suture) itself because the objective is intended for early skill learning and the assessment focus at this point is on the robotic manipulation. Criteria for surgical excellence can easily be added when it is appropriate to do so.

Conclusion

Notions of learning have gone beyond behaviorism to take situational context, learners, and the dynamics of the mind into consideration, but a need for objective measurement of learning remains. With technology and advances in instructional design, objectives-based assessments should continue to be useful for this purpose.

Gail Kopp

See also Assessing Learning in Simulation-Based Environments; Assessment of Problem Solving and Higher Order Thinking; Cognition and Human Learning; Criterion-Referenced Assessments; Norm-Based Assessments; Performance Assessment

Further Readings

Baker, E. L., Chung, G. K. W. K., & Delacruz, G. C. (2007). Design and validation of technology-based performance assessments. In J. M. Spector, M. D. Merrill, J. van Merriënboer, & M. P. Driscoll (Eds.), *Handbook of research on educational communications and technology* (3rd ed., pp. 595–604). London, UK: Routledge.

Jonnassen, D. H. (1991). Objectivism versus constructivism: Do we need a new philosophical paradigm? *Educational Technology Research & Development, 39*(3), 5–14.

Krathwohl, D. R. (2002). A revision of Bloom's taxonomy: An overview. *Theory Into Practice, 41*(4), 212–264.

Mager, R. F. (1997). *Preparing instructional objectives: A critical tool in the development of effective instruction* (3rd ed.). Atlanta, GA: Center for Effective Performance.

ONLINE MENTORING

Traditional mentoring (t-mentoring) has been considered to be the practice of transferring knowledge from a knowing, experienced person (mentor) to a younger, less experienced, or less knowledgeable person (protégé) through face-to-face formal or informal meetings. The importance of mentoring has been recognized in the literature as well as in business, psychology, and educational environments. Mentoring takes place in many different program settings and uses many different formats for many different reasons. In the United States, mentoring programs such as Big Brothers Big Sisters promote positive youth development to help youths avoid risky behavior such as drug and alcohol abuse and violence. icouldbe is a program that works with hundreds of schools to partner 7th- to 12th-grade students with mentors who provide them with career guidance, college information, and other valuable advice. MentorNet provides mentors to women and minorities in search of careers in the engineering field. Similar programs exist in many other countries (e.g., Youth in Action in the United Kingdom, the Australian Mentoring Network, and MentorIndia). Studies of traditional mentoring programs show that mentored individuals perform better on the job, advance more rapidly within the organization, and demonstrate more job and career satisfaction than do their nonmentored workmates. In the educational field, studies of traditional mentoring programs show that mentored college students report greater satisfaction with their educational experiences and are more likely to graduate than are nonmentored students.

Online mentoring involves the use of distance technology as the primary channel of communication; it is also referred to as telementoring, e-mentoring, virtual mentoring, cyber-based mentoring, Internet mentoring, or electronic mentoring. The use of technology now plays a significant role in mentoring students enrolled in online and hybrid courses. Online mentoring can apply tools such as e-mail, texting, audio or video conferencing, instant messaging, chat groups, virtual reality, and even other technologies such as wikis, blogs, podcasts, and social networks. The Internet provides support for personal as well as educational interactions. This entry discusses the origins of online mentoring, its advantages and problems, and its implications for higher education.

Origins of Online Mentoring

Online mentoring in education was first used for the professional development of teachers. This can be traced backed to the early 1990s in British Columbia, where a group of teachers who were experienced in using computers provided online support to novice users. In the United States, also in the 1990s, DuPont Corporation established a mentoring program to enhance leadership development of employees and for mentors and protégés to share knowledge, skills, and experiences. In 1993, the University of Texas launched an ambitious, online mentoring program for students. Hewlett-Packard began matching company staff with student protégés in 1995 in a project that integrated frequent e-mails with schoolwork. The International Telementor Center, founded in 1995, is a leader in the field of academic mentoring; it facilitates online mentoring relationships between professional adults and students worldwide; in 1998, the center was expanded to coordinate several company-sponsored online mentoring programs.

Online Mentoring: Advantages and Problems

The effects of a mentoring relationship are generally positive for both the mentor and the protégé. Mentoring, both online and traditional, involves sharing and transferring knowledge, wisdom, skills, and perspectives in an established, safe, and supportive relationship based on mutual trust, respect, and commitment for personal and professional growth, advancement, and development. The mentor is a guide, a counselor, a role model, an advocate, a confidant, a true friend. A mentor is someone who has a high desire to provide support, to lend a hand.

Advantages

Online mentoring has several advantages over traditional mentoring. With the changing nature of educational institutions and organizations, it may no longer be practicable or even advisable to have only one mentor. Online mentoring expands the opportunities to develop mentor-protégé relationships among those who are geographically apart. Online mentors can operate locally, regionally, nationally, or internationally. Online mentoring accommodates those who do not have time for traditional mentoring or who have lifestyles or situations that make face-to-face mentoring difficult. E-mails can be sent at any time and allow for convenient, frequent communication between mentors, protégés, and program coordinators. Potentially, online mentoring allows for more interaction between mentor and protégé than do many conventional programs, which accelerates knowledge transfer and provides a way to convey new learning.

Online mentors and protégés benefit by learning and using Internet communication technologies. In a social context, there are opportunities to network, to participate in teamwork, and to make use of a variety of social networking tools. Psychological benefits include (a) satisfaction from offering support and advice to others, (b) career and academic support, and (c) the opportunity to gain support from others. Some claim that online mentoring eliminates the personal bias that can come into play with face-to-face contact. Electronic communications might also mask differences between higher and lower status groups that might otherwise hinder communication. Actually, a new trend, referred to as "reverse mentoring," is emerging where the mentor is the younger participant in the relationship teaching and advising a mature protégé. Online mentoring generates an archive that can be used to evaluate the success of the program and that can serve as a reference for all parties. This archive can give mentors instant access to protégés' previous communications. Online mentoring offers the opportunity to make mentoring available to everyone, everywhere, anytime. Knowledge sharing flourishes beyond geographic, time, race, and age boundaries.

Problems

A number of potential problems are associated with online mentoring programs. Good technology infrastructure and support is needed, such as the establishment and maintenance of online databases or the creation of special mail groups. Time, effort, and costs can be a challenge. Students with poor basic skills can struggle with the task of communicating effectively in writing, which can become a chore for these students. This may limit the use of online mentoring for some at-risk students, and their behavioral and attitudinal problems may make online mentoring less effective than traditional mentoring. Communication between mentor and protégé may be limited to text, which can inhibit the development of trust, openness, and commitment.

Implications of Online Mentoring for Higher Education

The surge in nontraditional students and adult learners has brought with it changes to higher education, including (a) a shift toward career-oriented and work-training education, (b) a shortening of the time needed for degree programs, (c) an increase in online education, (d) changes in financial aid, (e) and more support for nontraditional students. One of the biggest changes in higher education has been the increase in online education. Online degree programs have been the key that allows many nontraditional students to fit higher education into their busy schedules. This creates a need for effective online mentoring.

Online mentoring could prove to be a means for persistence, retention, and graduation in higher education, and therefore it has special value for student affairs practitioners, counselors, faculty, academic administrators, adult and continuing educators, online students themselves, and all who are committed to making a difference in all undergraduate students' lives.

Conclusion

Although mentoring is a well-established approach to personal and career development, the use of online mentoring is still developing both within the workplace and education. The rapid increase in the number of schools, students, businesses, universities, and voluntary organizations going online will facilitate the expansion of online mentoring programs. It's likely the trend toward increased use of online mentoring will continue, given its advantages of not depending on a particular space, offering time for reflection, and retaining a permanent record for subsequent analysis.

Gloria Natividad

See also Asynchronous Tools and Technologies; Cultural Considerations in Technology-Enhanced Learning and Instruction; Information and Communication Technologies in Multinational and Multicultural Contexts; Internet: Impact and Potential for Learning and Instruction; Social Networking

Further Readings

Ensher, E. A., & Murphy, S. E. (2007). E-mentoring: Next-generation research strategies and suggestions. In B. R. Ragins & K. E. Kram (Eds.), *The handbook of mentoring at work: Theory, research, and practice* (pp. 299–322). Thousand Oaks, CA: Sage.

Mullen, C. A. (2009). Re-imagining the human dimension of mentoring: A framework for research administration and the academy. *Journal of Research Administration, 40*(1), 10–33.

Rowland, K. N. (2011). E-mentoring: An innovative twist to traditional mentoring. *Journal of Technology Management & Innovation, 7*(1), 228–237.

Scandura, T. A., & Pelligrini, E. K. (2007). Workplace mentoring: Theoretical approaches and methodological issues. In T. D. Allen & L. T. Eby (Eds.), *The Blackwell handbook of mentoring: A multiple perspectives approach* (pp. 71–96). Malden, MA: Blackwell.

Single, P. B., & Single, R. M. (2005). Mentoring and the technology revolution: How face-to-face mentoring sets the stage for e-mentoring. In F. K. Kochan & J. T. Pascarelli (Eds.), *Creating successful telementoring programs* (pp. 7–27). Greenwich, CT: Information Age Publishing.

Zey, M. G. (2011). Virtual mentoring: The challenges and opportunities of electronically-mediated formal mentor programs. *Review of Business Research, 11*(4), 141–152.

OPEN CONTENT LICENSING

Open content licensing is an alternative to traditional copyright licensing. In contrast to copyright, which restricts the use and distribution of content for the benefit of the copyright holder, open content licensing has been devised to make original content freely and more widely available to the general public. This entry first discusses the technological changes that led to open content licensing, the rationale for open content licensing, and examples of open content licenses. It then discusses the implications of open content licensing for education.

Educational institutions, government entities, and for-profit and nonprofit organizations have historically limited the public availability of content through means such as secure websites, proprietary databases, intranets, and learning/course management systems—each of which requires access codes and passwords available only to selected users. The secured content is unavailable to those without the proper memberships or funds. Although copyright does not necessarily prevent content from being accessed, it does provide its own form of content security by restricting what can and cannot be done with content. Copying a book, sampling a song, recording portions of a movie or accessing software source code are actions that typically can be performed only after obtaining permission from the copyright owner.

The advent and ubiquity of the Internet has changed the way that text, images, animation, audio, and video are delivered and accessed. People around the world can freely and easily receive content via a universal interface. Content for the Internet can also be created by users and shared to the world through video-sharing sites (e.g., YouTube, Vimeo, Flickr), social networking sites (e.g., Facebook, Twitter, LinkedIn), blogs, personal websites, and a myriad of other content sites. Copying an entire large printed book using a copy machine can be a long and laborious process, but users can copy and reproduce digital content that is identical in quality to the original. In addition, digitized content can be modified, added to, or edited.

Open content licensing capitalizes on the capabilities afforded by the Internet by providing a legal structure for the delivery and use of content by the general public that differs from traditional copyright. Technology makes content more easily and widely available and accessible from a usability perspective, and open content licensing makes content more easily and widely available and accessible from a legal perspective.

Rationale for Open Content Licensing

Advocates of open content licensing maintain that access to content, information, and education is a fundamental human right. As such, universal knowledge access is seen as a nationally and globally unifying mechanism that should be used to shrink rather than grow the digital divide. The cost of replicating digital information is considered to be so low that that content should rightly be made available to all people at no cost.

Another rationale for the promotion of open content is that intermediaries who market, sell, and distribute content often derive much greater financial benefit than do the authors or creators of the content. Others make the argument that copyright, which prohibits the free creation and distribution of new works derived from modifications of existing works, actually stifles, rather than promotes, true creativity.

A possible concern about open content licensing is that content creators and institutions may be denied profits rightly due them for their creative efforts. This could serve as a disincentive to content creation or sustainability because there may be little incentive to continue to develop, improve, or update the work. There may also be issues with quality control because many open content licensing options do not prevent works from being modified or applied in ways and for purposes that the original authors never intended. For instance, an author may be distressed to find that an original work has been modified with factually incorrect information or is being used to promote social, religious, or political views to which the author is opposed.

Examples of Open Content Licensing

Open Content License

An early (1998) version of an open content license, authored by David A. Wiley, is found at opencontent.org. The open content license was built using a framework known as the *5Rs*, which represents perhaps the most significant departure from traditional copyright restrictions. This license affirms the right to (a) *retain*, which allows users to make, own, and control copies of content, including downloading, duplicating, storing, and managing the content; (b) *reuse*, which allows users to use content in various ways and settings, such as in a face-to-face or online course, on a website, in a performance, or in a video; (c) *revise*, which allows users to translate content into another language or otherwise adapt or modify the content; (d) *remix*, which allows users to combine content with other open content to create a new or derivative work, such as in a mashup; or (e) *redistribute*, which gives users the right to share copies of the original content, revisions, or remixes with other users.

GNU General Public License

The GNU General Public License (GNU GPL) is the most popular license for free software and is available at gnu.org/licenses/gpl.html. The GNU GPL was created by Richard Stallman and is a product of the Free Software Foundation (also founded by Stallman). The Free Software Foundation promotes the development, use, and distribution of free software, which it defines as "free" if users of the program enjoy four essential freedoms: (1) the freedom to run the software for any purpose that the user wishes, (2) the freedom to analyze how the software works, and change it so it does what the user wishes, (3) the freedom to redistribute copies of the original software, and (4) the freedom to distribute copies of a user's modified versions of the software to others. Freedoms 2 and 4 require that users are able to access the software's source code.

The GNU GPL uses a strategy called *share-alike licensing* (also known as *copyleft*). This strategy requires that derivative works can only be distributed under the same licensing terms as the original work and is used to prevent free software from being transformed into proprietary software by individuals or organizations that restrict public access to changes made to the original software. Copyleft as described on the gnu.org website involves copyright law; however, instead of a means for restricting a program, copyleft becomes a means for keeping the program free and widely accessible without restrictions. As a result, the concept of free software gives all who have a copy the rights of ownership.

Creative Commons

The Creative Commons license was conceived originally by Lawrence Lessig and Eric Eldred, who were working together on a legal case to challenge the U.S. Copyright Term Extension Act. Creative Commons was based on the desire to apply the ideas of the Free Software Foundation and the GNU GPL beyond the realm of software programs and open source code. As explained by Lessig on the creativecommons.org website, the idea is to produce copyright licenses that the originators can use to announce the freedoms and restrictions that apply to their creative works. The meaning of a Creative Commons license is that some rights are reserved—which ones are determined by the copyright owner. Typical copyright law gives the copyright holder the exclusive right to make copies whereas a Creative Commons license may give the right to make copies to the public.

A Creative Commons license follows a predefined template that ensures that the content creator will retain the copyright and that any fair use, first sale, or free expression rights will not be affected by the license. Licensees who abide by the provisions of the Creative Commons license are awarded permission to copy, distribute, and display the work or perform the work in public. These users are also allowed to make a digital public performance of the work, such as a live webinar or webcast. Creative Commons licensees are required to obtain permission from the copyright holder for any uses outside of the Creative Commons license. Users must not alter the terms of the license or use technology, such as digital rights management, to restrict access to the content under the license. Users are also required to link to the Creative Commons license and keep all existing copyright notices intact.

In addition to the basic provisions of the Creative Commons template, the copyright holder can determine specific types of permissions or freedoms granted to the licensee. Each of the six license types requires users to give attribution to the copyright holder; however, the types differ in whether the licensee is allowed to use derivative works, whether the work can be used for commercial purposes, and whether a share-alike/copyleft license (i.e., requirement that derivative works must be released under the same license as the original work) must be deployed. The six Creative Commons licenses include (1) *Attribution,* which allows users to use the work any way that they like, as long as attribution is given to the copyright holder; (2) *Attribution-ShareAlike,* which allows users to use the work however they like, but they must give attribution and license any derivative work under a share-alike license; (3) *Attribution-NoDerivatives,* in which licensees must use the work as is, without modification, and must give attribution; (4) *Attribution-NonCommercial,* which specifies that the work must be used for noncommercial purposes, and attribution is given; (5) *Attribution-NonCommercial-NoDerivatives,* allowing users to use the work for noncommercial purposes, as is, and with attribution; (6) *Attribution-NonCommercial-ShareAlike,* in which the work must be used for noncommercial purposes, derivatives must be licensed under a share-alike license, and attribution is given to the copyright holder.

Implications of Open Content Licensing for Education

Open content licensing began during the early days of the World Wide Web. Online courses at the time were, by and large, websites created by faculty and were freely available to the public. The beginning of the 21st century saw the advent of secured sites and learning management systems, which placed educational content behind password-protected virtual walls. The second decade of the 21st century has given rise to an unprecedented skepticism of the value of higher education. Increasing costs of tuition, textbooks, and instructional materials—including publisher websites requiring paid access codes—have caused students and potential students to question the return on investment of attending colleges and universities and completing degree programs.

One reaction to this skepticism has been the increase in interest and use of open content. The success of the open content movement is evident in virtually every aspect of education. The Open Education Consortium (formerly the OpenCourseWare Consortium) has more than 200 higher education member institutions in more than 50 countries worldwide that make lesson materials used in their courses available freely to the public. Massive open online courses (MOOCs), many of which are free, now number in the hundreds. A growing number of K–12 schools, colleges, and universities are using open-source-based learning management systems (e.g., Moodle, Sakai), open-source content management systems (e.g., Drupal, WordPress), free textbook sites (e.g., Bookboon, OpenStax), and learning materials (e.g., Multimedia Educational Resource for Learning and Online Teaching [MERLOT], WebQuest). The largest encyclopedia in the history of the world, Wikipedia, is licensed through Creative Commons.

Anthony A. Piña

See also Open-Access Journals in Educational Technology; OpenCourseWare Movement; Open-Source Repositories for Learning and Instruction

Further Readings

Fitzgerald, B. (2007). *Open content licensing for open educational resources.* Brisbane, Australia: Organisation for Economic Co-operation and Development, Queensland University of Technology. Retrieved from http://www.oecd .org/edu/ceri/38645489.pdf

Guibault, L., & Angelopoulos, C. (Eds.). (2011). *Open content licensing: From theory to practice.* Amsterdam, Netherlands: Amsterdam University Press. Retrieved from http://www.ivir .nl/publications/angelopoulos/9789089643070_TEXT_HR _DRUK.pdf

Wiley, D. A. (n.d.). Defining the "open" in open content. Retrieved from http://opencontent.org/definition

Websites

Creative Commons: creativecommons.org
Free Software Foundation: fsf.org
GNU General Public License: gnu.org/licenses/licenses.html
Open Content License: opencontent.org

OPEN-ACCESS JOURNALS IN EDUCATIONAL TECHNOLOGY

Open-access journals in educational technology are a specific type of academic journal focused on educational technology. The type of scholarship academic journals publish can range from traditional empirical studies to literature reviews, position pieces, and book reviews. Open-access journals differ from traditional journals in several ways, including that readers can view articles online without a subscription. This entry describes academic journals and notes some that focus on educational technology. The entry then explains the difference between closed-access and open-access journals, discusses the pros and cons of open-access journals, and details controversies over open-access journals.

Articles in academic journals are usually peer reviewed. Peer review is a process in which two or more peers review a manuscript. The reviewers provide feedback to the authors and the editor and recommend whether the manuscript should be published, revised, or declined. Typically, an editor makes the final publication decision. Peer review is usually one key difference between academic journals (e.g., *Educational Technology Research and Development*) and professional magazines (e.g., *Educational Technology*) in a field. Some academic journals publish both peer-reviewed *and* nonpeer-reviewed articles (e.g., *TechTrends*). The peer review process is generally believed to increase the rigor and prestige of a publication and to help further advance a field of study. Despite these perceived benefits, many academics are quick to point out problems with the typical peer-review process (e.g., innovative thinking can be suppressed, it relies on busy unpaid volunteers, it can slow the publication process).

The field of educational technology has more than a hundred different academic journals. Some of these journals have a traditional research focus, such as *Educational Technology Research and Development*, the *British Journal of Educational Technology*, and *Computers & Education*. These three journals, in particular, are some of the oldest and generally accepted as the most prestigious journals in the field. Other educational technology journals, such as *TechTrends*, are more practitioner oriented, focusing less on reporting traditional research and more on reporting emerging trends and practices in the field. Other academic journals focus on a specific aspect of educational technology such as distance education (e.g., *The American Journal of Distance Education* or *The Internet and Higher Education*) or on educational technology in a specific context (e.g., the *Journal of Technology and Teacher Education* or the *Journal of Computing in Higher Education*).

Open Versus Closed Academic Journals

Traditional academic journals use a subscription model in which to access a specific journal, people either have to pay, usually in the form of a subscription, or have access to an institution (e.g., a university library) that subscribes to the journal.

As the Internet grew, academic journals began to be published online. Many of these early online academic journals (sometimes called e-journals) were free for anyone to access. Generally, there were no subscription fees to read the articles in these journals. As a result, online journals that were free to access began to be labeled as *open-access journals.*

Open-access journals have since grown in popularity. Currently there are more than 70 different educational technology or educational technology–related open-access journals. Two reputable open-access educational technology journals are *Journal of Educational Technology & Society* (first issue published in 1998) and *The International Review of Research in Open and Distance Learning* (first issue published in 2000). Other long-standing open-access journals related to educational technology are *First Monday* (first issued published in 1996) and the *Journal of Computer-Mediated Communication* (first published in 1995).

Some open access educational technology journals are indexed in the Social Sciences Citation Index (e.g., *Journal of Educational Technology and Society, The International Review of Research in Open and Distance Learning,* and *Australasian Journal of Educational Technology*). Over the years, some notable and respectable journals have chosen to become open access, such as the *International Journal of E-Learning & Distance Education,* and the *Australasian Journal of Educational Technology,* but other open-access journals have ceased publication.

Open-access journals may be perceived as free. However, open-access journals are usually subsidized by a group or institution (e.g., a professional organization such as the Association for Educational Communications and Technology [AECT] or the IEEE Computer Society, a society of the Institute of Electrical and Electronics Engineers) or by individual authors (e.g., through article publication fees) to cover publication costs.

For a number of years, a journal could clearly be identified as either open-access or not open-access (sometimes referred to as closed or as a closed-access journal). However, as demand for open-access to research has increased during the past decade, a number of variations of open-access have emerged:

Complete open access (sometimes referred to as gold open access): All articles are completely open access.

Delayed open access: Articles become open-access after a period of time (e.g., six months after publication).

Hybrid open access: Authors have the option to pay fees to make their article open access, or open access is allowed to members of a professional association.

A growing number of traditional publishers now offer some type of hybrid open access to authors.

Pros and Cons of Open-Access Journals

Open-access journals offer a number of benefits for educational technology researchers and practitioners alike. The most notable benefit of open access is that removing barriers makes it easier for readers to access literature in the field. This is especially important for practitioners whose employer might not subscribe to academic journals. Other benefits include a possible faster time from submission to publication. Traditional academic journals can often take longer than a year to publish an article. Open-access journals have the potential to publish articles faster, although some traditional publishers now publish accepted manuscripts online immediately after acceptance. Another perceived

benefit of open-access journals is that authors typically retain the copyright of their work rather than signing over copyright to their work to a publisher. Open-access journals also have the potential to increase the readership base for an article. For instance, the *Journal of Educational Technology & Society* has published hundreds of articles, including four articles with more than 20,000 downloads. Open-access journals are also often cheaper and easier to start up than traditional journals. Finally, and directly related to educational technology, open-access journals—largely because they are online—have the ability to publish different types of educational technology scholarship, whether that is more creative works or more design-based research. For instance, the *International Journal of Designs for Learning* publishes multimedia cases along with traditional articles.

Despite these possible benefits, researchers and practitioners must be aware of some possible shortcomings of open-access educational technology journals. The primary shortcoming is that open-access journals, despite growing in acceptance and popularity, are still viewed by many as being less rigorous and less prestigious than traditional academic journals. This perception keeps some academics from publishing their research in open-access journals as well as from reviewing for or reading open-access journals. Another drawback with open-access journals is that they can cease publication because of lack of financial sustainability, leaving authors without a permanent record of their scholarship (e.g., *Innovate: Journal of Online Education* closed after a few years of operation). Many open-access journals are not indexed as traditional journals are, limiting their influence; further, the majority of open-access journals are not indexed in *Journal Citation Reports,* leaving them without the SSCI impact factor. Another drawback, specifically for pre-tenured faculty, is that some colleges and universities view open-access publications as being inferior to traditional publications. Finally, open-access journals are sometimes associated, or perceived to be associated, with predatory publishers who try to make money off of author processing charges.

Controversy Over Open-Access Journals

Open-access journals and the larger open-scholarship movement continue to challenge traditional forms of scholarship. Although academics often resist change, the open-access movement has sparked a larger discussion about whether publicly funded research should be freely available to the public; some funding organizations have even begun requiring funded research to be published in an open-access format.

The rise of hybrid open-access options, in which an author can pay thousands of dollars to have his or her article published as open-access, has highlighted how much publishers can profit from the work of academics. Rather than pay what is perceived as exorbitant fees, some academics have chosen instead only to publish in open-access journals or those in which members of an association have open access with no author fees being charged. Other academics have chosen to self-archive their own work by placing earlier copies of their work on their own websites (called green open access) or by uploading their work to academic repositories (e.g., Academia or ResearchGate) or specifically to institutional repositories.

Conclusion

There are proponents of, and detractors from, open-access journals. Some glorify the open-access movement, and specifically open-access journals, and question why anyone would ever read or publish in a closed journal; others question why anyone would waste his or her time reading or publishing scholarship in what they perceived as a low-quality journal.

The future of academic journals is unclear, but there appears to be a place for both open-access and closed-access academic journals. Both academics and practitioners value electronic access and a faster time to publication.

Patrick R. Lowenthal

See also Open Content Licensing; OpenCourseWare Movement; Open-Source Repositories for Learning and Instruction

Further Readings

Anderson, T., & McConkey, B. (2010). Development of disruptive open access journals. *Canadian Journal of Higher Education, 39*(3), 71–87. Retrieved from http://prophet.library.ubc.ca/ojs/index.php/cjhe/article/view/477/506

Bohannon, J. (2013). Who's afraid of peer review? *Science, 342*(6154), 60–55. Retrieved from http://www.sciencemag.org/content/342/6154/60.full

Lowenthal, P. R., & Dunlap, J. C. (2012, July/August). Intentional web presence: 10 SEO strategies every academic needs to know. *EDUCAUSE Review Online.* Retrieved from http://www.educause.edu/ero/article/intentional-web-presence-10-seo-strategies-every-academic-needs-know

Oliver, M. (2012). The risk of open scholarship: Avoiding irony in the promotion of technology for scholarly communications. *Educational Technology, 52*(6), 22–25.

Perkins, R. (n.d.). *EdTech Journals.* Retrieved from http://www.edtechjournals.com

Priego, E. (2013, October). Who's afraid of open access? *The Comics Grid.* Retrieved from http://blog.comicsgrid.com/2013/10/whos-afraid-open-access

Prosser, D. C. (2005). Open access: The future of scholarly communication. *Cadernos de Biblioteconomia, Arquivística e Documentação, 1,* 6–20. Retrieved from http://eprints.rclis.org/10304/1/CadBAD105_Prosser.pdf

Ritzhaupt, A. D., Sessums, C. D., & Johnson, M. C. (2012). Where should educational technologists publish their research? An examination of peer-reviewed journals within the field of educational technology and factors influencing publishing. *Educational Technology, 52*(6), 47–56.

Veletsianos, G., & Kimmons, R. (2012). Assumptions and challenges of open scholarship. *The International Review of Research in Open and Distance Learning, 13*(4), 166–189. Retrieved from http://www.irrodl.org/index.php/irrodl/article/view/1313/2304

Zawacki-Richter, O., Anderson, T., & Tuncay, N. (2010). The growing impact of open access distance education journals: A bibliometric analysis. *Journal of Distance Education/Revue de l'Éducation à Distance, 24*(3). Retrieved from http://www.jofde.ca/index.php/jde/article/view/661/1210

OpenCourseWare Movement

The OpenCourseWare (OCW) movement is an initiative to freely open graduate and undergraduate course materials such as lecture notes, syllabi, reading lists, exam questions, simulations, and video recordings of lectures to anyone who has an Internet connection. Materials can be used and adopted for education uses under an open license. Hal Albenson has indicated that this initiative is a large-scale, organized instructional technology innovation. The movement can also be seen as creating crucial infrastructure for learning, which is one of the main concerns of the educational technology field. The OCW movement can be considered as a continuation of the open-access movement, which started in different fields such as software engineering (e.g., with open-source software such as Linux), journal publications (e.g., open-access journals such as *Journal of Educational Technology & Society*), and textbooks. This entry discusses how the OpenCourseWare movement developed, its advantages and disadvantages, and how it may develop in the future.

Development of OpenCourseWare Movement

This movement emerged in 1999 at the Massachusetts Institute of Technology (MIT), which attempted to position itself prominently within the e-learning milieu. MIT decided to open all its graduate and undergraduate course materials at no cost to anyone with Internet access. The MIT OCW initiative included materials that are generally organized in a one-semester course and used generally as supplementary material in traditional classrooms instead of materials prepared specifically for distance learners. By 2012, there were 2,150 courses published in the MIT OCW portal and 125 million visitors.

This movement was adopted in the United States and in many other countries including China, France, India, Japan, the Netherlands, Spain, Thailand, Turkey, and Vietnam. The MIT OCW has a number of mirror sites that include translation of course materials into different languages. The Spanish-language Universia, China Open Resources for Education (CORE) in China, or Turkish Academy of Sciences (TÜBA) Açik Ders in Turkey have translations of MIT courses in their respective languages. To promote the further spread and uptake of OCW throughout the world, the OpenCourseWare Consortium was established in 2008 with the participation of many higher education institutions and associated organizations from around the world. An independent nonprofit organization, the consortium has been continuously expanded. Members of the consortium have increased to about 350 and include various higher education institutions, associated consortia, organizational members, and corporate members, according to the OCW Consortium website.

The target audience can be divided into self-learners, students, and educators. Course materials have been used for different purposes by visitors. Self-learners mainly use course materials to explore topics outside their professional fields, review basic concepts in their professional fields, prepare for future courses of study, and keep current with developments in their fields. Students mainly use these materials to enhance their personal knowledge, complement a current course, or plan a course of study. Educators use these resources to improve their personal knowledge, learn new teaching methods, incorporate OCW materials into a course, and find reference materials for their students, according to MIT's 2011 OCW impact report.

The OCW movement can be seen as a subset of the larger initiative named *open educational resources* (OER). As indicated by Paul Albright, the OCW movement can be regarded as one of the most widely used models of OER. In this model, no interaction and no actual MIT degree is granted. It follows a very faculty-centric model in that faculty mainly provide the resources. The budget for the MIT OCW initiative has been sponsored by different external sources (e.g., the Andrew W. Mellon Foundation and the William and Flora Hewlett Foundation). Other OER initiatives, such as OpenLearn in the United Kingdom and OpenStax at Rice University, follow their own distinctive OER model. For instance, the general structure of the Connexions

model is decentralized, which means it is mainly based on end-user participation. OpenLearn, conversely, has a blended model, which means its content depends heavily on the Open University's course materials, but end users can contribute their own content in the LabSpace, as discussed by Engin Kursun and colleagues.

Open licensing is an indispensable part of this movement because it provides legal infrastructure for the initiative. This makes the movement different from other attempts because one can distribute, adopt, and remix technically and legally with this kind of license. Different open licenses such as Academic Free License, Creative Commons (CC), and GNU Free Documentation License are available. One of the most widely used and popular open licenses is CC because it has a simple structure easily understood by ordinary people and machines. The CC license basically consists of three layers: a legal code layer, a commons deed layer (known as the "human readable" version), and a machine readable layer. The first layer, legal code, is designed in a text format that most lawyers can understand. The second layer, commons deed, can be understood by most users. Finally, the last layer, machine readable, makes the licenses recognizable by software such as search engines and office programs.

Advantages and Disadvantages of OpenCourseWare

The OCW movement has a number of advantages for different stakeholders including self-learners, faculty members, and institutions. As indicated in the 2011 OCW impact report, self-learners are the main benefactors of these materials. Those resources can be used by disadvantaged self-learners, such as those living in rural communities or underdeveloped and developing countries where there are few centers of higher education. As for educators, it may increase their professional abilities and personal reputations; they can see what other colleagues are doing, and they can archive their own resources online. Finally, for institutions, the OCW movement can help develop curricula and can attract new students.

Although this movement has many benefits, there are also barriers that inhibit the development of the movement. As argued by Niall Sclater, resistance from faculty members can be regarded as one of the major barriers. Faculty members are concerned that their content will be used without attribution to them. Some faculty members fear that their content can be changed in a way they do not want. Another barrier is the sustainability of this movement in the long term because such projects require external support with funds for initial development of the resources and subsequent maintenance and updating of content, according to Cathy Casserly. The reusability of digital resources can be seen as another important barrier to the cost-effectiveness and sustainability of this kind of project; studies show that people are not willing to reuse others' materials and often prefer to use their own resources or those developed commercially.

Despite these benefits and inhibiting factors, there are also general criticisms about the OCW movement. As claimed by Paul Stacey, there is a lack of pedagogical value in some of the resources such as presentation slides because they are isolated from real classroom settings and lack the context to be meaningful for many self-learners. Sclater argues that there are few opportunities for students to interact with each other and that assessment and accreditation are questionable for this movement.

Future Development of OpenCourseWare Movement

An extension of the OCW movement has come with the recent development of massive open online courses (MOOCs), now offered by both for-profit and not-for-profit organizations. MOOCs are often free and come with high-quality self-learning materials (i.e., interactive activities, tests, and videos), and opportunities for students to interact with each other and, to some extent, with lecturers. Most importantly, successful participants can be certificated at the end of the course and courses are offered in a set period, such as one or two semesters. For instance, the nonprofit edX provides online courses in topics such as biology, history, computer science, and engineering from the world's top universities, such as MIT; the University of California, Berkeley; and Harvard University. Coursera and Udacity are for-profit companies that offer MOOCs that are generally free, although students may pay for certain courses or for a verified certificate. With MOOCs, though the numbers of registered students are high, there are concerns about course completion rates, which are rarely above 10%, according to Jon Billsberry. In addition, limitations on formative feedback and interaction with instructors are still an issue.

Selçuk Karaman and Engin Kursun

See also Open Content Licensing; Open-Access Journals in Educational Technology

Further Readings

Albenson, H. (2008). The creation of OpenCourseWare at MIT. *Journal of Science Education and Technology, 2*(17), 164–174.

Geser, G. (Ed.). (2007). *OLCOS roadmap 2012.* Salzburg, Austria: EduMedia Group. Retrieved from http://www.olcos .org/english/roadmap/

Johnstone, S. (2005). Open educational resources serve the world. *EDUCAUSE Quarterly, 28*(3), 15–18. Retrieved February 20, 2012, from http://www.educause.edu/ero/ article/open-educational-resources-serve-world

Johnstone, S. M., & Poulin, R. (2002). What is OpenCourseWare and why does it matter? *Change, 34*(4), 48–50.

Kozinska, K., Kursun, E., Wilson, T., McAndrew, P., Scanlon, E., Jones, A., & Cagiltay, K. (2010). Are open educational resources the future of e-learning? In S. Gulsecen & Z. Ayvaz Reis (Eds.), *Proceedings of the Third International Conference on Innovations in Learning for the Future 2010: e-Learning* (pp. 34–44). Istanbul, Turkey: Kultur University.

Lane, A. (2010). *Global trends in the development and use of open educational resources to reform educational practices.* UNESCO. Retrieved from http://unesdoc.unesco.org/ images/0019/001913/191362e.pdf

McAndrew, P., Santos, A., Lane, A., Godwin, S., Okada, A., Wilson, T., . . . , & Webb, R. (2009). *OpenLearn research report 2006–2008.* Milton Keynes, UK: Open University.

Organisation for Economic Co-operation and Development (OECD). (2007). *Giving knowledge for free: The emergence of open educational resources.* Paris, France: OECD Publishing.

Sclater, N. (2011). Open educational resources: Motivations, logistics and sustainability. In N. F. Ferrer, & J. M. Alfonso (Eds.), *Content management for e-learning* (pp. 179–193). New York, NY: Springer.

Stacey, P. (2007). Open educational resources in a global context. *First Monday, 12*(4). Retrieved from http:// firstmonday.org/ojs/index.php/fm/article/view/1769/1649

Websites

AECT Open Content Portal: https://sites.google.com/site/ aectopencontent/textbooks

Creative Commons: http://creativecommons.org

OpenCourseWare Consortium: http://www.ocwconsortium.org

Open-Source Repositories for Learning and Instruction

Technology and communication networks have transformed how instructional resources, documents, and media are stored and accessed. Instead of only maintaining traditional brick and mortar libraries, institutional efforts of the past two decades have created electronic or digital repositories, with the goal of making these instructional resources widely accessible. The profusion of many open-source repositories for learning and instruction stems from (a) the public's increasing demand for access to information, (b) the culture of designing and sharing Internet-housed media and instructional resources, and (c) the availability (for cost or gratis) of software to readily design, share, and customize these resources. Open-source culture anticipates that users will abide by copyright guidelines as media found in these repositories (sometimes labeled *digital libraries*) are used, customized, and redistributed for educational purposes.

As a result of the increasingly multimodal, sophisticated, and engaging capacities of technology to present and explain information within efficient or rapid communication networks, open-source repositories can achieve the promise of providing access to all sorts of information for learning and instruction. These repositories have been developed since the 1990s for a range of disciplines and diverse learners, via institutional or regional hosting, or for worldwide distribution. Developers, instructors, and students will find a broad range of content, due to a desire to provide several kinds of resources to promote educational goals across all age groups. To facilitate accessing the resources within repositories, the entries are indexed and there is a search tool and a list of categories on the repository's home page. Some repositories provide multiple parallel collections, aligned with selected languages, or through a link to a translation application. Often foundations, international organizations, businesses, and donations underwrite the repositories, so users have free access to these resources. Some repositories ask users to share information or pay a fee to gain access.

This entry discusses four types of open-source repositories for learning and instruction: commercial repositories, institutionally based repositories, state or regionally based repositories, and internationally focused repositories.

Commercial Repositories

Some of these repositories for learning and instruction are designed for use within course or learning management systems because of the potential benefit for, and expectations of, students and faculty. Desire2Learn and Blackboard (xpLor), often purchased by institutions, offer these additional elements or features for sharing learning content (faculty created and commercially provided). Pearson eCollege is designed specifically to customize an online learning environment for targeted instruction, so faculty and students can intentionally interact and access resources from diverse publishing entities within Pearson.

Institutionally Based Repositories

Many higher education institutions take pride in the libraries and artifacts they have collected over time, through their faculty's efforts and graduates' gifts. Some institutions, noting the potential of online learning opportunities, established these repositories to promote (a) specific research, (b) innovation, and (c) access to high-quality digital media for research and higher education. The National Science Foundation established the National Science Digital Library in 2000 to provide understandable descriptions and links to Web-based educational resources to align with the increasing role of the sciences in our society. Tufts University's Perseus Digital Library, in development since 1985, focuses on the culture, history, and literature of the Greco-Roman world. The Artstor Digital Library (often accessed via nonprofit institutions' subscription) provides researchers and instructors access to high-quality images of artwork and maps, across time periods and cultures, to enhance interdisciplinary scholarship and creation of instructional resources within copyright guidelines. Many nations, research libraries, and universities have established and maintain digital collections to increase access to unique artifacts and books.

State or Regionally Based Repositories

Some state-level education departments were early adopters of online learning and the infusion of technology in classrooms. They sought and received state funding to create repositories so pre-K–12 teachers and higher education faculty could share and customize instructional resources. State-funded higher education institutions were networked to provide, via course management systems, links to these repositories. Often, one of the state or regional higher education institutions assumed responsibility to manage the repository and offered selected links to other repositories to increase the access to these rich, unique research materials. Access to many U.S. public libraries is promoted by publicLibraries.com, including all 50 states and the District of Columbia's archives and official records, states' colleges and universities, obituary records, the presidential libraries, and noteworthy college and university libraries.

The Digital Public Library of America is a portal and platform that provides free access to more than 5.6 million digital resources from libraries, archives, and museums to facilitate the creation of responsive and unique instructional resources. Established in 2008, in California, the HathiTrust Digital Library provides access to millions of copyrighted, digitally preserved resources in the public domain for academic and research institutions. Ellyssa Kroski manages a blog for the Open Education Database where users can locate a state-by-state list of librarian-vetted repositories of instructional resources in the United States.

Internationally Focused Repositories

As communication networks connect the world, some repositories are designed to provide researchers and practitioners (especially in remote areas of the world) access to their digital instructional resources. The Ariadne Foundation, a member of the Global Learning Objects Brokered Exchange (GLOBE) Alliance, manages an accessible, digital collection of scalable learning resources, which serves researchers and institutions on most continents. The World Digital Library, supported by UNESCO, is a multilingual repository of sound, graphic, and print media from 8000 BCE until the present that links collections on six continents. The Multimedia Educational Resource for Learning and Online Teaching (MERLOT), developed in California in 1997, houses a peer-reviewed collection of online teaching and learning materials. This repository has evolved to offer training, Webinars, a journal, and a content-building tool and nurtures an online learning community. Its pages can be translated into 42 languages using Microsoft translator. To support educators and researchers in developing countries, the eGranary Digital Library contains more than 30 million indexed multimedia documents, accessed via Intranet Web sites. This repository is supported by several foundations, along with the U.S. Agency for International Development and the U.S. International Council on Disabilities. DMOZ, which comes from Directory Mozilla and is supported by AOL Search, is a human-edited directory of the Web with parallel pages in 22 languages. A partnership between the University of Maryland's Human-Computer Interaction Lab and the International Children's Digital Library provides access to children's literature to promote tolerance and understanding of diverse cultures. The site can be viewed in five languages and requires signing up for long-term access and use of this collection. Since 2007, the Open Educational Resources Commons has been curating, providing support services, and making available instructional resources from around the world. For the benefit of U.S. educators, the resources are tagged with Common Core State Standards and linked to the Learning Resources Metadata Initiative.

The Commonwealth of Learning (COL) promotes open access and open educational repositories for use around the world and especially in developing countries. Many resources are already available through COL to support a wide range of courses and skills. COL also sponsors the Open Schools Initiative and supports that effort with materials to support 17 subjects in six countries: Botswana, India, Lesotho, Namibia, Seychelles, and the Republic of Trinidad and Tobago. COL provides teacher guides, print-based and CD-ROM materials, multimedia artifacts, and other resources.

Implications of Open-Source Repositories for Learning and Instruction

Many different institutions and organizations have created and maintain these repositories for learning and instruction. Despite all these efforts, there are opportunities for redundancies and omissions. The repositories depend on funding and the capacity to digitize (with high quality) and warehouse the ever-expanding documentation of human innovation, creativity, and thought. Will the format for preserving or digitizing these collections remain the standard over time? Sustaining these repositories may depend on the largesse of foundations and the decision of institutions to allocate funds for this purpose.

Susan Farber

See also Digital Archives; Digital Curation; Transmedia in Education; Twenty-First-Century Technology Skills

Further Readings

Downes, S. (2007). *Models for sustainable open educational resources.* Retrieved from http://nparc.cisti-icist.nrc-cnrc.gc.ca/npsi/ctrl?action=rtdoc&an=5764249&lang=en

Wiley, D. (2006). *The current state of open educational resources.* Retrieved from http://opencontent.org/blog/archives/247

Wiley, D. (2007). *On the sustainability of open educational resource initiatives in higher education.* Retrieved from http://www1.oecd.org/edu/ceri/38645447.pdf

Yuan, L., MacNeill, S., & Kraan, W. (2008). *Open educational resources: Opportunities and challenges for higher education.* Retrieved from http://muele.mak.ac.ug/file.php/1/Student_Reading_Resource/oer_briefing_paper.pdf

Websites

Ariadne Foundation Collection: http://www.ariadne-eu.org

Artstor Digital Library: http://www.artstor.org/index.shtml

Commonwealth of Learning: http://www.col.org

Digital Public Library of America: http://dp.la

DMOZ: http://www.dmoz.org/about.html

eGranary Digital Library: http://www.widernet.org/egranary/

HathiTrust Digital Library: http://www.hathitrust.org/home

International Children's Digital Library; http://en.childrenslibrary.org

Library of Congress Digital Collections and Services: http://www.loc.gov/library/libarch-digital.html

LOUISiana Digital Library: http://louisdl.louislibraries.org

Minnesota Digital Library: http://www.mndigital.org

Multimedia Educational Resource for Learning and Online Teaching (MERLOT): http://www.merlot.org

National Libraries of the World: http://www.publiclibraries.com/world.htm

National Science Digital Library: https://nsdl.org

New York Public Library Digital Gallery: http://digitalgallery.nypl.org/nypldigital/index.cfm

North Carolina Learning Object Repository: http://explorethelor.org

Open Education Database: http://oedb.org/ilibrarian/250-plus-killer-digital-libraries-and-archives

Open Educational Resources Commons: http://www.oercommons.org

Princeton University Digital Library: http://pudl.princeton.edu

Texas Learning Object Repository: http://www.txlor.org

Tufts University's Perseus Digital Library: http://www.perseus.tufts.edu/hopper

WiderNet Project, home of eGranary: http://www.widernet.org

World Digital Library: http://www.wdl.org/en

ORGANIZATIONAL LEARNING AND PERFORMANCE

Traditional educational and instructional solutions in the workplace are aimed at improving the skills and knowledge of workers, but organizational leaders are ultimately interested in, and accountable for, performance results. In this sense, improving learning at the worker level adds value only to the extent that it measurably contributes to the attainment of worthwhile organizational performance objectives. Roger Kaufman argues that a critical distinction must be made between means and ends. It is important to recognize that educational technology concepts, tools, and products are some of the means organizations can use to improve learning at the worker level. However, these means should never be picked before carefully determining what organizational performance results we are responsible for accomplishing, what gaps exist between those desired results and current results, the causal factors contributing to those results, and finally, what solutions are appropriate, given the causes for existing gaps.

Performance data may indicate that a lack of skills and knowledge in a group of workers is not a factor, and in this case we must turn to other relevant solutions that, even though they may be outside the scope of learning, are still within the scope of performance. These include clear objectives, systematic job processes, and appropriate consequences. This systemic orientation is driven by relevant performance data at all levels of the organization and at all stages of organizational processes. Dale Brethower references Geary Rummler's work as being the quintessential example of how one

can continuously learn about, and improve, organizational performance, primarily by focusing on two key questions: "What are the variables that measure the results desired? What variables must we manage to achieve those results?" (p. 18).

Therefore, beyond a focus on individual learning, organizational learning and performance are concerned with the organization's ability to continuously improve itself based on timely performance data relevant to its ultimate, and en route, objectives. In this sense, organizational learning and performance are intricately linked to continuous improvement in that they involve monitoring key data and then using them to make ongoing adjustments. This entry first discusses how organizations learn from performance measurement and what performance indicators are measured. It then discusses performance monitoring and feedback systems and the outcomes of organizational learning.

Learning From Performance Measurement

A group of scientists, engineers, and economists at the Massachusetts Institute of Technology that constituted the MIT Commission on Industry Productivity specifically recommended that organizations must develop and use sound techniques for measuring and improving the efficiency and quality of their processes. This 1989 landmark study, published in part as *Made in America: Regaining the Productive Edge*, further stated that it is necessary to identify opportunities for progressive improvements in their performance.

Without accurate and timely performance feedback—provided by ongoing measurement and tracking of performance indicators—it becomes nearly impossible to efficiently and effectively see progress toward desired ends. It becomes equally difficult to make sound decisions about what to keep, what to change, and how. Performance feedback therefore provides a unique and crucial role in the improvement of human and organizational performance.

Most scholars and practitioners would agree about the importance of establishing performance objectives that provide strategic direction to our efforts. What is not as widely understood—and perhaps even practiced—is that without en route timely measurement of those objectives, organizations do not really know whether they are getting closer to or further away from those objectives, whether they are using the most efficient way to get there, or whether they are taking unnecessary twists and turns. In this sense, performance measurement is the compass that keeps an organization on course toward a desired destination, while providing the intelligence to make day-to-day decisions about how to best get there. Performance measurement can, nevertheless, speak both to effectiveness (Was the target destination reached?) and efficiency (Was the destination reached in the most economical way—whether in terms of time, cost, and other resources?).

Since the popularization of total quality management in the 1980s, the subject of performance measurement has been generating ever-increasing interest among academics and practitioners alike. Meaningful advances have been made on establishing performance management and measurement systems that track performance beyond the traditional financial measures. However, many companies still rely on financial measures as their primary index of performance, thus limiting their decision making to an incomplete—and often reactive—data set.

Moreover, without systemically measuring and tracking performance, an organization is not purposefully managing performance. In 1995, Geary Rummler and Alan Brache highlighted the central role of measurement in performance improvement. Rummler and Brache described the management function at the organizational and process levels as one that "involves obtaining regular customer feedback, tracking actual performance along the measurement dimensions established in the goals, feeding back performance information to relevant subsystems, taking corrective action if performance is off target, and resetting goals so that the organization is continually adapting to external and internal reality" (p. 21). Of course, sources of feedback can go beyond the traditional definition of *customer* to include all relevant stakeholders.

Performance measurement is not something done in addition to managing; rather, it is at the core of intelligent management. Measurement systems must be systemically linked to an organization's *value chain*, a term first proposed by strategy guru Michael Porter in 1985, to ensure purposeful measurement that feeds and supports management in obtaining top organizational performance. Moreover, performance measures must be set up such that they support coordinated performance improvement and management efforts. Managing any measure in isolation of the entire system could result in suboptimization of the entire organization.

Goals, Objectives, and Performance Indicators

The starting point for creating a performance measurement system from which organizational members can continuously learn and improve performance is identifying or verifying the ultimate ends the organization wants to accomplish. These ends are results, accomplishments, products, outputs, outcomes, or consequences (rather than the processes, activities, or resources to be implemented and used). Although

"ends" are what the organization exists to accomplish and deliver, "means" are how it goes about doing that. Means include processes, programs, projects, activities, resources, and a host of others things that the organization uses and does to accomplish the desired ends.

One useful framework for portraying this means and ends distinction is the organizational elements model (OEM), introduced by Kaufman in the 1960s. The OEM consists of five overarching elements (inputs, processes, products, outputs, and outcomes) in two major categories: ends and means. This is a useful conceptual framework for beginning to think about the relationships among different levels of results and between these results and the means used to accomplish them. According to Kaufman, the three levels of results are as follows:

1. *Strategic:* Long-term organizational results that ultimately benefit clients and society, often stated in terms of a consistent vision. James Collins, the leader of a management research center, and Jerry Porras, professor emeritus from Stanford University, provide a useful discussion of an organizational vision and define it as the organization's reason for being and the foundation for strategic planning and execution. Their recommended timeline for the achievement of strategic aims tends to be at least a decade.

2. *Tactical:* Shorter-term organizational results that help operationally define the vision, usually stated in terms of an organizational mission. The timeline for the achievement of such accomplishments tends to be set on an annual basis. It is not so much that the types of results sought change every year, but rather that there are concrete annual targets to reach.

3. *Operational:* The building-block objectives—perhaps at the department, unit, team, or individual level—that contribute to the accomplishment of the organization's mission. In settings such as the military, operations are used to describe the building-block results, as well as the processes used to produce them.

All levels of results must be aligned and identified in the context of strategic planning, alignment, assessment, monitoring, and evaluation. Desired results drive both the processes we employ and how we carry them out. Processes and inputs may be important to achieving results; however, performance goals and objectives exclusively concern results, not how they are achieved. Still, it is also important to highlight that when monitoring performance for purposes of feedback and improvement, task specificity, in the context of overall processes, is critical to measure to enhance organizational learning and performance improvement. That is, feedback should be specific to discrete tasks and describe which tasks should be modified, and how, to deliver desired results.

Performance Indicator Maps

Performance indicators are specific and concrete gauges of a result, process, or activity that allows us to make complex systems palpable and manageable. Much as the gauges on a car's dashboard provide a synopsis of its performance status, performance indicators provide organizations with the essential knowledge that could potentially help managers make effective decisions. These indicators are the basis for the data we track both now and into the future (in fact, continuously) that can be used as feedback to make decisions regarding specific actions for improvement. Successfully using this feedback then depends on how well feedback is provided to, and perceived by, those responsible for improving performance. If feedback is not perceived as important, and performance improvement actions are not specified, they will provide little support to users and might make performance worse. Clear performance indicator maps can increase the utility of feedback, which helps users take the right performance improvement actions today, to get desired results tomorrow.

Leading indicators, often called, *key performance indicators* (KPIs), should be tracked most often because these determine how likely it is that we will reach our established objectives. Therefore, understanding the relationships between lagging and leading indicators is critical and provides organizational members with valuable knowledge about the likely effects of their actions. If these relationships are not understood, it becomes difficult for organizational members to make sound decisions on a range of daily topics—for example, what services contribute more to desired results, the type of personnel required, scheduling of personnel, outreach activities to promote, budget allocation, and so on.

Performance Monitoring and Feedback

The proliferation of performance dashboards has raised awareness about the importance of simultaneously monitoring various performance indicators. Performance dashboards, or performance monitoring and feedback systems, are collective sets of metrics used to gauge performance and in turn manage and improve it. These dashboards support organizational learning by providing just-in-time feedback about relevant organizational variables and can support objective and proactive decision making that can lead to measurably improved performance. Although several studies have shown evidence that there is a positive relationship between monitoring and performance, results are still quite mixed, and in fact, in a 1996 meta-analysis of 131 rigorous studies, Avraham N. Kluger and Angelo DeNisi found that about one third of performance monitoring and feedback interventions had a negative impact on

performance. Important mediating factors found included task specificity and perceptions of those receiving the feedback. Specifically, results revealed that as data provided by feedback systems focused more on the performer overall, rather than on specific performer tasks, feedback effectiveness decreases. Further, the more ill-structured the task, the more important data about specific task elements (i.e., formative data rather than summative data) becomes.

Feedback is seen as a primary component in formative assessment and, when well designed, one of the factors that has the strongest potential to influence performance. Two important works highlight that delivery of the feedback is critical because different performers perceive feedback differently. Moreover, for feedback to be formative and improve performance, feedback should be clearly articulated and presented so that it invites learners' active engagement.

Perceptions of feedback are defined as the extent to which individuals believe that feedback is important, accurate, and useful, and *processing feedback* concerns how the individual processes the received feedback. If feedback is interpreted as irrelevant or not useful for task completion or functioning, individuals can react to feedback by ignoring, discounting, rejecting, and consequently not processing it. If individuals do not assign meaning to the received feedback, they will not use it to make the desirable changes for performance improvement.

Using Feedback for Improving Performance: Organizational Learning in Action

One of the critical contributions of monitoring performance is the feedback that it provides. The feedback loop represents the reiterative nature of tracking and adjusting. This reiterative tracking of vital sign messages ensures that decision makers and other performers have the organizational knowledge they require to make sound decisions and improve their own performance, as well as that of the organization. Providing continuous feedback about performance is part of a broader, and effective, communication system. If developed appropriately, feedback allows leaders and employees to track, manage, and, sometimes, forecast performance at opportune times. For example, such feedback may assist with the projection of future program costs or communicate exemplars, not promises, of anticipated outcomes. In this sense, it is very much like monitoring the vital signs of the organization.

Learning, as a gradual process, requires evidence en route to responding to emerging issues and to making anticipated revisions. Further, it is sought to capitalize on the creative and adaptive applications of stakeholders as the program progresses. Intermediate outcomes may then be used as information toward terminal outcomes.

According to Peter Senge, the real lesson of continuous improvement is in learning. Senge popularized the new learning organization as one that continuously, and proactively, shapes its future. This position diverts an organization's thinking away from control and toward improving the performance of the system. Learning and performance, therefore, are not events, but rather processes that require a constant influx of information. The information gained from continuous improvement efforts may be interpreted as signals that convert measurement to data—and when put into context, turned to knowledge—and decisions to actions. Joseph Juran warned that when en route data is not captured, and no obvious alarm signals are being heard, problems and otherwise predictable crises are left undetected. When the crisis does hit, organizations are quick to react, often leading to misalignment between problem and solution. Applying a systematic approach, organizations actively listen for signals and are in a solid position of aligning the opportunity or deficiency with the appropriate solution.

Juran and A. Blanton Godfrey note that decisions are required at different stages and only en-route data will supply the information supporting evidence-based decision making. For example, we should expect different performance immediately following implementation versus after six months of practice, integration, and acclimation. In another example, environmental factors such as customer needs, economic conditions, and political climate, to name a few, are moving targets; therefore, leaders acquire ongoing data to adapt to changing conditions. W. Edwards Deming refers to improvement as a never-ending effort that can only be acquired through statistical control. According to Deming, stability of a system is an achievement, the result of purposeful monitoring of vital signs. Such systematic processes document organizational performance over time, have a continuous frequency of measurement, and specify points at which decisions move into action.

Ingrid Guerra-López

See also Agent Technologies for Evaluation; Human Performance Technology; Information and Communication Technologies: Knowledge Management; System Dynamics; Systemic Change and Educational Technology

Further Readings

Black, P., & Wiliam, D. (1998). Assessment and classroom learning. *Assessment in Education, 5*, 7–75.

Brethower, D. (2009). It isn't magic, it's science. *Performance Improvement Quarterly, 48*(10), 18–24.

Brinkerhoff, R. O. (2005). The success case method: A strategic evaluation approach to increasing the value and effect of training. *Advances in Developing Human Resources, 7*(1), 86–101.

Carroll, W. (2008). The effects of electronic performance monitoring on performance outcomes: A review and meta-analysis. *Employee Rights and Employment Policy Journal, 12*(1), 29–47.

Collins, J., & Porras J. (1996, September/October). Building your company's vision. *Harvard Business Review,* 1–14.

Deming, W. E. (1986). *Out of the crisis.* Cambridge: Massachusetts Institute of Technology, Center for Advanced Engineering Study.

Gabelica, C., Bossche, P. V., Segers, M., & Gijselaers, W. (2012). Feedback, a powerful lever in teams: A review. *Educational Research Review, 7*, 123–144.

Guba, E. G., & Lincoln, Y. S. (1989). *Fourth generation evaluation.* Newbury Park, CA: Sage.

Guerra-López, I. (2010). Performance tracking and management systems. In R. Watkins & D. Leigh (Eds.), *Handbook of improving performance in the workplace: Vol. 2. Handbook for the selection and implementation of human performance interventions.* Hoboken, NJ: Wiley.

Guerra-López, I. (2013). Performance indicator maps: A visual tool for understanding, managing, and continuously improving your business metrics. *Performance Improvement Journal, 52*(6), 11–17.

Guerra-López, I., & Hutchinson, A. (2013). Measurable and continuous performance improvement: The development of a performance measurement, management, and improvement system. *Performance Improvement Quarterly, 26*(2), 159–173.

Hattie, J. A. (2009). *Visible learning: A synthesis of over 800 meta-analyses related to achievement.* New York, NY: Routledge.

Hattie, J., & Timperley, H. (2007). The power of feedback. *Review of Educational Research, 77*, 81–112.

Havnes, A., Smith, K., Dysthe, O., & Ludvigsen, K. (2012). Formative assessment and feedback: Making learning visible. *Studies in Educational Evaluation, 38*, 21–27.

Juran, J. M. (1981). Product quality: A prescription for the west. *Management Review, 70*(6), 8–15.

Juran, J. M., & Godfrey, A. B. (1999). *Juran's quality handbook* (5th ed.). New York, NY: McGraw-Hill.

Kaufman, R. (2000). *Mega planning.* Thousand Oaks, CA: Sage.

Kluger, A. N., & DeNisi, A. (1996). The effects of feedback interventions on performance: A historical review, a meta-analysis, and a preliminary feedback intervention theory. *Psychological Bulletin, 119*, 254–284.

Kulhavy, R. W. (1977). Feedback in written instruction. *Review of Educational Research, 47*, 211–232.

Porter, M. (1985). *Competitive advantage.* New York, NY: Free Press.

Rummler, G. A., & Brache, A. P. (1995). *Improving performance: How to manage the white space on the organization chart* (2nd ed.). San Francisco, CA: Jossey-Bass.

Senge, P. (1999). It's the learning: The real lesson of the quality movement. *Journal for Quality and Participation, 22*(6), 34–41.

Shute, V. J. (2008). Focus on formative feedback. *Review of Educational Research, 78*, 153–189.

PEDAGOGICAL AGENTS

With the advance of interface technology, animated on-screen characters have been increasingly used both in commercial and educational applications. The characters are used to simulate natural human *social* affordance and are called by different names, including interface agents, animated agents, embodied agents, virtual tutors, and pedagogical agents. Researchers from various disciplines have investigated the efficacy of character use in applications from the unique perspective of their disciplines, such as artificial intelligence, human-computer interaction, educational technology, and social psychology.

In educational technology, the animated characters that are often called pedagogical agents play a range of instructional roles to effect motivation and learning in computer-based tutoring systems. Some acknowledge that pedagogical agents could overcome some constraints and expand functionalities of conventional computer-based learning. This entry first discusses how pedagogical agents are used and how they can enrich learning. The entry then discusses the design of pedagogical agents and provides recommendations for future research and use of the agents.

Traditionally, computer-based learning environments (e.g., intelligent tutoring systems) have been tailored to meet a student's individual needs, focusing mainly on the cognitive processes of learning. However, in social cognitive theory, learning is not only a solo activity occurring inside one's mind, but is also influenced significantly by interactions with tools and others. Conventional computer-based learning environments often fail to provide situated social interaction that is regarded as a significant influence on both learning and motivation. Pedagogical agents can overcome this

limitation through simulated social interactions. Anthropomorphized pedagogical agents can promote a sense of social presence in educational applications that is otherwise missing. Therefore, pedagogical agents make instructional communication more social and natural. While interacting with a pedagogical agent acting as a tutor or co-learner, a learner may build a social and intellectual partnership with the agent. Pedagogical agents define computers as social-cognitive tools for learning and build social relations, share empathy, and model new beliefs and attitudes.

Enrichment of Computer-Based Learning

An Easy-to-Use Interface

Computers are often regarded merely as tools to perform tasks, but computer users tend to expect computers to behave like social entities. People unconsciously apply similar social rules and expectations to computers as they do to humans. Students *consciously* expect their pedagogical agent to be as competent and friendly as human instructors in the real world. Learners perceive and interact socially with pedagogical agents even when their functionality and adaptability are limited. From ample research during the last two decades, the general consensus is that the presence of a pedagogical agent can make learners' interaction with computers more social, natural, and easy. After working with an agent, learners across age groups have evaluated their learning experience as more enjoyable and more engaging and perceived the learning environment as less difficult and the technology as easier to use. Also, the learners have expressed stronger desire to continue to use the program and demonstrated higher interest in the material, compared with those learners working without an agent.

Agents as Socio-Cognitive Tools

Teaching and learning are highly social activities. Interactions with teachers, peers, and instructional materials influence the cognitive and affective development of learners. Traditionally, it is presumed that cognition exists inside an individual's mind and that the cognitive process occurs internally. When individuals perform intellectual activities, however, they dynamically interact with other participants, tools, and contexts, and this could facilitate enhanced performance or frame individuals' cognition and intellect. Therefore, interventions failing to address the social-cognitive dimension of learning might not accomplish their instructional goals.

Computer-based learning environments should be designed to afford this social-cognitive dimension. Pedagogical agents might share learners' cognition, functioning as cognitive tools. Pedagogical agents can be equipped with knowledge and skills that learners would not have or might perform simple and mechanical tasks to preserve the cognitive capabilities of the learner for higher mental activities. Agents can be designed to learn with the learner or they can take turns generating ideas. In this way, learners could build an intellectual partnership with the agents and enhance performance in computer-based learning.

Agents as Interaction Partners

Intellectual development is achieved when learners interact with others. The concept of the zone of proximal development (ZPD), developed by Lev Vygotsky, is at the center of learning and developmental processes. ZPD, the distance between a learner's actual development and his or her potential development when assisted by others, defines developmental functions that have not yet matured but are in the process of maturation. In collaboration with more capable others, learners can grow intellectually beyond the current limit of their capabilities. Also, as espoused by Jean Piaget, cooperation and free discussion enable us to acquire and construct knowledge. Cognitive conflicts that learners experience while interacting with others are an essential part of the intellectual development process. Interactions with others establish the favorable conditions for counteracting an individual's egocentrism. Clearly, agent-learner interaction would not be equivalent with human-peer interaction. Even so, a pedagogical agent that may or may not command advanced knowledge can still bring forth different perspectives to instigate learners' cognitive conflict in computer-based environments. When designed carefully, pedagogical agents simulate social and interactive contexts, providing support and sharing empathy.

Agents as Social Models

An individual's cognitive development is inevitably rooted in the social context where the individual is placed. Social modeling refers to psychological and behavioral changes that result from observing others in social contexts. Through vicarious experience, one acquires resources and expertise mediated through social models. Social modeling research illustrates how the presence of others and the roles they play can influence one's self-efficacy beliefs and social and intellectual functioning. The use of a pedagogical agent is valuable as a social model. A learner's positive affect enables the learner to face challenges and persist in learning. Simulated social relations and social interactions might mediate a learner's positive affect toward a learning task. For example, a pedagogical agent serving as a mastery model may demonstrate positive attitudes toward the task or the desired levels of performance so that a learner can learn vicariously. Or an agent may work along with a learner as a companion and even figuratively learn from the learner, serving as a coping model. Research finds that a less smart agent helps a low-performing learner to build confidence and encourages the learner to persist in the task. Similarly, pedagogical agents have been used as role models for females and ethnic-minority students who lack interest or confidence in succeeding in mathematics and science learning. These agents inspire the students to sustain efforts to accomplish each learning task and to continue with intellectual pursuit in the domain.

Pedagogical Agents Design

To promote building social relations between an agent and learner, the learner should perceive the agent as natural and believable. To this end, agent design often adopts human metaphors, rendering persona to pedagogical agents. Two design issues frequently arise in agent research: (1) specifying an agent's instructional role, and (2) defining the agent's personal attributes. First, pedagogical agents are designed to represent different human instructional roles, such as expert, tutor, mentor, or co-learner. For example, the agents *Steve* and *Adele* developed by the Center for Advanced Research in Technology for Education at the University of Southern California represent experts in naval engineering and medical diagnosis. These agents demonstrate expert knowledge in the domain and observe learners' performance to provide adaptive feedback. The agent

AutoTutor, developed by the Institute for Intelligent Systems at University of Memphis, engages learners in a dialogue and highlights their misconceptions to promote deeper reasoning.

A mentor agent might simulate the qualities of an ideal human mentor, including both professional expertise and a personal and caring demeanor. Nonetheless, the most popular use is to design an agent to be peer-like. An agent that functions as a simulated peer learns *with* the learner or serves as a coping model for challenging tasks. The simulated peer has been permuted flexibly to a peer tutor, a collaborator, a competitor, or even a troublemaker. *MathGirls,* developed by the Citizens Reutilizing Assistive Technology Equipment (CReATE) lab at Utah State University, embeds a female-peer agent that tutors middle-grade girls in mathematical concepts and encourages the girls to have positive attitudes toward mathematics learning and their self-efficacy in the learning.

The second issue inquires into what type of personal attributes (e.g., agent gender, ethnicity, personality, etc.) a designer should equip an agent with to stimulate relationship building between a learner and agent and, thereby, maximize the effectiveness of the program. This inquiry about personal attributes would make a worthwhile contribution to the increasing diversity in the learner population today. In classrooms, similar personal attributes of a learner and others often serve as influential factors for the efficacy of an instructional intervention. Given that learners interact with pedagogical agents as socially and naturally as they do with human instructors and peers, it seems natural to expect that a learner would be motivated to work with an agent sharing a similar attribute. Indeed, research shows that when an agent's personal attributes match the learner's, the learner tends to build a more developed social relationship with the agent, compared with when they do not match. That is, the learner perceives the agent more positively and prefers to continue with the agent. The learner also listens to the agent more carefully and takes the agent's instructional messages more seriously. Nevertheless, there are incidences when this developed relationship functions as a distractor from learning.

Seven constituents are necessary for the effective design of pedagogical agents to produce successful modeling effects. Grounded in human-computer interaction and social psychology research, the constituents include (1) agent competency, (2) interaction type, (3) affect, (4) gender, (5) ethnicity, (6) multiplicity, and (7) feedback. The effect of various permutations of the constituents on learners' perceptions, social judgments, self-efficacy, and learning have been investigated. To conclude, it seems improbable that a single, optimal agent would work well with learners diverse in cognitive and personal characteristics.

Reflections and Recommendations

With the increasing accessibility of advanced technologies in school and at home, the educational technology community has explored a variety of ways that use advanced technologies to help address educational challenges. When embodied pedagogical agents are introduced in the field, many researchers have viewed this technology merely as one variation of multimedia-based learning or a combination of multimedia (text, image, sound, video, etc.). However, during the last decade, studies have found consistently that agent presence is much more than a collective medium; rather, an agent plays a distinct social and affective role for a broad range of learners. Using an agent augments the bandwidth of a learner's interactions with computers and adds social richness to the interactions. In particular, youths today have grown up with everyday technologies and are often called *digital natives.* In their use of technologies, the boundary between real and virtual is often blurred; interacting with animated digital characters (e.g., avatars and agents) is becoming commonplace. Pedagogical agents could supply simulated teachers or peers for youths who grapple with learning challenges and serve as supplemental tools for teachers who are overloaded with daily demands.

Continued research efforts are needed to establish the effectiveness of pedagogical agents on both learner affect and cognition. A volume of research already attests to the effectiveness of pedagogical agents on promoting motivation and affective engagement in the learning process. However, the effectiveness of an agent on cognitive skill acquisition is still unclear. Some studies demonstrate that agents have produced significant cognitive gains including knowledge transfer, yet others fail to demonstrate this effect, even when they have established evidence for increased motivation. This conflicting trend sometimes promotes skepticism regarding pedagogical agent use, and, consequently, some researchers focus their research on affective development without expectation of cognitive skill changes. This implies that designers should judge the option carefully. Certainly, when an application is geared toward facilitating learners' positive affect, agent presence can be a robust choice, taking advantage of social affordance through the illusion of life.

In the face of inequity in science, technology, engineering, and mathematics (STEM) education, pedagogical agents might play a role in helping to achieve equity. The gender and ethnic inequity in this area is often attributed to the unsupportive learning context in schools and undesirable social influences such as stereotyping. This has led to growing awareness of the social and cultural aspect of females' and ethnic minorities' learning processes. More research is called for in designing effective learning technology for these students. The effective technology should support the students' identification with STEM and include specific features that stimulate their motivation. Pedagogical agents can be one such technology. A pedagogical agent acting as a role model might motivate female and minority students to STEM learning that is not typically popular but worth pursuing.

Research has shown that agent presence has a strong appeal for many females and ethnic-minority students and successfully elicits the students' social responses. These students' online learning experiences seem to relate closely to their everyday classroom experiences. Their positive experiences with their pedagogical agent are influenced largely by their marginalized experiences in the everyday STEM classrooms. Thus, it seems natural that minority students better identify themselves with the learning domain when working with an agent than when not. One important implication of this is that the careful observation of student characteristics and accurate understanding of challenges that students face in the classroom should be a primary step guiding the effective design and use of pedagogical agents.

Yanghee Kim

See also Affective Factors in Learning, Instruction, and Technology; Animated Agents in Learning Systems; Avatars and Agents in Virtual Systems; Cultural Considerations in Technology-Enhanced Learning and Instruction; Human-Computer Interaction; Virtual Tutees

Further Readings

Cassell, J., Sullivan, J., Prevost, S., & Churchill, E. (Eds.). (2000). *Embodied conversational agents* (Vol. 22). Cambridge, MA: MIT Press.

Graesser, A. C., Person, N. K., Harter, D., & Group, T. R. (2001). Teaching tactics and dialog in AutoTutor. *International Journal of Artificial Intelligence in Education, 12,* 257–279.

Gulz, A. (2004). Benefits of virtual characters in computer-based learning environments: Claims and evidences. *International Journal of Artificial Intelligence in Education, 14,* 313–334.

Johnson, W. L., Rickel, J. W., & Lester, J. C. (2000). Animated pedagogical agents: Face-to-face interaction in interactive learning environments. *International Journal of Artificial Intelligence in Education, 11,* 47–78.

Kim, Y., & Baylor, A. L. (2006). A social-cognitive framework for designing pedagogical agents as learning companions. *Educational Technology Research & Development, 54*(6), 569–596.

Kim, Y., & Lim, J. (2013). Gendered socialization with an embodied agent: Creating a social and affable mathematics learning environment for middle-grade females. *Journal of Educational Psychology, 105*(4), 1164–1174.

Kim, Y., & Wei, Q. (2011). The impact of user attributes and user choice in an agent-based environment. *Computers & Education, 56,* 505–514.

Moreno, R., & Flowerday, T. (2006). Students' choice of animated pedagogical agents in science learning: A test of the similarity attraction hypothesis on gender and ethnicity. *Contemporary Educational Psychology, 31,* 186–207.

Nass, C., & Moon, Y. (2000). Machines and mindlessness: Social responses to computers. *Journal of Social Issues, 56*(1), 81–10.

PEDAGOGICAL KNOWLEDGE

Today's teachers must use pedagogical knowledge, or a variety of approaches, strategies, and techniques, to teach functional and critical thinking skills related to information, media, and technology. Given the importance of mastering core content in many disciplines, these subjects must be interwoven with other 21st-century knowledge and skills (e.g., global awareness, multiple literacies, learning and innovation skills, information, media and technology skills, career skills, etc.). In other words, 21st-century pedagogy should provide students with multiple technological opportunities to learn related to their future academic and work lives. This entry first describes the theoretical and conceptual frameworks behind pedagogical knowledge as applied to technology. The entry then describes exemplar pedagogies that promote skills such as problem solving and critical thinking, collaboration and communication, and creativity and innovation, which are crucial skills for success in the 21st century.

Theoretical and Conceptual Frameworks

Technology has been used to support teaching and learning for several decades with mixed results. Several theoretical constructs undergird how individuals learn in technology-supported environments. For example, current learning theories such as constructivism, social constructivism, situated cognition, and communities of practice undergird the pedagogical choices and conceptual notions about teaching and learning with technology reviewed herein.

Technological Pedagogical Content Knowledge (TPCK or TPACK) has been identified as a framework for what is required to teach appropriately when using technology. TPCK, a new interpretation of Pedagogical

Content Knowledge (PCK), suggests that teachers need to know more than the content they teach; teachers also need to know how resources and activities may change when technology is involved. Thinking about learning and teaching with technology is important because teaching in traditional didactic ways may not be effective or appropriate when integrating technology into the curriculum.

Technology is often used in the classroom to replace, amplify, or transform instruction. This entry focuses on the last two. Teachers should focus on students' developing critical thinking skills so they will be able to use the power of various technologies to solve real-world problems and do useful work. To learn more than facts and procedural knowledge, new pedagogical models for using technology can be used to help students develop deep conceptual understanding through active engagement with academic content.

Exemplary Pedagogies Integrating Technology

Project-based learning (PBL) is a constructivist approach that promotes in-depth learning by placing students in situations where they must use inquiry-based tactics to solve real-world problems. Similarly, challenge-based and problem-based learning have proven to be successful pedagogical models in technology-rich settings. These pedagogies require teachers to design challenges, problems, or projects that require students to use critical thinking skills and work in teams to locate, analyze, and synthesize information to find answers to problems and share their findings. Throughout the process of challenge-based learning and problem-based learning, technology serves as a tool that supports students in researching and evaluating multiple sources of information, as well as analyzing and presenting data. In the process, students engage in amplified and sometimes transformational learning experiences that develop their critical thinking, communication, and collaboration skills.

Problem-based activities—including generating lists, narrowing of topics, outlining options, debating issues, and even voting—can take place in a virtual community. Wikis allow students to meet in virtual spaces to collaborate on projects and solve problems. Similarly, blogs can be used to promote communication skills as students write and share their writing with audiences beyond their teacher. When using PBL, students also can make use of other collaborative and social networking tools such as Skype, Google, Twitter, Instagram, and numerous other Web 2.0 tools that are available for 21st-century teachers and learners.

Wikis, blogs, podcasts, and numerous other tools for communication can promote collaboration locally and globally, as can participation in online *citizen science projects* (e.g., Cornell University's Great Backyard Bird Count or the National Aeronautics and Space Administration's numerous citizen science projects), which are typically supported by tools such as Skype, mobile phones, and other digital devices. Other Internet-based, data-gathering curriculum projects are available to teachers so their students collaborate to complete joint projects with students in classrooms around the world (e.g., ePals.com and iEarn.org). These websites promote collaborative research projects and global understanding and engage students in real-world activities similar to those scientists and social scientists undertake daily. Such projects exemplify how situated cognition and communities of practice represent pedagogy in the 21st century. They also have the potential to amplify and potentially transform pedagogy for 21st-century teachers and learners.

WebQuests and *virtual field trips* are additional constructivist, inquiry-based pedagogies that promote 21st-century knowledge and skills by leveraging what the Internet has to offer. WebQuest, developed by Bernie Dodge and others at the San Diego State University Department of Educational Technology, is an award-winning pedagogical tool and an example of a learning object, or a digital resource, that can be reused to support learning. Thousands of teachers have created and shared WebQuests, which are based on a common structure that focuses students on information teachers want them to encounter and evaluate; most but not all of the information teachers gather to create a WebQuest comes from the Internet. Relatedly, thousands of potential virtual field trip sites are available on the Internet so that students can visit and learn about things that might be too dangerous, too far away, too costly, or even impossible to experience in real life. Attesting to their value as a pedagogical tool to amplify student learning, Harold Wenglinsky has name virtual field trips as one of nine key implementation factors correlated with education success measures, such as disciplinary action rates, dropout rates, high-stakes test scores, Advanced Placement course enrollment, and graduation rates.

Many educators think computer and video games are a waste of time for students and cannot envision any benefits for using gaming as an appropriate pedagogy in school. However, cognitive and learning scientists have shown how the learning principles built into video *games, simulations,* and *virtual worlds* can be effective for teaching and learning content in K–12 classrooms as well as in university settings. For example, research has begun to demonstrate that engaging in games and simulations provides people (children, youths, and adults) with meaningful new experiences in virtual worlds that have the potential to transform and make people smarter and more thoughtful, compared with an environment that focuses on drill and practice, scripted curriculum, and high-stakes testing. The pedagogical principles inherent in games make learning meaningful for students by empowering them, requiring problem solving, and promoting deep versus shallow understanding.

Similar notions about transformational play are also based on research about using games for learning. Also called *epistemic games*, these kinds of computer games help players learn to think like professionals in particular careers (engineers, urban planners, doctors, journalists, etc.) by providing authentic tools and experiences needed for learning how these professionals understand the world. That is, these games position students to use and understand academic content to effectively resolve problematic scenarios, which may require learners to take on roles as scientists, doctors, reporters, and mathematicians who must learn the content of those disciplines to accomplish the tasks posed for them in the game. Epistemic games also provide new, back-end ways to assess individual learning as the game simulates a professional community's real world.

Conclusion

Many new foci for teaching with technology are emerging at this time (e.g., digital fabrication and social media); these and others have significant implications for both society and schools in the 21st century. As new tools for teaching and learning become available, they can be used to further enhance and transform current pedagogical frameworks and approaches. As a result, pedagogical knowledge should be viewed as a dynamic body of knowledge and skills. The goals, however, should always be to make learning effective, which often translates into student-centered and active learning aimed at supporting inquiry and problem-solving skills, critical thinking, collaboration, and communication.

John Dewey argued that learning and doing were tightly coupled and that learning occurs through activity when people try to accomplish real goals. This is the promise of using well-designed projects, games, and simulations as basic pedagogical approaches; when learners are engaged and motivated, they also learn. The same is also true for the other pedagogies discussed in this entry, all of which constitute current pedagogical knowledge.

Lynne Schrum and Barbara B. Levin

See also Constructivist Theory; Games to Promote Inquiry Learning; TPACK (Technological Pedagogical Content Knowledge); TPACK (Technological Pedagogical Content Knowledge): Implications for 21st-Century Teacher Education

Further Readings

Barab, S., Gresalfi, M., & Ingram-Goble, A. (2010). Transformational play: Using games to position person, content, and context. *Educational Researcher, 39*(7), 525–536.

Gee, J. P. (2003). *What video games have to teach us about learning and literacy.* New York, NY: Palgrave Macmillan.

Jonassen, D. H. (2000). *Computers as mindtools for schools: Engaging critical thinking* (2nd ed.). Upper Saddle River, NJ: Merrill.

Mishra, P., & Koehler, M. J. (2006). Technological pedagogical content knowledge: A framework for teacher knowledge. *Teachers College Record, 108*(6), 1017–1054.

Schrum, L., & Levin, B. B. (2012). *Evidence-based strategies for leading 21st century schools.* Thousand Oaks, CA: Corwin.

Solomon, G., & Schrum, L. (2010). *How 2, Web 2: How to for Educators.* Eugene, OR: International Society for Technology in Education.

Wenglinsky, H. (2005). *Using technology wisely: The keys to success in schools.* New York, NY: Teachers College Press.

PERFORMANCE ASSESSMENT

Performance assessment is the judgment of how well a task has been performed in relationship to a defined criterion or goal. Typically, the tasks are *authentic*: meaningful in a work environment, such as troubleshooting a computer network, creating a novel, teaching a lesson, or conducting a negotiation. Measurement of the task is often done by examination of a portfolio of work artifacts and end products (often after task completion), but may also include direct or indirect observation of work processes such as dialogues with coworkers or interactions with instrumentation systems. The context of the performance can be real-world or simulated. The performance assessment may determine if the performance is at or above a previously specified competency level, or it may describe, compare, or rank performance. Further, the purpose of the performance assessment may be to judge past performance, or it may be to infer a general competency or expertise that is believed to predict future performance of a class of tasks. This entry gives examples of performance assessments, explains how performance assessment differs from conventional testing, and discusses the design of performance assessments.

Table 1 illustrates a variety of examples of performance assessments.

It is important to understand how performance assessment differs from conventional testing of knowledge, skills, or abilities. Some of the most important differences are summarized in Table 2.

Table 1   Four examples of performance assessments

Goal	Task	Evidence	Criterion
Certify flight competence of airline pilots.	Flying an airplane (under a variety of conditions).	Cockpit observation by a check pilot using a rubric (checklist). Recorded interactions with cockpit controls.	Expert judgment of minimum acceptable performance level on each rubric observation, validated by data gathered from successful and problematic flights.
Identify the top sales person last quarter.	Closing sales contracts.	Last quarter's data on each sales person: contract value, cost of sales (Hale, 2010), customer satisfaction, mix of products/services sold.	Ranking of all sales people on all four forms of evidence.
Demonstrate mastery of technical skills in lab animal care.	Care of animals in a medical research lab.	Execution of routine procedures for animal care and cage maintenance. Execution of procedures for safety precautions in lab operations.	Correct, complete, and consistent procedure execution. Appropriate and correct application of safety precautions.
Identify performance gaps in skills of constructing evidence-based argumentation in high school (HS) physics.	Construct a chain of evidence-based arguments leading to a causal inference in the domain of HS physics.	A well-formed evidence-based argument leading to a causal inference within the domain of HS physics.	Defined criteria for a well-formed evidence-based argument, based on expert judgment.

Table 2   Common distinctions between conventional and performance assessment

Typical Feature	Conventional Testing	Performance Assessment
What is measured	Conclusion or answer to a specially constructed artificial task designed to sample a representative behavior from a domain that defines a body of knowledge, skill, or a trait/ability/aptitude. Often with minimal context.	Authentic whole task or subtask involving many discrete behaviors/steps/strategies (complex problem solving), in real or simulated contexts.
Answer types supported	Usually convergent reasoning (right/wrong, closed-ended).	Convergent or divergent reasoning, complex, ill-defined, taking into account contextualization and optimization.
Context of measurement	Individual, personal	Individuals may work individually or within groups, collaborative teams.
Measurement tools	Test questions, prompts	Rubrics applied to direct observations and work products. Direct data gathering from the performance environment (e.g., clickstream).

Source: Wellesley R. Foshay, based on distinctions in Pellegrino, J. W., Chudowsky, N., & Glaser, R. (Eds.). (2001). *Knowing what students know: The science and design of educational assessment.* Washington, DC: The National Academies Press.

Practitioners in education and training are showing increased interest in performance assessment, as their experience with conventional knowledge, skill, and aptitude testing has made them acutely aware of the limitations of conventional tests and as advances in cognitive science have placed renewed emphasis on complex cognitive skills such as expertise in ill-structured problem solving (Pellegrino et al., 2001). However, careful examination shows that performance assessments have a different mix of advantages and disadvantages when compared with conventional testing; neither strategy is superior in all respects. For example, the shortcomings of performance assessment include

- Difficulty and expense of administration
- Unreliability of scoring because of human rater error or bias
- Poorer validity or generalizability because of limited time and opportunity to sample extensively from a broad universe of knowledge and skill

These shortcomings often limit the use of performance assessment at scale and in high-stakes applications.

Advances in the theory of assessment show the way to improved, more rigorous methods of design and development of performance assessment. Evidence-centered design provides a rigorous framework for the development of performance assessment and has been successfully applied in digital learning contexts (Behrens et al., 2013). Evidence-centered design is portrayed as a progression through five layers:

1. Domain analysis: analysis of the properties of the performance in its environment

2. Domain modeling: conceptualization of key elements of the performance domain in terms of the assessment argument

3. Conceptual assessment framework: generation of student, evidence, and task models

4. Assessment implementation: development of reusable authoring tasks, scoring details, statistical models

5. Assessment delivery: execution of a four-process delivery architecture

Other examples of performance assessment development methods in training and certification are also available.

Although early models of performance assessment used a behavioral job task analysis framework, these modern design methods are based on a current theoretical framework drawn from cognitive science.

The assessment's integrity depends on a rigorous cognitive analysis of the domain knowledge structure and decision-making processes involved in the problem solving, which is often complex and ill structured.

Wellesley R. Foshay

See also Assessing Learning in Simulation-Based Environments; Assessment in Game-Based Learning; Assessment of Problem Solving and Higher Order Thinking; Cognitive Task Analysis; Workflow Analysis

Further Readings

Andrews, D. H., & Wulfeck, W. H. (2014). Performance assessment—Something old, something new. In J. M. Spector, M. D. Merrill, J. Elen, & M. J. Bishop (Eds.), *Handbook of research on educational communications and technology* (4th ed., pp. 303–310). New York, NY: Springer.

Behrens, J. T., Mislevy, R. J., DiCerbo, K. E., & Levey, R. (2010). An evidence centered design for learning and assessment in the digital world. Retrieved from http://www.cse.ucla.edu/products/reports/R778.pdf

Hale, J. (2010). Performance-based evaluation: Tools, techniques and tips. In J. L. Moseley & J. C. Dessinger (Eds.), *Handbook of improving performance in the workplace* (Vol. 3, pp. 179–199). San Francisco: Wiley/Pfeiffer.

Pellegrino, J. W., Chudowsky, N., & Glaser, R. (Eds.). (2001). *Knowing what students know: The science and design of educational assessment.* Washington, DC: The National Academies Press.

PERSONAL LEARNING ENVIRONMENTS

A *personal learning environment* or *PLE* is a learning technology that is designed around each student's goals or learning approach. A PLE can be described as a process that helps students organize the influx of information and resources that they are faced with on a daily basis into a personalized digital learning space or experience. The underlying principle of a PLE is that the student is put in charge of pedagogically designing his or her own learning environment. In a PLE, the student develops an individualized digital identity through the perceptual cues and cognitive affordances that the personalized learning environment provides, such as what information to share and when, who to share it with, and how to effectively merge formal and informal learning experiences. A PLE is primarily facilitated by cloud-based Web 2.0 technologies and services designed to help students create, organize, and share content; participate in collective knowledge generation; and manage their own meaning making. Examples of specific technologies used to create a PLE include Symbaloo, Evernote, and Personal Learning Environment Box (PLEBOX). This entry first discusses the origins of PLEs and how they provide for personalization. The entry then discusses how PLEs relate to self-regulation and how social media can be used in development of a PLE.

Origins of PLEs

Origins of the PLE concept can be traced back to research in artificial intelligence as early as 1976 and computer-supported collaborative learning (CSCL) in the 1980s and 1990s. In the 21st century, PLEs have been steadily gaining ground as an effective platform for student learning and have been described by scholars such as Brigid Barron, Stephen Downes, Tom Haskins, Scott Wilson, and Mark van Harmelen as individual educational platforms, self-initiated and interest-driven learning environments, unique creations of individual learners that help shape their knowledge and understandings, self-directed learning systems, and methods and tools that help students organize and self-manage their learning.

PLEs and Personalization

PLEs are increasingly addressing issues of learner control and personalization that are often absent in the institutional learning management system or LMS. The LMS is controlled by the institution's faculty and administrators leaving little room for students to create, manage, and maintain a personalized learning space that supports their own learning activities as well as connections to peers and social networks across time and place. In a PLE, the locus of control shifts away from the institution to individual students, helping them take control of their own learning and build a personal cyberinfrastructure and learning ecosystem that extends learning beyond the boundaries of the classroom, institution, or organization, using distributed and portable tools. In a PLE, the student *chooses* the tools that match his or her personal learning style and pace, and the student *decides* how to organize and manage the content to learn effectively and efficiently, hence, PLEs are individualized by design. Specifically, PLEs are built bottom up, starting with personal goals, information management, and individual knowledge construction, and progressing to socially mediated knowledge and networked learning. Consequently, PLEs can be perceived as a single student's educational or e-learning platform, allowing collaboration with other students and instructors and coordination of such interactions across a wide range of systems and learning communities.

PLEs, Self-Regulated Learning, and Social Media

PLEs empower students to take charge of their own learning; therefore, they are inherently self-directed, placing the responsibility for organizing learning on the individual. This requires the development and application of self-regulated learning skills. *Self-regulated learning* (SRL) refers to the degree to which students are able to become active participants of their own learning process and proactively engage in self-motivating and behavioral processes that increase goal attainment. SRL is also regarded as a set of skills that enable students to set learning or task goals, identify learning or task strategies needed to achieve those goals, and reflect on the efficacy of the strategies and processes that helped them achieve their goals. The relationship between PLEs and SRL is intuitive and interdependent and social media technologies have pedagogical affordances that can foster this relationship. Specifically, PLEs can be perceived as a pedagogical approach that facilitates SRL through the deliberate and strategic integration of formal and informal learning using social media technologies.

Social media technologies are being increasingly used by students for developing personal and social learning spaces or PLEs that start out as individual learning platforms, supporting individual knowledge construction, and evolve into social learning platforms or systems where knowledge is socially mediated. However, when students are put in charge of developing a PLE, they need pedagogical guidance and support, particularly if they do not possess SRL skills. With insufficient guidance, students may not be able to create a PLE that cultivates their independent learning skills and helps them achieve their learning goals. This is where the role of faculty becomes crucial. Faculty need to scaffold students in how to manage and navigate the content they create in a PLE and how to become effective organizers, analyzers, evaluators, and synthesizers of information as they gradually assume more responsibility for their own learning. Nada Dabbagh and Anastasia Kitsantas developed a pedagogical framework to assist faculty in scaffolding student PLE development using social media technologies. The framework is based on the pedagogical affordances of social media, namely the three levels of interactivity that social media enable: personal information management, social interaction and collaboration, and information aggregation and management.

Table I   Pedagogical framework to assist faculty in supporting student PLE development

	(Level 1) Personal information management	*(Level 2) Social interaction and collaboration*	*(Level 3) Information aggregation and management*
Social media sharing technologies (e.g., blogs, wikis, media sharing tools)	Faculty ask students to use a *blog* as a private journal to set learning goals and strategies related to course tasks	Faculty ask students to activate the blog sharing and commenting features to allow feedback from faculty and peers	Faculty ask students to use RSS feeds to aggregate other users' blogposts or content into their blogs to extend their learning
	Faculty ask students to use a *wiki* as a personal space for organizing and managing course content	Faculty ask students to activate the wiki's commenting and collaborative editing features to invite feedback and participation in organizational tasks	Faculty ask students to review the wiki's history and to reflect on the effectiveness of the process of organizing course content and its impact on their learning
Cloud based technologies (e.g., Google Calendar)	Faculty ask students to use a cloud-based calendar for personal time management of course tasks and learning goals	Faculty ask students to collaboratively use the cloud-based calendar for managing course-related team projects, activities, and tasks	Faculty ask students to archive personal and group calendars to enable self-evaluation and self-reflection on time management
Social networking sites (e.g., Facebook, LinkedIn)	Faculty ask students to create a personal profile on Facebook or LinkedIn related to their academic and career goals	Faculty ask students to link to communities and groups related to their learning goals and professional interests and to engage in relevant discussion	Faculty ask students to reflect on their social networking experience and to restructure their profile and manage their social presence accordingly

Sources: Adapted by Nada Dabbagh from Table 1 on p. 260 in Dabbagh, N., & Kitsantas, A. (2013). The role of social media in self-regulated learning. *International Journal of Web Based Communities (IJWBC)* [Special Issue], *Social Networking and Education as a Catalyst Social Change, 9*(2); and from Table 1 on p. 7 in Dabbagh, N., & Kitsantas, A. (2012). Personal learning environments, social media, and self-regulated learning: A natural formula for connecting formal and informal learning. *The Internet and Higher Education, 15*(1). Retrieved from http://dx.doi.org/10.1016/j.iheduc.2011.06.002.

At level 1 of the framework, personal information management, faculty can direct students to create a private learning space using social media technologies such as blogs and wikis and to populate this space with self-generated content for personal productivity or organizational learning tasks. This could include creating online bookmarks and media resources surrounding course topics and personal journals and calendars related to course assignments. These activities engage students in acquiring and applying SRL skills of goal setting and time management.

At level 2 of the framework, faculty can direct students to engage in social interaction and collaboration by sharing the content and task organization they created in level 1 with their peers and course instructors, thereby extending the PLE from a personal learning space to a social learning space. For example, students can be encouraged to enable a blog or wiki's commenting features, inviting instructor and peer feedback and informal knowledge sharing. Such activities promote self-monitoring and help seeking, both of which are SRL processes, and they prompt students to identify strategies needed to perform more formal learning tasks.

At level 3 of the framework, faculty can direct students to engage in content aggregation and synthesis using various social media tools and features prompting self-reflection and self-evaluation of their overall learning experience and leading to further customization and personalization of the PLE around their learning needs. These activities help students become better prepared for future educational and professional pursuits. Table 1 provides specific examples of how to apply the three-level framework in an educational context.

Nada Dabbagh

See also Cloud-Based Adaptive Systems; Personalized Learning and Instruction; System and Learner Control in Adaptive Systems; Technologies Supporting Self-Regulated Learning; Twenty-First-Century Technology Skills

Further Readings

Ash, K. (2013). "Personal Learning Environments" focus on the individual. *Education Week, 32*(32), S32, S34.

Barron, B. (2006). Interest and self-sustained learning as catalysts of development: A learning ecology perspective. *Human Development, 49*, 193–224. doi:10.1159/000094368

Dabbagh, N., & Kitsantas, A. (2012). Personal learning environments, social media, and self-regulated learning: A natural formula for connecting formal and informal learning. *The Internet and Higher Education, 15*(1), 3–8. Retrieved from http://dx.doi.org/10.1016/j.iheduc.2011.06.002

Dabbagh, N., & Kitsantas, A. (2013). The role of social media in self-regulated learning. *International Journal of Web Based Communities (IJWBC)* [Special Issue], *Social Networking and Education as a Catalyst Social Change, 9*(2), 256–273.

Downes, S. (2007). The future of online learning and personal learning environments. Retrieved from http://www.slideshare.net/Downes/the-future-of-online-learning-and-personal-learning-environments

EDUCAUSE Learning Initiative (ELI). (2009). *The seven things you should know about . . . personal learning environments.* Retrieved from http://net.educause.edu/ir/library/pdf/ELI7049.pdf

EDUCAUSE Learning Initiative (ELI). (2012). *The seven things you should know about navigating the new learning ecosystem.* Retrieved from http://net.educause.edu/ir/library/pdf/ELI7084.pdf

Haskins, T. (2007). PLE's down under. Retrieved from http://growchangelearn.blogspot.com/2007/09/ple-down-under.html

McLoughlin, C., & Lee, M. J.W. (2010). Personalised and self regulated learning in the Web 2.0 era: International exemplars of innovative pedagogy using social software. *Australasian Journal of Educational Technology, 26*(1), 28–43.

Valjataga, T., Pata, K., & Tammets, K. (2011). Considering students' perspective on personal and distributed learning environments. In M. J. W. Lee & C. McLoughlin (Eds.), *Web 2.0-based e-Learning: Applying social informatics for tertiary teaching* (pp. 85–107). Hershey, PA: IGI Global.

Van Harmelen, H. (2008). Design trajectories: Four experiments in PLE implementation. *Interactive Learning Environments, 16*(1), 36–46.

PERSONALIZED LEARNING AND INSTRUCTION

Personalization refers to a broad range of practices that involve making adjustments to learning activities and resources based on a number of parameters pertaining to individuals and groups of learners. The terms *learning* and *instruction* are both included to reflect the fact that some aspects of personalization occur in informal and unstructured environments not easily associated with instruction, which refers to those learning environments specifically designed and structured to support learning with regard to various goals and objectives. Related terms include *differentiated learning* and *individualized instruction*, although each of these has somewhat more specific meanings and usage. *Differentiated learning* and *differentiated instruction* refer to the practice of grouping students according to their ability levels and needs. The practice dates back to the days of one-room schoolhouses and relies on assessments to determine appropriate groupings. The basic notion was and is that learners could be grouped by their current abilities so that appropriate activities and resources for those learners could be used. Assuming that the groupings were appropriate and exhaustive, all learners could then receive appropriate support for learning.

Individualized learning and individualized instruction focus on specific individuals rather than groups. The basic notion is that each individual has specific needs and characteristics that should be accommodated in planning and implementing instruction. Formal individualized instruction has focused on learners with disabilities, with the requirement in many school systems in the United States to develop and follow individualized education plans (IEPs) for each student with a disability. IEPs were first required by the Education for All Handicapped Children Act of 1975, which was reauthorized in 1990 as the Individuals with Disabilities Education Act and reauthorized in 2004 as the Individuals with Disabilities Education Improvement Act. More informal individualized instruction involves one-to-one tutoring and at-home schooling, practices that are not necessarily associated with those with learning impediments.

The interest in personalized learning, broadly conceived to include differentiated and individualized learning and instruction, is based on the notion that instruction for larger groups is not as effective as one-to-one tutoring, as noted by Benjamin Bloom in a famous 1984 article. Many educators advocate personalized learning and instruction in some form, but there has been relatively little systematic and sustained progress on a large scale. In the 1990s, intelligent tutoring systems provided a technology-based response to Bloom's challenge that was successful in highly restricted contexts, such as operating a device, writing programming code, and solving simple arithmetic problems. In general, these systems did not achieve the two-sigma improvement, or two standard deviations above those who only received conventional instruction, found by Bloom in one-to-one tutoring situations. But they often achieved significant improvements over non-individualized instruction. This entry first discusses the rationale for personalization and the dimensions of personalization. The entry then provides examples of personalized learning environments and discusses implications of personalization for learning and instruction.

Rationale for Personalization

The rationale for personalizing learning and instructional experiences is twofold, involving both effectiveness and efficiency. The notion of efficiency involves the resources needed to achieve a particular result. In the case of learning, the relevant resources involve learners as well as those supporting the learning (instructors, instructional systems, learning resources, learning spaces, and so on). For the people involved, a critical factor in efficiency studies is the time required. In the context of learning, one focus is clearly the learner's time to achieve a desired outcome. For personalizing learning, the belief is that by identifying specific learner needs and requirements, the learner will be able to achieve a desired outcome in an optimally short time. By focusing on specific learner problems, a personalized learning system can address those problem areas and help the learner make progress efficiently. By identifying what a learner already knows and is able to do well, a personalized learning system can skip over learning activities that might bore the learner and not contribute to improved performance or understanding. Human tutors achieve these sorts of efficiencies by adjusting to individual learner needs and situations.

Effectiveness involves the ability to achieve a desired outcome. How does personalization contribute to effectiveness? The chain of reasoning in this case builds on prior research on learning. Two highly reliable predictors of learning outcomes are level of prior knowledge in the domain area and time on task. Given a fixed amount of time to master a specific learning task, those with higher levels of relevant knowledge are more likely to succeed than are those with lower levels of relevant knowledge. This claim involves the assumption of learning constructed around fixed periods and based on a competency model of learning. In many cases, personalization

allows the possibility of open-ended periods to gain competence and knowledge, especially when associated with informal learning situations. Still, the ability to respond to a learner's level of prior knowledge can enable that learner to achieve the desired outcome without becoming bored or feeling overwhelmed.

The more complex aspect of effectiveness is time on task because this involves multiple constructs, including attitudes, motivation, volition, self-regulation, emotional control, and more. The basic notion, however, is quite simple. The more time that a learner spends practicing tasks and solving problems, the more likely that learner is to achieve the desired level of competence. Unguided practice and problem solving without timely and informative feedback, however, is suboptimal. Many people spend countless hours playing golf or bowling but never improve. In addition to spending sufficient time on a learning task, what is needed to achieve effective learning is timely and informative feedback, which a human tutor or a personalized system can in principle provide.

However, one might ask, what is required to get learners to spend time on a learning task? This question leads to the concept of meaningful engagement. A person who believes that learning X is essential for achieving personal goal Y is likely to be willing to invest time in learning X. Sometimes, learners do not see a link between X and Y (even though such links might well exist) and, as a result, do not invest sufficient time in learning X. Motivation, interests, moods, attitudes, and other cognitive and noncognitive factors play a role in a learner's willingness to commit time and effort to a particular learning task. Again, one can observe that effective human tutors are adept in recognizing these factors and can make appropriate adjustments. As it happens, personalized learning environments are beginning to have the potential to make similar adjustments based on such things as learning analytics, dynamic feedback, and student modeling. Computer tutors are becoming more like human tutors, which makes the possibility of personalizing learning on a large scale a promising aspect for the future.

Dimensions of Personalization

Before reviewing examples of personalized learning environments and discussing the future of personalized learning and instruction, it is worth considering the various dimensions of personalization that have been implemented or might be possible to implement with new technologies. Personalized learning and instructional environments can be categorized according to various aspects of individual differences. A comprehensive review of individual differences pertinent to learning and instruction was provided in 1993 by David Jonassen and Barbara Grabowski. Table 1 is a selected representation of many individual differences that can form the basis for personalization.

Table 1   Dimensions of personalization

Category	Dimension	Implementation Approach
Cognitive	Prior learning in the subject	Test learners at the beginning; skip units already mastered and construct appropriate sequences
	Major area(s) of interest/inquiry	Link resources and activities to learner interests
	General problems encountered	Identify in advance problems likely to be challenging and provide additional support for them
	Specific problems encountered	Recognize specific problems and provide guided practice with feedback to build competence
	Self-efficacy	Gradually shift the burden to learners to generate self-assessments and build confidence as they progress
	Learning styles/preferences	Adjust presentations and groups to match learning styles and preferences
Affective	Motivation	Determine motivation levels and address issues via a virtual agent or direct contact with the learner
	General attitude toward subject	Address negative attitudes by showing benefits
	Specific attitude toward course	Recognize the legitimacy of this attitude and respond in a constructive way
	Self-esteem	Determine level of self-esteem and provide support to improve learner confidence and self-esteem
	Emotional maturity	Identify learner responses that reflect emotional states that inhibit learning and address those individually
Cultural	Preferred language	Respond in a learner's preferred language if possible
	Nationality/ethnicity	Adjust resources to recognize and respect national and ethnic differences
	Religious preference	Adjust resources to recognize and respect religious differences
Demographic	Age	Provide age-appropriate examples
	Gender	Consider gender when forming groups
	Location	Recognize the learner's location and integrate that with examples and resources to the extent possible
	Mobility	Recognize the learner's [in]ability to move and respond accordingly
Disability	Hearing impairment	Recognize and provide appropriate support
	Sight impairment	Recognize and provide appropriate support
	Movement impairment	Recognize and provide appropriate support
Personal	Values	Integrate into resources and activities when possible
	Sports	Integrate into resources and activities when possible
	Hobbies	Integrate into resources and activities when possible

Notes: Categories are only suggestive as many dimensions cut across multiple categories. Many of these dimensions can be tracked in a dynamic study profile and used in an automated system. This list is not intended to be an exhaustive list of all possible dimensions of personalization; rather, it is intended to suggest the breadth of those dimensions and the complexities involved in responding to them in support of learning and instruction.

The categories reflected in Table 1 are admittedly arbitrary and not mutually exclusive. These categories (cognitive, affective, cultural, demographic, disability, and personal) were selected because they represent the various ways that advocates of personalization have discussed the ways to achieve meaningful and effective individualization. The category of disabilities has long framed individualized learning because resources and support had to be devised to meet with various disabilities. The cognitive category is the one most addressed in emerging personalized learning environments and was the explicit focus of earlier intelligent tutoring systems. These earlier systems created dynamic profiles of learners based on material and tasks already mastered along with difficulties encountered and mistakes made to then generate learning activities and resources specific to that individual's cognitive needs in the context of a particular instructional sequence. The affective category has been partially explored for which kinds of pedagogical agents are likely to be appropriate for different learners. More recently, researchers have recognized that emotions influence learning with attempts to dynamically detect emotional states in individuals that might be hindering learning; motivational agents are then activated to help a particular individual overcome an undesirable emotional state, such as anxiety or boredom. In those personalized systems that attempt to be responsive to individuals, using the age, gender, nationality, language, and personal interests of the learner can enhance the effectiveness of pedagogical as well as motivational agents.

Another way to think about personalization is in terms of what is being personalized. It seems possible to customize such things as (a) content (e.g., by using examples relevant to a particular learner based on that learner's profile), (b) activities (e.g., by putting a learner in a small group of learners with similar interests with a task relevant to those interests), (c) feedback (e.g., using an agent to communicate personally to a learner about the performance), (d) objectives (e.g., by customizing specific objectives to meet individual learner interests consistent with overall learning goals), (e) goals (e.g., by asking learners to define goals or objectives and then configuring relevant resource and activities options), or (f) peers and tutors (e.g., allowing learners to select peer learners or tutors according to their interests). Some of these options involve issues of learner versus system control. As learners gain competence and confidence, it is often desirable to shift the locus of control from the system to the learner because this also contributes to the development of self-regulation skills and a sense of self-efficacy.

Consistent with the preceding list of things that might be personalized is the notion of who is doing the personalization—an automated system, a human instructor, or a learner. During an entire curriculum, this may vary; it may also vary from one lesson or unit of instruction to another. Research relative to the impact of varying who (or what) is doing the personalization, as well as what is being personalized and in which ways, is still in its infancy. However, contrary to those who advocate learner control and a very high level of personalization at all times, evidence suggests that those new to a task domain typically expect and require some external guidance and support, whereas very advanced learners can be successful with much less external guidance and support.

Different models have been proposed to support personalized learning that emphasize various factors and dimensions mentioned previously, as well as different school cultures and stages of learner engagement and decision making. Some models focus on successive stages of competency, whereas others focus on processes and activities involved in developing knowledge and expertise. In any case, moving from traditional classroom environments designed for larger groups of learners to instruction intended for small groups and individual learners is a major undertaking. Given that fact, one approach to implementing personalized learning and instruction is to take smaller steps rather than attempting a radical makeover of a system all at once. Smaller steps can include organizing parts of a course to involve personalized instruction. One such technique is to have an early part of a course implemented using a personalized approach to bring all learners up to a basic level of competence and familiarity with relevant concepts. Another approach is to implement personalized learning for individuals who may be quite advanced or who may require specific support or remediation. In short, there is no one way and no right way to personalize learning and instruction. Keeping in mind what works for each and every learner is important to guide implementation and refinements.

Examples of Personalized Learning Environments

Several kinds of systems and environments provide the type of personalization described earlier. One simple form of personalization can be implemented as a pedagogical agent that is constructed to meet learner expectations (with the learner possibly constructing the appearance of the agent) and to respond to an individual learner personally (e.g., by name and specific learning situation).

Another type of personalized learning environment is a cognitive tutor that is essentially an intelligent tutoring system that makes use of a cognitive model to provide feedback to students to complement and support problem-solving activities. Cognitive tutors and software to build cognitive tutors are available through Carnegie Mellon University's Cognitive Tutor Authoring Tools (CTAT) website.

At a higher level than a pedagogical agent or a cognitive tutor is a personalized learning approach for an entire degree program. Such a program has recently been implemented at Northern Arizona State University. That program is entirely self-paced (recall the earlier comments about fixed time to achieve mastery), competency-based, and adjustable to individual learners' prior knowledge and experience. Human mentors are provided to supplement the online courses and resources.

Implications of Personalization for the Future of Learning and Instruction

For technology-enabled personalization to make serious gains in the future, what is needed is the development of smart learning environments that include built-in learning analytics and a recommendation engine to respond to individual learning needs and to the needs of teachers to support their learners. Suppose, for example, that a middle school student in a physical science class is learning about magnetism and how it can be used to generate electricity; electromagnetism is typically taught in middle school science curricula and is identified at that level in the Next Generation Science Standards, which were developed by 26 states and several groups of scientists and teachers and serve as guidelines for what schools should teach at different levels. They include standard MS-PS2–5, which involves motion, stability, forces, and interactions. This standard, which can be construed in this context as a learning goal, is: "Conduct an investigation and evaluate the experimental design to provide evidence that fields exist between objects exerting forces on each other even though the objects are not in contact" (ExploreLearning). The clarification for teachers that accompanies this standard is that it can involve magnets and that student investigations can include firsthand experiences or simulations. The assessment is limited to qualitative evidence for the existence of electric and magnetic fields.

Many kinds of learning activities and lessons can be devised to support this standard. One way to begin could be to check to see if learners understood all of the relevant concepts; those who do not could be directed individually by a smart personalized environment to a mini-lesson aimed at developing the requisite knowledge. Some learning activities might involve electric motors while others might involve electrically charged strips of tape. In a nonpersonalized lesson in support of this goal, one kind of interaction experience would be devised for everyone in the class. In a personalized lesson, a variety of interaction experiences could be devised to support the particular interests of students. For example, a small group interested in how electric motors work might engage in an activity using magnets, copper wire, and a battery to create a motor; another group with interests in how simulations work might engage in a task to create or complete a simulation of an electric motor; other tasks involving magnetism could be devised to suit the interests of other groups of students or individual students.

To achieve such levels of personalization on a large and sustainable scale, a number of things are required, including a large repository of relevant lessons (with resources, activities, and assessments), data on students who have taken the lessons and how they performed, dynamic student profiles on those who might take the lesson, and a recommendation engine to match a particular individual's learning needs with what has worked for similarly situated students in the past. Although the means exist to create and deploy all these things, that has yet to be done, and issues regarding privacy and intellectual property have yet to be resolved.

Nonetheless, the future of personalized learning and instruction is quite promising. As more and more resources are put online, and more and more learners use those resources in pursuit of various learning goals and objectives, the ability to determine which resources are effective with which learners using learning analytics becomes a real possibility. It is conceivable that the one-to-one two-sigma learning improvements envisioned by Bloom in 1984 may be possible by the year 2024 through automated personalized learning environments and the benefits of dynamic learning modeling and learning analytics.

J. Michael Spector

See also Adaptive Learning Software and Platforms; Agent Technologies for Evaluation; Assistive Technology; Dynamic Student Profiles; Intelligent Tutoring Systems; Learning Analytics; Pedagogical Agents; Personal Learning Environments; Student Modeling; Technologies That Learn and Adapt to Users; Virtual Learning Environments; Virtual Tutees

Further Readings

Alfieri, L., Brooks, P. J., Aldrich, N. J., & Tenenbaum, H. R. (2011). Does discovery-based instruction enhance learning? *Journal of Educational Psychology, 10*(1), 1–18.

Bloom, B. S. (1984). The 2 sigma problem: The search for methods of group instruction as effective as one-to-one tutoring. *Educational Researcher, 13*(6) 4–16.

Bray, B., & McClaskey, K. (2013). A step-by-step guide to personalize learning. *Learning and Leading with Technology, 40*(7), 12–19. Retrieved from http://www.learningandleading-digital.com/learning_leading/201305#pg1

ExploreLearning. (n.d.). Next generation science standards—Science: Middle schools. Retrieved from http://www.explorelearning.com/index.cfm?method=cResource.dspStandardCorrelation&id=1891

Gibbons, M. (1970). What is individualized instruction? *Interchange, 1*(2), 28–52.

Izmestiev, D. (2012). Personalized learning: A new ICT-enabled education approach. Moscow, Russia: UNESCO. Retrieved from http://iite.unesco.org/pics/publications/en/files/3214716.pdf

Jonassen, D. H., & Grabowski, B. L. (1993). *Handbook of individual differences: Learning and instruction.* Hillsdale, NJ: Lawrence Erlbaum.

Psotka, J., Massey, L. D., & Mutter, S. A. (Eds.). (1988). *Intelligent tutoring systems. Lessons learned.* Hillsdale, NJ: Lawrence Erlbaum.

Spector, J. M. (2014). Conceptualizing the emerging field of smart learning environments. *Smart Learning Environments, 1.* Retrieved from http://www.slejournal.com/imedia/5770048871218301_article.pdf

Spector, J. M., & Anderson, T. M. (Eds.). (2000). *Integrated and holistic perspectives on learning, instruction and technology: Understanding complexity.* Dordrecht, Netherlands: Kluwer Academic.

Tomlinson, C. A. (1999). *The differentiated classroom: Responding to the needs of all learners.* Alexandria, VA: Association of Supervision and Curriculum Development.

Websites

Carnegie Mellon University's Cognitive Tutor Authoring Tools (CTAT) website: http://ctat.pact.cs.cmu.edu/index.php?id=examples

George Veletesianos's website on personalized pedagogical agents: http://www.veletsianos.com/category/pedagogical-agents

NASA page on magnetism activities for sixth- through eighth-graders: http://sunearthday.nasa.gov/2011/getinvolved/lp_68.php

Next Generation Science Standards: http://www.nextgenscience.org/next-generation-science-standards

Northern Arizona State University: http://pl.nau.edu

PHILOSOPHICAL PERSPECTIVES ON EDUCATIONAL TECHNOLOGY

See Educational Technology, Philosophical Perspectives on

PLANNING FOR TECHNOLOGY UPGRADES AND IMPROVEMENTS

The rapid pace of change in information technologies ensures that sooner or later they will have to be upgraded. Ray Kurzweil identified three factors driving rapid changes. Computer processors are becoming more powerful and dropping in price. Storage is becoming more abundant, faster, and cheaper. The capacity for transmitting information over the Internet is also becoming greater and faster at the same time it is becoming less expensive. All these changes are occurring at an accelerating rate. Taken together, these three factors lead to an unprecedented pace of change in technology.

To keep up, information technologies generally need to be upgraded every 3 to 5 years. However, technology should not be upgraded merely because newer technology is available or because everyone else is upgrading. Technology upgrades should be driven by requirements. If existing technology meets current and near-term requirements, then an upgrade may not be needed. If current technology does not meet current or projected requirements, then it is time to upgrade. It is generally a good idea to plan for both sets of circumstances. Equipment breaks and requirements change. Organizations can manage technology upgrades more effectively if they have a plan in place. This entry discusses the various types of technology that organizations must plan to upgrade and the factors to consider when determining how often to upgrade.

Types of Technology

One should consider four primary areas when upgrading technology: (a) infrastructure, (b) software, (c) peripherals, and (d) computers. Infrastructure refers to the essential systems and subsystems that allow technology to operate. Upgrades to infrastructure can be the most expensive but also the most economical upgrades in the long run. Software refers to the applications that run on the computers. Peripherals refer to all of those items that may be connected to a computer to extend its functionality. Upgrades to computers are what organizations most frequently consider when planning for technology improvements.

Infrastructure

Although infrastructure upgrades typically cost the most, they can affect every other part of a technology system. This makes them a good choice when looking to get the largest return on an upgrade investment.

Bandwidth is one important factor to consider when upgrading infrastructure. Increasing the amount and the speed at which wired and wireless networks carry information is important. As more organizations embrace the bring your own device (BYOD) philosophy, increasing wireless access becomes increasingly important. Providing more in-depth and accessible support for users is also important; this can include increasing help-desk staff and hours. Providing more training opportunities for users is a third important consideration; stand-alone tutorials on hardware and software can help with professional development. Replacing old furniture with ergonomically advanced designs may enhance productivity. Buildings built before the computer era may not have sufficient power or cooling capacity; when adding computers it may be necessary to increase both. Increasing server space and speed is yet another important consideration. Lastly, improving network security systems to reduce spam and cyber-attack threats is important to consider.

Software

Software upgrades often drive the need for hardware upgrades. New versions of software may not work with older computers. At the same time, new computers may not work with older software. It is important to ensure that software and hardware systems are compatible and that the decision to upgrade is requirements driven. Again, there are several considerations when upgrading infrastructure. First, new versions of operating systems are periodically released and companies stop supporting older versions of systems. Changing an operating system can affect every piece of software and hardware on a computer, so care should be taken to ensure compatibility. Second, older applications are updated and new applications are released regularly. Sometimes these releases can offer significant enhancements to productivity. Sometimes, however, the enhancements are merely cosmetic. Third, increasingly software is being offered as a service rather than a product.

Applications are not resident on a local computer but instead are served over the Internet and hosted in the cloud. Google Docs is a prime example of this. It is important to recognize that upgrades to systems that affect the entire organization can be economical, but they can also be disruptive. Accounting or financial systems, e-mail, Web hosting, personnel systems, and learning management systems affect the entire organization. Upgrading these systems may require significant retraining of personnel.

Peripherals

Often overlooked as an aspect of a technology environment are peripherals. These add-on devices enhance the functionality of main systems. They generally fall into two broad categories: input and output devices. Input devices include mice, keyboards, touch screens, microphones, cameras, and scanners. Output devices generally include printers (including 3D printers), monitors, speakers, and projectors. Upgrading these devices is typically less expensive than upgrading other parts of the system and can still have real benefits. A third category of peripherals is portable devices. Laptop and tablet computers, smartphones, and media recording and playback devices can all be upgraded relatively inexpensively.

Computers

By far the most commonly considered technology upgrade is an upgrade to computers. When one wants to upgrade a computer, there are three basic choices to consider: repair, refurbish, or replace. If current technology is not meeting the requirements because it is broken, then it may be best to simply repair it. This is a good idea if the technology is still under warranty or budget is limited. If the technology is out of warranty and budget is limited, it may be better to refurbish the equipment. Components of most computer systems can be upgraded without having to replace the entire system. The most common and efficient upgrade is to expand the amount of RAM in the computer. Replacing or adding a hard-drive is also common. As of this writing replacing a magnetic hard disk drive (HDD) with a solid-state drive (SSD) as the boot drive for a computer is a common way to increase the performance and extend the life of a system. If the technology is out of warranty and the budget is sufficient, then replacing the system is probably the best option.

When replacing a computer, the best strategy is to get the best affordable system that is consistent with the requirements of the organization. If the computer will be used primarily for routine tasks such as e-mail and word processing, then it doesn't need to be the most powerful computer available. If the computer will be used primarily for more resource-intensive tasks, such as video rendering, then a more powerful system is warranted. In either case, it is probably advantageous to consider systems that can be upgraded later. It is also worthwhile to consider backward compatibility. Does the new system need to work with older existing hardware and software?

The computers that are being replaced can still be useful. Many organizations use a cascade approach, in which the best computers are replaced regularly on a 3- to 5-year cycle, and are then used to replace the next tier of systems. In other words, say an organization maintains 99 desktop computer systems. It has identified 33 of these as needing to be high-end systems (tier one), 33 as standard systems (tier two), and 33 as low-end systems used primarily for e-mail and word processing (tier three). In a replacement year, the organization replaces the tier one systems with new systems, uses old tier one systems to replace tier two systems, and uses old tier two systems to replace tier three systems, which are given away or sold as surplus. This approach minimizes capital outlay for technology upgrades. The drawback is that the tier three systems are always 6 years old to begin with and are 9 years old at the end of their life cycle; however, they may still be sufficient for basic tasks. Chances are that many of these systems will cease to function before they are due to be replaced, or that they will be unable to function with enterprise-wide upgrades in software. They are long out of warranty, so fixing them may be more expensive than replacing them.

Another approach to replacing systems is to replace a portion of the total number of systems every year. On a 3-year replacement cycle, one third of the systems would be replaced every year. On a 5-year cycle, one fifth of the systems would be replaced every year. The categories of systems might still be differentiated into high-end, standard, and low-end, but rather than cascading the systems down to the next tier, one would instead replace the appropriate percentage in each category with new systems in that category. The benefit is that none of the systems are older than 3 years. Therefore, they are more likely to function with new software, less likely to break, and more likely to be under warranty if they do break. The disadvantage is that the cost is higher.

Stephen W. Harmon

See also Cyberinfrastructure for Learning and Instruction; History of Educational Technology

Further Readings

Garretson, C., (2010, April 22). Pulling the plug on old hardware: Life-cycle management explained. *Computerworld*. Retrieved from http://www.computerworld.com/s/article/9175832/ Pulling_the_plug_on_old_hardware_Life_cycle_management_ explained?taxonomyId=12&pageNumber=2

Kurzweil, R. (2005). *The singularity is near.* New York, NY: Viking.

PODCASTING FOR LEARNING AND INFORMATION SHARING

A *podcast* refers to a type of digital media that allows for automatic downloading of audio or video files over the Internet. This auto downloading capability, which is enabled through user subscription to a Really Simple Syndication (RSS) feed from the source site, distinguishes a podcast from a regular downloadable audio or video file on the Web. Podcasts are typically produced on a focused topic with consistent updates of new content or episodes. After user subscription, podcast content from the source site is directly delivered to the user's computer or mobile devices without him or her checking back to the site to seek updates. Podcasts include audio podcasts and video podcasts, the latter of which are also called videocasts or vodcasts and refer to podcasts that contain video clips in addition to audio content.

According to the Merriam-Webster dictionary, the first known use of the term *podcast* appeared in 2004. Journalist Ben Hammersley is credited with first coining the term in an issue of *The Guardian* newspaper. It is believed that the term was originated from the combination of Apple's music player, *iPod,* and *broadcast.* Because of its fast-growing popularity in areas such as news, music, and entertainment, *podcast* was selected as the Word of the Year in 2005 by the *New Oxford American Dictionary*. According to Gilly Salmon and Ming Nie, it was also in 2005 that podcasting started to catch the attention of educators. Despite its origin, the use of podcasts is not limited to iPods. Podcasts can be delivered on personal computers as well as on mobile devices other than iPod, such as tablets, mobile phones, and personal digital assistants (PDAs). As a result, podcasting is considered a type of mobile learning technology. It allows learning to occur anytime, anywhere in either formal or informal learning settings, such as in traditional classrooms, while traveling, or in a coffee shop. Podcasting is also considered a type of Web 2.0 social media technology because it provides an effective, convenient, and cost-effective way for users to create and distribute information on the Web, a characteristic shared by Web 2.0 technologies. As a newly emerged educational technology application, podcasting offers great potential to enhance teaching and learning in various settings. This entry first discusses how podcasting works and the use of podcasting in education. The entry then discusses the benefits of, and barriers to, podcasting in teaching and learning settings.

Podcasting Technology

Podcasting technology is cost-effective. A variety of free software programs are available for easily creating, distributing, and downloading a podcast. Anyone can create a podcast with a microphone, computer, audio recording and editing software, and a connection to the Internet. Examples of free audio recording/editing software include Audacity for Windows and Garageband for Mac. Examples of free video recording and editing software include Movie Maker for Windows and iMovie for Mac. Once an audio or video podcast is created, it can be published to a podcast hosting site such as Blubrry or a learning management system such as Blackboard.

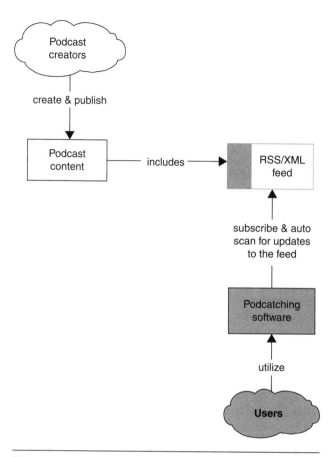

Figure 1   Podcasting technology

To allow automatic delivery of podcast content, subscription to an RSS feed is necessary. Based on the Extensible Markup Language (XML) format, an RSS file or feed is where new content is described by a podcast publisher. A standard RSS feed icon is a small, orange square with white radio waves inside. Other variations of the RSS feed format include orange rectangles (mostly) with such words as "RSS," "XML," or "Feed." Subscription to a feed can be made by simply clicking on an RSS icon, which will allow the user to select a preferred podcast reader or podcatcher program for downloading the podcast as well as receiving updated content automatically whenever it is made available. Examples of podcast readers include iTunes and Juice. Most Web browsers also have built-in RSS readers, including Live Bookmarks in Mozilla Firefox and Feeds in Internet Explorer. Podcasts downloaded to a computer via a podcatcher can be synched onto a mobile device such as a smartphone or tablet PC.

Educational Use of Podcasting

As asynchronously delivered content, podcasts have become increasingly popular in educational settings and have been widely used in K–12 schools and higher education in a variety of subject matter areas. For instance, Bard Williams provides various examples of the use of podcasts in mathematics, science, social science, English and language arts, fine arts, physical education, health, and wellness, and news and research, mostly in K–12 school settings. At the same time, Salmon and Palitha Edirisingha provide research-based examples of podcasting use in different subject matter areas in higher education. Podcasting can be integrated into different modes of learning, such as face-to-face courses, blended learning, and distance education. Although the length of podcasts can vary, researchers generally recommend that a podcast for learning should be no longer than 15 to 20 minutes because of relatively short human attention spans; this recommendation applies in both K–12 and higher education settings. Some educational podcasts produced are several minutes long in a style similar to digital storytelling or radio-style talk shows.

Mark J. W. Lee and his colleagues as well as some other researchers distinguish *learning through creating podcasts* from *learning from podcasts*, the former referring to learner-generated podcasts and the latter referring to instructor-generated podcasts. Instructor-generated podcasts exist in such forms as orientation to class activities, recorded lectures, supplementary material presentation, or summary feedback to learners. A well-known educational podcast site with recorded lectures is iTunes U where numerous universities have joined so their instructors can share course materials in the form of podcasting. Learner-generated podcasts, whether produced individually or in group settings, are less common. Advocates of this type of podcast argue that producing their own podcasts allows students to co-construct knowledge, and in so doing, makes learning more experiential, authentic, and learner-centered than listening to instructor-generated podcasts.

Benefits of, and Barriers to, Podcasting Use

Research in the field has documented a variety of benefits of using podcasts in teaching and learning settings. For example, podcasting provides a time-saving way of receiving learning content because the learner does not have to manually check through or monitor the source site to find relevant content. Podcasts are also considered learning objects that can be reused over time or across different courses. Other benefits that have been reported in the literature include, but are not limited to, the following: low cost, ease of use, flexibility (anytime, anywhere, on any device), learner control, enhanced feedback to learners, increased learner reflection, learner motivation, engagement with course content, and increased learner understanding of course content.

At the same time, barriers to the use of podcasts have also been documented in the literature. For example, in a review of audio podcasting use in K–12 and higher education settings, Khe Foon Hew identified several barriers to using podcasts encountered by both learners and instructors, including learner and instructor lack of familiarity with podcasts, technical problems accessing and downloading podcasts, failure to see the relevance of podcasts for learning and teaching subject areas, and instructors' lack of time for preparing the podcasts. However, according to Hew, the identified barriers are not very different than those of other computing devices such as laptops and handheld computers. Overall, with appropriate strategies to overcome the potential barriers, podcasting has great potential for enhancing teaching and learning.

Xiaoxia Huang

See also Digital Storytelling; Integrating Social Media Into Learning and Instruction; Learning Objects; Mobile Tools and Technologies for Learning and Instruction; Social Media in Elementary School Settings; Social Media in Higher Education; Social Media in Secondary School Settings; Web 2.0 and Beyond

Further Readings

Hammersley, B. (2004, February 11). Audible revolution. *The Guardian*. Retrieved from http://www.theguardian.com/media/2004/feb/12/broadcasting.digitalmedia

Hew, K. F. (2008). Use of audio podcast in K–12 and higher education: A review of research topics and methodologies. *Educational Technology Research & Development, 57*(3), 333–357. doi:10.1007/s11423-008-9108-3

Lee, M. J. W., McLoughlin, C., & Chan, A. (2008). Talk the talk: Learner-generated podcasts as catalysts for knowledge creation. *British Journal of Educational Technology, 39*(3), 501–521. doi:10.1111/j.1467-8535.2007.00746.x

Salmon, G., & Edirisingha, P. (Eds.). (2008). *Podcasting for learning in universities*. Maidenhead, UK: Open University Press.

Salmon, G., & Nie, M. (2008). Doubling the life of iPods. In G. Salmon & P. Edirisingha (Eds.), *Podcasting for learning in universities* (pp. 1–11). Maidenhead, UK: Open University Press.

Williams, B. (2007). *Educator's podcast guide*. Eugene, OR: International Society for Technology in Education.

Predicting Change and Adoption of Technology Innovations

Change is the process by which an organization or social system modifies its practices, beliefs, operations, values, or structures. One of the most common ways in which an organization or social system changes is through the identification, development, adoption, and use of new technologies. Innovative technologies have been adopted with great effect by organizations in many fields including banking, telecommunications, the military, medicine, and entertainment, to name only a few. There are also numerous examples of innovative technologies that have been adopted by educational and training organizations during the last several decades. Among the most notable of these have been programmed instruction, instructional films and radio, computer-based instruction, Web-based instruction, and mobile learning. These innovative technologies have allowed K–12 schools, colleges and universities, and other organizations to reach new learners, reduce the costs associated with education and training, make use of new and emerging learning theories and communication tools, allow for greater learner control and access to information, and create rich, flexible learning environments.

Although new educational technologies offer amazing potential benefits to both organizations and learners, there are potential problems and issues related to their adoption. It is common for newly adopted technologies to fail to be widely used by members of an organization or to be used inappropriately or ineffectively. Because the financial, human, and operational costs associated with technology are often high, the consequences of failed adoption can have a severe, long-term, negative impact on an organization. As a result, it is becoming increasingly important for administrators, technology managers, change agents, teachers, and other stakeholders to better understand the technology adoption process and to account for the factors that serve as enablers or barriers to successful adoption. This entry first discusses issues to consider in predicting the adoption of technology innovations and factors affecting the adoption of technology innovations. The entry then discusses how adoption of technology innovations leads to their implementation, diffusion, institutionalization, and finally their replacement or augmentation. The entry ends by discussing the implications of technology adoption for educational technology.

Those hoping to predict the adoption of innovative technologies should consider five broad issues: First, there is no single, unified, widely accepted theory of technology adoption. A large number of concepts and perspectives from widely diverse fields make up the theoretical foundation of change and adoption. Rather than studying or applying a single theory, change agents operate within the context of an expansive theory cluster originating in fields such as sociology, psychology, management, marketing, history, and political science, among others. The second issue to consider is that the adoption of a new technology has to be viewed as a process, not as an isolated event. Technology adoption, especially at the organizational or societal level, is often the result of a lengthy process that includes awareness, information gathering, competition between alternatives, trial and error, distributed decision making, the development of supporting technologies, and shifting market forces. All technologies, no matter how successful they ultimately become within the marketplace, undergo a period of rather slow adoption.

The third issue is that the adoption of any innovative technology is highly contextualized. Organizations in different sectors usually have vastly different cultures, policies, practices, and other characteristics that facilitate or impede adoption. Even similar organizations within the same area will experience the adoption process quite differently. For example, two elementary schools in the same district will likely have at least some different issues that affect the adoption of the same innovation in their schools. In addition, the characteristics of the technology itself and the nature of the change also affect adoption. Some small-scale innovations affect a relatively small number of people within an organization, but other more large-scale innovations affect everyone within an organization. Some innovations have more of a superficial or incremental impact and are used primarily to augment or enhance existing organizational processes, but others are more revolutionary, disruptive, and systemic and require significant modifications to an organization's existing processes or structure. The interaction between the characteristics of each specific organization and the characteristics of a specific technology creates a highly contextualized and idiosyncratic adoption situation.

Fourth, the end users play a critical role in the adoption process. Although the decision initially to adopt an innovation can be made by a small group of people, the effective use of that innovation is ultimately controlled by the end users. Technologies that are not appropriate, usable, reliable, superior to other options, or readily available will rapidly be modified, minimized, or discontinued altogether by the people within an organization. Technology adoption is largely a socially negotiated process. To predict the adoption of a technology innovation, change agents must understand the innovation from the perspective of the end users.

Fifth, both the immediate and distal outcomes of technology adoption are often wide ranging and unpredictable. The unintended consequences, both positive and negative, of an innovation can be difficult or impossible to anticipate. A current trend in the study of adoption and change is to take an ecological perspective of technological innovation. From this perspective, the introduction of a new technology within an organization is seen as analogous to the introduction of a new species within an ecosystem. The introduction of a new technology will invariably have profound impacts on the overall organization, often in seemingly unrelated and counterintuitive ways, and requires ongoing monitoring and maintenance.

Factors Affecting Adoption of Technology Innovations

Although predicting the adoption of new technologies can be difficult, highly contextualized, complex, and often unpredictable, several factors have been shown to enable or impede the adoption of technology innovations. Resources have consistently been shown to play a vital role in the adoption of a technology. This includes financial resources, human resources, intellectual and managerial resources, and technical resources. Many innovations require a large initial commitment of resources to be successfully adopted, as well as continuing resources. Resource allocation between competing innovations is also an important consideration. Although not sufficient in itself, the availability of necessary resources is an important factor in predicting the successful adoption of a technology. Infrastructure is another important predictor of success in technology adoption. Infrastructure refers to the supporting technologies that are required to make effective use of a new technology. Educational technology infrastructure can include teaching and learning facilities such as classrooms and labs, communication technologies such as servers, wireless networks, data management and security software, and mobile technologies; production capacity such as application software and peripherals; and workplace requirements such as offices, physical storage, heating and cooling systems, and office supplies, among many others.

Another factor that affects adoption is the nature of the social system and culture within an organization. An organization with a culture that is open to change, empowers risk taking and experimentation, encourages entrepreneurship, fosters collaboration, provides rewards and incentives, and supports shared decision making is more likely to experience successful technology adoption than are other organizations. In addition to organizational culture, the collective innovativeness of the members of an organization can be a strong predictor of successful adoption. Organizations with large numbers of innovators and early adopters are more likely to experience successful adoption than are organizations with large numbers of late adopters or laggards. Organizational policies are another factor that can predict the successful adoption of a technology innovation. Organizations with more fluid, less entrenched, more easily modified policies can more easily respond to changes brought about by innovative technologies and are often more successful in adopting technologies than are more structured or traditional organizations. Support is another commonly cited factor in facilitating the adoption of technology. Support includes training, both initial and ongoing, for personnel who will use the technology; technical support to install, maintain, repair, and upgrade the new technology and related technologies; and ongoing, meaningful administrative support by both frontline and senior-level management. Educational technologies also require pedagogical support for both staff and learners to ensure the innovation incorporates emerging and pedagogically sound practices that effectively foster learning.

Adoption, Implementation, Diffusion, Institutionalization, and Re-Innovation

Although much of the discussion in the field of educational technology to date has focused on the adoption of technologies, there is a growing realization that adoption is only one part of the overall change cycle. Adoption, the initial decision to begin using an innovation, is followed by implementation, the process of fostering the effective use of an innovation on a day-to-day basis. Implementation, also sometimes referred to as integration or utilization, must account for the numerous issues, both predictable and unpredictable, that threaten the continued use of an innovation after adoption. For example, an organization that adopts a training system delivered via mobile devices will have to account for issues such as new technical developments in the mobile industry, mobile software upgrades and compatibility issues, changes in service providers, and the modification of content from nonmobile platforms, among other issues, during the implementation phase. If an innovation is successfully adopted and effectively implemented, diffusion is the next consideration.

Diffusion is the process of ensuring that an innovation is more widely (or deeply) used within an organization. In our mobile learning example, diffusion could mean the use of mobile learning by more departments within the organization or for a larger percentage of the organization's overall training. It could also mean the use of mobile learning for training in higher order and more complex skills. Institutionalization, the next phase of the change cycle, involves a technology moving from being viewed as an innovation to being viewed as an accepted, stable, and routine part of the organization. For example, institutionalization (or routinization) would occur when mobile learning becomes the standard training method within an organization and most of the barriers to its use have been overcome.

Following institutionalization, an organization often finds it necessary to begin a process of re-innovation. This is the process by which an organization, having successfully adopted an innovation, seeks to adopt a new innovation to either replace or augment the existing technology. Re-innovation can be the result of a problem or an opportunity. For example, an organization that has successfully adopted, implemented, diffused, and institutionalized mobile learning will almost certainly come to find that mobile learning is no longer meeting its needs, that a new technology has been developed that enhances mobile learning, or that a completely new technology has been identified that has the potential to replace mobile learning.

Technology Adoption and Educational Technology

Educational technology and innovation are inseparable. Educational technologists create innovations as a routine part of their daily jobs. These innovations may be pedagogical, such as a new theory of assessment, or technological, such as a new computer-based training simulation. Every innovation affects people and organizations in many ways. These impacts can be large or small, superficial or profound, temporary or permanent. Even the smallest innovation, such as incorporating the use of social media into an online course, can have a large impact on the learners' achievement, motivation, and academic or occupational success. Large-scale, systemic innovations, such as moving all training or an entire degree program to an online format, represent important milestones in the development and growth of organizations, require the commitment of significant resources, and can have enormous consequences for everyone associated with the organization. In addition, innovations from other fields, such as social networking, adaptive and assistive technology, and emerging theories of cognition and motivation, affect the field of educational technology on a regular basis. To enhance adoption, educational technologists should strive to better understand the change process, to design and develop products that are both instructionally sound and technically strong, and to work with change agents to modify and adapt innovations to account for multiple adoption contexts.

Daniel W. Surry

See also Change Agency; Diffusion of Distance Education; Diffusion of New Technologies in the Workplace; Early Adopters; Innovators and Risk Takers in Education; Technology Integration

Further Readings

Ely, D. P. (1999). Conditions that facilitate the implementation of educational technology innovations. *Educational Technology, 39,* 23–27.

Fullan, M. (2007). *The new meaning of educational change* (4th ed.). New York, NY: Teachers College Press.

Hall, G. E., & Hord, S. M. (1987). *Change in schools facilitating the process.* New York, NY: State University of New York Press.

Rogers, E. M. (2003). *Diffusion of innovations* (5th ed.). New York, NY: Free Press.

Surry, D. W., & Ely, D. P. (2007). Adoption, diffusion, implementation, and institutionalization of educational innovations. In R. Reiser & J. V. Dempsey (Eds.), *Trends and issues in instructional design and technology* (2nd ed., pp. 104–111). Upper Saddle River, NJ: Prentice Hall.

Surry, D. W., Ensminger, D. C., & Haab, M. (2005). A model for integrating instructional technology into higher education. *British Journal of Educational Technology, 36*(2), 327–329.

PROBLEM- AND TASK-CENTERED APPROACHES

Problem- and task-centered approaches often refer to educational technologies designed to situate instruction in authentic or meaningful settings. Such approaches are organized around questions specific to the discipline where technology can serve as a medium for problem solving.

Problem- and task-centered principles are used to facilitate learning in a wide range of disciplines, such as medicine, science, law, business, and mathematics. For example, problem-centered learning in medicine requires students to work in groups to acquire skills needed to diagnose patient cases and integrate clinical knowledge required in practice. Inquiry-based learning in the sciences or humanities requires students to formulate explanations for a phenomenon under investigation by defining a question, seeking evidence, and outlining an argument. In legal and business education, case-based learning is used to encourage students to identify and summarize important information from selected cases and then present their cases to the classroom where the instructor provides feedback. Project-based learning activities in math and science require students to work together on joint projects where constructive feedback is provided to each other or by tutors or teachers.

Although these instructional approaches have been implemented in different domains, they share core assumptions that are organized around situating learning in meaningful situations. Students collaborate to solve problems, search topics under investigation, and discuss and reflect on the outcomes of their efforts.

This entry first briefly reviews the historical roots of problem- and task-centered approaches used to design educational technologies and outlines several mechanisms that account for learning in these situations. The entry presents an analysis of these tenets by drawing on research by Susanne P. Lajoie and Eric Poitras where problem- and task-centered frameworks guide the design of technology-rich learning environments (TREs) in several disciplines, including medicine, avionics troubleshooting, and history.

Theoretical Foundations of Problem- and Task-Centered Approaches

The origin of problem- and task-centered approaches to instruction can be traced back to constructivist theories of learning. Participation in valued activities within different domains is fundamental to how students learn. Proponents of constructivism suggest that learning is a process that involves others, such as peers or mentors, where collaborative activities can lead to higher reasoning levels. Students may change their own perspectives after engaging with others where they acquire new strategies. Lev Vygotsky introduced the construct of the zone of proximal development to explain how peers or mentors can facilitate knowledge construction. Within this framework, instruction is considered effective when it reduces the distance between what students are able to do on their own and what can be accomplished with the assistance of more knowledgeable peers.

TREs can provide such assistance when diagnostic assessment mechanisms are used to monitor learners' performance with the goal of improving learning. Dynamic assessment is used to provide scaffolding support to individuals. A physical scaffold is a temporary structure that helps one complete a job and is removed when a job is completed. Scaffolds in the educational context are also temporary and assistance is removed when no longer needed. Scaffolding is intended to help learners accomplish tasks that would otherwise be beyond their reach. When designing tools to scaffold learners, we must consider what should be supported, as well as when and how to support the learner and how to fade scaffolding when competence is demonstrated. Open-ended TREs, such as Web-based environments and social media platforms, where learners search across vast quantities of information, may require more attention to scaffolding.

Analyses of Problem- and Task-Centered Approaches to the Design of TREs

Problem- and task-centered approaches to the design of TREs have been researched extensively, with major shifts seen in the empirical literature pertaining to the use of scaffolds for learning in the design of TREs that use these approaches to learning.

The first research shift occurred in the early 1990s where researchers proposed the metaphor of using computers as cognitive tools with the aim of scaffolding learning processes. Cognitive tools refer to TREs that assist learners in accomplishing cognitive tasks by (a) supporting cognitive processes such as memory and metacognition, (b) sharing the cognitive load by supporting lower order processes so that learners can engage in higher order processing that would otherwise be out of their reach, and (c) enabling learners to generate and test hypotheses in the context of problem solving.

Several TREs have incorporated cognitive tools as a means to implement problem- and task-centered approaches to instruction. The Jasper series consists of interactive video-based narratives that anchor project-based learning in meaningful contexts where the Jasper character acts as an adult mentor who scaffolds student problem solving. Sherlock was a TRE that coached first-term airmen in the context of their avionics troubleshooting skills for repairing the F-15 aircraft. BioWorld provides a practice environment for medical students who are learning to diagnose patient cases.

Cognitive task analyses are the starting point for designing cognitive tools for improving proficiency within a particular domain. These analyses lead to the identification of skills that should be modeled and assessed during learning, where a TRE can compare less and more skilled actions for each type of problem. Cognitive tools can put into practice several principles of problem- and task-centered approaches to instruction by modeling the appropriate use of skills, providing opportunities for deliberate practice of problem-solving combined with feedback and opportunities for peer collaboration. The evaluation of these technologies can determine if there is evidence of emerging competence through better training and practice and if higher levels of engagement and satisfaction occur in these environments.

The second research shift occurred a decade later, when the scaffolding metaphor was extended to the use of computers as metacognitive tools. Computers as metacognitive tools refer to situations where students make choices in the context of an open-ended TRE, but receive computer support to regulate certain aspects of their own learning. Research programs using computers as metacognitive tools include those that help students learn about scientific concepts and complex historical situations, such as the following:

- *MetaTutor* was designed to assess and train students in the use of self-regulatory skills to help them study scientific topics, such as the human circulatory system.
- *Betty's Brain* was also designed as a metacognitive tool in that it implements a learning-by-teaching paradigm where students build a concept map of their knowledge as a first step in teaching an artificial agent what they know so that the agent can learn. If the agent fails a quiz, students reassess their own knowledge and redesign their concept map so that the agent will pass the test.
- *Crystal Island* is an inquiry-based game narrative where students learn about microbiology by investigating the cause of an illness spreading on an island.
- *The MetaHistoReasoning Tool* was designed to support students to regulate certain aspects of their learning by investigating the causes of complex historical events.
- *BioWorld* supports students in their monitoring of the diagnostic reasoning process during and after case resolution.

TREs can be used to study learning processes by creating profiles of self-regulatory strategy use while studying text or by modeling the development of domain-specific self-regulatory skills while investigating the causes of historical events. Educational technologies assess the use of regulatory skills primarily through the analysis of user interactions with system features stored in the log-file data; however, recent research aims to extend the range of sensors that are implemented in these systems. Research on students learning with Betty's Brain has shown that tools designed to scaffold self-regulated learning result in better learning outcomes. Students were able to build better concept maps about the topic under study when they monitor and self-regulate the content and quality of these concept maps.

Mechanisms of Learning With Problem- and Task-Centered Approaches

Scaffolding is a mechanism that aligns instruction with assessment by identifying the specific needs of learners and providing the right assistance needed to complete particular tasks. This section reviews the core assumptions of scaffolding (problematizing, structuring, and adapting) and how they guide the design of TREs in accordance with problem- and task-centered approaches.

Brian Reiser outlined a framework that explains how scaffolding can *problematize* and *structure* instruction. Software tools can be designed to promote learning by problematizing the subject matter when a learner's attention is drawn to critical aspects of the task that have not been performed adequately and that might otherwise be overlooked. At the same time, software tools can assist learning by structuring the task, reducing the amount of complexity and choice by creating an external representation of task constraints.

Problem-centered or task-centered approaches used in TREs can be designed to balance how instruction is problematized and structured. In the case of diagnosing patient cases in BioWorld, the subject matter is problematized through the case description. The patient exhibits symptoms that are indicative of an underlying disease; however, the nature of this disease is not immediately apparent to the learner. Therefore, the environment structures instruction by providing students with several tools. The chart allows students to order lab tests and monitor the vital signs while testing their hypotheses. The consult tool provides hints that are tailored toward their diagnostic activities. The library enables students to search for more information in relation to the diseases and lab tests. The feedback palette allows students to compare their diagnostic process to the solution process of an expert physician.

Valerie Shute and Diego Zapata-Rivera attribute the benefits of TREs that scaffold to their capability of *adapting* instruction to learner needs. TREs can provide stealth assessment, adapting instruction to the individual learner model. Adaptive TREs gather and analyze information about the learner to select and deliver the most suitable instructional content. As an example, inquiry-based TREs can be designed to adapt instruction to the specific needs of different learners. The Meta-HistoReasoning tool prescribes instructional content on the basis of the assessment of user interactions. Students first acquire skills by studying examples and categorizing the skill that is shown. The system tailors the delivery of examples on the basis of the estimates of future categorization accuracy for each type of skill. These estimates are provided by a prediction model that analyzes variables such as the time taken to categorize each example, the number of attempts taken to categorize an example, the type of skill that is shown in the example, and so on. Students then practice and refine disciplinary-based skills such as setting goals for their investigations. A pedagogical agent embedded in the system is designed to train students against confirmation bias by prompting them to consider alternative explanations and refute counterarguments. The prompts are chosen through a rule-based classifier that analyzes variables such as the rankings of the probability for each cause that led to the event under investigation, the claim and warrant that was selected by the students, and the number of sources that corroborate the evidence.

Conclusion

Problem- and task-based centered approaches to the design of educational technologies share common assumptions across disciplines. Namely, educational technologies can be designed to scaffold learning by supporting an individual as he or she solves problems through collaborative problem-solving activities of the group or by scaffolding individuals through technology. The power of scaffolding with technology was discussed in terms of promoting learning through dynamic and stealth assessment. The underlying mechanisms of scaffolding are problematizing, structuring, and adapting. These notions are critical in scaffolding learning with TREs across different disciplines.

Susanne P. Lajoie and Eric Poitras

See also Adaptive Learning Software and Platforms; Anchored Instruction; Case-Based Reasoning and Educational Technology; Cognitive Apprenticeship; Pedagogical Agents; Stealth Assessment

Further Readings

Hmelo-Silver, C. E. (2004). Problem-based learning: What and how do students learn? *Educational Psychology Review, 16*(3), 235–266.

Kinnebrew, J., Biswas, G., Sulcer, B., & Taylor, R. (2013). Investigating self-regulated learning in teachable agent environments. In R. Azevedo & V. Aleven (Eds.), *International handbook of metacognition and learning technologies: Vol. 26. Springer international handbooks of education* (pp. 451–470). New York, NY: Springer.

Krajcik, J. S., & Blumenfeld, P. (2006). Project-based learning. In R. K. Sawyer (Ed.), *The Cambridge handbook of the learning sciences.* New York, NY: Cambridge University Press.

Lajoie, S. P. (2009). Developing professional expertise with a cognitive apprenticeship model: Examples from avionics and medicine. In K. A. Ericsson (Ed.), *Development of professional expertise: Toward measurement of expert performance and design of optimal learning environments* (pp. 61–83). New York, NY: Cambridge University Press.

Lajoie, S. P., & Azevedo, R. (2006). Teaching and learning in technology-rich environments. In P. Alexander, & P. Winne (Eds.), *Handbook of educational psychology* (2nd ed., pp. 803–821). Mahwah, NJ: Lawrence Erlbaum.

Loyens, S. M. M., & Rikers, R. M. J. P. (2011). Instruction based on inquiry. In R. Mayer & P. Alexander (Eds.), *Handbook of research on learning and instruction.* New York, NY: Routledge.

Poitras, E., & Lajoie, S. P. (2013). A three-pronged approach to the design of technology-rich learning environments. In R. Atkinson (Ed.), *Learning environments: Technologies, challenges and impact assessment.* Hauppauge, NY: Nova Science.

Reiser, B. J. (2004). Scaffolding complex learning: The mechanisms of structuring and problematizing student work. *Journal of the Learning Sciences, 13*(3), 273–304.

Shute, V. J., & Zapata-Rivera, D. (2012). Adaptive educational systems. In P. Durlach (Ed.), *Adaptive technologies for training and education* (pp. 7–27). New York, NY: Cambridge University Press.

Williams, S. M. (1992). Putting case-based instruction into context: Examples from legal and medical education. *Journal of the Learning Sciences, 2,* 367–427.

PROFESSIONAL DEVELOPMENT TOOLS AND TECHNOLOGIES

The body of knowledge recognized and accepted by professionals in any field of study is often increasing, refined, and revised. Policies and procedures within organizations and government agencies change, sometimes with great frequency. *Professional development* refers generally to the process of remaining current in one's professional area of expertise, which includes functioning as a member of a professional community. Participation in professional development, or designing and delivering professional development, often requires the use of tools or technologies. As such, it is important to understand the tools and technologies used for experiencing, or designing, professional development. This entry first discusses tools and technologies commonly used in formal and informal professional development. The entry then discusses the design and development of professional development experiences and emerging trends in the technology used in professional development.

Participating in Professional Development

Individuals in fields such as education, health care, and law, among others, are required to maintain professional licenses to practice. The renewal of professional licenses often requires documented professional development. For example, as of 2013, teachers in the U.S. state of Georgia must maintain their professional certificate required for teaching school in Georgia. The certificate is renewed every 5 years by completing a minimum of 6 semester-hours of approved college credit, or 10 approved professional learning units. Lawyers in West Virginia, similarly, must complete a minimum of 6 hours of continuing legal education for every 2-year period they are practicing law. Requirements like these examples are common in many professions around the world.

Even if a license to practice is not required, maintaining extra certifications can be attractive in some professions. Performance improvement professionals have the ability to obtain the designation of certified performance technologist through the International Society for Performance Improvement. This designation requires recertification every 3 years, and the recertification process includes documentation of continued professional education.

The mandate, or encouragement, for continued professional development is an important element in ensuring that professionals are up-to-date on knowledge, policies, changes, and innovations in their field of practice. This is congruent with Etienne Wenger's work on communities of practice and how an individual progresses to become a full participant in a community. Professional development experiences can be classified into two high-level types: formal professional development experiences and informal professional development experiences.

Formal Professional Development

Formal professional development experiences are structured activities or courses offered specifically for professional development. They often are provided by school districts, institutions of higher education, professional organizations, government agencies, or foundations or groups with an interest in education. The format and mode of delivery for formal professional development experiences vary. The purpose here is to consider technology-based professional development, so this entry highlights experiences that use technology. Popular modes of delivery include (a) fully online, for-credit courses; (b) fully online courses for continuing education credits; (c) blended learning experiences that use online and face-to-face activities; and (d) webinars.

Fully online experiences are increasingly common because of the advantages of reaching a large potential audience with professional learning opportunities. If the experiences are designed as asynchronous, online activities, then they meet the needs of busy professionals, who can learn when they have time. Further, if experiences are offered in a self-paced format, then professionals may meet their learning needs any time, and anywhere, they choose.

Fully online course experiences and blended learning experiences typically use some form of learning management system (LMS) as an organizing structure for the experience. An LMS is a collection of Web-based tools and services where information is presented, resources are shared, and participants can interact with the course facilitator and classmates. The LMS also is used to track participation in the experience. If graded assignments are part of the professional development, then they can be submitted to facilitators through the LMS. Feedback can be returned to participants via the LMS as well.

Webinars are Web-based, synchronous experiences that use an online, Web conferencing tool. Common Web-conferencing tools include Adobe Connect, Blackboard Collaborate, and Cisco WebEx, but several other options are available. Professional organizations often provide webinar-based professional development experiences as a way to keep their members up-to-date with current skills and knowledge. The webinar format usually consists of one or more presenters delivering content though a shared presentation tool in real time. Webinars can include audio or video of the presenters and participants. Participants watch or listen to the presentation. Interaction in a webinar is a variable that is specified by the designer of the experience. There may be opportunities for questions from the participants, breakout discussion between participants, or interactivity between the presenters and participants via polling or direct questioning. Most Web-conferencing tools allow the sessions to be recorded, thus creating an archive of the session that can be viewed later. However, viewing the session after it has concluded removes the ability for interaction in the experience between other participants or the presenters.

Many different organizations offer formal professional development experiences such as those just described. Offerings from colleges and universities are easy to find, but they are not the only providers. Organizations such as the Public Broadcasting Service (PBS) and the National Aeronautics and Space Administration (NASA) in the United States and the British Broadcasting Corporation (BBC) in the United Kingdom have well-established presences in professional development.

PBS maintains TeacherLine, an online portal for teachers' professional development that offers online courses. Participants have the option to participate in courses covering a broad range of topic and content area choices, with options to earn continuing education credit, or graduate credit at selected universities. The courses are offered in various formats including self-directed options and are fee-based.

NASA's electronic Professional Development Network (ePDN) is an example of professional development offerings from a government agency. It is a partnership between NASA's Office of Education and the Georgia Institute of Technology. The ePDN offerings include science, technology, engineering, and mathematics (STEM)–related courses that follow either a facilitated or self-directed format. The courses are free. These well-structured course, or course-like, offerings are one type of professional development experience, but with growing online social networks, online tools, and services, it is possible to assemble your own collection of resources for professional development.

Informal Professional Development

Informal professional development refers to those experiences that an individual constructs, adapts, or chooses to participate in that are not offered specifically for the purpose of professional development. The number of opportunities to participate in informal professional development experiences has grown exponentially. This growth has come through the combination of nearly ubiquitous access to the Internet, increased ownership of Internet-capable devices, a wide array of online social networking services, and organization and curation tools.

Online services such as Twitter, Facebook, and Google+ enable an individual to subscribe to—known as *following*—any number of professional organizations, publications, news outlets, or other professionals as they desire. The sources followed will publish original information, make announcements, or share other resources deemed valuable to the professional community. It is possible to use any of these tools for personal, nonprofessional communication, but they allow a great deal of flexibility professionally because individuals are able to construct their own personal learning networks (PLNs). These tools allow an individual entry to a community of practice with the same trajectories described by Wenger, whereby members begin with establishing norms and collaborative relationships, develop a shared understanding of the profession, and finally produce shared resources available to each member of the community. For example, at the entry level, one might choose to simply be a consumer of the information available from his or her self-constructed PLN, observing practices, procedures, and learning terminology. Over time, one might move from only being a consumer of information shared in his or her PLN, to someone who understands the needs and fundamental beliefs of the community, and finally to someone who shares resources and contributes back to the professional community.

The success of one's PLN can be measured by the amount of useful information or professional networking that results from the PLN. Retaining and organizing the information harvested from a PLN presents a problem that must be solved so that the efforts of professional development experience can be retained and accessed in the future.

In addition to social networking options for professional development, a number of additional resources are available on the Internet, including websites, videos, audio files, blog posts, and more. A meaningful way to curate these assets is needed so that they can be preserved, recalled, and shared on demand.

Various tools exist for the curation of digital artifacts. An individual may choose to create his or her own ad hoc system of curation through a combination of computer-based tools or through computer programming expertise. There are, however, a growing number of online tools and services designed to let users manage collections of resources in personally meaningful ways. Tools such as Diigo, Evernote, and Pinterest, among others, allow users to save information about resources online, including websites and descriptions of the resources in searchable formats. Sites and services like this allow the user to categorize online resources into collections for specific purposes and may allow the ability to assign personally developed keywords for future reference. Some services, such as Evernote, provide options for digitizing resources such as photographs, audio, and documents that were not originally in a digital format, and to store them online. The development of a personal list of keywords for resources is often referred to as *tagging*. When a user *tags* a resource, the user is assigning one or more personally meaningful keywords or phrases to it so that it can be searched later, or shared with others for whom the resources and tags may be meaningful.

These organizational tools and services can be used for both formal and informal professional development. Through a simple choice of tags, it would be easy to filter a collection of resources into *formal* and *informal* experiences, if that distinction were needed.

Many tools and opportunities are available for individuals to assemble their own professional development experiences from resources intended for that purpose and from resources not specifically planned for that purpose. Whether designed as formal professional development experiences, or informal experiences, there is still a need for the creation of intentional professional development experiences. What is important in the design of these experiences?

Design and Development of Professional Development Experiences

There are many models and processes documented for the design of learning experiences. These generally fall under the heading of instructional systems design (ISD) processes. Designers of professional development should carefully study these processes and apply one that is congruent with the design team, the target learners, and the organization sponsoring the professional development. A complete description or review of ISD processes is beyond the scope of this entry, but a few suggestions for where ISD can assist designers are warranted. ISD will provide a structure for considering learner prerequisite knowledge, effective instructional strategies, technical details such as those related to the delivery mode, how learners will be assessed, and how the experience will be evaluated.

An important concept to be considered in the design and development of professional development experiences is accessibility. Accessibility in this sense refers to the degree to which the experience is designed and developed to maximize the number of individuals who can fully access and use the experience, regardless of disabilities or special needs. Often, the designers will not know who might be participating in their learning experiences, especially when they are designing and developing free and open resources. As such, it is necessary to use tools and best practices to create experiences that are accessible for groups such as those with visual or auditory impairments. In many instances, courses designed and developed for federal government or state government agencies must be developed with specified levels of accessibility.

In addition to accessibility concerns, developers must anticipate that their materials will be accessed from any one of an ever-changing list of devices. Anticipating the exact types of devices that users will apply to access materials online is not a realistic expectation, but designers and developers should anticipate that their products will be accessed from devices of varied screen size. Efforts should be taken to use development tools and practices that can easily accommodate the need to generate different versions of materials, or that can dynamically change the presentation of materials, to account for screen size.

The need for professional development will continue into the future, though how individuals participate in, or construct, their professional development experiences will continue to evolve. Some hints at changes in professional development are available by examining some emerging trends.

Looking Forward

Badging and massive open online courses (MOOCs) are trends that may prove to have significant effects on professional development. A badge is a digital token that represents that the bearer has demonstrated a skill or has completed an experience or project. Badges can be awarded by many entities, including individuals and professional organizations. Badges are in the early stages of development and acceptance, but some groups are experimenting with badges for teacher professional development. The HP Catalyst Academy is a collaboration between Hewlett-Packard, the International Society for Technology in Education, and the New Media Consortium that is offering free, online professional development for teachers in the STEM areas. Teachers who complete the Catalyst Academy experiences will be awarded badges indicating their various levels of completion. One issue under consideration regarding badging is who will serve as guarantor of badges. If badges gain acceptance, then they are likely to be an important aspect of professional development.

MOOCs are online courses delivered in formats that are supposed to be accessible by hundreds or thousands of students per offering. MOOCs are typically offered free of charge, without college credit, but some fee-based MOOC initiatives are in development that do include college credit. Many MOOCs operate outside of the college-credit model, so badging is commonplace with MOOCs. The combination of MOOCs and badging could have huge implications for professional development, if both of these trends prove that they can overcome the initial hurdles in their implementations and gain mass acceptance.

Charles B. Hodges

See also Distance Learning for Professional Development; Informal Learning Strategies; Integrated and Networked Mobile Devices for Learning and Instruction; Integrating Social Media Into Learning and Instruction; Personal Learning Environments

Further Readings

Duncan-Howell, J. (2010). Teachers making connections: Online communities as a source of professional learning. *British Journal of Educational Technology, 41*(2), 324–340.

Garet, M. F., Porter, A. C., Desimone, L., Birman, B. F., & Yoon, K. S. (2001). What makes professional development effective? Results from a national sample of teachers. *American Educational Research Journal, 38*(4), 915–945.

Guskey, T. R. (2000). *Evaluating professional development.* Thousand Oaks, CA: Corwin.

Loucks-Horsely, S., Stiles, K. E., Mundry, S., Love, N., & Hewson, P. W. (2010). *Designing professional development for teachers of science and mathematics* (3rd ed.). Thousand Oaks, CA: Corwin.

Wenger, E. (1998). *Communities of practice: Learning, meaning, and identity.* Cambridge, UK: Cambridge University Press.

PROGRAM EVALUATION

Program evaluation involves a systematic effort to report and explain what happened as a result of particular educational practices and instructional interventions. Introducing and integrating educational technologies is a situation involving a program or project that is typically evaluated to determine to what extent the effort succeeded. Critical questions that inform a program or project evaluation include the following:

- To what extent were the goals and objectives of the program or project achieved?
- Was the technology developed and deployed as planned?

- Was adequate preparation and training provided to those involved?
- Were the design, development, and deployment aimed at the problem(s) identified at the outset?

This entry provides an overview of program evaluation, stresses the significance of fidelity of implementation studies as they explain the findings in an impact study, presents a representative logic model, and describes formative and summative evaluation.

Definitions and Context

There are differences between programs and projects, both of which are covered in this entry. A typical educational technology project addresses a problem situation by introducing an intervention involving one or more technologies. A typical project has an overall goal and specific objectives; a project has a beginning (e.g., a problematic situation or a needs assessment) and an ending (e.g., a duration of months or a few years). A program shares many of the same attributes; however, a program is usually intended to continue and evolve, so the objectives are likely to change while the overall goal remains stable; moreover, the period associated with a program is longer than that associated with a project (e.g., years or decades); as a result, changes in the situation should be reviewed periodically. Projects sometimes result in the initiation of a program, so the two are closely related. Programs and projects typically change how tasks are performed, and, as a result, they may involve policies and procedures to guide practice and the use of new educational technologies.

Technology is the disciplined or systematic application of knowledge to solve a particular problem or achieve a goal of recognized benefit to a group or society. Educational technologies, then, involve the purposeful use of technology to achieve an educational goal. Examples include animated agents, design procedures and models, discussion forums, feedback mechanisms, intelligent tutors, interactive simulations, scaffolding to support learning, and so on.

Learning is characterized as stable and persisting changes in what an individual or group knows or is able to do (e.g., abilities, attitudes, beliefs, knowledge, skills, etc.). Instruction is typically defined as that which is designed to support or facilitate learning. Based on these common definitions, we can see that there are close connections between learning, instruction, and technology. Technology can support any of the activities normally associated with the design, development, or deployment of a learning environment or instructional system. Any aspect of the process of planning and implementing educational interventions is subject to evaluation, including a needs assessment as well as design and development processes. Evaluation, then, is not limited to just determining learning outcomes. Program evaluation is linked to the goals and objectives that motivated the effort and is essential for understanding the impact of projects and programs.

In conducting a program evaluation, the attempt is basically twofold: (1) to determine the extent to which the program or project met its goals, and (2) explain why that degree of success occurred. The former is usually accomplished through an impact study, and the latter is usually accomplished through a fidelity of implementation study. It is generally desirable to have a basis for assessing the progress achieved. This can be accomplished using a baseline study, a recognized benchmarking measure, comparison and control groups, analyses of significance and effect size, growth curve modelling, and so on. As such, evaluation studies represent an important kind of educational research and are frequently linked to research designs.

Impact and Fidelity of Implementation Studies

Despite more than 50 years of intensive empirical research, little evidence suggests that many educational technology interventions have significantly affected learning. A partial explanation for this discouraging finding is linked to inadequate evaluation research conducted on technology-based educational interventions. There has been a tendency to examine superficial indicators of impact without examining the nature and details of how the intervention was designed, developed, and implemented. Program and project evaluations have been summative in nature, focusing on three indicators of success: (1) Did the effort stay within budget? (2) Did the effort occur on schedule? and (3) Did the effort achieve intended outcomes? Such evaluations do not provide information or insight that could improve the effort while it is underway or explain the outcomes when it is completed. A summative evaluation only looks at learning outcomes when the effort is completed (and sometimes before its initiation). The analysis of the before and after research data often indicates that there is little impact on learning, although other summative indicators (on-time, within-budget) may reflect success.

In summary, a summative evaluation, though important, is not adequate and serves little real purpose without the support of a formative evaluation that examines how the effort is being implemented and offers feedback to project or program leaders with regard to improving the likelihood of success. Because project and program evaluation are aimed at the entire life of the effort, it is important to determine progress frequently and suggest

areas of strengths and weaknesses (i.e., perform ongoing formative evaluations). Formative evaluation is an evaluation that is intended to improve an intervention as it is being designed, developed, and deployed. In summary, a comprehensive program or project evaluation includes both formative and summative evaluation.

A formative evaluation is often cast as a fidelity of implementation study and is aimed at the activities associated with the intervention and the immediate results of those activities (the inputs column in a logic model, as seen in Figures 1 and 2). A summative evaluation is often cast as an impact study and is aimed at the program's or project's overall objectives, which are often learning outcomes (the outcomes column in a logic model, as seen in Figures 1 and 2). The primary goal of a comprehensive evaluation is to help ensure the success of the effort (formative evaluation); the secondary goal of a comprehensive evaluation is to report the extent to which the effort was successful and offer an explanation of that success (summative evaluation). The second part of the summative evaluation (an explanation of the degree of success) cannot be performed in the absence of a formative evaluation.

In many cases, there will be both internal and external examiners. The larger the effort, the more likely it is to have external evaluators involved. For example, many large National Science Foundation (NSF) and Institute of Education Sciences (IES) projects require an external examiner, as do most European Commission projects. When both internal and external examiners are involved, an internal evaluator sometimes focuses only on formative evaluation, while an external evaluator focuses only on summative evaluation. Sometimes, both kinds of evaluators focus on both kinds of evaluation, which might be considered the ideal practice when resources allow such an arrangement.

What distinguishes an internal evaluator from an external evaluator is not necessarily the source of funding for the evaluation; rather, the distinguishing factor is to whom the evaluator reports and is responsible. For example, on some European projects, external evaluators are paid by the commission and report to the commission and perform both formative and summative evaluations. On some NSF and IES projects in the United States, however, external evaluators are paid by the project but report to the funding agency (NSF or IES).

Logic Models

By way of summary, when conducting applied educational research, one may have a new technology that one believes will achieve desired outcomes. This situation is a prime target for evaluation as well as research. The questions of concern in a program evaluation are

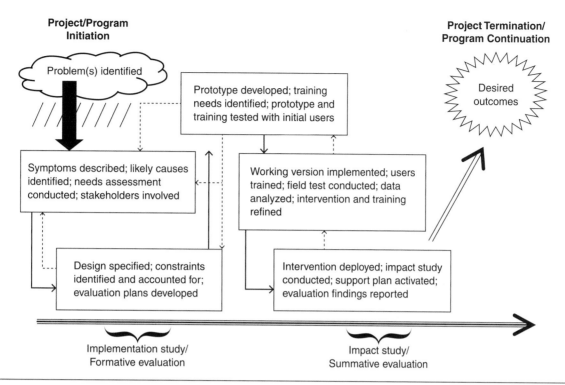

Figure 1   Implementation and impact studies

whether and to what extent an intervention (e.g., an innovative technology, a new learning environment, or a revised instructional system) achieves its intended aims, and why it succeeded or fell short in some way. As previously indicated, there are two kinds of studies associated with a program evaluation: a fidelity of implementation study (formative evaluation), and an impact study (summative evaluation) (see Figure 1). A logic model is used to explain the differences in these two kinds of research and evaluation studies and to show how what is being designed, developed, and deployed links the problem situation and desired outcomes together (see Figure 2). A logic model is a visual representation of (a) a problematic situation and the associated underlying problem, (b) implementation of an intervention intended to resolve the problematic situation, and (c) the desired outcomes and benefits of the intervention if it is successful. A theory of change (based on established theory, empirical research, best practices, and prior experience) explains why and how the intervention will lead from the problematic situation to the desired outcomes; the logic model is a representation of this theory of change (see Figure 2). The fidelity of implementation study is structured so that the results of various design, development, and deployment efforts are likely to explain the degree of success (as in high, medium, low, or superior, adequate, or marginal, and typically focusing on such variables as professional

development and technology support). Having these data is useful in explaining why and to what extent the effort was successful.

The problem description is important because that is the outcome of an analysis such as a needs assessment. Documenting the problem situation is an important step in a program evaluation. The desired outcomes of the effort should be directly linked to the goals and objectives that result from an analysis of the problem situation. The responsibility of program evaluation goes well beyond reporting outcomes and how resources were used. Program and project evaluation starts with an analysis of the problem situation. Who was involved in identifying needs and the likely underlying causes of the problem? Which stakeholders were involved? How and why were they selected? Did a divergence or convergence of views develop when analyzing the problem situation? Were the methods and instruments used to collect and analyze data reliable? If the problem identification process is incomplete or inadequate, then it is unlikely that subsequent implementation efforts will lead to the desired outcomes. Evaluators should examine all aspects of the program or project as it evolves, including early analysis and planning phases, to give meaningful formative feedback that will help the program or project succeed.

Most technology implementation efforts involve training users. Therefore, evaluators must observe and

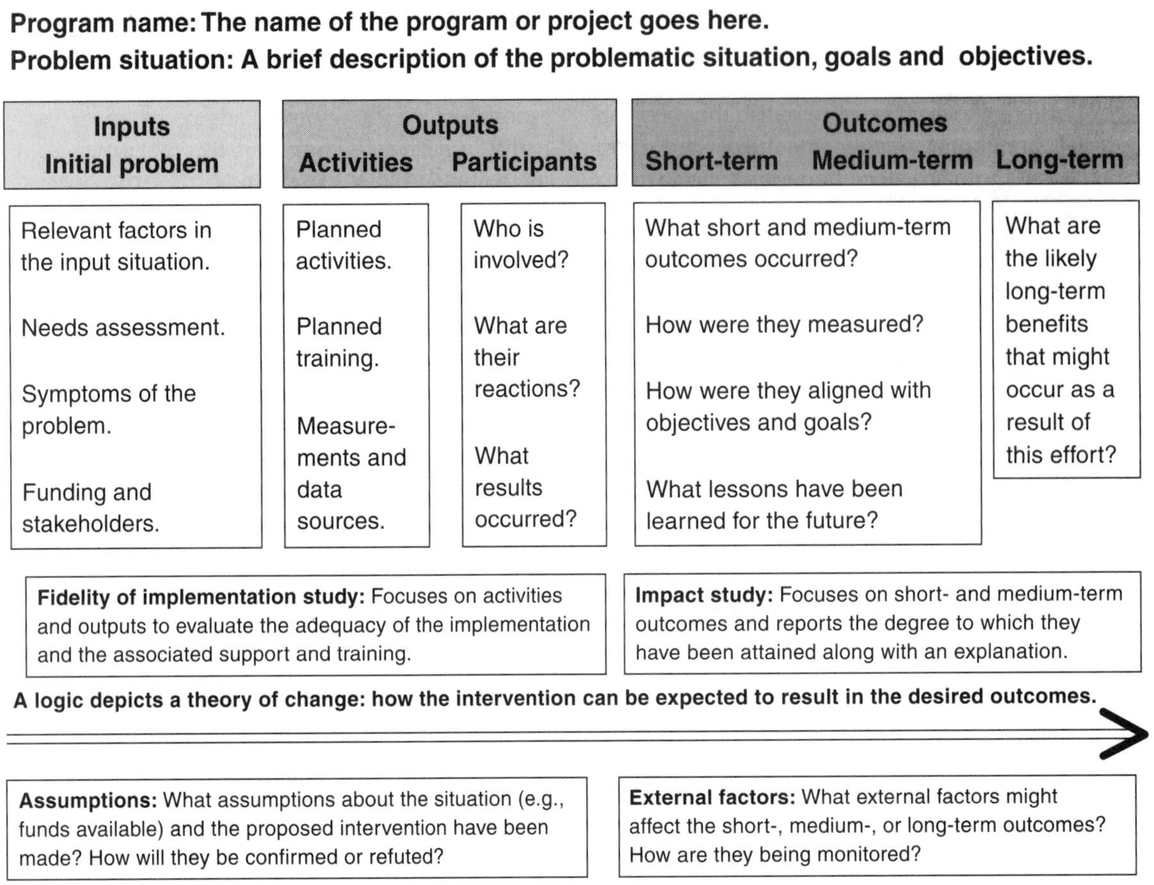

Program name: The name of the program or project goes here.

Problem situation: A brief description of the problematic situation, goals and objectives.

Inputs Initial problem	Outputs Activities Participants		Outcomes Short-term Medium-term Long-term	
Relevant factors in the input situation. Needs assessment. Symptoms of the problem. Funding and stakeholders.	Planned activities. Planned training. Measurements and data sources.	Who is involved? What are their reactions? What results occurred?	What short and medium-term outcomes occurred? How were they measured? How were they aligned with objectives and goals? What lessons have been learned for the future?	What are the likely long-term benefits that might occur as a result of this effort?

Fidelity of implementation study: Focuses on activities and outputs to evaluate the adequacy of the implementation and the associated support and training.

Impact study: Focuses on short- and medium-term outcomes and reports the degree to which they have been attained along with an explanation.

A logic depicts a theory of change: how the intervention can be expected to result in the desired outcomes.

Assumptions: What assumptions about the situation (e.g., funds available) and the proposed intervention have been made? How will they be confirmed or refuted?

External factors: What external factors might affect the short-, medium-, or long-term outcomes? How are they being monitored?

Figure 2   A logic model template

report the outcomes of training plans (how they were developed; how they were pilot tested) and actual training (who was involved, for how long, and with what results). Poor training often results in poor outcomes even when the technology involved is quite promising. Planning for change that inevitably results from an innovation or intervention and properly preparing users are critical for success. Program evaluators have a responsibility to report shortcomings and potential problem areas as the program evolves to avoid wasteful efforts. As stated earlier, a primary obligation of evaluators is to alert the implementation team and management of anything that might jeopardize the success of the effort. However obvious this may seem, it is somewhat rare to find a project or program that involves evaluators throughout the process in this way.

Evaluation and Research

An evaluation effort represents one kind of applied research; when an explanation is developed to explain what happened (or failed to happen), there is a need to have both quantitative data (typically associated with an impact study) along with qualitative data (often part of a fidelity of implementation study). Evaluation studies are typically mixed methods applied to research studies. Evaluators typically make use of the same tools and methods one generally finds in educational research. One difference pertains to the focus. Evaluation is focused on decisions made (and the consequences of those decisions) during the design, development, and deployment of an intervention with the aim of helping improve the effort so as to produce desired outcomes. Other forms of educational research are typically focused on answering questions that contribute to a body of knowledge or the development of theories to explain a range of phenomena (i.e., they have a more generalized focus). As one would expect, program and project evaluations often inform research about learning and instructional phenomena, so the distinction between educational technology program evaluation and educational technology research is fuzzy.

J. Michael Spector

See also Evaluation Research; Formative Assessment; Summative Assessment

Further Readings

Cronback, L. J. (1989). *Designing evaluations for educational and social programs.* San Francisco, CA: Jossey-Bass.

Louw, J. (1999). Improving practice through evaluation. In D. Donald, A. Dawes, & J. Louw (Eds.), *Addressing childhood adversity* (pp. 66–73). Cape Town, South Africa: David Phillip.

Potter, C. (2006). Program evaluation. In M. Terre Blance, K. Durrheim, & D. Painter (Eds.), *Research in practice: Applied methods for the social sciences* (2nd ed., pp. 410–428). Cape Town, South Africa: UCT Press.

Rao, V., & Woolcock, M. (2003). Integrating qualitative and quantitative approaches in program evaluation. In F. Bourguignon & L. Pereira da Silva (Eds.), *The impact of economic policies on poverty and income distribution: Evaluation techniques and tools* (pp. 165–190). Oxford, UK: Oxford University Press.

Rossi, P., Lipsey, M. W., & Freeman, H. E. (2004). *Evaluation: A systematic approach* (7th ed.). Thousand Oaks, CA: Sage.

Scriven, M. (1994). The fine line between evaluation and explanation. *Evaluation Practice, 15,* 75–77.

Spector, J. M. (2012). *Foundations of educational technology: Integrative approaches and interdisciplinary perspectives.* New York, NY: Routledge.

Spector, J. M. (2013). Program and project evaluation. In J. M. Spector, M. D. Merrill, J. Elen, & M. J. Bishop (Eds.), *Handbook of research on educational communications and technology* (4th ed., pp. 195–201). New York, NY: Routledge.

Suchman, E. A. (1967). *Evaluation research: Principles and practice in public service and social action programs.* New York, NY: Russell Sage.

Suppes, P. (1978). *Impact of research on education: Some case studies.* Washington, DC: National Academy of Education.

QUALITATIVE RESEARCH TOOLS FOR EDUCATIONAL TECHNOLOGY RESEARCH

Qualitative research tools (QRTs) used for educational technology research provide a robust set of techniques, strategies, and technologies for exploring what, why, and how. QRTs also provide rich descriptions of who, when, and where so that educational technologists gain a deeper understanding of the phenomena being studied. Techniques and strategies range from specific methods for data collection to strategies for data analysis and presentation. QRTs also use a broad range of technologies to address these core questions, from various tools enabling data capture to software for data organization and analysis. Understanding the best techniques, strategies, and technologies to use for a particular qualitative study is important for educational technology researchers so they can provide the most robust recommendations to inform design, development, and practice. This entry provides an overview of qualitative research, followed by a description of some of the major approaches to qualitative research. The entry concludes with an elaboration of the techniques, strategies, and technologies for conducting qualitative studies in educational technology.

What Is Qualitative Research, and Why Do We Need It in Educational Technology?

Educational technology research is deeply rooted in experimental and quasi-experimental studies. For the first few decades of research, the focus was on studying environments where control groups could be created, interventions could be implemented, and hypotheses tested. These types of studies dominated the field for many years and assisted educational technology researchers with improving the practices of the field.

Then, in the 1980s and 1990s, other types of studies started to appear in the mainstream research literature. In these studies, researchers sought to gain a more in-depth understanding of what was happening in educational environments from the perspective of those participating in the context. Techniques such as interviewing and observing started to appear more frequently as educational technology researchers sought to understand and build meaning in situ. Qualitative research, an approach that enables an in-depth exploration and study of people and phenomena in natural, real-world settings, came into its own in educational technology research.

Table 1 provides an overview of the key differences between qualitative and quantitative research.

As illustrated in Table 1, qualitative and quantitative research have key differences that can help the researcher determine the best approach depending on the goals and types of questions being asked in a study. Next we turn to some of the most common paradigms that guide qualitative research.

Paradigms for Qualitative Research

Fields of study are guided by paradigms and theories; qualitative research is no different. As indicated by Norm Denzin and Yvonne Lincoln, the list of paradigms is extensive, ranging from positivist to queer theory. Denzin and Lincoln, pioneers in the qualitative research field, indicate that four major paradigms provide structure for qualitative research: critical theory, feminist-poststructural, positivist/postpositivist, and constructivist-interpretive. The last two are described in

599

Table I   Key differences between qualitative and quantitative research

Research Characteristic	Qualitative Research	Quantitative Research
Overarching Purpose	Exploratory Discovery Understand in-depth	Hypotheses testing Causation Understand specifics
Goals	Interpret Understand Open to what comes	Test Measure Focal point
Researcher Roles	Closely involved Researcher as instrument	As little involvement as possible Researcher removed
Questions	Can change during study Questions often begin with What, How, Why	Set from the beginning Questions often begin with Do, When does
Data Collection Methods	Semi to unstructured Changeable as needed	Structured Established protocols
People Involved	Participants Typically small number	Subjects Large number
Results	Context specific Rich and robust details	Generalizable Focused and succinct

more detail because they have had the most influence on educational technology research.

Positivist/Postpositivist

The positivist/postpositivist paradigm focuses on a realist perspective with a leaning toward objectivity. A belief in "one reality" is often associated with this paradigm. Survey methods are often used by researchers following this paradigm, as are highly structured and systematic qualitative methods. Internal and external validity, along with reliability, are the primary criteria used for evaluating the veracity of the findings. Reports of a more scientific nature often result from studies following this paradigm. The positivist/postpositivist paradigm is perhaps the one that has received the most use in educational technology research because it is the next step away from the more traditional quantitative studies conducted in the field.

Constructivist-Interpretive

The constructivist-interpretive paradigm is in many ways on the opposite end of the continuum from the positivist/postpositivist paradigm. The constructivist-interpretive focus is on a relativist perspective with a belief in multiple realities. More naturalistic methods are used (e.g., interviews and observations) as the researcher and participant co-construct understanding. Evaluation of veracity of the research is based on

trustworthiness, credibility, confirmability, and transferability. Case studies are one primary way to represent the findings. This paradigm has also received attention in educational technology research particularly as researchers have sought to gain an in-depth understanding of a particular context (e.g., classroom, organization).

Techniques and Strategies for Qualitative Research

Many techniques and strategies are used in qualitative research to assist the researcher with developing understanding. Three areas are explored in this entry: (1) methods for data collection, (2) strategies for data analysis, and (3) strategies for data presentation.

Methods for Data Collection

As in all research, data collection methods in qualitative research are driven by the goals and questions posed for the overall study. Many methods can be used; three primary methods are discussed: (1) interviews/group interviews/focus groups, (2) observations, and (3) analysis of documents.

Interviews/Group Interviews/Focus Groups

Interviews, conducted individually or in groups, or focus groups (a specific methodology for group interviews) are primary methods used when the researcher is focused on getting the "story" from those involved in the phenomena being studied. Interviews can take place one-on-one with the researcher and participant. Group interviews and focus groups are created when the researcher talks with several participants at the same time. In each instance, a primary goal, as described by Irving Seidman, is to understand the experience of other people and the meaning *they* make of that experience.

The many advantages to using interviews in qualitative research include access to firsthand reconstruction of events and the depth of information gathered. There are also challenges associated with interviews/focus groups: gaining access, time commitment for the researcher and participants, and the time needed for the researcher to develop robust interviewing skills. That said, few methods enable the researcher to get more direct interaction with the participants.

Observations

Observations are also frequently used in qualitative research. Observation strategies range from more distanced and nonparticipatory observations to more intimate and fully participatory observations. Like surveys, a primary goal of observations is to understand the experience of other people; unlike surveys, observations seek to gain "in the moment" access as the experience is unfolding.

This latter goal is perhaps one of the greatest advantages of observations: They enable the researcher to see the experience as it is "lived" by others. There are challenges associated with doing observations; gaining access, the time commitment for the research and participants, and the honing of observations skills by the researcher among them. Particular challenges arise when the researcher is also a participant, perhaps most notably the researcher's ability to be both in and outside the experience at the same time. Similarly to interviews, the "in the moment" access that observations afford often outweighs the challenges.

Analysis of Documents

Documents, artifacts, and records (*documents* is used in this section to represent all three) are a rich source of information for qualitative researchers. Documents have not historically received a lot of attention by educational technology researchers seeking to do qualitative research, although that has changed, particularly in the last 15 to 20 years as researchers have turned to various Internet applications as a source of data (e.g., chat groups, online classes). A primary goal of using documents as data is to reconstruct what happened through artifacts created for or as a result of the event(s). Unlike interviews, documents are not a reconstruction of past events; instead, they serve as records of what was.

There are several advantages for using documents in qualitative research, including that they provide a record of past events and, often, easier access to this form of data, particularly in comparison to interviews and observations. Challenges include finding the documents and confirming the authenticity of the documents. Documents beyond those generated by chat groups or online classes may receive more attention by educational technology researchers as documents are increasingly available in electronic formats. Although electronic formats make finding the documents easier, this can make confirming authenticity even more challenging.

Strategies for Data Analysis

Once the data are collected, analysis begins. This is one perspective on how the analysis process occurs; another is that analysis starts as soon as data collection begins—and continues until all data are collected. Which path is taken is a decision for each qualitative researcher to make; the strategies used on either path are similar, starting with reading through the data (e.g., interview transcripts, observation field notes, documents). As the researcher reads through the data, taking notes or creating memos is recommended so that initial ideas about patterns and themes are captured.

After reading through the data, the researcher has several options for proceeding to the next level of data analysis. Joseph Maxwell provides a succinct overview of three primary approaches: (1) memos, (2) categorization, and (3) connections. Each is briefly described here.

Memos

Memos, or notes taken during the reading and rereading of the data, are an important analytic technique. Memos can capture insights related to the data; they also can help to stimulate further thinking about the data. Although the memos themselves become another source of data that need to be analyzed (e.g., through categorization), their value can often outweigh the development of additional data.

Categorization

This is the most frequently described analytic technique for qualitative data. Categorization involves searching for instances in the data that are similar and assigning a code to these instances so they can later be organized into larger patterns and themes. Constant comparison of the data is also often used to refine and revise codes, patterns, and themes as the data analysis process continues.

Connections

One of the criticisms often raised about categorization as a strategy for data analysis is that it fragments the data. Connecting strategies seek to keep the data in context so that relationships across aspects of the data can be identified. Rather than looking for similarities for coding, connecting strategies (e.g., narrative analysis) seeks to look at how pieces fit together to create the whole.

Strategies for Data Presentation

The presentation of qualitative data can take many forms, depending on the underlying paradigm of the study, goals, and research questions. Laura Ellingson provides a rich description of a continuum of representation of qualitative data. Two areas are explored in more detail in this entry because they are most relevant to educational technology research: (1) data presentation from more of a positivist/postpositivist paradigm and (2) data presentation from more of a constructivist-intrepretivist paradigm.

Data Presentation From a Positivist/Postpositivist Paradigm

The presentation of data in this paradigm frequently results in tables and charts as ways to summarize the data. The use of a "third person" voice may be common because the researcher is more distant from the results. Given the distancing of the researcher, the processes used to minimize bias are often highlighted, with more focus on the objectivity brought to the data analysis and presentation.

Data Presentation From a Constructivist-Intrepretivist Paradigm

The presentation of data in this paradigm often results in a more narrative representation, with reports of the participants' voices in thick, rich descriptions. First person is more common because the researcher's involvement in the research process is one of closer engagement. The subjectivity or standpoint of the researcher is an important consideration as his or her interpretation is highlighted.

Technologies for Qualitative Research

Many technologies, hard and soft, are used in qualitative research to assist the researcher with the overall process. Two areas are explored in this section: (1) tools for data capture and (2) software for data organization and analysis.

Tools for Data Capture

Many tools are used by qualitative researchers to capture data from interviews, observations, and documents. During the interview process, researchers may use audio or video recorders to capture their conversations with participants. The choice of which tool is best will depend on what is needed for the study; for example, if facial expressions and body language will assist the researcher in developing understanding, a video recording may be an important data source. The type of recorder, the need for an external microphone, and backup recording devices are all important considerations.

Observations may also be captured using video recording. Decisions such as having a still camera or walking around with the camera are important considerations. If the researcher is going to be in the same environment over time, more permanent video capturing equipment may be used. In contrast to the more sophisticated technologies, the researcher may choose to capture observations using pen and paper (or computer) with a protocol document to guide the observations.

Tools for capturing documents will vary depending on the document. Some documents will be in electronic format enabling easy access. Other documents may need to be copied, if that is an option; extensive notes may need to be made for documents where copies are not an option. Like an observation protocol, extensive protocols have been developed by organizations such as the Smithsonian Institution to assist with recording information about documents.

Regardless of the tool used—digital recorder, microphone, and so on—it is very important to check all equipment before use. Batteries can suddenly run out; microphones may not be connected properly. It is also recommended to have two devices for capturing interviews, video, and so on. This can eliminate considerable frustration should something happen to one of the technologies during data capture.

Software for Data Organization and Analysis

Qualitative data analysis software (QDAS) has its roots in the 1970s and 1980s as databases and word processors were developed for more day-to-day use. As Silvana de Gregorio and Judith Davidson describe in their detailed account of qualitative research and technology, the release of QDAS NUD*IST (non-numerical unstructured data indexing, searching, and theorizing, now called NVivo) and Ethnograph in the early 1980s brought the use of software for data organization and analysis to the fore for qualitative researchers. It also brought with it questions by qualitative researchers regarding whether to use or not use the tools, with researchers making individual decisions depending on preferences and resources.

Since then, many other software tools have been developed (e.g., HyperRESEARCH, MaxQDA) as well as the repurposing of other traditional productivity tools (e.g., word processing software, concept mapping software) for the organization and analysis of qualitative data. Most recently, Web 2.0 tools have greatly extended the resources available to qualitative researchers for data organization and analysis. For example, the ability to tag, blog, and share via wikis has opened a new era in QDAS that is beginning to be explored. The ease of access anywhere anytime is certainly one benefit of Web 2.0 tools; another is that teams of researchers can readily access the same data and update in real-time through tools such as Google Docs.

Implications of Qualitative Research Tools for Educational Technology

Qualitative research tools provide educational technology researchers with a robust set of options for conducting qualitative research. As the field continues to expand the paradigms and perspectives from which we view the world, the tools will also expand, enabling yet unknown understandings to unfold and new practices in educational technology to manifest.

Janette R. Hill

See also Case Study Research in Educational Technology; Design and Development Research; Design-Based Research; Evaluation Research; Experimental Research and Educational Technology; Instructional Design Research; Research in Schools

Further Readings

de Gregorio, S., & Davidson, J. (2009). *Qualitative research design for software users*. Maidenhead, Berkshire, UK: Open University.

Denzin, N. K., & Lincoln, Y. S. (Eds.). (2011). *The SAGE handbook of qualitative research*. Thousand Oaks, CA: Sage.

Ellingson, L. L. (2011). Analysis and representation across the curriculum. In N. K. Denzin & Y. S. Lincoln (Eds.), *The SAGE handbook of qualitative research* (pp. 595–610). Thousand Oaks, CA: Sage.

Maxwell, J. A. (2013). *Qualitative research design: An interactive approach* (3rd ed.). Thousand Oaks, CA: Sage.

Rapley, T. (2011). *Doing conversation, discourse and document analysis*. Thousand Oaks, CA: Sage.

Seidman, I. (2013). *Interviewing as qualitative research* (4th ed.). New York, NY: Teachers College Press.

Wolcott, H. F. (2001). *Writing up qualitative research* (2nd ed.). Thousand Oaks, CA: Sage.

Websites

QSR International, NVivo (software): http://www.qsrinternational.com/default.aspx

Qualis Research, Ethnograph (software): http://www.qualisresearch.com

Research Ware, HyperRESEARCH (software): http://www.researchware.com/products/hyperresearch.html

VERBI GmbH, MaxQDA (software): http://www.maxqda.com

Radio Frequency Identification in Education

Radio frequency identification (RFID) is the wireless recognition of, and communication with, uniquely identified electronic devices. RFID devices are commonly used in cell phones, car keys, building access systems, passports, and identification cards. This entry discusses how RFID works, its use in education, and controversy over RFID use and the privacy concerns it can raise.

Basic Technology

Each RFID device has its own identifier code, allowing it to *tag* a specific item or individual, so the devices themselves are commonly called *tags*. RFID codes are item specific, rather than universal product codes (UPCs) that only identify specific classes of items. While many identical products will have the same UPC, the code for each RFID tag is unique. The most common RFID identifier codes are International Mobile Equipment Identity (IMEI) and Media Access Control address (MAC). RFID devices are identified by *interrogators* or *readers* connected to RFID information processing systems.

RFID tags may be active or passive depending on whether they have their own power source. Passive RFID tags may be microscopic and may be embedded in credit cards, identification cards, or printed documents. Passive RFID tags are activated by electromagnetic induction when they pass through a magnetic field, called a *read field*, generated by the reader. Read fields may be three-dimensional, allowing them to record the bearer of an RFID tag as present when it passes through the read field in one direction and as absent when it passes through it again in another direction. Read fields for passive tags can range from 1 foot to more than 30 feet across, whereas self-powered RFID devices, such as satellite phones, have practically no distance limits. Physical spaces can be divided into *virtual rooms* to promote group learning projects, or serial learning, where students complete tasks in one area before moving on to another. With current technology, RFID readers for passive devices can identify as many as 1,500 tags per second.

The radio waves used by RFID systems can pass through most materials. The tags can also be hardened or encased in plastic so they won't be affected by moisture or most physical shocks.

Use in Education

The first uses of RFID systems in education were for identification and access cards used in lieu of keys or of cards with magnetic stripes. These systems are also used for tracking attendance of students in classrooms and laboratories. Passive RFID tags can track each student's arrival and departure times.

Inexpensive wireless keypads, or *clickers*, use embedded RFID tags that can be assigned to individual students. In a classroom setting, students can use clickers or other RFID communication devices to respond to questions asked by an instructor or projected onto a screen. The RFID information processing system can automatically analyze responses and present the aggregated statistics to the class as numbers or percentages, or it can grade and record scores of quizzes presented in this way. Larger clickers may include alphanumeric keypads that students can use to write text messages, or touch screens for drawing graphics. RFID-tagged devices can also be used to record student attendance at museum exhibitions, seminars, or other activities if these locations are equipped with RFID readers.

RFID and Individualized Learning and Assessment Methodologies

RFID devices and their integrated information systems can track the locations of individual students, and more importantly, they can analyze and record students' educational progress and other relevant information. Because of this, RFID-based learning assessment systems (RLASs) can be used to customize learning and assessment methodologies based on the needs and capabilities of the individual student. Students can be offered asynchronous classes, rather than classes where all students are taught at the same speed and assessed at the same times. Although the learning objectives may be the same for all students, individuals can choose different routes for achieving those objectives based on their own learning styles, skill sets, and previous knowledge. Group assessments must present the same questions or challenges to all students, so they are generally limited to only assessing basic capabilities. With RLAS, students can be provided feedback and additional learning resources based on their individual assessment responses. They can later be reassessed for knowledge or capabilities they lacked in earlier attempts, but not be reassessed for areas where they have already shown their mastery. This can allow learning and assessment activities to be integrated, resulting in improved teaching efficacy and assessment accuracy.

RFID systems, including RLAS, can allow students to achieve the successful attainment of all learning objectives, rather than just a required percentage of them. These systems can make the educational experience more interesting because its progression can be tailored to, and determined by, the individual student. Finally, the use of RLAS can decrease the motivation for cheating that results from assessments where outcomes are only recorded as points or percentages. When students perceive assessments as means for discovering their own weaknesses and for being guided toward resources to overcome those weaknesses, they are more likely to see assessments as valuable tools for achieving their goals rather than just as hurdles or barriers.

Advanced Tracking and Adaptive Response Systems

Tracking technologies are evolving rapidly. New devices track location and movement, acceleration, change in elevation, and rotation. When paired with Global Positioning System (GPS) devices and given adaptive communication capabilities (e.g., automatic switching between cellular, Wi-Fi, and Bluetooth) they can automatically adjust their functionality. For example, the M7 motion coprocessor chip in the Apple iPhone 5s can communicate via cellular networks when moving faster than 5 miles per hour, then switch to Wi-Fi networks when movement is less than that. Wi-Fi networks will provide different information than cellular does. If Bluetooth signals are detected, the device can attempt to pair with them. A student, given an assignment to visit an art exhibit on the second floor of a particular museum, might first receive driving or riding information (e.g., "Turn left on Austin Street, go three blocks and park or exit the bus."), then Wi-Fi ("The museum entrance is 50 feet ahead. Once you enter, take the elevator on your left."), the Bluetooth information ("The large sculpture near the door is . . ."). At the completion of the tour, perhaps after attending a required lecture at the museum, the tracking device can report the student's progress and provide directions for other assignments or opportunities.

Incidentally, random challenges at identification by a system such as Apple's Touch ID fingerprint identification system can prevent a lazy student from asking a friend to carry his RFID tracker with her.

Virtual Worlds, Role-Playing, and Avatars

Role-playing within simulated virtual worlds is a growing area of educational activity. A college student studying education might be assigned to play different characters in a virtual classroom (i.e., young or old teacher, male or female student, minority or handicapped student). The simulated classroom could be populated with the avatars of other education majors, who are wirelessly controlling movement and gestures, as well as speaking to each other in the virtual classroom. Avatars in other simulations might be police, firefighters, psychologists, surgeons, accountants, or business majors. In each case, the wireless tracking devices allow students to adopt avatars, enter and interact with the simulation and with other avatars, while assessing each student's performance as well as providing real-time feedback and suggestions.

Controversy

The basic strengths of RFID systems—the abilities to locate, track, and record information on individuals—have also been controversial, particularly because of concerns over privacy. Many people are wary of technologies that allow their locations to be tracked and their personal information to be recorded by others.

These fears have been amplified by popular media, such as films showing people being chased by adversaries able to track the locations of their automobiles, cell phones, and credit cards. Such fears are not unfounded. Hackers have been able to steal personal information from cell phones and computing devices. In 2013, the National Security Agency (NSA) confirmed that it conducted a test project to track the locations of Americans' cell phones. The development of adequate security technologies and privacy restrictions will be an important element in the development of RFID and RLAS systems. Perhaps the basic question is the extent to which individuals are able to effectively control which information about them is tracked, and who has access to the information collected. Clearly, however, the adoption of RFID tracking and analysis devices in educational environments can provide profound benefits.

Sherwood Bishop

See also Remote Sensing Technologies

Further Readings

Cooney, E. (2007). *The complete review of radio frequency identification* (1st ed.) Independence, KY: Cengage Learning.

Drona, V., Drona, S., Rusell, C., & Tabrizi, M. H. N. (2009). RFID-based learning assessment system. *WSEAS Transactions on Computers, 6*(8), 1109–2750.

Faas, R. (2013). *The M7 coprocessor in the iPhone 5s is a big deal.* Retrieved from http://www.computerworld.com

Lehlou, N. Buyurgan, N., & Chimka, J. R. (2009). An online RFID laboratory learning environment. *IEEE Transactions on Learning Technologies, 2*(4), 295–303.

Liang, Y., & Qiang, J. X. (2012). The design and implementation of interactive response system based on RFID and MAS technology. *Applied Mechanics and Materials, 182,* 716–720.

Nava, S. W., Chavira, G., Hervás, R., Villarreal, V., & Bravo, J. (2008). Towards simple interaction in the classroom: An NFC approach. In *Proceedings of the IADIS International Conference on eLearning* (pp. 279–286). Amsterdam, Netherlands: IADIS.

Savage, C. (2013, October). In test project, N.S.A. tracked cellphone locations. *New York Times.* Retrieved from http://www.nytimes.com/2013/10/03/us/nsa-experiment-traced-us-cellphone-locations.html

RECOMMENDATION ENGINES

Recommendation engines are specially designed systems that collect and store information (data) about a person that can be subjected to filtering and statistical analysis (analytics) to make recommendations about actions the individual could take or resources the individual could explore. For example, asking a person to name his or her three favorite musical groups provides a glimpse of the individual's taste in music. When this information is merged with other known information such as the person's age and address, a statistical profile can be generated to compare the individual's musical interests with millions of other people to make suggestions about other musical groups the individual might enjoy. Recommendation engines are one component of a larger trend known as *personalization technologies* that seek to use large data sets to improve the user experience by making recommendations.

Recommendation engines are generally proprietary because of (a) the unique data sets (i.e., customers, subscribers, credit records) that form the base of the system, (b) specially designed algorithms that are tested and refined by mining the data for statistically significant relationships, and (c) the way in which the system is designed to present customized recommendations to users. Recommendation engines have been implemented in a variety of 21st-century applications for the general public including personalized radio, book purchasing suggestions, and movie watching recommendations. Commercial interest in recommendation engines is driven by a desire to mine customer data to reveal behavioral dispositions that can be managed in ways that stimulate increased sales. Whereas technology users may readily appreciate the value of a recommendation engine for its efficiency in discovery, it is not always clear how a specific recommendation system works or how to correct or modify misguided recommendations. Experts believe that recommendation engines will be widely implemented in education as a means of personalizing the learning experience in ways that optimizes the quality of a learner's experience and improves educational outcomes. Before discussing the implications of recommendation engines for learning, this entry describes how these engines are used in daily life and how they work.

Recommendation Engines in Daily Life

In the early 21st century, the average citizen's encounter with a recommendation engine is likely to have occurred in one of three contexts. First, when an individual orders a book from the online retailer Amazon, the system provides a list of other book titles that might be of interest. This list of book recommendations is culled from the purchase history of other customers who purchased the same book. The assumption is that the purchases of other people with similar interests might also be relevant and result in additional purchases. Over time, the depth of data accumulated in the system, and the ongoing revision of the algorithms, has allowed the Amazon recommendation system to become more knowledgeable about the most desirable books on a topic (assuming volume of sales are an adequate metric of quality) than a typical human bookseller.

A second application of a recommendation engine is Pandora Internet Radio. This music recommendation engine is built on the Music Genome Project that began in 2000. The database at the core of the recommendation system was based on the work of experts in music theory who listen to and analyze contemporary songs. For each song, the experts coded 400 attributes such as composer/group, genre, rhythm, harmony, and lyrics. Users begin by selecting a favorite song or musical group (known as the *seed*) that becomes the basis of a personal radio station. Pandora populates the radio station by mining the database to play songs that have characteristics similar to those of the seed. The prediction algorithm is refined by allowing the user to use a thumbs-up or thumbs-down rating for each song, to adjust the algorithm accordingly in the pursuit of creating the perfect radio station.

Netflix, a media-streaming service, is another example of a recommendation engine that has affected the daily lives of many. Movies offer a rich context for metatagging such as actors, director, genre, topic, and more. Each of these tags offers a way to search for movies. The system maintains a history of all the movies each user has watched and allows users to assign a 1- to 5-star ranking to the movie. When Netflix recognized the implications of the shift in their core business from renting physical DVD copies of movies to streaming movies online, they also understood the value of transforming their movie recommendations to grow their customer base. This insight resulted in their sponsorship of a contest that began in October 2006, known as the Netflix Prize. The prize was $1,000,000 that would be awarded to the individual or team that could create a 10% improvement in the Netflix Cinematch recommendation system. Contestants were provided with a sample data set of more than 100 million 1- to 5-star ratings on nearly 18,000 movie titles from more than 480,000 randomly selected anonymous customers. On July 26, 2009, Netflix announced that the grand prize had been won by the BellKor's Pragmatic Chaos team with a verified 10.06% improvement in the Cinematch system. Technical details of the winning solution are publicly available on the Netflix Prize website.

Despite the increasingly routine use of recommendation engines in daily life, Eli Pariser has discovered that recommendation engines are being deployed in ways that many citizens do not know or understand. For example, he discovered that a colleague in New York City who worked on Wall Street was using Google to search for information on the April 2010 BP oil spill in the Gulf of New Mexico in the weeks following the accident. His colleague's first screen of search results provided links to news items concerning the financial impact the accident would have on BP. However, another colleague in Portland who conducted the same exact search, but was a known wildlife advocate, received search results that highlighted the environmental impact of the accident. Most citizens do not understand that Google has been personalizing search results for many years because of the extensive data they have about individuals as well as each individual's search history. Whereas this personalization can be appreciated from an efficiency perspective, it raises questions about how recommendation engines work, how data are collected without individuals' permission or awareness, as well as how corrections or changes can be made by an individual when his or her interests change.

How Recommendation Engines Work

Recommendation engines use one or more mathematical approaches for making predictions. Recommendations like those found on Amazon are based on *collaborative filtering*. Collaborative filtering is made possible because of a data set of the user's historical interests, preferences, and or purchases that can be correlated with other groups of individuals to create statistical affinity groups. The more factors that the user has in common with others in his or her affinity groups (e.g., both like the same kind of music, have similar socioeconomic status as judged by income or zip code, and share the same preferred clothing or shoe designers), the more likely the system can predict the user's preferences, such as political preference or the model of the automobile that he or she drives. This type of approach requires a significant amount of data about an individual to make accurate predictions, which has led to efforts known as *data mining* to gather data from many sources to create a digital profile about an individual.

A second approach used when designing recommendation engines involves *content-based filtering*. Pandora uses this type of approach as it creates a personalized radio station that has content similar to the original musical song/group (seed) the user identifies. When collaborative filtering and content-based filtering are combined, they are known as a *hybrid recommendation engine*.

Several recent developments suggest that data mining and recommendation engines are reaching new levels of influence and impact in U.S. society. Recently, Acxion, a data mining company, announced that it was providing consumers with the opportunity to view the data set, summarizing more than 150 variables, about their life (see AboutTheData.com). This action is comparable to a credit reporting service allowing consumers to see their credit report and correct any errors. In an infamous case study in recommendation engines, the retailer Target developed analytics that searched its customer database to predict which women might be pregnant to target coupons and sales of baby clothing, furniture, and other baby-related items. A father whose teenage daughter received one of these targeted mailing catalogs had an angry exchange with a Target store manager, suggesting that the retailer was trying to encourage his daughter to become pregnant. Subsequently, the father found out that his daughter was pregnant and apologized to the store manager who had no idea that the corporate office was engaged in this sort of data mining of customer data. The retailer had refined an algorithm that combined sales data about its customers to make a prediction that a woman may be pregnant.

Implications of Recommendation Engines for Learning

The evolution of recommendation engines in education is natural as businesses and educators search for new ways to increase academic achievement, particularly among groups of students who have historically demonstrated a significant achievement gap, such as students with disabilities, English language learners, students of color, and students living in poverty. However, given the sophisticated technical and mathematical knowledge needed to develop and implement recommendation engines, most educators will be relegated to roles of users rather than serving as expert advisors in the design of recommendation engines in education.

Readers interested in observing how recommendation engines have been implemented in the context of digital learning materials are encouraged to explore the systems of Vocabulary.com, Khan Academy, and Knewton. Whereas traditional curricula and instruction define one pathway for all students to achieve the learning outcomes, these types of personalized learning systems monitor student performance in real time and use collaborative and content-based filtering to make recommendations about optimal pathways. This approach brings a level of efficiency never before seen in education as students who demonstrate competency on small sets of performance tasks can then accelerate learning to topics that provide appropriate levels of challenges. Students who struggle can be routed through remedial pathways to provide just-in-time support. Advocates for personalization have proposed federal education legislation, the Each Child Learns Act, which defines the national interest in personalization technologies to improve the quality of 21st-century education. As the public becomes more comfortable with the concept of personalization through the application of personalized medicine, it is expected that the demand for personalized learning will continue to expand.

To date, there is limited research on the use of recommendation engines within K–12 education or higher education. As recommendation systems become more widely implemented, new opportunities for research and evaluation are expected. However, one significant obstacle researchers will encounter is how to gain access to proprietary data sets and data mining algorithms that distinguish the performance of each recommendation engine.

Dave L. Edyburn

See also Adaptive and Responsive Websites; Adaptive Learning Software and Platforms; Data Mining and Recommendation Engines; Learning Analytics; Technologies That Learn and Adapt to Users

Further Readings

Alliance for Excellent Education. (2012). Working draft of suggested legislation: The Each Child Learns Act. Retrieved from http://all4ed.org/reports-factsheets/working-draft-of-suggested-legislation-the-each-child-learns-act

Duhigg, C. (2012, February). How companies learn your secrets. *New York Times.* Retrieved from http://www.nytimes.com/2012/02/19/magazine/shopping-habits.html

Gaughran, D. (2013, February). Amazon's recommendation engine trumps the competition. Retrieved from http://davidgaughran.wordpress.com/2013/02/22/amazons-recommendation-engine-trumps-the-competition

Hill, K. (2012, February). Target isn't just predicting pregnancies: "Expect more" savvy data-mining tricks. *Forbes.* Retrieved from http://www.forbes.com/sites/kashmirhill/2012/02/24/target-isnt-just-predicting-pregnancies-expect-more-savvy-data-mining-tricks/

Ji, J., Liu, C., Sha, Z., & Zong, N. (2005). Personalized recommendation based on a multilevel customer model. *International Journal of Pattern Recognition and Artificial Intelligence, 19*(7), 895–916.

Layton, J. (2011). How Pandora Radio works. *How stuff works.* Retrieved from http://computer.howstuffworks.com/internet/basics/pandora.htm

Leavitt, N. (2006). Recommendation technology: Will it boost e-commerce? *Computer, 39*(5), 13–16.

Lin, Y., & Kim, C. (2013). Professional Development for Personalized Learning (PD4PL) guidelines. *Educational Technology, 53*(3), 21–27.

Pariser, E. (2011). *The filter bubble: What the Internet is hiding from you.* New York, NY: Penguin Press.

Silverman, M. (2011, November 4). How algorithms and editors can work together to burst the "filter bubble." *Mashable.* Retrieved from http://mashable.com/2011/11/04/eli-pariser-media-summit

Waddoups, M., & Alpert, F. (2005). Recommendation engines: What they are, an empirical investigation of frequency and type of use, and a guide for managers. *Journal of Website Promotion, 1*(4), 39–59.

Weinberger, D. (2012). *Too big to know: Rethinking knowledge now that the facts aren't the facts, experts are everywhere, and the smartest person in the room is the room.* New York, NY: Basic Books.

Websites

AboutTheData.com: https://aboutthedata.com

Amazon: www.amazon.com

Khan Academy: www.khanacademy.org

Knewton: www.knewton.com

Netflix: www.netflix.com

Netflix Prize website: www.netflixprize.com

Pandora: www.pandora.com

Vocabulary.com: www.vocabulary.com

REFLECTION AND PREFLECTION PROMPTS AND SCAFFOLDING

Reflection plays an important role in experiential learning, both cognitively and metacognitively. It has been widely discussed in the literature as an important approach for promoting learning and higher order thinking skills, developing professional practices, and facilitating and structuring learning through experiences. Preflection, as a precursor of reflection, is for learners to be consciously aware of the expectations associated with the learning experience, which is meant to enhance and enrich the reflection process. Meanwhile, prompts can be leveraged as the scaffolding mechanism for guiding reflection and preflection by offering both cognitive and metacognitive support to learners before, during, and after their learning processes.

This entry explores the research literature concerning reflection and preflection prompts as scaffolding in human-to-human and human-to-computer environments. The entry first differentiates reflection and preflection and clarifies their roles for learning, then explores the literature on reflection and preflection prompts and on prompts as scaffolding in human-to-human and human-to-computer environments. Finally, the entry discusses the potential future direction for research on reflection and preflection prompts as scaffolding to foster reflective learners.

Reflection, Preflection, and Learning

Reflection is a crucial part of experiential learning. From a psychological perspective, reflection is a form of mental processing—a form of thinking—that people use to fulfill a purpose or to achieve some anticipated outcome. Jennifer Moon suggested that it is applied for probing and understanding relatively complicated or unstructured ideas for which there is no obvious solution. Historically, John Dewey, who himself drew on the ideas of many earlier educators, such as Plato, Aristotle, Confucius, Lao Tzu, Solomon, and Buddha, is acknowledged by many, such as Neville Hatton and David Smith, to be a key originator of the concept of reflection in the 20th century. Dewey's basic ideas are seminal and indicate that reflection may be seen as an active and deliberative cognitive process, involving sequences of interconnected ideas that consider underlying beliefs and knowledge. Donald Schön, with a similar view in treating reflection as a response to a problem, made the distinction between "reflection-in-action" and "reflection-on-action": the former occurs while the learner is in the midst of the experience; such an analysis may arise because something unexpected has occurred and may change the outcome of the experience. The latter is a process that occurs after the experience has taken place and often provides clarification and insights through evaluation by one's self or with others.

Preflection is defined by Lynn Jones and Denise Bjelland as "the process of being consciously aware of the expectations associated with the learning experience." It will increase learners' capabilities for focusing on learning during subsequent concrete learning experiences and allow learners to prepare for learning. Preflection can be categorized into the third form of reflection besides reflection-in-action and reflection-on-action: It is "reflection-for-action," which is an expansion of Schön's reflection model and refers to the type of reflection that guides future action based on past thoughts and actions. The preparation for learning in advance will help learners better interpret the plethora of data and focus on aspects most important for their learning.

The ability to reflect has been associated with the higher levels of learning in a number of taxonomies of learning objectives. Benjamin Bloom's taxonomy places the process of reflection resulting in evaluation and critique as the highest educational objective. John Biggs described the process of reflection as indicative of the highest extended abstract level of learning in the structure of observed learning outcome (SOLO) taxonomy. With a mapping between SOLO levels and concepts of deep and surface learning, he concludes that reflection is indicative of deep learning. When reflection is missing from teaching and learning activities, only surface learning can result. Biggs uses this mapping to highlight where teaching and learning activities, such as those encouraging reflection, must be inserted to promote deep learning. Similarly, Moon has noted that the ability to carry out meaningful reflective learning is indicative of the highest level of deep learning, which she terms *transformative learning*. She suggested that the encouragement to be critically reflective and to engage in progressively higher levels of activities will move students up through the levels until transformative learning is possible. Reflection can also result in a variety of outcomes in problem-solving activities—for example, in the development of theory, the formulation of action plans, or the resolution of uncertainties. Reflection can also lead students to self-development, empowerment, and knowledge about their own feelings and emotions.

Prompts as Scaffolding

Prompts are essential instructional methods for guiding key processes of self-regulated learning. According to Thomas Lehmann and colleagues, prompts, being in the form of static questions, incomplete sentences, execution instructions, or pictures, graphics, and other forms of multimedia, can be used as scaffolding to guide the learning process, offering both cognitive and metacognitive support to students. In classroom settings, teachers can ask questions to guide students to carry out tasks in a more expert-like manner, to make self-justifications, self-explanations, and self-evaluations, and to acquire a better understanding of the kinds of questions they should be addressing in learning and problem-solving practices. Prompts can also be used in technology-enhanced learning environments to help direct students in reflection toward learning-appropriate goals.

A review of empirical studies reveals that different types of prompts can fulfill a number of cognitive and metacognitive functions, such as scaffolding student knowledge construction, knowledge integration, and ill-structured problem-solving processes. The research literature also suggests that prompts from teachers, peers, software, or texts can promote reflection by eliciting explanations. Michelene Chi and her colleagues indicated that questions that elicit self-explanations lead to improved understanding of texts. Elizabeth Davis suggested that students who provide explanations to other students' questions or who explain examples they find in their textbooks seem to strengthen connections among their ideas. Researchers in intelligent learning environments have recognized the importance of incorporating prompts into the design of intelligent learning environments. Mechanisms for supporting self-explanation, tutorial dialogue, or reflective dialogue have been prevalent in intelligent tutoring systems (ITS), in which the computer plays the role of tutor (e.g. Cognitive Tutor, AutoTutor). Longkai Wu and Chee-Kit Looi also

explored the role of tutee prompts in fostering the students to play the role of tutor and engage in reflective activities with the computer tutee.

Reflection and Preflection Prompts as Scaffolding

Moon suggests structuring reflection with questions to deepen the quality of reflection. By engaging in reflective activities such as responding to the reflection questions, learners build their understanding and locate the significance of their activity in a larger context. Thus, they are enabled to observe the meaning they have taken from the experience and discover the underlying qualities that made the experience significant. When the learner is prompted to deeper forms of reflection, it becomes possible for the learner to identify *learning edges*, that is, those questions or issues that the learner is seeking to understand to advance his or her work. In doing reflection stimulated by prompts, the learner can unpack the richness of the experience and evaluate which issues emerging from that experience need to be pursued. From an instructional point of view, as shown in Figure 1, prompts can be orchestrated as a request for reflection before, during, and after the learning process.

Debra Coulson and Marina Harvey have also stressed that the development of reflective skills is an iterative process that may be returned to at any time before, during, and after the experience to support learners in deepening their level and complexity of reflection. In addition to the timing of prompts, Maria Bannert noted that the method of prompting and the

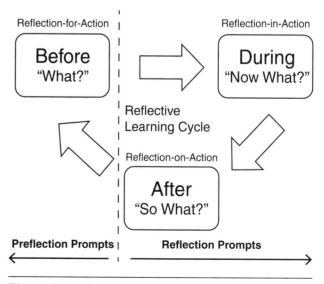

Figure 1 Reflection and preflection prompts in a reflective learning cycle

degree of specification can be personalized and adapted to the learners' needs. While investigating the time of prompting for successful learning, Davis found that prompting before the learning task facilitates the planning of required learning procedures, whereas prompting during the learning process helps the learner monitor and evaluate complex learning events. However, if timing does not meet the requirements of external support from the learners' perspective, prompts may result in increased cognitive effort and thus may hamper learning, as suggested by Lehmann and colleagues. According to Dean Falk, preflection prompts represent a strategy designed as a tool to enhance and enrich the reflection process, which involves posing questions to learners before a learning experience to help them develop a frame of reference through which they will be engaged. The goal is to make learners realize their own expectations and stereotypes with the anticipation that the learning experience will challenge and change their previous understandings and beliefs.

A layered learning framework, as shown in Figure 2, illustrates the interrelationship between the learning environment, the level and development over time of learner agency, and the level and type of teacher-led scaffolding required for each learning phase. Students are encouraged to build their understanding, confidence, skill, and agency as they move into, through, and out of their learning experiences. This framework acknowledges that the development of learners' reflective capacity is not a linear process: Students and teachers may focus on one phase, they may revisit phases, their agency and thereby their roles ebb and flow as teacher scaffolding is reduced and student agency increases.

In the context of an intelligent learning environment, Wu and Looi proposed three types of prompts across the tutoring phases to stimulate the learner to behave as a tutor in the process of understanding, monitoring, repairing misunderstandings, and self-explaining when dealing with complex and unfamiliar domains: pre-tutoring prompts (e.g., *What is your expectation of me? How do you plan to teach me?*), mid-tutoring prompts (e.g., *Can you explain the concept you taught me just now? Why do you teach me the relationship such as this one? Can you explain more? I thought what you taught me is not very related to the text above. Anything you want to say?*), and post-tutoring prompts (*Did I really learn from you? How will you evaluate your teaching work? What is the most important thing you have taught me? Did you also learn something from me after you taught me?*).

The metacognition instruction model called the Reflection Assistant, originated by Claudia Gama, focuses on the metacognitive skills: (1) problem

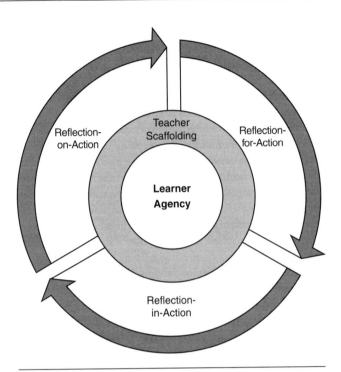

Figure 2　A framework for scaffolding reflection for learning through experience

Source: Chee-Kit Looi and Longkai Wu, adapted from Coulson, D., & Harvey, M. (2013). Scaffolding student reflection for experience-based learning: A framework. *Teaching in Higher Education, 18*(4), 405. doi:10.1080/1356 2517.2012.752726.

understanding and knowledge monitoring, (2) selection of metacognitive strategies, and (3) evaluation of the learning experience. Based on this model, Wu and Looi further incorporated the prompts adapted for four stages (Figure 3) into a learning-by-teaching process, such as familiarization (understanding and planning—e.g., *Can you read the learning objectives to identify the important parts?*), production (teaching and presenting inquiries and answers—e.g., *Can you tell me if my reasoning process is correct and give me a further explanation?*), evaluation (evaluating the performance—e.g., *What have you learned from me as your tutee?*), and post-task reflection (reflecting on learning-by-teaching experience—e.g., *What is your thinking after teaching me?*).

Conclusion

Effective reflection for learning through experience requires a capacity for understanding one's thinking and learning processes; critical self-awareness of values, beliefs, and assumptions; and an openness to alternative, challenging perspectives, as suggested by Coulson and

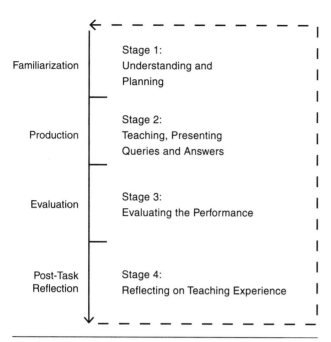

Figure 3   Stages for prompting in a reflective learning
cycle

Harvey. Reflection on metacognitive strategies and beliefs, which is one solution to remedy the overemphasis on content-driven strategies, has the potential to help learners analyze their learning process, adjust their learning strategies and beliefs, and become autonomous learners. The widely reported practice of using reflection to support learning through experience belies the complexity and higher order cognitive processes required for effective critical reflection and metacognition. Assigning reflection and preflection prompts is one possible strategy to effectively support learning through experience. As we advance our theoretical understanding of technology-enhanced learning processes, there will be better designs and applications of adaptive and personalized reflection and preflection prompts, as well as automated feedback, toward providing scaffolding for higher order learning.

Chee-Kit Looi and Longkai Wu

See also Adaptive Learning Software and Platforms;
Constructivist Theory; Games to Promote Inquiry Learning;
Learning by Modeling; Simulation-Based Learning

Further Readings

Bannert, M. (2009). Promoting self-regulated learning through prompts. *Zeitschrift für Pädagogische Psychologie, 23*(2), 139–145.

Biggs J., & Collis K. (1982). *Evaluating the quality of learning: The SOLO taxonomy.* New York, NY: Academic Press.

Bloom, B. S., Engelhart, M. D., Furst, E. J., Hill, W. H., & Krathwohl, D. R. (1956). *Taxonomy of educational objectives: The classification of educational goals. Handbook 1: Cognitive domain.* New York, NY: David McKay.

Chi, M. T. H., Siler, S., Jeong, H., Yamauchi, T., & Hausmann, R. G. (2001). Learning from human learning. *Cognitive Science, 25,* 471–533.

Coulson, D., & Harvey, M. (2013). Scaffolding student reflection for experience-based learning: A framework. *Teaching in Higher Education, 18*(4), 401–413. doi:10.1080/13562517.2 012.752726

Davis, E. A., & Linn, M. (2000). Scaffolding students' knowledge integration: Prompts for reflection in KIE. *International Journal of Science Education, 22(8),* 819–837.

Dewey, J. (1910/1933). *How we think.* Boston, MA: Heath.

Falk, D. (1995). Preflection: A strategy for enhancing reflection. *NSEE Quarterly, 13*(Winter).

Gama, C. A. (2004). *Integrating metacognition instruction in interactive learning environments* (PhD thesis). University of Sussex, Brighton, UK.

Hatton, N., & Smith, D. (1995). Reflection in teacher education: Towards definition and implementation. *Teaching and Teacher Education, 11*(1), 33–49.

Jones, B. L., & Bjelland, D. (2004). International experiential learning in agriculture. In *Proceedings of the 20th Annual Conference* (Vol. 20, pp. 963–964). Dublin, Ireland: AIAEE.

Lehmann, T., Hähnlein, I., & Ifenthaler, D. (2013). Cognitive, metacognitive and motivational perspectives on preflection in self-regulated online learning. *Computers in Human Behavior, 32,* 313–323. doi:10.1016/j.chb.2013.07.051

Moon, J. A. (1999). *Reflection in learning and professional development: Theory and practice.* London, UK: Kogan Page.

Rodgers, C. (2002). Defining reflection: Another look at John Dewey and reflective thinking. *Teachers' College Record, 104*(4), 842–866.

Schön, D. A. (1987). *Teaching artistry through reflection-in-action: Educating the reflective practitioner.* San Francisco, CA: Jossey-Bass.

Thillmann, H., Künsting, J., Wirth, J., & Leutner, D. (2009). Is it merely a question of "what" to prompt or also "when" to prompt? The role of presentation time of prompts in self-regulated learning. *Zeitschrift für Pädagogische Psychologie, 23,* 105–115.

Wu, L., & Looi, C. K. (2012). Agent prompts: Scaffolding for productive reflection in an intelligent learning environment. *Journal of Educational Technology & Society, 15*(1), 339–353.

REMOTE SENSING TECHNOLOGIES

Remote sensing can be defined as the art, science, and technology of obtaining reliable information about physical objects and the environment through the process of recording, measuring, and interpreting imagery and digital representations of energy patterns derived from noncontact sensors. Some definitions make specific references to the types of sensors and the wavelengths of electromagnetic radiation involved. Classic fields of application are topographic and thematic mapping, meteorology, climatology, oceanography, hydrology, and geology. New application fields include 3D mapping and environmental monitoring, as well as assessment and management support for catastrophic events.

The Electromagnetic Spectrum Used for Remote Sensing

The fact that elements have a characteristic interaction with electromagnetic radiation is used to build remote sensors. Every sensor is made of chemical elements that are sensitive to a specific range of electromagnetic wavelengths. The intensity of the radiation is then recorded by a calibrated sensor or set of sensors. The registered electromagnetic radiation also depends on the material composition of the objects from which it is reflected or emitted. Several regions of the electromagnetic spectrum are suitable for remote sensing. The ultraviolet section of the spectrum ranges from 0.1 to 0.4 μm and has the shortest wavelengths that can be used for remote sensing. The light that our eyes can detect is the visible spectrum covering a range from 0.4 to 0.7 μm. The next portion of the electromagnetic spectrum is the reflected infrared region with wavelengths from 0.7 to 3.0 μm followed by the thermal infrared domain with wavelengths from 3.0 to 100 μm, which records emission from the Earth's surface in the form of heat. The portion of the spectrum beyond the infrared range is the microwave region from about 1 mm to 1 m.

Taxonomy of Remote Sensing Systems

Remote sensing has come a long way from its origins in aerial photography and image interpretation. Remotely sensed information is recorded by digital sensors onboard satellite and airborne platforms and is computer-processed. The sensors can passively record emitted or reflected radiation from the Earth or act as their own energy source in an active mode. Common categories of remote sensing systems are shown in Table 1.

The quality and level of detail of the results and the possibility for exact differentiation and delineation of the observed phenomena depend largely on the accuracy with which the original image data are acquired. This accuracy depends on the resolution characteristics of the employed sensor. There exist four different types of resolution.

Table I Taxonomy of remote sensing systems

Recording Platform	Satellite/Shuttle		Aircraft/Balloon		Stationary	
Recording Mode	Passive (Visible, Near Infrared, Thermal Infrared, Thermal Microwave)			Active (Laser, Radar)		
Recording Medium	Analog (Camera, Video)			Digital (Whiskbroom, Line Array, 2D CCD)		
Spectral Coverage	Visible/ Ultraviolet	Reflected Infrared		Thermal Infrared	Microwave	
Spectral Resolution	Panchromatic 1 Band	Multispectral 2–20 Bands		Hyperspectral 20–250 Bands	Ultraspectral >250 Bands	
Radiometric Resolution	Low (<6 bit)	Medium (6–8 bit)		High (8-12 bit)	Very High (>12 bit)	
Spatial Ground Resolution	Very Low >250 m	Low 50–250 m	Medium 10–50 m	High 4–10 m	Very High 1–4 m	Ultra High <1 m

Source: Adapted by author from Ehlers, M. (2004). Remote sensing for GIS applications: New sensors and analysis methods. In M. Ehlers, H. J. Kaufmann, & U. Michel (Eds.), *Remote sensing for environmental monitoring: GIS applications, and geology III* (pp. 1–13). Bellingham, WA: International Society for Optics and Photonics.

Spectral Resolution

Charge-coupled device (CCD) cameras use an array of sensors that register electromagnetic radiation at different wavelengths. Because of the limited space on a CCD chip, only a limited number of sensor types can be arranged on one chip. Therefore, for *multispectral* imaging sensors, radiation can usually be recorded only in a number of discrete wavelength intervals, and a complete recording of a continuous spectrum is not possible. This can be achieved by imaging spectrometers or *hyperspectral* sensors with hundreds of very narrow spectral bands throughout the visible, near-infrared, and mid-infrared portions of the electromagnetic spectrum. Their very high spectral resolution facilitates fine discrimination between different targets based on their spectral response in each of the narrow bands. Because of the limited sensor space, however, this achievement comes at the expense of spatial resolution or ground coverage. A *panchromatic* sensor is a single-channel detector sensitive to radiation within a broad wavelength range. The physical quantity being measured is the apparent brightness of the Earth's surface targets. The advantage of broad-range single sensors is that they receive more energy and can in return use smaller CCDs, which results in higher spatial resolution.

Active sensors such as *radar* sensors emit coherent microwave radiation in a series of pulses from an antenna, side-looking at the Earth's surface perpendicular to the direction of the moving platform. When the energy reaches a target on the Earth's surface, some of the energy is reflected back toward the sensor. This backscattered microwave radiation is detected, measured, and timed. The time required for the energy to travel to the target and return back to the sensor determines the distance or range to the target. By recording the range and magnitude of the reflected energy, a 2D essentially black-and-white image of the surface can be produced through the platform motion. Because radar provides its own energy source, images can be acquired day or night. Also, microwave energy is able to penetrate through clouds and rain, making it an all-weather sensor.

Spatial Resolution

The smaller the sensor elements can be constructed, the more detail can be recorded. However, the elements have to be large enough to accumulate enough electromagnetic energy to provide a satisfactory signal-to-noise ratio. Highest spatial resolution can therefore be delivered by panchromatic sensors that record electromagnetic radiation over a single band covering a wide range of wavelengths, usually from the blue to the near infrared domain. High spatial resolution therefore comes at the expense of spectral resolution and vice-versa. Although we measure spatial resolution as ground sampling distance, the actual specific spatial resolution for passive sensors is determined by its solid angle or sensor-specific instantaneous field of view. In general, sensors onboard high-altitude platforms view a larger area but can only provide a low spatial resolution. For satellite systems, two major orbits are used for Earth observation. Geostationary satellites are placed in an orbit above the equator with the same speed as the Earth's rotation so that they can continuously look at the same place on Earth. These orbits have a distance of 36,000 km from Earth, so the spatial resolution has to be very coarse to allow enough energy to reach the sensors. Higher resolution is achieved by remote sensing platforms at much lower (400–1200 km) orbits that are basically aligned north to south. With the Earth's rotation from west to east, they cover most of the Earth's surface over a certain period.

Side-looking radar images have a very different geometry. They come with two different spatial resolutions: in-flight direction (azimuth resolution R_A) and perpendicular to it (ground range resolution R_G). R_A depends on the length of the antenna, the altitude of the platform, the sensor's specific wavelength, and the sensor's side-looking viewing angle. R_G is independent of the flying height and depends only on the temporal length of the microwave pulse. Better range resolution can be achieved by using a shorter pulse length, whereas smaller R_A values can be gained by increasing the antenna length D. This, however, is only possible to a certain degree, so that especially for radar images from space a very long antenna has to be simulated. This is achieved by using the Doppler effect of the forward motion of the satellite, thus increasing the azimuth resolution. This complex recording technique, called *synthetic aperture radar*, provides the only sensor with a spatial resolution independent of the platform's altitude.

Radiometric Resolution

The radiometric resolution characterizes the actual information depth that can be acquired in an image. The sensor's sensitivity to the intensity of the electromagnetic radiation determines the radiometric resolution. The higher the radiometric resolution of a sensor, the more sensitive it is to detecting finer details. The radiometric resolution is measured as the number of bits used for coding this range in binary format. The maximum number of brightness levels available depends on the number of bits used in representing the energy recorded. If a sensor uses 8 bits to record the data, there would be $2^8 = 256$ digital values available, ranging from 0 to 255. Current remote sensors produce signals with up to $2^{12} = 4,096$ gray levels.

Temporal Resolution

This parameter is the minimum time that exists between two recordings of the same area. For example, the revisit period of a satellite sensor is fixed by its orbit and lasts usually several days (e.g., 16–24). Therefore, the absolute temporal resolution of a satellite remote sensing system to be at the exact orbit a second time is equal to this period. Because of some degree of overlap in the imaging swaths of adjacent orbits for most satellites and the increase in this overlap with increasing latitude, some areas of the Earth can be recorded more frequently. Also, modern satellite systems are able to point their sensors to record the same area between different satellite passes separated by just a few days. Thus, the actual temporal resolution of a sensor depends on a variety of factors, including the satellite/sensor capabilities, the swath overlap, and latitude.

Manfred Ehlers

See also Augmented Reality; Avatars and Agents in Virtual Systems; Radio Frequency Identification in Education

Further Readings

Campbell, J. B. (2011). *Introduction to remote sensing* (5th ed.). New York, NY: Guilford.

Colwell, R. N. (1997). History and place of photographic interpretation. In W. R. Philipson (Ed.), *Manual of photographic interpretation* (2nd ed., pp. 33–48). Bethesda, MD: American Society for Photogrammetry and Remote Sensing.

Ehlers, M. (2004). Remote sensing for GIS applications: New sensors and analysis methods. In M. Ehlers, H. J. Kaufmann, & U. Michel (Eds.), *Remote sensing for environmental monitoring: GIS applications, and geology III* (pp. 1–13). Bellingham, WA: International Society for Optics and Photonics.

Jensen, J. R. (2006). *Remote sensing of the environment: An earth resource perspective* (2nd ed.). Upper Saddle River, NJ: Prentice Hall.

Lillesand, T. M., & Kiefer, R. W. (2007). *Remote sensing and image interpretation* (6th ed.). New York, NY: Wiley.

Natural Resources Canada. (2007). *Fundamentals of remote sensing: A Canada centre for remote sensing remote sensing tutorial*. Retrieved from http://www.nrcan.gc.ca/earth-sciences/geomatics/satellite-imagery-air-photos/satellite-imagery-products/educational-resources/9309

REPAIR THEORY

Repair theory is an attempt to explain how individuals learn procedural skills. Developed and expanded by Kurt VanLehn in the early 1980s, repair theory emerged during a time when researchers and educators were beginning to consider how personal computers could be used in an educational environment. Repair theory is significant in that it demonstrated, at the time of its publication, potential links between cognitive science, education, and computer science research. The theory also provided a framework for understanding the role technology could have in supporting learning. This entry introduces the premise of repair theory, explains significant tenets, and highlights the application of the theory to educational technology.

Definition

According to repair theory, the human mind is logical, like a computer, when engaged in procedural tasks. When all components of a procedure are known, the learner is able to perform the task. However, when a learner possesses a mistaken belief about a component of the procedure and cannot perform, the learner experiences an *impasse*. The learner attempts to resolve the impasse with strategies called *repairs*. Repairs do not necessarily lead to the correct response. These mistakes, then, are referred to as *bugs*. Repair theory suggests that bugs can be identified and predicted for certain procedures. Repair theory is linked to the areas of artificial intelligence and intelligent tutoring. The generation of the theory involved the development and use of computer programs to evaluate and respond to complex human actions.

Explanation

Repair theory provides a framework for understanding human thought process and the role of predictive analysis. The theory is supported by substantial data obtained from a study involving analysis of several hundred primary students' arithmetic tests. Through analysis of these tests, a substantial number of bugs, or errors, were identified and further validated. Results indicated that predictive models could be established for how a student might make a mistake in a given process. In essence, all known or expected bugs for a particular skill could be identified. Further, the theory suggests it is possible to predict what bugs will exist for procedural skills that have not yet been analyzed.

Development Overview

The theory was first proposed by John Seely Brown and Kurt VanLehn in an article titled "Repair Theory: A Generative Theory of Bugs in Procedural Skills," published in 1980 in the journal *Cognitive Science*. Later, VanLehn elaborated the theory in the book *Mind Bugs*, published in 1990. In the development of repair theory, VanLehn and Brown use computer programs Buggy and Debuggy to analyze hundreds of math problems solved by children in third, fourth, fifth, and sixth grades. Through these programs, it was possible to identify systematic bugs in the children's work, which then led to the development and proposal of the theory.

Elaboration

Central Concepts: Bugs and Repair

The concept of bugs is central to repair theory. Bugs are systematic, minor deviations from a correct procedure. They are complex, intentional actions that represent a learner's mistaken belief about the skill. VanLehn and Brown note the difference between bugs and slips. Bugs are intentional, whereas slips are errors in which the learner did something he or she did not intend to do.

Bugs are generated by two events: (1) the learner reaches an impasse, and (2) the learner consequently attempts to repair the impasse. For example, assume that a student never correctly learned a portion of a mathematical skill, such as what to do when subtracting from zero, as demonstrated in this equation:

$$\begin{array}{r} 50 \\ -\,42 \\ \hline \end{array}$$

Or, assume that the learner learned the rule and forgot it. The learner's attempt to follow the incomplete or impoverished procedure will result in an impasse. Unlike a computer, the learner will become inventive and will attempt to problem-solve a repair to the impasse. In doing so, the learner will execute the procedure in an erroneous way. For example, the learner may erroneously assume the answer demonstrated below, having not learned adequately how to decrement a zero:

$$\begin{array}{r} 50 \\ -\,42 \\ \hline 12 \end{array}$$

Because the learner lacks understanding of some portion of the procedural skills, the kind of repair that the learner performs is independent of how the erroneous procedure was derived originally. The repair the learner performs depends only on the impasse confronting him or her.

Instability of Bugs

Another central tenet is the instability of students' bugs. Repair theory introduces the concepts of *tinkering* and *bug migration*. Learners who tinker repair an impasse more than one way on a test. In other cases, students switch from one repair to another between tests. This phenomenon was termed *bug migration*. The implication of tinkering and bug migration is that learners' bugs are complex and sophisticated, and consequently there is a need for principled heuristics to identify and predict potential bugs.

Prediction of Bugs

Perhaps most significant to repair theory is the notion that all known or expected bugs for a particular procedural skill can be defined and even predicted. Doing so requires a framework, or heuristic, for defining how learners may arrive at repairs. This framework includes (1) a representation of a given procedure, (2) a set of deletion principles, (3) a set of repair heuristics, and (4) a set of critics.

Deletion refers to portions of the correct procedure that may be lost to the student. For example, deleted portions might reflect what facets of the correct procedure the student forgot or never learned. For bugs to be predicted, a set of principles for what facets could be deleted is first needed. Repair heuristics can propose any possible repairs that are then tested. A set of critics will filter out some repairs that are considered unreasonable.

By using such a framework, artificial intelligence, such as Debuggy used in Brown and VanLehn's original study, can identify students' bugs.

Intelligent Tutoring Systems

Repair theory provided the framework for VanLehn's work in the field of intelligent tutoring. Intelligent tutoring systems are designed to simulate a human tutor's behavior and guidance. Because these systems, like Brown and VanLehn's Buggy and Debuggy, are able to interpret student responses, they are able to identify areas of misunderstanding, provide guidance for understanding why, and offer hints to help the student improve his or her grasp of the material. Developed for both educational and professional settings to provide immediate and customized feedback, intelligent tutoring systems date to the early 20th century with the creation of "teaching machines" by Sidney Pressey. Intelligent tutoring and computer-assisted instruction (CAI) developed in popularity in the latter part of the 20th century with the increased availability of personal computers.

Two of VanLehn's notable projects in the area of intelligent tutoring are Andes and Why2-Atlas, programs focused on the area of physics. Using Andes, students create physics-related diagrams, enter equations, and define variables. Andes provides feedback and principle-based hints. Studies indicated that students who used Andes learned significantly more than did students who completed the same homework problems with paper and pencil. Using Why2-Atlas, students are presented with conceptual physics questions. Students would type narrative answers, which were then reviewed by the intelligent tutoring systems using dialogue in natural language with the intent of assisting students in realizing the mistakes in the answers. Results of studies comparing Why2-Atlas with a human tutor indicated the system was just as effective as a human tutor.

Intelligent tutoring systems can be expensive to develop, implement, and evaluate. However, developing platforms, including e-learning and distributed learning, offers improved opportunities for intelligent tutoring. Research in the area of intelligent tutoring focuses on the development of sophisticated dialogue capabilities and the capabilities for such systems to interpret, adapt, and respond to learners' different emotional states.

Sources of information regarding intelligent tutoring include the International Artificial Intelligence in Education Society, which organizes a biennial conference that provides opportunities for the exchange of information and ideas on related research, development, and applications. The Association for the Advancement of Artificial Intelligence sponsors conferences and symposiums and supports the publication of 14 journals. The biennial International Conference on Intelligent Tutoring Systems also provides opportunities to exchange ideas related to the subject.

Dustin L. Annan-Coultas

See also Games: Impact on Learning; Human-Computer Interaction; Intelligent Tutoring Systems; Virtual Tutees

Further Readings

Brown, J. S., & VanLehn, K. (1980). Repair theory: A generative theory of bugs in procedural skills. *Cognitive Science, 4,* 379–426.

VanLehn, K. (1982). Bugs are not enough: An analysis of systematic subtraction errors. *Journal of Mathematical Behavior, 3*(2), 3–71.

VanLehn, K. (1990). *Mind bugs: The origins of procedural misconceptions.* Cambridge, MA: MIT Press.

VanLehn, K. (Ed.). (1991). *Architectures for intelligence.* Hillsdale, NJ: Lawrence Erlbaum.

REPOSITORIES FOR LEARNING AND INSTRUCTIONAL APPS

A *content repository* is where digital artifacts are stored. Most repositories accommodate documents (e.g., PDFs), and many allow storage of media (e.g., video, images, audio) along with self-contained instructional modules (i.e., learning objects). The sites typically include the capability to search and filter content, ranging from simple keyword search to sophisticated Boolean searches. Although the use of content repositories is widespread across every knowledge-based discipline including business, industry, and government, this entry addresses the use of content repositories in K–12 and higher education. The entry first provides background on digital content repositories and sources of digital content. The entry then gives examples of digital content repositories now in use and discusses factors affecting the production and use of media found in the repositories. A table lists common features of digital content repositories.

Perhaps the first digital content repositories in education were located in university libraries and consisted of journal articles and similar publications that had been digitized. As articles began to be published in digital form, this use of digital content repositories in university libraries increased greatly and still forms a major component of library services.

In K–12 education, the earliest use of digital content repositories was for storing and disseminating lesson plans. Lesson plans are central to the teaching process in K–12, and it comes as no surprise that lesson plans form a type of currency that teachers trade and barter freely. Unlike the more formalized environment of the university library, however, the digital content libraries serving K–12 come in many varieties, from the low-tech repository consisting of links on a teacher's PortaPortal page, to full-blown databases containing thousands of plans.

As the use of educational media has increased, content repositories have evolved to accommodate the special requirements associated with these media, including integration with learning management systems (LMS, e.g., Blackboard, Canvas, Moodle). Indeed, the explosion of new media tools in the past 10 years has led to a profusion of the number and types of available content repositories, such that locating an artifact of interest can be quite difficult because of the sheer volume of sources to be considered. For example, a recent Web search on the term *digital content for education* yielded more than 840 million results.

Where Does Content Come From?

Content can be created, curated, or repurposed. *Content creation* has long been the purview of specially trained educational media specialists and instructional developers. However, advances in content creation tools along with the ever-increasing technical sophistication of students and teachers have led to remarkable capacity for the creation of original digital content for educational use by teachers and students.

Similarly, *content curation* has traditionally been practiced by librarians both in K–12 and higher education. Again, however, new tools for content curation have enabled curation via crowdsourcing, leading to a rapid rise in the breadth, depth, and quality of available resources. Consider, for example, the offerings at sites such as Pinterest, Learnist, Scoop.it, and a host of others.

Content repurposing involves taking content originally developed in one form (e.g., long-format video) and reconfiguring it for a different use (e.g., for the Web). Obviously, this process can be practiced only by organizations with large content holdings, such as Discovery Education and the Public Broadcasting Service (PBS). The latter's initiative, PBS Learning Media, has recast original video footage from past PBS shows into more than 30,000 digital resources, now accessed by more than 1 million educators.

Examples of Current Content Repositories

Content repositories may be maintained by state and federal agencies, universities, nonprofits, corporations, and discipline-focused associations. Agencies include state and federal governmental entities with a charter for content dissemination. The North Carolina Learning Object Repository (NCLOR), for example, is managed by the North Carolina Community College System and funded through the North Carolina state legislature. NCLOR provides access to thousands of resources and is accessible to all educators in the state of North Carolina. In addition, NCLOR serves as a gateway for a multitude of open source and special collections, including the National Repository of Online Courses (NROC), Annenberg Media Interactives, CK-12 Flexbooks, Cool Tools for Teaching Online, and others. At the federal level, resource repositories initiatives are supported by the National Aeronautics and Space Administration (NASA), the National Science Foundation (NSF), the National Oceanic and Atmospheric Administration (NOAA), and the Smithsonian Institution (Smithsonian Education), among many such agencies around the world.

Among universities, the Massachusetts Institute of Technology (MIT) is well known in the United States for its MIT OpenCourseWare initiative that makes course materials for its undergraduate and graduate classes freely available to all. Other university-based initiatives include the Harvard Open Learning initiative, the Harvard Natural Science Lecture Demonstrations Series, the Notre Dame University OpenCourseWare initiative, the Open Yale Courses initiative, the Princeton University Lectures, and the Stanford University Seminars. A general repository for higher education—Multimedia Educational Resource for Learning and Online Teaching (MERLOT) is maintained by a consortium of universities and is often touted as a model for repository service for higher education, offering 40,000 learning resources of various types and a strong content vetting system.

Among nonprofits, perhaps the best-known example is the Khan Academy. The Khan Academy provides a repository of free online materials (e.g., videos, interactive activities, teacher tools) in support of a quality education for everyone, anywhere in the world. In the past 2 years, it has delivered more than 350 million lessons and 1.7 billion exercise problems. Currently, it has 10 million users per month and 4 million exercise problems completed each day. The Khan Academy includes a wide variety of subjects for K–12 and higher education. Other nonprofits include PBS Learning Media and the British Broadcasting Corporation (BBC).

A variety of corporations offer repository-based educational materials for a fee. Discovery Education, for example, offers a popular video streaming service covering a wide range of topics for K–12 education. It also maintains a repository of hundreds of lesson plans available without charge, as does SAS Curriculum Pathways.

Discipline-focused associations include the professional associations for each of the major content disciplines in K–12 and higher education, including science, math, history and social studies, and English. The various associations offer a widely varying array of resources via their websites. Perhaps the best example of repository services among professional associations is ReadWriteThink, associated with the International Reading Association. Additional repositories can be found at NASA, the World Bank, and various European and Asian projects and agencies.

Factors Affecting Media Production and Use

To understand the use of content repositories, it is useful to consider the use within the overall context. In the last 10 years, educational media have transformed the learning landscape. The use of content repositories is inexorably tied to this increase in the importance and use of educational media in higher education and K–12 education. Increasingly, creation of original digital content by students and teachers will become a significant part of the educational experience, supplementing the current offerings. What factors influence this ever-growing role of educational media?

Policies

In 2012, the U.S. State Educational Technology Directors Association (SETDA) published a whitepaper—titled *Out of Print*—in which it recommended that K–12 schools migrate away from use of printed textbooks toward use of educational media. This migration is echoed in the U.S. Education Department's National Educational Technology Plan as well. This migration is a milestone in the history of public education, marking the transition to a new paradigm for teaching and learning.

Students as Content Creators

A number of researchers have chronicled student engagement in new media during the past 10 years and recognized their growing sophistication in media development. This evolution has been identified within formal education agencies as well. In the Educational Technology Plan for Virginia 2010–2015, for example, the Virginia Department of Education highlights the progression of learners from content consumers to content producers.

Improvement in Content Creation Tools

There has been a tremendous increase in the last 10 years in the availability of content creation tools for students and teachers. These tools have become more varied and powerful, even as they have become easier to use and less expensive. Indeed, many of the tools are available without charge. Many of the tools represent enhancements of offerings in traditional media categories (e.g., video, photography), whereas other tools constitute entirely new categories of media (e.g., augmented reality). Additional tools can be found at NASA, the World Bank, and various European and Asian projects, agencies, and providers.

New Technology Platforms/Ecosystems

Just as the nature of the content creation tools has become more varied, the technology environments in which they may be used has expanded. Once housed on traditional PC/Mac desktop and laptop computers, the technology platforms on which the tools operate have

expanded to include smartphones, tablets, and hybrid devices (e.g., so-called all-in-one devices). In addition, entire new ecosystems of applications and content have developed in support of these new platforms, including apps and app stores for iOS devices (Apple), Android devices (Google), and Windows devices (Microsoft). To take but one example of growth, Apple's App Store, launched in 2008 in support of the iPhone, by 2014 contained more than 1.2 million apps accessed by 75 billion downloads.

Open Content Initiatives/ New Forms of Copyright

Content creators are increasingly willing to make their materials available without cost for noncommercial use such as education through so-called open source initiatives. Beginning with software years ago (e.g., Linux), the open source movement has expanded to include academic resources as well. MIT, for example, makes its entire curriculum available to anyone interested in perusing its class content. The author of this entry uses open source textbooks in two of his undergraduate classes, including books published through the MacArthur Foundation and the National Research Council.

The impetus for much of the open content comes from the revised notion of traditional copyright captured in Creative Commons copyright. Unlike traditional copyright, which provides severe restrictions on the use of its content, Creative Commons copyright provides tiered protection of materials, allowing the author to make the content available to others under varying stipulations for use. For example, a Creative Commons agreement may allow consumers free and open use of the content but require attribution of the source, or it may limit use to noncommercial applications.

Although a Creative Commons approach has become common for textbooks, its use has so far been limited for creation and reuse of educational media. However, greater use is anticipated as media creation increases and the Creative Commons approach becomes more widely adopted in the schools.

New Models of Content Creation

As students become content producers, new models for content creation are created. One such model is proposed in the Educational Technology Plan for Virginia 2010–2015 in suggesting that schools partner with instructional design and media programs in higher education for the purpose of promoting media design and development skills in K–12 students. One such program—the educational Technology Apprenticeship

Program (eTAP), in development by Richard E. Ingram—seeks to partner university students in educational media programs with teachers in K–12 schools who do not have the time or expertise to create such media themselves.

New Educational Practices

One of the most interesting developments in educational practice has been the recent emergence of the teaching practice known as flipping the classroom. Although strictly speaking not a new practice, flipping the classroom has received significant attention in recent years for its potential to engage learners in new ways and optimize class time for deeper learning. A key component of flipping is the use of media (usually videos) that students view as homework. The purpose of the video is to provide the learner with the basic knowledge necessary to engage in higher order discussion and application of the topic during class time.

Common Content Repository Features

To make sense of this sometimes-bewildering array of repositories, it is useful to develop a set of descriptors that allow direct comparison of the offerings. These descriptors are presented in Table 1.

Table I Common content repository features

Feature	Description
Account Types	Types of users supported by the system including students, teachers, professors, publishers, local administrators, parents, guests, other
Portal Types	User-specific search, interface, and content delivery including students, teachers, parents, guests, other
Content	Subject coverage including type (subjects), levels (grades), breadth (number of topics), depth (enabling content)
Media Types	Types of content supported including lesson plans, video, images, audio, learning objects, collections, assessments, e-books
Content Grain Size	Size of content objects including small (Web-video, images, activities), medium (lesson plans), large (course, books)
Link Type	Local, remote, and special content including file, URL, collection (multiple related files)
Search Capability	Search options including by subject, grade, level, keyword, full-text
Cost	Cost for storing/accessing content (some repositories are free for the end user).
Support Sustainability	Likelihood of ongoing support including grant supported, member supported, institutionally supported
Content Ownership	Content ownership models including author own, Creative Commons
Metatagging	Options available for metatagging range from keywords to the minimal Dublin Core Metadata Element Set to comprehensive sets of standards (e.g., state standards, Common Core State Standards, professional standards, custom standard sets)
Metatagger	Person supplying metatags including author, publisher
Content Review Methods	Available review options including ranking, rating, comment
User-Created Content	User-created content supported including student, teacher
Content Vetting	Method used to ensure content quality including publisher reviewed, peer-reviewed, other
Content Sharing	Methods for sharing content including e-mail to friend, link to object, embedded code

(Continued)

Table 1   (Continued)

Feature	Description
Learning Registry	Exposes metadata to learning registry
Web Search Tie-in	Exposes metadata to Web search engines (Google, Bing)
Proactive Procurement	Proactive efforts to build the repository (e.g., targeted content creation contests)
Content Collections	Supports customizable content organization including personal library, shared library, playlist, playlist sharing
Customizable to Local Needs	Support local organizational schemes including class structure, unit guide, pacing guide
Community Support	Support for communities of practice including community network (link content collections to partners), content community (member notification based on content subject, grade, topic)
Badging	Supports recognized badging scheme (e.g., Mozilla)
Mobile Support	Supports operations via mobile devices
Integrate with LMS	Interoperates with industry-standard LMS
User Experience	Human factors associated with usage including usability, navigability, dynamism, guide for users

The Future

The era of new media brings with it a new consideration for repositories that can store and disseminate an ever-growing list of media types for an increasing variety of media usage. Traditionally, content repositories have been created by and for institutions and agencies, to serve content aligned with their mission. Increasingly, media-focused companies are repurposing their traditional format media for use on the Web, just as students and teachers are becoming content producers.

To help address this information overload, a new type of content repository is emerging—the *content hub*. A content hub is designed to store artifacts and to support the curation and collection of content of interest, wherever the content might be available on the Web, across disparate repositories and in various forms. The capability to reach across disparate sources is particularly important given the rise of new app-based ecosystems for content offered for iOS (Apple), Android (Google), and Windows (Microsoft) devices.

With the content hub comes customized content creation, curation, and storage designed for the individual teacher or student. This customization leads to a greater degree of personalization of the educational experience, consistent with a smaller grain size for content objects. The smaller grain size, in turn, supports greater flexibility in media usage, and along with

emerging offerings for designing individual learning pathways (e.g., Learning Ace), presages new possibilities for personalized instruction.

Finally, this personalization will not lead to learners isolated in the learning landscape, but rather to the development of learner-centered communities of practice (both virtual and real) that support teachers and students in the communities most aligned with their needs and interests. Traditional content repositories will continue to be important, but will be filtered through the lens of community-based content hubs designed primarily to support the learner.

Richard E. Ingram

See also Creative Commons; Digital Archives; Digital Curation; Intellectual Property; Internet: Impact and Potential for Learning and Instruction; Knowledge and Skill-Based Digital Badges; Learning Objects; Massive Open Online Courses; Media Literacies; Open Content Licensing; Open-Source Repositories for Learning and Instruction; Personal Learning Environments; Socially Constructed Virtual Artifacts; Transmedia in Education

Further Readings

Iiyoshi, T., & Kumar, V. (Eds.). (2010). *Opening up education: The collective advancement of education through open technology, open content, and open knowledge.* Boston, MA: MIT Press.

State Educational Technology Directors Association. (2012). *Reimagining the K–12 textbook in a digital age*. Retrieved from http://setda.org/web/guest/outofprintreport

U.S. Department of Education. (2010). *National educational technology plan 2010*. Retrieved from https://www.ed.gov/technology/netp-2010

Virginia Department for Education. (2010). *Educational technology plan for Virginia 2010–2015: Executive summary*. Retrieved from http://www.doe.virginia.gov/support/technology/edtech_plan/executive_summary.pdf

WikiEducator. (n.d.). *Exemplary collection of open eLearning content repositories*. Retrieved from http://wikieducator.org/Exemplary_Collection_of_Open_eLearning_Content_Repositories

Websites

Creative Commons: http://us.creativecommons.org

RESEARCH IN SCHOOLS

Research on educational technology in schools examines the impact of technology on teaching and learning. New technologies are being introduced at a rapid pace and school leaders need evidence-based research to determine what will best address the need to improve student learning and achievement.

This entry introduces the idea that there are multiple levels of educational technology research in school systems as well as limitations of research that are often found in authentic school research. A model of how one might approach research on educational technology is discussed. The model has been used in many countries to structure data collection and analysis to determine the impact of educational technology on achievement. Types of research designs that are plausible in schools are discussed, as well as a look to the future of research on emerging technologies.

Levels of School-Based Research

The impact of educational technology can be addressed at multiple levels of schooling. The International Association for the Evaluation of Educational Achievement (IEA) has conducted studies across many nations and has proposed that research can be conducted at three levels—macro (state or national level, large decision-making system), meso (district or school operational unit level), and micro (classroom or student teacher-learner level) (see Figure 1). The macrolevel may involve state, country, or district-level decision-making

systems, often related to policy. The mesolevel includes the school building level as well as the classroom or grade level. The microlevel often involves research targeting student-level data. Typically, a classroom teacher might conduct research at the microlevel, which may also be known as action research.

Limitations of Research on Technology in Schools

Even at the most narrow (micro) level, conducting research on such a broad and rapidly changing topic as educational technology in schools may limit the amount of learning that can be attributed to technology innovations. Changes can vary by the implementation from one classroom to another and one school to another. Educational technology research attempts to control for as many factors as possible but, according to Herbert J. Klausmeier and Richard E. Ripple, 37 different factors can contribute to a student's learning. For example, students who come to school having had nothing to eat since lunch at school the day before are not able to focus on learning because their basic needs have not been met. An interdependent set of variables that may or may not be well defined and attributing change to only one variable is difficult.

Research on the mesolevel and microlevel often requires a large number of indicators related to learning as well as "total cost of ownership." The purpose of gathering these data is often for data-driven decision making for strategic planning purposes. The

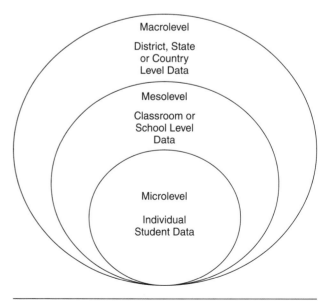

Figure 1   Simplified graphic of micro-, meso-, and macrolevels of school research

"total cost of ownership" compares the impact of the learning with the cost involved in implementing the technology-infused program.

Research regarding the effectiveness of educational technology is very important at the mesolevel because most large technology purchasing decisions are made at this level. For example, 1:1 laptop or tablet initiatives, with accompanying support and professional development, are often implemented at the school district or individual school level.

Research at the micro or classroom level is also very important to define and refine "what works." Action research in the classroom should involve true partnerships between practitioners and researchers in which the practitioner is part of the design of the research plan, not just the "beneficiary of the findings." For example, a science teacher may wonder whether the use of a program with a virtual frog dissection is effective in improving student's learning. The teacher may partner with a researcher to gather both content-related data as well as attitudinal data regarding the learning approach. The researcher can guide the teacher in setting up the research design and gathering data so that there is a treatment as well as a comparison group to produce stronger, more reliable results.

One practice-based research method focused on improving instructional outcomes is known as design-based research. Design-based research involves conducting iterative research on the components of the design process. Design-based research bridges formative and summative evaluation, removing the artificial distinction between focusing solely on the product rather than the process of learning.

Emerging Macrolevel Research: Data Driven Decision Making

Macrolevel research involves a large educational system such as a state, country, or school district. The macrolevel is often the level in which policies are created. Data driven decision making has as a goal to give timely, accurate feedback to teachers or others who are involved in implementing teaching goals and objectives. It implies that data are available at the time an instructional decision needs to be made to allow an informed decision to improve learning. Although it is typically used for achievement data at the school level, it can also be used by teachers at the classroom level. Technology is a tool that can allow this process to occur at an accelerated rate to inform classroom teachers as well as administrators and policy makers, allowing the timely improvement in instructional practices.

Emerging Mesolevel Research: Learning Analytics

Mesolevel research includes the school and classroom (teacher) level research. Increasingly, it is becoming common to gather the data using technology itself during the process of learning activities, and this is becoming manifest in a new type of research called *learning analytics*. The main idea behind learning analytics is to use data captured from students as an integral part of planning, designing, and assessing the learning experience to individualize instruction. Many companies such as Amazon and Google have been using these data metrics to tailor the shopping experience and target advertising based on user data on the Internet. These large volumes of data are being analyzed through statistical techniques that look for trends. Studying the impact of technology in schools is a new application of a technique that has been well established in other domains.

Emerging Microlevel Research: Formal Models of Technology Integration in Schools

Microlevel research in general addresses learning at the student level. Evidence to date indicates that simply adding technology to a classroom or school is not going to improve learning. The way in which it is implemented has the greatest impact. Thus, the focus on the activities conducted with the technology and the pedagogical approach are the focus of most research in this field. Formal models such as the will, skill, tool (WST) model of technology integration have been demonstrated as conceptionalization for research that addresses aspects of the effectiveness of educational technology and how it relates to other important aspects of the learning environment at the micro classroom level. Researchers in the United States, Africa, Germany, and Mexico have used the WST model to predict the amount of learning that can be attributed to technology-related intervention.

The WST model has been tested and shown to include the key components necessary to predict effective technology integration at the classroom level (see Figure 2). Will is measured as attitude, skill is the competency needed to use technology, and tool is measured as the access to the necessary tools to teach and learn with technology. The WST model predicts the level of technology integration as a function of attitude, competence, and access to technology.

Experimental and Quasi-Experimental Designs

Scholars such as Chris Dede have noted that issues of frequency, duration, and intensity determine whether an

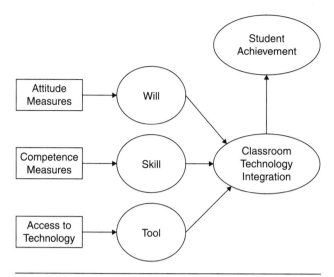

Figure 2 Simplified illustration of the will, skill, tool model for technology integration and student achievement

implementation of technology is effective in any given environment. Failure to focus attention on these issues is analogous to a physician giving every patient the same drug no matter his or her size, age, illness, or past medical history.

Yet it is difficult to conduct research in schools using the gold standard of experimental research, defined as randomized controlled studies. It is often not feasible to randomly select students for a treatment because it may interfere with instructional goals and objectives. When studying the learning that takes place in schools, researchers seldom have the luxury of randomly assigning students to a treatment or withholding instructional activities deemed to be "good." Even the best-funded, most carefully planned research project seldom complies with textbook design specifications after the data are gathered and cleaned. In pretest to posttest paired data acquisition, situations such as sampling and attrition are issues that are a threat to the outcome of the research. The major issues appear to boil down to what Donald T. Campbell and Julian Stanley in their classic short book *Experimental and Quasi-Experimental Designs for Research* called issues of internal validity and issues of external validity. The former have to do with whether one trusts that the research study or experiment was justified in the conclusion reached. External validity is concerned with whether the conclusions the researchers reached can be generalized outside the group used to produce the results. This is closely tied to sampling issues. Decision makers might hope a single, local finding would apply to their schools, but this may ignore differences in environments.

One common strategy to compensate for not being able to randomly assign students is to implement the treatment for one classroom while using other classrooms as comparison groups. The intention is to implement the treatment for the comparison classrooms later, after the research has been conducted. In this manner, research can be conducted using a quasi-experimental design while the learning of all participants is enhanced. For example, a school is given a set of probes to measure the quality of water in a nearby pond. The school principal would like to know whether this tool improves certain benchmark measures for the students who use the probes before reporting to the district, who may then purchase these probes for the entire district. Although it is likely that experiential learning is better and every student would benefit from the probes, research should be done to prove it by having a treatment and comparison group. The teachers in the comparison group are more likely to be willing to provide data to the researchers if they know they will soon also receive the probes.

Longitudinal Studies

Funding research that can be sustained long enough to show an impact continues to be problematic for schools. Most studies present cross-sectional rather than longitudinal student data. A typical project from the National Science Foundation or U.S. Department of Education will span 1 to 3 years and rarely longer than 5 years. Within that timeframe, it is not feasible to implement the intervention and follow up on a longitudinal basis 3 to 4 years later. Even if that is possible, often the standardized measures that may have been used will be different or the large amount of student attrition does not allow for long-term follow-up.

An example of a technology-infused project designed to include longitudinal research is the KIDS Project in Texas, funded by a $9.2 million federal Technology Innovation Challenge grant. Research on the KIDS Project showed its impact on students' reading achievement is on the order of 10% improvement per year compared with no technology implementation. Studies have shown it takes 2 to 3 years before a measurable gain results and many years longer to determine whether it had a lasting impact.

New Research Horizons

As new technology tools reach the K–12 learning environment, new research techniques will be necessary to capture data related to learning with these tools. The internationally recognized New Media Consortium New Horizons Report identifies and examines emerging technologies for their impact on teaching and learning. The report's researchers predicted in 2013 that in the next year cloud computing and mobile computing were likely to have a large impact on the teaching and learning environment. The report also categorized its examination of emerging technologies by which of these tools were likely to be adopted within 2 to 3 years, or within 4 to 5 years. The emerging tools the report identified included learner analytics, open content, 3D printing, and virtual and remote laboratories. Research on the impact of these tools may employ new forms of assessment and evaluation. Researchers should be concerned with the impact on learning, and they should be focused on a wider impact that includes such topics as ergonomics, age appropriateness, and a possible negative impact on society.

Other issues such as constant texting, bullying with technology tools, social media, multitasking, and social etiquette are emerging in schools and need to be addressed by unbiased researchers.

Conclusion

Although most K–12 students are considered digital natives, one cannot assume that these students have basic digital literacy skills. They may be able to text 60 words per minute while they are listening to music on their smartphones but they often lack fundamental skills such as file management or efficient Internet searching skills.

Perhaps the issue is not to determine whether we should include technology in the learning landscape but to realize it is a part of students' lives, both now and in their future work environment. Instead, the focus should be placed on what conditions and in which environments technology can best enhance learning. Research on educational technology should be driven by learning objectives and goals and how technology can help meet those goals—not by finding a new, cool piece of technology and wondering how one can use it for learning.

Rhonda Christensen

See also Evaluation of Educational Technology Competencies; Evaluation Research; Experimental Research and Educational Technology; Instructional Design Research

Further Readings

Agyei, D. D., & Voogt, J. M. (2011). Exploring the potential of the will, skill, tool model in Ghana: Predicting prospective and practicing teachers' use of technology. *Computers & Education, 56*(1), 91–100.

Campbell, D. T., & Stanley, J. C. (1963). *Experimental and quasi-experimental designs for research*. Chicago, IL: Rand McNally.

Christensen, R., & Knezek, G. (2002). Instruments for assessing the impact of technology in education. *Computers in the Schools, 18*(2), 5–25.

Dede, C., Honan, J. P., & Peters, L. C. (2005). *Scaling up success: Lessons learned from technology-based educational improvement*. San Francisco, CA: Jossey-Bass.

Johnson, L., Adams Becker, S., Cummins, M., Estrada V., Freeman, A., & Ludgate, H. (2013). *NMC Horizon Report: 2013 K–12 edition*. Austin, TX: New Media Consortium.

Klausmeier, H. J., & Goodwin, W. (1975). *Learning and human abilities: Educational psychology* (4th ed.). New York, NY: Harper & Row.

Marshall, G., & Cox, M. (2008). Research methods: Their design, applicability and reliability. In J. Voogt & G. Knezek (Eds.), *International handbook of information technology in primary and secondary education* (pp. 983–987). New York, NY: Springer.

Morales, C., Knezek, G., Christensen, R., & Avila, P. (Eds.). (2005). *The will, skill, tool model of technology integration. A conceptual approach to teaching and learning with technology*. Mexico City, Mexico: Instituto Latinoamericano de la Comunicacion Educativa.

Pelgrum, W. J., & Anderson, R. A. (Eds.). (1999). *ICT and the emerging paradigm for lifelong learning: A worldwide educational assessment of infrastructure, goals and practices*. Amsterdam, Netherlands: IEA.

S

SEAMLESS LEARNING

Seamless learning refers to the synergistic integration of learning experiences across a range of dimensions, such as spanning formal and informal learning contexts, individual and social learning, and across time, location, and learning media. The basic premise of seamless learning is that it is neither feasible nor productive to equip learners with all the knowledge and skills they need based on specific snapshots of an episodic time frame, location, scenario, or setting, which is what happens in much of formal education or instruction.

Traditionally, *formal learning* is defined as learning that happens at a fixed time following a predefined curriculum or plan. *Informal learning* means a mode of learning driven by self-interest outside of school environments and is emergent in nature. As learning happens continuously over time, learning experiences are being enriched when similar or related phenomena are studied or seen from multiple perspectives. In more formal settings, learners may acquire canonical knowledge about a subject or topic, while in more informal settings, learners experience the subject or topic in its natural settings or in different contexts, thus achieving more holistic notions of learning and literacy.

Designing for seamless learning requires enabling and supporting learners to learn whenever they are curious and to seamlessly switch between the different contexts. Learning can be facilitated or scaffolded by teachers, peers, or others in one context; yet at other times, it could be student initiated, impromptu, and emergent. Seamless learning also views learning as going beyond the development or acquisition of knowledge and skills to developing the capacity and the attitudes to learn seamlessly. This entry discusses the dimensions of seamless learning and the role of technology in creating a personal, seamless learning environment.

Dimensions of Seamless Learning

One seamless learning framework views learning spaces based on two dimensions or factors: physical setting and learning process as shown in the quadrant of Figure 1. Type I refers to planned learning in classrooms or formal settings, while Type II means planned learning outside of formal environments such as field trips. Type III refers to emergent learning happening outside of formal environments, mostly driven by learners' interests and initiatives. Finally, Type IV means emergent learning in formal environments, such as unplanned teachable moments and serendipitous learning.

In broadening this initial dichotomy of dimensions beyond this 2 x 2 model, Lung-Hsiang Wong and Chee-Kit

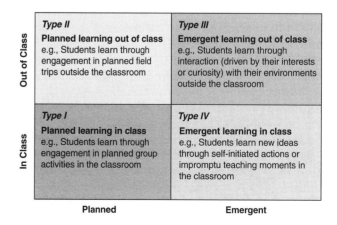

Figure 1 Matrix of learning spaces
Source: Chee-Kit Looi.

627

Looi listed 10 salient features or dimensions that characterize what *seamlessness* in a mobile seamless environment entails:

1. Encompassing formal and informal learning;

2. Encompassing individual and social learning;

3. Learning across time;

4. Learning across locations;

5. Ubiquitous access to learning resources such as online information, teacher-supplied materials, student artifacts, and student online interactions;

6. Encompassing physical and digital worlds;

7. Combined usage of multiple device types;

8. Seamless and rapid switching between multiple learning tasks, such as data collection, analysis, and communication;

9. Knowledge synthesis (prior and new knowledge as well as multiple levels of thinking skills, and/or multidisciplinary learning); and

10. Encompassing multiple pedagogical or learning activity models (facilitated by the teachers).

The framing of the design problem becomes either one of blurring the boundaries of the continuum along each or some of these dimensions or bridging the learning experiences across these continuums. One can frame the challenge faced by learning design practitioners as designing to bridge the gaps between two points on any of the continuum of each dimension.

Role of Technology in Seamless Learning

Learning occurs when a learner interacts with others and the environment across time and locations seamlessly through the use of the technology as a mediating tool. Mobile technology serves as a *horizontal technology* used to meet students' personal needs across multiple physical contexts. A mobile device can serve as a *learning hub* for individual seamless learners, as it can be carried by a learner to store and integrate all of the personal learning tools, resources, and self-created artifacts. Learners can foster their routine use of the learning hub to manage their own seamless learning. This allows a learner to seamlessly synthesize suitable learning resources that were picked up along the ongoing learning journey to mediate the latest learning task. Thus a learning hub should be the nucleus of a set of learning resources, a suite of affordances to support learning activities, and the learner's learning history (including stored resources and self-created artifacts).

The conventional notion of one device or more per learner can be expanded and interpreted as a division of labor strategy, wherein a learner may employ mobile devices with different form factors for different learning tasks or in different learning contexts. For example, smartphones are good tools for rapid learning tasks on the move, such as photo taking, note taking, quick communication, Web searches, and navigation. Whenever learners have free time, they can turn to notebooks or even desktop computers as plausible tools for carrying out more complex learning tasks such as data analysis, report writing, and learning in 3D virtual worlds.

The proliferation of cloud computing technology offers a broader view of the learning hub. A personal learning hub need not be associated with a hardware device. Instead, it may exist as a learner account that stores the learner history on a cloud-based, device-independent seamless learning platform that provides a suite of learning affordances. The combination of a cloud-based learning hub account, a smartphone for constant access, and additional notebook or desktop computers provide the technical setting needed for a personalized seamless learning environment.

Conclusion

Seamless learning can be fostered and scaffolded by appropriate design of learning across the various dimensions of learning. The ideal is for learners to internalize seamless learning as a learning disposition and attitude so that they become seamless learners in their own right. When they learn, they can find ways to integrate their own learning experiences across space, time, location, and the other dimensions, and to be able to self-regulate their own learning. Understanding technology-supported seamless learning is important for researchers, instructional designers, and practitioners who are interested in connecting formal learning and informal learning spaces in order to create rich and holistic learning experiences for the learner.

Chee-Kit Looi and Lung-Hsiang Wong

See also Informal Learning Strategies; Mobile Devices: Impact on Learning and Instruction; Mobile Tools and Technologies for Learning and Instruction

Further Readings

Chen, W. L., Seow, P., So, H.-J., Toh, Y., & Looi, C.-K. (2010). Connecting learning spaces using mobile technology. *Educational Technology, 50*(5), 45–50.

Looi, C.-K., & Wong, L.-H. (2013). Designing for seamless learning. In R. Luckin, P. Goodyear, B. Grabowski, J. Underwood, & N. Winters (Eds.), *Handbook of design in educational technology* (pp. 146–157). New York, NY: Routledge.

Milrad, M., Wong, L.-H., Sharples, M., Hwang, G.-J., Looi, C.-K., & Ogata, H. (2013). Seamless learning: An international perspective on next generation technology enhanced learning. In Z. L. Berge & L. Y. Muilenburg (Eds.), *The handbook of mobile learning* (pp. 95–108). New York, NY: Routledge.

Norris, C., & Soloway, E. (2002, August). Keynote speech. IEEE International Workshop on Wireless and Mobile Technologies in Education 2002, Växjö, Sweden.

Sharples, M. (2006). How can we address the conflicts between personal informal learning and traditional classroom education. In M. Sharples (Ed.), *Big issues in mobile learning* (pp. 21–24). Nottingham, UK: Learning Sciences Research Institute, University of Nottingham.

Sharples, M., McAndrew, P., Weller, M., Ferguson, R., FitzGerald, E., Hirst, T., . . . & Whitelock, D. (2012). *Innovating pedagogy 2012: Exploring new forms of teaching, learning and assessment, to guide educators and policy makers.* (Open University innovation report no. 1). Milton Keynes, UK: The Open University.

Stroup, W. M., & Petrosino, A. J. (2003). An analysis of horizontal and vertical device design for school-related teaching and learning. *Education, Communication & Information, 3*(3), 327–345.

Toh, Y., So, H.-J., Seow, P., Chen, W., & Looi, C.-K. (2013). Seamless learning in the mobile age: A theoretical and methodological discussion on using cooperative inquiry to study digital kids on-the-move. *Learning, Media and Technology, 38*(3), 301–318. doi:10.1080/17439884.2012.666250

Wong, L.-H. (2012). A learner-centric view of mobile seamless learning. *British Journal of Educational Technology, 43*(1), E19–E23.

Wong, L.-H. (2013). Enculturating self-directed learners through a facilitated seamless learning process framework. *Technology, Pedagogy and Education, 22*(3), 319–338.

Wong, L.-H., Chai, C.-S., Chin, C.-K., Hsieh, Y.-F., & Liu, M. (2012). Towards a seamless language learning framework mediated by the ubiquitous technology. *International Journal of Mobile Learning and Organisation, 6*(2), 156–171.

Wong, L.-H., & Looi, C.-K. (2011). What seams do we remove in mobile assisted seamless learning? A critical review of the literature. *Computers & Education, 57*(4), 2364–2381.

Zhang, B. H., Looi, C.-K., Seow, P., Chia, G., Wong, L.-H., Chen, W., . . . & Soloway, E. (2010). Deconstructing and reconstructing: Transforming primary science learning via a mobilized curriculum. *Computers & Education, 55*(4), 1504–1523.

SECOND SELF

In 1984, Sherry Turkle's book, *The Second Self,* appeared as an early look at computer culture and the human relationship with *smart* machines. Written at a time when the Internet was still a research project and computer interfaces were predominantly textual and often required programming skills, the book remains influential not only for its historic profile of a time when computers were rapidly entering U.S. mainstream culture, but because of the emergent social themes Turkle identified through her research on computer users of that period. These themes continue to resonate in debates about human cognition, identity, development, education, relationships, and dependence, with questions about how digital technologies are changing the human condition and the way we think about it. She argued that the computer was increasingly being seen not only as a tool but as a touchstone that was being used to define what it means to be human, how the mind *thinks,* and as an extension of one's self.

Turkle, a professor at the Massachusetts Institute of Technology (MIT) with a background in sociology and social psychology, went on to further develop the primary themes from *Second Self* in her more recent works, *Life on the Screen: Identity in the Age of the Internet* released in 1995, and *Alone Together: Why We Expect More From Technology and Less From Each Other* in 2011. She indicates we have moved from having computers influencing the ways we see ourselves to broader questions of how we live our lives in an age of digital ubiquity. While in the 1984 book Turkle attempted to present a neutral or questioning view of our relationship with computers showing both positive and negative interactions, her later works are more openly apprehensive about the potential to lose our humanness as we increasingly accept machines as meeting our innate needs for relationships and living in simulations rather than dealing with the challenges of direct interaction and emotional attachment to others.

Early Computer Cultures: Development, Identity, and Obsession

In *Second Self,* Turkle described the results of her ethnographic studies of computer users, examining how individual interactions with computers impacted development and identity. Written for a popular audience, the book includes anecdotes from individuals interviewed between 1976 and the early 1980s interspersed with commentary based on social theory to show how a computer was viewed as a *second self* or alter ego to humankind. The study included over 200 children and 200 adults, with a focus on what Turkle defined as differing computer cultures, including children, gamers, home computer owners, programmers, hackers, and experts in artificial intelligence. The individuals profiled in *Second Self* detailed both their interactions with digital devices and reflected on their perceptions of how those contacts made them think about themselves and others. Turkle noted that the language used to describe how computers function had begun to enter everyday conversations about human intelligence, including concepts like programming, memory, and information processing.

The initial focus of the book is on children, examining development and the shaping of identity through their stories about technology interactions. It begins with young children playing with digital toys of the time, such as Simon, a game in which children try to copy increasingly complex patterns of light and sound using four buttons, and Speak and Spell, a game of matching sounds or words to pictures. School-age children were interviewed while using programming to create images on a screen or move a turtle using Logo commands. Through their discourse, Turkle examined how younger children discussed what it meant to think as well as what it meant to be human, noting that they invariably examined smart machines from a perspective of intelligence, feelings, and morality with essential differences from people ultimately focused on the affective dimension.

Turkle contrasted this childhood focus on identity and forging categories to understand the world with older children's need for mastery and control, exhibited in the use of arcade games and computer programming. She suggested a duality with games establishing limited, rule-based scenarios as opposed to the originality and playful exploration of programming in which adolescents expressed themselves in creative ways. In one case, a female student stated programming a microworld allowed her to project a part of herself on the computer constructing a second mind. Turkle showed that computer programming allowed mastery for children and adolescents with differing personalities and talents. While some students were able to use these successes in applying skills learned to the real world as they matured, for others, the computer became an escape.

In examining the world of adults and computers, Turkle's study caught the transition from hobbyists building their own machines to home users who bought commercial computers because they needed tools for specific purposes, such as word processing or using modems to log in to bulletin board systems. She contrasted the early adopters who had an intimate connection to the computer's workings and system-level programming with the latter who were often frustrated by a system lacking transparency that had rules and limitations that were not always easy to understand. These adults in her study had multiple views of computers, with some suggesting computers were just mechanistic machines to those who viewed them as mysterious, complex, and autonomous. Turkle concluded that there was neither consensus on how computers might be seen in relationship to human intelligence while also proposing there was no single computer culture among adults.

The later sections of *Second Self* cover two cultures that Turkle indicated were more problematic in their viewpoints about computing and human relationships.

In reviewing hacker culture, she described this predominantly male group as being obsessive rather than antisocial. These individuals had taken mastery as the ultimate challenge, describing the relationship with computers as compulsive programming resulting in Zen-like states and an extension of one's mind to the machine, while pushing limits both of computer capabilities and of human bodies. Defined by competence and individuality rather than social values, the hacker culture challenged traditional roles and rules, but Turkle also noted that unlike other addictive hobbies, hacker culture could result in further education and lucrative careers.

In the final group discussed, Turkle examined the culture of experts in artificial intelligence (AI) as well as their graduate students. She argued this culture was steeped in scientism and examination of how the brain works based on machine metaphors, offering purely technical solutions to the mystery of the mind. With what she termed intellectual hubris underscored by lack of awareness of other disciplines, the AI experts proposed that intelligence is emergent from complex, programmed parts and lacks agency. At the extreme, she described students who denied free will and reasoning as being beyond personal control, without a *me*. She intimated that such extreme computational views of mind are seductive because they both fascinate and threaten our human distinctiveness.

Shaping Popular Culture: Philosophy, Psychology, and the Human Condition

Second Self is solely a study of U.S. culture and perceptions of technology within an American worldview. Although Turkle briefly discussed the digital divide and noted the international dimensions of limited access, the research reported was specific to one part of the society in which technology was most rapidly spreading. However, even within the United States and despite an increasing public fascination with and media attention to computers, at the time of the publication in 1984, only 8.2% of homes had a computer and these early machines could cost as much as an automobile, making the cultures described a specialized minority. One power of the study was the capturing of embryonic trends, examining multiple considerations that remain central in current thinking about mind, human nature, and the limitations of technology.

In the 20th-anniversary edition of *Second Self* released in 2005, Turkle added a new preface, epilogue, and extensive footnotes updating the study, noting that the computer remains an evocative object that continues to provoke self-reflection and creates a tension between virtual and physical worlds. She proposed that technology-centric concepts were shaping popular understandings of human nature and worldviews, extending earlier frames including Freudian psychology on the divided mind and Darwinian biological views of humans as organisms in the animal world. Interaction with computers, she argued, made the user consider deeper philosophical questions of self, personality, mortality, and even sensuality. In this respect, she saw her work as contributing to knowledge of computer cultures as well as leading to an understanding of the sociology of knowledge, with technology not as deterministic but being understood by the meaning people give to it.

Ellen S. Hoffman

See also Affective Factors in Learning, Instruction, and Technology; Cognition and Human Learning; Digital Identity

Further Readings

Turkle, S. (1984). *The second self: Computers and the human spirit.* New York, NY: Simon & Schuster.

Turkle, S. (1995). *Life on the screen: Identity in the age of the Internet.* New York, NY: Simon & Schuster.

Turkle, S. (2005). *The second self: Computers and the human spirit* (20th anniv. ed.). Cambridge, MA: MIT Press.

Turkle, S. (2011). *Alone together: Why we expect more from technology and less from each other.* New York, NY: Basic Books.

SELF-REGULATED E-LEARNING DESIGN PRINCIPLES

Research in the field of self-regulated learning (SRL) reveals that many learners have trouble managing and regulating their learning activities with e-learning systems. One vital factor in successful e-learning activities is learners' SRL abilities. Many studies have developed e-learning design principles that can encourage and support learners to self-regulate their e-learning, specifically actively processing e-learning contents and materials. These design principles are based upon the framework of SRL, which represents important concepts as phases and components. This entry first explains the concepts of SRL and research on SRL in e-learning environments. It then discusses e-learning design principles to promote students' SRL abilities.

Concepts of Self-Regulated Learning

Since Barry Zimmerman and Dale Schunk's publication of *Self-Regulated Learning and Academic Achievement: Theory, Research, and Practice* in 1989, three main

theories and models have explored the concept of SRL through investigating its components and processes. The most well-known SRL models developed by Zimmerman focus on the four main components of SRL: cognition, metacognition, motivation/affect, and behavior, which are also the four psychological attribute domains of self-regulated students. Cognition regulates cognitive strategies while learning and performing a task. Metacognition governs various metacognitive strategies to monitor and control cognitive processes. Motivation and affect include students' motivational beliefs such as self-efficacy and academic emotions about a learning task. Lastly, behavior involves monitoring one's own learning progress and actions, managing time and the learning environment, and requesting help and support. These four essential components of self-regulated learning can help students be more successful in their academic and professional endeavors.

Zimmerman continued to explore the process of SRL and suggested a cyclical model of SRL, which is composed of three phases in which certain SRL activities are performed, that is, the forethought phase (e.g., goal setting, planning, self-efficacy, outcome expectation, intrinsic interest/value, learning-goal orientation), the performance phase (e.g., imagery, self-instruction, attention focusing, task strategies, self-recording, self-experimentation), and the self-reflection phase (e.g., self-evaluation, causal attribution, self-satisfaction/affect, adaptive/defensive self-reaction). It allows us to define SRL as the degree to which learners are metacognitively, motivationally, and behaviorally active participants in their own learning.

Paul Pintrich's model, another leading model of SRL, proposes regulatory processes organized according to four phases: planning, self-monitoring, control, and evaluation. Within each of these phases, self-regulation activities are structured into four components: cognitive, motivational/affective, behavioral, and contextual.

In recent years, Zimmerman, Schunk, Pintrich, and other researchers have developed and applied their theories of self-regulation in learning contexts. Researchers analyze SRL as a combination of self-regulation, metacognition, and self-directed learning. SRL can be defined as a learning situation or process in which learners set their learning objectives, plan, conduct, regulate, and evaluate their learning activities independently to attain their goals.

Self-Regulated Learning in E-Learning Environments

The Web and developing technology have not only transformed learning and teaching activities and processes but also led to the rapid growth of the e-learning market worldwide. Studies have pointed out that isolated e-learning environments require self-regulation for effective learning. Reviewing SRL studies regarding online learning environments from 2003 to 2012, Chia-Wen Tsai, Pei-Di Shen, and Ya-Ting Fan indicated that many researchers have developed systems for implementing SRL in online learning and have explored the effects of SRL in online learning performance. SRL plays a critical role in improving learners' willingness to continue studying and in learning effects in e-learning environments.

David Jonassen and other colleagues suggested that the necessity of self-regulation in online learning environments may be even more important than in the traditional environment because of the less active role of the teacher. Learners must access the e-learning course independently and structure the time, pace, and strategy of their own learning processes. Also, Frederick B. King, Michael Harner, and Scott W. Brown hypothesized that

self-regulation of learning is more important in the e-learning context than in the traditional classroom context. Joan Whipp and Stephannie Chiarelli suggested that online learners use adapted SRL strategies, as indicated in Table 1.

The e-learning literature points out that successful online learners who have high self-regulation in their abilities to perform certain academic tasks tend to use more strategies and show higher task persistence than those who have lower self-regulation levels.

Developing Effective Principles for Learners

One important goal of both traditional and online educational systems is for students to learn to direct their own learning. Therefore, a key task for instructional

Table 1 Traditional and online SRL strategies

SRL Strategies	Traditional	Online
Forethought		
Goal setting and planning	Calendars and organizers; self-imposed deadlines; chunking work	Daily log-ons; coordination of online and offline work; planning for tech. problems
Performance and **Self-Observation**		
Organizing and transforming instructional materials	Note taking; outlining, underlining, or highlighting course texts; graphic organizers	Printing out course materials and discussions; offline composing and editing of postings; sorting discussion threads
Structuring the learning environment	Reducing distractions; relaxation techniques	Finding a fast computer and Internet connection; creating a psychological place for class
Help seeking	Phone, e-mail, or personal contact to get help from instructor or peers	Accessing technical expertise; peer contacts to reduce loneliness; Web-based helpers; using student postings as models
Self-monitoring and recordkeeping	Charts and records of completed assignments and grades	Multiple back-ups; tracking reading and writing for discussions; frequent checks of online gradebook
Self-Reflection		
Self-judgment	Using checklists and rubrics; using instructor comments and grades	Using an audience of peers to shape discussion postings
Self-reactions	Success based on academic performance	Success based on technical, social, academic performance

Source: Adapted from "Self-Regulation in a Web-Based Course: Case Study," by J. L. Whipp and S. Chiarelli, 2004. *Educational Technology Research & Development, 52*(4), 5–21.

designers and teachers is to develop effective principles or strategies that encourage and guide learners to actively participate and engage in their learning work.

Table 2 shows the e-learning design principles that promote students' SRL abilities in accordance with the suggested SRL components and processes. These principles were developed on the basis of the results of the research undertaken mainly between 2000 and 2013.

Cheolil Lim and Taejung Park

Table 2 Design principles for supporting SRL in e-learning environments

Components of SRL	Phases of the SRL Process		
	Forethought	*Performance*	*Reflection*
Cognition	• Support prior knowledge activation	• Offer learning support tools such as e-note, e-concept map for learning rehearsal, organization, and elaboration	• Give questions, feedback, or case studies to students for retrieving and applying acquired knowledge
	• Let students get engaged in task analysis	• Present online prompts, hints, and scripts for scaffolding to students	
		• Provide students with online discussion forums for composing, editing, and sorting postings	
Metacognition	• Guide students to set up goals/subgoals and plan the learning process	• Encourage students to use self-metacognitive questioning to comprehend the problem and use strategies for solving the problem	• Present self-evaluation forms for evaluating their own learning process/outcomes, behavior, and volition
	• Give advice or feedback to each student on his/her SRL diagnostic assessment	• Enable students to pursue their own goals but ask them to periodically verify how their stated goals relate to the learning task	• Offer e-portfolio for each student to review the records of his/her own work with self-monitoring and self-evaluating data
	• Provide course description, syllabus, assignments, and grades	• Allow students access to learning tracking system or log analyzer for self-monitoring	• Use e-progress to allow students to reflect on their learning progress
		• Introduce optional learning strategies to students for self-selection	
Motivation/Affect	• Provide students with the feeling of self-efficacy and technological efficacy	• Give students progression and attribution feedback to motivate students to keep going in their learning	• Provide students with opportunities for reflection about self-efficacy and technological efficacy
	• Encourage students to check their volition before they learn and give them feedback encouraging volition	• Inspire students to recognize and utilize self-efficacy and technological efficacy	• Let students freely express perceived satisfaction with learning environment

(Continued)

Table 2   (Continued)

Components of SRL	Phases of the SRL Process		
	Forethought	Performance	Reflection
Motivation/ Affect		• Offer synchronous and asynchronous communication tools to help students interact and collaborate with peers and to overcome a sense of isolation	
Behavior	• Let students check their learning goals	• Use LMS (learning management system) to enable students to easily and continuously check and record their learning process, activities, and learning outcomes and performance	• Present e-journal forms to students to freely write down reflections on their own learning
	• Offer e-calendar to allow students to plan time for learning	• Provide e-calendar for students to check and control their learning schedule	
	• Get students to check and structure learning environment	• Guide students to search for information and choose options from lists	
		• Construct online help seeking corner or help agents to encourage students to get support while learning	

See also Adaptive Learning Software and Platforms; Affective Factors in Learning, Instruction, and Technology; E-Portfolio Technologies; Human-Computer Interaction; Intelligent Tutoring Systems; Learning Analytics; Pedagogical Agents; Reflection and Preflection Prompts and Scaffolding; Synchronous Tools and Technologies; Web 2.0 and Beyond

Further Readings

Jonassen, D. H., Davidson, M., Collins, M., Campbell, J., & Haag, B. B. (1995). Constructivism and computer-mediated communication in distance education. *American Journal of Distance Education, 9*(2), 7–26.

King, F. B., Harner, M., & Brown, S. W. (2000). Self-regulatory behavior influences in distance learning. *International Journal of Instructional Media, 27*(2), 147–156.

Lim, C. (2005). Development and effects of a learning management system for supporting self-regulated learning. *Journal of Educational Technology, 21*(4), 77–100.

Pintrich, P. R. (2000). The role of goal orientation in self-regulated learning. In M. Boekaerts, P. R. Pintrich, & M. Zeidner (Eds.), *Handbook of self-regulation* (pp. 452–502). San Diego, CA: Academic Press.

Schunk, D. H., & Zimmerman, B. J. (1994). *Self-regulation of learning and performance: Issues and educational applications.* Hillsdale, NJ: Lawrence Erlbaum.

Tsai, C., Shen, P., & Fan, Y. (2013). Research trends in self-regulated learning research in online learning environments: A review of studies published in selected journals from 2003 to 2012. *British Journal of Educational Technology, 44*(5), E107-E110.

Whipp, J. L., & Chiarelli, S. (2004). Self-regulation in a Web-based course: Case study. *Educational Technology Research & Development, 52*(4), 5–21.

Zimmerman, B. J. (2002). Becoming a self-regulated learner: An overview. *Theory into Practice, 41*(2), 64–70.

Zimmerman, B. J., & Schunk, D. H. (Eds.). (1989). *Self-regulated learning and academic achievement: Theory, research and practice.* New York, NY: Springer-Verlag.

SEMANTIC WEB

The Semantic Web is an extension of the World Wide Web (WWW) in which information becomes more meaningful through well-defined concepts and systems enabling people and machines to work cooperatively. In the Semantic Web, machines can better understand and share the context in which information is being used by humans. This is achieved by improving interoperability at the system level and portability at the data level, thus creating a wide ranging infrastructure of semantically linked information that makes it easier to integrate, process, and publish data. This entry discusses the background and technological foundations of the Semantic Web, its uses in education, and its future prospects.

The Semantic Web initiative is a standardization endeavor within the World Wide Web Consortium aiming to provide the standards for representing and sharing machine-readable information on the Web. It emerged from the research traditions of knowledge representation, artificial intelligence, and information retrieval and has spread into areas such as knowledge management, library and documentation science, enterprise information management, and more recently into e-commerce and e-learning.

Semantic Web technologies are being utilized across a wide area of application areas including classification systems, knowledge bases, search engines, recommender systems, storage technologies, and metadata management. As Semantic Web standards attempt to change the ecosystem on the Web by building network effects around data, the Semantic Web has also been called Web 3.0, the Web of Data, Giant Global Graph, and Linked Data.

Technological Foundations of the Semantic Web

The core idea of the Semantic Web can be boiled down to the handy formulation: *things not strings.* This basically means that on the Semantic Web, machines are not processing words (strings) but concepts (things) to decipher their meaning in their particular context. This is achieved by embedding these concepts within so-called knowledge models or ontologies. They allow a machine to specify the context in which a certain meaning can claim validity. By doing this a machine is capable of distinguishing between the concept of *apple* as a fruit, a computer company, or a record label, thus improving the precision of a retrieval system. To achieve this, three methodological steps are obligatory:

1. *Use HTTP-URIs to name things:* On the Semantic Web, all things have a unique uniform resource identifier (URI), thus distinguishing ambiguous words from unique concepts. The idea behind this is to use HTTP-URIs—as we know them from the WWW—not just to address but also to name things via so-called namespaces. The HTTP-URI allows machines to dereference things and retrieve associated information, since an HTTP-URI can be linked to other HTTP-URIs according to the principles of hypertext.

2. *Link URIs using RDF:* By using RDF (Resource Description Format), HTTP-URIs are semantically linked to graphs. The tiniest graph is called a triple and is represented by the form of subject-predicate-value. Thus it is possible to express simple statements such as *Apple* (subject) *is a* (predicate) *fruit* (value), or *William Shakespeare* (subject) *is author of* (predicate) *King Lear* (value). Specific extensions of RDF—such as RDF Schema—allow linking millions of triples to create giant graphs and build highly expressive data webs. These graphs can be queried with the so-called SPARQL.

3. *Use ontologies to represent context:* Ontologies are domain-specific knowledge models that improve the semantic expressivity of RDF. Ontologies can take various forms and differ widely in scope and complexity. An ontology can range from a simple vocabulary (like DublinCore; LOM, for learning object metadata; or SCORM, for sharable content object reference model) that specifies the meaning of concepts within a certain knowledge domain, to highly expressive logic models that specify the relationships between concepts and classes and define logical constraints such as symmetries, transitivities, and inverse relationships. Commonly used standards for the latter case are the Simple Knowledge Organization System (SKOS) or the Web Ontology Language (OWL). From a technological perspective, ontologies lay the basis for a machine to disambiguate, infer, and reason over data, thus improving the linking, integration, coherent navigation, and discovery of knowledge sources.

At this point, it is important to draw a distinction between the Semantic Web and semantic technologies. While the latter denotes a wide range of technologies that are used to algorithmically derive meaning from information; that is, via data mining, natural language processing, reasoning, or tagging, the former should be understood as an endeavor to define standards for representing, linking, and sharing information. Hence, the Semantic Web provides the standards with which semantic data can be represented and published for further processing. Both technological strands complement each and are often symbiotically intertwined.

Semantic Web for Learning and Education

A learning situation is often characterized by a heterogeneity of knowledge sources and complex information management tasks. Software supported learning environments need to adapt to these specific circumstances, thus providing support to tutors and learners. Accordingly, Semantic Web technologies help to (1) represent learning content and organize learning repositories and digital libraries; (2) create adaptive platforms that support domain-specific learning situations, authoring, and exploration of instructional systems; and (3) build collaborative systems that enable sharable learning objects, learner models, and personalized learning designs.

Along the content value chain, Semantic Web technologies support the following:

- *Content acquisition* is mainly concerned with the collection, storage, and integration of data necessary to produce learning objects. In the course of this process, information and facts are being pooled from internal or external sources for further processing.
- *Content editing* entails all necessary steps that deal with the semantic adaptation, interlinking, and enrichment of data often performed via processes such as tagging or referencing to enrich learning objects.
- *Content bundling* is mainly concerned with contextualization and personalization of information. It can be used to provide customized access to learning objects, for example, by using metadata for the device-sensitive delivery of news items or to compile thematically relevant material into landing pages or dossiers, thus improving the navigability, findability, and reuse of information.
- *Content distribution* deals with the provision of machine-readable and semantically interoperable metadata via application programming interfaces (APIs) or so-called SPARQL endpoints. These can be designed either to serve internal purposes so that data can be reused within controlled environments (i.e., within or between classes) or for external purposes so that data can be shared between unknown users (i.e., as open data on the Web).
- *Content consumption* entails any means that enable a human user to search for and interact with content

items in a pleasant and purposeful way. This level mainly deals with end user applications such as search, recommendation, and filtering functionalities that provide personalized access to learning objects and enable adaptive information filtering.

Conclusion and Future Prospects

Semantic Web standards help to discover, create, reuse, and share information within specific learning situations. They expand our information management capabilities and support associated workflows on top of robust standards that have proven their practical value within various domains and application areas. But while the technological foundations of the Semantic Web are relatively simple, their application within networked and interoperable learning environments can reach a high level of complexity, making it difficult to manage and maintain such interconnected ecosystems, especially when external knowledge sources are volatile and do not comply with shared standards of technological and technical quality. This includes aspects such as the reliability and validity of data sources, their consistency, timeliness, and objectivity, as well as sufficient information on integrity, provenance, and licensing. Semantic Web technologies offer interesting approaches to tackle these issues and create a more robust information environment. Nevertheless, if and how Semantic Web technologies will shape future learning is less a question of technological feasibility then a question of educational policy.

Tassilo Pellegrini

See also Data Mining and Recommendation Engines; Disruptive Technologies; Emerging Educational Technologies; Knowledge Elicitation; Metatagging of Learning Objects and Apps; Natural Language Processing in Learning Environments; Web 2.0/3.0 in the Workplace

Further Readings

Alesso, H. P., & Smith, C. F. (2009). *Thinking on the Web. Berners-Lee, Gödel and Turing.* Hoboken, NJ: Wiley.

Berners-Lee, T., Hendler, J., & Lassila, O. (2001, May 17). The Semantic Web. *Scientific American.* Retrieved from http://www.scientificamerican.com/article.cfm?id=the-semantic-web

Dicheva, D., Mizoguchi, R., & Greer, J. (Eds.). (2009). *Semantic Web technologies for e-learning.* Amsterdam, Netherlands: IOS Press.

Heath, T., & Bizer, C. (2011). *Linked data: Evolving the Web into a global data space.* San Rafael, CA: Morgan & Claypool. Retrieved from http://linkeddatabook.com/editions/1.0/

Hitzler, P., Krötzsch, M., & Rudolph, S. (2009). *Foundations of Semantic Web technologies*. Boca Raton, FL: CRC Press.

World Wide Web Consortium. (2013). Semantic Web standards. Retrieved from http://www.w3.org/standards/semanticweb/

SERIOUS GAMES

Serious games (SGs) are games designed for a primary goal involving learning. SGs are a significant part of the broader concept of gamification, which involves using game elements in non-entertaining environments or situations to improve the user experience. SGs are receiving growing interest for use in training and education. Exploiting the latest simulation and visualization technologies, SGs are able to contextualize the player's cognitive experience in challenging, realistic environments. Play supports exercising freedom that can complement formal learning by encouraging learners to explore various situations, with few barriers of space and time. SGs can also simulate complex environments at relatively low costs, as well as simulate dangerous situations without exposing the user to danger. This entry first describes SGs and gives an overview of their use in education. It then discusses the history of SGs and ways of classifying them, how SGs are developed, how their design and use relates to pedagogical theories, and how they are used in instructional settings.

SGs can be for multiple players, which can support team building, collaboration, and cooperation. The widespread diffusion of mobile gaming opens new opportunities for learning and online socialization. Furthermore, a large and growing population is increasingly familiar with new typologies of games (e.g., brain-training games and intellectual challenges such as *Professor Layton and the Curious Village* and *Phoenix Wright: Ace Attorney*) and with new modalities of interactions (e.g., online collaboration, verbal commands, gesture-based control, social environments, family gaming). Moreover, several new games are cheap to produce and run on low-cost platforms.

There are currently thousands of SGs. Examples include *America's Army*, one of the first ones, and still used for military recruitment; *Building Detroit*, which is integrated with other multimedia material for education; the *Siege of Syracuse*, featuring virtual reconstructions in the cultural heritage domain; *CancerSpace* and *Re:Mission* in the health sector; *SimPort,* for management of harbor activities; *RescueSim*, a detailed simulation for the training of security forces; *Hands-On Equations 1 Lite*, for children's math instruction; *Renault Academy,* for training salesmen and dealers; the *Real Lives 2010* life simulation game; and, *Marketplace*, a business simulation for higher education.

Use of SGs for education and training introduces some concerns. For instance, intended learning outcomes, game objectives, and features (e.g., difficulty level, duration, aesthetic, interaction modalities) might not be well aligned. The suspension of disbelief, typically required in a game, may negatively influence the learning processes. Certain sociodemographic groups may feel excluded and frustration may be created by usability issues and competition. There is a risk of stressing extrinsic motivation (through competition, rewards, badges, etc.) while neglecting intrinsic motivation that is fundamental in the long term. Developing commercial games is extremely expensive, and educational institutions can rarely afford large game expenditures. Thus, the term *game* may create a mismatch with user expectations. A study by Jayshiro Tashiro reports that while there is insufficient evidence to know if current serious games may improve healthcare education, there is evidence that they may inculcate inadequate clinical pattern recognition. All these observations highlight the fact that SG design is a complex challenge, involving a variety of dimensions, and that use of SGs in educational settings should be properly organized.

History, Application Domains, and Taxonomies

Following from the differentiation between games for fun and games for learning, the term *serious game* was first used by Clark C. Abt. The *serious game* term in a digital context was first used in 2002 with the start of the Serious Game Initiative led by David Rejeski and Ben Sawyer.

SGs were initially conceived to train people for tasks in particular jobs, such as Army and sales personnel. With the diffusion of new devices (e.g., smartphones, tablets, various types of consoles), a variety of SGs has rapidly emerged for different types of users (students, adults, workers, etc.), with different applications and goals (instruction, training, advertising, politics, etc.) in different genres (arcade, first-person shooter, etc.). Taxonomies have been proposed classifying SGs according to different criteria, such as application domains, markets, skills, and learning outcomes. The SG classification proposed by Sawyer and Peter Smith features a matrix of two major criteria: market (the application domain) and purpose (initial purpose of the designer). Items in the first dimension include government, defense, marketing, education, and corporate. Items in the second dimension include adventure games, games for health, and games for training. A hypercube taxonomy has been developed by Michael Kickmeier-Rust, with the following dimensions:

Purpose—ranging from fun and enjoyment to training and learning.

Reality—ranging from imitation of real and fictitious contexts to proving abstract visualizations, such as in *Tetris* and similar games.

Social Involvement—ranging from single player games to massively multiplayer games.

Activity—ranging from active game types (e.g., action games or those with a physical activity dimension such as the *Nintendo Wii*) to passive game types (where at the end of this continuum the passive perception of a movie is situated).

A worldwide collaborative classification of SGs selected these classification dimensions:

- *gameplay*, referring to games with fixed goals to achieve and core rules;
- *purpose*, which can refer to, for example, education, information, marketing, advertising, subjective message broadcasting, training, goods trading, and storytelling;
- *market*, which is used to refer to the general theme of the game, with the categories entertainment, state and government, military and defense, healthcare, education, corporate, religion, culture and art, ecology, politics, humanitarian and caritative, media, advertising, and scientific research; and
- *audience*, which is broken into age groups, the general public, professionals, and students.

More structured databases of educational SGs have been by projects such as Imagine, ENGAGE (European Network for Growing Activity in Game-based learning in Education) Learning, and GaLA/Serious Games Society (SGS). The GaLA (Game and Learning Alliance) SG Knowledge Management System includes a number of descriptors that are useful for conducting SG studies, including

- *description/classification*, which refers to the genre, platform(s), application domain, learning curve, effective learning time, play mode, player assessment, provision of feedback, and others;
- *analysis of game components*, which refers to the user interface (UI), rules, goals, entity manipulation (i.e., player activities that change the status of objects in the game), and assessment, providing a detailed specification of the game mechanisms;

- *pedagogy*, which details both the games' theoretical frameworks (constructivism, objectivism, personalism, etc.) and outcomes, including cognitive, psychomotor, and affect outcomes, and soft skills;
- *deployment,* or how the game is used, specifying settings such as target users (age, specific categories of persons, school level, etc.); target topics; prerequisites for use, if any (cognitive, content-related, domain related, psychomotor, etc.); and context of use (e.g., formal education, corporate training);
- *technologies employed for the development*, including the game engine, development tools and platforms, and AI algorithms; and
- *metrics* provided to allow an assessment of SGs along dimensions such as learning effectiveness, efficiency, and fun level.

SG Development: A Multidisciplinary Challenge

In order to develop and deploy effective tools for learning, it is necessary to consider all the stakeholders (users, educators, families, researchers, developers, and industries) and the whole cycle from research to market. One must also consider a complex mix of disciplines and technologies, such as artificial intelligence (AI), human-computer interaction (HCI), networking, computer graphics and architecture, signal processing, Web-distributed computing, and neurosciences. User benefits are at the center of the process. When designed with instructional and learning goals in mind, SGs should provide quality content and be strongly grounded in pedagogy and the sciences of learning. Figure 1 sketches the complexity of the various disciplines and factors involved in proper SG development.

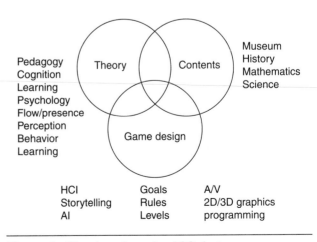

Figure 1   The three kernels of SG design

Pedagogical Theories and Models

Games can be used to motivate students. However, instructional effectiveness involves other aspects that can be analyzed in light of pedagogical and learning theories.

The design and use of digital serious games has a theoretical foundation in constructivist learning theories, which stress that knowledge is created through experience while exploring the world and performing activities. The implications of such theories for game design involve the creation of virtual environments, typically 3D, where the player can gain knowledge through exploration and practice (e.g., manipulating objects), possibly in collaboration with other people.

Constructivism stresses the importance for the learners to build their own knowledge. However, guidance is also needed, in particular for novices. Learning is a complex activity that requires time and several steps that have to be supported by various tools and generally have to be guided in order to be meaningful or compelling for the learner without wasting time and energy. Maps, landmarks, contextualized helps, and lists of objectives with status information are game elements that can be employed to avoid cognitive overload.

Another important theory is *flow*, based on Mihaly Csikszentmihalyi's foundational concepts. As the result of more than three decades of commercial competition, most of today's video games deliberately include and leverage the eight components of flow: concentration, challenge, skills, control, clear goals, feedback, immersion, and social interaction. In order to maintain a user's flow experience, the game's activity must balance the inherent challenge and the player's ability to address and overcome it. If the challenge is beyond that ability, the activity becomes so overwhelming that it generates anxiety. On the other hand, if the challenge fails to engage the player, the player loses interest and quickly tends to get bored. Serious games designed to educate also should balance the challenge with the user's ability to meet the challenge.

Personalism is another fundamental pedagogical theory that tends to consider education as a human relationship between a child (learner) and an adult (teacher) who introduces the child to reality. Centrality of the person stresses user-centered design. Other specific implications from SG design may involve (a) presence of real-world hooks (e.g., territorial gaming), (b) references inside the game, (c) a dialogue between learner and teacher, and (d) game analytics to provide detailed information about performance that could be analyzed by the teacher in order to advise on possible improvements and corrective actions.

Two complementary pedagogical models seem particularly useful to analyze SGs: (1) Bloom's revised taxonomy, which is the most popular cognitive approach to SG evaluation; and, (2) Kolb's experiential learning model, which puts experience at the center of the learning process. Good SGs and simulations should allow users to have significant experiences, thus typically supporting the experiential learning pedagogical paradigm.

Deploying SGs

SGs are being used in a variety of training and educational settings ranging from elementary schools (e.g., with games for mathematics and foreign languages) to universities (e.g., in particular with games for business management, logistics, and manufacturing). Extensively gamified courses are also being deployed. Even the use of commercial-off-the-shelf (COTS) games (e.g., *Civilization*, *SimCity*) is being considered for instruction, given their popularity and cost-effectiveness. COTS are not tailored to specific instructional goals but can be molded for use in education.

When selecting commercial games or SGs, typical criteria include the following:

- ability to cover the needed topics for the target students with a range of abilities and needs satisfaction of basic pedagogical principles;
- satisfaction of basic usability criteria;
- license costs; and
- possibility for students to play at home, or on a laptop or mobile device.

In order to describe and analyze the educational characteristics of each game, which is a fundamental step for selection, use of Bloom's revised taxonomy and of Kolb's learning stages has been investigated. Jannicke Baalsrud-Hauge and colleagues proposed a framework for the proper integration of games in education, supporting different goals in different steps of a formal education process. While based on experience in business games, this framework can be employed in other subjects.

Concerns have emerged about an extensive use of videogames, in particular by youngsters. This is to be kept in consideration also in the case of educational games, in particular when considering concerns about children becoming hyperstimulated and whether they can distinguish between virtuality and reality. Addressing these concerns requires responsible adults managing the education process as well as the use of games with a user-centered design that considers all stakeholders, starting with parents.

The SandBox SG model

SG design involves devising and using proper mechanics and models. As an example, this section describes the sandbox serious game (SBSG) model, which relies on a generalization of task-based learning theory. The model invites players to perform cognitive tasks contextually while exploring information-rich virtual environments. The model defines games (e.g., treasure hunts) that are set in realistic virtual worlds (typically 3D) enriched with embedded educational tasks implemented as minigames that can be instantiated out of a set of predefined templates. This approach simplifies the authoring work, allowing an approach similar to the mind-maps concept, where a topic can be subdivided into a hierarchy of items. Tasks or minigames (played through a virtual smartphone interface) allow the player to focus on a specific item or topic in the environment. Each task or minigame involves very short introduction and conclusion texts that complement and reinforce the task experience through plain verbal knowledge. Discussing a lab-user test aimed at verifying the acquisition of cultural heritage knowledge, a study reports that games appear particularly suited for supporting the study of images, especially of iconography. Compared to reading a text, a game forces the player to focus more strongly on problems, which favors knowledge acquisition and retention. Learning complex concepts requires an investigative attitude, which can be spurred by well-designed games. Good design involves usability, graphic appeal, appropriate content, and the presence of connections that a player must discover in the content. Players should be asked to pay attention to and reason about their whole game activity—including the relationships between the game content, the brief introduction, and concluding texts.

When designing an SG, the definition of levels is a major aspect. In general, novice learners and users need guidance, while advanced users can benefit also from experimentation. Thus, as a general rule, the lower levels should involve rich game elements that drive the user along an instructional path, while higher levels can be more like simulations, where the player who has already developed some reliable knowledge structures can exercise freedom in exploring a field.

In any case, an effective application of SGs for education and training demands appropriate metrics, analytics, tools, and techniques for in-game user assessment. This is a distinctive point for educational serious games. Assessment is key for games in education, since knowing and understanding what was learned is the basis for appropriate treatment. Proper assessment requires continuously tracking the user in all game activities, providing appropriate feedback and also supporting adaptivity and personalization. Assessment should be done in real-time and without interrupting the user's flow (as in stealth or embedded assessment). This can be achieved in particular by measuring elements such as learning outcomes and engagement, considering the twofold nature of SGs as compelling games that achieve precise educational goals. Learning analytics and game analytics are the tools now being developed in order to improve game design and to provide feedback to the player based on actual gameplay data.

Adaptivity to different learner profiles is a capability that is difficult to provide by human teachers in large classes. As a consequence, it represents a significant added value for a system able to support efficient learning and teaching.

Devices such as stereo cameras, eye trackers, tablets, smartphones, pointing devices, motion sensors, sensors related to the central and peripheral nervous systems (e.g., galvanic skin response, heart rate, neuronal activity), among others, present opportunities to develop innovative solutions for continuous user monitoring and assessment.

However, due to the complexity of human nature and individual differences, an objective and systematic assessment of learner behavior and performance remains highly difficult. In addition, data analyses and evaluation methods taking into account the nature of SGs are still underdeveloped.

Conclusion

SGs aim at improving learning processes by providing attractive, motivating, and effective tools. So far, effectiveness of SGs has been shown by recent studies, but the potential of SGs for instruction—in particular, providing compelling plots and contexts where players can effectively and efficiently acquire new knowledge and skills and accurately verify progress—is still far from being fulfilled. There is a growing need for scientific and engineering methods and tools for efficiently building games to provide effective learning experiences. The development of new generation SGs requires exploitation of advanced technologies (in fields such as artificial intelligence, human-computer interaction, modeling and simulation, neurosciences, virtual reality, etc.,) and accurate studies on the design of game formats, mechanics, and dynamics so that games can fulfill both education and entertainment goals, which is difficult to achieve in a single design.

Alessandro De Gloria,
Francesco Bellotti, and Riccardo Berta

See also Games: Impact on Interest and Motivation; Games: Impact on Learning; Games and Transformational Play; Games in Business and Industry Settings; Games in Elementary and Middle School Settings; Games in Higher Education; Games in Medical Training; Games in Military Training; Games to Promote Inquiry Learning; Gamification

Further Readings

Baalsrud Hauge, J., Bellotti, F., Berta, R., Carvalho, M. B., De Gloria, A., Lavagnino, E., . . . & Ott, M. (2013). Field assessment of serious games for entrepreneurship in higher education. *Journal of Convergence Information Technology, 8*(13), 1–12.

Bellotti, F., Berta, R., & De Gloria, A. (2010). Designing effective serious games: Opportunities and challenges for research. *International Journal of Emerging Technologies in Learning, 5*, 22–35.

Connolly, T. M., Boyle, E. A., MacArthur, E., Hainey, T., & Boyle, J. M. (2012). A systematic literature review of the empirical evidence on computer games and serious games. *Computers & Education, 59*(2), 661–686.

Doucet, L., & Srinivasan, V. (2010). Designing entertaining educational games using procedural rhetoric: A case study. In S. N. Spencer (Ed.), *Proceedings of the 5th ACM SIGGRAPH symposium on video games* (pp. 5–10). New York, NY: Association for Computing Machinery. doi.acm.org/10.1145/1836135.1836136

Gee, J. P. (2003). *What video games have to teach us about learning and literacy.* New York, NY: Palgrave Macmillan.

Greitzer, F. L., Kuchar, O. A., & Huston, K. (2007). Cognitive science implications for enhancing training effectiveness in a serious gaming context, *ACM Journal of Educational Resources in Computing, 7*(3), 1–15.

Howell, K., Glinert, E., Holding, L., & Swain, C. (2007). How to build serious games. *Communications of the ACM, 50*(7), 44–49.

Prensky, M. (2003). *Digital game-based learning.* New York, NY: Paragon House.

Shute, V. J, & Ke, F. (2012). Games, learning, and assessment. In D. Ifenthaler, D. Eseryel, & X. Ge (Eds.), *Assessment in game-based learning: Foundations, innovations and perspectives* (pp. 43–58). New York, NY: Springer-Verlag.

Wouters, P., van Oostendorp, H., van Nimwegen, C., & van der Spek, E. D. (2013). A meta-analysis of the cognitive and motivational effects of serious games. *Journal of Educational Psychology, 105*(2), 249–265.

Zyda, M. (2005, September). From visual simulation to virtual reality to games. *IEEE Computer, 9*. Retrieved from http://www.computer.org/csdl/mags/co/2005/09/r9025-abs.html

Websites

Serious Game Classification: http://serious.gameclassification.com

SIMULATED SYSTEMS FOR ENVIRONMENTAL PLANNING

Sustainable management of a region's valuable environmental assets requires comprehension of alternative ways that these resources will function into the future depending upon different policy and investment choices. Environmental resources must be understood and treated as complex systems that are part of regional and global networks. Simulated systems for environmental planning serve as planning support systems that simulate future environmental change associated with alternative futures resulting from present day decisions. These tools are included here because they utilize simulation, an important educational technology methodology, to educate citizens and stakeholders to assist with environmental decision making in public forums. These systems use visualization to produce output in formats that enable users to easily perceive trends and intuitively visualize results through the use of educational multimedia such as graphs, moving images, and motion pictures generated from the data displayed with computer generated imagery (CGI). A number of these important systems have been developed by professors and students in a higher education setting, where they are also utilized for teaching and learning. This entry provides information about the critical need for support with environmental planning today and about how these simulated systems can help. It discusses the components of the systems and their workflow and explains how they are used in tandem with facilitated planning processes. It presents the land-use evolution and impact assessment model (LEAM), as an example of such a simulated system.

The Crucial Role of Environmental Planning

The global need for sustainability is a critical and challenging issue today involving complex interdependencies among social, political, and technical domains. Important discussions are now taking place around the world related to climate change, water quality and quantity, air quality, habitat fragmentation, and energy sources and consumption patterns among other environmental issues. Climate change has been attributed by a number of observers to land use. Past development has often sparked a series of unanticipated environmental consequences. Patterns of urban and regional development undertaken without thorough consideration of possible outcomes can cause harm by degrading critical environmental resources, negatively affecting public and species health. Simulated systems for environmental planning are in their infancy but are increasingly available for use by communities and governmental decision-making bodies to estimate the impacts of development when utilizing planning processes to address natural resource and environmental concerns.

Environmental planning is an interdisciplinary activity with an enormous scope and impact on public welfare. It encompasses environmental design, sustainability, natural resource management, urban and regional planning, social and economic development, and infrastructure systems. It comprises growth, development, and evolution of urban and rural areas and responsive and effective management during crisis and disasters. Related environmental issues include water, air, and noise pollution; transportation; economic and housing characteristics; wetlands; endangered species and their habitats; public health and toxicity; and flood zones susceptibility and coastal zones erosion, among other topics.

Definition of Simulated Systems in Environmental Planning

A simulated system for environmental planning is a computer system that imitates the operation of a real-world environmental system. It consists of two components: a *model* representing the key features of the selected physical system and the *simulation* itself, which "runs" the model and represents the operation of the system over time, resulting in outputs that help users to visualize and understand the environmental impacts of various choices. The model is made up of the algorithms and equations that capture the behavior of the system being modeled, while the system constitutes the actual running of the program containing the equations and algorithms. The scale of events and variables that can be simulated by computer simulations can far exceed anything possible using traditional paper and pencil mathematical modeling, hence their usefulness for exploring the performance of systems too complex for noncomputerized analytical solutions such as environmental systems.

Simulated systems for environmental planning serve as planning support systems that simulate future environmental changes associated with alternative futures resulting from differing strategies. Each system is used in tandem with a corresponding process that assesses the future development on the environment through

- characterizing ecosystem features and resources,
- forecasting future changes, and
- assessing how these future changes will affect environmental resources.

These simulated systems make it possible to carry out this process with extremely detailed quantitative and systematic analyses of regional and urban dynamics. They provide an enhanced ability to systematically challenge conventional wisdom and preconceived notions because of the emergence of unintended consequences during the computer simulation process.

Simulated systems for environmental planning are planning support systems. Different systems vary in the types of planning processes they are best suited to support. While all such processes are iterative, some systems provide more transparency, supporting decision making that is more collaborative and inclusive. Systems also differ in their requirements for data preparation; the composition, type, and underlying data structure of the models used; and the formats for visualization of the output data such as multimedia to effectively communicate findings to stakeholders.

Example: Land-Use Evolution and Impact Assessment Model (LEAM)

The purpose of LEAM, as stated on its website, is to enable others to make better future land-use decisions through helping them to understand the relationships between human economic and cultural activities and biophysical cycles from a changing land-use perspective and to recognize that these interacting systems behave in very complex and dynamic ways. The development and applications of LEAM are conducted and managed by a team of faculty, staff, and students at the University of Illinois at Urbana-Champaign (UIUC). The team has expertise in substantive issues, modeling, high performance computing, and visualization from the Departments of Landscape Architecture, Urban Planning, Geography, Economics, Natural Resources and Environmental Sciences at UIUC, the National Center for Supercomputing Applications at UIUC, the United States Army Corps of Engineers, and private industry.

LEAM is designed to simulate future land-use change as a result of alternative policies and development decisions. It was developed to coordinate complex regional planning activities and aid in regionally based thinking, decision support, and policy establishment. Recently LEAM has been used in combination with transportation and social cost models to capture the effects land use has on transportation demands and social costs.

The first incarnation of LEAM was developed in the Department of Urban and Regional Planning at UIUC in the late 1990s with funding from the National Science Foundation. Its popularity led to technology licensing and commercialization. Since 2003, when the LEAM group was formally founded, LEAM and its planning and decision support tools have been used throughout the United States and abroad.

LEAM utilizes a modeling approach that uses cellular automata and other technological advances in spatial simulation modeling to help improve a community's ability to make ecologically and environmentally sound decisions. It is intended to enable users to capture stochastic influences and view the reported probable consequences of intended events in a scenario-based visual format comprehensible by local experts, decision makers, and stakeholders.

There are two major parts in the LEAM framework: a land-use change (LUC) model and urbanization impact models. The LUC is the core of LEAM and is used to answer the question "How does land use change with specific assumptions or policies?" The urbanization impact models further analyze urban land-use change answering questions related to the results of the land-use question under consideration, such as the meaning of the resulting land-use change and its effect on a number of factors including water quality, air quality, traffic, property values, and so on.

After models are created, dialogue with planners, policy makers and other participating community members and stakeholders takes place. Feedback is acquired through use of questions eliciting satisfaction with the modeling results as well as proposed alternatives and suggestions for revised strategies. These comments are used as feedback input to the models and may result in running additional scenarios in the LUC model.

In the creation of the LUC model, the forces—or drivers—that may contribute to land-use change are explicitly quantified; this makes it possible to evaluate the potential for land-use transformation in a particular scenario. These drivers represent the interactions between the urban system and surrounding landscape. Each driver is developed as an independent submodel that can be calibrated before being run simultaneously with the other LEAM drivers in the computer simulation process. Vacant or developable lands can be transformed into one of three types of urban cells: residential, commercial and industrial, and urban open space. Driver submodels address urban dynamics as influenced by regional economics, social factors, transportation infrastructure, proximity to city centers, geographic factors, neighboring land uses, and spontaneous growth. LEAM has an open architecture and modular design that makes it simple to incorporate extra drivers.

LEAM uses maps based on the U.S. Geological Survey's National Land Cover Data to replicate the land-use conditions in the area being considered. The model similarly uses the same resolution map to simulate the socioeconomic, parcel-by-parcel decision making influencing urban growth patterns. Each driver

contributes to the calculation of the development potential of each grid cell and can be weighted to represent the local influence as appropriate. This modeling process is used to determine the overall growth potential of each land cell. Modeling also occurs in the next phase to provide population and economic trends over time. A regional input-output econometric model is applied. If needed to determine various regional demands, results can be further used in allocation models. This makes it possible to adjust the development potential of each cell to real probability to meet regional demand.

Ultimately, a Monte Carlo stochastic simulation is conducted to select the cells that are best suited to be developed for urban growth. Stochastic models are those that use random number generators to model chance or random events. LEAM developers have chosen this method because they feel that the Monte Carlo simulation provides a fairer means of selection, makes it possible to run the simulation in parallel mode, and provides a visually realistic pattern.

The LEAM modeling environment makes it possible to model and test environmental, economic, and social system impacts of alternative scenarios including different land-use policies, growth trends, and unexpected events. These scenarios are built around various decision-maker hypotheses that play a strong role in the human process portion of the simulation workflow. As output, LEAM delivers visual representation(s) of each scenario's outcome; possible formats include simulation movies, maps available through a built-in mapping tool, graph or chart displays, or raw data. These visual representations provide an intuitive means for collaborative decision makers to understand the results of different strategies that have been hypothesized and serve as input for discussion and group decision making. As land-use changes from one type to another during the computer simulation runs, they often impact other elements in the model. The LEAM Framework is able to track and integrate these changes through impact models.

LEAM makes it possible to determine the consequences of additional developments in a particular part of a community and the perhaps unforeseen regional impact of changing conditions such as new roads. Questions on the impact of growth policies on the social well-being and environmental health of existing residents can be considered. The most important feature of LEAM, according to its creators, is its emphasis on a "collaborative approach and the democratization of results" (Ruth, 2006, p. 199).

LEAM is a dynamic work in progress; this is the case with other prominent simulation systems for environmental planning including UrbanSim, an open source simulation system supported by the National Science Foundation and U.S. Environmental Protection

Agency, which has been regularly revised since 1998 and is used throughout the world. GoldSim, a dynamic, probabilistic simulation software, has been in development since 1990 and has been extensively used for high-profile environmental risk analysis.

With the acceleration of computing power and increasing acceptance of the need for environmental innovation and planning, it is probable that simulated systems for environmental planning and their affiliated technologies and processes will continue to evolve and be increasingly used.

Deborah Elizabeth Cohen

See also Multimedia and Image Design; Simulation-Based Learning

Further Readings

Deal, B., & Pallathucheril, V. (2009). Sustainability and urban dynamics: Assessing future impacts on ecosystem services. *Sustainability, I,* 346–362. Retrieved from www.mdpi.com/journal/sustainability

Iacono, M., Levinson, D., El-Geneidy, A. (2008). Models of transportation and land use change: A guide to the territory. *Journal of Planning Literature, 22*(4), 323–340. Retrieved from http://nexus.umn.edu/Papers/MTLUC.pdf

Ruth, M. (2006). *Smart growth and climate change: Regional development, infrastructure, and adaptation.* Northampton, MA: Edward Elgar.

Sun, Z., Deal, B., & Pallathucheril, V. (2009). The land use evolution and assessment model: A comprehensive urban planning support system. *Urisa Journal, 21*(1), 57–68.

Waddell, P. (2002). UrbanSim: Modeling urban development for land use, transportation and environmental planning. *Journal of the American Planning Association, 68*(3), 297–313.

Websites

GoldSim, Monte Carlo simulation software for decision and risk analysis: http://www.goldsim.com

Land use evolution and impact assessment model (LEAM): http://www.leam.illinois.edu/leam

UrbanSim, a software-based simulation system for supporting planning and analysis of urban development: http://www.urbansim.org

Simulation Applications in Engineering Education

Simulation refers to a methodology to build usually complex mathematical or logical models to imitate the operations of real-life systems. These simulation models can be static or dynamic, deterministic or stochastic, and discrete or continuous, as argued by Averill Law.

Simulation can be used for several different purposes: For example, it is a technique that enables one to evaluate functions when mathematical forms of these functions are not available. Furthermore, simulation can be used to investigate different scenarios through the *what-if* analysis; that is, change one or more data in the simulation model and analyze the effects of these changes on the performance measures. Moreover, simulation can be used to find better working conditions for systems, which satisfy some limitations on the resources (i.e., optimization). However, simulation is time consuming. A further disadvantage of simulation is that if the models are stochastic, the performance measures are only estimated through some sophisticated statistical techniques up to certain measures of accuracy (i.e., variances). Therefore, analytical techniques are preferable to simulation, if they are available. Jack Kleijnen discusses sophisticated statistical tools for simulation and the various uses of simulation. This entry first discusses different types of simulation models and why simulation is important in engineering education. It then gives examples of simulation games used in engineering education.

An example of dynamic, stochastic, and discrete models is a queuing model. As an example of a queuing model, one can think of the simulation model for a supermarket, where customers arrive and do their shopping. For such systems, it is usually assumed that as soon as the customers finish shopping, they join the queue of a cashier and wait for their turn. Whenever the cashier finishes serving the customer currently in service, that customer leaves the supermarket, and in the simulation language, the cashier becomes idle. Then, instantaneously, the service of the first customer in queue, if there are any, starts, and the cashier becomes busy again; this is what is called the first-in-first-out queue discipline. Depending on the studied systems, the next customer to be served can be the last one in the queue, the one with the shortest processing time in the queue, and so forth. One could use a what-if analysis, changing the first-in-first-out queue discipline to last-in-first-out, and analyze its effects on the average delay in the queue.

For the supermarket model, one usually does not know the times between the arrival of successive customers or their shopping times; in fact, one can only observe and collect certain realizations of these times. Therefore, the interarrival and the shopping times form the *stochastic* components of the supermarket simulation model. Furthermore, building simulation models requires the definition of some state variables, which are the variables that describe the system at a particular point in time. For the supermarket model, if one is interested in estimating the expected delay time in queue and the expected utilizations of all cashiers, then possible state variables consist of the number of customers in the queue and indicators showing whether the cashiers are idle or busy at a particular time. Obviously, these state variables change *dynamically* in time, and the changes occur at *discrete* points in time by the occurrences of two types of events, namely the arrival and the departure of a customer. This finishes the description of one type of simulation, which is known as *discrete-event dynamic simulation* in the academic literature.

There are also dynamic, deterministic, and continuous simulation models. These models are typically formulated through a complex, *deterministic* system of differential equations, which is not analytically solvable. A typical example is the predator-prey model, where one considers two interacting populations, say, rabbits and foxes. The dynamics of the system are determined by the births and the deaths of both populations. The state variables can be the two population sizes at a particular point in time, and these variables change *dynamically* in time. Furthermore, different from the discrete-event simulation, the changes in the state variables (i.e., population sizes) occur *continuously* in time; as an analogy, one can think of the population size as the water level in a tank at a particular time point, with water coming in the tank as the birth rate and water going out of the tank as the death rate. This finishes the description of another type of simulation, which is known as *system dynamics simulation* in the literature.

Another type of simulation is *Monte Carlo simulation,* which refers to a scheme of generating pseudorandom numbers for solving *stochastic* or *deterministic* problems that are analytically unsolvable (e.g., a system of complex integrals). For Monte Carlo simulation, time has no role; therefore, different from the previous models, the Monte Carlo models are *static*.

Why Is Simulation Important in Engineering Education?

Engineering is a practicing profession, which is devoted to harnessing and modifying the three fundamental resources available for the creation of all technology, namely energy, materials, and information. The overall goal of engineering education is to prepare students to practice engineering, that is, to deal with the forces and materials of nature. Thus, instructional laboratories have been an essential part of undergraduate and, in some cases, graduate programs.

Lyle Feisel and Albert Rosa have argued that information technology has dramatically changed laboratory education. The nature and practices of laboratories have been changed by two new technology-intensive automations, namely simulated laboratories and remote laboratories. Considering that in education, simulation has been used to provide illustrations of phenomena that are hard to visualize, such as electromagnetic fields, laminar flow in pipes, heat transfer through materials, and electron flow in semiconductors, and that it is possible to develop reasonably accurate mathematical models of these physical phenomena, it is natural that simulation experiments have been used as an adjunct to or even as a substitute for actual laboratory experiments.

The general uses of simulation in engineering education and its advantages are discussed below.

* It is possible to use simulation as a prelab experience to give students some idea of what they will encounter in an actual experiment. This improves laboratory safety by familiarizing students with the equipment before actually using it, and it can also result in significant financial savings by reducing the needs on real and expensive laboratory equipment, as discussed by Feisel and Rosa.

* It is possible to use simulation as a substitute for actual laboratory experiments and then assess students' learning by comparing the performance of students who used simulation and those who used physical laboratory experiments. John Campbell and his colleagues found that the students who used simulation scored higher on a written exam. After they had done the simulation, these students were also required to perform two physical laboratory experiments. Judged on the basis of time needed to complete these experiments, the two groups performed about the same, although the times of the students who used the simulation exhibited a significantly higher variability.

* Simulation is useful for experimental studies of systems that are too large, too expensive, or too dangerous for physical measurements. As an example, one can think of a manufacturing company that is contemplating the purchase of an expensive machine but is not sure whether the potential gain in productivity would justify the purchase cost. A careful simulation study that simulates the company as it currently is and as it would be if the machine were purchased can satisfactorily answer this question.

* Simulation is a learning-by-doing technique that incorporates an element of fun in the learning process.

* Simulation enables dynamic participation of the students, and it gives immediate feedback to the students, which can help with connecting theory and practice to encourage students' understanding of the subject.

Simulation Games in Engineering Education

A simulation game consists of elements like score, performance rating, conflict, and payoff, and simulates a real-world situation for decision making or alternative evaluation. Simulation games are important in engineering education because they enable the players to experience cooperation and teamwork without the risk of expensive mistakes. Amit Deshpande and Samuel Huang discuss several simulation game applications in engineering education.

An example is the beer distribution game, known as *beergame*, developed by a group of professors at MIT Sloan School of Management in the early 1960s. The aim of the game is to meet customers' demands for beer through a multistage supply chain by minimizing the sum of backorder and inventory costs. Another example is the industrial waste management game developed by Yukio Hirose and his colleagues. The aim of the game is to make players understand the social dilemma between individual interest of hazardous dumping and the social cost of purifying pollution and find a monitoring and sanction system for illegal dumping.

Ebru Angun

See also Learning With Simulations; Model-Based Approaches; Simulation-Based Learning; System Dynamics; Technology-Facilitated Experiential Learning

Further Readings

Campbell, J. O., Bourne, J. R., Mosterman, P. J., & Brodersen, J. A. (2002). The effectiveness of learning simulators in electronic laboratories. *Journal of Engineering Education, 91*(1), 81–87.

Deshpande, A. A., & Huang, S. H. (2009). Simulation games in engineering education: A state-of-the-art review. *Computer Applications in Engineering Education, 19*(3), 399–410.

Feisel, L. D., & Rosa, A. J. (2005). The role of the laboratory in undergraduate engineering education. *Journal of Engineering Education, 94*(1), 121–130.

Hirose, Y., Sugiura, J., & Shimomoto, K. (2004). Industrial waste management simulation game and its educational effect. *Journal of Material Cycles and Waste Management, 6,* 58–63.

Kleijnen, J. P. C. (2007). *Design and analysis of simulation experiments*. New York, NY: Springer-Verlag.

Law, A. M. (2014). *Simulation modeling and analysis* (5th ed.). New York, NY: McGraw-Hill.

SIMULATION-BASED LEARNING

Technology is entering educational practice at an increasing pace, even more so in recent years due to the influence of tablet technology and associated Web-based applications. One particular type of technology that is gaining in popularity is computer simulations. Computer simulations are computer programs that have a computational model of a system or a process as their core. The system or process that is modeled normally has a natural world origin and the model that is created is usually a simplification (i.e., reduction and abstraction) of the real-world phenomenon. When learning with simulations, learners interact with the model through an interface that allows them to change values of input variables and observe the effects of these changes on output variables. Simulations for learning are now available on a large scale, covering many domains that include physics, chemistry, biology, astronomy, medicine, and psychology.

The basic value of computer simulations is that they bring content into the classroom in an interactive and dynamic way. Students can directly interact with the domain and experience the content *in action* and simulations react dynamically to the actions of the students. This level of interaction with the domain is not offered in traditional, text-based forms of instruction. Often-cited practical advantages compared to real-world interactions are that students can work at any place and any time, that there are no (harmful) consequences of their interventions, and that simulations can be cheaper, which allows students to do experiments they could never do in real practice. Compared to interacting with the real world, simulations can also enhance the learning process by simplifying the underlying model so that it comes within reach of students' understanding. These simplifications include changing time scales so that processes that otherwise would be too slow or fast can be observed and investigated, changing size scales so that processes that otherwise would be too large or small can be investigated, and "augmenting reality" so that invisible components (e.g., light rays) become visible.

Basically, computer simulations can be used to acquire conceptual domain knowledge or domain-related skills. In the latter case, we speak of *experiential learning*, where the simulation presents a virtual representation of a domain in such a way that students can practice a specific procedural skill. When students acquire conceptual knowledge with a simulation, they do not follow a specific procedure but engage in a process of *inquiry learning*. Simulations then offer students the opportunity to test hypotheses they have developed for the domain by performing (virtual) experiments. In these situations, simulation-based learning may also have the goal of acquiring inquiry skills. The rest of this entry focuses on the relative effectiveness of simulations for the acquisition of procedural skills, conceptual knowledge, and inquiry skills.

Learning Skills in Simulations Versus Learning in the Real World

Skills are an important instructional goal in curricula that can range from nursing to management to flying airplanes. Simulations can offer a real-world-like situation with an increasing level of fidelity. Nowadays, these types of simulations are often characterized as serious games. Examples are simulations or games in which a metro station is simulated and students have to learn how to act in case of emergencies or a virtual ticket booth at which students can learn how to act as cashiers. In some cases of experiential skill learning, the underlying model can stay completely hidden for the students, who only have to learn the procedure; but in other cases, they also need to understand how the model works, for example in making a diagnosis in medicine or engineering. An important principle for experiential learning in simulated rather than real environments is that this allows students to receive more extensive experience with the skill to be learned.

Compared to learning in real situations, simulations can support learning independent of place and time, can present critical situations that may not occur frequently in reality, and can create situations that would be too expensive or dangerous in reality. The main principle behind this approach is that an element of practice is necessary in the learning of skills. This practicing of skills requires variation in tasks and confrontation with critical tasks; by not having to rely on the natural and possibly rare occurrence of specific situations, simulations offer the best opportunity for appropriate practice. Further, simulations can help to speed up or slow down skills so that practice can take place more deliberately and moments of reflection may be built in. Overall, research shows that students do acquire relevant skills in these kinds of procedural simulations but would also need additional practice in real-life circumstances.

Simulation-Based Learning Compared to Traditional Instruction

A central question is whether inquiry learning with computer simulations is more effective than traditional, teacher-presented and written material-based expository interventions. One study that compared different instructional approaches was conducted by Tessa Eysink and colleagues. In this work, students received instruction about the domain of probability theory that took one of four different approaches: (1) hypermedia learning in which the information was presented directly to students by text and animations, and they were only free to move through the material in a network kind of

way; (2) observational learning in which the material was shown to the students by a (virtual) agent who explained principles and demonstrated calculations; (3) self-explanation-based learning in which learners received (partially) worked-out problems and had to present explanations of the solutions; and (4) inquiry learning with a computer simulation in which students could change variables (e.g., number of runners in a race) and could observe how that changed the probability of particular outcomes (e.g., the order of the first three winners of the race). A total of 624 students participated in this study in which the material in all conditions covered the same topic and was computer delivered to exclude teacher effects, and the participants' performance was measured with the same test covering different types of knowledge.

The outcomes of this study showed that the two approaches that asked students to generate content themselves (self-explanation-based learning and simulation-based inquiry learning) led to better performance. This was true for all types of items on the posttest but especially apparent on items measuring deeper types of knowledge such as transfer; overall explanation-based learning yielded the highest results, but students who engaged in simulation-based learning performed best on far transfer items (knowledge or skills further removed from the context of the learning environment).

A number of meta-analyses and overview studies have appeared that all confirm these results: Inquiry learning (based on simulations) leads to higher levels of acquisition of domain knowledge than more direct forms of instruction. Most of this work focuses on learning domain knowledge, which means that there are relatively few studies that have examined the acquisition of inquiry skills. Within the work that has looked at inquiry skills, particularly the work by David Klahr, most attention is given to the design of experiments and even more specifically to investigating whether students are able to acquire the heuristic of varying only one variable at a time. This work shows that in order to become proficient at designing experiments, students benefit from explicit instruction along with experience with investigations.

There is one caveat that needs to be mentioned when the positive effects of inquiry learning are emphasized. All work, including the meta-analyses, points to the fact that open, free discovery is not effective and inquiry only realizes its virtues when it is embedded in an instructional support structure. Traditionally, investigations can be guided by the teacher, but in simulation-based learning, the software can also provide this kind of support.

Support or guidance is needed because students often experience difficulties with the processes that constitute inquiry, such as creating hypotheses, designing experiments, and so forth. The support offered can have different levels of directedness, leaving more or less initiative to the learner. In an overview, Ton de Jong and a colleague distinguished different types of guidance that include

- performance dashboards, which analyze students' log files or online products and present them with overviews of their own behavior, such as showing students their experimentation behavior;
- prompts, which are simple reminders to carry out a certain action without any further information on how to perform the action;
- heuristics, which are guidelines on how to carry out a specific process (e.g., not to vary too many variables at the same time);
- scaffolds, which are software tools that help students to perform a specific learning process (e.g., a tool that helps students make a summary of the domain and generate research questions); and
- direct presentation of information, which is needed when students are not themselves able to generate knowledge.

These types of guidance support students in an increasingly directive way and range from simply informing students without giving any direction on what to do to directly presenting what should have been discovered. All types of guidance seem to help students in improving their inquiry skills; the research challenges are currently in finding which type of guidance is most effective when and for which types of students and domains. Most probably, the most optimal environments would combine different types of guidance and would also use a process of fading, in which the guidance is gradually made less directive or even disappears.

Simulation-Based Learning Compared to Physical Laboratories

Simulation-based inquiry learning can be compared not only to direct instruction but also to learning in traditional hands-on laboratories that similarly support inquiry learning. In this case, the simulation presents a virtual representation of the wet laboratory. De Jong and colleagues have presented a brief review of the different affordances of physical and virtual laboratories. In both cases, students are invited to perform investigations, but virtual laboratories offer the possibility of reducing the complexity of the real situation, of enabling quick and frequent experimentation without extensive preparation of equipment, and of *augmenting*

reality by showing invisible elements such as vectors, electric currents, and light rays.

Comparisons of learning effects of physical and virtual learning environments, overall, show that virtual laboratories are as effective as or more effective than physical laboratories in comparable circumstances. Physical laboratories, however, also have specific affordances that make them a valuable teaching approach; they offer students experience with real equipment and students can more naturally experience the presence of measurement errors. Recent work shows that combining physical and simulated labs, either sequentially or side by side, may lead to even better results than using a simulated lab alone. This may be attributed to the fact that students must abstract from different representations. The literature seems to suggest that if used in sequence, it may be more effective to use the virtual laboratory first. In all cases, the effect of learning with laboratories, like the effects of learning with other types of simulations, depends heavily on the use of an adequate guidance structure.

Practical Implications

Learning from simulations offers an interesting alternative for traditional (text-based, laboratory-based, or real-life) instruction. In addition to the advantages mentioned earlier, simulations also offer great opportunities to further enhance collaboration between students. For example, in performing investigations students must decide which hypotheses to test, which values of variables to change, and so forth, which gives them very natural hooks for collaboration and negotiation.

If implemented, however, simulations should be embedded in sufficient guidance. Simulations that are available for teachers often do not offer that guidance in the software itself, and scenarios that support the teacher in providing students with this guidance themselves are often also not available. For simulations to have a real impact in our educational structure, it is necessary for these scenarios (online and offline) to be further developed. Another condition for the educational uptake of simulations is that curricula must be adapted to include simulation-based learning. Not only should guidance be offered to support the simulation, but it is also necessary to determine the most appropriate place of the simulation in the curriculum. In this regard, it is not yet fully determined whether the simulation should precede or follow a more direct form of instruction, resulting in a blended form of learning, or whether it can even completely replace it. Other aspects that may hinder the increased use of simulations in the classroom are a lack of computer facilities and software that is not stable. However, these final practical limitations may disappear soon.

Ton de Jong

See also Experiential Learning

Further Readings

Alessi, S. M., & Trollip, S. R. (2001). *Multimedia for learning: Methods and development* (3rd ed.). Boston, MA: Allyn & Bacon.

de Jong, T. (2006). Computer simulations: Technological advances in inquiry learning. *Science, 312,* 532–533. doi:10.1126/science.1127750

de Jong, T. (2010). Instruction based on computer simulations. In R. E. Mayer & P. A. Alexander (Eds.), *Handbook of research on learning and instruction* (pp. 446–466). New York, NY: Routledge.

de Jong, T. (2010). Technology supports for acquiring inquiry skills. In P. Peterson, E. Baker, & B. McGaw (Eds.), *International encyclopedia of education* (pp. 167–171). Oxford, UK: Elsevier.

de Jong, T., & Lazonder, A. W. (2014). The guided discovery principle in multimedia learning. In R. E. Mayer, J. J. G. van Merriënboer, W. Schnotz, & J. Elen (Eds.), *The Cambridge handbook of multimedia learning* (2nd ed., pp. 371–390). Cambridge, UK: Cambridge University Press.

de Jong, T., Linn, M. C., & Zacharia, Z. C. (2013). Physical and virtual laboratories in science and engineering education. *Science, 340,* 305–308. doi:10.1126/science.1230579

Eysink, T. H. S., de Jong, T., Berthold, K., Kollöffel, B., Opfermann, M., & Wouters, P. (2009). Learner performance in multimedia learning arrangements: An analysis across instructional approaches. *American Educational Research Journal, 46,* 1107–1149. doi:10.3102/0002831209340235

Furtak, E. M., Seidel, T., Iverson, H., & Briggs, D. C. (2012). Experimental and quasi-experimental studies of inquiry-based science teaching: A meta-analysis. *Review of Educational Research, 82,* 300–329. doi:10.3102/0034654312457206

van Joolingen, W. R., & de Jong, T. (1991). Characteristics of simulations for instructional settings. *Education & Computing, 6,* 241–262. doi:10.1016/0167-9287(91)80004-H

Rutten, N., van Joolingen, W. R., & van der Veen, J. T. (2012). The learning effects of computer simulations in science education. *Computers & Education, 58,* 136–153. doi:10.1016/j.compedu.2011.07.017

Scalise, K., Timms, M., Moorjani, A., Clark, L., Holtermann, K., & Irvin, P. S. (2011). Student learning in science simulations: Design features that promote learning gains. *Journal of Research in Science Teaching, 48,* 1050–1078. doi:10.1002/tea.20437

Smetana, L. K., & Bell, R. L. (2012). Computer simulations to support science instruction and learning: A critical review of the literature. *International Journal of Science Education, 34,* 1337–1370. doi:10.1080/09500693.2011.605182

SITUATED LEARNING

Situated learning, as defined by Jean Lave and Etienne Wenger, is a model of learning rooted within a community of practice. It is a process of interaction and relationship around a specific domain and which occurs within a social, cultural, and historical context, resulting in spontaneous learning. This entry first discusses the backgrounds of Lave and Wenger and the development of the situated learning model. It then discusses the precursors of situated learning and impact of situated learning. Finally, it discusses the implications of situated learning for instructional design.

Jean Lave and Etienne Wenger

Lave and Wenger each brings to the development of the model of situated learning rich, diverse academic preparation and professional research and experiences. Lave earned her PhD from Harvard University (1968) in social anthropology and is professor emerita of geography at the University of California, Berkeley. She is an expert in social learning, and her work in situated learning is strongly informed by her ethnographic studies in apprenticeship. Lave initiated development of the model that became situated learning by determining that housewives were able to conduct mathematical calculations while doing comparison shopping that they could not repeat in a classroom environment.

Etienne Wenger earned his PhD from the University of California, Irvine in artificial intelligence (1990). While Wenger was employed by the Institute for Research of Learning (now the Institute for Research of Learning and Development), he worked with Lave researching apprenticeships with individuals and in settings, including Yucatec midwives, Vai and Gola tailors in Liberia, naval quartermasters, meat cutters, and nondrinking AA members. Together the two derived additional principles and a more robust model of situated learning. Their seminal work, titled *Situated Learning: Legitimate Peripheral Participation,* was published in 1991.

Development of Situated Learning Model

Lave proposed that learning does not occur in isolation but rather occurs in relationship with others, through social interaction and spontaneous, appropriate activities within an authentic context. This activity is embedded within what Lave called a *community of practice* or CoP. A CoP serves as the authentic context and within it has tasks that align with real-world situations with a focus of being in some specifically identified and bound-aried domain. The activities, tools, interactions, and conversations within that CoP produce context-specific types of artifacts that are uniquely bounded by the culture of the CoP.

Lave's model was deepened through collaboration with Wenger. In their 1991 book, they proposed the concept of *legitimate peripheral participation,* suggesting that those novices who seek entrance to a community of practice typically enter from the periphery, participating from a *speak about* rather than a *speak within* perspective.

In order to master skills more deeply and move toward expertise and central participation as an expert within the CoP, the individual must learn the contextual language, normative behaviors, and other contextual factors of the CoP. Their resulting thinking and behaviors will increasingly reflect the unique characteristics of the CoP.

According to Lave and Wenger, three factors must exist for situated learning to occur:

1. *Domain:* A domain or system of thinking and doing must be clearly identifiable.

2. *Community of Practice:* Wenger defines a CoP as people who share concerns about something they do and want to learn how to do it better. He further states that CoPs are formed by people who engage in collective learning in a shared domain of interest.

3. *The Practice:* There must be specifically, contextually placed interpersonal engagement and activity that results in the way things are done or practiced within the CoP.

Lave and Wenger also list the four keys to newcomer success within the CoP:

1. Access to all that community membership entails;

2. Involvement in productive activity;

3. Learning the discourse of the community, including talking about and talking within a practice; and,

4. Willingness of the community to capitalize on the inexperience of newcomers.

The ongoing result within the community is a reciprocal learning process that perpetually redefines the individual and the group as it moves forward in time and space.

The Precursors to Situated Learning

The theoretical foundation for situated learning derives from various branches of psychology. Behaviorism suggests that behaviors originate as the direct response to observed stimuli. Social learning theory expands upon this theory, that while observation is important, behavior is the result not only of observation but also internally negotiated processes. Albert Bandura's social cognitive theory carries this notion further, with behavior being the result of continuous interactions between the individual, personal environment, and personal behaviors. Constructivism, derived from the work of Jean Piaget and others, posits (a) that cognitive development precedes learning, and (b) that it is based on the premise that learning is first an internally negotiated active construction process based in personal experience and hypotheses that one tests through social interaction and negotiation with others. Problem-based learning, first introduced in medical education, focuses on learning through the acquisition and application of knowledge and skills required to solve a problem. In affordance theory, the world is viewed as consisting of shapes and spatial relationships that have meaning in terms of the possibilities they afford to those who have access to them. Lev Vygotsky suggested that social interaction is a precursor to learning, with learning being strongly situated within and mediated through the cultural and other aspects of one's environment. In Vygotsky's perspective, an individual learns through being in a zone of proximal development (ZPD), or the sphere of influence and availability of a person who has learned more than the individual and is further ahead in terms of the specific knowledge and skill.

Each of these theoretical perspectives has led to the evolution of situated learning of being a description of contextual learning, with various influential individuals within that context who provide, through social interaction, related observation, and demonstration of behaviors the information an individual needs to learn. Legitimate peripheral participation can be viewed as a pure form of Albert Bandura's social learning and social cognitive theories. People observe others' behaviors within an environment, potentially interact with them, and are influenced by those interactions and observations.

As individuals persist in these interactions, they move from the periphery to a more central role within the context and eventually if they remain, they serve as experts within the system. Thus, in line with Vygotsky, social interaction is seen as the precursor to learning, and learning is the direct, spontaneous result of those kinds of interactions over time.

Influence of Situated Learning

As the result of the identified tenets of situated learning, the subsequent notions of situated cognition and cognitive apprenticeship emerged. Cognitive apprenticeship focuses on the apprenticeship of imparting knowledge and skill from a master to a novice through modeling, a key tenet of Bandura's social learning theory.

Two specific areas of life have been strongly impacted by situated learning. The first is in organizational learning, and the second is in formal school education settings. Situated learning provides guidance to organizations in terms of how to develop a learning organization in which informal learning as well as more formally structured learning opportunities occur as the result of an intentionally designed environment that supports spontaneous learning.

Research of formalized school education and applications of situated learning to the work of teachers and students in the classroom suggest that classroom learning can achieve CoP results provided it involves the entire system (e.g., teachers, students, people from the business community and the local community, and the community accessed through the Internet) in the learning experience, mirroring as completely as possible the real environment in which students live.

Implications for Instructional Design

Clearly the application of situated learning provides a different perspective and approach to learning, in that it portrays the value and utility of communities of practice and how to move from the periphery—a legitimate perspective—to the center, where expertise has been and is reciprocally fostered. How can situated learning inform instructional design practice? Provided here is an example that begins the discussion on the multiple potential applications of this model of learning.

Face-to-face training in corporate and other settings is often devoid of CoP design and often tends toward a highly structured and directive approach. Situated learning activity can be designed within a classroom such that tables or groups serve as small, developing communities of practice that in turn revolve around the other groups within the larger classroom, leading to a full-group situated learning laboratory. Intentionally designing activities to leverage the strengths (affordances) of various individuals in the group enables a cross-pollination of the diverse capabilities and strengths of group members. Including within this environment a deftly and exceptionally well-designed, authentically represented, and highly integrated story within the curriculum, which requires authentic group construction of artifacts and the cross-pollination of capabilities within each small group and the one larger CoP, builds group cohesion and fosters a greater level of trust and cooperation that—depending on the length of the curriculum—can be carried forward into participant work lives.

Suzanne J. Ebbers

See also Activity Theory; Cognitive Apprenticeship; Constructivist Theory; Engaged Learning; Learning With Simulations; Organizational Learning and Performance; Simulation-Based Learning; Virtual Teams

Further Readings

Bandura, A. (1977). *Social learning theory.* Upper Saddle River, NJ: Prentice Hall.

Bandura, A. (1986). *Social foundations of thought and action: A social cognitive theory.* Englewood Cliffs, NJ: Prentice Hall.

Barrows, H. S. (1996). Problem-based learning in medicine and beyond: A brief overview. *New Directions for Teaching and Learning, 68,* 3–12.

Collins, A., Brown, J. S., & Newman, S. E. (1987). *Cognitive apprenticeship: Teaching the craft of reading, writing and mathematics* (Technical Report No. 403). Urbana: Centre for the Study of Reading, University of Illinois.

Gibson, J. J. (1977). The theory of affordances. In R. E. Shaw & J. Bransford (Eds.), *Perceiving, acting and knowing.* Hillsdale, NJ: Lawrence Erlbaum.

Lave, J. (1988). *Cognition in practice: Mind, mathematics and culture in everyday life.* Cambridge, UK: Cambridge University Press.

Lave, J., & Wenger, E. (1991). *Situated learning: Legitimate peripheral participation.* Cambridge, UK: Cambridge University Press.

Vygotsky, L. S. (1978). *Mind in society: The development of higher psychological processes.* Cambridge, MA: Harvard University Press.

SKILL DECOMPOSITION

In instructional design, skill decomposition is the activity of first identifying the end goal of a learning event in terms of what the learner should *see* and be able to *do* as the result of the learning events and activities, and next, breaking down the component skills into smaller and smaller increments of skill and attendant knowledge. The latter decomposition effort continues until the skills are at such a rudimentary level that it would be a pragmatically wasted effort to continue further. Engagement in skill decomposition typically begins with a needs assessment or analysis, during which time performance challenges are identified and the gap between current and desired results due specifically to insufficient skill is identified.

Once the target skills-focused objective(s) is or are identified, the work of decomposing, or breaking down, the skill ensues. This analysis activity and breakdown of a skill typically occur in a flowcharted format. Flowcharting software is used to build out visual representations of decomposed skills. Prioritizing skill decomposition as a central instructional design activity is key to achieving effective skills-based learning as the result. Lack of precision in this vital task will result in no clearly defined and sequenced learning objectives, no order to the learning process, no ability to assess learning, and no effective impact on the organization. In this entry, the basics of skill decomposition are discussed, followed by a discussion of principled skill decomposition based on Jeroen van Merriënboer's 4C/ID (four component instructional design) model. A brief case-based example of skill decomposition is provided to highlight the basic process of skill decomposition.

Skill Decomposition Basic Terminology

As is the case in goal theory, one cannot move in the direction of breaking down a skill into its component parts in order to build a model of the learning design if the desired end result is left undefined. Skill decomposition begins with the identification of the end learning result, which is in the form of a behavior or skill that can be demonstrated. This end result is also called the *target objective*. Once defined, skills are broken down into their constituent human capabilities so that they can then be organized in a way that builds that end, or target objective. There are a number of human capabilities that can be combined in various ways to achieve desired learning outcomes. Such human capabilities include verbal knowledge, attitudes, motor skills, cognitive strategies, and a hierarchical building-block group of intellectual skills. Intellectual skills can be further categorized in terms of discrimination, concrete concepts, defined concepts, rules, and problem solving (in order of increasing complexity). The ability to decompose skills resides in a deep understanding of the meaning of each of these capabilities and the ability to break down each task—no matter how complex—into a hierarchically developed flowchart portraying human capability linkages, concurrencies, decision steps, and sequences. These human capabilities, each with their capability verb used in developing learning objectives, are provided in Figure 1.

Building Block Results

To decompose a skill, one must ask what the various human capabilities are that, when combined, will instill the target skill. As those capabilities are identified *at a first lower level* as enabling objectives, they must be configured appropriately according to what must be learned first, second, and so on, with each prerequisite skill being sequenced further and further to the left and down when flowcharted. Once this second level of human capabilities is flowcharted and aligned to the

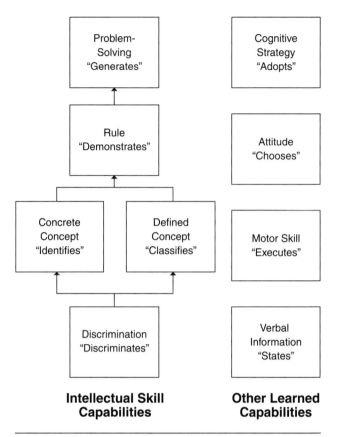

Figure 1   Human capabilities and associated verbs

target objective, this level of enabling objectives then becomes a list of target objectives and the process repeats. Depending on the complexity of the skill to be demonstrated at the end of the instruction, this process can be repeated a number of times, and the flowcharting can be quite complex.

The emphasis in skill decomposition has been on demonstration of skills and affiliated knowledge and attitudes learned, but human capabilities include verbal knowledge and attitudes, neither of which are skills per se. Through careful definition of learning objectives and decomposition of the target objective(s), it will be possible to visibly see and hear concrete evidence that the learner has acquired specific knowledge or attitude.

Decision Points in Skill Decomposition

In addition to accurately configuring relevant human capabilities in the flowchart, decision steps are important. Decision steps, typically portrayed in the flowchart as a diamond shape, usually ask the designer to respond to a yes/no answering algorithm, and the flowchart arrows send the content in one of two directions, as seen in Figure 2.

Making the Right Investment

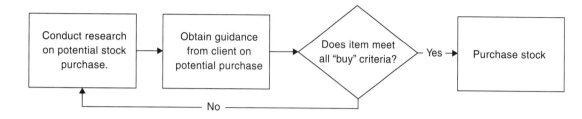

Figure 2   Portrayal of yes/no decision points

Prerequisite and Entry Skills

Prerequisites are those skills that must be acquired before subsequent skills are instructed. Prerequisite skills are identified in flowcharts as coming from either or both the lower levels of the decomposed skill portrayal and include essential prerequisites (component skills that must be learned prior to performing the target learning objective) and supportive prerequisites (skills and related knowledge that build capacity to achieve the target skill faster, easier, or more effectively).

At some point in the skill decomposition process, the instructional designer—usually with assistance from subject matter experts—determines that the target audience must enter the learning event with a minimum and specific set of knowledge, attendant skills, and attitudes, per the flowcharted hierarchy of skills and as acquired during the needs assessment or analysis. The skills are usually delineated on the flowchart with a dotted line, in which those skills below the dotted line are considered entry skills.

Vertical and Horizontal Relationships

Vertical flowcharted relationships of skills include the target skill (at whatever level one begins) and the enabling, or prerequisite skills, which feed into it from below. Horizontal relationships, on the other hand, are either *transposable* (the ordering is inconsequential), *simultaneous* (one occurs at the same time as the other), and *temporal* (one occurs first before the next).

Skill Decomposition Analyses

Skills can be decomposed through a procedural or information-processing analysis, and through a learning-task analysis. The procedural analysis breaks down the skill into a sequential flowchart of tasks to be performed.

The learning-task analysis portrays decomposition of all prerequisite skills in addition to the decomposition of the skill itself, therefore providing a clear understanding of all skills and associated knowledge and attitudes that the learner must possess at entry or that must be incorporated within the learning event to effectively achieve learning outcomes.

The 4C/ID Model and Skill Decomposition

Jeroen van Merriënboer's 4C/ID Model specifies the process of learning complex cognitive skills. The human capabilities previously discussed serve as the framework for skill decomposition efforts but are subsumed into declarative knowledge and procedural knowledge. Declarative knowledge includes verbal knowledge, concepts, strategies, and intellectual skills that make up a subskill. Procedural knowledge includes the task(s) to be accomplished, very much in line with the description earlier of a procedural task analysis.

The 4C/ID Model most clearly specifies that the end result of learning *at any level* of the decomposed skill hierarchy is the demonstration of a skill package that incorporates all related knowledge, motor skills, and attitudes. The model also provides a methodological framework for precise placement of decomposed recurrent tasks (tasks that always occur in basically the same manner, no matter what the circumstances surrounding them) and nonrecurrent tasks (those tasks that can be more heuristic in nature), as well as just-in-time information (that information that must be provided at the specific point in time that it is required in order for the individual to be able to accomplish the task), supportive information (information supporting the learning of nonrecurrent tasks), and procedural information (information that supports the learning of recurrent tasks).

Target Objective: As the result of this training, learner will generate a decomposed skill by flowcharting out all human capabilities in appropriate order and connections, ensuring that prerequisite skills are identified and the entry level skill set is identified.

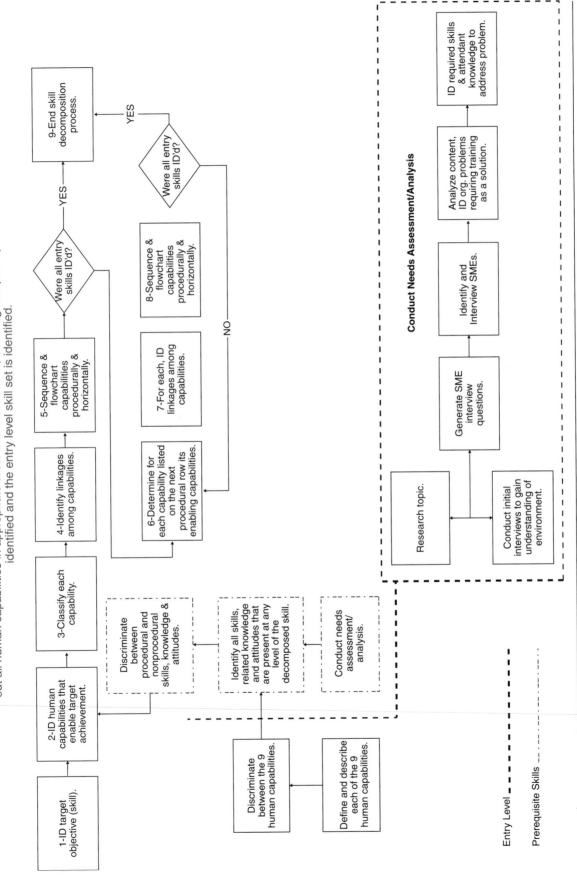

Figure 3 Decomposition of the skill

Decomposition of the Skill

This section provides a target objective of skill decomposition, along with a flowcharted diagram of that decomposed skill and explanatory information to assist in understanding the decomposition process. As the result of this training sequence, the learner will generate a decomposed skill by flowcharting out all human capabilities in appropriate order and connections, ensuring that prerequisite skills are identified and the entry-level skill set is identified. This constitutes the target objective.

Figure 3 provides on the top row a list of Steps 1 through 9 that would ultimately be the process being instructed. The items presented in boxes bounded by a dot-dash-dot-dash sequence are skills that would be prerequisite to the learning of the process. The way this would be interpreted would be as follows:

In order to achieve *2-ID human capabilities that enable target achievement,* one must (from bottom to top) (1) conduct a needs assessment/analysis, (2) identify all skills, related knowledge, and attitudes that are present at any level of the decomposed skill, and (3) discriminate between procedural and nonprocedural skills, knowledge, and attitudes.

Note that these items are bounded by a dark dotted line, below the words *Conduct needs assessment/analysis* and to the left of the dot-dash boxes. These items would be considered *entry-level skills* that the learner would possess prior to joining the training.

Lastly, the entire process of conduct needs assessment/analysis is bounded by the dark dotted line. The ability to do this process would also be considered a prerequisite skill and beyond the scope of learning how to decompose a skill, as portrayed in the flowchart.

Suzanne J. Ebbers

See also Cognitive Task Analysis; Elaboration Theory; Four-Component Instructional Design (4C/ID); Instructional Design Models; Think-Aloud Protocol Analysis; Workflow Analysis

Further Readings

Bloom, B. S., Engelhart, M. D., Furst, E. J., Hill, W. H., & Krathwohl, D. R. (Eds.). (1956). *Taxonomy of educational objectives: The classification of educational goals: Handbook 1: Cognitive domain.* New York, NY: Longman.

Gagné, R. M., Briggs, L. J., & Wager, W. W. (1992). *Principles of instructional design* (4th ed.). Fort Worth, TX: Harcourt Brace Jovanovich.

Jonassen, D. H., Tessmer, M., & Hannum, W. H. (1999). *Task analysis methods for instructional design.* Mahwah, NJ: Lawrence Erlbaum.

Mager, R. F. (1984). *Goal analysis* (2nd ed.). Belmont, CA: David S. Lake.

Reigeluth, C. M. (1999). The elaboration theory: Guidance for scope and sequence decisions. In C. M. Reigeluth (Ed.), *Instructional-design theories and models, Volume II. A new paradigm of instructional theory* (pp. 425–453). Mahwah, NJ: Lawrence Erlbaum.

van Merriënboer, J. J. G., & Dijkstra, S. (1997). The four-component instructional design model for training complex cognitive skills. In R. D. Tennyson, F. Schott, N. M. Seel, & S. Dijkstra, S. (Eds.), *Instructional design: International perspectives, Volume 1: Theory, research and models* (pp. 427–445). Mahwah, NJ: Lawrence Erlbaum.

van Merriënboer, J. J. G., & Kirschner, P. A. (2007). *Ten steps to complex learning: A systematic approach to four-component instructional design.* Mahwah, NJ: Lawrence Erlbaum.

SOCIAL MEDIA, IDENTITY IN

Social media are attractive technologies in an online learning setting because they enable Internet-based communication and sharing among users, who often form communities. To participate, social media users create online identities. Identity, in this context, refers to the combination of text and visual elements that in combination come to distinguish a particular social media user and allow each user to be individually identified and described. A social media identity typically starts as a simple username, but with each interaction that occurs online, additional information is amassed about an identity.

Within the realm of educational technology, social media identities are an important and yet often overlooked topic. When instructors ask students to use social media, pedagogy, learning, and motivation are likely their primary concerns. However, when students sign up for a social media account they are creating a digital footprint. Those digital footprints will develop and change over time as they engage in different forms of online sharing and interactions via social media. The issue of a persisting digital footprint raises privacy and identity management concerns. Ideally, both instructors and students actively consider their desired digital footprints and adjust the content and nature of their social media-based interactions accordingly. This entry first discusses the elements of social media identity and options for users in selecting a social media identity. It then explains how users perform social media identity and construct it with other users. It concludes by discussing privacy concerns involved with using social media and guidelines for using social media in K–12 schools, higher education, and the workplace.

Elements of Social Media Identity

A social media identity is constructed and communicated in a variety of ways. The username is perhaps the first and most consistently visible part of a social media identity. Certain social media tools allow users to pick any name that suits them for a username, often resulting in usernames of fantasy characters or ones that communicate elements of the user's identity (e.g., sports fan or fashion enthusiast); some tools, such as Facebook and LinkedIn, require users to register under their real names.

Many social media tools further allow users to create a profile, in which personal information may be shared. Standard profile information may include a photo or avatar, e-mail address, geographic location, other demographic information, and personal favorites (e.g., books or websites). Profiles might also list system-generated information, such as lists of people with whom the user is connected or networked and recent items that the user has shared. Additionally, some social media tools like blogs allow for further personalization, such as choosing a background and page layout and adding links and widgets.

Finally, identity is communicated and constructed in every interaction that a user has. Using Facebook as an example, each time an individual indicates a *like* for an item or checks in at a location, indicating physical presence, that user is contributing additional information that gets incorporated into the user's social media identity. Elements of an online identity such as the username and avatar may generate a first impression, but every piece of information publicly shared further develops that identity.

Identity Options

There are three key identity options for users of social media. The first, and most readily apparent, is to create an online identity that largely reflects one's actual identity. This option is a good choice for adult learners who wish to use social media for professional development and networking purposes, and a number of social media tools (e.g., Facebook, LinkedIn) expect users to sign up and interact using their real names. Other tools are more flexible. In these cases, the decision to use a real name might indicate the desire to use social media for professional networking or marketing purposes and to connect one's online and offline identities, whereas the decision to not use a real name might indicate the desire for privacy or communicating a different identity.

Pseudonyms are a good choice for individuals who do not wish to have their social media-based interactions appear when their real name is searched online, or who otherwise wish to establish an online identity that is separate from their real identity or who wish to create an online identity centered around an alternate identity. To create a pseudonym, the user simply needs to choose a preferred username. To fully maintain a pseudonymous identity, the user then needs to be careful about self-disclosure, either omitting identifiable details, altering details, or using pseudonyms and fictitious information.

Anonymity is the third identity option, which brings with it a combination of freedom and limitations. True anonymity online is difficult to achieve; many social media tools require that users register with a unique username. Individuals may choose nonrevealing names and avoid self-disclosure, but unique usernames still mean that all of an individual's contributions and activities can be aggregated. However, some media, such as blogs and discussion forums, can be set to allow anonymous contributions. When multiple individuals interact in the same space as anonymous participants, it can be difficult to distinguish among comments and responses. In these situations, readers may struggle to follow threads of the online conversation. Furthermore, anonymity can in some contexts result in incivility, as respondents and participants may feel free to express opinions and make statements that they would not contemplate in a nonanonymous comment. For these reasons, anonymity generally is not recommended in an educational setting.

Many people maintain multiple, separate social media identities. By doing so, they are able to keep different parts of their online and offline lives separate. For example, a person might use one username (likely a real name) for professional purposes and a pseudonym when interacting online in a hobby-based community. In a class context, learners who already have established online identities may wish to create secondary ones for school purposes. Keeping learning experiences separate from other life experiences and ensuring they do not show up in a search for the learner's real name may make some learners more comfortable.

Performativity and (Co)Construction of Online Identity

Social media identity is something individuals perform. In other words, users select among the details of their lives, selecting photographs, actions, moods, and thoughts to share and, collectively, paint the image that they wish to project. Because identity unfolds and changes over time, its development is essentially a performance that runs in tandem with everyday life. For some users, this performance is a rather intentional one, whereas for others it is a tacit one.

Although each individual performs a social media identity, that identity may be coconstructed by users and the members of their social networks. For example, a user's Facebook Timeline, which is essentially a profile, typically combines contributions from the user but also from the user's friends. People viewing the profile come to understand who this person is from the combination of performed identity elements and friend-contributed elements.

Privacy Concerns and Guidelines

When requiring students to create an online identity, instructors need to be sensitive to individual privacy concerns. Most K–12 schools have clear social media policies that govern whether and what types of social media accounts might be used in the learning context. For example, teachers and students might be restricted to either password-protected closed social media communities designed specifically for K–12 users or a shared class account controlled by the teacher. These policies are necessary because K–12 students are minors and teachers are responsible for their safety.

In higher education, similar social media guidelines generally do not exist. Typically, adult learners are considered responsible enough to manage their own privacy and self-disclosure. However, this may not always be the case. When social media are used in higher education, students may benefit from instructor modeling and guidance on developing and maintaining an appropriate social media identity.

In corporate or other professional settings, social media guidelines for employees are becoming increasingly popular. Companies may be concerned with how their employees represent them online as well the security of proprietary information. These concerns may apply not only when the employee is acting in a professional capacity on the behalf of the company (e.g., providing technical support via social media or leading a webinar for clients) but also may extend to personal use of social media. Should social media be used as part of professional development or training, even for employees who do not typically use social media as part of their jobs, employees should be made aware of the guidelines.

Vanessa P. Dennen

See also Digital Identity; *Second Self;* Social Media and Networking; Web 2.0 and Beyond

Further Readings

boyd, d. m., & Ellison, N. B. (2007). Social network sites: Definition, history, and scholarship. *Journal of Computer-Mediated Communication, 13*(1), 210–230. Retrieved from http://onlinelibrary.wiley.com/doi/10.1111/j.1083-6101.2007.00393.x/pdf

Dibbell, J. (1999). *My tiny life: Crime and passion in a virtual world.* London, UK: Fourth Estate.

Rheingold, H. (1993). *The virtual community: Homesteading on the electronic frontier.* Boston, MA: Addison Wesley.

Subrahmanyam, K., & Šmahel, D. (2011). *Digital youth: The role of media in development.* New York, NY: Springer-Verlag.

Thomas, A. (2007). *Youth online: Identity and literacy in the digital age* (New literacies and digital epistemologies, vol. 19). New York, NY: Peter Lang.

Turkle, S. (2011). *Life on the screen: Identity in the age of the Internet.* New York, NY: Simon & Schuster.

SOCIAL MEDIA AND NETWORKING

Social media use Internet-based technologies and tools to allow users to share and exchange information. As users engage with these technologies, they become connected to others due to the social nature of the tools. They become networked to people, metaphorically similar to the existing network of hardware, software, and wires that physically makes this possible. At the most proximal level, these networked connections are familiar. A person might have a friend on Facebook or an acquaintance following him on Twitter. The promise and challenge of such networks, however, is that the networking quickly becomes exponential. A person might soon be connected with a friend of a friend, might get a follower based simply on her online interests, or might meet new people through a free online course.

An online user might not know someone who has taught in a foreign country but is very likely to know someone who knows someone who has taught in such a situation. Such connections can occur through a variety of social networking tools such as blogging and online games and simulations; they can be intentional connections (e.g., someone chose to add someone) or unintentional (e.g., someone who is in the same forum). Such social media–based networks can lead to positive or negative outcomes; oftentimes users do not make use of these networks in a way that would fully realize their potential. The social media tools and the networking that results are important to educators because they offer new opportunities to enhance teaching and learning at both the student and teacher level. This entry first defines networking and discusses the benefits and drawbacks of using social media for networking. It concludes by discussing research on social media and networking and potential future research directions.

Understanding Networking and Social Media

There is a popular networking concept that argues that any two people on earth are essentially always connected by six or fewer degrees of separation. Many people first heard of this concept through a game called

Six Degrees of Kevin Bacon, where people would name an actor and try to connect her to Bacon through her film roles with the fewest number of connections. The point is that networking is not a novelty of the digital age. Business leaders and educators have long capitalized on the power of making and using connections.

However, the digital age has produced technologies that either directly promote social connectivity or draw on those connections for a variety of reasons. For instance, people might join Facebook to connect or stay connected to current and past friends and acquaintances. They might join LinkedIn to seek employment. There are also indirect uses of social media. Here, the technologies are not solely for the purpose of connecting but rather connecting for a purpose. Popular commercial sites mine user data to suggest products that similar users have bought. And, some companies use crowdsourcing to fund innovative technology projects. There are positive and negative ways that social networking intentionally or unintentionally impacts education.

The Positive Impact of Social Media and Networking

Researchers have provided evidence of a number of important factors in the learning environment. For instance, learners benefit from the support of a more knowledgeable other. Students are often under the tutelage of one instructor, or at least one instructor per content area. However, research in mentoring suggests that people benefit from seeing multiple mentors. One positive aspect of social media is that it provides access to networks of mentors and more knowledgeable others, many of whom more closely match the ethnicity, gender, or other characteristics of the learner.

Getting access to content in a variety of ways is also an important factor for learners. Social networks provide opportunities for learners to get both remedial and advanced support in styles that match their learning preferences. This support for learning is not just for students. Teachers consistently require sustained professional development. Research has provided evidence that these networks provide content and mentors for those learning or those teaching.

A third key area is related to learners graduating and finding jobs. In the learning process, social networks can provide learners with opportunities to engage others who are legitimately participating in the contexts in which the students will enter. They provide anchored instruction for students who are attempting to apply what they are learning. And, through the use of social media tools, students can more quickly post their résumés or find connections to employers.

The Negative Impact of Social Media and Networking

There are two major challenges for educators regarding social media and networks. First, although students come into learning environments with a grasp of how to use social media tools, they do not often understand the long-lasting impact of networking. Although it is easy to use these tools to find a potential employer, it is just as easy for employers to search social media tools to find out about the habits and preferences of students and future employees.

A second key challenge has to do with indifference. Some educators just do not understand the potential value of networking through social media. At best, they teach how not to use it; at worst, they fail to provide any significant instruction. Learners are left unscripted as to the potential positive impact of using these tools to connect with others either during their learning process or upon graduation.

The Proactive Aspect of Social Media and Networking

Much of what is written about social media and networking relates to the individual. There are positive and negative impacts of using social media on the learner and the teacher. However, it is worth noting that there are significant, potentially negative or positive outcomes on educational organizations through the use (or lack of use) of social media. Many schools are now finding ways to build better home-school partnerships through social media. They also realize that many constituents now get their news online. They use their networks to seek information about schools, teachers, and curricula. Positive, proactive means of building or supplementing existing organizational networks with social media can have a positive impact on the physical and digital culture of an organization. Failure to connect through these networks that are ubiquitous in the lives of the learners (and their families) can result in a disconnect between the culture of the school and the culture of those who attend the school.

Existing and Future Research

There is very limited research on the role of social media and networking in education. Much of this research has focused more directly on the tool that is being used (e.g., Twitter), rather than a broad conversation of the impact of social networks. The research does suggest that the use of social media and networking can create feelings of belonging and social identity, which can positively or negatively impact the learning environment. A second finding is that social media can both enhance and change existing social networks. These changes or enhancements are powerful and have led to deeper explorations of the role of social network analysis.

Researchers have suggested that more research needs to be completed in this area. That research should be situated under a deeper understanding of the relationship between existing and future networks as impacted or enabled by social media. It should attempt to understand the use of social media for network building and how that might change how people view networks and network creation and maintenance in the future. Finally, more research needs to examine teaching and learning within these networks through the use of social tools.

Richard E. Ferdig

See also Blogs as a Communication Tool; Collaboration and Social Networking; Collaborative Communication Tools and Technologies; Digital Literacy and Adult Learners; Information and Communication Technologies: Competencies in the 21st-Century Workforce; *Second Self;* Social Media, Identity in; Social Media in the Workplace; Social Networking; Web 2.0 and Beyond; Web 2.0/3.0 in the Workplace

Further Readings

boyd, d. m., & Ellison, N. B. (2008). Social network sites: Definition, history, and scholarship. *Journal of Computer-Mediated Communication, 13*(1), 210–230. Retrieved from http://onlinelibrary.wiley.com. doi/10.1111/j.1083-6101.2007 .00393.x/pdf

Hampton, K. N., Goulet, L. S., Rainie, L., & Purcell, K. (2011). *Social networking sites and our lives.* Pew Research Center's Internet & American Life Project. Retrieved from http:// www.pewinternet.org/2011/06/16/social-networking-sites-and-our-lives

Kaplan, A. M., & Haenlein, M. (2010). Users of the world, unite! The challenges and opportunities of social media. *Business Horizons, 53*(1), 59–68.

Kietzmann, J. H., Hermkens, K., McCarthy, I. P., & Silvestre, B. S. (2011). Social media? Get serious! Understanding the functional building blocks of social media. *Business Horizons, 54*(3), 241–251.

Kietzmann, J. H., Silvestre, B. S., McCarthy, I. P., & Pitt, L. F. (2012). Unpacking the social media phenomenon: Towards a research agenda. *Journal of Public Affairs, 12*(2), 109–119.

LeNoue, M., Hall, T., & Eighmy, M. A. (2011). Adult education and the social media revolution. *Adult Learning, 22*(4), 4–12.

Merchant, G. (2012). Unraveling the social network: Theory and research. *Learning, Media and Technology, 37*(1), 4–19.

Rosen, D., Barnett, G. A., & Kim, J. H. (2011). Social networks and online environments: When science and practice co-evolve. *Social Network Analysis and Mining, 1*(1), 27–42.

SOCIAL MEDIA IN ELEMENTARY SCHOOL SETTINGS

Social media are Internet-based technologies designed to be used by more than one person. Social media includes any online technology used to enable people to collaborate, including (a) social networking tools; (b) blogs, microblogs, video blogs; (c) work collaboration tools; (d) virtual immersive environments; (e) mobile tools, platforms, and applications; (f) shared media; (g) social bookmarking; and (h) shared workspaces. Social media in the education sector has become popular as an instructional tool in the classroom. Social media can extend learning, model effective communication, and help young learners develop. Social media is part of many university activities and used in some secondary school settings. However social media is not yet used or planned for use in many elementary schools. A recent study in the United States found that public schools typically ban access to many popular social media sites. The most prevalent reason that elementary schools avoid the use of social media is concern for students' safety online. The key to Internet safety lies in responsible usage. This entry discusses the impact of social networking on young learners, the advantages and disadvantages of its use in education, and how social media can be used in instruction.

Christine Greenhow argues that social networking expanded students' abilities by providing practice in relevant 21st-century skills such as collaborative learning and interactive technology integration. She lists four other benefits of social media in education:

1. Meeting various students' needs, including emotional and cognitive support

2. Challenging students to express themselves to multiply their audience

3. Fulfilling various social learning functions (e.g., peer support for creative endeavors, help with school-related tasks)

4. Building students' communication and technology skills and understanding different points of view

Social media fits into Abraham Maslow's hierarchy of needs, which includes self-actualization, esteem, belonging, safety, and physiological needs. Specifically, social media builds social awareness and promotes social learning, which contribute to the top parts of Maslow's hierarchy.

Pros and Cons of Social Media

Prior to using social media in an elementary school setting, teachers, students, staff, and parents should be prepared to use social media. Many social networking tools are open source, which poses safety issues such as hacking and possibly exposing learners' identities. It is vital that schools and social media users understand the liability of using social media. Internet filters can block educational websites. Filters can also protect schools from illegal downloads of music and images. Internet filters should be used as a management tool, in accordance with a social media policy that sets boundaries for what is acceptable and unacceptable in simple and easily understood language.

Charlie Osborne stated the following advantages and disadvantages related to social media:

Advantages

Familiarity: Many students use social networking.

Promotion of digital citizenship: Students need to learn acceptable online behavior, which is critical in subsequent studies and activities.

Sharing learning materials: Sharing resources is made easy with social networking sites and tools.

Differentiation: Varied types and formats of information can appeal to different learning styles.

Authentic learning: Social media can support learning as it occurs outside the classroom.

Disadvantages

Change: Social media platforms and content change rapidly, creating a need for schools and teachers to continuously monitor them.

Time management: Teachers and students can spend too much time with social media at the expense of other learning activities.

Cyberbullying: Social media platforms can be an outlet for inappropriate personal attacks on students.

Technology divide: Students who do not have devices and access outside the classroom can easily be disadvantaged.

Stuart Davidson recommended seven steps for using social media for communicative and educational purposes:

1. Inform parents and make sure to welcome their opinions

2. Have clear objectives as to why the school is implementing social media

3. Make sure social media policies are established that involve community stakeholders, parents, students, and staff

4. Provide students with digital citizenship training

5. Make sure parents or guardians have agreed to allow their children's photos to appear on social media platforms

6. Use social media to the children's advantage—use for math investigation or grammar competition

7. Employ a way to quickly stop spreading gossip or rumors

Using Social Media for Instruction

Karmen Erjavec conducted a qualitative study of students using Facebook for informal learning. The study consisted of 60 participants. The researchers analyzed semistructured interviews, think-aloud responses, and the content of Facebook profiles. The results indicated that a majority of participants saw a connection between their use of Facebook and the knowledge and skills they felt their teachers valued. The results also indicated that participants used Facebook to learn about technology and support their formal learning. Erjavec's study results showed that participants used Facebook to obtain validation and as a collaborative tool.

Elementary schools can use interactive response systems such as whiteboards in their classrooms. Ways to use interactive whiteboards in the classroom include

- international virtual field trips;
- student achievement documentation;
- problem-solving collaboration;
- displaying multimedia presentations and lessons that include podcasts and vodcasts (video podcasts); and
- recorded lessons that can be used for reinforcement, substitute teachers, and flipped learning.

Social media in an elementary setting can be used as a language tool. Using social media in the classroom provides an authentic classroom audience. Sharon Smaldino and her colleagues stated that when students are developing literacy and communication skills, interactive tools and social media can offer opportunities that reinforce traditional classroom practice. Backchannels are tools that create dialogue online during an activity. Backchannels can engage learners in a classroom discussion. The teacher can ask students a question to gauge their understanding of a topic prior to teaching. The students will respond to the question online and see their classmates' responses. This can create dialogue, as well as informal data for the teacher to adjust the lesson as needed. Students can access the dialogue after the class and continue the conversation outside of the classroom.

Social media can be used to build research skills early in a student's schooling. Learners can conduct trend searches on specific keywords. Students also could create relationships with peers with similar interests. In addition, elementary school students can benefit from virtual environments and *gamification* that have integrated social media functionality. Elementary learners can gain *badges* that recognize an accomplishment; these are appealing to young learners. For example, the teacher can create a spelling competition and students with high scores can be given a badge. With social media, students can also learn by doing—for example, by providing feedback, asking questions, and sending feedback through podcasts and video clips.

Learners need to develop skills in using collaborative tools. Collaboration is a required lifelong skill. Collaborative tools allow learners to integrate independent thinking into group activities. Collaborative tools such as a wiki, a website that allows users to create and edit content, allow students to constantly add new information. As a result, the learner is engaging in content creation. A wiki is one way for students with writing weaknesses to improve their skills in sharing information with classmates or other people. Wikis can be used for individual assessment projects. Students can upload their project to the wiki and link their profiles. Students can share their notes and edit their notes. The wiki allows them to be a peer teacher. There are other ways wikis could also be used for elementary learners:

- as a fan club for a favorite artist, historical figure, or author;
- for virtual tours of various places;
- as a special topic encyclopedia; or
- for detailed and illustrated descriptions of cycles (e.g., the water cycle).

Mobile applications are inexpensive and widely available. Mobile applications allow differentiation and individualized learning for learners with various learning needs. The advantages of mobile applications include cost-efficient learning and instructional flexibility (learner or teacher choices). Mobile applications vary in user experiences. For example, learners with a reading deficit can download an audio book or practice basic reading skills without bringing attention to their deficit. Learners could record their teacher using audio or video and listen to the information after class. The learners could also submit verbal summary projects, or take pictures in their community to demonstrate understanding of the lesson.

Courtney L. Teague

See also Apps for Use at the Elementary Level; Disruptive Technologies; Engaged Learning; Twenty-First-Century Technology Skills

Further Readings

American Society for Training and Development. (2011). *Social learning.* Retrieved from http://www.astd.org/Communities-of-Practice/Career-Development/~/media/Files/Certification/Competency%20Model/SocialLearning1.ashx

Bumgardner, S., & Knestis, K. (2011). *Social networking as a tool for student and teacher learning.* Retrieved from http://www.districtadministration.com/article/social-networking-tool-student-and-teacher-learning

Chandler, E. (2013). *10 tips for engaging pupils and parents in e-safety and digital citizenship.* Retrieved from http://www.theguardian.com/teacher-network/teacher-blog/2013/nov/18/10-tips-digital-citizenship-esafety-pupils-parents

Connolly, M. R. (2011). Does social networking enhance or impede student learning? Social networking and student learning: Friends without benefits. In P. M. Magolda & M. B. Magolda (Eds.), *Contested issues in student affairs: Diverse perspectives and respectful dialogue* (pp. 122–134). Sterling, VA: Stylus.

Davidson, S. J. (2013). *Social media in primary schools.* Retrieved from http://stuartjdavidson.com/social-media-in-primary-schools

Erjavec, K. (2013). Informal learning through Facebook among Slovenian pupils. *Scientific Journal of Media Education, 41*(21), 117–126.

Greenhow, C. (2008). Commentary: Connecting formal and informal learning experiences in the age of participatory media: Commentary on Bull et al. *Contemporary Issues in Technology and Teacher Education, 8*(3), 187–194.

Osborne, C. (2012). *The pros and cons of social media classrooms.* Retrieved from http://www.zdnet.com/blog/igeneration/the-pros-and-cons-of-social-mediaclassrooms/15132

Smaldino, S. E., Lowther, D. L., & Russell, J. D. (2012). *Instructional technology and media for learning* (10th ed.). Boston, MA: Pearson.

SOCIAL MEDIA IN HIGHER EDUCATION

Social media refers to various technologies, typically Internet driven, that allow users to create, share, exchange, and review content and ideas. This sharing of content and ideas takes place through photo-hosting sites, texts, online communities, multiplayer games and simulations, online shared courses, discussion forums, blogs, wikis, social media networks (e.g., LinkedIn or Facebook), and distribution tools (e.g., Twitter or e-mail lists). These technologies have impacted almost every aspect of daily life from business to personal and from shopping to learning.

Higher education has been impacted in two key ways. First, faculty in higher education are now working with students who are well versed in the use of social media. This can lead to positive and negative outcomes for teaching and learning environments. Second, given the ubiquity of the tools and their use by students in higher education, colleges and universities are attempting to leverage these technologies to improve learning. The results have been mixed. Success stories include schools and faculty who are rethinking their content and the distribution channels to reach students. Challenges include schools that block access in attempts to protect students as well as students who do not completely understand the social aspect of these new tools. Educational technologists must find ways to capitalize on the ubiquity of such tools for teaching and learning in higher education. This entry first discusses the ways that social media can be used in teaching and learning in higher education and some of the challenges presented by its use. It then discusses research findings on social media use in higher education and the implications for educational technologists.

The Promise of Social Media in Higher Education

There are many reasons why social media have a place in teaching and learning in higher education. Perhaps the most straightforward reason is that most current undergraduate and graduate students have grown up with social media. Studies have provided evidence that students in their late teens and early 20s do everything from ordering food to finding roommates through social media. As such, if the technologies are already ubiquitous in the lives of the students, educators posture that it is prudent to attempt to reach these students through these same channels. Unlike other educational tools that might only be used in the higher education setting (e.g., the textbook), students come to the learning environment already versed in the use of social media tools.

A second reason for the value of social media in higher education is that some researchers have begun to argue that today's students not only seek and exchange knowledge this way, they also think differently because of access to these tools. Students who

spend all day reading and writing limited character texts or tweets might find it incomprehensible to sit and listen to two-hour lectures.

Perhaps most importantly, the promise of social media rests in what the field understands about how people learn. Researchers have provided evidence that learners benefit from the scaffolding and support of more knowledgeable others. These more knowledgeable others could be other students or teachers and mentors outside of the traditional classroom. Social media can also make content available to students at all hours of the day to support their remedial and advanced learning needs. Social media fulfill many of the stated needs of learning environments that support all learners.

The Challenges of Social Media in Higher Education

Although there is great promise in the use of social media for learning in higher education, there are also many challenges. First, students enter higher education with great familiarity with social media tools. However, just because students are familiar with how to use the tool does not mean that students understand the tool or understand how to use the tool for learning. For instance, many students spend hours on social media sites posting photos, videos, and textual descriptions of events and happenings that may gain them social standing or prowess but end up hurting them as they graduate and seek jobs. News stories unfortunately abound of students who graduated and were hired, only to have their offers rescinded when a scandalous story or photo resurfaced. Some employers now even check social media sites prior to offering jobs to students.

Moreover, students might be familiar with a tool but be unaware of its use in teaching and learning. They might spend a morning posting on a discussion forum for their personal interests, and yet be unaware of how to use that same tool to carry on a conversation with classmates. The bigger problem is often that universities and colleges often fail to recognize that just because students use the tools does not mean they know the broader impact of the tool.

A second challenge is that many students have grown up with social media tools. They can post videos, blogs, and tweets. However, faculty and staff in colleges and universities are not necessarily so well equipped. More professional development needs to take place to help faculty and staff understand student use of existing tools, the benefits and dangers of such tools, and the integration into education. Without this training, there will be more evidence of schools that ban certain tools on campus, effectively throwing out the baby with the bathwater.

The Research on Social Media in Higher Education

Research findings evaluating the use of social media in higher education have typically been positive, although the study outcomes have been mixed. Some research has highlighted how these tools have brought a social aspect to learning. One of the potential concerns about the research is that many studies are self-reported or student-reported valuation studies, highlighting whether the students "liked" the social media integration. Some studies have also found students who feel some sense of ownership of the tools as private and social media rather than tools for universities and colleges.

Perhaps the most important finding from the research relates to the differentiation of the tools defined as social media. In other words, researchers have found value not by studying whether social media works in higher education, but by whether certain tools (e.g., blogs, wikis) work in higher education. These studies have provided specific examples of when and how specific social media can be used to teach or learn given content.

Implications for Educational Technologists

Although there are research studies that provide both positive and negative outcomes when using social media in higher education, almost every study acknowledges two key things. First, social media are ubiquitous in the lives of learners. Second, social media can be used to fulfill some of the pedagogical goals of faculty and staff in universities and colleges. Given these two factors, educational technologists need to focus on a few key topics. They need to understand how students are being taught to protect themselves and others from risks that social media present, such as bullying and posts that could harm job prospects. They also need to understand the importance of training faculty and staff, many of whom will be unaware of the social and educational potential of such tools given that they themselves have not used them for personal reasons. Finally, educational technologists need to recognize that, given the ubiquity of these tools, the focus should not be on whether they should be used in higher education, but on the best ways in which to capitalize on their existing use.

Richard E. Ferdig

See also Apps for Use in Higher Education; Collaborative Communication Tools and Technologies; Disruptive Technologies; Games in Higher Education; Integrating Social Media Into Learning and Instruction; Massive Open Online Courses; Social Media, Identity in; Social Media and Networking; Social Networking; Web 2.0 and Beyond

Further Readings

Andrews, T., Tynan, B., & Backstrom, K. (2012). Distance learners' use of non-institutional social media to augment and enhance their learning experience. In M. Brown & J. E. Hartnett (Eds.), *Ascilite 2012: Future challenges, sustainable futures* (pp. 25–28). Wellington, New Zealand: Australasian Society for Computers in Learning in Tertiary Education.

Bonzo, J., & Parchoma, G. (2010). The paradox of social media and higher education institutions. In L. Dirckinck-Holmfeld, V. Hodgson, C. Jones, M. de Laat, D. McConnell, & T. Ryberg (Eds.), *Proceedings of the 7th International Conference on Networked Learning 2010* (pp. 912–918). Lancaster, UK: University of Lancaster.

Dabbagh, N., & Kitsantas, A. (2012). Personal learning environments, social media, and self-regulated learning: A natural formula for connecting formal and informal learning. *The Internet and Higher Education, 15*(1), 3–8.

Hrastinski, S., & Aghaee, N. M. (2012). How are campus students using social media to support their studies? An explorative interview study. *Education and Information Technologies, 17*(4), 451–464.

Hung, H.-T., & Yuen, S. C.-Y. (2010). Educational use of social networking technology in higher education. *Teaching in Higher Education, 15*(6), 703–714.

Jacobsen, W. C., & Forste, R. (2011). The wired generation: Academic and social outcomes of electronic media use among university students. *Cyberpsychology, Behavioral and Social Networking, 14*(5), 275–280.

Johnson, J., & Maddox, J. (2012). Use of social media in graduate education: An exploratory review for breaking new ground. *Journal of Higher Education Theory and Practice, 12*(3), 87–93.

Rios-Aguilar, C., González Canché, M. S., Deil-Amen, R., & Davis, C. H. F., III. (2012). *The role of social media in community colleges: A survey report from the Center for the Study of Higher Education at the University of Arizona and Claremont Graduate University.* Retrieved from http://www.academia.edu/1491571/The_Role_of_Social_Media_in_Community_Colleges

Tay, E., & Allen, M. (2011). Designing social media into university learning: Technology of collaboration or collaboration for technology? *Educational Media International, 48*(3), 151–163.

Tess, P. A. (2013). The role of social media in higher education classes (real and virtual): A literature review. *Computers in Human Behavior, 29*(5), A60–A68.

SOCIAL MEDIA IN SECONDARY SCHOOL SETTINGS

In 2012, the American Management Association conducted a survey of 768 managers and executives of various companies on the importance of critical thinking, creativity, communication, and collaboration (the 4Cs). The ability to successfully use the 4Cs was a desired skill employers look for but often find lacking in new graduates. The surveyed executives suggested that schools would have a better chance at effectively ingraining these skills in students than would companies after graduates are hired.

The importance of students leaving their K–12 education with the 4Cs is acknowledged by schools, but the difficulty comes with figuring out how to embed and teach these concepts in the modern classroom. A tried and true method has always been to tie learning to the interests of students, which is why secondary schools have begun to look at social media as one possible method to teach the 4Cs. Social media can be defined as ways for users to interact, communicate, and collaborate on various topics through the Internet. This entry first discusses the use of social media by teenagers and details the concerns about and benefits of the use of social media in secondary schools. It then discusses some examples of social media and how educators have used them.

There is no denying the impact of the Internet and social media on the modern teenager. A 2012 survey by the Pew Research Center found 95% of all teens between the ages of 12 and 17 were online. The same survey reported that 81% of all online teens use some form of social media, with 67% of teen social media users visiting a networking site daily. Considering that connecting students to real-world experiences is a common practice in K–12 schools, it should not be surprising to find schools expanding lessons and reaching out to their students through social media. Of course, with every opportunity, there are challenges that must be overcome.

Concerns About and Benefits of Social Media in the Secondary Setting

Many of the concerns schools have with students in a face-to-face setting will translate to online behavior, such as bullying and harassment. Interestingly, online harassment is not as prevalent as it is offline, but cyberbullying is far more common, with the possibility of severe consequences for the teens involved. *Sexting,* or the sharing of sexual images electronically, is concerning for schools as well. In 2009, 15% of teens who own cell phones said they received a sexual image of someone they know through text, while 4% said they have sent an image of their own. Some states in the United States have passed laws to curb sexting among minors.

A final concern revolves around privacy and the sharing of personal information online. The information placed on the Internet never truly disappears. There is a concern that students often lack the foresight to see how one inappropriate photo posted might impact their future. However, a 2012 Pew survey showed that 60% of teenage Facebook users kept private accounts. The naive assumption is that a private account is a secure account. A privacy setting for a social media site is simply not enough of a barrier to keep personal information from becoming public.

While cyberbullying and inappropriate postings are serious concerns, there are also benefits of social media to students. Social media offer communication and collaboration workspaces that can be customized to fit many learning situations. Certain social media sites allow for personalization along with plug-ins that can enhance the experience through wikis, forums, and more. With or without these plug-ins, social media sites can effortlessly promote communication and collaboration among users. Students have the ability to share projects and information with classmates, work both asynchronously and synchronously in groups, and have the opportunity to engage in meaningful discourse, all while working virtually.

Further, the socialization aspects of social media should not be ignored. Social media allow students to interact with their peers in a setting that might be preferable to face-to-face settings. Sharing ideas and participating in online discussions could help these students become more comfortable with social interactions. If proper rules are set up, social media can give students chances to practice being respectful, tolerant of others, and have proper online etiquette. These benefits give students the opportunity to amplify classroom learning through the use of modern technologies.

Examples of Popular Social Media

There are a wide variety of social media applications that can be accessed from the classroom. The following non-exhaustive list offers examples of popular technologies.

Social Networks

Social networks allow users to share information while maintaining relationships and can be used both asynchronously and synchronously. The most recognizable of these sites is Facebook, with over 1 billion monthly users. LinkedIn is another well-known social network, focused primarily on professional connections. Leveraging this popularity, some secondary schools have created pages dedicated to specific classes, services (such as student counseling), and various student groups.

Microblogging

Microblogging is the ability to publish communication asynchronously and synchronously, usually using no more than 140 characters. Twitter and Plurk, popular microblogging sites, can be used for multiple purposes. Teachers have used microblogging to communicate quick reminders to students and to get students to participate and engage in discussions.

Blogs

Usually described as a virtual journal, a blog is an asynchronous method of publishing writings that can remain private or be made public. For the classroom, using an educational site such as Edublogs allows students opportunities to reflect and share, letting their peers comment and begin whole class discussions. It some cases, educators have used blogs to model language learning and proper paragraphs for nonnative speakers.

Wikis

To understand and grasp the impact of wikis, there is no need to look any further than Wikipedia. With over 76,000 active contributors, this popular site allows people to read, edit, and add to a collective knowledge database of more than 31 million articles in multiple languages, including over 4.5 million articles in English, as of 2014. Student wikis, created through sites such as Wikispaces, can be used in much the same way in an asynchronous manner. Collaboration and the sharing of ideas can be a basic focus for classroom wikis.

Video

YouTube is the leading site in the video-sharing category. Boasting more than 1 billion unique user visits each month, this asynchronous site allows users to upload videos and leave comments in a discussion thread. Other video services include TeacherTube (more directed to educators) and Vimeo. For the classroom, video can be used simply as a visual resource. However, students can also post their own class-related videos and have their peers leave comments.

Social Bookmarking

Using popular tools such as Delicious or Diigo, social bookmarking allows users to collect and share websites with other users asynchronously. For the classroom, teachers can set up bookmarks for students who then have the ability to visit and annotate with notes that can be pushed out to the class. Social bookmarks can help collaboration among students as they share information.

Conclusion

The rise of social media gives schools another opportunity to use a real-world connection with their students. The benefits are plentiful, allowing for collaboration and communication opportunities both in and out of the classroom. Depending on the social media tool selected, students can share videos, writing, and photos while allowing others to comment and interact. While the socialization aspects are powerful, educators should strongly consider the online safety of young teens before venturing into social media. If not supervised properly, social media can open students up to cyberbullying and leaving a negative digital footprint, both of which could have strong, lasting effects.

Social media has become ingrained into the teenage lifestyle. As with other cultural touchstones, schools should not be afraid to make an educational connection. If the concerns are addressed properly, the benefits could be significant for both the students and the schools.

David Adelstein and Michael K. Barbour

See also Blogs as a Communication Tool; Collaborative Communication Tools and Technology; Social Media, Identity in; Social Media and Networking; Wikis as a Collaboration Tool

Further Readings

Churchill, D. (2009). Educational applications of Web 2.0: Using blogs to support teaching and learning. *British Journal of Educational Technology, 40*(1), 179–183.

Gao, F., Luo, T., & Zhang, K. (2012). Tweeting for learning: A critical analysis of research on microblogging in education published in 2008–2011. *British Journal of Educational Technology, 43*(5), 783–801.

Hew, K. F., & Cheung, W. S. (2013). Use of Web 2.0 technologies in K–12 and higher education: The search for evidence-based practice. *Educational Research Review, 9*, 47–64.

Johnson, L., Smith, R., Levine, A., & Haywood, K. (2010). *2010 horizon report: K–12 edition*. Austin, TX: The New Media Consortium. Retrieved from http://www.nmc.org/pdf/2010-Horizon-Report-K12.pdf

Jones, T., & Cuthrell, K. (2011) YouTube: Educational potentials and pitfalls. *Computers in the Schools, 28*(1), 75–85.

Lenhart, A. (2009, December 15). *Teens and sexting*. Washington, DC: The Pew Internet & American Life Project. Retrieved from http://www.pewinternet.org/~/media//Files/Reports/2009/PIP_Teens_and_Sexting.pdf

Lenhart, A., Purcell, K., Smith, A., & Zickuhr, K. (2010). *Social media and young adults*. Washington, DC: The Pew Internet & American Life Project. Retrieved from http://www.pewinternet.org/Reports/2010/Social-Media-and-Young-Adults.aspx

Madden, M. (2012, February 24). *Privacy management on social media sites*. Washington, DC: The Pew Internet & American Life Project. Retrieved from http://pewinternet.org/Reports/2012/Privacy-management-on-social-media.aspx

Madden, M., Lenhart, A., Cortesi, S., Gasser, U., Duggan, M., & Smith, A. (2013, May 21). *Teens, social media, and privacy*. Washington, DC: The Pew Internet & American Life Project. Retrieved from http://pewinternet.org/Reports/2013/Teens-Social-Media-And-Privacy.aspx

Madden, M., Lenhart, A., Duggan, M., Cortesi, S., & Gasser, U. (2013). *Teens and technology 2013*. Washington, DC: The Pew Internet & American Life Project. Retrieved from http://www.pewinternet.org/Reports/2013/Teens-and-Tech.aspx

O'Keefe, G., & Clarke-Pearson, K. (2011). The impact of social media on children, adolescents, and families. *Pediatrics, 127*, 800–805. Retrieved from http://pediatrics.aappublications.org/content/127/4/800.full.html

SOCIAL MEDIA IN THE WORKPLACE

Social media allows people to interact with each other on the Internet using Web applications, such as Facebook, Twitter, and Second Life. With social media, people can create, reuse, and exchange user-generated content—photos, videos, reviews, or articles—on sites such as Instagram, YouTube, Trip Advisor, and Wikipedia.

Social media is deployed on many types of hardware devices, which vary according to screen size, user interface, and degree of mobility (desktop, laptop, tablet, smartphone, etc.). User preference and constraints imposed by work situations suggest an optimal or possible device for a certain task. Web 2.0 provides the software foundation or platform for social media. Web 2.0 thus enables readers to be writers, or *prosumers*, a term coined by Alvin Toffler.

In using a new generation of technology to support learning, two dilemmas must be resolved: (1) the ultimate goal of an educational technology; and (2) the main criteria for its measure of success, whether it supports learning. However, this goal may not be attained (and sometimes is not even aimed for) in a workplace setting, where business goals take precedence. Another dilemma is that although employees need a certain amount of socializing in order to bond and function as teams, socializing is considered as a distraction during the workday, and excessive distractions shorten the time spent on work.

The key to these dilemmas is to find the right balance between working, learning, and socializing. This entails building educational technology on existing work practices and integrating with appropriate social media. The main challenge for this extension and integration is not the technology per se, but to make the use of it persist, engaging the employees, and supporting learning on demand. Another challenge is to decide whether to mandate the use of social media. In contrast to institutions of higher education, e-learning and social media in companies are sometimes optional rather than mandated because the companies wish to provide employees with alternative ways to access information (e.g., paper-based catalogs in addition to Internet search) to cater to different age groups and personal preferences. As long as there are multiple ways to access required information, both with and without social media, and employees do not engage excessively in socializing with family and friends, a policy of discretionary use of social media in the workplace can be successfully implemented. It is the pedagogical framing, integration with work, and organizational implementation that needs special attention for social media to succeed as an educational technology in workplace settings.

Employees use social media productively at work when it helps them locate required information, seek knowledgeable individuals to answer questions, to learn about the skills and functions of others in the organization, and to boost work performance. The rest of this entry goes into more detail. First, it classifies types of social media as a learning environment. Then it provides an overview of findings from workplace studies and presents technology components and emerging trends.

Social Media in the Learning Environment

Social media gives rise to two types of learning environments: (1) integrated learning environment and (2) social learning environment. Mike Atwood used the term *integrated learning environment* (ILE) in 1991 to describe the integration of an intelligent tutoring system in a work organization. Its use was inspired by Gerhard Fischer's notion of an integrated domain-oriented design environment, consisting of a design environment for content creation and a hypertext system for generalized information about content creation, with prototypes created for different application domains (kitchen design, computer networks, telephone services, etc.). In the era of the World Wide Web, ILEs mean that task-specific work tools are integrated with a shared space for users to find the right content at the right time for accomplishing a work task without disruption, but leaving room for *reflection-in-action*, a concept for learning on demand coined by Donald Schön. When empowered by Web 2.0, users also contribute their own content to supplement missing or crudely rendered information. Julita Vassileva used the term *social learning environment* (SLE) to describe the following additional functionality: (1) support learners to connect with the right people (right for the context, learner, purpose, and educational goal), and (2) motivate and give incentives for people to learn.

Examples of ILEs include using YouTube to search for instructional videos to provide help and guidance and wiki systems for reading, writing, discussing, and tagging Web articles. Examples of SLEs include customer engagement platforms such as Get Satisfaction, which provides tools for a company to crowdsource the development of new ideas or to reach out to its customers in a joint effort to improve the company's products or services; LinkedIn, a large business-oriented social media network, which allows people to maintain a list of contacts with whom they have some level of relationship; and online courses in the virtual world Second Life, in which role playing is used to simulate human resources and social relations.

Social Media in Workplace Studies

In a large bibliometric analysis of 324 articles on workplace e-learning published in leading journals between 2000 and 2012, Bo Cheng and colleagues identified six recurring research themes based on the keywords, titles, and abstracts of these articles; one theme was "social media in informal learning," which was identified with knowledge sharing among peers in companies. The study suggests that social media is an important topic in e-learning research, but among the six themes, it had the most fragile topics, indicating a theme under development. The finding aligns with the notion of social learning environment described earlier.

Grete Netteland conducted a three-year e-learning implementation and adoption study in a telecom company in Scandinavia to determine why the implementation process failed. The study adopted a sociocultural perspective on the analysis and used aspects of Yrjö Engeström's cultural-historical activity theory (CHAT) to identify problems. Netteland identified six main problems: (1) hardware and software resources, (2) execution of implementation tasks, (3) management control, (4) information sharing, (5) allocation of time to accomplish e-learning, and (6) relevance to work and previous knowledge. SLEs address problems with information sharing and ILEs address relevance to work and previous knowledge.

Social media is gradually replacing or supplementing e-learning and knowledge management in many organizations. Andrew McAfee coined the term *Enterprise 2.0* to mean Web 2.0 applied within an organization. The inadequacy of knowledge management systems to capture tacit knowledge, such as traces of everyday work activities, triggered his inquiry into finding new solutions. McAfee made a distinction between two types of information and communication technology: channels (e-mail and instant messaging) and platforms (corporate intranets and websites and information portals); and his studies and survey indicate that although channels (particularly e-mail) are used more, platforms retain traces of work better.

When Enterprise 2.0 tools extend outside the boundaries of a company, they have the potential to involve a larger community of collaborators to join forces with company employees to develop novel ideas of mutual interest. Don Tapscott and Anthony Williams refer to this as *mass collaboration* and provide two paradigmatic examples: the Linux operating system (an open source model of collaboration in which users identify bugs and propose patches to improve the system), and Wikipedia (involving domain-expert users to create specialized content through short articles).

Technology Components and Trends

Today's Web applications sometimes contain features and mechanisms that go beyond an interactive and collaborative Web 2.0. With a semantic Web framework (Web 3.0), social media becomes adaptive and may complete actions for the user. For example, when users are *tagging* webpages with keywords (metadata) to describe and organize the contents for searching and browsing, search engines can adapt to user preferences. Furthermore, based on the actions taken by past users on related items, a *recommender system* can make suggestions to a new user regarding an item on a webpage (book, movie, etc.). A *reputation system* is a related mechanism that computes a reputation score for an item based on direct feedback from users (likes, dislikes, reviews, etc.); these interactions help users make decisions about the item. Reputation systems are also used to promote specialized privileges. For example, a user with a high reputation score in one of Get Satisfaction's online communities may be promoted to champion and be paid part time to help other customers.

Another mechanism, *information delivery*, means to decide between different strategies for presenting information to users: (a) proactively (automatically computed ahead of time based on the user's interaction history), (b) reactively (computed immediately after an action that triggered a need for information), and (c) on request (user searches manually for information).

An example of a combination of proactive and reactive ways of information delivery is the Rich Site Summary (RSS). An RSS feed automatically sends a summary of a website to an RSS reader (a Web application for viewing) after an update has occurred on the site. Finally, *learning analytics* is a set of mechanisms for unleashing the educational potential of social media, frequently implying a normative perspective by combining statistical analysis and predictive modeling. One goal with learning analytics is to go beyond simply using the Web for problem solving and mirroring of activity by stimulating learners to reflect on their actions, achievements, and patterns of behavior in relation to others and to learn from it.

Gerhard Fischer distinguished three *learning strategies* for social media learning environments: (1) fix-it level (learning does not delay work, but little understanding is required), (2) reflect level (temporary interruption, fragmented understanding), and (3) tutorial level (systematic presentation of a coherent body of knowledge, substantial time requirements). Researchers are attempting to find the right balance of these learning strategies for social media in the workplace.

Anders I. Mørch

See also Education in Workplace Settings; Integrating Social Media Into Learning and Instruction; Social Media and Networking; Social Media in Higher Education; Web 2.0/3.0 in the Workplace

Further Readings

Cheng, B., Wang, M., Mørch, A. I., Chen, N.-S., Kinshuk, & Spector, J. M. (2014). Research on e-learning in the workplace 2000–2012: A bibliometric analysis of the literature. *Educational Research Review, 11,* 56–72.

Fischer, G. (2013). A conceptual framework for computer-supported collaborative learning at work. In S. P. Goggins, I. Jahnke, & V. Wulf (Eds.), *Computer-supported collaborative learning at the workplace* (pp. 23–42). Heidelberg, Germany: Springer-Verlag.

Grudin, J., & Palen, L. (1995). Why groupware succeeds: Discretion or mandate? In H. Marmolin, Y. Sundblad, & K. Schmidt (Eds.), *ECSCW'95 Proceedings of the Fourth Conference on European Conference on Computer-Supported Cooperative Work* (pp. 263–278). Norwell, MA: Kluwer Academic.

McAfee, A. P. (2006). Enterprise 2.0: The dawn of emergent collaboration. *MIT Sloan Management Review, 47*(3), 21–28.

Netteland, G. (2008). *E-learning for change in a large organization* (Unpublished PhD thesis). Department of Information Science and Media Studies, University of Bergen, Norway.

Schön, D. A. (1983). *The reflective practitioner: How professionals think in action.* New York, NY: Basic Books.

Tapscott, D., & Williams, A. D. (2008). *Wikinomics: How mass collaboration changes everything.* London, UK: Penguin Group.

Toffler, Alvin. (1980). *The third wave.* New York, NY: Bantam.

Vassileva, J. (2008). Toward social learning environments. *IEEE Transactions on Learning Technologies, 1*(4), 199–214.

Social Network Analysis

Social network analysis (SNA) is a methodology to map and examine relationships between various units within a network. SNA can also be viewed as a method of social inquiry, suggests Barry Wellman, which focuses on analysis of relationships between individuals as the primary mechanism for understanding network and individual behavior. Stanley Wasserman and Kathleen Faust propose SNA as a distinctive research perspective that focuses on relational concepts. The big shift in perspective offered by SNA is the ability to study a phenomenon or process *relationally,* that is, examining units and the relationships between units in a process or entity.

For example, historical notions of learning have focused on the individual, suggesting that isolating the abilities of individual learners can lead to improved understanding of how to engender learning. A social network view, conversely, might suggest that learning is better understood by examining the learner in the context of the various relationships and communities the student is engaged with. If we take a student who has difficulties learning math, one approach might be to test the student's motivation and knowledge and then design a specific program of instruction to teach the student math. An SNA perspective would suggest trying to look at the student's current activities, knowledge, and relationships and to identify how and where math might be introduced in a natural and relational manner. For example, can math be introduced as part of the student's customary game playing or interaction with family and friends? SNA should be viewed as an important additional tool to help clarify how individual behavior and learning is affected by relationships to other individuals. This entry first identifies important components and metrics of social networks. It then discusses how SNA is used to understand dynamics of learning environments and the implications of SNA for learning.

Concepts and Variables Within Social Network Analysis

The simplest components of a social network consist of sets of *nodes* interconnected by sets of *ties,* and a specific network structure is identified as a configuration of particular sets of *relations* between *nodes,* as suggested by David Knoke and Song Yang. Figure 1 is a simple depiction of a social network. Assuming *A* and *B* are friends, and *B* is friends with *C, D,* and *E,* Figure 1 depicts that social network. Each of the individuals is a *node* or *actor* in an SNA; each node is linked by a tie or *relation.*

Assume that *A, B, C, D,* and *E* each have other friends, and as is often the case, some of them are also friends with each other. Such an extended network is depicted in Figure 2.

Within a given network configuration, measures of *centrality* (which deal with individuals) or *density* (which deal with the group) can be generated. *Centrality* refers to the prominence of a node's role within the network. A prominent node is one that is the recipient or initiator of a large number of ties within the network. In Figure 2, *B* would be considered a prominent node in the network because of high involvement in many relations. By contrast, *H* and *I* would be considered to have low prominence. Centrality has various measures, including *degree* and *betweenness. Degree centrality*

measures the extent to which a node is connected to other nodes in the network. The higher a node's degree centrality, the more prominent it is in the network. *Betweenness* centrality measures the extent to which a node lies between other nodes in the network. Thus, even nodes with low-degree centrality can act as intermediaries or gatekeepers between different parts of a network. In Figure 2, *A* and *B* both have high *betweenness* centrality, since information would have to go through *A* and *B* to disperse to the entire network.

Density represents the level of linkage between all nodes in a network (the number of existing ties divided by all possible ties). Density is an important measure of social networks since it can reveal information flow within the network. *Cliques* consist of highly interconnected members within the network, where every member of the clique is connected to the other members within the clique. In Figure 2, the subgraphs *AKL* and *CFG* would both be considered cliques. *Cliques* offer important insights into social networks by allowing researchers to focus on the effects of a closed subgroup on the flow of information into and outside the clique, as well as the specific impacts of cliques on member behavior.

Using Social Network Analysis in Learning Environments

SNA has been used in different disciplines, including biology, economics, sociology, organizational development, and political science, to understand how complex relationships can influence the behavior of groups and individuals. Learning environments can also be viewed as complex networks of individuals and their relationship with other individuals in the environment. Learning environments include formal (institutional, e.g., an online course) and informal spaces (noninstitutional and public, e.g., online forums to manage weight).

In formal learning environments, SNA has been used to understand and document interaction within the classroom. Jonathan Guryan and colleagues have developed software for handheld devices that can track data pertaining to interaction and discussion between peers. Using SNA, such data allow us to understand how peers interact and how such interaction affects their development. Kai Hakkarainen and Tuire Palonen used SNA to analyze the intensity of the discourse within two classrooms. SNA allowed these researchers to track and analyze conversations between students and identify the level of participation among students as well as gender differences in participation.

Similar approaches can be used in formal or informal online learning environments. The growth of online education provides researchers with various types of

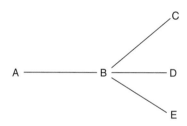

Figure 1   Simple network sociogram

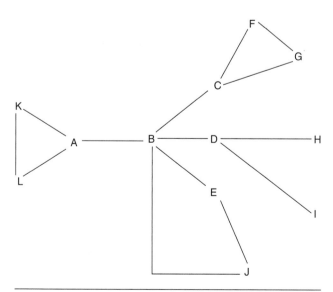

Figure 2   Extended network sociogram

online data that can reveal the processes occurring within the learning space. For example, within a formal online class, SNA can be used to identify the *density* of interactions between students and instructor and identify if there are specific designs or interactions that foster higher density. Higher density could suggest greater engagement in ideas and interaction, both of which are crucial to learning. In addition, SNA can help identify the activity level of students. Specifically, if there are students with high centrality (many connections to other students), then it may be incumbent on the instructor to identify whether the student's prominence supports or hinders learning. Conversely, SNA can also help instructors identify and track students with low centrality (which might indicate low engagement) to provide increased opportunities for engaging with other learners. Identifying and examining the role of cliques within the course can also be useful to understand how groups function to advance (or hinder) learning within the clique and the larger network.

With the increased use of online and mobile tools, educators and researchers are interested in understanding how learning or knowledge building occurs in informal online environments. Concurrently, there is renewed interest in the notion of *communities of practice,* proposed by Jean Lave and Etienne Wenger, which suggests that learning occurs through engagement in communities that form around a specific skill or practice. When viewed using SNA, online social networks offer rich potential to illustrate many facets of learning and knowledge building, including (1) how individuals interact within a network and what impact that has on group thought and behavior; (2) which individuals or groups are central to the network in acting as gatekeepers for information or resources; (3) how gatekeepers affect dissemination of information within the community and the value of information that is disseminated; (4) what established norms and implicit rules guide the network and what impact they have on quality of information and resource dissemination. These facets have significant impact in informing our understanding of how individuals learn, develop knowledge, and modify behavior in informal environments, as well as how specific structures of networks including centrality of certain authority figures and cliques, affect the quality and validity of information within a network.

Implications of Social Network Analysis for Learning

The ability to document and parse the impact that social networks can have on the behavior of an individual may provide fundamental insights into how people learn informally and how such learning can be supported in formal educational environments. Given SNAs' ability to help researchers refine and reveal particularities of individual and network behavior, future educational technologists and researchers should be prepared to understand and use this methodology to assist design and assessment.

Priya Sharma

See also Social Media, Identity in; Social Media and Networking; Social Media in Elementary School Settings; Social Media in Higher Education; Social Media in Secondary School Settings; Social Media in the Workplace

Further Readings

Guryan, J. E., Jacobs, B., Klopfer, E., & Groff, J. S. (2008). Using technology to explore social networks and mechanisms underlying peer effects in classrooms. *Developmental Psychology, 44*(2), 355–364.

Hakkarainen, K., & Palonen, T. (2003). Patterns of female and male students' participation in peer interaction in computer-supported learning. *Computers & Education, 40*(4), 327–342.

Knoke, D., & Yang, S. (2008). *Social network analysis* (2nd ed.). Thousand Oaks, CA: Sage.

Lave, J., & Wenger, E. (1991). *Situated learning: Legitimate peripheral participation.* New York, NY: Cambridge University Press.

Wasserman, S., & Faust, K. (1994). *Social network analysis: Methods and applications.* New York, NY: Cambridge University Press.

Wellman, B. (1988). Structural analysis: From method and metaphor to theory and substance. In B. Wellman & S. D. Berkowitz (Eds.), *Social structures: A network approach* (pp. 19–61). New York, NY: Cambridge University Press.

SOCIAL NETWORKING

Social networking is a phenomenon in which individuals use Internet-based tools to communicate with each other, sharing both text-based and multimedia-based information. Social networks have been increasingly used in educational contexts to support learning, professional development, and extracurricular functions. A wide variety of social networking tools are available, and they generate a great deal of data that can be used to better understand how people interact and learn online.

Although social networks have been referred to as communities, Lee Rainie and Barry Wellman, in their 2012 book titled *Networked,* suggest that social networks are not the same as communities, but rather, they represent the diverse groups of people who somehow touch our lives. At the core of social networking is the network itself: the group of people to whom an individual is somehow connected. These connections represent existing relationships (e.g., family and friends who wish to connect online), people with a shared affiliation (e.g., a group of people who all belong to the same organization), or people with a shared interest. Each person's network is unique. This entry first discusses the use of social networking tools in education and details the characteristics of some popular social networking tools. It then discusses the analysis of data generated by online social networks.

Social Networking in Education

The social networking movement has paralleled the growth of online and blended learning, and social networking tools have attracted the attention of many educators. Several of these tools are popular among K–12 and university students, and using them for instructional purposes might interest those students. Additionally, these tools can readily be used to facilitate learner-centered interactions that easily incorporate Web-based media or to help students interact with experts and practitioners, extending their learning experience beyond the traditional classroom and class community. Finally, social networking has been used to support a great deal of informal learning and professional development among working professionals.

Educational use of social networking tools differs across learning context. In K–12 settings, preference is generally given to tools that are made specifically for use with that market and that offer some form of security or privacy to keep children safe. Related to this safety concern, many schools have policies that do not allow student use of popular social networking tools for school purposes. In some higher education cases, social networking tools are being used in lieu of or in conjunction with a university-supported learning management system. A social networking tool might become the backbone of a course, or it may simply be used for individual assignments. In some corporate settings, social networking tools may be heavily used by individuals when engaged in informal learning, professional development, and job-related networking.

The concept of personal learning networks is heavily associated with social networking. A personal learning network is the network constructed by an individual with the explicit intent to support learning. For example, a person might choose to follow certain experts online or to make connections with people in similar jobs because these are people who might share useful knowledge or who might be contacted for assistance when a specific knowledge need arises. The underlying theories related to personal learning networks include connectivism and social constructivism.

Popular Social Networking Tools

There are many social networking tools available on the Internet. Most of these tools are free for anyone to use, although some have premium versions with added features and storage capability. Many of the tools are created for general social networking purposes, not education-related ones. However, educational versions of some tools have been designed, providing safe, private spaces in which students can interact.

Facebook, the most widely used social networking tool, had its founding moments at a university. Visualized and created by Mark Zuckerberg and his friends when he was a student at Harvard University, Facebook was originally intended to be an electronic version of the paper-based facebook created and circulated by many universities to help students network with each other. It rapidly expanded from Harvard to other schools and eventually was opened to the general public. It remains a tool that is primarily used to support informal social networking interactions, although many businesses have used it to support social marketing as well.

People who are networked with each other on Facebook are called *friends*, regardless of their real-life relationship. All Facebook friendships are reciprocal, with one person initiating the friend request and the other accepting or rejecting it. Friendship on Facebook allows people to see what their friends post. Each Facebook member has a Timeline (formerly a Wall), which is a webpage on which their status updates, photos, life events, friendships, and other Facebook activities may appear in reverse chronological order. Although school-related use and teacher-student friendship is largely banned in secondary education, in higher education some educators have begun using Facebook as a learning management system in their courses. Facebook also is heavily used to support the activities of student groups and extracurricular events. Many universities are using Facebook and other social networking tools to help recruit students and stay in touch with alumni.

Google+ was created several years after Facebook began to dominate the social networking market. Released in 2011 by Google and integrated with Google's other tools, G+ allows users to place individuals in their network in circles and share information with those circles. G+ does not require reciprocity in the networking relationship. In an education setting, circles have been used to connect students working on a project together and Hangouts, a multiuser video chat tool, has been used for virtual instruction.

LinkedIn is a social networking tool that primarily supports professional networking and interactions. Individuals on LinkedIn are identified by their names, their organizational and institutional affiliations, and their connections with others. A person's LinkedIn profile is essentially an online resume, and networked users can endorse each other for skills and provide recommendations. LinkedIn also includes group spaces where individuals can engage in asynchronous discussions.

Twitter is a microblogging tool, allowing individuals to share messages of 140 characters or less. These message may include URLs, allowing them to link to more extensive and media-rich content. Twitter users can follow each other's posts in nonreciprocal relationships. Additionally, there is the option to search for topically aggregated posts. Twitter had been used to support individual broadcasting, brief conversations, and scheduled chat sessions. In an educational context, Twitter has been used to connect classrooms with experts via chat, to develop classroom community, and for professional development.

Edmodo is an education-specific social networking platform. Edmodo functions as a learning management system with a social networking feel to it that allows teachers, students, and parents to interact around a course context. Edmodo is a closed system, limiting access to appropriate individuals in the interest of keeping students safe and their education-related records private.

The tools mentioned above are heavily used in North America. Some, such as Facebook and Twitter, have a large number of users worldwide. Additionally, there are some country, region, and language-specific social networking tools. For example, Cyworld is a large social network in South Korea; the Google-run Orkut gained a large audience mostly in Brazil and Asia; Renren and Weibo are popular in China. Additionally, there are tools used by specific sectors of the population who share a common interest, such as Academia.edu, which is a network that connects academic researchers, as well as tools that focus on sharing a particular type of media while at the same time enabling the development of social networks among users, such as YouTube (video sharing), Flickr (photo sharing), and Slideshare (slide sharing).

Social Network Analytics

Social networks generate a tremendous amount of digital data about things like who interacted with whom, when they interacted, what they shared, what they read, and what they liked. These data can then be analyzed, either as big data sets to determine overall user trends or as smaller or individualized data sets to learn more about users in a particular group. In education, these data can help educational researchers learn more about the interaction and information sharing habits of productive students. Teachers might use some of this data to assist with both formative and summative assessment.

Vanessa P. Dennen

See also Social Media, Identity in; Social Media and Networking; Social Network Analysis; Web 2.0 and Beyond; Web 2.0/3.0 in the Workplace

Further Readings

boyd, d. m., & N. B. Ellison. 2007. Social network sites: Definition, history, and scholarship. *Journal of Computer-Mediated Communication, 13*(1), 210–230. Retrieved from http://onlinelibrary.wiley.com/doi/10.1111/j.1083-6101.2007.00393.x/pdf

Greenhow, C., Robelia, B., & Hughes, J. E. (2009). Web 2.0 and classroom research: What path should we take now? *Educational Researcher, 38*(4), 246–259.

Jenkins, H., Clinton, K., Purushotma, R., Robinson, A. J., & Weigel, M. (2006). *Confronting the challenges of participatory culture: Media education for the 21st century.* Chicago, IL: The John D. and Catherine T. MacArthur Foundation.

Rainie, L., & Wellman, B. (2012). *Networked: The new social operating system.* Cambridge, MA: MIT Press.

Vela-McConnell, J. A. (1999). *Who is my neighbor? Social affinity in a modern world.* Albany: State University of New York Press.

SOCIALLY CONSTRUCTED VIRTUAL ARTIFACTS

Virtual artifacts refer to nonphysical objects created either in the human mind or in the digital environment such as the Internet, intranet, cyberspace, or virtual reality. Virtual artifacts that are constructed through social collaboration are called *socially constructed virtual artifacts*. Virtual artifacts have become an essential cultural phenomenon and are affecting physical world events and people's lives. In the education sector, virtual artifacts have become an emerging teaching and learning tool, especially in the incorporation of digital technology in learning institutions. Thus, an understanding of how virtual artifacts are constructed socially and how this affects education is vital in handling the incorporation of the current technology phase in the social learning community. This entry first discusses the social construction and historical development of virtual artifacts. It then discusses the theory behind socially constructed virtual artifacts and the implications of socially constructed virtual artifacts for education.

In the digital environment, physical artifacts are objects such as desktop computers, keyboards, mice, printers or other computer peripherals, personal digital assistants (PDAs), mobile phones, tablets, and other communication devices. Virtual artifacts could be in the form of computer programs, software applications, animations, hyperlinks, social sites, or social software, among other artifacts. Virtual spaces and places could also be considered as artifacts. Virtual artifacts are abstract in nature and cannot exist physically but could resemble real-life artifacts. Thus, real-life objects and the environments could be simulated virtually in digital environment such as computer games or 3D animations. Simulations, such as those in the form of animation, could have educational value. For example, students could observe and learn how rain or tornados are formed in a science lesson using animations. In another example, through 3D computer games like *The Sims,* students could learn about life management. Primarily, particular corporations (e.g., software developers) or individual parties were responsible for developing these artifacts. For example, Microsoft Corporation developed Microsoft Office and Mark Zuckerman developed Facebook. However, since the introduction of Web 2.0 (e.g., dynamic websites and highly accessible and publishable social media) in the early 2000s, more and more virtual artifacts were constructed through collaborative initiatives by a particular knowledge community or people who share common interests in knowledge and solutions. Wikipedia, an encyclopedia that anyone can edit, is an example of a platform to which any individual could contribute in sharing information about any particular topic for public reference. Certain blogs could also be constructed by a group or community to share information on topics of common interest or discuss a solution to a problem. Wikipedia or other blogs as described here are examples of socially constructed virtual artifacts.

Historical Development of Virtual Artifacts

Virtual artifacts are not new and in fact coexist with humanity in the form of imaginary worlds and characters described in fables and stories. Imaginary artifacts became more sophisticated when they began to be described through advanced visual presentation such as television, film, and photography. Virtual artifacts have even become interactive through current digital technologies and impressively became independent entities existing outside the human mind. Artifacts in general play an important role as learning tools in learning communities where through the process of reification and dual process of participation, learners could negotiate meanings and share common repertoire. Participation involves combined acts of communication such as doing, talking, feeling, thinking, and having a sense of belonging. Reification is the process of giving form to the learning experience by producing objects that reflect these learning experiences. In the physical educational world, using appropriate teaching and learning tools is crucial to facilitate cognitive development and skills development among learners.

Theoretical Development of Socially Constructed Virtual Artifacts

The social construction of virtual artifacts could be further described by theories such as social construction of technology (SCOT). SCOT was introduced by Trevor Pinch and Wiebe Bijker in 1984. The theory could explain the reason and the construction process of the artifacts. According to SCOT, the creation of a social artifact is based on three elements. First, the artifact is subjected to *interpretive flexibility.* This refers to how an artifact could be interpreted differently by different individuals or groups of people. Pinch and Bijker also pointed out that the second element, *relevant social groups,* also determines the construction of the artifact. This means that an artifact could be constructed by different groups of people that share the same meanings for the particular artifact (e.g., consumers, advertisers, engineers, sales agents). Conflicts of construction could arise as each group struggles to control the artifact's design based on its respective interpretation and definition of the problem (assuming that the artifact could solve the problem). The third element is when the conflict is settled after the construction of the artifact reaches *stabilization.* This is the point where the social groups have come to a mutual view of the problem, which then results in the final design of the artifact. In other words, the meaning given by the relevant social group determines the design of the artifact.

Bijker pointed out the bicycle as a classic example to illustrate this theory. When the bicycle was first introduced in the 1800s, the public initially received it with a high degree of interpretive flexibility. The relevant social groups at the time had different opinions about the bicycle. Young men saw it as a fun machine to race, while women and the elderly saw it as a dangerous machine. After the invention of the pneumatic tire, the construction of the bicycle reached stabilization. Air-filled tires could be designed into different sizes to provide a smooth ride for children, elderly people, and women. At the same time, bicycles with bigger tires were designed for young men to race. The conflict was resolved by an artifact (pneumatic tire) and the basic design of the bicycle is what we see today.

However, further development of the SCOT theory revealed that the interpretive flexibility of an artifact could resurface at the user level of the technology. An example given by Kline and Pinch in their study was that in the rural United States in the early 1900s the automobile, which in cities was used for personal transportation as designed, developed new functions in farming areas. The users (farmers) redefined new meanings into the automobile technology. The American farmers not only used the motor car for personal transportation but it was used to transport their farm products in and out of their farms to retailers. The basic design of the car was redesigned into tractors and pickup trucks to suit their purpose. Even the motorcar engines were converted into stationary power source to process their farm products or facilitate their farming chores. The engines were used as corn shellers, water pumps, wood saws, corn or wheat grinders, and for many other purposes. The design and the use of the artifact (the automobile) are flexible to change, as certain groups of users were able to see beyond the manufacturers' vision.

The same principle applies largely in the present construction of virtual artifacts used socially in the digital environment. An example would be the Internet. The Internet was first designed for military communication but has evolved since and robustly by the present social communities as a means of group or personal communication. Today, the Internet has redefined the landscape of the global economy, politics, and culture, integrating both the physical context and virtual world. Gone are the days of waiting in line to pay utility bills and conduct banking transactions. People are increasingly opting for online purchasing rather than doing their shopping at physical departmental stores. In short, virtual artifacts have essentially become a cultural phenomenon and are affecting physical world events and people's lives.

Implications of Socially Constructed Virtual Artifacts for Education

In effective delivery of teaching and learning, the types and suitability of teaching and learning tools are essential components. Similarly, in incorporation of technology in education, besides physical artifacts (e.g., laptops, keyboards, mobile phones, printers, fax machines, and others), proper virtual artifacts for teaching and learning should be determined. Types of virtual artifacts for education should be based not only on the learning process but also on other factors such as learners' cultural and economic background, their knowledge of technology, their learning environment, and their motivation to use

technology. Besides these, learners' awareness, which include learners' knowledge of their roles, activities, responsibilities, and social connections, would determine their level of participation in the learning process via the virtual environment.

Virtual learning environments not only provide an alternative communication system for learners, but also virtual spaces are more flexible compared to the physical learning environment. For example, in a virtual environment, learners could create and manipulate places to suit their current social and learning situations, such as a virtual meeting place for a specific social group or a virtual forestry environment to observe and discuss ways to conserve natural resources. In real life, the creation of these places would be impossible or extremely difficult because of the cost and time involved. The flexibility of virtual spaces could also allow the learning community to continuously build and restructure the spaces according to evolving needs.

Saedah Siraj

See also Collaboration and Social Networking; Collaborative Learning With Technology; Learning Objects; Social Networking; Virtual Worlds; Web 2.0 and Beyond; Wikis as a Collaboration Tool

Further Readings

Ho, C. M., & Nelson, M. E. (2012, May). Students' construction of a virtual museum for multimodal meaning-making: The case of a pilot intervention. In *Proceedings of the 9th Hawaii International Conference on Education* (pp. 4353–4364). Honolulu, HI: Hawaii International Conference on Education.

Keefe, D. F., & Laidlaw, D. H. (2013). Virtual reality data visualization for team-based STEAM education: Tools, methods, and lessons learned. In R. Shumaker (Ed.), *Virtual, augmented and mixed reality: Systems and applications* (pp. 179–187). Heidelberg, Germany: Springer-Verlag.

Pinch, T. J., & Bijker, W. E. (1984). The social construction of facts and artefacts: Or how the sociology of science and the sociology of technology might benefit each other. *Social Studies of Science, 14*(3), 399–441.

Weiss, J., Nolan, J., Hunsinger, J., & Trifonas, P. (Eds.). (2006). *International handbook of virtual learning environments.* Heidelberg, Germany: Springer-Verlag.

STEALTH ASSESSMENT

When assessment is seamlessly woven into the fabric of the learning or gaming environment so that it's virtually invisible—blurring the distinction between learning and assessment—this is stealth assessment. It is intended to be invisible, be ongoing, support learning, and remove (or seriously reduce) test anxiety while not sacrificing validity and consistency. A good way to describe stealth assessment is with a metaphor. Consider the way that businesses were run before the onset of barcodes in the mid-1970s. Before barcodes, businesses had to close down once or twice a year to take inventory of their stock. But with the advent of automated checkout and barcodes for all items, businesses today have access to a continuous stream of information that can be used to monitor inventory and the flow of items. Not only can a business continue without interruption, but the information obtained is far richer than before, enabling stores to monitor trends and aggregate the data into various kinds of summaries, as well as to support real-time, just-in-time inventory management.

Now think about approaches to assessment in schools today. They are usually divorced from learning where the typical educational cycle is *Teach. Stop. Administer test. Loop back with new content.* But with stealth assessment, schools would no longer have to interrupt the normal instructional process at various times during the year to administer external tests to students. Instead, assessment would be continual and invisible to students, supporting real-time, just-in-time instruction. This entry first discusses the relevance of stealth assessment to education and how stealth assessment uses the assessment design framework known as evidence-centered design. It then gives a brief example of stealth assessment.

Relevance of Stealth Assessment

Why is stealth assessment relevant to education right now? Constructing such seamless and ubiquitous assessments across multiple learner dimensions, with data accessible by diverse stakeholders, could yield several educational benefits. First, the time spent administering tests, handling make-up exams, and going over test responses is not particularly conducive to learning. Approximately 10% of class time is currently spent on assessment activities. Given the importance of time-on-task as a predictor of learning, reallocating that 10% into activities that are more educationally productive is a potentially large benefit that would apply to almost all students in all classes.

Second, by having assessments that are continuous and ubiquitous, students are no longer able to cram for an exam. Although cramming provides good short-term recall, it is a poor route to long-term retention and transfer of learning. Thus, standard assessment practices in school lead to assessing students in a manner that is in conflict with their long-term success. With a continuous assessment model in place, the best way for students to do well is to do well every day. And though

this statement sounds tautological, it is not how most classes are structured. By moving students toward a model where they will retain more of what they learn, we are enabling them to better succeed in cumulative domains such as mathematics and science, which are essential to our nation's economic health.

The third direct benefit is that this shift in assessment mirrors the national shift from evaluating students based on the number of years they have occupied seats at a desk to evaluating students on the basis of acquired competencies. A growing number of states are requiring students to pass a high-stakes final exam in order to graduate from high school. While increasing numbers of educators are growing wary of pencil-and-paper, high-stakes tests for which students must prepare, this shift toward ensuring students have acquired "essential" skills fits with the idea of continuous, stealth assessment.

The remainder of this entry provides an overview of evidence-centered design (which undergirds stealth assessment) and describes briefly an example of a game that has three stealth assessments running within it.

Stealth Assessment and Evidence-Centered Design

Stealth assessment uses an assessment design framework referred to as evidence-centered design, formalized by Robert Mislevy, Linda Steinberg, and Russell Almond in the late 1990s. In general, the primary purpose of any assessment is to collect information that will allow the assessor to make valid inferences about what people know, believe, and can do, and to what degree (collectively referred to as *competencies* in this entry). Accurate inferences of competency states support instructional decisions that can promote learning. Evidence-centered design (ECD) defines a framework that consists of several conceptual and computational models that work in concert. The framework requires an assessor to (a) define the claims to be made about learners' competencies, (b) establish what constitutes valid evidence of the claim, and (c) determine the nature and form of tasks or situations that will elicit that evidence. Each of these models is now described.

Three Main Models in ECD

Competency Model

The first model in a good assessment addresses this question: What collection of knowledge, skills, and other attributes should be assessed? Variables in the competency model (CM) describe the set of personal attributes on which inferences are based. The term student (or learner) model is used to mean an instantiated version of the CM—like a profile or report card, only at a more refined grain size. Values in the learner model express the assessor's current belief about the level on each variable within the learner's CM.

Evidence Model

The second model is the evidence model, which asks, "What behaviors or performances should reveal those constructs identified and structured in the CM?" An evidence model expresses how the student's interactions with, and responses to, a given problem constitute evidence about competency model variables. The evidence model (EM) attempts to answer two questions: What behaviors or performances reveal targeted competencies? What's the statistical connection between those behaviors and the CM variable(s)? Basically, an evidence model lays out the argument about why and how observations in a given task situation (i.e., student performance data) constitute evidence about CM variables.

Task Model

The third model addresses the kinds of tasks or situations that should be created to elicit those behaviors that comprise the evidence. A task model (TM) provides a framework for characterizing and constructing situations with which a learner will interact to provide evidence about targeted aspects of knowledge or skill related to competencies.

As learners interact with tasks or problems during the solution process, they are providing a continuous stream of data that is analyzed by the evidence model. The results of this analysis are data (e.g., scores) that are passed on to the competency model, which in turn updates the claims about relevant competencies. In short, the ECD approach provides a framework for developing assessment tasks that are explicitly linked to claims about personal competencies via an evidentiary chain (e.g., valid arguments that serve to connect task performance to competency estimates) and are thus valid for their intended purposes.

Brief Example of Stealth Assessment

Physics Playground (developed by Empirical Games and formerly known *as Newton's Playground*) is a computer-based game with 2D physics simulations for gravity, mass, potential, kinetic energy, transfer of momentum, and so on. The goal of all 75 levels in the game is to guide a green ball over to hit a red balloon. Everything in the game obeys the basic rules of physics. Using the mouse, players draw colored objects on the screen, which "come to life" when drawn. These objects apply Newtonian mechanics to get the ball to the balloon, and they include simple machines such as levers, ramps, pendulums, and springboards.

Three stealth assessments are coded deeply into the game: measuring creativity, conscientiousness, and qualitative physics understanding. Competency and evidence models were created for each of the constructs. This entailed, per construct, about a 10- to 12-month literature review, then structuring the main competency variables into a model. Evidence was defined as the things a person did in the game that would provide information about particular competency variables. Task models provided a blueprint for creating all of the levels in the game. Levels increased in difficulty across the seven different playgrounds, and each level focused on eliciting evidence related to particular aspects of Newton's laws of motion.

For instance, conscientiousness was modeled with four main facets: persistence, perfectionism, organization, and carefulness. For the persistence facet, a set of observables was defined (i.e., behaviors in the game providing relevant evidence) that included the following: time spent on unsolved levels, number of restarts of a level, and number of revisits to unsolved levels. The game automatically tallies this information in log files that are then analyzed by the stealth assessment machinery. The difference between answering self-report questions about persistence (e.g., "I always try my hardest") and actually exerting substantial effort when trying to solve a hard problem in the game is a clear example of the expression *Actions speak louder than words*. And they do.

Conclusion

In addition to the direct benefits to education described earlier, there are some indirect benefits as well. For example, the current capacity to assess students is often limited in that it is based on a relatively small number of test items. In moving toward a seamless assessment model, one will be able to more accurately assess students since there will be access to a much broader collection of the student's learning data. More accurate assessments will enable better support for student learning across a range of important educational areas.

Valerie J. Shute

See also Assessing Learning in Simulation-Based Environments; Assessment in Game-Based Learning; Assessment of Problem Solving and Higher Order Thinking; Engaged Learning; Games and Transformational Play; Learning Analytics; Measuring Learning in Informal Contexts; Twenty-First-Century Technology Skills

Further Readings

Messick, S. (1989). Validity. In R. L. Linn (Ed.), *Educational measurement* (3rd ed., pp. 13–104). New York, NY: Macmillan.

Messick, S. (1994). The interplay of evidence and consequences in the validation of performance assessments. *Education Researcher, 23*(2), 13–23.

Mislevy, R. J. (1994). Evidence and inference in educational assessment. *Psychometrika, 59*, 439–483.

Mislevy, R. J., Steinberg, L. S., & Almond, R. G. (2003). On the structure of educational assessment. *Measurement: Interdisciplinary Research and Perspective, 1*(1) 3–62.

Shute, V. J., & Ventura, M. (2013). *Measuring and supporting learning in games: Stealth assessment.* Cambridge, MA: MIT Press.

Shute, V. J., Ventura, M., Bauer, M. I., & Zapata-Rivera, D. (2009). Melding the power of serious games and embedded assessment to monitor and foster learning: Flow and grow. In U. Ritterfeld, M. Cody, & P. Vorderer (Eds.), *Serious games: Mechanisms and effects* (pp. 295–321). Mahwah, NJ: Routledge.

STRUCTURAL LEARNING THEORY

Structural learning theory (SLT) is a deterministic theory that aims to explain, predict, and direct the behavior of individual subjects on specific problems in given domains. It covers knowledge representation, methods for constructing same, cognitive processes, knowledge assessment, and interactions between agents (e.g., teachers and students). This entry first discusses how in SLT, structural analysis is used to hierarchically represent higher and lower level knowledge with arbitrary levels of precision. It then discusses how these representations, together with SLT's universal control mechanism and each individual's processing capacity and processing speed, make it possible to infer individual knowledge and predict human behavior. Finally, the entry outlines how SLT can be used to build tutoring and adaptive learning systems.

Structural (Domain) Analysis

Structural analysis (SA) is a systematic method for constructing arbitrarily precise representations of what needs to be learned to master any given domain. To-be-learned competencies are represented in terms of cognitive constructs referred to as SLT rules. Each SLT rule consists of a procedural hierarchy operating on a data structure hierarchy. Both are represented formally in terms of abstract syntax trees (ASTs). Cognitively speaking, data

ASTs represent increasingly automated encodings (directly perceived data) and corresponding (to-be-decoded) data generated therefrom. SLT rules may be thought of as hierarchies of equivalent programs, each with its own (hierarchical) data structure. In effect, SLT rules represent hierarchies of increasingly automated to-be-learned procedures operating on data at various levels of abstraction. Procedures higher in a hierarchy are simpler than those lower but operate on relatively complex data structures. Lower level procedures are more complex operating on simpler data.

Given a well-defined problem domain, the first step in SA is to specify SLT rules (cognitive constructs) that account for behavior in that domain. These SLT rules represent competences a subject matter expert (SME) believes should be learned for success—simultaneously at all levels of abstraction. SLT rules have no direct relationship to what may be in human brains. SA is a systematic method for identifying (cognitive) constructs that make it possible to explain, predict, and direct student behavior.

SA begins by selecting a prototypic set of problems in some domain. These prototypes represent what an SME believes adequately represents the range of behavior students are to perform. The first step is to assign a name to the top level operation along with its input and output parameters. Given the domain of solving linear equations, one top level operation might be *solve (equation: ; solution)*; another might be *solve (: equation;)*. The input-output parameter *equation* in the latter represents the equation before and after solution.

The next step is to create an SLT rule (hierarchy) sufficient for solving all problems judged similar to the prototype. As detailed in a U.S. patent (8,750,782) issued June 10, 2014, a small number of data and corresponding procedural refinement types are sufficient. Allowed data refinements are component, prototype, category, and dynamic. Corresponding procedure refinements are sequence, parallel, iteration (Repeat . . . Until, While . . . Do), selection (If . . . Then, Case), and interaction (callback). Furthermore, SMEs may construct any number of equivalent SLT rules (cf. borrowing and equal additions methods for column subtraction). The same top-down process is repeated for each prototype.

In ill-defined domains, SLT rule(s) in turn serve as prototypes for higher order problem(s). SME must then construct a (higher order) SLT rule for each prototype. The process of SA can be continued indefinitely. As a practical matter, however, SMEs rarely go beyond first-level higher order SLT rules.

Higher order rules in SLT are analogous but very different from learning mechanisms in production system based theories. SLT rules, higher as well as lower order, are not *de novo* but rather derived from given domains. Chaining corresponds to one kind of higher order SLT rule. Generalization and case-based reasoning are others.

SA ensures a full and adequate account of behavior associated with any given domain, whether expert, neophyte, or anywhere in between. Moreover, SLT rule-based accounts are cumulative. They can incrementally be extended to accommodate extended domains.

Individual (Student) Knowledge

SLT rules and higher order rules derived via structural analysis provide an arbitrarily precise foundation for operationally defining individual knowledge. Each node in an SLT rule (hierarchy) defines a subset of problems or subproblems associated with the SLT rule. Higher level nodes define more complex subproblems while lower level node subproblems are less complex. Terminal nodes in column subtraction, for example, might include the subtraction facts or deciding whether a top digit is less than a bottom digit, for example. Higher level nodes correspond to such things as subtracting columns whether or not they involve regrouping (borrowing).

Success on higher level nodes necessarily implies success on all subordinate nodes. Conversely, failure on a subproblem implies failure on all higher level nodes. In effect, higher level nodes correspond to relatively complex skills. Lower level nodes correspond to relatively basic skills. Terminal nodes correspond to prerequisites assumed on entry. In effect, representing knowledge hierarchically as SLT rules makes it possible to quickly pinpoint individual knowledge. Equivalently, this makes it possible to determine what any given learner can and cannot do at each stage of learning.

Cognition

Mastery of any nontrivial domain requires learning both lower and higher order SLT rules. In SLT, the use of SLT rules is controlled by SLT's universal control mechanism (UCM). UCM is recursive in nature. It operates completely independently of the SLT rules and higher order rules whose use it controls.

Given a problem, UCM seeks an SLT rule whose goal matches the problem goal and whose input matches the problem givens. If exactly one SLT rule matches, the SLT rule is applied. If not, UCM directs the search for SLT rules whose ranges (outputs) include SLT rules that match the problem. If a unique match is found, the (higher order) SLT rule is applied and a new SLT rule is generated. Newly derived SLT rules are added to the learner's limited capacity processor. Control then reverts to the original problem goal. When a newly

derived SLT rule matches the problem, it is applied and the problem solved. As necessary, UCM directs searches to still higher levels until a match is reached or memory capacity is reached. (When more than one SLT rule matches, higher order rules play a role analogous to motivation—selecting the rule deemed most appropriate or otherwise preferred.)

True to its deterministic core, SLT also assumes each individual has a fixed processing capacity common over all tasks. A series of experiments by Donald Voorhies and Joseph Scandura showed that some students have a processing capacity of 5, others 7, for example. Aside from health, extreme age, and other physiological changes, processing capacity is assumed to remain relatively constant. (Miller's *magic number 7 +/- 2* was based on group averages.) Constraints on working memory may be relaxed in practice, wherein subjects are assumed to have the benefit of pencil and paper or other external memory aids.

A final assumption in SLT—a fixed processing speed—has only anecdotal support. Some individuals characteristically react quickly (whether correctly or otherwise). Others are more measured. These characteristics tend to remain stable over long periods of time. Experimental data addressing this assumption would obviously be welcomed, with the caveat that empirical testing requires a very different paradigm. The use of averages would completely miss the point because processing speed varies considerably with degree of mastery. Controlling for such differences requires significant pretraining.

Instructional Systems

Hierarchical representation of knowledge as SLT rules makes it possible to quickly infer with arbitrary degrees of precision what any individual does and does not know at each point in time. Accordingly, SLT provides a rigorous foundation for building dynamically adaptive (aka "intelligent") tutoring systems. Tutoring involves ongoing interaction between tutors and students: presenting information, receiving responses, evaluating responses, making inferences about what the student does and does not know, and defining the best way forward.

Adaptive learning systems are gaining attention. Most work on adaptive learning goes under the rubric *learning analytics* (LA). The latter derive from advances in *big data* technologies, correlations between multiple data bases. Aside from privacy issues, LA has a major limitation. Correlation between subject matters does not necessarily imply causation. As a deterministic theory, causation is the foundation on which SLT rests. SLT is further distinguished from other cognitive theories (e.g., ACT-R, or adaptive control of thought-rational) that almost universally rely on data averaged over individuals.

The AuthorIT authoring and TutorIT delivery systems build directly on SLT, and the patented methods derived from SLT, are discussed earlier in this entry. AuthorIT provides automated assistance for SA, making it possible for SMEs to represent to-be-acquired knowledge hierarchically with arbitrary degrees of precision. AuthorIT has been used to develop a broad range of dynamically adaptive tutorials. TutorIT takes knowledge representations as input and automatically determines what each individual does and does not know at each point in time, with the goal of delivering precisely the information needed by the student when it is needed until the student has mastered the material to be learned.

Joseph M. Scandura

See also Adaptive Learning Software and Platforms; Cognitive Task Analysis; Intelligent Tutoring Systems; Learning Analytics; Learning Analytics for Programming Competencies; Learning Analytics for Writing Competencies

Further Readings

Durnin, J. H., & Scandura, J. M. (1973). An algorithmic approach to assessing behavior potential: Comparison with item forms and hierarchical analysis. *Journal of Educational Psychology, 65,* 262–272.

Miller, G. A. (1956). The magic number 7 plus or minus 2: Some limits on our capacity for processing information. *Psychological Review, 63,* 81–97.

Newell, A., & Simon. H. A. (1972). *Human problem solving.* Englewood Cliffs, NJ: Prentice Hall.

Novak, E. (in press). A dynamically adaptive TutorIT tutorial for basic statistics skills. *Technology, Instruction, Cognition & Learning.*

Scandura, J. M. (1971). Deterministic theorizing in structural learning: Three levels of empiricism. *Journal of Structural Learning, 3,* 21–53.

Scandura, J. M. (1973). *Structural learning I: Theory and research.* London, UK: Gordon & Breach.

Scandura, J. M. (1974). The role of higher-order rules in problem solving. *Journal of Experimental Psychology, 120,* 984–991.

Scandura, J. M. (1977). *Problem solving: A structural/process approach with instructional implications.* New York, NY: Academic Press.

Scandura, J. M. (2005). AuthorIT: Breakthrough in authoring adaptive and configurable tutoring systems? *Technology, Instruction, Cognition & Learning, 2–3,* 185–230.

Scandura, J. M. (2007). Knowledge representation in structural learning theory and relationships to adaptive learning and tutoring systems. *Technology, Instruction, Cognition & Learning, 5,* 169–271.

Scandura, J. M. (2011). What TutorIT can do better than a human, and why—Now and in the future. *Technology, Instruction, Cognition & Learning, 8,* 175–227.

Scandura, J. M. (2013). Dynamically adaptive tutoring systems: Bottom-up or top-down with historic parallels. *Technology, Instruction, Cognition & Learning, 9,* 146–155.

Scandura, J. M. (2013). Introduction to Dynamically Adaptive Tutoring: AuthorIT Authoring and TutorIT Delivery Systems. *Technology, Instruction, Cognition & Learning, 1,* 137–145.

Scandura, J. M. (in press). Adaptive Learning: How it is learned or what is learned? *Technology, Instruction, Cognition & Learning.*

van Merriënboer, J. J. G., & Sweller, J. (2005). Cognitive load theory and complex learning: Recent developments and future directions. *Educational Psychology Review, 17,* 147–177.

Websites

AuthorIT and TutorIT: http://www.TutorITweb.com

STUDENT MODELING

Student modeling is the process of creating a dynamic representation of students' personal attributes so as to provide individualized support in the learning process. The resulting profile is typically called *student model* or *learner model*. Student modeling has several parallels with user modeling, which is widely used in the commercial sector to create personal profiles of users. After discussing the use of student modeling in learning applications, this entry describes its various components and then examines both the role of student modeling in emerging learning environments and the use of learning analytics.

Use of Student Modeling in Learning Applications

In contrast to a typical learning management system that provides the same course content, activities, and interactions to all students, adaptive and personalized learning systems attempt to customize learning experiences for individual students by adapting the learning environment to their individual characteristics, competencies, interests, and needs. By doing this, these systems aim at improving learning outcomes while fostering better learning efficiencies and effectiveness. To be able to do that on an ongoing basis, these systems need to not only know as much as possible about the students but also about any changes in students' individual attributes.

Student models are, therefore, key to every adaptive and personalized learning system.

Historically, student models have been used in intelligent tutoring systems, with earlier systems focusing primarily on competency improvement for students. Later realizations of adapting learning to individual student behavior, preferences, and other characteristics evolved earlier learning systems into adaptive and personalized learning systems. Although researchers and implementers have frequently used the terms interchangeably, there are differences in the ways that adaptive learning systems and personalized learning systems play a role in improving learning experience; these differences impact the information needed in their respective student models. On the one hand, adaptive learning systems emphasize providing different course content, activities, and other aspects automatically to different students, focusing primarily on performance and progress in a course. On the other hand, personalized learning systems attempt to customize courses to suit individual student characteristics, including prior performance and progress but also interests and other relevant factors that influence learning.

Various Components of Student Modeling

Being part of a variety of learning applications, student modeling requires different types of information about the students. Major components of student modeling are described below. Depending on the type of application, certain components play a more prominent role than others.

Demography Component

The demography component includes primarily static information that can be used by the adaptive and personalized learning systems to initiate adaptive processes. Information gathered through the demography component of student modeling typically includes a student's name, gender, student ID, begin time of study, grade, study program, and contact information.

Competency Component

The competency component of a student model contains information about a student's domain competence. Several variations are used depending on the purpose and the situation in which the student model will be used. Four types of student models have been commonly used: overlay student model, differential student model, perturbation student model, and constraint-based student model.

Overlay Student Model

In an overlay type of student model, the knowledge of the student is assumed to be a subset of an expert's knowledge at any point in time. The bigger the difference between student's knowledge and expert's knowledge, the bigger is the lack of student's skills and knowledge. Adaptive systems target this difference to analyze what and how to provide instruction to the individual student. Different variations are possible in the overlay model, ranging from binary type where the only information recorded is whether a concept is learned or not, to a more granular approach where system records how much of the overall knowledge is learned.

Differential Student Model

Differential student models evolved from overlay student models. A differential student model separates the domain knowledge into learned and not learned components for each student.

Perturbation Student Model

Perturbation student models represent a next step in student modeling. A perturbation student model not only contains what each student has learned and how it is different from an expert's knowledge, but it also records the misconceptions a student may have. These misconceptions are recorded separately and are known as a buggy model or an error model.

Constraint-Based Student Model

Constraint-based student models record domain knowledge and student knowledge in the form of a set of constraints. These constraints portray the fundamental rules and concepts of the domain.

Cognitive Component

The cognitive component of a student model focuses on the cognitive resources of a student and then model cognitive processing of individual students to enable adaptive and personalized learning systems to customize learning experience to suit the specific cognitive abilities of a student. Known as a *cognitive trait model*, this component models various cognitive abilities or traits of the students, such as working memory capacity, inductive reasoning skills, associative learning skills, and information processing speed. These traits are the innate abilities that are persistent in terms of time and consistent across a variety of domains and tasks. Consequently, the results of cognitive trait modeling not only remain useful for a long period of time but are also transferable to different learning systems.

Cognitive trait modeling infers students' cognitive abilities through monitoring of students' actions in the learning systems. All student actions are recorded in the student behavior history. A trait analyzer subcomponent takes the logged information in the behavior history for a student and performs a cognitive analysis of that student's actions, using various clues gleaned from the cognitive psychology literature, to determine the level of cognitive abilities of that student.

Various cognitive abilities affect learning experience in different manners, and therefore modeling of different cognitive abilities enable learning systems to adapt learning experience precisely to the individual students. Some examples include the following:

Working memory capacity. Working memory capacity affects students' learning process in a variety of ways because it affects various tasks needed during learning, including the use of natural language, such as comprehension, production and recognition of declarative memory, and acquisition of skills. Determination of an individual student's working memory enables learning systems to ensure formation of higher order rules in the student's learning process and to prevent learning activities from overloading the storage system of working memory.

Inductive reasoning skills. Inductive reasoning skills enable students to construct concepts from examples. During the learning process, students look for known patterns in the new concepts and use them to abstract theoretical underpinnings. Students with higher inductive-reasoning skills typically recognize a previously known pattern much faster and with more ease to generalize higher order rules. As a result, the working memory load is reduced, and the learning process becomes more efficient.

Associative learning skills. The associative learning skills enable linking of new knowledge to existing knowledge. The association process entails pattern matching encompassing discovery of the existing information space, analysis of the relationships between the existing and new knowledge, and then transferring new knowledge in the long-term memory. To be able to assist the association processes during the student's learning, the learning systems need to customize the learning experience in such a way so as to assist the recall of learned information, clearly show the relationships of new concepts to existing ones, and facilitate the creation of associations by providing information of related domain area.

Information processing speed. Information processing speed identifies how fast learners acquire the information

correctly. Learning systems consider this information to ensure correct pace of learning for individual students.

Behavioral Component

The behavioral component of student modeling gathers information about student behavior in the learning process, including how students use the system, which particular functionality and types of content they use more often, and the various functionalities and various types of content for learning.

Course-Related Information

The behavioral component typically identifies which course the student is in and the history of previous courses. It also contains data about the preferred services of each student, including how much time a student spent in each service, when that service was used, and which services the student used most.

Types of Content

The behavioral component also gathers information about the learning objects viewed by the students and the learning activities individual students completed, to enable the learning system to infer patterns about student preferences for the type of content and associated learning activities. In addition, student interactions with other students and teachers are also analyzed, typically in discussion forums, to relate the context of learning with student understanding of the domain content.

Interest Levels

The behavioral component includes information on current interest levels as well as a past history, to enable the learning system to contextualize learning experiences accordingly. Interests are generally measured in terms of strong interest (if a student showed interest more than once in a specific concept), weak interest (if a student showed interest in the concept only once), and disinterest (if a student rejected learning about the concept for the majority of requests). The interest levels of students play an important role for learning systems to plan and recommend navigation among concepts during the learning process. They also affect the way learning systems assign problems, and further adaptations can be provided in peer-to-peer discussions by annotating certain inputs as useful from students with similar interests.

Social Closeness

Social closeness is inferred by the behavioral component to enable the learning system to adapt students' interactions with others. It includes information about the level of familiarity between students, whether and how much they know each other, whether they have learned together previously, and whether they are willing to learn together again. It also attempts to find out the general preferences of students for collaboration, in terms of whether they like to work and learn together with other peers.

Learning Styles

Students' learning styles are inferred to analyze how students perceive, gather, and process learning materials. Different students have different ways of learning, affecting their learning process and consequently the learning outcome. There are multiple ways to define and classify learning styles, and different models are available that suit different needs and requirements of the learning systems. Similarly, there are multiple ways to infer students' learning styles. Two predominant approaches are collaborative student modeling and automatic student modeling. *Collaborative student modeling* acquires information directly from students through some sort of direct questioning, such as through interviews or questionnaires. *Automatic student modeling* attempts to infer students' learning styles by monitoring their behavior in the learning system and mapping that behavior to various aspects of learning styles. While collaborative student modeling enables learning systems to gather sufficient data at the start of learning to be able to provide adaptivity immediately, it suffers from problems related to consuming students' time for non-subject-related tasks (e.g., completing a questionnaire or taking part in an interview that has nothing to do with the subject the student wants to learn), the subjective nature of responses, and the need for a repeated data collection task to infer any changes in learning styles since previous data collection. Automatic student modeling suffers from the cold-start problem, where sufficient data is available only after the system has monitored students' actions in the system for a longer period of time, which means no adaptivity is possible during that time period. A hybrid approach is used by many learning systems, where initial data is collected through collaborative student modeling, which is then verified and maintained through automatic student modeling.

Ubiquitous and Mobile Learning

The exponential growth of wireless technology in recent years, increasing availability of high bandwidth network infrastructures, advances in mobile sensor technologies, and the popularity of handheld devices have opened up new opportunities for education. Mobile and ubiquitous learning environments have started to emerge to overcome the restrictions of classroom or workplace-restricted learning and extend e-learning by bringing the concepts of anytime and anywhere to reality, aiming at providing people with better educational experiences in their daily living environments. The learning process in such environments includes the real-life experience augmented with virtual information and the social interaction of the learners with others either through face-to-face discussions or through social media. Such a rich mixture of different types of media, along with the changing context of learning, has created additional demands on student modeling.

To accommodate adaptivity and personalization in ubiquitous and mobile learning environments, student modeling requires information about current location of students, history of past movement, what learning objects students explored in those locations, and what associated learning activities they completed (or attempted to complete). The learning system uses this information to customize the learning experience for the next set of learning objects and activities as students navigate through the environment.

Location information is typically identified and stored as GPS (global positioning system) coordinates, identity of base stations of cellular networks, or access points for Wi-Fi broadband wireless networks. It can even be in the form of a textual description, such as postal code or address as well as name of the place.

The location information is used by the learning systems in a number of ways to customize the learning experience of students. It is used to identify students in the vicinity of each other to create face-to-face learning groups. It is also used to contextualize the learning experience by detecting those real-life objects in the surroundings of the student that could be used in the current learning process and the learning activities that could be created using those objects.

Learning Analytics

An emerging area of student modeling is learning analytics. Learning analytics is about analyzing learning patterns in various yet related levels of granularity. Technologies now exist to track the learning processes students undertake to achieve their learning goals and outcomes. Tracking of learning processes comprises monitoring of a network of learning activities that lead to a measurable chunk of learning. The learning system can then provide just-in-time feedback to individual students (and inform instructors, if required) as and when pedagogically valid issues are identified automatically in the learning process.

Kinshuk

See also Adaptive Learning Software and Platforms; Design and Creation of Adaptive Educational Systems; Intelligent Tutoring Systems; Learners and Instructional Control in Adaptive Systems; Personal Learning Environments; Personalized Learning and Instruction; System and Learner Control in Adaptive Systems

Further Readings

Graf, S., Kinshuk, Zhang, Q., Maguire, P., & Shtern, V. (2012). Facilitating learning through dynamic student modelling of learning styles: An architecture and its application for providing adaptivity. In P. Isaias, D. Ifenthaler, D. G. Sampson, & J. M. Spector, *Towards learning and instruction in Web 3.0: Advances in cognitive and educational psychology* (pp. 3–16). New York, NY: Springer-Verlag.

Graf, S., Lin, T., & Kinshuk. (2008). The relationship between learning styles and cognitive traits—Getting additional information for improving student modelling. *Computers in Human Behavior, 24,* 122–137.

Hong, H., & Kinshuk. (2004). Adaptation to student learning styles in Web based educational systems. In L. Cantoni & C. McLoughlin (Eds.), *Proceedings of World Conference on Educational Multimedia, Hypermedia & Telecommunications* (pp. 491–496). Chesapeake, VA: Association for the Advancement of Computing in Education.

Kumar, V., Graf, S., & Kinshuk. (2011). Causal competencies and learning styles: A framework for adaptive instruction. *Journal of e-Learning and Knowledge Society, 7*(3), 13–32.

STUDENT RESPONSE SYSTEMS

Student response systems (SRSs), sometimes called personal response systems (PRS) or classroom performance systems (CPS), are electronic, generally wireless, means of communicating between instructors and students. While typical applications involve the use of simple wireless keypads (*clickers*) by each student in a classroom setting to respond to questions posed by instructors, SRS use is not limited to physical classrooms. As educational technologies and classrooms evolve, the purposes and functions of SRSs are evolving as well. This entry first discusses the technology needed for classroom SRSs, the background of these systems, and their use in classrooms and online classes. It then discusses the benefits and drawbacks of SRSs and developing trends in the systems' use.

Basic Classroom Technology

The keypads are small, handheld transmitters, typically with five to 15 buttons or keys. They can transmit on radio waves (*rf*) or infrared light (*ir*). Other than the keypads, classroom SRSs require a computer, an rf or ir receiver, software, technical staff for system installation and maintenance, and training for instructors and students.

History and Contexts

The antecedents of SRSs were hardware-based audience response systems, first used in the early 1960s. Audiences in specially equipped theaters used hard-wired keypads to record their responses to various versions of unreleased commercials or motion picture endings. By the mid-1960s educators began experimenting with their use in classrooms, but they were not available for general classroom use until early in this century. In the last few years, the popularity of SRSs, and the variety of vendors, has grown rapidly.

Use in Classrooms

The most basic uses of classroom SRSs are for student polling (including taking attendance) and learning assessment. Instructors can pose questions verbally or via a projection screen, and individual student responses are aggregated and analyzed and can be instantly presented to the class, either as tables or graphs. Results can be used for group decision making (e.g., choosing a test date) or integrated into lectures (e.g., "Do you think Statistics 1401 should be a prerequisite for this class?"). The most common format of SRS use for learning assessment is multiple-choice quizzes, with students allotted a specified time to answer each question. Some clickers have LCD screens and alphanumeric keyboards to allow composition of short answers.

Another common use of an SRS is for enhancement of student participation. Students can use their keypads to ask questions or respond to questions during a lecture, with aggregated or anonymous responses displayed on a large screen. This can increase participation by overcoming student fear of asking a silly or stupid question or publicly answering a question incorrectly. Students can be required to respond to questions in order to increase attention.

Smartphones, laptops, tablet computers, and other multipurpose computing devices can be used, with appropriate software, to achieve many of the functions of dedicated keypads. However, these devices also present some limitations. First, all students do not own smartphones or portable computers. Their cost is much higher than the cost of designated classroom keypads, and the students most likely to lack these devices are those who can least afford them. Second, these devices are multifunctional, so students are more likely to be tempted to play games, tweet during class, or look up answers to quiz questions.

Use With Hybrid and Online Classes

Applying the SRS definition to hybrid and online classes emphasizes the meaning of *system* in the term. While e-mail could be considered a simple type of SRS, it does not provide the more important functions of an SRS, such as aggregation and broadcasting of responses, response analysis, and automatic grading and reporting. Three online systems that provide the function of response broadcasting are forums, chat rooms, and Web-conferencing software.

Forums allow instructors or students to post statements or questions online. Responses from others are added over time and remain accessible for the life of the forum. Forums are typically divided into topics, allowing for members to easily search posts by subject.

Chat rooms operate in real time, allowing organic discussions among the participants. Names of participants who are currently logged on are listed, so questions may be directed to specific people. An active chat room may provide a quick source of information in a stimulating and even fun environment, but without oversight, conversations may wander and normative arguments may overwhelm the chat. Empty chat rooms are also a problem. If there is no one else online, students will leave.

Web-conferencing software, such as Skype, Open-Meetings (Apache open-source software) and Adobe Connect, can also provide real-time conversations between participants in different locations, with the addition of video feeds. The video can be a presentation broadcast from a central location, individual comments from participants, or a combination of both. Participants use the video cameras on their individual computers, but they can provide audio comments and see video from others if they don't have such cameras. When used with hybrid or online classes, these systems can replicate classroom discussions, as well as be prescheduled to provide for online office hours or study and review sessions.

Online assessment tools can also be used for anonymous polling, for learning assessment, and for interactive education as well. For example, individual feedback can be written for each possible response to multiple-choice questions so that students will receive an explanation of exactly why each response they chose is wrong or can receive kudos and additional information when they choose the correct answer.

Student Response Systems: Pros and Cons

There are pros and cons to each of these technologies. Classroom-based SRSs by nature require students to be together in a room and to focus on one topic or task at a time. The cost of system installation and maintenance may be prohibitive. The training requirements for appropriate SRS use by instructors are considerable. Students will likely resent having to pay for a device that is only used for taking attendance or for occasional quizzes. Instructors need training in polling, question design, and other skills for integrating SRS into their classes.

There are numerous keypad designs, each appropriate for different classroom tasks, so a student may be required to buy more than one of these devices, even if an institution designates one vendor for all systems. The keypads typically cost from $25 to $75 each, and sometimes an annual software license fee ($10 to $20) is also required. Some institutions subsidize the cost of the keypads. Each student must register the device, a process that may be complex. Further complications may arise from lost or nonfunctioning keypads, dead batteries, and so forth, so instructors also need training in basic SRS troubleshooting and maintenance. Dealing with these problems will use valuable instructor time, and sometimes class time as well.

As mentioned above, while most students already have smartphones or other portable computing devices, the multifunction capabilities of these devices as well as their cost for students who don't already have them, are problematic. Nonetheless, the simplicity and dependability of these systems are improving and their prices are falling. They are very useful for simplifying student assessment and improving classroom communication and involvement.

Future Development

Several complementary trends are contributing to the future development of SRSs.

- The ubiquity of student response systems is increasing along with improving capabilities and rapidly decreasing prices.
- Almost all institutions of higher learning, and most public schools, now provide, or are planning, campus-wide wireless networks.
- Most textbooks are now available in digital form, and publishers generally provide slide presentations, flash cards, and other digital content along with their books.
- Solid-state, touch sensitive displays and virtual keyboards are rapidly becoming less expensive. They can be built into a classroom desk and sealed for protection from liquid spills or other contamination but easily removed and repaired when necessary.

The confluence of all of these changes is likely to result in the merging of multipurpose computing devices and stand-alone student response systems. A virtual touch-sensitive keypad can be projected on the device's screen. Instructors will be able to easily modify their functionality during class. Except when instructors prohibit specific functions, students will be able to access their personal files and notes, search the Internet, and initiate or respond to inquiries with the instructor and other students, from a keypad at their classroom desk or using their personal portable computing device.

Sherwood Bishop

See also Engaged Learning; Radio Frequency Identification in Education

Further Readings

Bruff, D. (2009). *Teaching with classroom response systems: Creating active learning environments.* Hoboken, NJ: Wiley.

Clark, R. C. (2007). *Developing technical training: A structured approach for developing classroom and computer-based instructional materials* (3rd ed.). San Francisco, CA: Pfeiffer.

Freeman, M., Bell, A., Comerton-Forde, C., Pickering, J., & Blayney, P. (2007). Factors affecting educational innovation with in class electronic response systems. *Australasian Journal of Educational Technology, 23*(2), 149–170.

Marzano, R. J. (2006). *Classroom assessment and grading that work.* Alexandria, VA: Association for Supervision & Curriculum Development.

Petersohn, B. (2008). *Classroom performance systems, library instruction and instructional design: A pilot study.* Retrieved from http://digitalarchive.gsu.edu/univ_lib_facpub/35

Wankel, C., & Blessinger, P. (2013). *Increasing student engagement and retention using classroom technologies: Classroom response systems and mediated discourse technologies.* Bingley, UK: Emerald Group.

SUMMATIVE ASSESSMENT

Assessment in the field of education focuses on the measurement of student learning. The gauge or yardstick used for measurement may take a variety of forms, and effective assessment often involves the use of multiple forms of assessment as a basis for educational decision making. This entry first discusses summative assessments and their relationship to formative and benchmark assessments, then explains the scoring and analysis of summative assessments. Common uses of summative assessments, such as their relationship to school accountability, their use in the Response to Intervention process, and the role they play in entrance to college also are considered.

Summative assessments are assessments of learning, which sum up what a student has learned at a particular point in time. An assessment that is given at the end of a course or grade level and is used for the purposes of determining that a student has mastered the skills and learning necessary to proceed to the next level as well as for the purposes of assigning a final grade is a summative assessment. Standardized achievement tests also are summative assessments, and schools frequently use the Iowa Test of Basic Skills or the California Achievement Test to measure students' achievement in selected subjects, such as reading, math, and science. State-developed achievement tests based on state-developed standards or the Common Core State Standards also are summative assessments.

Summative assessments frequently are called "assessment *of* learning," a phrase developed by Rick Stiggins, founder and executive director of the Assessment Training Institute. In writing about assessment, he makes the distinction between assessments *of* learning, which provide evidence of achievement for public reporting, and assessments *for* learning, which serve to help students learn more by informing students of their progress toward reaching standards or learning targets.

Data collected from summative assessments or assessments *of* learning report student achievement at a given period of time. Data from state tests, college entrance tests, and other summative assessments give educators, as well as state officials, community members, and parents, a picture of what a student or groups of students have learned; report whether or not students have exceeded, met, or are below standards; and are used to compare students or groups of students. A summative assessment may be a multiple-choice test, in which test items are aligned to specific standards or criteria, or a rubric-graded performance assessment, which uses a rubric that is aligned to specific standards or criteria to determine achievement.

Summative assessments frequently are normed, standardized, or standards-based assessments with scores reported as percentiles or stanines for specific subject areas. Norm-referenced summative assessments rank students according to how well they performed in relation to other students. The normed tests are developed by administering the test to a nationwide sample, or norm group. Students taking the test are then ranked in quartiles or stanines according to how well they did in relation to the norm group.

Summative assessments become standardized when they are administered to students under uniform conditions so that students' performances may be compared and not influenced by differing conditions, such as the length of time used for completing the test. Standardization of protocols for the administration of a summative assessment is important in determining the assessment's validity, or the concept that test questions measure what they are intended to measure, and the assessment's reliability or consistency of test results. Depending upon the content, a standardized summative assessment may or may not be standards based.

Summative assessments become standards-based when they are made up of a series of questions or tasks that are directly aligned with a specific set of standards. In general, questions on standards-based assessments are content based. Multiple-choice questions ask students to select a correct answer from a series of possibilities. Performance assessments, such as essays, ask students to demonstrate or show what they have learned and are evaluated using a standards-based rubric. Both multiple-choice and performance-based assessments assess the standards-based content the students have been taught.

Summative assessments complement the use of formative and benchmark assessments. While summative assessments measure what a student has learned over a specific period of time, formative assessments, sometimes referred to as assessments *for* learning, measure learning and progress toward meeting standards in order to adapt teaching to meet the immediate learning needs of students. Data from formative assessments are collected minute to minute and day to day and used by teachers, learners, or their peers to make decisions about next steps in instruction. Data from formative assessments are based on questions and products that are closely tied to a standards-based curriculum and help teachers make microinterventions that may include teaching a target lesson to an entire class, providing special help to individual students, or changing instructional pacing or materials in the curriculum.

In tracking student progress over time, such as a grading period or a semester, schools often give benchmark assessments or common final exams. Benchmark assessments are common assessments in that all teachers of a particular grade or subject give the same test at approximately the same time. The use of common benchmark assessments help to enhance student achievement of all students because data from common benchmark assessments help teachers and school leaders identify students' strengths and weaknesses and thus provide specific macrointerventions and resources to remediate the weaknesses.

Benchmark assessments often serve the purpose of being both formative and summative. They are summative assessments in that they may serve as a quarter or semester exam and receive a grade. The same benchmark assessment also may be a formative assessment in that it provides information to teachers and administrators on how a student or group of students is progressing toward meeting standards. Often benchmark assessments are used to predict how students will fare on summative state assessments or graduation tests.

Formative and benchmark assessments are complementary to summative assessments in that they provide teachers and school leaders with data to monitor students' progress toward standards, provide interventions to increase student learning, and ultimately help students achieve a higher score on high-stakes summative assessments such as state tests of standards. Summative assessments complement formative and benchmark assessments in that they provide assurances to teachers, school district leaders, parents, and community members that the local curriculum and assessments are aligned with standards and levels of achievement outside the school or district. In other words, formative and benchmark assessments assess student progress toward local learning targets and standards that are being taught to students and provide data that show what students have or have not learned. Normed summative assessments assess students' knowledge in given subject areas or standards and provide data that show how individuals or groups of students rank or compare with others in their local school, state, or nation.

In general, the information teachers and other educators gain from various kinds of assessments, be it formative, benchmark, or summative assessments, student discussion, or student body language, has long been the power that drives the numerous adjustments educators make to teaching and learning activities. Effective teachers use assessment of student achievement to advance student learning as well as report student progress. They make assessment a valuable teaching and learning tool (1) by articulating to their students the achievement targets their students are expected to achieve; (2) by transforming those expectations into assessment exercises and scoring procedures that accurately reflect student achievement; (3) by using assessment results as a source of information for adjusting curriculum and instruction; and (4) by using assessment results to communicate to students and parents areas of strength and weakness and ways to improve.

Assessment of student learning is nothing new. The word *assess* dates back to the Medieval Latin word, *assidere*, which means to sit by or attend, and attending to students' learning by using a variety of assessment strategies always has been a trademark of good teaching. Assessments show educators what students know before instruction begins, whether or not students understand the lesson while it is being delivered, as well as what, if anything, students have learned from a lesson or a series of lessons. What is new is that assessments are now being used to hold teachers and schools accountable more than ever before. What students have or have not learned is published in local newspapers, school report cards are sent home to parents on a regular basis, and schools that fail to make adequate yearly progress (AYP) under the federal No Child Left Behind law face serious consequences. Clearly under No Child Left Behind teachers are being held accountable for student learning as well as teaching.

Scoring and Analysis of Summative Assessments

The results of summative assessments frequently are reported in assessment subscores, such as a vocabulary score for reading, or by standard. Often a test analysis procedure known as item analysis is used and test items are aligned to a subscore category or a specific standard. When the assessment is scored, test items for each subscore category or standard are combined into a percentage score for the subscore category or standard.

By reviewing an item analysis by subscore or standard report, one can determine how an individual student or a group of students performed on a specific subscore category or standard. Thus data from these reports can be used to monitor or report a student's attainment of subscore categories or key standards. By monitoring attainment of subscore categories or key standards, educators have useful information to make adjustments to curriculum and instruction. By reporting students' attainment of subscore categories or key standards, educators, parents, and school officials know whether students have met or exceeded educational targets and are able to make decisions regarding a school's effectiveness as well as a student's ability to succeed in college.

No Child Left Behind has mandated that the data analysis process include the disaggregation of data by subgroup. As a result, the collection and analysis of summative assessment data on state-mandated summative assessments is done in conjunction with demographic data, which includes gender, ethnicity, income level, language background, and special needs. Because overall averages gathered from student assessment data can hide learning problems of specific subgroups, it is useful when the data is disaggregated in order to describe the achievement level of each subgroup tested. By disaggregating the data, educators are able to examine how various subgroups are progressing toward subscore categories and standards and identify subgroups that may be experiencing difficulty with a particular subscore category or standard. Reviewing disaggregated data allows educators to identify next steps for low achieving subgroups and begin to close achievement gaps.

Summative Assessments and School Accountability

In terms of accountability, standards-based state tests are summative assessments that validate what schools, teachers, local curriculum, instructional practices, and local assessments are doing to prepare students to meet and exceed standards as well as the challenges of the future. However, accountability at the local school level is strongly influenced by the school's ability to collect and use local formative and benchmark assessment data to inform instruction and help students learn. Thus the primary forces in accountability are not only the state or the federal government, but also school and district leaders who are responsible for building and promoting an instructional program based upon common, standards-based curricula and assessments that produce reliable formative, benchmark, and summative data so that teachers have the means to guide each student's learning experiences. Used together, data from formative, benchmark, and summative assessments provide a comprehensive picture of what students know and where there are gaps in their learning.

Summative Assessments and Response to Intervention (RTI)

Response to intervention (RTI) is a model of academic intervention that provides early, systematic assistance to children who are having difficulty learning. RTI seeks to prevent academic failure through early intervention, frequent progress monitoring, and research-based instructional interventions for children who continue to have difficulty. The RTI assessment plan for progress monitoring

- identifies students at the beginning of the year who are at risk or who are experiencing difficulties, as well as students who have reached benchmarks and who need to be challenged;
- monitors students' progress during the year to determine whether at-risk students are making adequate progress in critical skills and to identify any students who may be falling behind or need to be challenged;
- informs instructional planning in order to meet the needs of individual students; and
- evaluates whether the intervention provided is powerful enough to help students achieve grade-level standards by the end of each year.

The RTI assessment plan is achieved using four types of assessments during the school year:

1. *Screening assessments* provide quick formative measures of overall ability and critical skills known to be strong indicators that predict student performance.

Administered to all students as an initial baseline, these assessments help to identify students who do not meet or who exceed grade level expectations.

2. *Progress monitoring assessments* are brief, periodic formative assessments given to determine whether students are making adequate progress and to analyze and interpret gaps in achievement.

3. *Diagnostic assessments* are more lengthy formative assessments that provide an in-depth, reliable assessment of targeted skills to help diagnose and plan more powerful instruction or interventions.

4. *Outcome assessments* are group-administered summative assessments of important outcomes, such as state standards. Outcome assessments are often used for school, district, or state reporting purposes. These tests are important because they give school leaders and teachers feedback about the overall effectiveness of their instructional program.

Summative Assessments and College Entrance

Acceptance to a college or university often is determined by standards-based summative assessments that evaluate students' academic readiness for college. The ACT measures college and career readiness using verbal and mathematical achievement. The SAT measures literacy and writing skills that are needed for academic success in college as well how well the student analyzes and solves problems.

These tests typically are taken by high school juniors and seniors and are believed to provide a better indicator of success in college than high school grades alone. Because there are substantial differences in funding, curricula, grading, and difficulty among U.S. secondary schools, these assessments are intended to supplement secondary school records and help college admission officers put local data, such as course work, grades, and class rank, in a national perspective.

Nancy W. Sindelar

See also Criterion-Referenced Assessments; Diagnostic Feedback in Formal Educational Settings; Diagnostic Feedback in Informal Educational Settings; Educational Data Mining; Formative Assessment; Measuring and Assessing Literacy Skills; Measuring and Assessing TPACK (Technological Pedagogical Content Knowledge); Norm-Based Assessments, Performance Assessment

Further Readings

Fuchs, D., Compton, D. L., Fuchs, L. S., & Bryant, J. (2008). Making "secondary intervention" work in a three-tier responsiveness-to-intervention model: Findings from the first-grade longitudinal reading study at the National Research Center on Learning Disabilities. *Reading and Writing: An Interdisciplinary Journal, 21,* 413–436.

Sindelar, N. W. (2010). *Assessment-powered teaching.* Thousand Oaks, CA: Corwin.

Sindelar, N. W. (2011). *Using test data for student achievement: Answers to No Child Left Behind and Common Core Standards* (2nd ed.). Lanham, MD: Rowman & Littlefield.

Stiggins, R. (2002). Assessment crisis: The absence of assessment for learning. *Phi Delta Kappan, 83*(10), 758–765.

Stiggins, R. (2002). Assessment for learning. *Education Week, 21*(26), 30, 32–33.

Wiggins, G. (1993). *Assessing student performance: Exploring the purpose and limits of testing.* San Francisco, CA: Jossey-Bass.

SYNCHRONOUS TOOLS AND TECHNOLOGIES

Synchronous tools are technologies used to mediate real-time communication in various forms, including instant messaging, voice-over-internet protocol (VoIP), and video conferencing. Online learning has become a more and more popular and pervasive learning format in the global and digital age; therefore, the demand to adopt synchronous tools and technologies to support real-time interaction in the learning process has been increasing.

Interactions occurring in an online learning environment can be categorized according to (1) interaction between participant learners and content, (2) interaction between the instructor and participant learners, and (3) interaction among participant learners. The first type of interaction (learners-content) usually is mediated through asynchronous tools because learners need time to read, reflect, comprehend, and respond to the content. Synchronous technology can facilitate instructor-learner and learner-learner interactions. Synchronous tools allow the instructor to provide real-time communication, enable all participants to present and communicate simultaneously, and enhance participants' sense of community and connectedness. Since participant learners from all over the world may participate in an online learning environment, they often will never see their classmates face to face; therefore, it is extremely important to help them form a learning community in which they feel a sense of belonging. Once the sense of community is established, members can interact with one another as they engage in the learning process. The sense of community is strongly related to participant learners' online learning satisfaction.

Tools to Support Learning

Immediate interaction and social connectedness are at the heart of learning. Immediate interaction occurs between the instructor and learners or between learners and learners. Through real-time discourse, faculty can gauge students' understanding of the topic, make necessary changes to instruction, mediate confrontation, and allow students to discuss, debate, share, and exchange their perspectives. Real-time discourse is common in the traditional face-to-face classroom. In the online learning environment, the instructor can manage immediate communication through the synchronous tools and technologies. Immediate communication between participants can be mediated through text-based, audio-based, video-based, webinar-based, and 3D virtual environment tools.

Text-based synchronous tools such as Internet Relay Chat (IRQ) and chat rooms are the most commonly used communication technologies because of their low technology requirements. Text-based chat rooms, which are used as personal communication tools, have been adopted by educators to support communication among learners in the online learning environment. The use of synchronous text-based tools is appropriate for stimulating in-depth discussion and for maintaining a relatively high protection of the participants' identities. Many learning management systems, such as Blackboard and Moodle, provide built-in chat room modules. Participants who are slow in typing or who are non-native speakers may have difficulty in joining text-based mediated sessions as naturally as they would in face-to-face sessions. Sometimes parallel communication occurs in a text-based chat room if there are many participants, and this makes it challenging for participants to follow all of the conversation themes.

Audio-based synchronous tools, such as Skype and Google Talk, are ideal for conducting informal conversations and meetings and for providing just-in-time support. Instructors can provide immediate feedback through audio-based sessions. However, only one presenter can speak at a time, and the conversation session may be dominated by only a few. All participants can communicate simultaneously in text-based chat rooms.

The video-based synchronous tool has been frequently adopted by the public, especially after improvements in network connectivity and the emergence of mobile devices. Before computer technology became pervasive, many universities used closed-circuit television to deliver one-way lectures on campus. Now a video-based tool allows participants to communicate through two-way audio, video, and text data. Common video conferencing tools are Skype, Google Hangout, and Microsoft Lync. Service providers allow a certain number of participants to connect through video conferencing simultaneously. Video-based synchronous tools enable a communication form that approximates to face-to-face communication. Therefore, video-based tools are quite often used to connect a group of participant learners with subject experts or special guests.

Through video communication, the participants can interact with the presenters in a real-time format.

Synchronous tools can enable one or two forms of communication simultaneously. Learning is restricted to text and aural communication. Even though video-based tools allow participants to view each other, the interaction is limited. It is challenging for an instructor to provide multilayered interactive learning experiences using these synchronous communication tools.

Recent advancements in technology have pushed the emergence of webinar synchronous technology, referred to as interactive Web conferencing. Webinar technology provides real-time, point-to-point communication; therefore, it can offer connection between the instructor and multiple participants in different locations and enable interactivity among all participants. Thus, webinar technology makes it possible to establish or strengthen social presence of all participants. The most frequently adopted webinar technologies in higher education and industry are Elluminate and Adobe Acrobat Connect. In addition to text, audio, and video communication tools, webinar technology provides a variety of features that allow instructors to promote interaction and meaningful pedagogical practices, such as group discussions and collaborative learning. These features include

- desktop application sharing, which allows sharing applications with participants and demonstrating procedures and functionality;
- co-Web and document browsing, which allows sharing documents or Web browsing windows with participants so that the group is viewing the same content for discussion;
- electronic whiteboard, which allows multiple participants to collaboratively develop content through text or graphics simultaneously; this feature is useful for brainstorming or facilitating the development of flowcharts or concept maps;
- polling, which enables the moderator to poll participants to assess their understanding of a specific topic, get feedback, or facilitate participants' discussion;
- breakout session, which allows the moderator to assign participants to several sub-rooms so each group can work on a unique task; each sub-room has access to its own whiteboard and communication tools to facilitate the group work; and
- recording and archive capability, which allows the recording and archiving of sessions for future use.

Another form of synchronous communication is mediated through the interaction between avatars in a virtual 3D environment. Second Life is a frequently adopted online virtual environment to support learning and training. Each participant creates an avatar, which serves as a surrogate when participants interact with one another in the virtual 3D environment. Real-time interaction in Second Life can be mediated through texts, audio, body language of the avatars, and the interaction among the avatars. If the instructor has the privilege of building and modifying the virtual environment, the instructor can create instant feedback when the participants' avatars interact with certain objects in the virtual environment, such as simulation effects. Participants can observe the phenomena simultaneously and discuss it as a group while enjoying the immersive and situated learning experience.

Voice, video, and animation data demand more network bandwidth compared with text data. Network bandwidth and the reliability of the service providers affects the quality of the synchronous session mediated through audio, video, webinar, or 3D environment tools.

Compared with asynchronous communication tools, synchronous tools and technologies have certain benefits, including support of dynamic and immediate interactions. The instructor not only can interact with individual participant learners through multiple formats of communication simultaneously but also can allow participants to collaborate with each other. Synchronous technology allows participants to provide immediate feedback and makes it convenient to exchange constructive feedback and provide voluntary help to others. Moreover, the real-time interaction can help participant learners establish their social presence and create a sense of a learning community. These elements are important in a healthy and successful online learning environment.

The adoption of synchronous tools and technologies also raises issues. As with face-to-face interaction, synchronous communications environments can be dominated by certain participants and leave learners who need time to process information out of the discussion. In the face-to-face classroom, learners can express their opinions through nonverbal signals or social cues, but it is difficult to give individual attention or observe each participant's reaction when using synchronous tools. Also, synchronous tools require that all participants need to attend the session concurrently; this may limit the participation of some learners. Another concern is the availability of a high-speed and reliable Internet connection. The interaction mediated through webinar tools relies on a stable high-speed connection. Slow Internet speed delays data transmission and can result in low audio and video quality.

Educational Use of Synchronous Tools and Technologies

Synchronous tools and technologies have been widely adopted to support asynchronous online learning. The most common use of synchronous tools is to deliver lectures and presentations. To increase participant learners' cognitive attention during the learning, instructors need to apply effective and appropriate pedagogical strategies.

Synchronous technologies have been adopted as an effective and popular tool with which to support language learning because language acquisition depends on immediate interaction between the instructor and the learners. Synchronous communications technology supports the development of most cognitive aspects of language learning. Synchronous tools offer teachers greater immediacy. Learners can be connected with a native-language speaker who is located in a remote place or even in a different country. Learners' facial expressions and lip movements in sync with the oral communication also help the instructor to correct learners effectively, especially their pronunciation.

New technologies make it possible to connect learners with experts anywhere in the world at low cost. More and more universities and organizations allow students to take courses together and share resources and expertise, and many of these institutions encourage students to exchange their perspectives, diverse backgrounds, and cultural and learning experiences. Synchronous technologies support this type of collaboration or communication, using the format of an instructor teaching multiple participant learners either in the same room or in two locations, each with multiple learners. Lectures or presentations can be archived and disseminated to other learners who are interested in the same topic.

Synchronous technologies can effectively support decision making. When a group needs to work on a problem, especially an ill-defined problem that might have many solutions, the group members need to discuss details, ask questions, make clarifications, assign roles and tasks, set up plans, and evaluate work. These processes require a great amount of spontaneous communication and have to be mediated through synchronous technologies.

Synchronous tools can also be adapted to facilitate group work and peer tutoring. Learners can engage in deep conversation to build on each other's ideas, share and construct knowledge, and practice reasoning skills.

Many online learning instructors use synchronous tools to provide virtual office hours. The main course is delivered through asynchronous tools with a self-path learning environment. Virtual office hours enable the instructors to meet with participant learners who have questions or concerns through text-based or audio-based chat rooms on a regular basis. Virtual office hours can reduce online learners' anxiety or confusion, help learners with weak self-regulation skills, and strengthen a sense of community.

Limitations of Synchronous Tools and Technologies

Even though synchronous tools and technologies provide advantages in supporting online learning, there are problems and challenges with their use. Synchronous tools can support factual information and conceptual knowledge but are not so easily used to support instructors in conveying procedural knowledge (e.g., demonstrating how to use a specific application). Even with advanced webinar features, such as desktop sharing and instant audio/visual communication, it is still difficult to monitor participants' learning progress and provide meaningful, real-time feedback. Procedural knowledge requires accurate performance of sequences of tasks. The instructor needs to make sure that participants are successful in previous steps before moving on to the next step. Current synchronous technologies are not especially good at monitoring and providing personalized feedback to individual learners when complex procedural tasks are involved.

Some learners tend to be quiet in face-to-face classrooms. Participant learners who are introverted or who lack self-regulation skills may be reluctant to participate in both a classroom setting and in an online, real-time discussion. Some learners with special learning needs (such as those who are unfamiliar with technology, type slowly, or need more time to digest information or develop responses) may experience difficulty in asynchronous learning environment. Synchronous technologies may create heavy cognitive loads and a sense of urgency for some, which will inevitably cause interference with their willingness to participate and make progress. Instructors need to develop a variety of strategies to engage learners to participate in the learning process.

When there are many students involved in a synchronous learning situation, a teacher-centered approach is likely to be used; this may not be as optimal as a more student-centered approach that could be possible when asynchronous tools are also involved.

Another common issue is lack of knowledge and practice with a particular technology. The instructor needs to go through training sessions to master the features provided by synchronous tools and technologies as well as pedagogical strategies. The synchronous session relies on network speed and reliability. If the instructor plans to apply different pedagogies, especially student-centered pedagogies, the participant learners need to know how to use all these features and need to have access to a reliable network as well. If any participant learners have technology problems, they may have to interrupt the session to seek help from the instructor. Nonetheless, synchronized tools and technologies provide greater instructor immediacy for effective learning in the online learning environments. They have greatly improved the online learning quality and enriched the online learning experiences.

Shiang-Kwei Wang

See also Collaborative Communication Tools and Technologies; Distance Learning for Professional Development; Interactive Webinars; Internet: Impact and Potential for Learning and Instruction

Further Readings

Allmendinger, K. (2010). Social presence in synchronous virtual learning situations: The role of nonverbal signals displayed by avatars. *Educational Psychology Review*, 22, 41–56. doi:10.1007/s10648-010-9117-8

Johnson, G. M. (2006). Synchronous and asynchronous text-based CMC in educational contexts: A review of recent research. *TechTrends*, 50(4), 46–53.

Martin, M. (2005). Seeing is believing: The role of videoconferencing in distance learning. *British Journal of Educational Technology*, 36(3), 397–405.

Murphy, E., & Ciszewska-Carr, J. (2007). Instructors' experiences of web based synchronous communication using two way audio and direct messaging. *Australasian Journal of Educational Technology*, 23(1), 68–86. Retrieved from http://www.ascilite.org.au/ajet/ajet23/murphy.html

Park, Y. J., & Bonk, C. J. (2007). Is online life a breeze? A case study for promoting synchronous learning in a blended graduate course. *MERLOT Journal of Online Learning and Teaching*, 3(3), 307–323.

Wang, C. X., Jaeger, D., Liu, J., Guo, X., & Xie, N. (2013). Using synchronous technology to enrich student learning. *TechTrend*, 57(1), 20–25.

Wang, S.-K. (2008). The effects of a synchronous communication tool (Yahoo Messenger) on online learners' sense of community and their multimedia authoring skills. *Journal of Interactive Online Learning*, 7(1). Retrieved from http://actxelearning.pbworks.com/f/7.1.4.pdf

Wang, S.-K. & Hsu, H.-Y. (2008). Use of the webinar tool (Elluminate) to support training: The effects of webinar-learning implementation from student-trainers' perspective. *Journal of Interactive Online Learning*, 7(3), 175–194. Retrieved from http://www.ncolr.org/jiol/issues/pdf/7.3.2.pdf

SYSTEM AND LEARNER CONTROL IN ADAPTIVE SYSTEMS

An adaptive system refers to a learning environment in which the learner is placed at an appropriate level by the system, which determines the appropriate level based on the learner's learning performance. More advanced adaptive systems identify the learning style to provide appropriate strategies. In an adaptive system, the system is in control. The adaptive feature of the system is to trace and record each individual learner's specific learning performance and traits in order to diagnose the learner's learning deficiencies and identify the most appropriate content and learning methods for the learner at each learning stage.

A learning environment can also be designed for the learner to control where the learner is allowed to choose where to start and what, when, and how to learn. When the learner has the control, the system is called an adaptable system. The adaptable feature of the system is to provide a variety of options and tools for the learner to choose so the learner will be able to adopt the best personal approach for learning to reach a maximal learning status.

A learning system can be both adaptive and adaptable, such as one that uses system control to record learning performance and provide feedback along with options for the learner to select. There are a variety of adaptive and adaptable learning (intelligent) systems. While some are comparatively simple, others can be extremely complex. Adaptive/adaptable learning systems include some CAI (computer-assisted instruction) learning systems. These can be Web-based online learning systems. This entry first discusses different types of adaptive and adaptive/adaptable CAI learning systems and Web-based adaptive/adaptable learning systems. It then discusses how adaptive/adaptable learning systems are designed.

Types of Adaptive/Adaptable CAI Learning Systems

CAI can be designed as an adaptive system through which learners are placed at an appropriate learning level after taking a placement test, for example. The system determines the learning level of the learner through analyzing the learner's test results. The learner takes instruction and then another test. The system keeps analyzing the learner's test results and places the learner at a higher or lower learning level based on learning performance. This example is used to illustrate system control in a simple adaptive learning system. The placement of the learner is determined by the system. Enabling system control are programmed modules (usually based on subject matter experts' insights) and if/then rules, such as a module for generating test items based on a learner's current level, a module for checking learning deficiencies (e.g., comparing responses to deficiency criteria), and providing a recommendation for the next learning level for that particular learner. It is not always necessary for the learner to complete all the items on a test for the system to determine an appropriate level of placement. As long as certain criteria are met while the learner takes the test, the system is able to determine where the learner should be placed.

A variety of common CAI learning systems are designed as learner control systems in which learners can choose a level or next module. In a learner-control CAI, the system is designed with branches at different levels with a variety of subareas. Learners usually do not take the placement test at the beginning because the system is not in control so the data will not be analyzed or utilized. Learners can access instructional modules (small units of instruction) at different levels to determine where to start. They can also change the level based on their own learning experience.

When an adaptive CAI learning system is integrated with learner control, the system is also adaptable. The adaptive/adaptable CAI learning system can be designed for learners to take expert advice that the system provides. TICCIT (time-shared, interactive, computer-controlled information television) in the early 1970s was a system that has the design of learner control where the learner is advised by the system before determining the display strategies and a level for learning. With the system-control feature, TICCIT evaluates what the learner has done and provides advice or suggestions based on the learner's learning pattern and performance. With the learner-control feature, learners are provided with the opportunity of choosing what they are going to learn instead of the system placing the learners at a particular learning level without providing a choice for learners' preferences.

Web-Based Adaptive/Adaptable Learning Systems

There are many types of Web-based learning or e-learning systems. Alan Mustafa analyzed 52 different types of e-learning systems and categorized them into eight groups based on their adaptability, adaptivity, and personalization. There are also various types of learner controls. M. David Merrill categorized them into external and internal learner controls. Therefore, a variety of Web-based systems and learner control learning systems can have various adaptive and adaptable features.

In a Web-based adaptive learning environment, the system is more intelligent than what was previously described. Instead of placing a learner at an appropriate level of the predesigned instruction, the system needs to match the learner's learning level and traits with the appropriate learning level and instructional methods. This can be done through a variety of types of instruction online with the appropriate navigation path to direct the learner to the right resources where the appropriate level of instruction is delivered in an appropriate method that matches the learner's learning level and style to help the learner learn in this more advanced learning environment. Alternatively, the system can make an adjustment of the instructional module for the learner based on the information collected from the learner's behavior of learning and preferences. In a

Web-based adaptive/adaptable learning environment, the system does not directly adjust instructional modules for the learner; based on the information available through interaction with the learner, the system provides opportunities for the learner to adjust or select learning modules to allow the learner to make changes.

Multimedia provides many learning opportunities. Easy access to various online learning resources offers learners the opportunity to choose what is needed to accomplish their learning goals. Learning is better supported when the learning environment serves various learners with different learning characteristics and different learning goals. In a system-control learning system integrated with learner control, learners have the control of when, what, and how to learn to accomplish their own learning goals at their own paces and through their own processes. This is an adaptive/adaptable learning environment in which the learners explore, design, and construct knowledge. They also make sense of their learning by using the adaptive/adaptable system as a tool to accomplish their own learning goals. Moreover, the design of this system considers the learner's social context so learners are in a learning environment where they may discuss and work with their real or simulated peers. Advanced Web-based adaptive/adaptable learning systems that diagnose the learner's learning deficiencies and place the learner at the appropriate learning level or allow learners to form their own learning models are still rare, although this is an important emerging area of educational technology.

Design of Adaptive/Adaptable Learning Systems

Good design of adaptive/adaptable learning systems is not possible without the collective intelligence and efforts of experienced and insightful professionals. The instructional part of design requires complex and detailed analyses, appropriate and accurate sequencing of instruction, and sophisticated design of instructional strategies based on instructional and learning theories. Without instructional/learning theories as guidance, a good design of instruction is a haphazard enterprise. The design of Web-based adaptive/adaptable learning systems requires principled guidance. Instructional theories, learning theories, and models, such as Robert Gagné's nine instructional events, M. David Merrill's first principles of instruction, Lev Vygotsky's theories of socioculturalism and the zone of proximal development, Albert Bandura's social learning theory, and others are helpful in the design of effective Web-based adaptive/adaptable learning systems.

Feng-Qi Lai

See also Adaptive Learning Software and Platforms; Component Display Theory; Human-Computer Interaction; Instructional Transaction Theory; Open-Source Repositories for Learning and Instruction; Personal Learning Environments; Self-Regulated E-Learning Design Principles; Social Media and Networking

Further Readings

Kelly, D. (2008). Adaptive versus learner control in a multiple intelligence learning environment. *Journal of Educational Multimedia and Hypermedia, 17*(3), 307–336. Retrieved from http://wenku.baidu.com/view/76043d 353968011ca3009138.html

Merrill, M. D. (1980). Learner control in computer based learning. *Computers & Education, 4,* 77–95. Retrieved from http://mdavidmerrill.com/Papers/TICCIT_Paper[OCR].pdf

Merrill, M. D. (1984). What is learner control? In R. K. Bass & C. Dills (Eds.), *Instructional development: The state of the art, II* (pp. 221–242). Dubuque, IA: Kendall/Hunt.

Mustafa, A. (2011). *Impact of learner control on learning in adaptable and personalized e-learning environments* (Doctoral thesis). University of Greenwich, London, UK. Retrieved from http://gala.gre.ac.uk/7143/1/Alan_Mustafa_ Impact_of_learner_control_2011.pdf

SYSTEM DYNAMICS

System dynamics refers to a technology to model complex systems created by Jay Forrester. It also represents a way to think about complex systems, as argued by Peter Senge. A complex dynamic system is one with many components that interact in ways that change the observed behavior of the system over time. An example is our solar system. One can think of the sun, the planets, and their orbiting satellites as the components. All of these components are moving with their movements determined by the physical laws of nature (e.g., gravity). If one wishes to place an object in orbit around one of these components (a system intervention), one must understand the dynamics of the entire system. Many complex and dynamic systems allow for the direct manipulation of one or more factors or components that influence the behavior of the system. An example is a supply-chain system in which a corporation orders raw materials to produce items (supply) based in part on past, current, and projected orders (demand). The number of orders changes over time, and there can be a delay in getting raw materials and producing the product. The complexity of managing such delays and changes in demand requires understanding internal feedback loops (e.g., receiving more orders creates an increase in demand for raw materials, which eventually leads to more production, which can reduce the number of pending and anticipated orders). There is a cost associated with overproduction (e.g., excess inventory storage, which can also affect price) as well with underproduction (e.g., unsatisfied customers, which can affect demand), so such dynamic and deep understanding is critical for efficiency. Many other examples of complex and dynamic systems that require decision making and policy formulation can be found in nearly every human enterprise. As a consequence, understanding the complexities of a system (delays, nonlinear relationships, internal feedback, etc.) is a highly valued competency in many decision-making and problem-solving task domains. As such, understanding complexity and tools and technologies used by system dynamics professionals is pertinent to many educational technology applications.

System Dynamics Models and Representations

The fundamental model used in system dynamics is called a stock and flow model. However, in order to create such a model, system dynamicists typically engage in a knowledge elicitation process and create an initial causal loop diagram (aka a causal influence diagram). Both can be useful in supporting learning and instruction, as argued by Marcelo Milrad and colleagues, and the stock and flow model can serve as the basis of an interactive simulation when the components are mathematically specified, according to John Sterman.

A causal loop diagram is intended to represent all of the major factors and their relationships that are involved in a complex and dynamic system. While its primary use is in eliciting information from experts about the system, it is also used to convey information to others about how a complex system operates. In addition, the process of developing a causal loop diagram has been shown to be an effective indicator of how well someone understands the complexities of a problematic situation and, as a consequence, can be used for assessment and feedback to support the learning process. Figure 1 is a simplified causal loop diagram representing a population model. Note that two death rates are included—one for adults and one for children. The person developing the diagram could have included additional death rates (e.g., to explicitly represent infant mortality rates or death rates for adolescents). The point here is twofold: (1) first, there is typically not a single correct representation for a complex and dynamic situation, and (2) the representation should include components that might be targets for human intervention. With regard to the latter, it could easily be imagined that proper prenatal care might impact infant mortality

rates; therefore, it could be argued that this relationship should be made explicit in the figure. The purpose and projected use of the representation is an important consideration. A general advantage of a causal loop diagram is that it supports a holistic view of a complex and dynamic system in a single figure represented on a single page or screen. Such representations address a common deficiency in human reasoning—namely, the tendency to ignore significant portions of a complex system, as shown by Dietrich Dörner as well as by Peter Senge. As Figure 1 indicates, delayed effects can also be represented, which is an additional challenge; all too often, humans expect to see nearly instantaneous effects of a decision or action, but real systems often involve significant delays. Positive and negative feedback loops are depicted through the use of influence indicators. In Figure 1, a plus sign indicates a change in the same direction between the connected nodes, while a minus sign indicates a change in the opposite direction between the connected nodes. In general, a loop with an odd number of minus signs is a negative feedback loop (aka a balancing loop), while a loop with an even number of minus signs is a positive feedback loop (aka an escalating loop). The loop connecting children and maturing adolescents is a balancing loop as there is one minus sign in that loop.

Once a causal loop diagram has been created, a system dynamicist can then transform that into a stock and flow diagram (aka a stock and flow model) and include mathematical equations to represent the various stocks (accumulators—things that can be enumerated), flow rates, variables, and any constants that might be presumed to govern the situation. Figure 2 shows a stock and flow diagram for the population model depicted in Figure 1. Note that nearly all of the same components from the causal loop diagram appear in the stock and flow diagram. What typically happens, however, is that additional variables and stocks appear as the simpler causal loop diagram is elaborated and transformed into the basis for a mathematically driven simulation model.

A mathematically elaborated stock and flow diagram can serve as the basis for an executable simulation that shows how all of the components change over time or how the behavior changes when certain critical variables are manipulated. What cannot be represented in a causal loop diagram are the effects of nonlinear relationships among system components, but stock and flow diagrams that are mathematically based can do just that. Understanding the impact of nonlinear relationships in a complex system is a particular shortcoming of human reasoning. Stock and flow models can address that weakness in human decision making and policy formulation and support learning about complex systems. As scholars such as Pål Davidsen and John Sterman have argued, stock and flow models inform a number of so-called

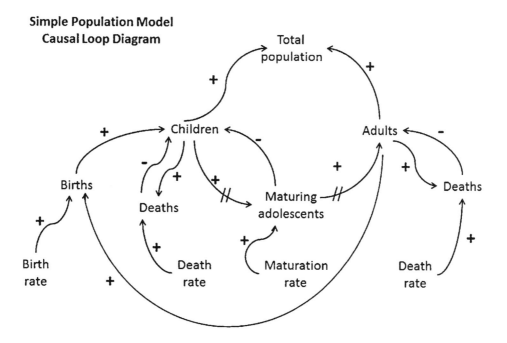

Legend: the arrow indicates the direction of influence; a minus sign indicates that a change in the source node tends to produce a change in the opposite direction in the destination node; a plus sign indicates a change in the same direction; slash indicates a significant delay.

Figure 1   Sample causal loop diagram

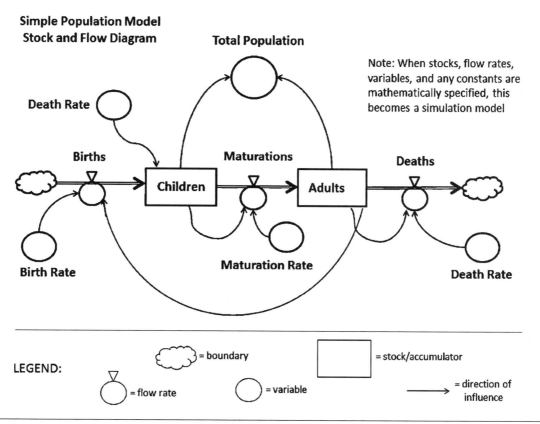

Figure 2   Sample stock and flow diagram

management flight simulators that are designed to allow users to manipulate one or more critical components in order to achieve a desired outcome, such as a stable and sustainable population growth. When the critical components are changed, the behavior of the system changes, and users can see the consequences of making a particular decision or following a particular policy.

Management flight simulators have been developed for such areas as business growth and expansion, diffusion of innovation, economic planning, educational modeling, environmental planning, inventory management, supply-chain decision making, and more. To be effective, the underlying stock and flow models need to be accepted as reasonably reflective of reality in terms of (a) surface validity (consistent with expert views), (b) extreme condition response (react to extremes as would the actual system), (c) sensitivity response (sensitive to the same critical variables as the actual system), and (d) predictive validity (consistent with actual data when such data exist).

System Dynamics-Based Learning Environments

System dynamics can be used to support learning and instruction in addition to supporting decision making and policy formulation as already indicated. Just as there are two kinds of representations of complex systems used by system dynamicists, there are two basis ways that these representations can support learning: (1) learning with models and (2) learning by modeling. Either type of model (causal loop or stock and flow) can be used to support either type of learning. The former approach (learning with models) is primarily aimed at learning declarative knowledge (facts and concepts) associated with a complex system. A causal loop diagram can be used to depict the basic relationships among critical system components and, as a consequence, can support learning which components are critical and how specific components are related to other components, which can also be supported using a stock and flow model. In addition, a causal loop diagram can help a learner identify specific positive and negative feedback loops. A system without active negative feedback loops is usually considered a system that is out of balance; learning the concept of balancing loops can be supported at least in part with a causal loop diagram or with an executable stock and flow simulation model.

Likewise, a stock and flow diagram can also be used to support learning facts and concepts. For example, an executable stock and flow diagram can be used to help learners identify which variables seem to have a significant impact on system behavior in various circumstances. By changing one or more variables and observing system behavior, a learner can develop such

an understanding. In addition, stock and flow diagrams can help learners understand the nature and extent of delayed effects. Moreover, by allowing learners to manipulate one or more key variables, a stock and flow model can help learners realize the impact of nonlinear relationships on system behavior; such effects are often counterintuitive as humans are more accustomed to reasoning about linear relationships.

In addition to learning with models, students can develop even deeper understanding by creating models. A learner can be provided with a description of a complex system or problem situation and be asked to create either a causal loop diagram or, for more sophisticated learners, a stock and flow model. As shown by J. Michael Spector, a causal loop representation is particularly helpful in assessing how learners are conceptualizing complex systems and situations, especially in comparison with regard to an earlier representation or that of a domain expert. Because learning is fundamentally about change, representations of a learner's models before and after instruction are particularly helpful in determining progress of learning. Because change in a particular direction is desired (e.g., similar to expert thinking), comparison of a learner's representation (causal loop diagram or stock and flow diagram) with that of an expert is also useful in helping to determine progress of learning.

When feedback can be provided while a learner is working on a complex problem situation, that learning activity or experience can be especially meaningful. For example, comparing a learner's model with that of an expert can reveal that the learner is missing a critical component, and feedback can be immediately provided in the form of either a query (e.g., "How might component X affect this model?") or a follow-on activity (e.g., "What are the differences and similarity between your representation and this one?").

In addition to supporting meaningful assessments, learning by modeling can be a highly engaging means of promoting inquiry-based learning (learning what happens when and why). It is important to realize that one cannot simply expect those new to a complex domain with little or no knowledge of system dynamics to begin creating very good causal loop diagrams or stock and flow models. However, one can help learners develop the capacity to create meaningful representations of complex systems by a graduated set of activities that involve active modeling. Asking students to transform a text-based description of a complex system or problematic situation into a causal loop diagram could be an initial step. Such an initial step need not involve any of the language of causal loops or system dynamics. Rather, it is possible to simply present the problem situation, ask learners to indicate the key factors influencing the situation, describe each factor, indicate how those factors are related, and describe those relationships. That is in fact the essence of an annotated causal loop diagram, and it can be depicted as such, either by the learner or by a support system. The learner is then in a position to reflect upon the diagram and compare it with diagrams created by others. This would be a simple learning by modeling activity.

With students who know something about stock and flow diagrams, a relatively simple learning by modeling activity would be to present a partially complete stock and flow model along with data about system behavior. The learner can then be asked to provide the missing parts of the model in order to account for the reported behavior. A more challenging activity would be to provide the learner with a robust causal loop diagram and data about actual system behavior and have the learner create a stock and flow model that when executed provides data consistent actual data.

Implications of System Dynamics for Learning

Systems thinking and system dynamics representations in the form of causal loop diagrams and stock and flow models can support learning in and about complex and dynamic systems and problematic situations. While it is unlikely that most students, decision makers, and policy developers will become system dynamicists, there are effective ways to promote critical thinking about complex problems using the tools and techniques developed for system dynamics. Highly interactive simulations can be based on mathematically based stock and flow diagrams. Just-in-need feedback can be provided to students when representing their problem conceptualizations in a form consistent with a causal loop diagram. Holistic views of complex systems can also be promoted using causal loop diagrams. When the learning goal is to promote a deep understanding of the structure and behavior of complex and dynamic problem situations, then it is appropriate to consider integrating the tools and techniques of system dynamics.

J. Michael Spector

See also Adaptive Learning Software and Platforms; Constructivist Theory; Games to Promote Inquiry Learning; Learning by Modeling; Simulation-Based Learning

Further Readings

Davidsen, P. I. (2000). Issues in the design and use of system dynamics based interactive learning environments. *Simulation & Gaming: An Interdisciplinary Journal of Theory, Practice and Research, 31*(2), 170–177.

Dörner, D. (1996). *The logic of failure: Why things go wrong and what we can do to make them right* (R. Kimber & R. Kimber, Trans.). New York, NY: Metropolitan Books.

Forrester, J. W. (1961). *Industrial dynamics*. Cambridge, MA: MIT Press.

Milrad, M., Spector, J. M., & Davidsen, P. I. (2003). Model facilitated learning. In S. Naidu (Ed.), *Learning and teaching with technology: Principles and practices* (pp. 13–27). London, UK: Kogan Page.

Senge, P. (1991). *The fifth discipline: The art of the learning organization*. New York, NY: Doubleday.

Spector, J. M. (2000). System dynamics and interactive learning environments: Lessons learned and implications for the future. *Simulation & Gaming, 31*(4), 528–535.

Spector, J. M. (2010). Mental representations and their analysis: An epistemological perspective. In D. Ifenthaler, P. Pirnay-Dummer, & N. M. Seel (Eds.), *Computer-based diagnostics and systematic analysis of knowledge* (pp. 17–40). New York, NY: Springer-Verlag.

Sterman, J. D. (1994). Learning in and about complex systems. *System Dynamics Review, 10*(2/3), 291–330.

Systemic Change and Educational Technology

Instructional technologies are critically important for creating systemic change in school districts. Charles Reigeluth and others have written extensively about these technologies and how they can be used to transform education. Instructional technologies applied in a piecemeal fashion cannot create the kind of changes needed to transform school systems to comply with the requirements of our knowledge age society. These technologies should be applied within the context of principles of systemic change if education systems are to be transformed. This entry first discusses school districts as whole systems and the differences between piecemeal change and systemic change in school districts. It then discusses in detail why piecemeal changes fail to improve school districts and outlines the principles of systemic change.

School Districts as Whole Systems

School districts are whole systems. A system is a collection of parts that interact synergistically to produce outcomes. Michael Beer identified and defined parts of organizations as systems. These parts are described in this section using school districts as the context.

External Environment

All school systems exist within an environment. The environment provides financial, technical, human, and information resources. The environment also has stakeholders.

People

School systems are staffed by people who have individual needs, interests, abilities, and expectations for their career. Those human variables (needs, interests, and so on) create a complex web of relationships in a school system that is profoundly affected by system dynamics.

Organization Culture

Just as individuals have personalities, school systems have cultures. Organization culture has a powerful influence on how people think and behave. The culture is a systemwide mental model for how a school district should function, about how educators should do their work, and about how children should be educated. The culture also significantly shapes the internal social infrastructure of a school system (i.e., the reward system, communication processes, among others).

Organization Structures

Organization structures are created to guide human behavior in systems. Structures include policies, handbooks, job descriptions, information management systems, and the physical layout of buildings. These structures are also part of a system's internal social infrastructure referred to in the prior section.

Dominant Coalition

All school systems have a small group of people with significant influence on how the system functions, on how and what decisions are made, and on what is valued or not valued within the system. Dominant coalition members are the enforcers of the system's culture. They have a significant influence on the system's internal social infrastructure. They also use sociopolitical skills to advance their agenda for the system. The coalition can either support or hinder any effort to create and sustain systemic change.

Human Outputs

System dynamics (that is, the relationships between and among the components described earlier) create psychological and emotional consequences for educators that include motivation, job satisfaction, clarity of goals, and commitment to the organization. If the system dynamics are positive, then those consequences should be positive (e.g., high motivation, high job satisfaction). If the dynamics are negative, then those consequences will likely be negative (e.g., low motivation, low job satisfaction).

Organizational Outcomes

School systems provide educational services to children. Children are expected to leave school systems with attitudes, concepts, and skills that will help them lead successful lives. If the educational outcomes are evaluated by external stakeholders as being below expectations, then the system will be evaluated as being in need of improvement. If external stakeholders evaluate the outcomes as meeting or exceeding expectations, then the system will be evaluated as a high-performing system.

Feedback

Evaluations of organizational outcomes yield feedback that influences the level of future resources provided to the system. Negative evaluations could result in a system receiving fewer resources. Positive evaluations could result in a system receiving more resources.

Piecemeal Change Versus Systemic Change in School Districts

Piecemeal Change

The dominant approach to improving school systems is piecemeal change. This approach aims to improve education by implementing a swarm of disconnected changes such as spending more money, lengthening the school day or school year, providing parents with school choice options, and so on. Piecemeal attempts to fix schools focus on pieces of the system with the belief that if the broken pieces (e.g., the low performing schools) are fixed then the whole system will improve. Piecemeal efforts to fix schools and school systems have not succeeded.

Many in the field of systems thinking believe that school systems and their schools do not need fixing because they are not broken. In fact, they are performing exactly as they were designed to perform within the framework of an Industrial Age paradigm. If fundamentally different and better results from school systems are desired, then efforts to improve education must go beyond reform efforts to conceive whole new systems designed for the knowledge age society. To do this requires educators and policy makers to adopt and use principles of systemic change.

Systemic Change

Definitional Confusion

Kurt D. Squire and Charles M. Reigeluth identified different definitions of *systemic change*. Reigeluth and Francis M. Duffy commented on these different definitions. They are as follows.

Statewide policy systemic change. Systemic change used in this context creates statewide changes in tests, curricular guidelines, teacher-certification requirements, textbook adoptions, funding policies, and so forth that are coordinated to support one another. This meaning is how policy makers typically think of systemic change.

Districtwide systemic change. From this perspective, systemic change produces changes in curricula or programs instituted throughout a school district. This is how PreK–12 educators typically think of systemic change.

Schoolwide systemic change. People holding this view of systemic change focus on what happens inside individual school buildings. Systemic change in this context is any change or program instituted throughout a school. This meaning is how educators participating in groups such as the Coalition of Essential Schools typically think of systemic change.

Ecological systemic change. From this point of view, systemic change is based upon a clear understanding of interrelationships and interdependencies within a system and between the system and its external environment. This definition recognizes that significant change in one part of a system requires changes in other parts of that system. This definition of systemic change subsumes all the other three definitions, and it is how systems thinkers like Russell Ackoff, Bela H. Banathy, Duffy, Merrelyn Emery, Ronald E. Purser, Reigeluth, and Peter Senge view systemic change.

The first three definitions apply principles of systemic change, but they are not truly systemic. The fourth definition represents systemic change.

Why Piecemeal Change Fails

Ackoff said that it is pure folly to improve parts of a system. He said that not only will the entire system fail to improve by improving the parts, but it is likely that this piecemeal focus will actually cause the system's performance to deteriorate.

Ackoff also described how systems function. Those descriptors enlighten us about why piecemeal change fails to improve whole systems. The eight descriptors adapted for school systems are

1. The whole system has one or more defining properties or functions; for example, a defining function (i.e., a system's main purpose) of a school district is to educate students.

2. Each part in the system (e.g., each school in a district) affects the behavior of the whole system; for example, a couple of low-performing schools in a district can drag down a whole school district.

3. There is a subset of system parts that are essential for carrying out the main purpose of the whole system but they cannot, by themselves, fulfill the main purpose of the system; for example, teachers and classrooms in a single school building are essential parts of a school system and they are necessary for helping a school system fulfill its main purpose, but these "parts" cannot and never will be able to do what the whole system does.

4. There is also a subset of nonessential parts that help the system fulfill its main purpose; for example, in a school system these important, but nonessential parts include school and community relations, pupil personnel services, among others.

5. When a system depends on its environment for resources it is said to be an "open system." A school district is an open system.

6. The way in which an essential part of a system affects the whole system depends on its interaction with at least one other essential part; for example, the effect a single school has on the whole district depends on the interaction that school has with other schools in the district. Let us say that a school district is organized as prekindergarten through 12th Grade. This means the work process for that district is 13-steps long (PreK–12th Grade). Now, let us say that district leaders are concerned about the performance of their high school (which represents a subset of the system). The high school contains Grades 9–12. Then, let us say that the performance of that high school is dragging down the overall performance of the district on state assessments. According to Ackoff's description of how systems function, it would be a mistake to focus improvement efforts only on the high school because that high school's performance is affected by at least two other subsets of schools (i.e., the elementary and middle schools that "feed" kids into those high schools). Since all essential parts of a school system interact and affect each other, it would be reasonable and "systemic" to examine and determine how these parts are affecting the performance of the high school. Focusing improvement only on the high school would be a nonsystemic and, therefore, piecemeal approach to improvement.

7. A system cannot be divided into its individual parts without loss of its essential properties or functions. For instance, the dominant approach to school district improvement is called *school-based* or *site-based improvement.* This approach has had the consequence

of deconstructing school systems into their aggregate parts (individual classrooms, schools, and programs). Further, individual classrooms, schools, and programs do not and never will provide children with a total education. When efforts are made to improve a school system in this way—by disaggregating it into its individual parts—a system's effectiveness deteriorates rapidly.

8. Because a system derives its effectiveness from the synergistic interaction of its parts rather than from what the parts do independently (i.e., the whole is always greater than the sum of its parts), when efforts are taken to improve the individual parts (as in piecemeal change), the performance of the whole system deteriorates. This is one reason why school-based improvement and piecemeal change have generally failed to improve schooling.

Principles of Systemic Change

Ackoff's descriptors of how systems function provide a framework for identifying 15 principles of systemic change.

Principle 1: Seek systemic change, not piecemeal change.

Principle 2: Adopt a systemic change methodology that provides strategies and tactics for creating systemic change along three pathways—(1) transform the core and support work processes, (2) transform the internal social infrastructure, and, (3) transform the system's relationship with its broader environment.

Principle 3: Integrate the systemic change methodology into the system's permanent structures, policies, and procedures and create a permanent budget line to fund systemic change.

Principle 4: Help educators unfreeze their mindsets (attitudes) to consider how to reimagine the instructional core (i.e., the relationship between teachers, students, and curricular content), their system's internal social infrastructure, and how their system interacts with its external environment.

Principle 5: Provide educators with real-world examples of new mental models for transforming their systems.

Principle 6: Assess the readiness of the system to engage in systemic change.

Principle 7: Secure expert guidance to implement systemic change.

Principle 8: Identify and train formal and informal leaders within the school system to lead systemic change.

Principle 9: Gain political support for creating and sustaining transformational change.

Principle 10: Identify sources of internal and external funds to sustain systemic change.

Principle 11: Assess communities' needs, expectations, and dreams for their school systems.

Principle 12: Identify a starting point for systemic change that has the potential to create a huge ripple effect throughout the system. This is called a high-leverage starting point.

Principle 13: Transform the central administration (or senior administrator office) to support the systemic changes happening throughout the school system.

Principle 14: Realize that systemic transformation will not happen unless there is personal transformation, which means that educators' mindsets (their attitudes toward systemic change) and their mental models (their preferred processes, and so on, for educating children) must also change.

Principle 15: Seek enduring revolution through persistent evolution. Daniel Kim, a renowned systemic-change expert, pointed out that one of the laws of systems thinking states that "slower is faster." He said most change efforts that try to create a revolution fail because they attempt to impose an artificial set of improvements in an arbitrarily short period of time.

Conclusion

Instructional technologies are critical components for transforming school systems to comply with the requirements of the knowledge age. If these technologies are adopted and used in a piecemeal fashion, it can be predicted that they will not create the kinds of changes needed to transform school systems. If these technologies are adopted and used as part of a systemic-change effort, then it can be predicted that they can and will help educators and policy makers to realize the dream of moving our education system and its component school systems out of the Industrial Age paradigm and into the knowledge age paradigm.

Francis M. Duffy

See also Design and Creation of Adaptive Educational Systems; Organizational Learning and Performance; Personal Learning Environments; Personalized Learning and Instruction; Predicting Change and Adoption of Technology Innovations; System Dynamics

Further Readings

Ackoff, R. L. (1999). *Re-creating the corporation: A design of organizations for the 21st century.* New York, NY: Oxford University Press.

Ackoff, R. L. (2001). *A brief guide to interactive planning and idealized design.* Retrieved from http://www.ida.liu.se/~steho/und/htdd01/AckoffGuidetoIdealizedRedesign.pdf

Banathy, B. H. (1996). *Designing social systems in a changing world.* New York, NY: Plenum Press.

Beer, M. (1980). *Organization change and development: A systems view.* Santa Monica, CA: Goodyear.

Duffy, F. M. (2010). *Dream! Create! Sustain!: Mastering the art and science of transforming school systems* (Leading Systemic School Improvement Series). Lanham, MD: Rowman & Littlefield.

Duffy, F. M., & Reigeluth, C. M. (2008). The school system transformation (SST) protocol. *Educational Technology, 48*(4), 41–49.

Emery, M., & Purser, R. E. (1995). *The search conference: A comprehensive guide to theory and practice.* San Francisco, CA: Jossey-Bass.

Kim, D. H. (2001). *Organizing for learning: Strategies for knowledge creation and enduring change.* Waltham, MA: Pegasus Communications.

Reigeluth, C. M., & Duffy, F. M. (2006). Trends and issues in P–12 educational change. In R. A. Reiser & J. A. Dempsey (Eds.), *Trends and issues in instructional design and technology* (2nd ed., pp. 209–220). Upper Saddle River, NJ: Prentice Hall.

Reigeluth, C. M., & Karnopp, J. R. (2013). *Reinventing schools: It's time to break the mold.* Lanham, MD: Rowman & Littlefield.

Senge, P. M. (1990). *The fifth discipline: The art and practice of the learning organization.* New York, NY: Doubleday.

Squire, K. D., & Reigeluth, C. M. (2000). The many faces of systemic change. *Educational Horizons, 78*(3), 145–154.

TABLET DEVICES IN EDUCATION AND TRAINING

Tablet devices are handheld computers, with a display of 7 to 10 inches that doubles as the touch-sensitive interface using fingers or a specific stylus or pen. Compared to laptops or netbooks, tablets are small, light, and have a longer battery life of up to 10 hours. They are ready to use almost immediately after switching on. They serve for surfing the Internet and may be extended with additional hardware such as a keyboard and software applications. The combination of intuitive operation (through an intuitive-user interface), a wide range of functions, high mobility, and permanent Web access makes tablets an interesting learning tool for schools and universities. This entry first discusses tablet technology and how tablets are used in education. It then discusses the benefits and challenges of tablet use and the results of research on tablet use in education.

Tablet Technology

By the sixth decade of the 20th century, Alan Kay and others were working on the concept of portable computers with touch interfaces. Nowadays, tablets boast an integrated microphone and speech recognition, a photo/video camera, a compass, a GPS (global positioning system) chip, Wi-Fi functionality, Bluetooth, cell phone network chip, and an accelerometer. An early milestone was the development of handwriting recognition software by Charles Erlbaum, as seen in Apple's Newton, which was launched in 1993. In the same year, Toshiba unveiled its Dynapad T 100 X, which might be considered the first tablet. In 2001, Siemens introduced the SIMpad, already successful for

a short period in an industrial context, but it was only when Apple presented its first iPad in 2010 that the worldwide breakthrough began. According to Apple statistics, it took just 28 days to sell the first million devices worldwide and, as of April 2014, 211 million iPads had been purchased. But Apple's market leadership did not last long, as competitors developed similar tablets such as Samsung's Galaxy Tab, Amazon's Kindle, and Microsoft's Surface.

Hardware and Software

Operating systems for tablets are normally adaptations of the companies' smartphone operation systems, such as iOS (by Apple) or Android (by Google). Microsoft adapted its new Windows 8 operating system for its Surface tablet. Additional to inbuilt functionality, so-called apps may be purchased and installed to extend the software of all tablets. The range of available apps is extremely wide and numerous, but each is specific to an operating system and therefore incompatible with those of rival tablets using other operating systems.

Educational Use of Tablets

Because of their adaptability, many users perceive their tablets as a personal device and thus, unlike with desktop systems, there is no way to support all users fully. When tablets are used in education, students tend to have a device of their own and, as well as using it for education, make use of it outside school in their leisure time.

Access. With the help of browser software, students with a tablet can undertake investigations using the Internet and obtain up-to-date and authentic information wherever they are. This is helpful when outdoors, in a museum or at a historic site, and history or geography lessons take on a new quality through mobile learning. When published as e-books, textbooks can be updated as often as required and offer multimedia content beyond text and illustrations. This is not only more efficient, but the digital format means searching is much easier than with a printed book.

Exploration. Interactive apps such as The Elements allow explorative access to information and support discovery learning. Virtual molecule construction kits permit experiments in building molecules and offer direct feedback; dangerous chemical experiments can be simulated; microscopic biological cell structures can be explored; and apps such as Circuit Lab allow students to test electrical circuits. Invariably, benefits include direct feedback and the option to undertake learning at a student's own speed. In addition, recording videos of physical education classes and analyzing these with the help of Video Physics helps students to discern their own body movement, while apps such as The Waste Land or Explore Shakespeare offer authentic, playful, and emotional ways of learning in literature lessons.

Production. Integrated and additional apps support the production of learning materials by the students, another effective way of learning in the sense of teaching learning. The app Explain Everything explains how to make simple videos; Creative Bookbuilder or Book Creator let students create their own books with integral photos, videos, hyperlinks, and so on and to export them as an e-book to share with others. With the help of Garage Band, music production is simple, as is video editing with iMovie.

Reflection. Documenting topics with the help of the notes facility, virtual card indexes such as Evernote, Wikis, Mindmaps, and learning diaries give learners the ability not only to capture ideas but to reflect on their learning process. In summary, it is the combination of possibilities and varieties in usage that makes tablets interesting for learning. They combine functionalities, subjects, and topics, at school and at home. Studies show that the benefits are intensified if students possess a tablet of their own.

Benefits and Challenges of Tablet Use

Critics accuse tablets of being no more than the learning machines B. F. Skinner used and propagated in the middle of the last century, following behavioristic paradigms. This misunderstanding illustrates the essential and central role of pedagogic concepts when using tablets as tools. Like all tools, they are of no benefit without good ideas. The most appropriate way of

learning with tablets is in an open, project-oriented classroom in which students work and collaborate in groups, discussing topics, trying out things, producing and presenting material, and working on authentic materials. Scientific research has shown that this way of learning creates high motivation, investigation, interest, high learning quality, and sustainability, and that students take responsibility for their learning. It is not the technology that is foregrounded but the abilities and competencies of the learners. Tablet devices foster the so-called 21st-century skills that Tony Wagner summarizes as critical thinking and problem solving; collaboration across networks; leading by influence, agility and adaptability, initiative, and entrepreneurialism; effective oral and written communication, accessing and analyzing information; curiosity; and imagination.

Besides the benefits, teachers and researchers also found some disadvantages. Using tablets with Internet access may pose a distraction for students who will wish to check e-mail or social media. Again, this is not a technical problem but a question of negotiating media competences with the students and looking for solutions so that self-discipline and self-organization become a learning result. In addition, the issue of different operating systems and subsequent incompatibility continues to pose a challenge.

Evaluation of Tablet Use in Educational Practice

Since the introduction of the iPad in 2010, the use of tablets in schools and universities has been evaluated by researchers. Major studies include one on 10 different schools using 650 devices in Victoria, Australia; a study in cooperation with eight schools in Scotland using 370 devices; and a study on the use of 1,400 devices in schools in Boyne City, Michigan.

The results of these studies are similar, independent of language, culture, or type of school. The use of tablets in itself is highly motivating, even after the initial period, because students feel competent and self-guided in their learning. It is also motivating for teachers because seeing the achievements their students have made by using tablets opens up new methods of teaching. Tablets support individual learning; even weaker or students with disabilities benefit from using these devices. It has become obvious that roles in the classroom change. Students work together more, supporting each other, while the teacher relinquishes the role as organizer of the learning process and becomes more of an enabler, supporter, facilitator, and mentor. Parents found themselves more integrated with what is happening in school; the division between learning in school, doing homework, and leisure time shifted so that learning became a more holistic experience. Giving all students their own tablets is more effective than using classroom sets because of the personalization of the tablets and the chance to use them at home. Also, Wi-Fi access seems to be essential to appropriate use of tablets. The most important finding is that, rather than a tablet being a miracle cure for problems in education, the use of tablets can make a difference in improving learning.

Frank Thissen

See also Collaborative Learning and 21st-Century Skills; Collaborative Learning With Technology; Twenty-First-Century Technology Skills

Further Readings

Burden, K., Hopkins, P., Male, T., Martin, S., & Trala, C. (2012). *iPad Scotland evaluation.* Hull, UK: University of Hull.

Clark, W., & Luckin, R. (2013). *iPads in the classroom. What the research says.* London, UK: Knowledge Lab.

Johnson, L., Adams Becker, S., Cummins, M., Estrada, V., Freeman, A., & Ludgate, H. (2013). *NMC horizon report: 2013 higher education edition.* Austin, TX: The New Media Consortium. Retrieved from http://www.nmc.org/pdf/2013-horizon-report-HE.pdf

Pegrum, M., Oakley, G., & Faulkner, R. (2013). Schools going mobile: A study of the adoption of mobile handheld technologies in western Australian independent schools. *Australasian Journal of Educational Technology, 29*(1), 66–81.

TECHNOLOGIES FOR CRITICAL THINKING DEVELOPMENT

The 21st century is driven by the knowledge revolution. The manufacturing-based economy of the 19th and early 20th centuries has given way to an economic model that values creativity and knowledge creation. The knowledge revolution challenges educational institutions at every level to harness the skills and knowledge required to utilize the latest technologies—Internet browsing, Web resources, social media, gaming and simulation technologies, and so on—to develop and enhance critical thinking skills. *Critical thinking* is defined as self-regulated cognitive activity that applies multiple sources of information—evidence, inference, systematic methods, and context. Instructors and instructional designers have embraced educational technologies as a way to engage learners in critical thinking processes. Educational technologies include (a) personal computing devices as well as the software and applications that make them connect with others and enhance productivity,

(b) video and online games, (c) learning management systems, (d) social media, and more. This entry discusses how all of these technologies can promote critical thinking and student-centered learning.

Critical thinking emerged as a core construct of educational thought and reform starting in the early decades of the 20th century. John Dewey emphasized the importance of thinking as a distinct, vital, and teachable skill that serves not only the individual learner but also society as a whole. Edward Glaser identified five distinct actions that support the development of critical thinking: (1) recognition and definition of a problem, (2) data gathering and testing of assumptions about the problem, (3) development of possible explanations, (4) testing of one or more hypotheses and verification of outcomes, and (5) proposal of final conclusions. Richard Paul and Linda Elder built on this definition of critical thinking to determine the qualities of the critical thinker, emphasizing the notions of open mindedness and the process of continuous assessment of currently held assumptions, ideas, and expectations. In addition, the critical thinker exhibits effective communication skills, is intrinsically motivated and embraces standards of excellence, and is also a problem solver who rejects cultural biases related to race, gender, or ethnicity.

Critical Thinking and Educational Technologies

Since the beginning of the Industrial Age, forward-thinking educators have embraced new technologies as a way to bring education to more people as well as to people who have been traditionally underserved. More recently, computer-assisted learning developed alongside the availability of personal computers in the 1970s and 1980s.

Internet connectivity has transformed the field of educational technology, especially with regard to critical thinking. The combination of personal computers and high-speed Internet has produced a powerful relationship between learning, interactivity, and the construction of new knowledge along with problem solving. Web 2.0 technologies allow learners to collaborate in powerful ways in asynchronous as well as synchronous environments. Some applications allow for instructor guidance (e.g., wikis), while others are driven entirely by learners without instructor interference (e.g., language learning sites). Learning management systems (LMSs) qualify as Web 2.0 technologies although they are managed by learning institutions as part of courses offered to enrolled students; LMSs allow instructors and learners to interact outside of class, thus breaking down the traditional time constraints that have defined instructor-learner relationships. In addition, LMSs encourage the development of a learner-centered instructional model in which instructors guide the learner through the instructional events, facilitate interaction within the LMS and in the classroom environment, and evaluate the learner's mastery of instructional goals. Critical thinking skills are supported in an LMS context, encouraging the development of extrinsic motivation in the learner and providing tools for problem solving. Learning management systems also support critical thinking skills by supporting transparency in the evaluation stage of instruction; learners have access to their grades and any instructor feedback so that they can incorporate feedback into subsequent assignments.

Game-Based Learning as a Driver of Critical Thinking

Game-based learning has a long pedagogical history; children learn through games from infancy and continue to learn through play throughout their young lives. Video games and multiuser online games have attracted the attention of educational researchers and instructional designers due to their characteristic ability to engage their users in what are often complicated scenarios involving the acquisition of technical language, the understanding of complicated plot lines, and the adoption of sophisticated characters. More importantly for the development of critical thinking, video game users engage in the application of strategies to solve problems and to advance to more challenging levels of the game. Educational game researchers and developers propose that all disciplines, from K–12 to university level, can benefit from game-based learning; much of this game-based learning involves online interaction with fellow learners, instructors or facilitators, and the game content itself.

Theoretical frameworks that support game-based learning in online environments include social constructivism and flow theory. Social constructivism, developed by Lev Vygotsky, supports a game-based approach to learning due to its emphasis on learning within social settings; learners construct knowledge and solve problems collaboratively while using a shared system of language and artifacts. Mihály Csíkszentmihályi developed the concept of *flow*; flow taps into the immersive power of video games to keep the user engaged at a high enough level to eliminate distractions and generate high levels of enjoyment.

Social Media and Critical Thinking

The rise of social media, and particularly social network sites (SNSs), offers new opportunities for educators to develop instructional events that capture the power of collaboration to enhance and support learning. An SNS is defined as a Web 2.0 application, in mobile or desktop modalities, that permits account holders to create public or semipublic profiles, make connections to individuals, groups, companies, and institutions. Users can also expand their network "reach" by making new connections through their current network—in other words, making new friends through connections with current friends. A defining characteristic of SNSs, and of Web 2.0 in general, is the power of users to generate their own content. This active development of online content challenges learners to reject passive learning behaviors and to embrace active ones. Education research related to SNSs and student learning has linked the social constructivism of Vygotsky, with its emphasis on collaborative problem solving, with the affordances of Web 2.0 applications such as SNSs and wikis. The challenges related to implementing instruction within an SNS environment, or any other Web 2.0 environment, include privacy (especially with K–12 students); technical skills (instructors as well as students); access to the Internet outside of the school environment; and the speed of change that is inherent in Web 2.0 technologies, including cost, platform, and user interface.

Implications of Educational Technologies for Critical Thinking

Critical thinking retains its place as a core competency of all levels of education and has been a focus of legislators, parents, educators, and the general public; the rapid transition from an industrial economy to a knowledge economy means that the ability to think critically earns a premium in the marketplace. The educational technologies within the reach of educators and students have led to the phenomenon of ubiquitous learning—learning that takes place without thought to place or time. Student-centered learning is supported by these new Internet-driven technologies as students collaborate with fellow learners as well as instructional staff. Instructors as well as students will continue to be challenged by technological change that requires constant learning and relearning; critical thinking is supported by this challenge as instructors learn along with their students to master new technologies and use them productively.

Shelly Wyatt

See also Collaborative Learning With Technology; Constructivist Theory; History of Educational Technology; Social Media and Networking; Social Networking; Web 2.0 and Beyond

Further Readings

boyd, d. m., & Ellison, N. B. (2008). Social network sites: Definition, history, and scholarship. *Journal of Computer-Mediated Communication, 13,* 210–230. Retrieved from

http://onlinelibrary.wiley.com/doi/10.1111/j.1083-6101
.2007.00393.x/pdf

Dede, C. (2009). Immersive interfaces for engagement and
learning. *Science, 323*(5910), 66–69.

Dewey, J. (1938). *Experience and education.* Indianapolis, IN:
Kappa Delta Pi.

Facione, P. A. (1990). *Critical thinking: A statement of expert
consensus for purposes of educational assessment and
instruction.* Retrieved from http://assessment.aas.duke.edu/
documents/Delphi_Report.pdf

Glaser, E. M. (1941). *An experiment in the development of
critical thinking.* New York, NY: Columbia University.

Jonassen, D. H., Davison, M., Collins, M., Campbell, J., &
Haag, B. B. (1995). Constructivism and computer-mediated
communication in distance education. *The American Journal
of Distance Education, 9*(2), 7–26.

Lavin, R. S., & Claro, J. (2005). Wikis as constructivist learning
environments. *Proceedings of the Japan Association for
Language Teaching, Japan* (pp. 9–13). Retrieved from http://
www.pu-kumamoto.ac.jp/~rlavin/mainsite/page26/page29/
files/page29_1.pdf

Paul, R., & Elder, L. (2008). *The miniature guide to critical
thinking: Concepts and tools.* Retrieved from http://think
.hanover.edu/Resources/MiniGuidetoCT.pdf

Rollett, H., Lux, M., Strohmaier, M., Dösinger, G., &
Tochtermann, K. (2007). The Web 2.0 way of learning with
technologies. *International Journal of Learning Technology,
3,* 87–107.

Rosen, L. D. (2010). *Rewired: Understanding the iGeneration
and the way they learn.* New York, NY: Palgrave Macmillan.

Vygotsky. L. S. (1978). *Mind in society: The development of
higher psychological processes.* Cambridge, MA: Harvard
University Press.

TECHNOLOGIES FOR GIFTED STUDENTS

The National Association of Gifted Children defines a *gifted person* as a person who demonstrates a high level of (a) aptitude to learn and/or reason and (b) performance. This aptitude and performance can be in any domain (academic, athletic, etc.). Individuals who are gifted demonstrate outstanding levels of aptitude or competence. These individuals typically function at or above the top 10% of the general population. Areas where giftedness might be demonstrated include any structured area of activity with its own symbol system (e.g., mathematics, music, language) or set of sensorimotor skills (e.g., painting, dance, sports). Because of their abilities, gifted students have unique intellectual, academic, and social needs that often require modifications in curricula, strategies, and resources. This entry first discusses opportunities that technology presents for gifted students. The entry then discusses how technology can serve as a motivator, the impact of technology on creativity, and potential changes in the brain as a result of using certain types of technology. Finally, the entry discusses some of the ways technology impacts the teaching of gifted children.

Del Siegle states that technology applications can address many of the characteristics of gifted learners, such as the capacity for depth and complexity, knowledge transfer, quick processing, and inductive learning. Technology is an ideal medium for gifted students, who can collect, analyze, synthesize, and present information using (a) the Internet to retrieve data and information, (b) spreadsheets to analyze data, (c) word processors to communicate the implications of their findings, and (d) multimedia presentation software to generate presentations of their findings.

Technology has afforded gifted students many opportunities, such as access to the Internet, potential for distance learning, the option of using a multitude of learning platforms, ready access to research tools, and an increase in opportunities for social interactions. However, technology has opened new issues and concerns such as a digital divide between gifted students who have ready access to technology and those who do not. For the gifted, many of the outcomes of increased and improved technology usage have yet to be determined as new 21st-century technologies rapidly emerge and inundate the lives and learning options of individuals who are gifted.

Because of the information available through the Internet, gifted students are provided numerous opportunities to consider the information trends presented through data, providing an opportunity for in-depth inductive and deductive analysis. According to Siegle, there are subcategories of gifted students who excel in the use of technology and technology applications. Gifted students who possess technological prowess can be appropriately challenged to encourage interest in learning, to grow in knowledge, and to engage in learning opportunities that address these unique abilities. Such technological giftedness may be expressed through expertise and passion toward computer programming or innovative use of software and hardware. Gifted students who are skilled in programming can use codes or computer languages to generate computer and Web applications. Highly capable technology consumers are efficient and effective in applying existing software and hardware packages in innovative and creative ways. Other gifted students may exhibit their giftedness through their skill in troubleshooting, assisting peers and teachers with using technology, and through their self-taught engagement with computers and peripherals. All types of technologically gifted students will likely find learning more motivating and applicable if advanced technological opportunities are a part of their curriculum.

Technology as a Motivator

Although technology by itself may not be motivating, there does seem to be a relationship between the availability of technology and the motivation to learn for gifted students. Brian Housand identifies technology applications that tend to support specific characteristics of gifted students. Examples of these characteristics and abilities include time and resource management, project planning and follow-through, collaboration and cooperation, and curiosity.

The Impact of Technology on Creativity

Generation Z (aka the Net Generation) consists of students born in the mid-1990s or thereafter. Generation Z students view technology as an essential tool for day-to-day existence. In addition, the impact of technology on the creativity of Generation Z is obvious. Generation Z has already demonstrated technology-based creativity through the development of apps and programs that help to define today's technology. Mitchel Resnick suggests viewing the computer more as a paintbrush and less as a technological device. With the large multitude of digital devices that can be accessed at any time, mobile devices can be viewed as Swiss Army knives. At this point in time, it may be too early to determine the overall impact that technology will have on creativity. However, more technological tools that afford opportunities to engage in creative activities are available than ever before.

Neural Differences

As a result of new technologies, the definition of giftedness is evolving. Research on the impact of technology on the mind and the activity in the brain has shown that neuroplasticity is a core process. Neuroplasticity is the brain's ability to reorganize itself by forming new neural connections throughout life. Neuroplasticity allows the neurons in the brain to adjust in response to new situations or to changes in the environment. The pathways in the brain are actually changed. Brain reorganization takes place through mechanisms such as axonal sprouting in which axons grow new nerve endings to form new neural pathways to accomplish a needed function. Because technology requires users to respond to a new set of learning experiences that are totally unprecedented, there may be changes in the neural pathways of the brain as a result of technology. As a result, the definition of gifted may have to be modified to keep up with new knowledge about the brain.

Adaptations in the brain are made frequently through physical or mental activities. Neural pathways can be weakened or disappear through inactivity. The ways that information is synthesized through experience impact the synaptic activity in the brain and [re]structure responses to various stimuli. Technology may indeed impact the actual structure of the brain. Researchers have found that distinctive neural pathways had developed in Internet users, specifically the dorsolateral prefrontal cortex. Technology allows a greater understanding of the brain.

Technology Trends in Teaching

Technology can provide opportunities for acceleration. Curriculum-based assessment measures a student's mastery of the curriculum in various subject areas. Once mastery is determined, gifted students can learn missing skills and advance rapidly through the curriculum. Technology makes teaching tools such as curriculum-based assessment readily available providing efficiency for teachers and gifted students.

However, technology use in the classroom for gifted students has a downside. Many teachers feel threatened by gifted students who have superior technology skills. Some teachers may not have the technology skills to effectively integrate technology into the classroom. In addition, many teachers feel challenged to keep up with ever-advancing technology trends. This technology challenge is particularly apparent when dealing with gifted students because gifted students tend to be drawn into the latest technology and have the mental ability to keep up with new trends with ease.

Although technology offers many learning opportunities, there are drawbacks. Through the Internet, it is very easy to find unsavory sites, exploitive situations, and individuals of questionable character. Monitoring the technology use of young gifted children who often have technology skills far superior to their parents and teachers can be a challenge. In addition, children who are different are often the subjects of harassment and bullying. The Internet can provide opportunities for harassment and bullying that are difficult for parents and teachers to monitor.

As one visits gifted classes in various school districts, it becomes apparent that some classrooms have more technology than others. The digital divide is an issue. It is important to determine if a lack of opportunities impacts the outcomes of gifted students as well as other students.

Technology offers new career options for gifted individuals. Areas that offer potential job opportunities in the future include environmental engineering, Global Positioning System technology, and digital fabrication. It is very difficult to keep the curriculum in schools updated to address the workforce needs of the future. The situation is exacerbated with gifted individuals who tend to progress through the curriculum at a more rapid pace.

Conclusion

Technology offers gifted students many learning opportunities that are likely to increase as society undergoes a knowledge explosion. Technology may actually impact the way the brain functions providing new insight into giftedness. Society will be challenged to provide appropriate learning opportunities for the gifted that allow these students to enter the workforce of the 21st century and reach their full potential.

Tandra Tyler-Wood

See also Assessment of Problem Solving and Higher Order Thinking; Cognition and Human Learning; Conditions of Learning; Neuroscience and Learning

Further Readings

Carr, N. (2010). *The shallows: What the Internet is doing to our brains.* New York, NY: Norton.

Eriksson, G. (2012). Virtually there—Transforming gifted education through new technologies, trends, and practices in learning, international communication and global education. *Gifted Education International, 28*(1), 7–18.

Housand, B. C., & Housand, A. M. (2012). The role of technology in gifted students' motivation. *Psychology in the Schools, 49*(7), 706–715.

Pascual-Leone, A., Amedi, A., Fregni, F., & Merabet, L. B. (2005). The plastic human brain cortex. *Annual Review of Neuroscience, 28,* 377–401.

Resnick, M. (2006). Computer as paintbrush: Technology, play, and the creative society. In D. Singer, R. Golikoff, & K. Hirsh-Pasek (Eds.), *Play = Learning: How play motivates and enhances children's cognition and social-emotional growth* (pp. 192–208). New York, NY: Oxford University Press.

Siegle, D. (2004). Identifying students with gifts and talents in technology. *Gifted Child Today, 27*(4), 30–34.

Siegle, D. (2005). *Using media and technology with gifted learners.* Waco, TX: Prufrock Press.

TECHNOLOGIES FOR PERSONS WITH DYSLEXIA

Dyslexia is a specific learning disability with neurological origin. It is characterized by difficulties with accurate or fluent word recognition and by poor spelling and decoding abilities. In some literature, dyslexia is referred to as a specific reading disability and dysgraphia as its writing manifestation only. Here we follow the standard definitions of the *International Statistical Classification of Diseases (ICD-10)* and the *Diagnostic and Statistical Manual of Mental Disorders (DSM-IV)*, where dyslexia is listed as a reading and spelling disorder (*ICD-10*) or a reading disorder and a disorder of written expression (*DSM-IV*).

Since dyslexia is a learning disability that affects language, the available technologies can be divided into tools to assist reading, tools to assist writing, and other tools to support people with dyslexia. We selected only technologies specifically designed for people with dyslexia, and from them, we gave priority to the ones that are supported by user studies.

Reading Software for Dyslexia

The following are six specific reading tools for people with dyslexia:

1. *ClaroRead* is available for various platforms to support reading and writing. It includes an extra package for people with dyslexia, *ClaroView*, which is a color tool. The authors of this entry did not find evidence of user studies performed for the design or testing of this tool.

2. *Firefixia* is a Mozilla Firefox extension, especially designed to apply predefined features supporting people with dyslexia. It was designed on the basis of research done with participants with dyslexia and tested with four participants.

3. *IDEAL eBook Reader* is an e-book reader for Android, which includes specific settings for displaying books for people with dyslexia. Those settings are based on a user study of 23 participants with dyslexia.

4. *DysWebxia Reader* is an e-book reader for iOS for displaying books and documents for people with dyslexia. The settings of the tool are based on a set of studies using eye tracking with more than 100 participants with dyslexia.

5. *SeeWord* provides customization capabilities to improve Microsoft Word. It was also specifically tested with twelve students with dyslexia.

6. *Text4all* is a Web service that allows users to adapt text from existing webpages. The settings of the service take into account previous studies with this target group.

Even though the use of complicated language has been extensively pointed out as one of the key problems for this target group, all the existing applications—except for

Table 1   Comparison of reading software

| Software | Font | Size | Brightness | Color | Spacing | | | | Width | Synonym | TtS |
					char	word	line	para			
Kindle	yes	yes	yes	yes	no	no	yes	no	yes	no	yes
iBooks	yes	yes	yes	yes	no	no	no	no	no	no	yes
ClaroRead	yes	yes	no	yes	yes	no	yes	yes	no	no	yes
Firefixia	yes	yes	no	yes	yes	no	yes	no	yes	no	no
IDEAL	yes	yes	yes	yes	yes	yes	yes	yes	no	yes	yes
SeeWord	yes	yes	no	yes	yes	no	yes	no	no	no	no
Text4all	yes	yes	no	yes	yes	no	yes	no	no	no	no
DysWebxia	yes	yes	yes	yes	yes	yes	yes	yes	yes	yes	no

Text4all and *DysWebxia Reader*—at this time only alter the design of the text. *Text4all* and *DysWebxia Reader* also offer simpler synonyms on demand to the reader.

Writing Software for Dyslexia

Supportive writing technology for people with dyslexia includes spell checkers and word-prediction software programs.

A word-prediction program is an application that generates a list of possible words given the first letters of a word. Word-prediction software can improve word recall, spell correction, and automaticity in spelling, being therefore appropriate for dyslexic users. There is a long list of products available in the market. Those specifically aimed at users with dyslexia include the following:

Co:Writer analyzes writing in real time and offers word choices based on grammar. The program deciphers phonetic and invented spellings and misspellings with reversed or missing letters. It is also adaptable to new domains by providing the program with a domain-specific document.

Penfriend predicts the next word in the text based on a dictionary of known words, grammatical categories, and context. The program also allows the writer to hear the words before choosing one.

WriteOnline is a tool that incorporates prediction and text-to-speech technology to help people with dyslexia. Other tools are available such as word banks to help expand the user's vocabulary.

A spell-checker is a computer program that identifies misspelled words and may suggest a suitable replacement for them. There has been considerable research and development in spell-checking technology over the years, but spell-checkers for users with dyslexia have been proposed only recently. Jennifer Pedler found out that in a sample of 577 spelling mistakes produced by people with dyslexia, just over half were simple errors; the rest were multierrors and word-boundary errors. Typically a spell-checker will search for each typed word in a dictionary, and in case the word is not found, the program will try to insert, remove, substitute, or swap letters to see if the modified word is in the dictionary. The dictionary or list of correct words used by spell-checker applications may be based on an available dictionary or derived from a corpus of correct spellings. Spell-checkers can also rely on lists of commonly confused words created by computing similarities among words in a dictionary using a distance function. Suggesting a word from this list as a plausible substitute for the typed word may be based on syntax (e.g., part of speech tag of the two words) or on a probabilistic model. Precomputed confusion lists are sometimes not required when a big data set is available that can be used to model word-in-context usage. Alberto Quattrini Li, Licia Sbattella, and Roberto Tedesco have argued that spell-checkers for people with dyslexia need to adapt to the specific user, as is possible with PoliSpell, which can take into account the particular errors made by the user.

With spell-checkers for users with dyslexia, one specific feature identified in the literature as desirable is that, when there are multiple alternatives for a given target misspelled word, the correct one is one of the first options given. This feature addresses the fact that users with dyslexia may lack phonological processing and reading skills that are needed to decode and comprehend each suggestion in the list or to navigate between multiple windows to find the right substitute. Because comparing multiple alternatives to the misspelled word requires word-recalling capabilities, a dyslexic user may struggle with a long list of possible substitutes.

Additionally, JollyMate is a tool that provides handwritten character recognition to detect miswritten characters.

Other Tools

There are other tools that support the learning process of people with dyslexia. *GG Rime* and *GG Phoneme* are two games whose goal is to provide training on grapheme-phoneme connections. The player hears either sounds or words and has to match them to visual targets (letters and sequences of letters) displayed on the screen. *GG Rime* includes rhyming word families to reinforce grapheme-phoneme connections. *Alphabetics* provides different types of games to support grapheme-phoneme connections in English and Spanish. Luz Rello, Clara Bayarri, and Azuki Gorriz created *Dyseggxia*, a game with word games based on dyslexic errors in English and Spanish. The game was tested with 48 children with dyslexia between six and 11 years old, and children between nine and 11 years significantly decreased their spelling error rate. Heikki Lyytinen and colleagues created the computer game *Literate*, later called *GraphoGame*, which was developed to identify children at risk of having dyslexia before school age in Finland. Its exercises are aimed to help children connect graphemes (letters) and phonemes (sounds) to improve reading. Lyytinen and colleagues conducted two user studies with 12 and 41 children between six and seven years old with very promising results. Children who used *Literate* improved their accuracy in grapheme-phoneme connections, reading words, and naming phonemes after playing for less than four hours.

Horacio Saggion and Luz Rello

See also Adaptive Learning Software and Platforms; Human Performance Technology; Learning by Modeling

Further Readings

de Santana, V. F., de Oliveira, R., Almeida, L. D. A., & Ito, M. (2013). Firefixia: An accessibility Web browser customization toolbar for people with dyslexia. In *Proceedings of the 10th International Cross-Disciplinary Conference on Web Accessibility* (Article 16, pp. 1–16). New York, NY: Association for Computing Machinery.

Gregor, P., Dickinson, A., Macaffer, A., & Andreasen, P. (2003). SeeWord—A personal word processing environment for dyslexic computer users. *British Journal of Educational Technology, 34*(3), 341–355. doi:10.1111/1467-8535.00331

Kanvinde, G., Rello, L., & Baeza-Yates, R. (2012). IDEAL: A dyslexic-friendly ebook reader. In *Proceedings of the 14th International ACM SIGACCESS Conference on Computers and Accessibility* (pp. 205–206). New York, NY: Association for Computing Machinery. doi:10.1145/2384916.2384955

Khakhar, J., & Madhvanath, S. (2010). JollyMate: Assistive technology for young children with dyslexia. In *Proceedings of the 2010 12th International Conference on Frontiers in Handwriting Recognition* (pp. 576–580). Washington, DC: Institute of Electrical and Electronics Engineer Computer Society. doi:10.1109/ICFHR.2010.95

Kyle, F., Kujala, J., Richardson, U., Lyytinen, H., & Goswami, U. (2013). Assessing the effectiveness of two theoretically motivated computer-assisted reading interventions in the United Kingdom: GG Rime and GG Phoneme. *Reading Research Quarterly, 48*(1), 61–76.

Li, A. Q., Sbattella, L., & Tedesco, R. (2013). PoliSpell: An adaptive spellchecker and predictor for people with dyslexia. In S. Carberry, S. Weibelzahl, A. Micarelli, & G. Semeraro (Eds.), *User modeling, adaptation, and personalization* (pp. 302–309). Berlin, Germany: Springer-Verlag. Retrieved from http://link.springer.com/chapter/10.1007/978-3-642-38844-6_27

Lyytinen, H., Ronimus, M., Alanko, A., Poikkeus, A.-M., & Taanila, M. (2007). Early identification of dyslexia and the use of computer game-based practice to support reading acquisition. *Nordic Psychology, 59*(2), 109–126. doi:10.1027/1901-2276.59.2.109

Pedler, J. (2007). *Computer correction of real-word spelling errors in dyslexic* (Doctoral thesis). Birkbeck, University of London, London, UK. Retrieved from http://www.dcs.bbk.ac.uk/research/recentphds/pedler.pdf

Rello, L., & Baeza-Yates, R. (2014). Evaluation of DysWebxia: A reading app designed for people with dyslexia. In *Proceedings of the 11th Web for All Conference*. Retrieved from http://www.taln.upf.edu/content/biblio/676

Rello, L., Bayarri, C., & Gorriz, A. (2012). What is wrong with this word? Dyseggxia: a game for children with dyslexia. In *Proceedings of the 14th International ACM SIGACCESS Conference on Computers and Accessibility* (pp. 219–220). New York, NY: Association for Computing Machinery. doi:10.1145/2384916.2384962

Topac, V. (2012). The development of a text customization tool for existing Web sites. In *Text Customization for Readability Online Symposium*. Retrieved from http://www.w3.org/WAI/RD/2012/text-customization/t8

TECHNOLOGIES FOR PERSONS WITH HEARING IMPAIRMENTS

Instructors or instructional designers must give consideration to the needs of hearing impaired learners in the target population when designing instructional messages and strategies for education or training. Technologies for the hearing impaired include personal technologies (e.g., cochlear implants, hearing aids, wireless assistive listening systems), note taking and sign language interpreting services, captioned media, equipment with universal design features, and speech-to-text technologies for basic sensory access to information used to support learning. Learners with hearing impairments range in age and are different from one another with respect to hearing loss, language levels, first languages, socioeconomic circumstances, and additional disability conditions. These learners may benefit from well-designed visual or text representations of sound information and a variety of technologies and services to support their learning. This entry provides an overview of the current state of technologies and alternative representations of auditory information that may be used to reduce barriers to learning for classroom and online instruction.

Hearing loss is among the most common disabilities and occurs in all cultures and age groups. As much as 13% of the U.S. population of school age or older are known to be deaf or hard of hearing and similar demographics are found in other countries. Following the 2006 United Nations Convention on the Rights of Persons with Disabilities, many countries adopted laws similar to those already in place in the United States such as the Americans with Disabilities Act (ADA) and Individuals with Disabilities Education Act (IDEA) that prohibit discrimination, guarantee inclusive education and training, and require public accommodation to allow participation. Accommodations for the hearing impaired may require the use of Universal Design for Learning principles, amplification, or a variety of technologies and services to provide information both aurally and visually. Without this support, deaf or hearing-impaired learners with equal intellectual ability may lag behind their peers in all areas of education and training.

Reducing Barriers to Learning

Universal Design for Learning, as defined by the Center for Applied Special Technology (CAST), is a framework for designing curricula that reduce barriers and optimize support for learners. Within this framework are three principles: (1) multiple methods of representation to allow the information to be perceptible and comprehensible for learners, including those who communicate in a variety of languages (e.g., American Sign Language); (2) multiple methods for learners to take action and communicate what they know; and (3) multiple methods of engaging and challenging learners.

Three classroom situations can make hearing difficult for anyone but become barriers to learning for those with a hearing impairment: (1) distance between listener and speaker or sound source, (2) competing noise, and (3) poor room acoustics. Often, these situations occur at the same time, causing strain and exhaustion for learners. After determining the learners' functional limitations, such as the extent of the hearing impairment, their fluency with languages (e.g., English or American Sign Language) and the learning outcomes, the instructor or instructional designer can then select technology and modify or design appropriate media. For both classroom and online instruction, using hearing assistive technology systems and providing information both orally and visually can help overcome these barriers. The goal is to provide perceptible and comprehensible information through real-time interpreting, text transcript, or other methods to allow learners to interact, collaborate, and communicate in learning environments as fully as other learners.

The choice of assistive technologies depends on the type and degree of hearing loss and if the person uses a hearing aid or a cochlear implant. Many hearing aids and cochlear implants have a telecoil (t-coil) that acts as a wireless link to telephones, televisions, computers, MP3 players, and hearing assistive technologies such as personal listening systems.

Technologies

Personal Listening Systems

There are two kinds of personal listening systems that carry amplified sound using electromagnetic signals, FM (frequency modulation), or infrared signals, and are received by a headset or a telecoil in a hearing aid worn by the learner. To receive the signal, the learner must switch their hearing aid to the telecoil setting. The first type, an audio induction or hearing loop commonly used in England, is a loop of cable that generates an electromagnetic field around an area such as an auditorium. The second type, a one-to-one communicator, uses a microphone for the instructor that sends an FM signal directly to the hearing aid telecoil. This type is more common in the United States.

Class Notes

Providing notes and other written materials, sign language interpretation, and having notes taken and in the classroom or online can help make sound content available to learners with hearing impairments by converting it into text or visible form. Adults and older children who read can benefit from Computer Assisted Notetaking (CAN) or Computer Assisted Real-time Transcription (CART). Both of these services rely on both technology and human note takers. Note takers record a message as it is spoken and send it to a learner's computer or to a projector, when more than one learner can benefit. A condensed form of the teacher's message is provided by CAN, while CART provides the message verbatim. These services may be provided either locally or remotely.

Sign Language Interpreting

If a user is fluent in a sign language (French, British, Spanish, or American Sign Languages), and sign language interpreters are available locally, assistive technologies may not be necessary. But when interpreters are unavailable locally, remote interpreters, using live audio and video feeds, can see the deaf person and interpret instructor lectures or telephone conversations in real time. The Video Relay Service (VRS), or Video Interpreting Service (VIS), requires a videophone or combination of video camera, computers with high-speed Internet access, and Web conferencing or video conferencing software. Advances in hardware and software also allow VRS service via wireless services. The equipment currently required is 3G or higher wireless service, and a personal computer (PC), tablet computer, or smartphone with video calling capabilities.

Captioned Media

Providing captions for educational media is one method for providing an alternative for sound. Open captions are visible to everyone, but closed captions (CC) are not visible until turned on using a remote (or through a caption decoder for older equipment). Most recently produced media provide captions, but if media is not marked *CC,* the Described and Captioned Media Program may have a captioned version of the media available for instructors. The program provides a searchable database of their media library, guidelines, and links to captioning tools on the Web for those who need to caption their own media and a list of captioning service vendors.

Online Instruction

Online instruction may take place either synchronously or asynchronously using a variety of communication methods including threaded discussions, text or voice chat, telephone conversations, audio, video, or Web conferencing, and multimedia. Where information is transmitted aurally, it will need to be converted to a perceptible and comprehensible form. This may be done using methods discussed earlier, as well as whiteboards for synchronous communication and collaboration using Web conferencing and speech-to-text software. When using Web conferencing, and sign language interpreters are available either locally or remotely, a webcam can be used for signing while the instructor or students speak. When the online instruction involves telephone conversations, Telecommunication Devices for the Deaf (TDDs) can be used, allowing hearing-impaired learners to make or receive telephone calls. Alternatively, some learners use text messaging on mobile phones or computers for the same purpose.

Speech-to-Text and Other Technologies

Speech-to-text software (such as Dragon Naturally-Speaking, E-Speaking) has long been used to make text transcriptions from audio recordings. There are now smartphone apps (Dragon Dictation, Voice Assistant) that allow real-time captioning of telephone conversations. Using similar speech recognition technologies, voicemail transcription software (from Google Voice, Twilio, and others) allows deaf and hearing-impaired users to read their voicemails, rather than listen to them. Similar speech-to-text technology is being integrated into Web conferencing systems currently under development. Universal design features in newer computers that are particularly useful for hearing impaired learners include light signaler alerts that flash the computer screen when an alert sounds.

Jeanne L. Anderson

See also Adaptive Learning Software and Platforms; Assistive Technology; Instructional Design Practice; Message Design for Digital Media; Universal Design

Further Readings

CAST. (2011). *Universal design for learning guidelines version 2.0.* Wakefield, MA: Author. Retrieved from http://www.udlcenter.org/aboutudl/udlguidelines

Described and Captioned Media Program. (2013). *About DCMP.* Spartanburg, SC: Author. Retrieved from http://www.dcmp.org/about-dcmp#mission

Hasselbring, T. S., & Glaser, C. H. W. (2000). Use of computer technology to help students with special needs. *The Future of Children, 10*(2), 102–122.

Hersh, M. A., & Johnson, M. A. (Eds.). (2003). *Assistive technology for the hearing-impaired, deaf and deafblind.* New York, NY: Springer-Verlag.

Stifter, R., Rangel, F., & Reed, R. (2001, June). *Integrating technology and literacy: Digital video dictionary.* Presented at the Instructional Technology and Education of the Deaf Symposium 2001, National Technical Institute for the Deaf Rochester, NY. Retrieved from https://ritdml.rit.edu/bitstream/1850/1231/99/RStifterPaper06-25

Suppalla, S. J., Wix, T. R., & McKee, C. (2001). Print as primary source of English for deaf learners. In *One mind, one language: Bilingual language processing* (pp. 177–190). Oxford, UK: Blackwell.

U.S. Department of Education. (n.d.). *Building the legacy: IDEA 2004.* Retrieved from http://idea.ed.gov/explore/view/p/root

U.S. Department of Justice. (2010). *Americans with Disabilities Act Title III Regulations.* Retrieved from http://www.ada.gov/regs2010/titleIII_2010/titleIII_2010_regulations.htm#a303

Technologies for Persons With Physical Disabilities

Physical disabilities (PDs) are a wide range of impairments related to movement and strength. Physical disabilities include terms such as *orthopedic impairments*, *severe or multiple disabilities*, and other health impairments. Accessible electronic and information technology (EIT), along with assistive technology (AT), can reduce barriers and offer opportunities for students with PDs to benefit from established curricula and to participate in the same classroom activities as their peers.

Assistive technology is defined as any item, equipment, or system used by students with disabilities to perform tasks that would otherwise be difficult or impossible. Accessible EITs are software applications, multimedia, and websites that can be used directly by people with a wide range of abilities and are compatible with AT devices. Accessible EITs were developed using principles of universal design. This entry discusses EITs that allow people with physical disabilities to use the computer and EITs that provide assistance with communication for those with a disability involving speech or language.

The student's unique circumstances dictate selection of appropriate technology. This is determined though assistive technology assessments that involve collaboration between the student with PDs, teachers, parents, assistive technology specialists, occupational therapists, speech and language pathologists, and physical therapists. General principles are to choose devices and software that are compatible with student needs, integrate EIT with AT, and support participation in the curriculum. Technology considerations are one of several decisions that make participation possible. Students also need to be able to get to the classroom and to sit and move about comfortably. Legislation in the United States and many other countries guarantees students with disabilities access to physical space in schools through accessible structures such as elevators, ramps, water fountains, restroom facilities, and doorways. Many students use these structures along with power-assisted chairs and added equipment, such as trays and mounts for computers, laptops, and book stands. For students who do not use wheelchairs, considerations include appropriate seating and access to learning tools.

Computer Access

Many students with physical disabilities are able to use the computer by customizing the settings and options that are available in operating systems of both Mac OS and Microsoft Windows machines. These options can be saved to a user's login, applied as default settings, or saved for exporting to other machines. The settings are accessed through Universal Access settings (Macintosh) or Ease of Access Center (Windows). Both systems offer similar accessibility options for individuals with physical barriers.

Keyboard options can be set to ignore repeated keystrokes or to slow down the keyboard acceptance rate. The sticky (or latch key) setting allows the student to press keys sequentially in order to access the modifiers (e.g., *shift-control* or *alt*), thus allowing one finger typing. The toggle key setting emits a tone when pressing the lock keys (caps lock, num lock, or scroll lock). An onscreen keyboard displays options for selection with a mouse, pointer, or other device by clicking, scanning, or hovering. Speech recognition, included in newer operating systems, uses voice rather than the keyboard to dictate documents and control the computer.

Mouse options are also available. Mouse keys allow the pointer to be controlled with the numeric keypad. Button configuration settings switch the primary and secondary buttons for right- or left-handed use. The speed of the double click can be slowed, and the student can use the click lock feature to highlight and drag instead of holding down the mouse button.

Touch screens, available on tablet devices, smartphones, and laptops, have special appeal for students lacking the motor skills to use a mouse and keyboard because they use gestures (taps, swipes, or other movements) to control interactions. Gestures can be configured with the assistive touch feature, or control can be changed to one finger, stylus, or switch input.

Some students experience physical barriers that cannot be accommodated by customizing computer settings and will need to consider using alternate input devices such as special purpose keyboards, speech recognition software, and switches. Expanded keyboards have larger keys in an enlarged surface area. Some devices feature keys that must be physically pressed; others are flat surfaces that are customizable for an alphabetical or a QWERTY layout. Minikeyboards offer smaller keys over a smaller surface area. They accommodate students with a smaller range of motion or who might only have the use of one hand and are available with standard keys or a pressure sensitive membrane. Other keyboard options are available to users who only have the use of one hand but who have adequate finger dexterity. Half of QWERTY keys are able to produce two letters. For example, using a right handed keyboard, the student types the letter *l* by pressing its key; the letter *s*, which corresponds to ring finger placement on the left side of the keyboard, is produced by holding the space bar while pressing the letter *l*. One-handed DVORAK keyboards place frequently used letters on the home row and use a similar two-letter system. Chorded keyboards use fewer keys to type letters and commands using a combination of keystrokes, similar to chords on a musical instrument. On-screen keyboard programs have a variety of features, such as a customizable keyboard layout, scanning options, and word prediction and word completion settings.

Voice recognition software programs are used for hands-free operation of the computer and most application programs. These programs have a higher degree of accuracy and a greater ability to recognize the idiosyncrasies of an individual student's voice than the standard voice recognition settings available in the operating system. Full-featured voice recognition programs also include voice output and dictionaries with specialized vocabulary for scientific terms and math formulas. Voice recognition programs come in two formats. The continuous speech format recognizes sentences and is used by individuals with consistent articulation. The discrete speech format requires a short pause between words. It is used by individuals whose speech is inconsistent, slurred, or strongly accented.

Switches can be customized to interact with the most convenient movable body part and are used in place of mouse input. Trackball and joystick switches are on stationary platforms that allow the student to use minimal hand and arm movements to control the cursor. Students who cannot use their hands have other options. Direct selection switches use a physical movement to move the cursor and to make a selection. With head pointing direct selection systems, the student wears a headset or a reflective dot. An infrared or an optical sensor attached to the computer recognizes the user's movement and responds by changing the cursor location or enabling a selection. Eye-gaze switches use a camera that identifies the location of the retina to move the cursor. Selections are made by dwelling, hovering, or blinking. Other options include single switches combined with scanning programs that move the cursor systematically and automatically to locations on the screen. Whether a student uses direct selection or a single switch with scanning depends on the extent of spinal,

head, neck, and hand control. Direct selection requires some dexterity in order to move the cursor to the desired location, whereas a single switch only requires one movement to select what is on the screen.

Augmentative and Alternative Communication

Sometimes a physical disability affects a student's ability to speak, as with some forms of cerebral palsy or brain injury. Augmentative and alternative communication systems (AAC) are then used to supplement or replace speech for users with severe speech or language problems. Unaided AAC systems are signs and gestures; aided systems include electronic devices. Electronic AAC systems are devices that consist of a screen with language-based icons and a speech-generating device (SGD) that provides voice output. Most electronic AAC systems are contained in devices specifically designed for that purpose, and many have options that interface with standard computer operations or have wireless communication and Internet features built in. With advances in software development and technology, touch-screen devices are also emerging as alternatives for AAC hardware.

Conclusion

Assistive technology, when paired with accessible EIT, allows participation in the general education curriculum for students with physical disabilities. The challenge for teachers is to use and integrate these tools to ensure positive learning outcomes. The ultimate goal of technology use for students with physical disabilities is to enhance learning opportunities, foster participation and independence, and promote empowerment.

Kathleen S. Puckett

See also Assistive Technology

Further Readings

Dell, A. G, Newton, D. A., & Petroff, J. G. (2012). *Assistive technology in the classroom: Enhancing the school experiences of students with disabilities* (2nd ed.). Boston, MA: Pearson.

Websites

AbleData: http://www.abledata.com/abledata.cfm?userstyle=1&
EASTIN (European Assistive Technology Information Network) Association: http://www.eastin.eu/en-GB/searches/products/index

TECHNOLOGIES FOR PERSONS WITH VISUAL IMPAIRMENTS

Visual impairments include a wide range of disabilities related to sight, or how one uses vision to learn and interact with the world. The term *low vision* describes students who read print but may depend on optical aides for greater acuity or ease of obtaining information. *Functionally blind* describes students who do not use their vision for learning. They may perceive light or color and are able to use residual vision—some awareness of an object—to move around in their environment. Students who are *totally blind* do not receive any meaningful input—light, color, or object awareness—using vision. Students who are either functionally or totally blind must use auditory and tactile means to learn. Most students with visual impairments have some vision, from light perception alone to varying degrees of acuity. While accurate figures are not available, it is estimated that approximately 10% of students with visual impairments are totally blind. Technology can provide a powerful array of tools for these students.

The Individuals with Disabilities Education Improvement Act in the United States states that assistive technology (AT) must be considered for every student for whom an individualized education program (IEP) has been developed. *AT* is defined as a broad range of software, hardware, and services that includes an array of technologies that are flexible enough to be used for many different purposes. Continuing advancements in technology means that students, teachers, and parents can use or modify what is readily available to enhance opportunities to read, write, and access information.

The abilities to navigate a computer desktop, use word processing software and other commonly used software programs, use the Internet to search for specific information, send e-mails, and participate in online learning are common educational goals for students with visual impairments. Therefore, instruction may include methods for accessing appropriate assistive technology devices such as text to speech, Braille translation embossers and displays, electronic note takers, screen magnification software, video magnifiers, and optical character recognition (OCR) systems.

Readily Available Applications

All standard computers have customizable options and settings that are included in the operating system. Settings for vision barriers include screen magnification, audio alerts, screen readers (e.g., VoiceOver or Narrator), and adjustments to the display (high contrast settings, color settings, animation controls, and size and shape of the blinking cursor). Speech recognition, available on newer computers, allows users to use voice rather than mouse and keyboard to control the computer and use applications. Some users, however, cite limited capabilities of these settings and choose to add software programs for magnification, screen reading, and speech recognition.

Recent advancements in touch-screen tablets and smartphones have made them accessible to people with visual impairments. These devices can be configured with a combination of multiple touch gestures and screen reading. Gestures such as taps, drags, flicks, or rotors (a two-finger rotation as if one is turning a dial) are used to navigate screens and make selections while the screen reader announces the location.

Specialized Devices and Software

Accessibility features have reduced the cost of technology for students with visual barriers and are often as effective as specifically designed equipment. Some applications have limited capabilities, however, and must be supplemented with adapted hardware or software.

A Braille translator is a software product that converts computer text into Braille code. The text can then be printed using a piece of hardware called a Braille embosser, or it can be presented tactilely using a refreshable Braille display. A refreshable Braille display is a strip with Braille input keys and a single line of round-tipped dots that display a line of text in Braille and then refreshes. Newer versions are Bluetooth-enabled for wireless interface with the computer or with other devices, such as smartphones.

An electronic note taker is a specially designed personal digital assistant (PDA). Note takers enable students to input information using Braille keys or a QWERTY keyboard and to retrieve information in refreshable Braille or synthesized speech. Most note takers include an appointment calendar, an address book, a word processor, e-mail, Internet, media players, and a GPS receiver. Some students are replacing the electronic note taker with a smartphone paired with a refreshable Braille display, citing lower cost and convenience as factors in their decision.

While screen readers are available through accessibility options in standard computer operating systems, students may need advanced functions (e.g., reading math equations or locating text) that are offered in screen-reading software programs. A variety of screen reader options include commercially produced, open source, and Web-based applications. Choice depends on cost, computer platform, voice quality, keyboard command structure, the ability to customize the output, and other usage issues. Web-based screen readers are often used to increase the accessibility of public machines where one does not have permission to install custom software.

Screen magnification software enlarges text and graphics on the computer monitor. While a limited version is available in computer operating systems, full-featured screen magnification includes options such as greater magnification capabilities, adjustable views of a magnified and unmagnified portion of the screen, horizontal or vertical panning, and visible pointers or cursors. Some screen magnification programs have screen-reading functions.

Video magnifiers are electronic devices that use a camera and a viewing screen or monitor to magnify material. Video magnifiers can be used to read print, look at photographs and illustrations, read prescription and other product labels, complete forms, or complete close work. The more advanced models allow the user to change color, contrast, and background.

Obtaining Accessible Text

IDEA 2004 established (a) a standard file format for accessible instructional materials, (b) the National Instructional Materials Accessibility Standard (NIMAS), and (c) the National Instructional Materials Access Center (NIMAC) repository at the American Printing House for the Blind (APH). The APH maintains a database of sources that school districts may use to obtain accessible texts. One such source is Bookshare, which offers literature and textbooks online in accessible formats. Bookshare is free to K–12 and postsecondary students in the United States as a result of funding from the U.S. Office of Special Education Programs. Digital versions of out-of-copyright books and books in the public domain can be obtained from Project Gutenberg. Digital books can also be purchased from online commercial sources for use with e-readers, but their accessibility is variable. Some digital books are compatible with screen reading software; others are not.

Scan and read software programs use a scanner and OCR software to convert print to digital text that can be read with text-to-speech (TtS) software. Commercial programs vary in their features; some have integrated OCR features, while others rely on OCR conversion software that is available with many scanners. Most of these software programs offer an array of additional literacy supports, such as dictionary, thesaurus, and translation capacities as well as features for note taking, summarizing, and outlining. Open source TtS software could also be used when text is already in a digital format.

Mobile readers are handheld devices that combine a camera with OCR technology to convert text to speech. Most include a stand so that large documents and multiple pages of content can be scanned, converted, and stored for later use. These devices will accept and read digital text from a variety of accessible file formats. Mobile reader technology is also available as a software application for smartphone or tablet computer. These applications use the device's camera with OCR software and TtS to read the contents of a document aloud. Versions of this application have features that recognize and return audible messages for receipts, denominations of currency, and colors; some will read multiple languages, translating text to the preferred language of the user.

Emerging Technology

Numerous software applications (apps) for smartphone and tablet computers have the potential to make life more convenient for students with visual impairments. These apps combine camera with screen readers, GPS systems, bar code and QR readers, or databases to provide functionality for learning and activities of daily living. Some apps are free, others require a fee, and not all work as intended. As technology and software continue to improve, their use may eventually replace some stand-alone devices.

A 3D printer is an emerging technology with the potential to help students with visual impairments. It could be used to print three-dimensional representations that a student who is blind could examine in order to better understand its configuration. Advances in this technology are rapidly developing and are becoming affordable and available for school use.

Conclusion

No single technology application is appropriate for everyone. Even students with the same visual loss may use different forms of technology based upon their unique needs. Selection depends on assessment of needs and the educational tasks that are being required. Teachers, parents, vision specialists, and other professionals should work with students to make informed choices in considering the multiple options available. The ultimate goal of technology integration is successful learning, which is highly dependent on the manner in which technology is used.

Kathleen S. Puckett

See also Assistive Technology

Further Readings

Manduchi, R., & Kurniawan, S. (Eds.). (2012). *Assistive technology for blindness and low vision*. Boca Raton, FL: CRC Press.

Websites

Bookshare: http://www.bookshare.org
Project Gutenberg: http://www.gutenberg.org

TECHNOLOGIES FOR STUDENTS WITH ATTENTION DEFICIT DISORDER

Technologies for students with attention deficit disorder (ADD) are tools designed to level the playing field in education for a student with such a disability. ADD is commonly referred to, or considered akin to, attention deficit hyperactivity disorder (ADHD), or identified as one type of ADHD (i.e., the inattentive type as opposed to the hyperactive-impulsive type). For the purposes of this entry, ADD and ADHD are considered interchangeable, and the term *ADHD* will be used throughout to be more consistent with current literature and practice. ADHD is a disability recognized in schools under the 2004 Individuals with Disabilities Education Act (IDEA)—the law governing the education of students with disabilities in the United States—through the category of Otherwise Health Impaired. Students identified as having ADHD who do not qualify under IDEA are still protected and can receive accommodations through Section 504 of the 1973 Rehabilitation Act.

Technologies for students with disabilities are referred to as assistive technology; assistive technology must be considered for *all* students with a disability under the Individuals with Disabilities Education Act. The IDEA of 2004 generally defines *assistive technology* as something—whether a device, tool, or product—that benefits a student with a disability; the benefits can include improving or increasing the student's capabilities as well as maintaining the individual's ability to perform an academic or functional task. According to A. Edward Blackhurst, assistive technologies represent one specific type of educational technology among such other categories as teaching technology, medical technology, productivity technology, information technology, and instructional technology. Although assistive technology represents only one facet of educational technology, it can be a critical element in the educational experiences and success of students with disabilities. This entry provides an overview of technologies for students with ADHD, including technology to address academic challenges as well as technologies that specifically address and compensate for the unique challenges faced by students with this disability.

ADHD

The Centers for Disease Control and Prevention (CDC) define ADHD as a neurobehavioral disorder, commonly defined by characteristics of hyperactivity, impulsivity, and the inability to maintain sustained focus on individual tasks. In most cases, mental health professionals diagnose ADHD based on symptoms for hyperactivity and inattention, as outlined in the American Psychiatric Association's *Diagnostic & Statistical Manual for Mental Disorders*, 5th edition. ADHD is typically identified at a young age in children, with symptoms often lasting into adulthood and impacting the individual's experiences at home, in school, and in their greater community.

Current prevalence rates from the CDC suggest 11% percent of American school-age children in 2012 received a medical diagnosis of ADHD—translating to roughly 6.4 million children ages 4 to 17 with the disability. To date, no singular cause for ADHD has been identified. However, generally accepted possible risk factors aligned with the disability are identified including, but not limited to, genetics, lead poisoning, tobacco and alcohol use during pregnancy, and premature birth.

Although ADHD can present itself in different ways for individuals, common characteristics in children do exist. Richard Gargiulo outlined the common characteristics in students with ADHD across the three main facets of the disability: hyperactivity, inattention, and impulsivity. Academic and behavioral traits of hyperactivity may include constant fidgeting and restlessness, inability to stay seated, and excessive talking. With respect to inattention, children may exhibit short attention spans, careless mistakes, poor listening and organizational skills, or the inability to complete tasks in their entirety. In the classroom, impulsivity can be identified in children if they consistently blurt out answers, interrupt their peers, or struggle with waiting for permission to engage in activities. Students with ADHD alone or those with a comorbid disability (e.g., learning disabilities) also can display challenges in academic areas, such as with reading (e.g., decoding and comprehension) and mathematical performance (e.g., computation and problem solving).

Assistive Technology

Assistive technology as defined in federal law is ambiguous; many are left to wonder what is assistive technology and what is not. Dave Edyburn categorized assistive technology into three levels, although some consider it to have four levels:

1. No-tech: no technology but rather more instructional strategies (e.g., mnemonics),

2. Low-tech: typically tools not requiring a power source, lower in cost, and require less training (e.g., pencil grips, grip balls, seat cushions),

3. Mid-tech: typically tools that require batteries (e.g., calculators), and

4. High-tech: typically computer-based tools associated with higher costs and more training required (e.g., speech-to-text or text-to-speech software, and mobile devices such as iPods).

For the most part, it is not important if educators agree that a particular *technology* is an assistive technology as long as the technology helps a student with ADHD gain access to educational resources or achieve success in learning or independence.

Examples of Assistive Technology

Students with ADHD can benefit from assistive technology designed specifically to address the unique needs of these students. Examples of such technology include tools that provide additional stimulation and or allow for movement, such as seat cushions (i.e., filled with beans, gel, air), fidget toys that can be played with in one's hand (e.g., Silly Putty, Play-Doh, squeeze ball, Koosh ball), or even lap weights or weighted vests. Sensory simulation technology, such as color (e.g., color overlays, colored text, color tracking of text) and sound (e.g., text read aloud, music) can also benefit students with ADHD. According to Sydney S. Zentall, Kinsey Tom-Wright, and Jiyeon Lee, sensory stimulation technology supports the optimal simulation theory, which suggests individuals with ADHD suffer from a lack of stimulation in their respective environment.

In addition, technology for students with ADHD may include self-monitoring tools. While traditionally low-tech options of paper and pencil were used for self-monitoring or self-regulation, more high-tech options are being implemented in schools. For example, teachers can use student response systems (i.e., clickers) as well as mobile devices (e.g., iPods, iPads) to engage students in more high-tech self-monitoring. Beyond self-monitoring, tools that provide prompting can also benefit students with ADHD. For example, the WatchMinder is a watch that allows up to 30 different alarms and reminders to be set, in addition to 65 advanced programmed messages (e.g., take medication, pay attention). Of course, smartphones and other mobiles devices can also be programmed to provide prompting through alarms and reminders.

Given the potential for comorbidity between students being identified with ADHD and other disabilities (e.g., learning disability), technology to support students with learning challenges in the academic content domains can also benefit students with ADHD. For example, for students who struggle with reading, text-to-speech (e.g., NaturalReader), digital or e-text textbooks, and books on tape can easily be incorporated in classroom activities. Likewise, for students who struggle with writing—including spelling, handwriting, and written expression—technology such as graphic organizers to plan and organize one's writing (e.g., Inspiration or Kidspiration), word processors and speech-to-text software to produce one's writing (e.g., Dragon NaturallySpeaking), and spelling and grammar checks to revise and edit one's writing (e.g., Grammarly) can be beneficial. Finally, with regard to mathematics, manipulatives—concrete and virtual (e.g., the National Library of Virtual Manipulatives)—calculators, and computer-assisted instruction can support students who struggle with computation and problem solving.

Conclusion

When assistive technology is adopted in the classroom, students with ADHD greatly benefit from access to such tools to support their learning. That is, technology can serve as a prosthesis—whether as a cognitive prosthesis, as suggested by Edyburn, or in the case of students with ADHD, even a behavioral prosthesis. In other words, with the use of specialized technology, students with ADHD are capable of completing tasks that were once challenging, such as sustaining focus, recalling specific details, or fully completing academic tasks.

Emily C. Bouck and Rajiv Satsangi

See also Assistive Technology; Mobile Assistive Technologies; Technologies for Persons With Dyslexia; Technologies to Enhance Communication for Persons With Autism Spectrum Disorder

Further Readings

American Psychiatric Association. (2013). *Diagnostic and statistical manual of mental disorders* (5th ed.). Arlington, VA: Author.

Blackhurst, A. E. (2005). Historical perspectives about technology applications for people with disabilities. In D. Edyburn, K. Higgins, & R. Boone (Eds.), *Handbook of special education technology research and practice* (pp. 3–30). Whitefish Bay, WI: Knowledge by Design.

Centers for Disease Control and Prevention. (2013). *Attention-deficit/Hyperactivity disorder (ADHD)*. Retrieved from http://www.cdc.gov/ncbddd/adhd/index.html

Edyburn, D. L. (2005). Assistive technology and students with mild disabilities: From consideration to outcomes measurement. In D. L. Edyburn, K. Higgins, & R. Boone (Eds.), *Handbook of special education technology research and practice* (pp. 239–270). Whitefish Bay, WI: Knowledge by Design.

Gargiulo, R. (2012). *Special education in contemporary society: An introduction to exceptionality*. Thousand Oaks, CA: Sage.

Individuals with Disabilities Education Improvement Act (IDEA), Amendments of 2004, 20 U.S.C § 1400 *et seq.* (2004). Retrieved from http://www.ed.gov/policy/speced/leg/idea/idea.pdf

Zentall, S. S., Tom-Wright, K., & Lee, J. (2013). Psychostimulant and sensory stimulation intervention that target the reading and math deficits of students with ADHD. *Journal of Attention Disorders, 17*, 308–329. doi:10.1177/1087054711430332

Websites

Grammarly: http://www.grammarly.com
National Library of Virtual Manipulatives: http://nlvm.usu.edu
Natural Reader: http://www.naturalreaders.com

Technologies in Arts Education

Arts education is the body of pedagogical theory, practice, and institutions that inform, encode, and teach the arts and its creative expression. Arts education reflects its context embedded within society and culture, including the use of various technologies. These technologies are a complex combination of discursive, material, social, and sensory performances. These performances influence pedagogy through their encoding of artistic, sociocultural habits and practices. The arts consist of dance, music, theater, and the visual arts.

Technology in the arts is a multidimensional set of relations between technical, intellectual, environmental, and sensory elements. Elliot Eisner pointed out that the arts (a) engages us to create multiple levels of interpretation, (b) enables us to see and construct worlds, (c) assists us in making judgments, (d) affords us the ability to consider unanticipated possibilities, and (e) allows us to feel and reach into poetic and aesthetic capacities. Technologies are materials, tools, and processes, which assist and augment creative expression and expand abilities to learn about our worlds and ourselves. This entry discusses pedagogical theories of technology in arts education, the challenges and constraints of technology in arts education, and how technology is influencing arts education in the 21st century.

Pedagogical Theories of Technology in Arts Education

Technology in arts education has evolved through a variety of philosophies, theories, and epistemologies. From the industrial age of the 20th century to the information and knowledge (analytic) age of the 21st century, technologies emphasize, leverage, and extend our senses and how arts education locates, represents, and assesses information. Sensory perception in the arts and technology plays an active role in idea development, which is critical for teaching and learning. Sensory perception and active knowledge construction are especially critical in considering arts education and technology. Arthur Efland argues that the arts are places of meaning making through communication in which cognitive structures are formed and acquire meaning in support of learning. As a result, he asks us to consider an integrative approach to cognition to help harmonize the conflicting tendencies in the practices and policies of arts education.

Therefore, objectivist and constructivist theories and cognitive orientations in learning are significant for technologies in arts education. These include symbolic processing, sociocultural perspectives, and individual constructs of personal views of reality. Symbolic processing is a cognitive process that is assembled around domains of knowledge. The process blends intuition and intellect but artificially separates the individual from his environment and cultural context. A sociocultural perspective proposes a socially constructed reality in and through communication processes. This perspective establishes knowledge as cultural content, which is organized around social purposes rather than by disciplines. An individually constructed viewpoint emphasizes that reality is assembled from an individual's own making and doing. These three orientations support human agency and meaning making for teaching and learning with technology in arts education.

Challenges and Constraints of Technologies in Arts Education

In traditional computing environments, such as desktops and laptops that emerged in the late 1990s, educators could choose to interact with computers in educational settings. However, the advance of wireless communication, computing power, portable devices, and seamless user interfaces have accelerated the inclusion of these technologies in the arts education environment. This pervasiveness and acceptance of technologies are referred to as ubiquitous computing, and in an educational context, this is called *ubiquitous learning*. Consequently, arts education changes as society engages with technology and its expanding forms of sensory rich media. Social media and mobile devices influence teaching and learning in the arts. Learning has changed as distributed processing enhances the infrastructure of connectivity, networking, and dynamic information. Technological infrastructures alter the way arts educators and arts students connect and interact and how they express themselves and collectively engage in the arts' sensory, intellectual, and cultural processes.

The changes due to *new media* spawn new tools, modes of representation, and styles of discourse, as technology interfaces with pedagogical methodology. The arts engage with technology to question sensory experiences, cultural expressions, and historical paradigms, including modernist and postmodernist philosophies of aesthetics and art. For example, new media arts often exist outside the historical ideologies of cultural institutions, such as museums and schools. These types of institutions typically reinforce definitions of the arts as original, unique, provocative, expressive, and valuable beyond a pedagogical or persuasive function. Several issues resulting from the integration of technologies into an arts-based environment and arts educational practice include (a) broadening of the range of representational models and modes, (b) reshaping spatial and temporal boundaries, (c) building collective knowledge, and (d) altering the balance of agency.

These issues confront the boundaries of traditional art categorization and challenge pedagogical models, such as the visual arts Discipline Based Art Education (DBAE) with its four categories of production, criticism, aesthetics, and history. There are additional considerations specific to arts education, such as technologies' role in constructing meaning through a mediated interface, and the complex issues that are raised on creativity, agency, and authorship. Likewise, theater, dance, and music educators creatively and critically develop pedagogy balancing the performative modes of live and remote audiences across different media (e.g., television, streaming Internet media, and virtual reality). Technology in arts education in support of teaching and learning involves tools, techniques, and cultural representations. A cultural approach is the boundary at which technology (tools and media) and culture (beliefs, values, and assumptions) converge. That is, technology conceptualized as an interface is a cultural process, bridging human, machine, and hybrid forms, resulting in a combination of sensory and semiotic relationships. This approach enables arts education to focus on artworks and their

expressions, which facilitates the exploration of communication, knowledge processes, and cultural conventions.

The exploration from a cultural interface approach reveals multiple and often conflicting ways to consider technology and arts education pedagogy. For instance, arts education engages cultural conversation about technology to mobilize teaching and learning through

(a) *multimodality,* which is the human-machine interaction using multiple modes of input/output as part of the ways we come to know;

(b) *convergence,* which is the relationship among media audiences, producers, and content;

(c) *remediation,* which is the relationship between newer and older media;

(d) *embodiment,* which is the exploration of the physical, social being, and technology; and

(e) *relational context,* which is the use, concepts, and interpretation of technology in particular contexts within our lived experiences.

For example, VoiceThread is an application that provides multimodal conversations in the cloud, which pedagogically supports reflexive and emotional social interaction, improves Web presence, and engages students in multiple literacies simultaneously (e.g., text, audio, and visual). Educational practice evolves in response to technological changes in terms of multimodality, convergence, remediation, embodiment, and the relationality of the aesthetic and intellectual life around interconnected technologically rich cultural arts products and expressions.

Contemporary Context

Three characteristics of technology in arts education that support teaching and learning are technology as tools, technology as rules, and technology as systems. Extending the object world of technology tools into the world of culture provides a contextual understanding of technology in our everyday lives. The social and technical encoding that occurs through the arts and technology blurs the actual and virtual and shapes the identity of artists, audiences, technical processes, and aesthetic possibilities. The current ubiquity of technology in our educational and social environment subtly obscures and complicates how media translate our social, cultural, and educational experiences. The technologies in the arts are places of articulations, assemblages, and augmentations in which cognitive processes are crafted and make meaning. Technologies and the arts harness and constrain human learning and agency by challenging the boundaries of our senses and changing the way we experience the world. Technology in arts education provides expanded applications in teaching and learning to support the creation, production, and distribution of expressions and imaginings that define identity in the 21st century.

Michelle Tillander

See also Information, Technology, and Media Literacies; Personal Learning Environments; Social Media and Networking; Ubiquitous Learning

Further Readings

Bolter J. D., & Grusin, R. (1999). *Remediation: Understanding new media.* Cambridge, MA: MIT Press.

Efland, A. D. (2004). *Art and cognition: Integrating the visual arts in the curriculum.* Reston, VA: National Art Education Association.

Eisner, E. W. (2002). *The arts and the creation of mind.* New Haven, CT: Yale University Press.

Ito, M. (2013). *Hanging out, messing around, and geeking out: Kids living and learning with new media.* Cambridge, MA: MIT Press.

Jenkins, H. (2008). *Convergence culture: Where old and new media collide.* New York, NY: New York University Press.

Jones, C. A. (2006). *Sensorium: Embodied experience, technology, and contemporary art.* Cambridge, MA: MIT Press.

Kress, G. (2003). *Literacy in the new media age.* New York, NY: Routledge.

Lovejoy, M. (2004). *Digital currents: Art in the electronic age.* New York, NY: Routledge.

Sefton-Green, J. (Ed.). (1999). *Young people, creativity and new technologies: The challenge of the digital arts.* New York, NY: Routledge.

Sweeny, B. (Ed.). (2010). *Inter/actions Inter/sections: Art education in a digital visual culture.* Reston, VA: National Art Education Association.

Thompson, K., Purcell, K., & Raine, L. (2013). *Arts organizations and digital technologies.* Washington, DC: Pew Internet and American Life Project. Retrieved from http://pewinternet.org/Reports/2013/Arts-and-technology.aspx

Tufte, E. R. (1990). *Envisioning Information.* Cheshire, CT: Graphics Press.

Technologies in Humanities Education

All three of the main terms in the title of this entry have long and contentious histories. While there is some general understanding, there is no unanimity about the definitions of the terms *technology, humanities,* or *education.* Although some scholars explicate technology as a form of inquiry, or as a mode of being, technology is more commonly understood as some sort of tool including not only physical objects and systems, but also methods and institutions. The National Endowment for the Humanities specifies that the humanities include the study of languages, literature, philosophy, history, ethics, comparative religion, and humanistic aspects of the social sciences. They are often understood as the core and foundation of education. The exact nature of education has been on the intellectual agenda at least since Plato's *Meno,* in which Socrates presents the view that learning is remembering, and Plato's *Apology,* in which Socrates claims never to have been a teacher. More recently, Paolo Freire introduced the distinction between the *banking model* and the *critical model* of education. Most humanities educators believe that education is a process whereby knowledge, skills, and values are developed within individuals and communities. This entry first discusses the relationships between new technologies and the humanities, including whether technology affects the content and values of the humanities. It then discusses how new technologies are used to deliver humanities education, to promote interaction among students, and to assess students and faculty. It concludes by discussing some concerns about technologies in humanities education.

Values and Teaching Technologies

Two of the most important technologies over the history of the humanities have been physical objects (texts and other artifacts) and methodology (a pedagogical approach such as the Socratic method). Socrates wrote no works of philosophy. In Plato's *Phaedrus,* Plato presents Socrates as arguing that it is only through the give and take of dialogue and questions that knowledge is gained. Texts are of limited use because they present inert words as reality and knowledge as fixed, giving the reader the illusion of knowing in some cases. Plato argues that reliance on texts fails to encourage the questioning and interacting characteristics of knowing and learning. The underlying assumption of Plato's argument is that a particular technology—written text, in this case—is not neutral; some technologies are better suited to some purposes because they cohere with the sort of activity undertaken. Plato's position coheres with later claims that technology is value laden. This poses a central issue for humanities education in a world of rapid technological innovation: Do humanities teachers adopt new technologies toward their traditional tasks, leaving the content and values essentially unchanged, or do the new technologies fundamentally change the work of the humanities, the nature of education, or both?

The Digital Humanities

Digital humanities is a *technologized* form of humanities scholarship characterized by utilizing information technology tools. It is a contested term, taken to apply variously to (a) the application of new technologies to traditional humanities scholarship, such as digitalizing archives and using keyword searches to start research; (b) using the traditional questions and methodologies of the humanities to analyze digital media and technologies; (c) developing a new form of scholarship that arises out of the new technologies and which addresses fundamentally new questions and texts; and (d) combinations of those. The digital humanities movement has been focused on scholarship, but with the launch of digital pedagogy journals such as *Hybrid Pedagogy* and *The Journal of Interactive Technology and Pedagogy* in 2011, an explicit focus on using digital technologies to transform teaching and learning has emerged.

Distance Education in the Internet Era

The rapid growth of home and mobile computing over the past 35 years has been accompanied by efforts to move education online and to deliver courses, and even entire degree programs, at a distance. In 1993, Jones International University, offering undergraduate and graduate degrees, became the first fully accredited virtual university, or university to exist fully online. Today distance education takes place largely online although the mode of delivery and the nature of the course can vary. Online courses might be offered through course management systems, such as Blackboard or Sakai, that provide an online learning environment, through other Web-based services including blogs and video-hosting services, or through virtual worlds such as Second Life. Online courses can be versions of traditional courses with fairly limited numbers of students and with a professor who has significant autonomy concerning course design and content.

Humanities Course Delivery

Recent technological innovations have entered humanities courses, often to simultaneous fanfare and disdain, including new texts, new forms of interaction, and new models for organizing the course. The past 200 years of technological innovation has produced a wealth of new texts for humanities scholars and teachers, from photographs and mass-printed newspapers to popular music and film and underground publications. For some teachers, these new texts are primarily valuable as ways to engage student interest, and for others, the new texts are worthy of study in their own right. Digital technologies are also giving new access to traditional texts. One of the most striking examples is the DM project at Drew University, led by English faculty member Martin Foys and computer science faculty member Shannon Bradshaw. DM supports the study and annotation of images and texts. DM has focused largely on medieval maps and scrolls, but it also includes Old English, Latin, and French manuscripts.

New technologies, such as e-mail, wikis, blogs, and discussion forums, have also changed the forms of interaction by students, allowing for greater sharing of thoughts and resources as well as creating new possibilities for developing and presenting individual and collective work. *The Stanford Encyclopedia of Philosophy,* which started in 1995 and now averages over 950,000 accesses each week, is one example of using new technologies to develop and disseminate first-quality academic resources. A final, and very important, instance of technologies shaping humanities courses is the notion of the flipped classroom. Traditional classes focus on first-exposure learning in class through lecture and discussion, and then students return to texts and study for processing the material. A flipped classroom makes first exposure through encountering texts and other artifacts, prior to and outside the class, and synthesis and analysis are developed in class. Technologies that allow the delivery of traditional lecture material online facilitate these new modes of teaching.

Technology in the Humanities Classroom

Technology in the humanities classroom has largely meant tools for presenting the texts and other learning materials to a class. One aspect has been presenting visual images or sound to supplement traditional lecture and discussion. For many decades in the 20th century, this meant filmstrips, 16mm movies, and finally videotapes. Available resources were limited to those in the institutional library. Today these images are available on DVD, or more likely through some form of streaming media, which, when coupled with new sources of media such as the TED and TEDx conferences, greatly expand the range of options available in the classroom. The most prevalent technology in a classroom in the early 21st century is some sort of presentation software, usually PowerPoint. More recently, Pecha Kucha–style presentations promise to use increased structure and images to create greater focus and engagement. Technology also holds the promise of a more learner-centered classroom, with students using personal electronic devices, from using clickers to take quizzes and interact with professors to working with smartphones, tablets, and laptop computers to do in-class research and to interact with course material.

Assessment

New technologies have fostered new forms of assessment, both of students and of professors. Electronic grading of essays ranges from using editing tools within a word processing program, to electronically aided assessment such as found on Turnitin and EssayTagger, to complete computer-based automatic essay scoring. Students are also using new technologies to evaluate professors, courses, programs of study, and academic institutions. The best known and most used is Rate My Professors.

Concerns

Concerns about new technologies in humanities education range from a fear that technology will facilitate cheating and misrepresentation to a worry that instructors will become agents of technology and surveillance. The concerns include both value-neutral worries about whether professors understand the technical aspects of the technology, to value-laden considerations of how technology changes the interactions, texts, and thinking within the humanities. Plagiarism is a major concern, and as cut and paste is combined with the ever-expanding range of resources available online, faculty worry about the increased ease of cheating (value-neutral) as well as whether the very notion of illicit copying itself is fading (value-laden). Some institutions have adopted antiplagiarism technologies such as Turnitin in an attempt to use a technological tool to address a technologically enhanced problem. Some new e-book technologies allow professors to monitor student reading and study habits, a process compared to "Big Brother" by one academic dean. Others are concerned that new technologically mediated forms of communication mean not just that faculty and classmates are more accessible (value-neutral) and that professors are deluged with ever-more questions, but that interactions are more superficial, briefer, and less likely to engage substantive issues (value-laden). These latter concerns are part of a more general concern that reliance on electronic media is reshaping human attention spans and abilities to think critically, feel deeply, and form long-term affectional relationships.

Craig Hanks

See also Information and Communication Technologies for Formal Learning; Technology Support for Conceptual Change

Further Readings

Bartscherer, T., & Coover, R. (Eds.). (2011). *Switching codes: Thinking through digital technology in the humanities and the arts.* Chicago, IL: University of Chicago Press.

Bowen, J. A. (2012). *Teaching naked: How moving technology out of your college classroom will improve student learning.* San Francisco, CA: Jossey-Bass.

Cameron, F., & Kenderdine, S. (Eds.). (2007). *Theorizing digital cultural heritage: A critical discourse.* Cambridge, MA: MIT Press.

Cohen, D. J., & Rozenzweig, R. (2005). *Digital history: A guide to gathering, preserving, and presenting the past on the Web.* Philadelphia: University of Pennsylvania Press.

Dubnjakovic, A., & Tomlin, P. (2010). *A practical guide to electronic resources in the humanities.* Oxford, UK: Chandos Publishing.

Hoffman, S. J. (Ed.). (2010). *Teaching the humanities online: A practical guide to the virtual classroom.* Armonk, NY: M. E. Sharpe.

Lunenfeld, P., Burdick, A., Drucker, J., Presner, T., & Schnapp, J. (2012). *Digital_humanities.* Cambridge, MA: MIT Press.

Moss, M. (2011). *Education and its discontents: Teaching, the humanities, and the importance of a liberal education in the age of mass information.* Plymouth, UK: Lexington Books.

Russo, J. P. (2005). *The future without a past: The humanities in a technological society.* Columbia: University of Missouri Press.

Schacht, P. (2008). Rowing alone: Technology and democracy in the humanities classroom. *The International Journal of Technology, Knowledge, and Society, 4*(5), 61–68.

Schreibman, S., Siemens, R., & Unsworth, J. (Eds.). (2007). *A companion to digital humanities.* Malden, MA: Blackwell.

TECHNOLOGIES IN MATHEMATICS EDUCATION

Technologies in mathematics education refer to a wide variety of technical tools, including both hardware and software, utilized to support mathematical computation, representation, exploration, sense making and reasoning, and communication in a classroom environment. In K–12 and postsecondary education, basic four-function calculators coexist with scientific calculators, graphing calculators, next-generation handhelds, tablet apps, powerful integrated mathematical learning environments, and Web-based computational knowledge engines. In principle, the National Council of Teachers of Mathematics (NCTM) views technologies as essential tools in mathematics education because they enhance the accessibility of mathematical ideas and improve students' mathematical understanding. This entry describes the technologies used in mathematics education and discusses the emergent perspectives and recent trends in the use of these technologies.

Calculators

Calculators remain a primary handheld technology in school mathematics. Basic four-function calculators are mainly used in the elementary schools while scientific and graphing calculators are used in the middle and secondary schools. Despite recurring calls to question the use of calculators in the early grades and certain domains of mathematics, research has consistently shown that pedagogical uses of calculators promote students' problem-solving skills without hindering their computational skills.

Since the 1980s, the research community has established the significance of multiple representations in mathematics education in embracing diversity in mathematical thinking and pedagogical intervention. In summer 2007, Texas Instruments released its next-generation calculator TI-Nspire, featuring a linked multirepresentational environment that includes algebra, geometry, and spreadsheet pages. These computer-like calculators can be interconnected via a corresponding navigator system for a classroom network that supports assessment and communication. As a powerful pedagogical tool, these next-generation handhelds support the reconceptualization of school mathematics toward exploration, modeling, and social collaboration.

Dynamic and Interactive Mathematics Learning Environments

Dynamic and interactive mathematics learning environments (DIMLEs) emerged in the 1980s and gained fresh momentum at the turn of the 21st century because of the rapid advances of computer technologies and the corresponding theoretical developments regarding the nature of mathematical cognition, particularly the importance of dynamically linked multiple representations and didactical and mathematical modeling. While a few time-honored commercial DIMLEs, such as Geometers' Sketchpad (since 1991) and Cabri (since 1986), continue to be popular among mathematics educators, open-source DIMLEs such as GeoGebra (since 2002) also became freely accessible to the community of mathematics education. These DIMLEs went far beyond their microworld predecessors in the 1980s, integrating algebra, geometry, spreadsheets, data analysis, computer algebra systems (CAS), and programming in an interactive and dynamic system. They also have built-in Web-friendly utilities for exporting user constructions to Web-ready files. In light of Java portability, the new DIMLEs have consistent user interfaces and functionality

across various platforms, including Web Start features that allow the user to open a fully functional DIMLE within a Java-enabled browser. They are interactive because they allow users to manipulate mathematical objects for instant feedback. They are dynamic because the multiple representations are interconnected and allow for a continuous simulation of mathematical processes. Pedagogically, DIMLEs keep track of a user's construction protocol, which allows for diagnostic assessment and troubleshooting.

Students in the middle and secondary grades in general embrace the use of DIMLEs and demonstrate insightful, albeit frequently nontraditional, mathematical understanding. Research, however, has unveiled the challenges of DIMLE integration in school mathematics. There exists strong consensus among mathematics educators and researchers that the use of DIMLEs, which may include next-generation calculators, changes the epistemological nature of mathematics and traditional practices of mathematics teaching and teacher education. The real challenges may have come from the educational culture and established patterns of mathematical belief and classroom practice. Nonetheless, these emergent DIMLEs, especially the open-source ones, have positioned themselves to provide equitable and democratic access to powerful mathematical experiences to students from across the world.

DIMLEs such as GeoGebra are designed primarily for educational purposes, grounded in educational research on student learning and emergent theories of mathematical cognition. They stand in between ready-made virtual manipulatives, which target specific mathematical concepts in an applet, and computational environments such as Mathematica and Maple, which provide a wide range of tools and languages for advanced mathematical and scientific computation. In fact, DIMLEs are frequently employed to create personalized Web-accessible virtual manipulatives such as those at GeoGebraTube.com.

Programming Environments

With the advance of digital technologies, there have been constant calls to integrate computer programming into mathematics education. In reality, however, there have been few large-scale curricular integration endeavors in school mathematics; programming to learn mathematics continues to be a tantalizing vision for the future. Technically, an upgraded version of the classic Logo programming environment developed in the early 1980s is freely available on the Internet. In 2004, Scratch, a 21st-century upgrade of Logo, emerged from the Lifelong Kindergarten Group of the MIT Media Lab, featuring the use of visual programming blocks. Research and development around Scratch have led to new theoretical perspectives on young learners' computational thinking in a design-based learning environment.

Emergent Perspectives on Technologies in Mathematics Education

There is no doubt that mathematics classrooms in general fall behind other social institutions in terms of technology integration. Powerful digital technologies are frequently used to address traditional curricula, thus trivializing students' mathematical experience and contributing to the controversy about technology use in mathematics education. Research and theory development in the past three decades have established a few promising perspectives on the transformative use of technologies in mathematics education.

Technologies Have Become Infrastructural

The infrastructural view of technologies in mathematics education was proposed by James Kaput and his colleagues, who argued that digital technologies were beginning to serve as the technical foundation for professional communities and as necessary agencies or partners in mathematical reasoning and problem solving. Technologies are assuming an essential yet invisible role in mathematical practices, transforming the very nature of students' mathematical experience.

Technologies Enable Generative Designs

Generative design is a promising perspective on technology integration proposed by Walter Stroup and his colleagues, who argue for the generative affordances of new classroom networking technologies for orchestrating individual creativity and collective diversity. In a playful manner, students express, test, and revise their emerging ideas iteratively, generating new knowledge in a social environment that embraces diversity and open-ended problem solving.

Technologies Support Experimental Mathematics

Computational technologies are particularly powerful for exploring and demonstrating dynamic mathematical processes. A modeling perspective on mathematics education has gradually found its way into the mathematics education community. While proofs and deductive reasoning are still desirable, a new form of experimental mathematics is taking shape that takes advantage of computers to run complicated or time-consuming computations in search of errors and patterns. Modeling with mathematics is thus stipulated as one of the eight professional standards for mathematical practice in the Common Core State Standards for Mathematics.

Trends and Strategies

Mathematics education is a unique field where traditional paper and pencil and straightedge and compass may well continue to coexist with advanced handheld and computer-based learning environments, serving the pedagogical and developmental needs of mathematics teachers and their students. A variety of ancient tools, such as the abacus, slide rule, and protractor, have been transformed by touch technologies into interactive iPad and Android apps. There is a growing need to explore the alignment of mathematical content with technological tools. Mathematics educators are encouraged to include both mathematical tasks that are dependent on technology use and those that are independent of technologies in order for students to appreciate the affordances of technologies, promote metacognitive skills, and develop habits of seeking mathematical insight. Ahead of mathematics educators is a promising prospect that embraces diversity in technology use, mathematical thinking, and teaching and learning communities.

Lingguo Bu

See also Constructivist Theory; Design-Based Research; Learning by Modeling; Learning with Models; Tools for Modeling and Simulation; TPACK (Technological Pedagogical Content Knowledge); TPACK (Technological Pedagogical Content Knowledge): Implications for 21st-Century Teacher Education

Further Readings

Ball, L., & Stacey, K. (2005). Teaching strategies for developing judicious technology use. In W. J. Masalski & P. C. Elliott (Eds.), *Technology-supported mathematics learning environments* (pp. 3–15). Reston, VA: National Council of Teachers of Mathematics.

Borwein, J., & Devlin, K. (2009). *The computer as crucible: An introdcution to experimental mathematics.* Wellesley, MA: A. K. Peters.

Brennan, K., & Resnik, M. (2012). New frameworks for studying and assessing the development of computational thinking. In *Proceedings of the American Educational Research Association (AERA) Annual Conference.* Retrieved from http://info.scratch.mit.edu/Research

Heid, M. K. (1997). The technological revolution and the reform of school mathematics. *American Journal of Education, 106,* 5–61.

Hembree, R., & Dessart, D. J. (1992). Research on calculators in mathematics education. In J. T. Fey & C. R. Hirsch (Eds.), *Calculators in mathematics education* (1992 NCTM yearbook; pp. 23–32). Reston, VA: National Council of Teachers of Mathematics.

Kaput, J., Noss, R., & Hoyles, C. (2002). Developing new notations for a learnable mathematics in the computational era. In L. D. English (Ed.), *Handbook of international research in mathematics education* (pp. 51–75). Mahwah, NJ: Lawrence Erlbaum.

Lesh, R., & Doerr, H. M. (Eds.). (2003). *Beyond constructivism: Models and modeling perspectives on mathematics problem solving, learning, and teaching.* Mahwah, NJ: Lawrence Erlbaum.

Martinovic, D., & Karadag, Z. (2012). Dynamic and interactive mathematics learning environments: the case of teaching the limit concept. *Teaching Mathematics and Its Applications, 31*(1), 41–48.

Stroup, W. M., Ares, N. M., & Hurford, A. C. (2005). A dialectic analysis of generativity: Issues of network-supported design in mathematics and science. *Mathematical Thinking and Learning, 7,* 181–206.

TECHNOLOGIES IN MEDICAL EDUCATION

The integration and utilization of various types of technological resources have the potential to enhance knowledge acquisition in the field of biomedical sciences. Medical education varies throughout the world but is often described using three main components: undergraduate medical education (UGME), graduate medical education (GME), and continuing medical education (CME). UGME aims to provide a solid foundation in preclinical (basic science) and clinical studies that facilitate the goal of becoming a physician. Upon completion of UGME, many physicians pursue GME residencies or fellowships that focus on a clinical subspecialty such as psychiatry or neurology. CME is unique in that it offers an opportunity to continually refine skills in support of facilitating lifelong learning. CME activities are provided in a number of modalities (i.e., audio, video, online programs, journal clubs, webinars) and through a variety of entities (professional organizations, hospitals, medical education agencies, and educational institutions).

Educators' use of technology to enhance knowledge acquisition varies because of (a) complexity of content and associated learning objectives, (b) the extent to which collaboration is incorporated, and (c) preferred assessment strategies. Medical educators must meet the needs of a diverse audience who are used to just-in-time learning, obtaining information on demand, and learning and collaborating with peers; they thrive on interactive learning and feedback. This presents a need for technology and educational initiatives to be paired in a way that addresses the diverse learning needs of this audience. This entry first discusses the use of various kinds of technology in medical education, including online modalities, simulations, and mobile applications. It then discusses the use of technology for learning communities in medical education and changes in classroom instruction as a result of new ways of using technology.

Online Modalities

Incorporation of online learning in medical education often includes (1) integrating technology in the form of multimedia based tutorials or videos, (2) authoring and collaboration tools, and (3) incorporation of learning management systems (LMSs) to support collaboration and communication. To support a hybrid learning approach, multimedia tutorials shared via the Internet are often used in conjunction with didactic materials to supplement concepts and information acquisition and integration. This blended approach is common in medical education and utilizes technologies with which students are familiar. Collaboration and authoring tools (e.g., Skype, Google Hangouts, Google Drive) are also technologies used for sharing and discussing ideas as well as for team-based projects. An LMS offers opportunities to collaborate, initiate discussion, share information, and develop a learning community.

A more recent innovation is the incorporation of health information technologies (i.e., electronic health records) in order to broaden students' physician-patient communication skills and further develop core competencies within medical education using an evidence-based approach.

Low-, Mid-, and High-Fidelity Simulation

Simulations are often used to facilitate learning and increase interactivity among health professionals. Low-fidelity simulations are those that provide opportunities for learning and interaction but do not have the ability to closely replicate reality, as compared to their high-fidelity counterparts. Examples include problem-based scenarios or the use of a noncomputerized mannequin or specific body part. Role playing and engagement with arts-based opportunities are examples of mid-fidelity interventions that aim to enhance empathy, improve communication and presentation skills, and expose learners to relevant social, cultural, and spiritual factors.

High-fidelity simulations include using virtual or human patients in situations that closely imitate reality and wherein clinical debriefing is integrated into the learning. Both virtual and human patient simulations are used to provide a more realistic representation of what a physician would experience in reality. High-fidelity simulations offer a multitude of learning opportunities to aid in skill and knowledge acquisition. Incorporating real-world experience as it pertains to diagnosis, treatment, and physician-patient communication enables learners to refine their clinical reasoning abilities and enhance critical thinking skills. The question remains as to how medical simulations will evolve as new and powerful technologies continue to emerge.

Mobile Applications

Utilization and integration of mobile resources in medical education supports a variety of needs, including access to evidence-based information and resources and the utilization of productivity tools. Mobile applications (apps) are integrated into curricula in order to provide an additional means by which learners are able to communicate with one another, reflect on information presented, and learn additional ways of obtaining evidence-based information on demand. Mobile apps can foster collaboration, improve productivity, help identify new ideas, and support surveys that lead to further improvements.

For educators, mobile technology integration enables educators to arrange learning opportunities that meet the diverse needs of their students. For learners, mobile technology provides an opportunity to see various ways to access information, make meaningful use of data, cultivate collaboration, and build discussion among peers. Examples of mobile apps commonly integrated into curricula include Poll Anywhere, Popplet (for mind mapping), resource intensive databases such as Mobile PubMed (provides access to biomedical science literature), Eponyms, and Evernote (annotating articles).

Health science students utilize a variety of mobile devices and need the ability to retrieve quality evidence-based information on demand. Integrating mobile apps at various stages in health sciences curricula provides learners a foundation of knowledge from which they can build upon and helps to generate a sense of familiarity with a variety of technological resources that can be used in order to work effectively, efficiently, and collaboratively, in clinical environments.

Learning Communities and Social Networks and Resources

The creation of learning communities and integration of technology in continuing medical education and graduate medical education is often overlooked. The former aims to bolster communication and collaboration and offers an arena for further inquiry and debate. The latter aims to address refinement of skills and knowledge with respect to clinical knowledge and application. Both venues involve networks created to build and support lifelong learners. To what extent and how these are technologically integrated depends on the organization or governing body. For development of learning communities, wikis, blogs, learning management systems, and various other systems are created to facilitate interaction between and among community members. Technical features include the use of text-based and visual chats, publication widgets, RSS (rich site summary) feeds, polling, discussion threads, and the ability to upload media and files. Learning communities are a popular element to incorporate in medical education as they offer an opportunity for sharing of ideas in an interprofessional manner, with professionals from different teams collaborating, in order to meet the needs of the diverse and changing patient population with whom they interact.

Health science professionals engage in collaboration and further their personal learning via social mechanisms using social media tools (e.g., YouTube, Facebook, Twitter) and social networks (e.g., Research-Gate, Causes, and Sermo). The social outlets in which students participate are those that have the ability to link to the latest information and research, offer the opportunity to receive and provide feedback and comments, and have integrated opportunities to develop collaborations with others in a field of inquiry.

Conclusion

Currently, the methods just described are the primary methods of technology integration in medical education. An instructional paradigm shift has been seen whereby the traditional didactic instructional approach has slowly started moving toward one of a flipped-classroom or blended model where didactic information is provided to learners ahead of time and in-person class time is dedicated to discussion, analysis, critical appraisal, and collaboration with peers. This hybrid model supports the utilization of technology to support principles of active and engaged learning and is one that promotes self-regulated inquiry and the development of lifelong learning skills. Both technology and medical sciences are changing at a rapid pace, therefore it is critical to consistently evaluate current and new technological innovations to determine their applicability and value-added potential to the medical education experience.

Nandita S. Mani

See also Emerging Educational Technologies; Engaged Learning; Learning With Simulations; Mobile Devices: Impact on Learning and Instruction; Mobile Tools and Technologies for Learning and Instruction; Simulation-Based Learning; Social Media in Higher Education

Further Readings

de Jong, N., Savin-Baden, M., Cunningham, A. M., & Verstegen, D. M. (2014). Blended learning in health education: Three case studies. *Perspectives on Medical Education, 3*(4), 278–288. doi:10.1007/s40037-014-0108-1

Fleming, A., Cutrer, W., Moutsios, S., Heavrin, B., Pilla, M., Eichbaum, Q., & Rodgers, S. (2013). Building learning communities: Evolution of the colleges at Vanderbilt University School of Medicine. *Academic Medicine, 88*(9), 1246–1251. doi:10.1097/ACM.0b013e31829f8e2a

George, D. R., & Dellasega, C. (2011). Use of social media in graduate-level medical humanities education: Two pilot studies from Penn State College of Medicine. *Medical Teacher, 33*(8), e429–e434. doi:10.3109/0142159x .2011.586749

Hamstra, S. J., Brydges, R., Hatala, R., Zendejas, B., & Cook, D. A. (2014). Reconsidering fidelity in simulation-based training. *Academic Medicine, 89*(3), 387–392. doi:10.1097/ acm.0000000000000130

Motola, I., Devine, L. A., Chung, H. S., Sullivan, J. E., & Issenberg, S. B. (2013). Simulation in healthcare education: A best evidence practical guide. AMEE Guide No. 82. *Medical Teacher, 35*(10), e1511–e1530. doi:10.3109/01421 59x.2013.818632

Prober, C. G., & Khan, S. (2013). Medical education reimagined: A call to action. *Academic Medicine, 88*(10), 1407–1410. doi:10.1097/ACM.0b013e3182a368bd

Teri, S., Acai, A., Griffith, D., Mahmoud, Q., Ma, D. W. L., & Newton, G. (2013). Student use and pedagogical impact of a mobile learning application. *Biochemistry Molecular and Biology Education, 42,* 121–135. doi:10.1002/bmb.20771

TECHNOLOGIES IN SCIENCE EDUCATION

Technology is an artifact that should not be singled out but rather integrated with content and with pedagogy. Science, technology, engineering, and mathematics (STEM) broadly include the disciplines addressed in this entry. Integrating technology into science, engineering, and mathematics can make these disciplines exciting and innovatively transformative. Although many technologies are used in science education, this entry focuses on those that are currently important and those that are emerging and likely to become important in the near future. The entry first discusses the use of serious educational games, simulations, and alternate reality. It then discusses the use of next-generation technologies such as robotics, three-dimensional (3D) printing, haptic and biological feedback devices, and holograms.

SEGs, Simulations, and Alternate Reality

One transformative technology in education has been serious educational games (SEGs). A derivative of the serious games genre (games developed for training purposes and not necessarily entertainment), serious educational games are designed and developed to assist with teaching and learning in K–20 settings.

Some argue that SEGs fall under the larger virtual learning environment (VLE) canopy, which also covers 3D multiuser platforms (e.g., SecondLife, Active Worlds, OpenSim), simulations, and alternate and augmented reality. SEGs, as with any game, have rules and a taxonomy that inform gameplay. There is typically continuous or frequent feedback to the user. SEGs differ from commercial games by having educational goals and embedded assessments. SEGs are meant to be educational and, therefore, should formatively and summatively assess the user and provide feedback so the user can progress to the end of the game and achieve desired learning outcomes. The endgame in SEGs is generally a learning objective or a series of learning objectives, similar to what might be found in a traditional lesson or unit plan.

Simulations are similar to games, and although they too provide feedback to the end user, they do not have rules and taxonomy like games. Simulations also mimic the real world, whereas SEGs often mimic hypothetical settings and immerse the user in ill-structured problem solving.

3D multiuser platforms are generally used for mass communication purposes (i.e., meetings and distance learning) but could infuse either or both SEGs or simulations. These platforms allow for sometimes thousands of simultaneous users to interact with one another and with the environment. Because users choose or create their own avatars (digital representations of themselves), the notions of race, gender, ethnicity, language, and extrovert/introvert are not directly applicable.

Alternate reality games are mobile games played on a ubiquitous device such as a mobile phone, MP3 player with Wi-Fi, or a tablet device. Alternate and augmented reality gaming are currently two different fields with a moderate amount of overlap, but many see them merging in the future. Alternate reality is a form of gaming that uses the real world as part of the game narrative and game structure. It leverages websites, cell phones, pay phones, physical structures such as building and billboards, and so on, as part of the game experience. To date, it has been primarily used as a marketing vehicle for video games and movies, but pervasive social gaming is another area where alternate reality holds great potential.

Augmented reality superimposes or embeds a layer of digital media throughout the physical environment, which is viewed and interacted with via a mobile device. There are two forms of augmented reality currently available to educators: (1) location-aware and (2) vision-based. Location-aware augmented reality presents digital media to learners as they move through a physical area with a GPS-enabled device. The media (i.e., text, graphics, audio, video, 3D models) augment the physical environment with narrative, navigation, or academic information relevant to the location. Vision-based augmented reality presents digital media to learners after they point their device's video camera at an object (e.g., QR code, 2D target).

These two forms of augmented reality leverage several smartphone and tablet technologies (i.e., GPS, video camera, object recognition, and tracking) to create immersive learning experiences within the physical environment, providing educators with a novel and potentially transformative tool for teaching and learning. Augmented reality games are often based in environmental science because it is easy to create a scenario about the outside world where players will interact.

An interesting combination of all of the aforementioned technologies is something called modular serious educational games (mSEGs); mSEGs are games that begin in a computer-seated environment but evolve to an augmented reality platform in a cyclic narrative. The narrative of the game is of the action and adventure genre and allows the learner to begin playing on the computer. After attaining a desired skill or learned content, the player is given instructions to move beyond the seated class with a mobile device. The narrative continues through the augmented reality module until the desired skill of learned content is attained and instructions are given to the player to move back to the seated computer to load the next game level. The cycle continues until the ultimate learning objective is met.

The Next Generation

As progress occurs in integrating technologies into science education, technologies that are not currently being widely used in the classroom but are being introduced to the workforce are one place to look for likely opportunities. Such technologies as robotics, three-dimensional (3D) printing, haptic and biological feedback devices, and holograms represent emerging technologies of relevance to science education. Serious educational games, simulation, virtual worlds, and other current technologies now integrated in science education are likely to change significantly as new technologies emerge. It is not very clear what technology in science education will look like in 20 years due to the rapid pace of innovation in technology in general.

Seen in other disciplines, robotics is a technology, or series of technologies, slowly occupying the science education space. Like SEGs, robotics are fun and engaging ways to immerse students in science content and seamless pathways of connecting to future STEM careers. 3D printing is one of the technologies that appears to be a toy for students but if used correctly can allow students to design prototypes on a computer and print those prototypes to test their functionality. 3D printing has the potential to move students to the design phase and introduce engineering problems much earlier in a curriculum than was previously possible. Problem solving and design skills are prevalent in the Next Generation Science Standards recently released in the United States.

Haptic feedback devices allow students to feel the world around them, that is, imagine intermolecular forces about the subject in chemistry. Teachers generally draw on a board or show a simulation, but with a haptic feedback device, students can feel these forces themselves and potentially gain deeper insight into things not readily visible or easily experienced directly. As costs continue to plummet on haptic feedback devices, they will certainly be integrated more in science learning.

Biometrics is the technology used to recognize humans based on specific physical or behavioral traits. These technologies help computer software understand the physical and emotional state of learners. Physical traits such as facial expression, heart rate, skin moisture, and body temperature can be used to create detailed reports of student understanding and performance.

The last technology to be mentioned in this entry is perhaps more distant than the others in terms of integration into science education—namely, holograms. The notion of presence and immersion through distance learning can be amplified with the likeness of an instructor seemingly standing in front of the learner at home or in a distant classroom. The same notion can be applied to holograms of devices and entire situations. As noted, this technology is still in its infancy though it holds great potential for science education, bringing simulations to an entirely different level.

The key piece to technology integration in learning, specifically in science learning, is that technology-facilitated instruction is likely to be effective when it is student centered, providing levels of individual engagement and empowerment not previously possible without the technology. Teacher-centered use with students watching is less likely to promote deep learning or develop insight and understanding than having students use the technologies themselves. If the ultimate goal of education is to prepare the next generation of skilled workers and informed citizens, then giving students control of their learning with technologies is critical. Thinking computationally, solving problems like an engineer, and designing objects and solutions according to scientific principles can be well supported with new and emerging technologies.

Leonard A. Annetta

See also Serious Games; Simulation-Based Learning; TPACK (Technological Pedagogical Content Knowledge); TPACK (Technological Pedagogical Content Knowledge): Implications for 21st-Century Teacher Education

Further Readings

Annetta, L. A. (2008). *Serious educational games: From theory to practice.* Amsterdam, Netherlands: Sense Publishers.

Annetta, L. A. (2010). The "I's" have it: A framework for educational game design. *Review of General Psychology, 14*(2), 105–112.

Annetta, L. A., Minogue, J. A., Holmes, S., & Cheng, M.-T. (2009). Investigating the impact of video games on high school students' engagement and learning about genetics. *Computers & Education, 53*(1), 74–85

Clark, D. B., Nelson, B. C., D'Angelo, C. A., Slack, K., & Martinez-Garza, M. (2010). SURGE: Integrating Vygotsky's spontaneous and instructed concepts in a digital game. *Proceedings of the Ninth International Conference of the Learning Sciences* (vol. 2, pp. 384–385). Chicago, IL: International Society of the Learning Sciences.

Folta, E. (2010). *Investigating the impact on student learning and outdoor science interest through modular serious educational games: A design-based research study* (Doctoral dissertation). Retrieved from North Carolina State University Institutional Repository, http://repository.lib.ncsu.edu/ir/bitstream/1840.16/6136/1/etd.pdf

Hines, P. J., Jasny, B. R., & Merris, J. (2009). Adding a T to the three R's. *Science, 323,* 53.

TECHNOLOGIES SUPPORTING SELF-REGULATED LEARNING

The ubiquity and widespread use of advanced learning technologies (ALTs) poses numerous challenges for learners. Learning with these nonlinear, multirepresentational, open-ended learning environments typically involves the use of a multitude of self-regulatory processes such as planning, reflection, and metacognitive monitoring and regulation. Unfortunately, learners do not always monitor and regulate these processes during learning with ALTs, which limits these environments' effectiveness as educational tools to enhance learning about complex and challenging topics and domains such as science, math, and medicine. This entry provides an overview of ALTs that support self-regulated learning (SRL). It also gives examples of key self-regulatory skills used when learning with ALTs, provides brief examples of four contemporary ALTs that are designed to support SRL, and discusses implications for the future of ALTs and SRL.

Self-regulation comprises a set of key processes that are critical for learning about conceptually rich domains with ALTs such as open-ended hypermedia environments, intelligent tutoring systems, multiagent systems, serious games, and other hybrid systems. Learning with ALTs involves a complex set of interactions between cognitive, affective, metacognitive, and motivational (CAMM) processes. For example, regulating one's learning involves analyzing the learning context, setting and managing meaningful learning goals, selecting which learning strategies to use and when, monitoring whether the use of these strategies is effective in meeting the learning goals, monitoring and making accurate judgments regarding one's emerging understanding of the topic and contextual factors, and determining whether there are aspects of the learning context (e.g., engaging in help seeking by interacting with either a human tutor or an embedded pedagogical agent) that could be used to facilitate learning.

During self-regulated learning, students need to metacognitively monitor and accurately judge whether they understand what they are learning and perhaps modify their plans, goals, strategies, and efforts in relation to dynamically changing contextual conditions. In addition, students must also monitor, modify, and adapt to fluctuations in their motivational and affective states and determine how much social support (if any) may be needed to perform the task. Also, depending on the learning context, instructional goals, perceived task performance, and progress made toward achieving the learning goal(s), they may need to modify certain aspects of their cognition, metacognition, motivation, and affect (e.g., regulate confusion induced by a complex science diagram in a hypermedia system).

Exemplifying the Role of SRL With an Advanced Learning Technology

The complex nature of self-regulatory processes is best exemplified by providing an example of learning with a multiagent, adaptive, hypermedia learning environment such as MetaTutor. In a typical learning session, a student is asked to learn about the human circulatory system for two hours with the system. The environment contains over 40 multimedia pages with hundreds of paragraphs containing thousands of words with corresponding static diagrams. Each of these representations of information is organized in a principled fashion, similar to sections and subsections of book chapters, thus allowing students to navigate freely throughout the environment.

Imagine a self-regulated student who analyzes the learning situation, sets meaningful learning goals, and determines which strategies to use based on the task conditions. The student may also generate motivational beliefs based on prior experience with the topic and learning environment, success with similar tasks, contextual constraints (e.g., provision of adaptive scaffolding and feedback by an artificial pedagogical agent), and contextual demands (e.g., a time limit for completion of the task, finite instructional resources). During the course of learning, the student may monitor and judge whether particular strategies (e.g., summarizing) are effective in meeting his learning subgoals, evaluate his emerging understanding of the topic, determine which pages and diagrams are relevant vis-à-vis a current learning goal, and make the necessary adjustments regarding his knowledge, behavior, effort, affect, and other aspects of the learning context.

Ideally, the self-regulated learner will make adaptive adjustments, based on continuous metacognitive monitoring and control related to the standards for the particular learning task and these adjustments will facilitate decisions about what, when, how, and why to regulate. In addition to cognitive and metacognitive processes and generating motivational beliefs, learners must also monitor and control their motivation and emotions. For example, self-regulating learners need to monitor negative affect such as confusion, frustration, and boredom that may impact learning and performance. Sometime after the learning session and depending on a variety of factors (e.g., the nature and objective of the task, the role of the ALT) the learner may make several cognitive, motivational, and behavioral attributions that affect subsequent learning. This scenario represents an idealistic approach to self-regulating one's learning with an ALT. Unfortunately, there are vast amounts of evidence that empirically demonstrate that the typical learner does not engage in these complex adaptive CAMM processes during learning with ALTs. As such, the educational potential of these environments is severely limited.

Examples of ALTs Designed to Support SRL

This section provides a few examples of recent ALTs that have been designed to support SRL across age groups and domains. The aim is to illustrate how different researchers have conceptualized assumptions and models of SRL in their ALTs. Examples of ALTs designed to support SRL include Roger Azevedo and colleagues' MetaTutor, a multiagent, adaptive hypermedia learning environment; Gautam Biswas and colleagues' Betty's Brain, an agent-based environment for teaching middle school students about ecology; and, James Lester and colleagues' *Crystal Island—Outbreak*, a narrative-based and inquiry-oriented serious game learning environment for science.

MetaTutor is a multiagent, intelligent hypermedia learning environment that presents challenging human biology content. The system is both a *learning tool* designed to foster self-regulation and a *research tool* used to collect trace data on CAMM processes deployed during learning. The system supports several learning strategies including prior knowledge activation, goal setting, evaluation of learning strategies, integration of information across representations, content evaluation, summarization, note taking, and drawing. It also scaffolds specific metacognitive processes, such as judgments of learning, feelings of knowing, content evaluation, and monitoring progress toward goals. The system includes four PAs (pedagogical agents), which guide students and prompt them to engage in planning, monitoring, and strategic learning behaviors. The agents also provide feedback and engage in a tutorial dialogue to scaffold students' selection of appropriate subgoals, accuracy of metacognitive judgments, and use of particular learning strategies. Learners express metacognitive judgments and learning strategies through a palette of actions. For example, they can click a button to indicate they want to make a statement about their understanding of a page and then indicate on a scale that their understanding is poor. They can also indicate that they want to summarize the content of that page and type their summary in a text box. Students are prompted to self-assess their understanding and are then given a brief quiz. Results allow PAs to provide microadaptive feedback according to the calibration between students' confidence of comprehension and their actual quiz performance.

Betty's Brain, an ALT that helps students learn science by constructing causal-concept map models, is based on the learning-by-teaching paradigm, where the system has students take on the role and responsibilities of being the teacher to a virtual student named Betty. Biswas and colleagues provide evidence from classroom studies conducted with elementary school children and discuss the generation of hidden Markov models (HMMs) that capture students' aggregated behavior patterns, which form the basis for analyzing students' metacognitive strategies in the system. They also provide ample evidence on the use of sophisticated computational methods to analyze SRL behaviors. These methods stand to contribute to our existing conceptions and framework of metacognition and SRL and are related to the current work on assessing and modeling metacognitive knowledge and skills.

Crystal Island—Outbreak is a serious game environment developed and tested by Lester and colleagues and presents their extensive research on narrative-centered learning environments that provide engaging, story-centric virtual spaces that afford opportunities for discreetly embedding pedagogical guidance for content knowledge and problem-solving skill acquisition. Students' abilities to self-regulate learning significantly impact performance in these environments and are critical for academic achievement and lifelong learning. Their work explores the relationship between narrative-centered learning environments and self-regulation for science learning and literacy skills. Empirical support from a series of studies with hundreds of middle school students provides evidence that narrative-centered learning environments are particularly well suited for simultaneously promoting learning, engagement, and self-regulation.

Conclusions and Future Directions

To support self-regulated learning, ALTs need to be designed based on sound assumptions, frameworks, models, and theories of self-regulated learning. Emerging theoretical frameworks—that is, externally regulated learning, co-regulated learning, and socially shared regulated learning—also need to be considered. These frameworks are already impacting the use of and research on ALTs. A principled, theoretically based foundation is the key to the design of these systems in order for them to support and foster students' SRL.

Learning Context Issues

Future work in the area of SRL and ALTs needs to address several outstanding issues. First, issues related to the *learning context* need to be clearly described and accounted for by the learner and the ALT. In this category, variables of interest that need to be addressed include the following:

- the constituents of the learning context (e.g., human agents, artificial agents, nature, characteristics, and interdependence of the personal, physical, embodied, and virtual spaces);
- the learning goals (e.g., provision of challenging learning goals, self- or other-generated goals, duration allocated to completing the learning goals);

- the accessibility of instructional resources (e.g., accessibility to these resources to facilitate goal attainment, engaging in help-seeking behavior, and scaffolding while consulting resources);
- dynamic interactions between the learner and other external or in-system regulating agents (e.g., pedagogical agents' roles, levels of interaction, types and timing of scaffolding and feedback, and embodiment of modeling and scaffolding and fading metaphor behaviors); and
- the role of assessment in enhancing performance, learning, understanding, and problem solving (e.g., the type of assessment, the timing of assessment, and whether the assessment tests metacognitive knowledge and regulatory skills, or conditional knowledge for the use of SRL skills).

CAMM SRL Issues

The second set of issues is related to *learners' cognitive, affective, metacognitive, and motivational CAMM SRL knowledge and skills.* There are several issues that need to be addressed, including the following:

- What self-regulatory strategies are students knowledgeable about? How much practice have they had in using them? Are they successful in using them? Do they know they use them successfully?
- How familiar are students with the tasks they are being asked to complete? Are they familiar with the various aspects of the context and learning system they are being asked to use?
- What are students' levels of prior knowledge? How do individual differences impact their knowledge of and use of CAMM SRL processes? What impact will the context and learning system have on a learner's ability to self-regulate?
- Do students have the necessary declarative, procedural, and conditional knowledge essential to regulate their learning? Will the ALT offer opportunities for learning about these complex processes? Will the environment provide opportunities for students to practice and receive feedback about these processes?
- What are students' self-efficacy, interest, task value, and goal orientations, which may influence their ability to self-regulate?
- Are students able to monitor and regulate their emotional states during learning? If they are not able to do so, then should we use artificial agents to train learners to accurately detect, monitor, and regulate emotions as part of the overall learning process? How do we design ALTs that are sensitive to fluctuations in learners' motivational and affective states?

Characteristics of ALTs

The last set of issues that should be addressed in future research is related to the characteristics of ALTs:

- the instructional goals and the structure of the system: for example, using a hypermedia system to acquire a mental model of a science topic, engaging in a tutorial dialogue with an intelligent virtual human to refine a misconception, or using inquiry strategies to understand a particular scientific phenomenon.

- the role of multiple representations: What kinds of external representations are afforded by the ALT? How many types of representations exist? Are they associated with each other (to facilitate integration) or are they embedded in some random fashion (potentially causing extraneous cognitive load)? Are the representations static (e.g., diagram), dynamic (e.g., animation), or both? Are students allowed to construct their own representations? If so, how are they used—for example, by the system or some other external regulating agent to demonstrate to oneself and others (peers, teachers, artificial agents) one's understanding of complex phenomena like genetic code; to assess emerging understanding; to communicate with others (both internal and external to the ALT) such as manipulating an open learner model to indicate to the system that its beliefs about one's metacognitive monitoring are not correct? Or, are the representations just artifacts that may show the evolution of students' understanding, problem solving, learning, and so forth? Or is the purpose for learners to off-load their representations to increase working memory?

- the types of interactivity between the learner and ALT (and other contextually embedded external agents): Are there different levels of learner control? Is the system purely learner controlled and therefore relies on the learner's ability to self-regulate or is the system adaptive in externally regulating and supporting students' self-regulated learning through the use of complex AI algorithms that provide SRL scaffolding and feedback?

- the types of scaffolding: What is the role of externally regulating agents? Do they play different roles (e.g., scaffolding, modeling)? Is their role to monitor or model students' emerging understanding, facilitate knowledge acquisition, provide feedback, or scaffold learning, for example? Do the levels of scaffolding remain constant during learning, fade over time, or fluctuate during learning? When do these agents intervene? How do they demonstrate their interventions (e.g., conversation, gesturing, facial moves, dialogue system)? Lastly, how can we use emerging technologies like augmented reality to enhance learners' ability to understand, acquire, internalize, share, use, and transfer CAMM SRL knowledge, processes, and skills?

In sum, these are just some of the most relevant issues that need to be addressed by interdisciplinary researchers as we consider the future design and use of ALTs for self-regulated learning.

Roger Azevedo, Michelle Taub,
and Nicholas Mudrick

See also Animated Agents in Learning Systems; Avatars and Agents in Virtual Systems; Intelligent Tutoring Systems; Learners and Instructional Control in Adaptive Systems; Self-Regulated E-Learning Design Principles; System and Learner Control in Adaptive Systems; Technologies That Learn and Adapt to Users; Virtual Learning Environments

Further Readings

Azevedo, R., & Aleven, V. (Eds.). (2013). *International handbook of metacognition and learning technologies.* New York, NY: Springer-Verlag.

Azevedo, R., Harley, J., Trevors, G., Feyzi-Behnagh, R., Duffy, M., Bouchet, F., & Landis, R. S. (2013). Using trace data to examine the complex roles of cognitive, metacognitive, and emotional self-regulatory processes during learning with multi-agent systems. In R. Azevedo & V. Aleven (Eds.), *International handbook of metacognition and learning technologies* (pp. 427–449). New York, NY: Springer-Verlag.

Azevedo, R., Moos, D. C., Johnson, A. M., & Chauncey, A. D. (2010). Measuring cognitive and metacognitive regulatory processes used during hypermedia learning: Issues and challenges. *Educational Psychologist, 45*(4), 210–223.

Biswas, G., Leelawong, K., Schwartz, D., & Vye, N. (2005). Learning by teaching: A new agent paradigm for educational software. *Applied Artificial Intelligence, 19,* 363–392.

Graesser, A. C., D'Mello, S. K., & Strain, A. C. (2014). Emotions in advanced learning technologies. In R. Pekrun & L. Linnenbrink-Garcia (Eds.), *Handbook of emotions and education* (pp. 473–493). New York, NY: Taylor & Francis.

Greene, J. A., & Azevedo, R. (2009). A macro-level analysis of SRL processes and their relations to the acquisition of sophisticated mental models. *Contemporary Educational Psychology, 34,* 18–29.

Kinnebrew, J. S., Biswas, G., Sulcer, B., & Taylor, R. S. (2013). Investigating self-regulated learning in teachable agent environments. In R. Azevedo & V. Aleven (Eds.), *International handbook of metacognition and learning technologies* (pp. 451–470). New York, NY: Springer-Verlag.

Lester, J. C., Mott, B. W., Robison, J., Rowe, J., & Shores, L. (2013). Supporting self-regulated science learning in narrative-centered learning environments. In R. Azevedo & V. Aleven (Eds.), *International handbook on metacognition and learning technologies* (pp. 471–483). New York, NY: Springer-Verlag.

White, B., Frederiksen, J., & Collins, A. (2009). The interplay of scientific inquiry and metacognition: More than a marriage of convenience. In D. J. Hacker, J. Dunlosky, & A. C. Graesser (Eds.), *Handbook of metacognition in education* (pp. 175–206). Mahwah, NJ: Lawrence Erlbaum.

Winne, P. H., & Hadwin, A. F. (2008). The weave of motivation and self-regulated learning. In D. H. Schunk & B. J. Zimmerman (Eds.), *Motivation and self-regulated learning: Theory, research, and applications* (pp. 297–314). Mahwah, NJ: Lawrence Erlbaum.

Zimmerman, B. J., & Schunk, D. H. (Eds.). (2011). *Handbook of self-regulation of learning and performance.* New York, NY: Routledge.

Technologies That Learn and Adapt to Users

Adaptability is one of the most important benefits of learning enhanced by computer technologies because it allows for adjusting the learning materials, instructions, feedback, and learning strategies based on learners' needs and ability. The programmability and high-speed computation features of computers enable developed learning systems to take learners' personal factors, such as their knowledge levels, preferences, and learning styles, into consideration while interacting with them. Moreover, during the learning process, the learning system can even analyze system logs to evaluate the learning status of individual users so that personalized guidance or feedback can be provided to them readily. The ultimate goal of such systems and features is a personalized learning environment. This entry discusses the strategies for developing adaptive learning mechanisms and potential research questions on adaptive learning.

There are several strategies for developing adaptive learning mechanisms.

Content adaptation: providing or recommending personalized learning content based on individual learners' personal factors. For example, some researchers have represented learning materials with learning objects, which are small and constructive units of learning content. The learning systems select and compose the learning objects for individual learners based on their up-to-date learning status, which can include knowledge levels, learning progress, or even learning interests.

Interface adaptation: adapting the interface of the learning systems for individual learners. For example, some researchers have tried to provide different forms of user interfaces based on individual learners' learning styles or cognitive styles, which refer to how individuals think, perceive, and process information.

Feedback adaption: providing instant learning guidance or feedback based on the current learning status of individual learners. For example, some learning systems are able to evaluate and diagnose the learning difficulties of individual learners by analyzing their answers to some questions and providing hints or supplementary materials to them.

The advancements in computer and communication technologies in the past decades have significantly influenced the studies of adaptive learning. In particular, the growth and popularity of the Internet have encouraged the development of Web-based adaptive learning systems in which webpages are treated as the basic units for presenting learning contents, and the way of linking pages provides a new form of adaptability. In such webpage-oriented adaptive learning, content adaptation is accomplished by generating personalized webpages based on learners' knowledge levels and learning status (e.g., browsed pages and average browsing time), while interface adaptation is achieved by modifying the layout of the learning content on each webpage. Among various adaptation strategies for Web-based learning, adaptive navigation could be the most commonly adopted. There are several ways of supporting adaptive navigation on the Web, including personalized navigation path recommendation, the provision of personalized link annotations, and personalized link hiding.

The recent popularity of mobile, wireless communication and sensing technologies has further enabled a new opportunity for conducting adaptive learning; that is, the learning system is able to adapt the learning content and learning tasks and provide instant guidance and feedback based on real-world environments in which the learners are located. For example, in a mobile learning activity, the students were guided by the learning system via a mobile device with wireless communication and sensing facilities to observe butterfly ecology. Once the students approached a learning target (e.g., an area where a particular species of butterfly or a specified butterfly food plant is found), the learning system showed the corresponding learning tasks and hints to them. In another study, the learning system could even recommend personalized learning paths in the real world.

Table 1 summarizes the technologies, adaptation strategies, personal factors, and environmental factors for developing adaptive learning systems. The paradigm shifts of computer and information technologies have

Table 1   Technologies, strategies, and personal factors of adaptation

Waves of Technology Advancement	Adaptation Strategies	Personal Factors
Wave I: Personal Computer	Content adaptation (by representing learning materials with constructive objects) Interface adaptation Feedback adaptation	Profiles Preferences Learning portfolios
Wave II: The Internet/Web	Content adaptation (by generating personalized webpages) Interface adaptation (by modifying the layout of Web content) Feedback adaptation Adaptive navigation (by modifying the links between webpages)	Profiles Preferences Learning portfolios RSS feeds Social media Subscriptions and memberships
Wave III: Mobile Technology	Contextual adaptation (by adapting the learning content and tasks based on real-world contexts) Interface adaptation Feedback adaptation Learning path adaptation (by providing real-world learning path recommendations)	Profiles Preferences Learning portfolios Real-world contexts

brought adaptive learning from computer-assisted learning to Web-based learning and contextual learning.

It can be foreseen that with the help of those new technologies, richer information related to individual learners can be considered, and more effective adaptive learning systems can be developed. In addition, it is expected that, in the near future, the following research issues of adaptive learning will be investigated:

- the effects and interactions of adopting multiple personalization factors (e.g., knowledge levels, learning interest, and learning styles) on learners' performance and perceptions;
- the impacts of incorporating adaptive learning strategies into emerging e-learning systems, such as digital game-based learning systems, virtual learning environments, mobile and ubiquitous learning systems, and augmented reality-based learning systems; and
- the development of innovative adaptive learning systems by utilizing new factors, such as eye-tracking messages, brain waves, real-world behaviors, and emotional information.

Nian-Shing Chen and Gwo-Jen Hwang

See also E-Portfolio Technologies; Learners and Instructional Control in Adaptive Systems; Learning Analytics; Personal Learning Environments; Personalized Learning and Instruction

Further Readings

Chiou, C.-K., Tseng, J. C. R., Hwang, G.-J., & Heller, S. (2010). An adaptive navigation support system for conducting context-aware ubiquitous learning in museums. *Computers & Education, 55*(2), 834–845. doi:10.1016/j.compedu.2010.03.015

Chu, H.-C., Hwang, G.-J., & Tsai, C.-C. (2010). A knowledge engineering approach to developing Mindtools for context-aware ubiquitous learning. *Computers & Education, 54*(1), 289–297. doi:10.1016/j.compedu.2009.08.023

Graf, S., Liu, T.-C., & Kinshuk. (2010). Analysis of learners' navigational behaviour and their learning styles in an online course. *Journal of Computer Assisted Learning, 26*(2), 116–131. doi:10.1111/j.1365-2729.2009.00336.x

Hwang, G.-J., Sung, H.-Y., Hung, C.-M., Huang, I., & Tsai, C.-C. (2012). Development of a personalized educational computer game based on students' learning styles. *Educational Technology Research & Development, 60*(4), 623–638. doi:10.1007/s11423-012-9241-x

Mampadi, F., Chen, S. Y. H., Ghinea, G., & Chen, M. P. (2011). Design of adaptive hypermedia learning systems: A cognitive style approach. *Computers & Education, 56*(4), 1003–1011. doi:10.1016/j.compedu.2010.11.018

Reategui, E., Boff, E., & Campbell, J. A. (2008). Personalization in an interactive learning environment through a virtual character. *Computers & Education, 51*(2), 530–544. doi:10.1016/j.compedu.2007.05.018

Romero, C., Ventura, S., Zafra, A., & de Bra, P. (2009). Applying Web usage mining for personalizing hyperlinks in Web-based adaptive educational systems. *Computers & Education, 53*(3), 828–840. doi:10.1016/j.compedu.2009.05.003

Tseng, S.-S., Su, J.-M., Hwang, G.-J., Hwang, G.-H., Tsai, C.-C., & Tsai, C.-J. (2008). An object-oriented course framework for developing adaptive learning systems. *Educational Technology & Society, 11*(2), 171–191.

Technologies to Enhance Communication for Persons With Autism Spectrum Disorder

The *Diagnostic and Statistical Manual of Mental Disorders,* 5th edition, categorizes the challenges faced by individuals with autism spectrum disorders (ASD) as focusing on two domains: (1) impaired social communication and interaction and (2) restricted, repetitive behaviors and fixed interests. Such challenges have far-reaching implications for the ways that individuals with ASD interact within their social, educational, professional, and personal environments. Additionally, people with ASD have been considered to have difficulties with executive functioning, or the organizational aspects of cognition. Such challenges may mean that areas such as problem solving, planning, and working memory are negatively affected in people with ASD. The possibilities afforded by emerging advance technologies and social media provide a crucial tool in the living and sharing of experiences and understandings of people with ASD that would not have been possible previously. Similarly, technology may provide a mechanism through which to manage some of the challenges posed by differences in executive functioning. Technology can therefore potentially act as both a mediator of communication and a tool for intervention and strategies to promote the development of self-management.

Mobile and Tablet Devices

While utilizing technology as a learning tool is not new, technological advances in mobile devices, particularly tablets, have opened up new possibilities to address pertinent communication challenges and barriers faced by children with ASD, particularly those who are nonverbal. Capitalizing on their sensitivity to visual stimuli, various forms of augmentative and alternative communication (AAC) that use visual cues and picture cards, such as Picture Exchange Communication System (PECS), are frequently used to teach and assist individuals with ASD who have little or no speech to communicate and express their needs. More advanced technological features of mobile and tablet devices, including touch screens, microphones, and camera capabilities, allow for more creative and personalized exploration of AAC and educational tools for children with ASD. Research carried out by Elizabeth Lorah and colleagues have indicated that a high percentage of children with ASD demonstrate a preference for tablet-based AAC compared to low-tech picture exchange and traditional PECS. Mobile and tablet devices have also been found to be comparable substitutes for speech-generating devices (SGDs), which are generally bulky and very expensive. Others found that the use of tablets such as iPads increased the pretend-play dialogue utterances of children with autism while they were engaged in play. The use of tablets was shown to decrease challenging behavior and to increase the level of academic engagement among children with autism.

Social Media and Other Community Sites

Social media and community sites can act as platforms to enhance an individual's personal and professional relationships. Two of the sites that are especially valuable for persons with ASD are Facebook and YouTube.

Facebook

Facebook is a social media tool that enables users to connect in an online space. Users can develop friendship networks by requesting and accepting "friends." Research suggests several benefits of this management of social relationships, particularly for people with ASD. Such online communication draws on alternative communication styles in the development and maintenance of friends and acquaintances, ones that do not require the deciphering of nonverbal communicative exchanges.

Facebook provides an opportunity for making and maintaining friendships in ways that can be supportive for people with ASD. Eric Chen, an ASD advocate, reports that because social networking sites such as Facebook often include photographs as well as names of users, these sites make it easier to recall names and serve as tools to overcome challenges of name and face recognition—skills that draw on effective executive functioning. Chen also suggests that social networking sites facilitate social communicative exchanges because the text record of online exchanges enables users to plan for and engage in social activities more effectively. Such possibilities suggest that meaningful alternative friendships may develop and be managed within the applications of new technologies.

YouTube

YouTube is both a media repository and a mechanism for social networking. As such, it presents a unique opportunity for self-presentation and self-expression online. Video blogs can be created by individuals and distributed within a host site that attracts millions of viewers. Dana Rotman and Jennifer Preece argue that a key characteristic of the YouTube online community is that of face-to-face mediated interaction, and it is this visual self-presentation and visual viewing of others that is key in differentiating this media from more textual online communities. People with ASD have been shown to capitalize on this unique medium in broadcasting the image and representation of themselves that they want to portray. The number of video blogs posted by people with ASD demonstrates their embrace of YouTube as a communication tool, as does the creation of YouTube channels by individuals with ASD. Such representations therefore have important impacts on the understandings concerning the capabilities of people with ASD and the wider autistic advocacy movement.

In addition to providing possibilities for self-broadcast, YouTube is also an important tool for social networking. One of the key challenges faced by people with ASD is that of social communication. By removing the face-to-face complexities associated with relationships between individuals, YouTube can play a key role in the development of communities. Such communities can serve to provide support and guidance for individuals.

Online Tools in the Workplace

Reasonable connectivity coupled with opportunities for telework may mean the negotiation of work places is a more manageable enterprise for some people with ASD. Such technological developments enable both the connectivity of people socially as described above, and also the sharing of professional expertise demonstrated by tools such as Stack Overflow.

Stack Overflow

Stack Overflow is a question and answer community site aimed at IT professionals. Users can post programming problems for which members of the community suggest solutions. What makes Stack Overflow unique is that participants within the community can build their reputation and status by being active members within the community. What makes Stack Overflow unique is that all of this is managed online; such a tool, therefore, has far-reaching implications for work-based exchanges and collegial relationships for workers with ASD, who may find more traditional face-to-face exchanges difficult.

Interactive Virtual Technologies With Multiple Sensory Inputs

Proponents of play in children clearly point out how imaginative, symbolic, and creative play is important and crucial for the development of children. While the tendency to play is innate for typical children, children with ASD may struggle with imaginative and symbolic play. The efforts to integrate and synergize creative play with interactive virtual technologies (i.e., multitouch systems, multiple sensory inputs such as Wii game console, Kinect, interactive whiteboard) have brought forth exhilarating possibilities for the ASD community. Others have created educational games on multitouch tabletops to support development of social skills as well as collaborative interaction among children with ASD. Anne Marie Piper and colleagues pioneered and developed a project called SIDES (Shared Interfaces to Develop Effective Social Skills), a cooperative tabletop game that focuses on teaching children with ASD who are high functioning to negotiate, take turns, listen actively, and develop perspective-taking skills. It was found that the games built confidence in the participants while providing an engaging experience for them. Multitouch tabletops have also been shown to be useful with young children with ASD (5–8 year olds). Utilizing multiple inputs including touch and voice, the Trollskogen project developed by Ru Zarin and Daniel Fallman provides a range of applications to improve and strengthen various aspects of communication skills in young children. These include using fingers to paint stories on the table, moving virtual pictograms and symbols on the table to form sentences, and encouraging voice input via a microphone to help children improve speech-related skills.

Conclusion

The technologies discussed above indicate just a few examples of the potentials afforded by technology for people with ASD. The impacts of such technologies are far reaching, impacting the cognitive, social, and educational world of individuals with ASD, and additionally the world of work for some adults with ASD.

Helena Song and Charlotte Brownlow

See also Assistive Technology for Persons With Autism Spectrum Disorder; Collaboration and Social Networking; Mobile Assistive Technologies; Repositories for Learning and Instructional Apps; Social Media in Elementary School Settings; Tablet Devices in Education and Training

Further Readings

American Psychiatric Association. (2013). *Diagnostic and statistical manual of mental disorders* (5th ed.). Washington, DC: Author.

Chen, E. (n.d.). *Using Facebook for aspies*. Retrieved from http://iautistic.com/autistic-facebook-autism.php

Lorah, E. R., Tincani, M., Dodge, J., Gilroy, S., Hickey, A., & Hantula, D. (2013). Evaluating picture exchange and the iPad as a speech generating device to teach communication to young children with autism. *Journal of Developmental and Physical Disabilities 25*, 637–649.

Piper, A. M., O'Brien, E., Morris, M. R., & Winograd, T. (2006). SIDES: A cooperative tabletop computer game for social skills development. In *Proceedings of the 2006th Conference on Computer Supported Cooperative Work* (pp. 1–10). Retrieved from http://graphics.stanford.edu/~merrie/papers/sides_cscw.pdf

Rotman, D., & Preece, J. (2010). The "WeTube" in YouTube: Creating an online community through video sharing. *International Journal of Web Based Communities, 6*(3), 317–333.

van der Meer, L., Kagohara, D. M., Achmadi, D., O'Reilly, M. F., Lancioni, G. E., Sutherland, D., & Sigafoos, J. (2012). Speech-generating devices versus manual signing for children with developmental disabilities. *Research in Developmental Disabilities, 33*, 1658–1669.

Zarin, R., & Fallman, D. (2011). Through the troll forest: Exploring tabletop interaction design for children with special cognitive needs. In *Conference on Human Factors in Computing Systems (CHI 2011)* (pp. 3319–3322). New York, NY: Association for Computing Machinery.

TECHNOLOGIES TO SUPPORT ENGINEERING EDUCATION

This entry describes technologies that support engineering education, such as 3D printing, computer-assisted design, electromechanical systems and instrumentation, and control systems. Engineering education is one of four disciplines within STEM (science, technology, engineering, and mathematics) education. While science and mathematics are commonly regarded as core subjects in schools, engineering has had a less prominent role in K–12 education. However, engineering is increasingly used to teach science in context. This can increase students' depth of understanding, allowing them to apply scientific knowledge to real-world contexts while providing them with useful workforce skills.

Engineering education involves construction and testing of physical products. Advances in rapid prototyping have facilitated this hands-on approach to engineering education. In industry, rapid prototyping involves use of manufacturing technologies that allow a model or prototype to be quickly developed. Advanced manufacturing technologies such as 3D printing are accelerating the design process. These technologies are now becoming affordable, allowing them to be employed for engineering education in schools. Some of these technologies are shown in Table 1.

Rapid prototyping can involve disparate disciplines such as digital fabrication (which draws upon the discipline of mechanical engineering), electromechanical systems and instrumentation (which draws upon electrical engineering, among other disciplines), and control systems (which draw upon computer science and computer engineering). A new engineering discipline, *mechatronics*, encompasses all of these disciplines. This entry discusses

Table 1 Representative educational technologies in selected engineering fields

Engineering Discipline	Engineering Technology	Undergraduate Engineering	K–12 Engineering Education
Digital fabrication (mechanical engineering)	Additive fabrication	Industrial 3D printer	Desktop 3D printer
	Subtractive fabrication	Laser cutter	Computer-controlled die cutter
	Subtractive fabrication	Industrial CNC machine	Desktop CNC machine
	CAD software	SolidWorks / AutoCAD Inventor	Autodesk 123D Design
Electromechanical systems and instrumentation (electrical engineering)	Sensors	Industrial sensors	Vernier / PASCO science sensors
	Actuators	Motors and solenoids	SparkFun Inventor's Kit
	A/D and D/A conversion	myDAQ	PicoBoard / LEGO Mindstorms
Control (computer science)	Control software	LabVIEW	LabVIEW for Mindstorms / Scratch
	Processor	Propeller microprocessor	Arduino

tools now available in all of these disciplines that can be used in instruction in K–12 education as well as undergraduate courses.

Digital Fabrication (Mechanical Engineering)

Digital fabrication can encompass a series of manufacturing tools that can include (a) additive manufacturing tools such as 3D printers and (b) subtractive manufacturing tools such as laser cutters and computer-controlled milling machines known as CNC (computer-numerical control) systems. Many of these tools now have consumer counterparts that make them more accessible.

Additive Manufacturing

Several dozen manufacturers now offer desktop 3D printers for prices approaching a thousand dollars, considerably less than their industrial counterparts. This emerging market is leading to more affordable tools for engineering education programs. While various 3D printing technologies exist, most relatively affordable desktop 3D printers employ a similar method. A filament of plastic is drawn from a spool into a heated nozzle. As the plastic melts and is extruded through the nozzle, a computer program moves the nozzle to deposit drops of plastic at precisely specified locations. The 3D printer builds a shape layer by layer through this process. In addition to a lower initial cost, the filament used by desktop 3D printers is less than the cost of the filament used by their industrial counterparts.

Other 3D printing technologies will become available in educational settings in the future. For example, a process that uses a laser to solidify a thin layer within a tank of liquid resin, offering higher resolution than filament extrusion, may become increasingly affordable.

Figure 1 A student and his mentor design a 3D-printed catapult

Source: Nigel Standish.

Subtractive Manufacturing

Other manufacturing technologies subtract rather than add material. For example, a laser cutter can cut precisely guided shapes in plastic or wood creating objects in the same manner that a cookie cutter cuts out shapes in a layer of dough. Laser cutters can quickly cut out a gear in plastic or wood for an engineering class but are expensive industrial machines that require supervision for safe operation. Computer-controlled die cutters are the educational counterpart of laser cutters. These tools cut shapes out of card stock, and cost less than $300 each. Many of the operations of a laser cutter can be simulated with a computer-controlled die cutter.

Computer-controlled milling machines, known as CNC (computer numerical control) machines, can mill 3D objects out of metal. The consumer counterpart can perform similar operations on a smaller scale using materials such as soft wood or foam.

Computer-Assisted Design

Regardless of the production manner, objects are created with computer-assisted design (CAD) programs that allow a shape to be drawn, or by scanning (i.e., digitizing) an existing physical object. The file can then be sent to the 3D printer in a manner similar to the way that a word-processed document is sent to a 2D printer. SolidWorks and AutoCAD Inventor are among the CAD programs used in industry; both have educational licensing discounts for students. In addition, the growth of desktop 3D printers has resulted in a number of CAD programs for novices, such as Autodesk 123D Design.

Industrial CAD applications can be adapted for use as learning tools. Increasingly intelligent CAD tools can suggest solutions that can support and scaffold student learning. Some CAD tools are being designed to support education. Energy3D is an example of a specialized CAD tool developed for engineering design learning. The 3D user interface allows students to design buildings on the computer that can be fabricated and evaluated for energy efficiency. FabLab ModelMaker is another program designed for educational environments. This program allows students to quickly design a prototype using a computer-controlled die cutter before committing to the final production with a 3D printer.

Electronic Mechanical Systems and Instrumentation (Electrical Engineering)

An array of related disciplines is required to unlock the full potential of a 3D printer. When objects with moving parts are combined with microcontrollers, stepper motors, actuators, sensors, and controls, advanced manufacturing projects can be developed.

Educational tools such as the National Instruments myDAQ provide students with an analog-to-digital (A/D) interface to convert analog signals from a sensor to a digital signal read by the computer and a digital-to-analog (D/A) converter to control motors and actuators that can act on sensory input. Inexpensive A/D and D/A electronic boards allow young students access to these tools. For example, the PicoBoard, developed in the Massachusetts Institute of Technology (MIT) Media Laboratory, provides A/D inputs for collection of data generated by sensors (light, sound, temperature, etc.) at a price of less than $50. Educational communities have also formed around the Arduino microcomputer and other inexpensive computing platforms such as the Raspberry Pi. Sites such as SparkFun have been established to provide support with ancillary A/D and D/A controllers.

Control Systems (Computer Engineering)

Digital hardware requires a programming environment. A number of environments have been developed to provide scaffolding for programming, and several of these can be used to access hardware. The origins of these environments can be dated to the development of the computer language Logo, a variant of the computer programming language LISP (list processing), developed at Bolt, Beranek, and Newman and subsequently popularized by Seymour Papert. One of Papert's contributions involved interactions with real-world objects, supporting creation of scripts that could be used to control an educational robot known as a turtle for its hemispherical shape. Close collaboration with the LEGO company led to LEGO TC Logo, allowing Logo scripts to control user-built LEGO creations with motors and sensors.

Scratch, developed in the MIT Media Lab, is a modern-day descendent of Logo. It uses code blocks to create scripts by dragging blocks of code into the script. Hardware interfaces, such as the PicoBoard, have been engineered to work with some versions of Scratch, allowing students to experience real-world control.

The Laboratory Virtual Instrument Engineering Workbench (LabVIEW) is representative of an educational interface designed for data acquisition, instrument control, and industrial automation. Block diagrams can be used to build virtual representations of equipment and program them. The LEGO Mindstorms educational environment can be controlled by a simplified version of LabVIEW. Conceptually, LEGO Mindstorms is influenced by earlier work with Logo and Scratch. However, LabVIEW is used in real-world industrial automation processes, providing more direct alignment between engineering education and industrial engineering. Later versions of LEGO Mindstorms software and hardware (NXT and EV3) combine the data acquisition features of LabVIEW (including real time data logging and an oscilloscope mode) with the computer-control programming of robots built with LEGO intelligent motors and sensors and the EV3 Intelligent Brick.

Conclusion

Advances in emergent technologies make rapid prototyping increasingly feasible in both undergraduate engineering courses and in K–12 schools. Consumer counterparts of these industrial technologies can be used to teach K–12 subjects in the context of engineering design, illustrating practical applications of theoretical knowledge, while simultaneously providing students with workforce development skills.

Glen Bull and Joe Garofalo

See also Emerging Educational Technologies; Internet of Things; 3D Printing and Prototyping; Twenty-First-Century Technology Skills

Further Readings

Anderson, C. (2012). *Makers: The new industrial revolution.* New York, NY: Random House.

Bull, G., Chiu, J. L., Berry, R. Q., & Lipson, H. (2013). Advancing children's engineering through desktop manufacturing. In J. M. Spector, M. D. Merrill, J. Elen, & M. J. Bishop (Eds.), *Handbook of research on educational communications and technology* (4th ed., chap. 54). New York, NY: Springer-Verlag.

Clough, G. Wayne (chair). (2005). *Educating the engineer of 2020: Adapting engineering education to the new century.* Washington, DC: National Academies Press.

Gershenfeld, N. A. (2005). *Fab—The coming revolution on your desktop—From personal computer to personal fabrication.* New York, NY: Basic Books.

Lipson, H., & Kurman, M. (2013). *Fabricated: The new world of 3D printing.* Indianapolis, IN: Wiley.

Papert, S. (1980). *Mindstorms: Children, computers, and powerful ideas.* New York, NY: Basic Books.

Quinn, H., Schweingruber, H., & Keller, T. (Eds.). (2011). *A framework for K–12 science education: Practices, crosscutting concepts, and core ideas.* Washington, DC: National Academies Press.

Websites

Energy3D: http://energy.concord.org/energy3d/
FabLab ModelMaker: http://www.aspexsoftware.com/educationalsoftware/fablab.htm
Make to Learn: http://maketolearn.org/explore/

TECHNOLOGY, PEDAGOGY, AND THE LEARNING SOCIETY

Lifelong learning plays a key role in continuous personal and professional development. Digital technologies facilitate such learning and can be used to bridge science and practice. Because information and communication technologies (ICTs) are such important tools for learning and knowledge creation through innovation, it is important for learners to have skills that enable them to use these technologies. Personal and professional development can be improved and transformed through the use of ICT and, in particular, can make significant contributions to lifelong learning in the digital age. This entry first examines characteristics of the new learning society that is evolving as a result of digital technology. It then describes ways in which this technology has allowed for new forms of knowledge creation and is changing the nature of pedagogy. It concludes with a look at the framework of authentic learning, with the goals of enabling, engaging, and empowering, and suggests that the continued evolution of such learning will require a flexible and visionary perspective on applications of digital technology to teaching and learning.

The Learning Society

Digital technology is now a primary source of knowledge construction and learning at both the individual and collaborative levels, and it provides a powerful foundation for lifelong learning. The integration of digital technology and the services that it provides helps achieve such lifelong learning imperatives as social inclusion and self-sustainability, all of which contribute to ongoing learning in a wide range of broader areas related to knowledge, practical action, collaboration, coexistence, adaptability, innovation, and creativity. Digital technology thus underpins what might be referred to as a *learning society*.

Productivity, both for individuals and society more broadly, requires that learning be both individualized and collaborative. The use of ICTs has made possible an adaptive and eclectic pedagogy. The relevance of the available technologies and associated services lies in their power to connect learners and enhance social inclusion and adaptability in a fast-changing environment. ICTs also promote metacognition that allows learners to reflect on the cognitive process and to identify new strategies for gaining knowledge.

The diversified applications of the emerging technologies in the teaching and learning context have an impact on three significant components for success in

real life: productivity in learning, skills development, and socialization. Productivity in learning, skills development, and socialization can be nurtured by the use of ICTs and are important elements in continuous development.

As individuals adapt to the digital age, emerging technologies reshape both their roles and responsibilities as digital citizens, their relationship to others and to society generally, and their capacity to contribute productively to society as individuals and as members of informal and formal organizations. There is now an intensified need to clarify the roles of the modern digital citizen and define the necessary skills to be acquired from early childhood through full maturity. Key to this is the definition of what we mean by digital literacy in an educational context, in terms of such issues as computer basics, security, privacy, user-generated contact, and the entire notion of what might be termed *digital lifestyles*, along with the more traditional concepts of discourse, collaboration, and metacognition. All these aspects need to be considered and then included in the learning process with the use of technology supported by the appropriate pedagogies.

Pedagogy

Adapting to this new digital age requires a consideration of many factors, not least of which are the issues of social integration and self-esteem. Both individual and institutional development need to be based not only on adaptation to the new medium, but also on the use of the new medium as a tool for adaptation itself. The Web is key to sharing, exchanging, and constructing knowledge. Interactivity for collaboration is needed, along with team-based and community-based engagement, and can be driven by technology. In this respect, the notion of *tech-variety* for motivating learners increases social integration and self-esteem in the digital age. It would seem, therefore, that technology is at the heart of continuous development in the modern age and a key driver of the construction of knowledge and social integration for the learning community.

The control of content has been decentralized to allow everyone to collaborate, create, publish, and share information. Establishing networks plays a significant role in the learning and teaching process. Learning becomes the result of connected, shared information of learners. In addition, knowledge creation relies on connected learners' experiences and backgrounds. Social networks and Web 2.0 and Web 3.0 applications are concrete examples of how people are socialized through technology and provide examples also of how we can create learning platforms for professional improvement.

Web 2.0 uses social media and other tools including wikis, blogs, video/image sharing sites, multiplayer video games, and texting applications (apps) that enable information sharing, social communication, and collaboration. Web 3.0, also known as the Semantic Web, extends the possibilities for collaboration and shared knowledge creation. Treating the Internet as a giant database, Web 3.0 will be able to gather and analyze data in response to user queries, taking into account user characteristics and the context of the query.

As today's technologies are used for continuous development, they are changing the fundamental character of pedagogy through such innovations as electronic classrooms, flipped classrooms, course management systems, cloud learning, and e-books within different learning platforms. The application of mobile learning opens up rich ways of learning and teaching that enhance differentiated learning that takes into account the diverse needs of individual learners.

Peer learning has a major role to play in facilitating the ongoing development and learning that will contribute to the development of the skills and knowledge needed for the learning society. As emerging technologies take root, the relationships between individualized learning on the one hand and peer learning and group learning on the other are becoming more dynamic, in tandem with the increasingly facilitative role of the tools available. Digital storytelling allows learners to share knowledge and to reflect their understandings as they gain information and construct knowledge both individually and collectively.

The Three Es and Authentic Learning

In the digital age, a key issue is whether and how students are leveraging emerging technologies for learning through the three Es—enabling, engaging, and empowering. Taking into account possible approaches to this, such as mobile learning, online and blended learning, and e-textbooks, it becomes crucial to understand how emerging technologies can adopt and adapt these three Es of education and to what extent they fulfill their objectives. Of particular significance in this era is the use of mobile learning to increase the effectiveness of the learning process. Mobile learning devices, such as cell phones, smartphones, laptops, MP3 players, and tablets, all have vast potential to foster further engagement in the learning process.

Online and blended learning provide a natural forum for collaboration and sharing ideas. They have a number of specific benefits such as scheduling, control of learning, working at one's own pace, and ease of reviewing and sharing classroom materials that can enrich

both learning and socialization as well as supporting more personalized learning. Blended learning allows students to participate in a traditional school environment and also follow classes through an online mode. Course management systems help both students and teachers make the transition from the virtual learning world to discussions and further work in the physical classroom. Differentiated learning requires programs and tools to present materials in a creative way at a more individualized level.

There is an intensified need to internalize media and information literacy skills. 3D content and e-textbooks also facilitate further learning opportunities by providing real-life context and allowing learners to understand the world outside the classroom. Technology is also a cognitive tool within the framework of authentic learning. Although authentic learning is not new, the value of authentic activity supported by emerging technologies needs to be addressed.

Within the authentic learning framework, successful and stable learning needs to be achieved through collaboration, discussion, project-based activities, grappling with problems, and engaging in higher order thinking to solve these problems. In the digital age, new learning is accompanied by new ways of learning, and the emerging technologies are an ideal platform for realizing the goals of enabling, engaging, and empowering.

Simulations, digital gaming, and social networking technologies all increase opportunities for learning, collaboration, and knowledge sharing, which in turn promote skills development and socialization. Global trends such as mobile and cloud learning, adaptive learning, asynchronous learning, blended learning, course management systems, differentiated learning, digital storytelling, e-books, e-learning, flipped classrooms, electronic classrooms, gamification, massive open online courses, and virtual learning are all aspects of alternative learning environments in the digital age. It thus seems clear that there cannot be one solution to pedagogical issues; rather, an eclectic approach, integrating multiple technologies and tools, is the best option to foster learning, skills development, and socialization.

Looking more closely at some of these tools, adaptive learning engages software that can be managed according to students' learning needs; in asynchronous learning, students can participate at any time of day and from any place using online resources. Web-based learning environments (e-learning) allow interaction between learners and tutors, and through the electronic classroom, multimedia devices further enhance learning. In flipped classrooms, students watch videos or use other instructional materials at home, then discuss them in class. Digital games and gamification provide alternative learning and socialization opportunities. Extensive open online courses provide another possible solution to enhance personal and professional development processes for learners of all ages. Synchronous learning is based on a real-time learning environment and situation where two-way communication and interaction occur. The virtual learning environment can further support exams and assignments; mobile and cloud learning are presenting still more additional learning opportunities. It should be clear, therefore, that there is a vital need to choose from, use, and merge as appropriate the large number of alternative tools available for fostering learning, skills development, and professional learning in the digital age.

Therefore, both policy makers and teachers need to develop an eclectic paradigm that not only integrates new pedagogies with emerging technologies in educational settings but also adopts a visionary approach to doing so in order to develop those settings into adaptive, authentic, and interactive environments.

Zehra Altınay and Fahriye Altınay

See also Activity Theory; Collaboration and Social Networking; Collaborative Communication Tools and Technologies; Technology Integration

Further Readings

Atwell, G., & Hughes, J. (2010). *Pedagogic approaches to using technology for learning; literature review.* Life Long Learning UK. Retrieved from http://webarchive.nationalarchives.gov .uk/20110414152025/http://www.lluk.org/wp-content/ uploads/2011/01/Pedagogical-appraches-for-using-technology-literature-review-january-11-FINAL.pdf

Benseman, J. (2006). Moving towards lifelong learning in rural New Zealand: A study of two towns. *Journal of Research in Rural Education, 21*(4), 1–11.

Bozalek, V. (2011). An investigation into the use of emerging technologies to transform teaching and learning across differently positioned higher education institutions in South Africa. In *Changing demands, changing directions: Proceedings ascilite 2011 Hobart* (pp. 156–161). Retrieved from http://www.academia.edu/2717914/An_investigation_ into_the_use_of_emerging_technologies_to_transform_ teaching_and_learning_across_differently_positioned_higher_ education_institutions_in_South_Africa_2

George, V. (2010). *Emerging technologies in distance education.* Edmonton, AB, Canada: Athabasca University Press.

Godwin-Jones, R. (2011). Emerging technologies: Mobile apps for language learning. *Language Learning and Technology, 15*(2), 4–11.

Motteram, G. (Ed.). (2013). *Innovations in learning technologies for English language teaching.* London, UK: British Council.

O'Grady, A., & Atkin, C. (2006). Choosing to learn or chosen to learn: The experience of skills for life learners. *Research in Post-Compulsory Education, 11*(3), 277–287. doi:10.1080/13596740600916484.

van Weert, T. J. (Ed.). (2010). *Education and the knowledge society: Information technology supporting human development.* New York, NY: Kluwer Academic.

Technology and Information Literacy

Technology and information literacy refers to literacy that utilizes an individual's ability to use technology to identify, access, organize, manage, integrate, evaluate, create, and communicate information. The term *technology and information literacy* can be defined as a hybrid between technology literacy and information literacy.

Technology Literacy

Technology literacy can be defined as the ability of an individual, working both independently and with others, to responsibly, appropriately, and effectively use technology tools to access, manage, integrate, evaluate, create, and communicate information.

The Importance of Technology Literacy

Humans thrive in a technological world. The use of the terms *Bronze Age, Iron Age, Industrial Revolution,* and *Information Age* to designate major periods in history highlights the importance of technology to culture. Technology is ubiquitous and affects most parts of our lives. Technology allows individuals to perform their daily tasks and supports their ability to make informed decisions. With this in mind, digital citizens must have a clear basic understanding of how technology impacts the world in which they exist. No longer can individuals merely acquire technological literacy naturally through their everyday routines. Technology literacy has become a driving factor and key piece of curricula in education. As recognized by organizations such as the National Academy of Engineering, the National Research Council, and the International Technology Education Association in the United States and similar organizations in other countries, technological literacy is essential for all people living in the increasingly technology-driven world.

Characteristics of a Technologically Literate Individual

Experts in technology, engineering, and science have attempted to define the characteristics of a technologically literate individual. The three broad categories for characteristics are

1. Knowledge,

2. Ways of thinking and acting, and

3. Capabilities.

Knowledge

Technologically literate individuals understand that technology involves systems (groups of interrelated components) designed to collectively achieve a desired goal. Technologically literate individuals understand that technology involves more than easy access to facts and information; it requires the ability to interpret and synthesize facts and information.

Technologically literate persons recognize the pervasiveness of technology in everyday life, its risks, and benefits. They are familiar with the core concepts and scope of technology. Technologically literate persons understand that technology reflects the values and culture of society and that technology is the result of human activity or innovation. Technologically literate persons understand that technology results in both planned and unplanned consequences, acknowledge that solutions often involve tradeoffs, and may accept less of one quality in order to gain more of another quality.

Ways of Thinking and Acting

Technologically literate persons are problem solvers who consider technological issues from different points of view and relate them to a variety of contexts and ask pertinent questions of themselves and others regarding the benefits and risks of technology. Technologically literate persons appreciate the interrelationships between technology and individuals, society, and the environment.

Capabilities

Technologically literate persons incorporate various capabilities and behaviors found in engineers, artists, designers, crafts persons, technicians, sociologists, and others that are interwoven and act synergistically (e.g., design, collaboration, evaluation). Technologically literate persons understand and appreciate the importance of fundamental technological developments.

Information Literacy

Information literacy can be defined as the ability to identify what information is needed, understand how the information is organized, identify the best sources of information for a given need, locate those sources, evaluate the sources critically, and share that information. It is the knowledge of commonly used research techniques.

The Importance of Information Literacy

Information literacy is critically important because everyday life involves a growing overabundance of information, most recently via the Internet. Some information is authoritative, current, and reliable, while other information is biased, out of date, or even misleading and false. Ways of gathering, using, and manipulating information will continue to expand. Information literacy skills may be used for academic purposes, such as research papers and group presentations, or these skills may be used on the job, to find, evaluate, use, and share information. In addition, information literacy skills play a role in important consumer decisions, such as buying a home or choosing a doctor.

Characteristics of an Information Literate Individual

Organizations such as the American Association for Higher Education and the Council of Independent Colleges in the United States and similar organizations in other countries have endorsed characteristics (standards) of the information literate individual. The information literate person

- determines the nature and extent of information needed;
- accesses the information effectively and efficiently;
- evaluates information and its sources and incorporates the information into his or her knowledge base and value system;
- uses information effectively; and
- understands the economic, legal, and social issues surrounding the ethical and legal use of information.

The Big6 Model

An information literacy model that has gained prominence is the Big6 Model. This six-stage information literacy model is used to solve problems and make decisions by

1. Identifying information research goals (task definition),

2. Seeking information (information seeking strategies),

3. Locating and accessing information (location and access),

4. Using information (use of information),

5. Assembling relevant, credible information (synthesis), and

6. Reflecting (evaluation).

One final conception of information literacy, rooted in library instruction and directed at lifelong learning, is illustrated by the elements identified by the American

Association of School Librarians (AASL) and the Association for Educational Communications and Technology (AECT). They identify three categories (information literacy, independent learning, social responsibility), nine standards, and 29 performance indicators that describe the information literate student. The categories and standards are the following:

Information Literacy

1. The student who is information literate accesses information efficiently and effectively.

2. The student who is information literate evaluates information critically and competently.

3. The student who is information literate uses information accurately and creatively.

Independent Learning

1. The student who is an independent learner is information literate and pursues information related to personal interests.

2. The student who is an independent learner is information literate and appreciates literature and other creative expressions of information.

3. The student who is an independent learner is information literate and strives for excellence in information seeking and knowledge generation.

Social Responsibility

1. The student who contributes positively to the learning community and to society is information literate and recognizes the importance of information to a democratic society.

2. The student who contributes positively to the learning community and to society is information literate and practices ethical behavior in regard to information and information technology.

3. The student who contributes positively to the learning community and to society is information literate and participates effectively in groups to pursue and generate information.

Melding Technology Literacy and Information Literacy: Implications for the Future

With the barrage and increased importance of technology in our daily lives, and in order for individuals to thrive in an information-rich and technology-inundated world, information literacy is rarely defined without considering technology. With this in mind, the National Higher Education Information and Communication Technology (ICT) Initiative developed a definition of literacy in general for the 21st century. ICT proficiency is the ability to use digital technology, communication tools, or networks to define an information need; to access, manage, integrate, and evaluate information; to create new information or knowledge; and to be able to communicate this information to others. The ICT proficiency model encompasses key components of ICT proficiency within the context of cognitive and technical skills and social and ethical considerations. Seven processes were identified by ICT Initiative as critical components of ICT. These identified processes reflect the wide range of uses for ICT. To be proficient in ICT individuals must be able to

1. Use ICT tools to identify and appropriately represent an information need;

2. Know how to collect and retrieve information;

3. Organize information into existing classification schemes;

4. Interpret, summarize, compare, and contrast information using similar or different forms of representation;

5. Reflect to make judgments about the quality, relevance, usefulness, or efficiency of information;

6. Generate new information and knowledge by adapting, applying, designing, inventing, or representing information; and

7. Convey information and knowledge to various individuals and/or groups.

As the information explosion continues to swell and as technology continues to have a greater impact on our lives, there will be a growing demand for technology, information, and ICT literacy. The ability to understand, utilize, and share a variety of technologies and the information resources they make available to us continues to be increasingly critical. Some have argued that only those who are ICT literate have power over their futures, and those who are not ICT literate are only left with diminished power and limited opportunities. The disparity of ICT haves and have-nots may create a gap in our society. To avoid this rift, it is important to ensure that all individuals acquire the 21st-century literacy skills that our technology and information-driven modern society demands.

Marcus D. Childress

See also Information, Technology, and Media Literacies;
Information and Communication Technologies:
Competencies in the 21st-Century Workforce; Information
and Communication Technologies: Knowledge Management;
Media Literacies; Twenty-First-Century Technology Skills

Further Readings

American Library Association. (1989). *Presidential Committee on Information Literacy: Final report*. Chicago, IL: Author. Retrieved from http://www.ala.org/ala/mgrps/divs/acrl/publications/whitepapers/presidential.cfm

Association of College and Research Libraries. (2000). *Information literacy competency standards for higher education*. Chicago, IL: Author. Retrieved from http://www.ala.org/ala/mgrps/divs/acrl/standards/standards.pdf

Educational Testing Service. *ICT Literacy Assessment—Information and Communication Technology*. Princeton, NJ: Author. Retrieved from http://www.ncahlc.org/download/annualmeeting/05Handouts/GSUN0145k_Egan.pdf

International ICT Literacy Panel. (2002). *Digital transformation: A framework for ICT literacy* (A report of the International ICT Literacy Panel). Princeton, NJ: Educational Testing Service. Retrieved from http://www.ets.org/Media/Tests/Information_and_Communication_Technology_Literacy/ictreport.pdf

Technology Integration

Current definitions of technology integration comprise using computer- or digital-based tools to support teaching and learning in today's K–12 classrooms. Unlike most definitions, this one is not fixed, as the goals for technology integration continue to evolve. For example, when desktop computers were first introduced into K–12 classrooms in the early to mid-1980s, integration was aimed at teaching students how to use BASIC or Logo programming languages to make the computer accomplish simple tasks. In the mid- to late-1990s, integration emphasized increasing students' productivity skills through the use of common software programs such as word processing and spreadsheet applications.

Today, the integration process focuses on putting digital devices into the hands of K–12 students to facilitate their collaboration with local and distant peers to solve authentic problems. Although early proponents believed that computers would transform education, there is a growing recognition that students and teachers must *partner* with technology in order to achieve the kinds of educational changes initially envisioned. Today, few would disagree that pedagogical and technological issues must be addressed simultaneously for meaningful integration to occur. As such, promoting best practice and effective pedagogy are considered key to effective technology integration. Given this, the topic of technology integration intersects with nearly every other topic in this encyclopedia, as integration (i.e., meaningful technology use) is the ultimate goal of the various applications and tools explored in this work. This entry first discusses the introduction of computer technology into schools and shifts over time in its use by schools. It then describes how teachers adopt and use technology and details the factors that encourage or inhibit technology integration. Finally, it discusses the current focus on technology as part of a student-centered pedagogy.

Historical Perspective

When personal computers first entered the K–12 schools in the early 1980s, they were generally treated as a new subject in the curriculum; that is, students took computer literacy classes to learn such things as how to boot a computer, load software, and use the keyboard. Schools rushed to add computer teachers to their personnel rosters, computer labs to their facilities, and computer classes to their curricula. Because the computers themselves were not very powerful and the available software was extremely limited, computer classes tended to focus on teaching students how to use the programming language, BASIC, which came preloaded on the computers. Given this emphasis on programming, instructional computing was regarded as highly technical and, thus, typically placed within the mathematics curriculum.

As instructional software improved and schools began placing one or two computers into each teacher's classroom in the early 1990s, computers were typically used to provide remedial, supplemental, or enrichment instruction for individual or small groups of students. The development of computer-assisted instruction, or CAI, software made this goal readily achievable. As software quality improved, teachers began using these drill-and-practice and tutorial programs as surrogate or substitute teachers in order to facilitate differentiated instruction within their increasingly diverse classrooms.

Over time, educators gradually shifted their emphases from helping students learn *about* or *from* technology to helping them learn *with* technology. This was advanced by the publication of David Jonassen's textbook, *Computers in the Classroom: Mindtools for Critical Thinking*. Educators focused on helping students learn how to use the same productivity tools used in the workplace (e.g., word processing, spreadsheet, database, programs) to create high-quality products that were visually appealing, easily edited, and simple to reproduce. Jonassen built on this idea to advocate that students use technology as a *cognitive partner* to access and analyze information, interpret and transform that information into personal knowledge, and then to represent that knowledge to others. In effect, technology enabled learners to think in ways that were impossible without the tools, thus transforming the learning process to one that was more student driven and student centered.

About this same time, widespread access to the Internet and the growth of Web-based information reinforced this shift in perspective away from thinking about the computer primarily as a delivery or productivity tool to viewing it as a resource tool and communication device. The term *information literacy* replaced *computer literacy* to represent what students needed to know and be able to do with resources accessed via these new and emerging technology tools. This shift toward finding, analyzing, creating, and sharing information encouraged educators to focus more on how technology could support learning, rather than requiring students to learn basic skills that would quickly become outdated. The term *technology-enabled learning* advocated by current educators, especially in Europe, represents this shift in emphasis from *teaching* to *learning* with technology.

With the emergence of Web 2.0 applications in the mid-2000s, this shift has continued, allowing both teachers and students to create and share information via what is now considered to be a *participatory* Web. Furthermore, the ability to access this information on a variety of mobile devices has distributed technology-enabled learning across time and place and among teachers and learners. These changes toward social and mobile learning will undoubtedly impact the *next* definition of technology integration.

Teacher Adoption and Use

When personal computers first arrived in the K–12 schools, access was extremely limited. As such, early efforts focused on building infrastructure in the schools, including updating wiring and retrofitting specific spaces for computer labs or classroom computer stations, as well as providing teacher training and increasing technical support. However, depending on funding available, as well as local stakeholder interest and support, these efforts occurred in fits and starts. As a result, computers, especially networked computers, were unevenly distributed among schools—a phenomenon that continues to this day. This made it difficult to determine whether integration was occurring, as it was generally believed that teachers could not initiate the integration process until all the necessary resources were in place.

In an effort to circumvent this problem, Apple launched its *Classrooms of Tomorrow* (ACOT) project, with the goal of documenting what happens when teachers and students have ubiquitous access to technology. Early results were somewhat surprising to the researchers: When teachers in these classrooms started using technology, there was very little change in their classroom practices. For the most part, teachers used technology in ways that worked best with their own, typically traditional, teaching methods. However, as teachers gained confidence and skill with the technology, and as they witnessed changes in their students' motivation, performances, and interactions with each other, a shift toward more student-centered uses occurred.

These findings led to the development of a number of stage models, which described the adoption and implementation stages through which teachers progressed as they moved from initial technology adoption to full integration, or from novice to accomplished users. The general idea behind these developmental models was that teachers' uses evolved as they gained experience. Furthermore, the general consensus was that it took five or six years for teachers to accumulate enough experience to use technology in ways described by the top levels in these models—that is, to *transform* teaching and learning. In line with the educational reform efforts of the time, it was generally agreed that a transformed pedagogy relied on the constructivist paradigm, which enabled authentic learning within situated, social contexts. As such, the expectation was that teachers would use technology as a tool to engage students collaboratively, in authentic problems of the discipline, in order to construct deep and connected knowledge. However, based on recent results of both national and international surveys, this goal has not yet been achieved in the majority of teachers' classrooms.

Factors Impacting Technology Integration

It is almost impossible to talk about technology integration without discussing the barriers that have impeded its progress. Although early advocates believed that adding technology to teachers' classrooms would prompt changes in the way teachers taught, research findings have consistently demonstrated that this is not the case. To examine this disconnect, researchers have investigated the various barriers and enablers observed to impact teachers' classroom uses of technology.

To classify these numerous barriers, Peggy Ertmer distinguished between first-order barriers, which are external to the teacher (e.g., resources, training, support) and second-order barriers, which are internal (e.g., attitudes and beliefs, knowledge and skills). Historically, school districts' efforts focused, almost exclusively, on eliminating first-order barriers, with the majority of efforts directed toward increasing access, support, and training. Consequently, schools have reported remarkable gains: Student-computer ratios have been dramatically reduced while infrastructure, training, and support have been substantially increased to facilitate teachers' efforts.

However, despite these extensive efforts, teachers' instructional uses, even today, remain relatively unchanged. Reported uses still tend to be low level—those that support traditional, teacher-directed instruction such as using PowerPoint to present a lesson or searching the Web for information resources. Although most teachers and schools have shifted away from implementing classroom activities designed for students to learn *about* technology, students in today's classrooms still tend to learn *from* technology, using it primarily as a delivery tool. Given this, attention recently has turned to the role second-order barriers, including teachers' self-efficacy, knowledge, and pedagogical beliefs, play in the integration process.

Teacher Knowledge

It is generally agreed that in order to use technology to facilitate student learning, teachers need a set of knowledge and skills that build on and intersect with those initially defined by Lee Shulman: content knowledge, pedagogical knowledge, and pedagogical content knowledge. This additional knowledge has been conceptualized in a variety of ways, with TPACK (technological pedagogical content knowledge) being the most widely used. These models of teacher technology knowledge are based on the idea that technology integration depends, ultimately, on teachers' knowing which technology tools to use to best support students' learning of specific content. Although more work is needed to validate the TPACK framework, it provides a useful label for describing the unique knowledge base teachers need in order to use technology to support meaningful content-based pedagogies.

Teacher Self-Efficacy

Although it is recognized that knowledge of technology is *necessary* for teacher's technology use, it is not *sufficient* if teachers do not feel confident using that knowledge to facilitate student learning. In fact, some research has suggested that self-efficacy is more important than skills and knowledge, as it has been demonstrated to be one of the strongest predictors of teachers' technology use. To increase teachers' confidence, a number of strategies have been found to be effective, including mastery experiences (personal, successful experiences with technology), vicarious experiences (observing others be successful), and persuasion. In addition, when teachers observe how technology facilitates student success, confidence also increases.

Teacher Pedagogical Beliefs

In addition to knowledge and confidence, teachers also must value technology as an instructional tool, which typically relates to their beliefs about effective teaching and learning. In general, teacher beliefs are classified as traditional or constructivist. Whereas traditional teaching approaches emphasize teacher explanations and students' repetitive practice, constructivist approaches emphasize the construction of student knowledge through experiences with authentic problems. Many studies have confirmed that teachers with more constructivist beliefs use technology more frequently and in more challenging ways. Similarly, teachers who readily integrate technology tend to have more constructivist beliefs. Researchers have explained this relationship by hypothesizing that teachers use technology in ways that fit within their existing belief systems. That is, if teachers perceive that technology addresses important instructional and learning needs, the perceived value will be higher and subsequent use more likely. Conversely, if a teacher fails to sense alignment between the technology's purpose and specific classroom goals, she is likely either to not use the technology at all or to use it in ways that support the traditional activities with which she is more comfortable.

Because beliefs are considered to be precursors to action, it is commonly agreed that in order to affect changes in teachers' practice, we must first facilitate changes in the beliefs that underlie that practice. As such, second-order barriers, including teacher beliefs, are now being described as the true gatekeepers to technology integration. This is supported by the observation that while some teachers with few resources (those who have a high level of first-order barriers) have achieved high levels of integration, teachers with many resources but strong traditional beliefs have been observed to limit their students' technology uses. This pattern has been consistently observed, even in technology-rich schools, suggesting that integration is as much, if not more so, about pedagogy than technology.

Current Focus on Pedagogy

Since the 1980s, there has been a persistent call, not only for teachers' increased use of digital technologies, but also for more constructivist uses of technology in the classroom. The new goal for technology integration comprises teachers using technology to support 21st-century teaching and learning. Thus, in a 21st-century classroom, technology plays a more integrated role, serving as a cognitive tool, as originally proposed by Jonassen, to facilitate authentic student learning. In these classrooms, it is the students, not the teacher, who use the technology, specifically to support their efforts as researchers, designers, and problem solvers.

It is important to remember that the ultimate goal of technology integration efforts is not that teachers embrace technology, per se, but that they embrace the type of pedagogical approaches that benefit from meaningful and authentic technology use. This, then, suggests the need to downplay the tools (as these are constantly changing anyway), in favor of student-centered pedagogies that take full advantage of the tools, especially those that target the 21st-century skills that are deemed critical for our students' futures.

Peggy A. Ertmer

See also Mindtools; Technology and Information Literacy; TPACK (Technological Pedagogical Content Knowledge); TPACK (Technological Pedagogical Content Knowledge): Implications for 21st-Century Teacher Education; Twenty-First-Century Technology Skills; Web 2.0 and Beyond

Further Readings

Becker, H. J. (2000). How exemplary computer-using teachers differ from other teachers: Implications for realizing the potential of computers in schools. *Contemporary Issues in Technology & Teacher Education, 1*, 274–293.

Dwyer, D. C., Ringstaff, C., & Sandholtz, J. H. (1990). *Teacher beliefs and practices part 1: Patterns of change. The evolution of teachers' instructional beliefs and practices in high-access-to-technology classrooms* (ACOT Report #8). Cupertino, CA: Apple Computer.

Ertmer, P. A. (1999). Addressing first- and second-order barriers to change: Strategies for technology integration. *Educational Technology Research & Development, 47*(4), 47–61.

Ertmer, P. A. (2005). Teacher pedagogical beliefs: The final frontier in our quest for technology integration? *Educational Technology Research & Development, 53*(4), 25–39.

Jonassen, D. H. (1996). *Computers in the classroom: Mindtools for critical thinking.* Columbus, OH: Merrill.

Koehler, M. J., & Mishra, P. (2009). What is technological pedagogical content knowledge? *Contemporary Issues in Technology and Teacher Education, 9*(1), 60–70.

Shulman, L. S. (1986). Those who understand: Knowledge growth in teaching. *Educational Researcher, 15*(2), 4–14.

Tondeur, J., Hermans, R., van Braak, J., & Valcke, M. (2008). Exploring the link between teachers' educational belief profiles and different types of computer use in the classroom: The impact of teacher beliefs. *Computers in Human Behavior, 24*, 2541–2553.

U.S. Department of Education, Office of Educational Technology. (2010). Transforming American education: Learning powered by technology: National Educational Technology Plan 2010. Retrieved from http://www.ed.gov/technology/netp-2010

Voogt, J., & Pareja Roblin, N. (2012). A comparative analysis of international frameworks for 21st century competences: Implications for national curriculum policies. *Journal of Curriculum Studies, 44*, 299–321.

Zhao, Y., & Cziko, G. A. (2001). Teacher adoption of technology: A perceptual control theory perspective. *Journal of Technology and Teacher Education, 9*, 5–30.

TECHNOLOGY KNOWLEDGE

Technology knowledge reflects an individual's awareness of and ability to apply the affordances of technology to solve problems. Given the proliferation of technology throughout many aspects of daily life, the emphasis on the development of technology knowledge has become more pervasive as well. In K–12 settings, opportunities to learn about and apply technology are made available within specialized courses and curricula, as well as integrated across disciplines as an important component of the learning process. The learning framework developed by the Partnership for 21st Century Skills includes a specific focus on technology knowledge in the form of information, technology, and media skills. This entry defines technology knowledge, discusses its importance, and discusses ways of assessing technology knowledge.

Beyond school settings, the need for the application of technology knowledge is a common expectation across job settings and sectors. No longer is expertise regarding technology limited to specific professions. In a 2008 report, the United Nations Educational, Scientific and Cultural Organization (UNESCO) indicated that information literacy and information and communication technologies (ICT) skills are important and should be seen as a basic human right. The report further indicates that technology empowers individuals in all walks of life to seek, evaluate, use, and create information effectively to achieve personal, social, occupational, and educational goals.

Defining Technology Knowledge

The process of defining what is meant by technology knowledge is somewhat challenging, given the many perspectives and stakeholder groups that have an interest in its definition. Differing terms have been used to define one's technology knowledge, with a common synonym being technology literacy. As the International Technology Education Association has noted, the term *technology* originates from the Greek word *techne* for art, artifice, or craft; technology literally refers to an act of making or crafting, but it more generally refers to a diverse collection of processes and knowledge used to extend human abilities and satisfy human needs and desires.

Definitions of technology knowledge tend to focus on different dimensions of this construct. Don Ihde describes three such dimensions: (1) knowing about how technology functions, (2) knowing the theoretical principles that underlie a given functionality of technology, and (3) and knowledge through technology, or *praxis* knowledge.

The National Research Council (NRC) generated a seminal report in 1999 defining three aspects of technology knowledge: fundamental concepts, contemporary skills, and intellectual capabilities. Fundamental concepts relate to one's understanding and application of general technological operations. For example, one may have conceptual knowledge of how an operating system works (no matter the platform) or how a network functions. Contemporary skills reflect specific knowledge for a given technology, such as an individual software program or a proprietary network design. While fundamental concepts remain consistent over time, contemporary skills are constantly changing with each new technological innovation. The final component of technology knowledge, intellectual capabilities, represents the ability to apply information technology in a variety of complex situations and to understand the consequences of using a particular technology.

Perhaps the most challenging aspect of technology knowledge is to develop intellectual capabilities that exemplify higher order life skills. Such skills include problem solving, managing ambiguity, collaboration, communication across stakeholders, and anticipation of change. Other technology stakeholder groups also emphasize the importance of one's ability to use technology to solve problems. The NRC contends that while it is possible to maintain knowledge in each of these individual facets of technology knowledge, *fluency with information technology* (FITness) is only established when one has developed capacity across all three components.

Assessing Technology Knowledge

With the proliferation of technology throughout society, a variety of approaches have emerged to measure technology knowledge in a wide range of settings. From early grades through higher education and beyond, different organizations have created mechanisms through which to gauge an individual's awareness of and competence with technology. For example, the Educational Testing Service (ETS) offers the *iSkills* examination as a comprehensive assessment tool as a means to measure various facets of technology knowledge, including the aforementioned intellectual skills. According to ETS, the test includes sections that measure the ability to navigate, understand, and analyze information. The ETS contends that the *iSkills* assessment is designed to help universities evaluate students' critical thinking skills in a digital environment.

The European Computer Driving License (ECDL) was established in 1996 with the aim of raising digital literacy throughout Europe. Due to its popularity, countries outside of Europe became interested and so in 1999, the International Computer Driving License (ICDL) was established to administer a similar certification worldwide. According to the ECDL, certificates are awarded after demonstration of skills and knowledge in ICTs through the completion of exams at approved test centers.

The ETS *iSkills* exam and the International Computer Driver License are examples of assessment mechanisms used to determine individual skills and knowledge through objective testing strategies. Other stakeholder groups provide more general guidance for assessing technology knowledge through the provision of related standards.

The International Society for Technology in Education (ISTE) developed the ISTE Standards (formerly the National Educational Technology Standards) and offers guidance for assessing learning, teaching, and leading in the digital age. These standards go beyond knowing about technology to focus on the application of technology using higher level thinking skills. For example, the ISTE Standards for Students include technology operations and concepts, as well as creativity and innovation, communication and collaboration, research and information fluency, critical thinking, problem solving, decision making, and digital citizenship.

Another international organization with an interest in the development of technology knowledge in the educational sector is the United Nations Educational, Scientific and Cultural Organization (UNESCO). In 2008, UNESCO developed the Information and Communication Technologies Competency Framework for Teachers (ICT-CFT). This framework, revised in 2011, was designed to provide a scaffold upon which countries around the world could support teachers' effective use of ICT in their classrooms. The UNESCO ICT-CFT focuses on three main approaches: technology literacy, knowledge deepening, and knowledge creation.

While the aforementioned organizations offer standards for technology knowledge that are broad in scope and applicable across disciplines, the International Technology Education Association (ITEA) maintains specific standards for the development of specialized technological skills and abilities. Designed to span the K–12 curriculum, the ITEA standards include the study of the nature of technology, the role of technology in society, the technological design process and related abilities, and specialized learning outcomes from different business sectors. Along with the aforementioned organizations, the ITEA provides guidance for the development and assessment of technology knowledge identified as critical among its constituent group members.

Conclusion

The interest in defining, developing, and measuring technology knowledge continues to grow as technological innovations become increasingly pervasive and integral to everyday life. As these innovations continue to influence human performance on a global scale, so will their evolution impact how technology is defined and adopted.

Barbara B. Lockee and Kwame Ansong-Gyimah

See also Information, Technology, and Media Literacies; Information and Communication Technologies: Competencies in the 21st-Century Workforce; Information and Communication Technologies: Knowledge Management; Media Literacies; Technology and Information Literacy; Twenty-First-Century Technology Skills

Further Readings

Educational Testing Service. (2013). *The iSkills assessment.* Retrieved from http://www.ets.org/iskills/about

European Computer Driving License Foundation. (2013). *Our history.* Retrieved from http://www.ecdl.org/index.jsp?p=94&n=170

Ihde, D. (1997). The structure of technology knowledge. *International Journal of Technology and Design Education, 7,* 73–79.

International Society for Technology in Education. (2007). *ISTE standards: Students.* Retrieved from http://www.iste.org/docs/pdfs/20-14_ISTE_Standards-S_PDF.pdf

International Society for Technology in Education. (2012). *ISTE NETS: The standards for learning, leading, and teaching in the digital age.* Retrieved from http://www.iste.org/standards

International Technology Education Association. (2007). *Standards for technological literacy: Content for the study of technology.* Reston, VA: Author.

National Research Council. (1999). *Being fluent with information technology.* Washington, DC: National Academies Press.

Partnership for 21st Century Skills. (2009). *P21 framework definitions.* Retrieved from http://www.p21.org/storage/documents/P21_Framework_Definitions.pdf

United Nations Educational, Scientific and Cultural Organization. (2011). *ICT competency framework for teachers.* Paris, France: Author. Retrieved from http://unesdoc.unesco.org/images/0021/002134/213475E.pdf

Zuppo, C. M. (2012). Defining ICT in a boundaryless world: The development of a working hierarchy. *International Journal of Managing Information Technology, 4*(3), 13–22. doi:10.5121/ijmt.2012.4302

Technology Support for Conceptual Change

Conceptual change has been among the most important aspects in education for the last few decades. There is no specific definition of conceptual change given its complex and unpredictable nature. However, from the learning perspective, conceptual change can be generally referred to as the process whereby learners change or alter their initial understandings or beliefs to become more closely aligned with scientifically held understandings of the concepts. From a broader perspective, conceptual change can also be referred to as the change in the understanding of the concepts learners have and the conceptual framework that encompasses these concepts. Conceptual change can take different forms, from ordinary change such as weak restructuring to more radical change, which usually requires change across ontological categories. This entry discusses how conceptual change occurs, the role of technology in conceptual change, the use of modeling to support conceptual change, and the implications of modeling for conceptual change.

Although conceptual change can occur unintentionally, researchers argue that meaningful learning takes place when conceptual change is intentional. When learners are guided by their awareness of a need to change, knowing what to change, and wanting to change, conceptual change becomes a learning goal. In the recent developments in the field of conceptual change, there has been a shift away from regarding conceptual change as a personal cognitive process change arising from specific instruction such as cognitive conflict strategy as the main mechanism for conceptual change. There is now more of an emphasis on examining the implications of the design of instruction and curricula on conceptual change and investigating how contextual influences such as motivation, epistemological beliefs, and sociocultural perspectives influence and impact the change to account for the complex nature of conceptual change. Traditionally, conceptual-change research focused on science education, documenting and describing the process of change in students' misconceptions toward more scientifically held understandings. In recent years, most researchers have argued that for conceptual change to occur, what needs to be changed are not isolated misconceptions but the naive and domain-specific theories embedded in larger theoretical frameworks from which they obtain their meaning.

Role of Technology in Conceptual Change

Technology can play a critical role in fostering conceptual change. Specifically, it encourages learners to externalize and manipulate their internal conceptual models in order to construct or revise their conceptual understanding. When fostering conceptual change with technology, learning is meaningful, effortful, dynamic, and engaging. For intentional conceptual change to occur there must be substantial conceptual engagement. When learners engage in self-regulation and analyzing, evaluating, and synthesizing the new information into their current existing knowledge framework, they think deeply about their arguments and counterarguments, thus leading to the possibility of a conceptual change. Technology provides a platform for such conceptual engagement. It not only provides a platform for cognitive conflict or cognitive dissonance; through distributed cognition, learners may also focus on performing specific cognitive tasks for deep understanding. Depending on the affordances and roles they play, technology may engage learners differently, requiring them to exercise various cognitive skills, but the ultimate outcome is intentional conceptual change.

Supporting Conceptual Change With Modeling Tools

There are many different types of models, such as physical models that represent phenomena in the world, and conceptual models, or rather mental models, which may include abstract models (mathematical models), representational models (the central function of models used in science), and hypotheses and theoretical models (models constructed with theoretical principles). When engaged in modeling, learners create or revise their conceptual understandings. Building models as compared to using prebuilt models is considered to be more productive in fostering conceptual change as learners own the models and assume epistemic agency when creating them, thus creating stronger motivation to produce a sound and logical model. When engaging in technology-based modeling activities, learners externalize their thinking, making it visible for scrutiny. Because modeling supports varied deep-level cognitive processes such as hypothesis testing, inferring, predicting, evaluating, analysis, and most importantly causal reasoning, it is one important learning activity that could potentially invoke conceptual change. Various modeling tools support different types of modeling, depending on the context that they are modeling.

Modeling Domain Knowledge

There are a few direct benefits to modeling domain knowledge. Firstly, domain knowledge presented in school textbooks is mostly arranged and organized in a linear fashion. Such presentation impedes learning as learners are not made aware of the complex nature of the knowledge and the underlying semantic networks of their knowledge systems. The first step for conceptual change to occur is whether the learners are aware that there are contradictions in their learning. Modeling helps learners to visualize their knowledge structures for better comprehension, and when learning is visible, learners can identify their naive understanding or misconceptions more effectively, thereby noticing contradictions. Secondly, being aware that there are conflicts in learning is not always adequate for conceptual change to happen. Learners who have low interest or domain knowledge may not perceive a real need for change. However, when engaging in intensive modeling activity, then the chances of learners developing the need to change are higher as there is ownership of the learning.

When modeling domain knowledge, learners explicate and analyze what they already know, make adjustments to their current conceptual framework to provide better understanding of the current knowledge, or make refinements to it in order to incorporate new knowledge. Common tools for such purposes include technology-based concept mapping tools. Currently, a variety of such tools are capable of providing learners with a platform for nonlinearity modeling, which helps learners understand the complex associations of the domain knowledge that they are modeling, as shown in Figure 1. Concept mapping is one of the most common activities in schools and it can be used across various disciplines, thereby supporting a variety of classroom learning. Concept maps are composed of nodes, which are usually concepts or ideas, and links, which are statements of relationships that connect the ideas. With concept maps, learners identify the important and related concepts and make meaningful relationships to connect them. Such a process helps learners to represent and understand the underlying structures of the concepts that they are trying to learn. Without a strong understanding of the intricate interrelationships of

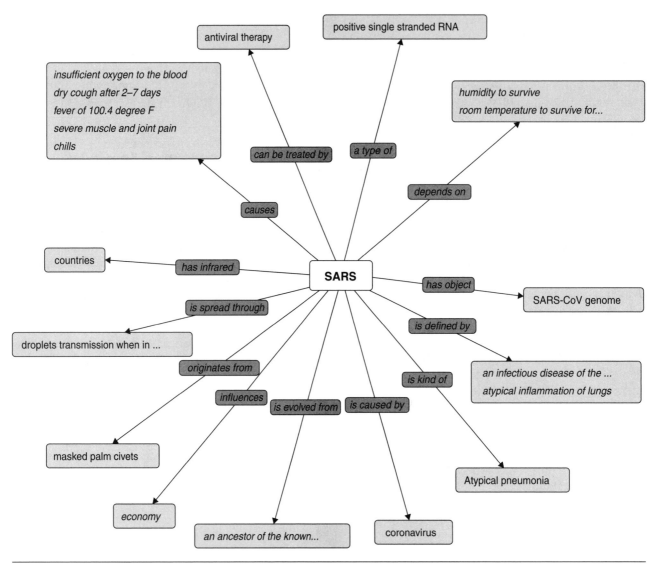

Figure 1   Modeling domain knowledge

concepts, it is probably impossible to form or revise an existing conceptual framework that is meaningful.

Modeling Systems

One of the common hurdles learners face is understanding content because, most often, content is presented in an inconsistent manner, opposed to how learners think. This creates problems for learners, especially when the content is highly complex and the ideas are abstract, and thus they are not able to grasp the interconnectedness of the information. Engaging learners in systems modeling helps them develop systemic perspectives on how phenomena are intricately related to each other. One of the most important triggers for conceptual change is perturbations regarding one's conceptions. When modeling a complex system, learners will come across situations where they experience cognitive conflicts. To resolve these perturbations, the learner must engage in a series of experimentation, questioning, discussion or other types of high engagement in order to compare rival naive theories, leading to possible conceptual change. As pointed out by many researchers, learners' naive understandings or misconceptions are most often entrenched beliefs and thus are difficult to revise or correct because these beliefs are part of the larger theoretical framework that explains the daily phenomena they observe. Systems modeling provides a platform for learners to comprehend the dynamic and complex nature of phenomena, challenge their belief systems, and create ownership of their learning.

Systems modeling tools enable the learner to describe rules related to populations of entities. Learners model systems by identifying individual elements of the system and describing their behavior. Traditionally, research on modeling tended to emphasize quantitative representation, meaning to represent phenomena in terms of mathematical formulas that involve the manipulation of variables and performing algebraic transformations using equations to solve the unknown.

Systems modeling tools such as STELLA and Powersim allow learners to build dynamic simulation models in the form of causal loops. The relationships of the variables are indicated by equations, and learners may run the models and observe the changes in the model over time. Using a set of building block icons such as stocks, flows, converters, and connectors, learners build an initial model that represents their understanding of the system. They build the model and determine the relationships of these factors by inputting mathematical equations. Next, they can test their dynamic models and engage in an iterative process of refining and modifying their models. Contemporary researchers argue that qualitative models are equally important as they help learners to understand the underlying systems that they are modeling, providing justifications for analysis.

When engaging in systems modeling activities, learners determine variables and manipulate the parameters to understand the system that they are modeling (see Figure 2). Figure 2, which is part of a larger diagram, shows a dynamic systems model built to capture the complex nature of the social studies learning system. It represents the interactions of students' structural knowledge, essential skills, teachers' instructional practices, and the goals of social studies. Regardless of whether learners are modeling domain knowledge or modeling cognitive systems or natural systems, modeling activities using technology-based tools enables them to externalize their thinking, making abstract understanding explicit so that they may reflect upon their knowledge, effectively identify their own learning gaps, and resolve perturbations created while engaging in the modeling activities.

Modeling Socially Constructed Knowledge

Community building tools are fast becoming an integral part of classroom learning in helping build learning communities and schools. While some of these tools were built with the intention of learning in mind, such as the Knowledge Forum and Edmodo, others such as Facebook were created for social interactions but have since been integrated into school curricula. They can be conceived as modeling tools as learners collaboratively model a topic of discussion. When activities are collaborative in nature and are supported by the relationships among learners as well as the intentionally created supporting environment, conceptual change may occur, even for very young learners. Regardless of the different features embedded in these platforms, they can provide learners with sociocultural support that encourages open-mindedness as an individual learner and multiple perspectives on various issues. The process of conceptual change in this sense refers to the ability to synthesize from a wider and broader perspective.

In more controlled learning communities, the learning environment is intentionally designed to support meaningful collaborations, and learners are provided with various forms of scaffolding to help them stay engaged. Usually, these learning communities have common learning goals and a specific purpose to achieve. Most interactions among members are closely monitored and mediated by facilitators who can be experienced members or teachers. Conceptual change in such an environment can be individual or social within the community.

In more controlled learning communities such as the Knowledge Forum, learners perceive ideas as improvable and learn to respect and value ideas according to their contributions to the group's knowledge base. The ideas proposed by learners, regardless of how naive they are, are considered as valuable and meaningful contributions, and initial ideas that may lack scientific explanations are regarded as a crucial starting point in the process of constructive idea improvement. Using scaffolding phrases such as "My theory is . . . ," "I need to understand . . . ," "My theory cannot explain . . . ," or "A better theory is . . . ," learners are supported in advancing their metacognitive and epistemic capacity by constantly examining their understanding. As learners scrutinize their own messages as well as those of their peers, they consciously pay more attention to the way in which they articulate their thoughts and make efforts to refine and improve their writing; this develops in learners the capacity to critique and improve ideas based on the criteria of a knowledge discipline. When learners build a verbal model of the topic that they are discussing, they engage in processes of individual as well as social conceptual change.

The pervasiveness of social media tools in the education context is drastically changing the way in which learners build their knowledge and will potentially invoke widespread conceptual change. There are practically no boundaries to these platforms, and activities are no longer constrained by common learning goals or specific tasks; rather, members are drawn to the interactions based on common interest and thus the dynamics of these communities are extremely strong. Unlike the more controlled learning communities, learners' ideas

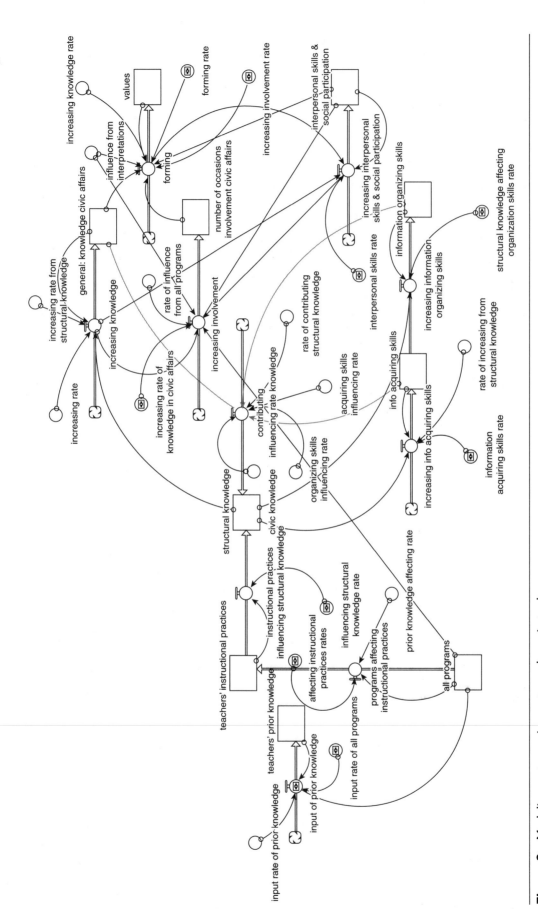

Figure 2 Modeling system using systems dynamic tool

and conceptions in open communities such as Facebook are constantly and rapidly exposed to the challenges posed by the community members or even others outside the community. There is little or no scaffolding in terms of verbal modeling of discussion; the driving force for change depends on how appealing the common interest is to the members.

As such media are highly efficient in delivering the most recent information around the world and bringing masses together based on common interest, they have the potential to influence our belief systems instantaneously and to achieve large-scale conceptual change within a short period of time. Such change includes change in the conceptions of democracy, human rights, and freedom of speech defined by the social groups. For instance, in some Asian and Middle Eastern countries where governments were once considered as unchallenged and the ultimate authoritative bodies, users of social media are questioning the governments' roles, functions, and actions. The formation of online communities not only creates a set of group beliefs or social beliefs but also influences an individual's own identity and belief system.

Implications of Modeling for Conceptual Change

This entry presents how technology as a modeling tool could foster conceptual change. For intentional conceptual change to occur, learners must know that there are contradictions or deficiencies in their knowledge structure, highlighting a need for change. Modeling as a highly engaging activity potentially creates awareness in learning and motivation for change. Different technologies engage learners differently, but the ultimate outcome is conceptual change. To effectively integrate model building activities into teaching and learning, one must be fully aware of the implications of the technologies that are being used and how conceptual change could be defined and assessed in that specific context.

Chwee Beng Lee

See also Model-Based Approaches; Simulation-Based Learning; System Dynamics

Further Readings

Jonassen, D. H. (2008). Model building for conceptual change. In S. Vosniadou (Ed.), *International handbook of research on conceptual change* (pp. 676–693). New York, NY: Routledge.

Lee, C. B. (2010). The interactions between problem solving and conceptual change: System dynamic modelling as a platform for learning. *Computers & Education, 55*(3), 1145–1158.

Lee, C. B., & Jonassen, D. H. (Eds.). (2012). *Fostering conceptual change with technology: Asian perspectives.* Singapore: Cengage Learning.

Spector, J. M. (2000). System dynamics and interactive learning environments: Lessons learned and implications for the future. *Simulation & Gaming, 31*(3), 457–464.

Vosniadou, S. (2007). The conceptual change approach and its re-framing. In S. Vosniadou, A. Baltas, & X. Vamvakoussi (Eds.), *Reframing the conceptual change approach in learning and instruction* (pp. 1–16). Amsterdam, Netherlands: Elsevier.

Vosniadou, S. (2008). *International handbook of research on conceptual change.* New York, NY: Routledge.

TECHNOLOGY-ENHANCED INQUIRY LEARNING

Inquiry learning (aka inquiry-based learning) is a range of educational approaches in which students collect and interpret information to address real-world problems. Technology-enhanced inquiry learning refers to the use of educational technologies to support student learning in inquiry settings. This entry provides (a) a definition of inquiry learning, (b) a discussion of educational technologies that can support information access and cognition in inquiry learning, and (c) a discussion of implications of technology-enhanced inquiry learning for education.

Inquiry Learning

In inquiry learning, students center their learning around an authentic, ill-structured problem, defined as a problem (a) with no clear solution or solution path, (b) that relates to students' communities or lives, and (c) that requires use of the tools and processes of the discipline to solve. Students need to collect data, seek out and read pertinent information, and synthesize found information to either describe the problem more thoroughly or solve it. A combination of contingent teacher support and student self-direction of learning is required for success in inquiry approaches. Central to inquiry instruction is the ability to create arguments in support of problem solutions. Addressing real-world problems is desirable, not only to prepare students for a workplace environment in which they will be paid to solve problems, but also because of the deeper learning that many posit arises from inquiry approaches.

Inquiry-Based Learning in K–12 Settings

In the United States, the importance of inquiry learning approaches was highlighted in 1996 with the release of the National Science Education Standards, developed by the National Research Council. A more recent set of standards that is now being implemented in many states, the Common Core State Standards, stresses the importance of inquiry learning approaches for all subjects. Inquiry learning can lead to the learning of content, problem-solving skills, and self-directed learning skills.

Inquiry learning is widely used in such subjects as science, social studies, English, and mathematics. Inquiry learning approaches used in science include problem-based learning, project-based learning, and design-based learning. Each of these approaches involves authentic, ill-structured problems. Differences lie in the ultimate output required of students. In project-based learning and design-based learning, students need to produce a product, such as a video or a model car, that accomplishes a goal. In problem-based learning, students need to develop and defend a problem solution. Inquiry learning in social studies often involves students addressing important historical, political, and societal questions through analysis of primary source historical documents. In mathematics, inquiry learning often takes the form of model-eliciting activities in which students need to construct and revise mathematical models that explain authentic problems.

Educational Technologies for Inquiry Learning

In technology-enhanced inquiry learning, educational technologies are not content-delivery mechanisms, but rather tools to facilitate students' engagement in the process of inquiry. Such educational technologies can be seen as largely being of two types: those that aid information access and those that aid cognition.

Information Access

Technology can give students access to a wide range of data on which to base inquiry. For example, technology can organize and give students access to data on microevolution of finches on the Galapagos Islands and to primary source documents from the civil rights era. A large project that does this in science is Web-based Inquiry Science Environment (WISE), which contains many units in which students can investigate science content.

When technology is used for information access, instructional designers gather original documents and other information that students can explore during inquiry. This is meant to facilitate information access and to ensure that students are exposed to the right type of information. Information access can be accomplished through establishment of a database with which

students engage during classroom learning or it can be integrated into a virtual world with which students engage exclusively during the course of their learning.

Databases

In WISE, students address a variety of scientific problems by investigating embedded resources and data. For example, one such problem centers on deformed frogs; in it, students can read different data related to the problem. In *Alien Rescue*, middle school students need to find a suitable planet in the solar system for various stranded aliens. Students can access information about possible planets as well as what the aliens need.

Virtual Worlds

Quest Atlantis is a computer game in which middle school students adopt avatars and can complete quests in which scientific problems need to be solved. Within the quests are scientific data that students can use to accomplish the quests. In *River City*, middle school students adopt avatars and investigate why residents of a town are sick. Students have access to scientific clues that point to possible reasons for the sickness and need to make and test hypotheses about the cause.

Cognition Aids and Scaffolding

Unaided K–12 students often do not have the skills to look beyond surface details of problems, critically evaluate evidence, evaluate arguments, understand multivariable systems, and evaluate their own thinking processes. Teachers play a critical role in supporting student learning in inquiry settings, and indeed, may be the single greatest influence on student success in such settings. One of the most crucial types of teacher support in inquiry learning is scaffolding. Scaffolding is one-to-one, contingent support that helps students engage in and gain skill at authentic problem solving. However, in a class of 30 students, one teacher cannot provide all needed support on a one-to-one basis. Technology in the form of computer-based scaffolding can supplement teacher support. Scaffolding can be differentiated from traditional instruction in that scaffolding helps students build skills as they are performing those same skills while engaging with authentic problems. Scaffolding can help students model the problem, collect and organize pertinent information, and develop a solution.

Scaffolding for problem modeling. For example, Model-It software helps students graphically model scientific problems. This in turn can help students see the variables involved in the problem, and how such variables interrelate. This is crucial because beginning problem solvers often struggle representing problems

Scaffolding for evidence interpretation. In the Persistent Issues in History project, Web-based resources serve as scaffolds to help students interpret primary source documents about the civil rights era to address the question of what should have been done after Martin Luther King Jr.'s assassination to promote a more just society. This is important because students often struggle interpreting evidence appropriately.

Scaffolding for solution development. The shared hypothesis scratchpad is a scaffold that contains a hypothesis template in which students can collaboratively select variables, how they relate, and any restrictions. Students can then test the generated hypotheses. This helps students move beyond simple descriptions to solutions of the problems.

Implications of Technology-Enhanced Inquiry Learning

In response to the development of the Common Core State Standards in the United States, many K–12 teachers will be eager to implement inquiry learning activities. As technology can serve as a great enabler of inquiry learning, there will likely be a rise in the use of technology-enhanced inquiry learning at the K–12 level. Due to the shift in job requirements in many industrialized nations, a comparable move to inquiry learning at the university level may also be expected. Thus, careful consideration of this line of research is essential.

Brian R. Belland

See also Cognitive Apprenticeship; Collaborative Learning With Technology; Problem- and Task-Centered Approaches

Further Readings

Belland, B. R. (2014). Scaffolding: Definition, current debates, and future directions. In J. M. Spector, M. D. Merrill, J. Elen, & M. J. Bishop (Eds.), *Handbook of research on educational communications and technology* (4th ed., pp. 505–518). New York, NY: Springer-Verlag.

National Research Council. (1996). *National science education standards.* Washington, DC: National Academies Press.

Crippen, K. J., & Archambault, L. (2012). Scaffolded inquiry-based instruction with technology: A signature pedagogy for STEM education. *Computers in the Schools, 29*(1/2), 157–173. doi:10.1080/07380569.2012.658733

Jonassen, D. H. (2003). Using cognitive tools to represent problems. *Journal of Research on Technology in Education, 35*(3), 362–381.

Kali, Y., & Linn, M. (2008). Technology-enhanced support strategies for inquiry learning. In J. M. Spector, M. D. Merrill, J. J. G. van Merriënboer, & M. P. Driscoll (Eds.), *Handbook of research on educational communications and technology* (3rd ed., pp. 145–161). New York, NY: Taylor & Francis.

Kolodner, J. L., Camp, P. J., Crismond, D., Fasse, B., Gray, J., Holbrook, J., . . . & Ryan, M. (2003). Problem-based learning meets case-based reasoning in the middle-school science classroom: Putting Learning by Design(™) into practice. *Journal of the Learning Sciences, 12*(4), 495–547. doi:10.1207/S15327809JLS1204_2

Krajcik, J., Blumenfeld, P. C., Marx, R. W., Bass, K. M., Fredricks, J., & Soloway, E. (1998). Inquiry in project-based science classrooms: Initial attempts by middle school students. *Journal of the Learning Sciences, 7,* 313–350.

Linn, M. C., Clark, D., & Slotta, J. D. (2003). WISE design for knowledge integration. *Science Education, 87*(4), 517–538. doi:10.1002/sce.10086

National Governors Association Center for Best Practices, & Council of Chief State School Officers. (2010). *Common core state standards.* Retrieved from http://www.corestandards.org/the-standards

van de Pol, J., Volman, M., & Beishuizen, J. (2010). Scaffolding in teacher-student interaction: A decade of research. *Educational Psychology Review, 22*(3), 271–296. doi:10.1007/s10648-010-9127-6

TECHNOLOGY-FACILITATED EXPERIENTIAL LEARNING

As opposed to passive learning, experiential learning is a process of knowledge creation through learning experience transformation, according to David A. Kolb. Through transformative reflection, concrete experience derived from learning activities is translated into new concepts that are tested by students and used for future problem solving. According to Kolb, the key elements of this approach are (a) *concrete experience* (doing), (b) *reflective observation* (observing), (c) *abstract concept formation* (thinking), and (d) *active experimentation* (planning to test a new concept in a new situation). The process of learning from experience is also referred to as *learning by doing* (a term created by John Dewey and discussed in the works of Thomas M. Duffy, Donald J. Cunningham, and others) and *experience-based learning.* M. David Merrill has often said in many presentations that people learn what they do. This entry discusses the general approaches of experiential learning, the affordances of technology for experiential learning, and design principles for the use of technology in experiential learning.

Experiential learning has been further developed as an instructional strategy in which learners acquire knowledge through making meaning of their experience(s) in learning task engagements that occur in real-world settings (e.g., field trips, internships, and community service work). Learning tasks are typically designed using authentic and ill-structured problems. At the elementary school level, an example of experiential learning is studying biology in the field rather than reading books; students directly observe and interact with plants or animals. In this case, a learning task can be a report that estimates the impact of pollution on plants along with a plan to protect the local environment. When students write reports alone or in collaboration with others, they need to reflect and interpret what they have observed and recorded in the field in the light of prior knowledge. By making sense of their observations and reflections, they construct new knowledge.

Another example is the participation of civil engineering students in authentic building projects. Involvement in real-world projects creates valuable opportunities for the students to apply and test theoretical knowledge acquired from their structured learning and, more importantly, to build professional skills. Students learn directly from engineers how to design and carry out solutions in the context of a real project. These kinds of learning opportunities are virtually impossible in traditional classrooms. New knowledge and skills are developed through deliberate practice in a discipline-specific approach to solving problems encountered in a given project.

Technology can play an important role in supporting experiential learning, especially since the development of the Internet, social networking technologies, virtual realities, and mobile computing. A close examination of technology-facilitated experiential learning, therefore, has both practical and theoretical implications.

Technology Affordances for Experiential Learning

The affordances offered by technology-facilitated learning environments and corresponding potential for interactivity are fundamentally transforming the nature of learning and teaching at all levels. With regard to experiential learning, technology can be leveraged to support the four key elements of experiential learning.

Technology can simulate real-life problem solving contexts. Virtual reality (VR) technology is able to simulate laboratory settings, workplaces, or natural environments where learners are engaged in re-created sensory experiences (e.g., virtual touch, sight, and smell). VR technology can locate students in a virtual environment where they not only manipulate objects but also navigate novel surroundings. VR is particularly useful in cases where learning situations are not accessible, dangerous, or expensive to explore. For example, the VR website Second Life has been used to enable multiplayer games, virtual clinical tours, simulated experiments, and implementation of patient scenarios in medical and health education, among others.

Technology can capture students' learning experiences outside the classroom, which can facilitate reflective practices. Apart from taking notes, learners can make use of camera or sound-recording tools to keep an account of their learning activities in detail, for both sharing and reusing these experiences. The high portability of multimedia capture devices (e.g., digital cameras, smartphones, and digital voice recorders) allows students to conveniently create videos, audio, or photos of outdoor observations or for data collection. These digital artifacts serve as a basis for continuous reflection.

Technology can augment the physical learning environment with context-aware digital information. Augmented reality (AR) technology is capable of pushing location-specific digital information (e.g., texts, pictures, or videos) to mobile devices based on user inputs or GPS (global positioning system) tracking data. A new information layer over the physical world is generated to enrich user experience. When students visit a heritage site for history study, for instance, related learning materials (e.g., photos of historical events and a quiz) can be automatically pushed to their tablet PCs or mobile phones through AR technology to stimulate further inquiry or exploration.

Technology can be effective media to support group collaboration and discussion. Social media technology (e.g., cloud-based storage, blogs, wikis, and mobile phones) supports sharing of materials, discussion, and collaborative work. For example, Google Drive is capable of supporting group authoring of a report and presentation slides and a collaborative analysis of data saved in spreadsheets.

Technology can foster ongoing reflection through the creation and sharing of artifacts. Content creation and publishing tools and technologies (e.g., blogs, digital storytelling, digital portfolio system, and social networking websites) have been used to encourage students to describe and share their learning experiences, such as internships, lab sessions, or community service. Blogs can be used to facilitate reflection during student internships for the reason that a blog is a good medium to encourage both personal narrative and social interaction.

Technology is capable of creating a seamless learning experience that can take place anywhere at any time. Typically experiential learning involves student participation in learning activities situated across different spaces. Personal mobile devices like smartphones can provide students with ubiquitous access to information and tools to perform a variety of learning activities individually or collaboratively across different situations as well as across virtual and physical spaces, as argued by Lung-Hsiang Wong and Chee-Kit Looi. In the aforementioned case of biology study at the primary school level, each student could be equipped with a smartphone to capture information, receive learning materials pushed by AR technology, and stay connected with others. The captured information is then brought back to the classroom for discussion, reflection, and drafting final reports. In such a way, seamless learning is enabled in multiple dimensions and at different levels.

Technology can enable various modalities of knowledge representation, which facilitates the transformative process of learning experience conceptualization. Multimedia technology allows students to create multimodal content for knowledge representation. In addition to text, students can represent ideas through video, audio, pictures, and any forms of their combination. Digital storytelling is one method of digital multimedia production by which students could share aspects of their learning experiences. Digital storytelling has been used to design learning activities in order to promote reflective practices, knowledge construction, and communication skills.

Technology can also offer a way to address various emotional needs that arise during learning. Social media technology can serve as a platform to cultivate a supportive learning environment. An online learning community can offer a safe venue where students are free from emotional burdens resulting from negative predispositions to learning in real-world settings and can celebrate their achievements and recharge their emotional batteries to keep motivated. Social media technology has been proven to be effective to support emotional engagement while learning. Social networking websites (e.g., Facebook) in general can lead to flexible, casual, and emotional expression and a feeling of connectedness, all of which are fundamental components for development of group dynamics of a learning community.

Design Principles of Technology-Facilitated Experiential Learning

As proposed by Scott Donald Wurdinger and Jennifer Louise Bezon, five general approaches of experiential learning are

1. Project-based learning—engaging in a project to produce a presentation, product, or performance;

2. Problem-based learning—working out a solution to a specific problem assigned by a teacher, individually or in a group;

3. Service learning—applying curriculum knowledge to serve the needs of a community;

4. Place-based education—learning in local environment or society; and

5. Active learning—empowering students to take an active role in learning activities.

Several design principles underpin these five approaches, and technology empowers learners through autonomy and self-regulation in all five approaches. First of all, knowledge and skills are mainly gained from hands-on experiences in learning activities, such as project participation, workshops, community service, field trips, internship and so forth. Direct experience as the source of meaningful and engaging learning requires efforts for careful design. One model to support student-centered learning experience, suggested by Daniel Churchill, is called RASE, for resources, activity, support, and evaluation. In the context of experiential learning, *resources* can include reading materials, guidelines, rubrics, software, hardware, funding, and so forth that are used throughout the learning process. *Activity* that leads to learning outcomes through yielding direct experiences should be designed to be hands-on, inquiry-based, and in most cases collaborative in real-world settings. *Support* can be joint supervision of community partners and teachers, academic support from peers, logistic aids from institutions or governments, and any other form of assistance, to ensure removal of possible learning barriers and drive students to go beyond existing levels of knowledge and skills. *Evaluation* should be formative in nature, putting primary emphasis on scaffolding for the sake of improving learning outcomes. In the RASE model, technology can serve as a resource in support of the three other pedagogical components. What's more, the increasingly high mobility of computing devices makes it possible to create seamless, ubiquitous, and situated learning experiences across a variety of situations.

Continued reflection upon earlier learning experiences is vital for knowledge construction. Reflection bridges theoretical knowledge with practices bidirectionally. Effective reflection entails higher order thinking (e.g., analyzing, evaluating, synthesizing, and creating) about what students are doing and observing so that they can turn experience into knowledge. Furthermore, reflection helps students develop awareness to plan, monitor, and regulate the learning process. Reflection activities such as journal writing, group discussion, storytelling, and student narrative should be continuous, challenging, and contextualized, as suggested by Eyler Janet and Giles Dwight. Access to the reflections of others benefits students in developing deeper understanding of their shared learning experiences. Students can share their observations, ask questions, seek help and suggestions, and discuss with others. To reinforce reflection, technology can be used to record learning experiences, document reflection, enable sharing and reflective discussion, as well as for multimodal and multimedia expressions.

The teacher takes the role of a facilitator, monitoring and guiding students to explore the problem relatively independently, building students' confidence to apply knowledge in various learning contexts, providing formative assessment and stimulating constant reflections. Technology can be a tool for teachers to monitor students' learning activities, offer personalized feedback, distribute learning materials, and evaluate students' learning outcomes. For example, it is often challenging and labor intensive to monitor internships. To address this issue, teachers could require students to develop digital learning portfolios to demonstrate learning progress and regularly offer suggestions on the students' learning artifacts.

Learning activities are student centered and directed. Emphasizing knowledge construction and application in real-life settings, much autonomy and freedom are given to students to play an active role in the learning process, such as identifying problems, analyzing, drawing up plans, making decisions, and evaluating solutions, in order to achieve the intended learning outcomes. A variety of personalized learning tools (e.g., mobile technology, blogs, and social bookmarking websites), enable students to take control over and manage learning processes to a large degree, individually or in groups. With the assistance of technology, students can have a great deal of autonomy to structure personal learning environments and determine the content and the pace of learning. They organize themselves in a range of social networks of common interests to exchange ideas and help each other. They interact with people they choose when they have problems to solve or when they are willing to share resources or ideas and are not limited to discussing ideas with teachers and fellow students but can also reach out to field experts, practitioners, and any others with common learning interests.

Experiential learning involves social and emotional engagement. Social interaction is an essential element of experiential learning, given that learning activities often take place in social contexts outside the classroom. Collaboration is also necessary to solve a complex problem or accomplish a project. Social interaction not only leads to cognitive but also emotional engagement; consequently, social interactions can facilitate learning processes. No matter whether students experience failure or success, a channel to express and share emotions should be in place to turn both success and failure into opportunities for learning as well as opportunities for motivation and encouragement. Social media technologies can be applied as media to support communication, collaboration, and sharing, but they can also be used to meet the emotional needs of students emerging during learning (e.g., expressing feelings and exchanging emotional supports).

Conclusion

It is increasingly evident that experiential learning is an effective method of promoting knowledge construction, effective application of knowledge, and transfer of learning. In real-world settings, students play an active role in exploring and experimenting with new concepts through problem solving activities. Students can benefit from experiential learning in terms of learning skills, thinking strategies, domain knowledge, and professional skills. The use of experiential learning has been expanded over educational and training areas of medicine, engineering, social studies, humanities, and science.

Technology can undoubtedly be leveraged to facilitate the key elements underpinning experiential learning. Technology-facilitated experiential learning features the use and integration of affordances of different technological tools to influence how students experience problem-solving processes and translate experience into knowledge through reflection. Care should be taken to match affordances of a technology with the pedagogical requirements of an experiential learning activity.

Jie Lu

See also Augmented Reality; Mobile Tools and Technologies for Learning and Instruction; Social Media and Networking; 3D Immersive Environments; Web 2.0 and Beyond

Further Readings

Churchill, D., King, M., Webster, B., & Fox, B. (2013). Integrating learning design, interactivity, and technology. In H. Carter, M. Gosper, & J. Hedberg (Eds.), *Electronic dreams: Proceedings 30th ascilite Conference* (pp. 139–143). Sydney, Australia: Australasian Society for Computers in Learning in Tertiary Education.

Duffy, T. M., & Cunningham, D. J. (1996). Constructivism: Implications for the design and delivery of instruction. In D. H. Jonassen (Ed.), *Handbook of research for educational communications and technology* (pp. 170–198). Mahwah, NJ: Macmillan.

Eyler, J., & Giles, D. (1996). *A practitioner's guide to reflection in service-learning: Student voices & reflections.* Nashville, TN: Vanderbilt University.

Kolb, D. (1984). *Experiential learning: Experience as the source of learning and development.* Englewood Cliffs, NJ: Prentice Hall.

Sobel, D. (2005). *Place-based education: Connecting classrooms and communities* (2nd ed.). Great Barrington, MA: The Orion Society.

Wong, L.-H., & Looi, C.-K. (2011). What seams do we remove in mobile-assisted seamless learning? A critical review of the literature. *Computers & Education, 57*(4), 2364–2381. Retrieved from http://hal.archives-ouvertes.fr/docs/00/69/62/39/PDF/Wong-2011.pdf

Wurdinger, S. D., & Bezon, J. L. (2009). Teaching practices that promote student learning: Five experiential approaches. *Journal of Teaching and Learning, 6*(1), 1–13.

THINK-ALOUD PROTOCOL ANALYSIS

Protocol analysis is a rigorous methodology for eliciting verbal reports of thought sequences of data on thinking, reasoning, problem solving, reading, and learning. The study of thinking reemerged with the cognitive revolution and information processing theories of psychological phenomena in the 1950s. In the new research approach to the study of thought processes, participants were asked to *think aloud,* leading to a new type of verbal reports of thinking that differed from the earlier intro-spective methods and became the core method of protocol analysis. Traditionally, verbal reports of all types are collected from humans, ranging in expertise, while performing tasks in their domain such as diagnosing a mammogram, solving a physics problem, reading a history text, solving a math problem, writing a computer program, and so on. The verbal data has been used to capture and understand the underlying cognitive processes and structures that differentiate expert from novices.

This entry first outlines the fundamental assumption underlying think-aloud protocol analysis and describes the major differences between several types of verbal data. It then gives an example of the use of concurrent think-aloud data using a hypermedia learning task and briefly describes the steps involved in analyses of verbal data. It concludes by discussing the advantages and disadvantages of using think-aloud protocol analysis.

Fundamental Assumptions and Issues Underlying Think-Aloud Protocols

One of the most common methods in the study of thinking, reasoning, problem solving, and learning is to elicit verbal reports. Verbal data stems from a long research tradition in psychology rooted in the work of William Chase, Herbert Simon, Anders Ericsson, and Micki Chi.

This entry focuses on concurrent think-aloud protocols and not on other types of verbal reporting, such as retrospective protocols. First, it should be emphasized that verbal reporting methods differ in important ways. For example, in concurrent think-aloud protocols, the participants are instructed to verbalize the problem information to which they are attending. By contrast, in structured interviews, questions are usually carefully crafted to focus on a specific topic or scenario and are often sequenced in a meaningful order. Explanations are sometimes given to questions generated by a peer, by oneself, or by an experimenter, and they can be retrospective and reflective. As such, they represent different ways to collect verbal reports and are the target of ongoing debates such as those over whether giving verbal reports actually changes one's processing of the task, or whether different knowledge elicitation methods elicit different kinds of knowledge from the participants. Not only can verbal reports be collected in several different ways, they can be collected within the context of any number of other tasks, such as a perception task, a memory task, or a sorting task.

According to Ericsson and Simon, *protocol analysis* is used to identify and measure problem-solving processes. In protocol analysis, the think aloud requires individuals to provide verbal reports of their thoughts *simultaneously* as they solve a task. This focus on simultaneous thinking aloud is a strict requirement of protocol analysis in order to identify the contents of students' working memory as directly as possible. The contents of working memory are of primary interest because they are associated with executive functioning. Working memory is the memory location where attentional resources are allocated when individuals seek to solve problems and, therefore, this is the memory location of interest for measuring (and acquiring evidence to support inferences) about a student's problem-solving processes.

Despite strict guidelines outlined by Ericsson and Simon for conducting concurrent think alouds, there are common concerns that are frequently used to criticize them as valid data sources. For example, *reactivity* is a common concern and involves the act of asking someone to verbalize personal thoughts during an activity. Reactivity is problematic because if think-aloud protocols change the cognition of interest, then verbal reports may misrepresent one's understanding of the contents of individuals' minds. A second concern often cited is known as nonveridicality, meaning that the act of asking someone to verbalize thoughts does not provide access to the cognition of interest. Nonveridicality is a problem because if think-aloud protocols do not identify and measure the cognition of interest, then verbal reports may again misrepresent our understanding of the contents of individuals' minds. Therefore, both reactivity and nonveridicality are serious concerns that can undermine the use of concurrent think alouds. However, Ericsson and Simon's review of the empirical research leads to the conclusion that reactivity and nonveridicality can be avoided when the concurrent think alouds are conducted as they prescribe.

There are two common procedural violations in protocol analysis that can lead to reactivity and nonveridicality, including waiting long after the task is completed to ask individuals to verbalize their thoughts about how they solved the task (instead of obtaining simultaneous vocalization) or instructing or allowing students to rationalize or conjecture as to how they think they solved the task. Waiting too long to record an individual's thoughts after the task is solved casts doubt on whether what is being reported did, in fact, occur while solving the task. In addition, instructing or allowing students to conjecture as to how they think they solved the task reflects an individual's belief about what happened and may not necessarily reveal the contents of working memory.

Using Think-Aloud Protocols to Capture Self-Regulated Learning With Hypermedia

This section provides an illustration of the most basic steps involved in performing protocol analysis. It outlines the procedure of conducting think-aloud protocol analysis in a hypermedia learning task typically used by Roger Azevedo, Jeffrey A. Greene, Daniel C. Moos, Jennifer G. Cromley, and their colleagues to examine the temporal unfolding of cognitive and metacognitive self-regulatory processes during learning about a complex science topic with a hypermedia system. A full description of the procedure of think-aloud protocol analysis can be found in the works of Ericsson and Simon.

The first steps involve the selection of the individuals and the task. In the example in this entry, this includes college students with low prior knowledge of the human circulatory system as the individuals and learning about the circulatory system with a hypermedia system as the task. Prior to engaging in the learning task, each individual is administered a pretest, and following the task, each participant is administered a posttest, and both are used to measure learning gains of the topic. After the pretest, the researcher provided instructions for the learning task, which included a global learning goal: *Make sure you learn about the different parts and their purpose, how they work both individually and together, and how they support the human body.* Participants were given a tour of the system, illustrating navigation and search functions. During this tour the researcher also told the participant that the circulatory system, heart, and blood articles were three

potentially helpful articles. Following this, the participant was trained on how to think aloud while using the hypermedia system. This was accomplished by showing the participant a video clip of a student performing a concurrent think-aloud protocol while solving two math problems. Three issues are worth highlighting: Researchers should provide more than one example during training, the examples used to demonstrate the techniques should not be in the domain or topic of interest, and participants should be allowed to practice the think-aloud technique prior to engaging in the task.

During the learning session, the participant was given a certain amount of time to use the system to learn. While navigating the system, the researcher may remind the individual to verbalize, if the participant was silent for more than three seconds (e.g., Say what you are thinking). Ericsson and Simon emphasize this issue; however, researchers are warned that they should not be prompting excessively. During the task, the individual continues to provide concurrent think alouds until the task is complete. Following the task, individuals are administered a posttest, debriefed, and thanked for their participation. The next step is the preparation and analyses of the verbal data.

Coding Think-Aloud Protocols From Self-Regulated Learning With Hypermedia

The most challenging aspect of verbal report methods is data analysis. More specifically, this involves several steps including transcribing, coding, recoding, and analyzing the verbal data. For example, in a typical problem solving task (e.g., diagnosing a mammogram), think-aloud protocols are analyzed in the context of the cognitive task, which requires a cognitive task analysis, in order to know the knowledge states, problem-solving operators, and problem-solving strategies (e.g., means-end analysis) that are to be used to segment individual statements (e.g., the main abnormality is in the right breast where there is a large, well-circumscribed lesion). However, this is more complicated using a hypermedia-learning task because of using self-regulated learning as a theoretical framework and individuals are allowed to navigate freely throughout the environment for 40 minutes.

Table 1 provides a snippet of a coded and segmented concurrent think-aloud transcription. It should be emphasized that a major issue is the development and testing of a theoretically based coding scheme and the training needed to accurately transcribe, segment, and code think-aloud protocols. Again, there are standard rules and procedures that researchers need to follow when transcribing (e.g., what to do with unintelligible recorded speech, how to differentiate between verbal data and reading from the context), segmenting (e.g., how does one determine the beginning and end of a segment?), and coding (e.g., at what level of specificity does the data need to be coded?) verbal data.

In this example, the segments are in the first column, the second column contains the utterances from the participant, and the third column includes both the macrolevel SRL (self-regulated learning) codes related to *planning, metacognitive monitoring,* and *cognitive strategy,* as well as microlevel codes related to SRL (i.e., summarizing, feeling of knowing, identifying the adequacy of information). This snippet reveals that this participant monitored both her understanding of the topic (circulatory system) and the relevancy of the environment's content. For example, she decided to hyperlink to the heart article after identifying that she had

previously learned information in the circulatory system article (Segment 5). She continued to monitor her understanding (Segments 7 and 9) and then eventually used the strategy of summarization (Segment 11). This snippet represents a few seconds during the 40-minute hypermedia-learning task. Coded transcriptions not only provide accurate descriptions of *what* learners do, but also *when* they do it, *what* occurs before and after each behavior, and *how often* each behavior occurs over the course of a learning task. Coded think-aloud protocols can be examined to understand the deployment of cognitive and metacognitive self-regulatory processes during learning, quantified within and across individuals (and experimental

Table 1   Example of a segmented and coded concurrent think-aloud transcription with micro and macro SRL codes

Segment	Utterance Transcribed From Participant During Learning With Hypermedia	[Micro SRL] and Macro SRL Codes
1	I am going to start with the circulatory system just because I am already there...	[No Code]
2	...and I'm just reading the introduction...circulatory system...it also known as the cardiovascular system and it deals with the heart...it transports oxygen and nutrients and it takes away waste...	[Summarizing] *Strategy Use*
3	...um, it does stuff with blood and I'm kind of remembering some of this from bio in high school, but not a lot of it, um...	[Feeling of Knowing] *Monitoring*
4	**Reads:** *The heart and the blood and the blood vessels are the three structural elements and the heart is the engine of the circulatory system, it is divided into four chambers.*	[No Code]
5	I knew this one, two right and two left...the atrium, the ventricle and the left atrium, and the left ventricle...	[Feeling of Knowing] *Monitoring*
6	...okay start the introduction [of the heart], just kind of scout it out real quick...and there's a section called function of the heart...and it looks like it will give me what I need to know...	[Identifying Adequacy of Information] *Monitoring*
7	...um...introduction, oh that's just basic stuff that we've been doing	[Feeling of Knowing] *Monitoring*
8	**Reads:** *Structure of the heart has four chambers*	[No Code]
9	We did that...	[Feeling of Knowing] *Monitoring*
10	**Reads:** *The atria are also known as auricles. They collect blood that pours in from veins.*	[No Code]
11	So, it looks like the first step is atria in the system and then the veins	[Summarizing] *Strategy Use*

Source: "Measuring Cognitive and Metacognitive Regulatory Processes Used During Hypermedia Learning: Issues and Challenges," by R. Azevedo, D. Moos, A. Johnson, and A. Chauncey, (2010). *Educational Psychologist, 45*(4), 216.

Note: SRL = self-regulated learning.

conditions, depending on specific research questions and hypotheses), correlated with learning outcomes and other performance measures, and used to design advanced learning technologies.

Conclusion

Think-aloud protocol analysis is a well-established and rigorous method used for decades to study cognitive processes used by individuals during thinking, reasoning, problem solving, learning, and reading. There is vast research literature that spans across age groups, domains, topics, and learning and training environments that has laid a solid foundation for the study of cognitive phenomena. Think-aloud protocol analysis requires extensive training in the use of various methods. It is a time-consuming method and requires precision; otherwise, the data may distort the cognitive phenomena being examined and lead to invalid results. When used properly, the technique offers many benefits including detailed task-specific process models, delineation of a myriad of knowledge states, problem-solving operators, strategies, and so on that can be used to generate hypotheses and design learning and training systems.

The technique also has some disadvantages such as (1) being time consuming to collect, transcribe, code, recode, and analyze; (2) requiring extensive training of coders; (3) dealing with missing data due to an individual being silent, and technical issues stemming from poor-quality recording; (4) segmenting, coding, and analyzing the data is not always straightforward since there may not be enough context needed to code a particular segment; (5) coding may be hampered if the coding scheme does not have enough codes to account for the utterances or is not stable because it has not been tested and expanded throughout piloting; and (6) dealing with process data that is seldom normally distributed therefore challenging the use of inferential statistics. Most the time think-aloud data need to be time stamped and triangulated with other process data (e.g., log-file and screen-capture video of user-system interactions, gaze behaviors from eye tracking) that were collected concurrently in order to add additional context that will facilitate inferences about the underlying cognitive phenomena. Lastly, once coded, think-aloud data can lead to new hypotheses, experimental manipulations, and design of learning and training systems.

Roger Azevedo, Michelle Taub,
and Nicholas Mudrick

See also Assessment of Problem Solving and Higher Order Thinking; Cognition and Human Learning; Cognitive Task Analysis; Experimental Research and Educational Technology; Human-Computer Interaction; Intelligent Tutoring Systems; Knowledge and Skills Hierarchies; Knowledge Elicitation; Learning Analytics; Repair Theory; Self-Regulated E-Learning Design Principles; Stealth Assessment; Student Modeling; System and Learner Control in Adaptive Systems

Further Readings

Azevedo, R., Cromley, J. G., Moos, D. C., Greene, J. A., & Winters, F. I. (2011). Adaptive content and process scaffolding: A key to facilitating students' self-regulated learning with hypermedia. *Psychological Test and Assessment Modeling, 53,* 106–140.

Azevedo, R., Moos, D. C., Johnson, A. M., & Chauncey, A. D. (2010). Measuring cognitive and metacognitive regulatory processes used during hypermedia learning: Issues and challenges. *Educational Psychologist, 45*(4), 210–223.

Chi, M. T. H. (2006). Laboratory methods for assessing experts' and novices' knowledge. In K. A. Ericsson, N. Charness, P. Feltovich, & R. R. Hoffman (Eds.), *Cambridge handbook of expertise and expert performance* (pp. 167–184). Cambridge, UK: Cambridge University Press.

Ericsson, K. A. (2006). Protocol analysis and expert thought: Concurrent verbalizations of thinking during experts' performance on representative tasks. In K. A. Ericsson, N. Charness, P. Feltovich, & R. R. Hoffman (Eds.), *Cambridge handbook of expertise and expert performance* (pp. 223–242). Cambridge, UK: Cambridge University Press.

Ericsson, K. A., Charness, N., Feltovich, P., & Hoffman, R. R. (Eds.). (2006). *The Cambridge handbook of expertise and expert performance.* Cambridge, UK: Cambridge University Press.

Ericsson, K. A., & Simon, H. A. (1993). *Protocol analysis: Verbal reports as data* (Rev. ed.). Cambridge, MA: MIT Press.

Feltovich, P. J., Prietula, M. J., & Ericsson, K. A. (2006). Studies of expertise from psychological perspectives. In K. A. Ericsson, N. Charness, P. Feltovich, and R. R. Hoffman (Eds.), *Cambridge handbook of expertise and expert performance* (pp. 39–68). Cambridge, UK: Cambridge University Press.

Greene, J. A., & Azevedo, R. (2009). A macro-level analysis of SRL processes and their relations to the acquisition of sophisticated mental models. *Contemporary Educational Psychology, 34,* 18–29.

Greene, J. A., Robertson, J., & Costa, L.-J. C. (2011). Assessing self-regulated learning using think-aloud methods. In B. J. Zimmerman & D. Schunk (Eds.), *Handbook of self-regulation of learning and performance* (pp. 313–328). New York, NY: Routledge.

3D IMMERSIVE ENVIRONMENTS

3D immersive environments (3DIE) refer to technologies in which the user is immersed and uses an avatar to interact with the environment, animated agents, and artifacts. Many 3DIEs allow multiple users and communication occurs via chat messaging or audio as part of scenarios intended to foster learning activities that are often game like or role-playing. There are several terms used to describe 3DIE systems, such as *virtual worlds, virtual learning environments, multiuser virtual environments (MUVE), computer games or serious games, immersive simulations,* and so on. Examples used for educational purposes include *Quest Atlantis, Whyville, EcoMUVE,* and *Omosa Virtual World.* This entry discusses the history of 3DIEs, gives some examples, and discusses learning successful approaches in 3DIEs.

Historical Overview

In terms of the history of 3DIEs, there has been interest in using the representations of 2D and 3D simulations and games with their collaborative and motivational aspects for educational purposes for many years. As Margaret E. Gredler noted a decade ago, despite the extensive development of 2D simulations and games for over 40 years, most projects only reported anecdotal evidence or personal impressions about the effectiveness of these systems and few provided research evidence that documented important learning outcomes.

By the mid-1990s, computer advances made 3D visualizations and virtual reality (VR) environments viable and prototype immersive 3D VR simulations for learning were developed, such as *ScienceSpace.* 3D VR systems typically involved specialized VR equipment in which the learner used stereoscopic head-mounted displays (HMD) with sound and perhaps haptic devices for kinesthetic feedback. Research at the time suggested these approaches might provide *value-added* learning over 2D simulations. However, 3D VR systems in the 1990s were very expensive due to the need for high-end computer graphics processing and specialized ancillary equipment such as stereoscopic LCD shuttered glasses or head-mounted display (HMD) units. Consequently, the research findings of important learning outcomes associated with 3D VR systems, while theoretically important, had no practical impact on regular classroom practices.

Since early 2000, there has been increasing interest in 3D computer games (actually a simulation of a 3D environment displayed on a 2D computer screen, sometimes called 2.5D to differentiate from true visually immersive 3D virtual experiences). The interactivity and engagement in commercially available computer games has attracted millions of users around the world and created a large economic market that is driving further technological and design developments in this area. Academics such as James Gee argued that many of the features of computer games were well suited to support many of the research recommendations about learning knowledge as well as a range of attitudes, skills, and dispositions of relevance in real-world settings.

However, a critical look at the research to date on computer games and learning suggests the case for how games support learning of school-oriented knowledge and skills has been and remains equivocal. Over a decade ago, it was found that while commercial games provide a forum for learning knowledge and skills, there is a mismatch between the content in commercial games and the traditional school curricula. There have been other issues related to 3DIE games, such as the impact of violence, gender images, and the displacement of other activities by excessive gameplay.

Over the last decade or so, there has been a shift from trying to repurpose commercial games for use in schools (which has not been very effective, as discussed earlier) to developing 3DIE systems that are game-like but specifically designed for use in schools. While research involving 3DIEs such as these has been encouraging, there remain concerns about the relatively modest findings of learning gains with these systems, especially for learning science subjects. The general consensus at this time is that future research is warranted to further explore the potential of various approaches for developing 3DIEs. More generally, learning designers should carefully examine educationally successful approaches of 3DIEs both in terms of the technology features and of the types of learning and teaching activities used with these systems.

Examples of 3D Immersive Environments

In this section, three examples of 3DIEs are briefly discussed that have been the focus of educational research demonstrating their effectiveness in helping students learn important knowledge, skills, and attitudes. One of the more extended programs of research into learning with 3DIEs is *Quest Atlantis* (QA). The developers refer to QA as an educational multiuser virtual environment (MUVE) that allows students to travel in a virtual space to perform in-class or after-school educational activities, talk with other students and mentors, and build virtual identities. Research involving QA has documented significant learning gains in a variety of school subjects including social studies, science, and language learning. QA is now being further developed as part of the *Atlantis Remix* project.

An example of a commercially viable 3DIE is *Whyville,* which is described as a virtual world geared to preteen and teenage girls and boys from 8 to 16. The *Whyville* educational Internet site engages users in a variety of topics in science, business, art, and geography, and has a base of millions of users considered *citizens.* *Whyville* is a virtual world where the avatars of the citizens role play as they engage in their world, which has its own newspaper, senators, beach, museum, city hall and town square, suburbia, and even its own economy with "clams" earned by playing educational games. Educational research has demonstrated important learning outcomes in areas such as health and identity, and the website has received numerous awards such as the National Parenting Publication Award Gold Award in 2008.

A more recently developed 3DIE is the EcoMUVE project at Harvard University, which combines elements of learning in a virtual learning environment with augmented reality (AR) in which the virtual experiences overlay an actual local pond. Students virtually explore the ecology of the pond, collect virtual data, and then engage in inquiry at the real pond. Special probeware has been designed to facilitate collection of real data at the pond and comparison with the virtual data students have collected. Research has demonstrated significant learning on water quality variables, feed webs, abiotic and biotic resources, and graphing.

Learning Approaches in Successful Educational Virtual Worlds

The pedagogical designs of many educationally successful 3DIEs are explicitly or implicitly guided inquiry approaches based on a social constructivist model of learning by doing. The use of online scaffolding to support the learners is common, and linking of cycles of online activities in the 3DIE with classroom-based teacher-led instruction has been found to be very effective.

The sense of immersion that the learner experiences is also important. There are various techniques that may be used to evoke the sense of immersion, such as the use of graphics, sounds, perceptions of moving in an environment, touching objects, and so on that are associated with various types of embodied sensory inputs. There are also social communication aspects of immersion, such as text or audio interactions between avatars, personalization of the avatar, flexibility, and agency in the story scenario, and feedback mechanisms for the learner to view progress or movements in the virtual environment.

However, it is important to realize that students do not automatically learn in 3DIEs. We are still relatively early in the research necessary to fully understand what types of knowledge, skills, and dispositions may be most efficaciously learned through activities involving 3DIEs versus other types of learning experiences and technological tools. Related, further research is need to identify the theories of learning, the types of learning and teaching activities, the assessment approaches that are most appropriate for 3DIEs, and the overall place of these learning tools and approaches in broader curricular sequences in various subject areas. Still, the promise is great for 3DIEs to be a central tool in the suite of advanced educational technologies that will enhance learning of important 21st-century knowledge and skills.

Michael J. Jacobson

See also Adaptive Learning Software and Platforms; Constructivist Theory; Games: Impact on Learning; Games to Promote Inquiry Learning; Haptic Technologies to Support Learning; Learning by Modeling; Simulation-Based Learning; Training Using Virtual Worlds; Video Games and Student Assessment; Virtual Learning Environments; Virtual Worlds

Further Readings

Barab, S. A., Thomas, M., Dodge, T., Carteaux, R., & Tuzun, H. (2005). Making learning fun: Quest Atlantis, a game without guns. *Educational Technology Research & Development*, 53(1), 86–107.

Dawley, L., & Dede, C. (2014). Situated learning in virtual worlds and immersive simulations. In J. M. Spector, M. D. Merrill, J. Elen, & M. J. Bishop (Eds.), *The handbook of research for educational communications and technology* (4th ed., pp. 723–734). New York, NY: Springer-Verlag.

Duncan, I., Miller, A., & Jiang, S. (2012). A taxonomy of virtual worlds usage in education. *British Journal of Educational Technology*, 43(6), 949–964.

Gee, J. P. (2003). *What videogames have to teach us about learning and literacy.* New York, NY: Palgrave Macmillan.

Honey, M. A., & Hilton, M. (Eds.). (2011). *Learning science through computer games and simulations.* Washington, DC: The National Academies Press.

Jacobson, M. J., Kim, B., Miao, C., Shen, Z., & Chavez, M. (2010). Design perspectives for learning in virtual worlds. In M. J. Jacobson & P. Reimann (Eds.), *Designs for learning environments of the future: International learning sciences theory and research perspectives* (pp. 111–142). New York, NY: Springer-Verlag.

Kirriemuir, J., & McFarlane, A. (2004). *Literature review in games and learning* (Report 8). Bristol, UK: Futurelab.

Klopfer, E., Osterweil, S., & Salen, K. (2009). *Moving learning games forward.* Cambridge, MA: MIT, Education Arcade.

McLellan, H. (2004). Virtual realities. In D. H. Jonassen (Ed.), *Handbook of research for educational communications and technology* (2nd ed., pp. 461–497). Mahwah, NJ: Lawrence Erlbaum.

Young, M. F., Slota, S., Cutter, A. B., Jalette, G., Mullin, G., Lai, B., . . . & Yukhymenko, M. (2012). Our princess is in another castle: A review of trends in serious games for education. *Review of Educational Research*, 82(1), 61–89.

3D PRINTING AND PROTOTYPING

3D printing, or computer-aided additive manufacturing, creates physical objects from digital files by generating very small layers of material that build up to a final form. 3D printing is a technological innovation that differs from older computer-controlled subtractive manufacturing techniques where objects are shaped by removing material from large pieces. With a 3D printer, one can make almost anything, including jewelry, circuits, food, and even artificial organs. In educational settings teachers can use 3D printers to help students create and design a variety of educational objects such as recreations of historical artifacts, complex art forms, scientific models, and even cheaper versions of lab materials. 3D prototyping involves iteratively making three-dimensional solutions to problems, finding places for improvement, and then refining and revising solutions. 3D printing and prototyping has been used in both undergraduate and graduate engineering education contexts. Recent innovations in technology, as well as a growing emphasis on science, technology, engineering, and mathematics (STEM) in precollege and informal settings, demonstrate the potential that 3D printing and prototyping can have in many educational contexts. This entry first provides an overview of the development of 3D printing technologies and elaborates on current uses in educational settings. It then discusses the future potential of 3D printers as well as barriers to integration with educational settings.

3D printing can be thought of as an extension of inkjet printing but instead of printing a single layer of ink, 3D printers print material. A 3D printer creates objects by adding material in successive layers, gradually building up the object in three dimensions by placing what are essentially two-dimensional cross-sections of the object on top of each other. Voids can be created in the object by adding a different support material that is later removed by post processing, such as using chemicals to dissolve the support material while leaving the rest of the object intact. This gives a 3D printer the capability to produce complex multipart assemblies that are fully assembled, something that would be difficult to achieve and require multiple steps through other means.

Users create objects to be 3D printed through computer-aided design (CAD) software. CAD software allows users to design and create virtual objects. Common examples of CAD software include AutoCAD, Pro-Engineer, and Google SketchUp. Once a user creates a design, the virtual object is converted into a standard computer format (such as the stereolithography, or STL, de-facto standard format) and processed by the 3D printer.

Rapid prototyping with 3D printing generally refers to the ability to make models of final designs quickly and with high quality. Although many fields have used rapid prototyping of objects as part of design processes before the invention of the 3D printer, rapid prototyping technologies such as 3D printers enable complex designs to be quickly fabricated for high resolution testing and revision. Instead of waiting weeks or months for prototypes, similar if not higher quality objects can be printed in days or hours.

Contemporary 3D printing has roots in industrial manufacturing and rapid prototyping. Prior to 3D printing, parts were usually made via *subtractive* methods (as opposed to the *additive* method utilized by a 3D printer), such as milling or grinding, which reduced larger starting pieces of material to form shapes. 3D printing first arose in the 1980s in industrial settings, and, as such, was cost prohibitive for regular consumers. Now, in the 21st century, hobbyist and home models of 3D printers are available at a price that many individuals and educational institutions can afford. These include machines from open-source projects such as RepRap and Fab@Home, as well as commercial offerings such as those from Afinia and Cubify. While not as fast or robust as an industrial model costing tens of thousands of dollars (or more), these hobbyist and home models (costing a few thousand dollars or less) allow regular consumers the ability to engage in the same rapid prototyping and custom fabrication that were previously only available in industrial settings. Designs created for the at-home 3D printer can also be processed by an industrial 3D printer, giving individuals the capability to send their designs out to an industrial 3D printer for mass production. Companies now offer 3D printing services for individuals who want to create their own custom 3D printed objects but do not have access to a 3D printer.

The use of 3D printers in education represents an experiential approach that enables students to learn through designing and fabricating objects, aligning with both constructivist and constructionist learning frameworks. Constructivist perspectives of learning hold that students actively build understanding through interactions with instructors, peers, and the environment. Constructionist perspectives of learning, such as those put forth by Seymour Papert, view building personally relevant artifacts as augmenting learning. In this way, 3D printing can augment learning by enabling students to easily build and fabricate personalized objects that enable them to share, add, refine, and revise their designs as well as their ideas. Typically, students learning through design at any level can get too focused on minor or superficial issues of prototyping. Spending more time on prototyping means that students devote less time to understanding larger concepts or other processes of learning by design such as revising and reflecting upon the objects. With 3D printers, educators have found that students can spend less time on prototyping and devote more time to learning material.

Because of the cost, the most frequent use of 3D printers in formal education has been in university settings with undergraduate and graduate students. Now with the technology becoming more pervasive and the price point more accessible, there are opportunities to expand into precollege school settings. In order for 3D printers to be accessible and useful in a formal setting, especially in K–12, there needs to be appropriate 3D-printing hardware and accessible CAD software, as well as curricula that effectively integrate design and prototyping.

Many students in university engineering and architecture programs across the country have access to commercial-grade 3D-printing technologies. Use in engineering programs involves becoming acquainted with advanced manufacturing technologies used in industry as well as creating high-quality design projects. Engineering design focuses on iteratively developing solutions to problems, making the use of 3D printing a natural fit for prototyping solutions. Typically 3D printers are alongside other computer-controlled manufacturing technologies such as computer-controlled die cutters and laser cutters. These machine shops or *fabrication labs* can be found in many engineering departments. In addition to having access to the physical hardware, most engineering programs suggest that students learn how to use commercial CAD software such as Pro-E or Autodesk Inventor so that they have those skills moving into the workforce. Many undergraduate engineering programs also incorporate design into their curriculum. Although traditionally engineering programs have only incorporated design into upper-level courses, many programs now encourage incorporating design projects for first- and second-year courses to increase engagement and to help students become acculturated to the field of engineering from the beginning.

Hardware, software, and curricula are available in higher education settings, and numerous examples exist of students using 3D printers as part of engineering courses. For example, undergraduate students have printed a complete drone airplane and models of zero-emissions homes as part of final class projects.

Use of 3D printers in higher education also extends to architecture and studio arts. Architecture students use 3D printers to construct 3D models of spaces and projects. Students in studio art classes have used 3D printers to build elaborate sculptural pieces. Other faculty offer classes in creativity and fabrication, such as Neil Gershenfeld's How to Make (Almost) Everything at the Massachusetts Institute of Technology and Michael Eisenberg's Things That Think at the University of Colorado Boulder.

The use of 3D printers in precollege formal education settings is just developing. The price point of 3D printers such as the Afinia or RepRap has now become affordable for K–12 classrooms. Software packages such as SketchUp and FormZ make CAD modeling accessible to younger students. Additionally, other software such as Fab@School and Energy3D has been specifically designed for younger students to develop CAD modeling skills. However, few K–12 classrooms currently have curricula that incorporate design and prototyping. With the increasing emphasis of engineering in precollege settings, educational organizations have put forth standards that incorporate engineering design. This emphasis on engineering design in science classrooms provides the perfect opportunity for 3D printing to become as ubiquitous as traditional printers in K–12 classrooms.

Classrooms that use 3D printers have had students engage in modeling or some sort of product design project. For instance, high school students have printed 3D models of proteins as part of biology classes. Other high school students in engineering classes have created technology enclosures. Universities and local school districts have joined efforts to integrate additive manufacturing into science classrooms.

3D printing and advanced manufacturing techniques have already made a huge impact on informal learning settings. The increasing popularity of *maker* culture (people who like to invent, create, and prototype in their spare time) demonstrates the potential of 3D printers for use in other informal learning contexts. A huge community of *makers* as well as *makerspaces* has popped up in the last decade. Makerspaces and *hackerspaces* are open community labs where people of similar interests come together to make all kinds of objects or things. Makerspaces typically have various kinds of fabrication technologies along with 3D printers. Students of all ages have made and shared various kinds of designs. Websites such as Thingiverse enable people around the world to share and build upon the designs of others using a 3D printer. Maker activities have the potential to get all kinds of students interested in STEM. Researchers are just beginning to understand how learners can develop traits such as perseverance and grit as well as STEM engagement in these settings.

Potential of 3D Printing

Because 3D printing enables anyone to print anything anywhere, different educational models and paradigms can now be carried out in and out of school settings. Rapid prototyping using 3D printing, combined with open source projects on the Internet, facilitate product refinement on a large scale. This can be thought of as a crowdsourced cottage industry. Crowdsourcing activity has been seen in other open source domains, such as open source software development, where the global community contributes to continually refine computer software. Now, with 3D printing, individuals in the global community can print physical objects from open source projects and refine, redesign, or integrate them in novel ways. Examples of this include an open-source 3D-printed robot used to teach electrical engineering, FM radio and speakers used to teach electricity, and even jewelry that is based on mathematical ratios.

Incorporating 3D printers and prototyping into college and precollege settings enables students to get authentic engineering experiences that are in demand for the growing advanced manufacturing industry. In STEM domains, students can use 3D printers to print out sophisticated models of complex systems. 3D printing can help make abstract concepts or ideas, like molecules or proteins, more concrete for students by providing physical models of phenomena. Students can use 3D printers to express themselves artistically through complex sculptural elements. Similarly, teachers can use 3D printers to create customized equipment that they may not have been able to find or afford before. For instance, teachers can create things such as physical models of complex mathematical shapes, machines for physics education, or anatomical models for biology.

3D printing also has the potential to increase diversity and involvement in educational activities through the creation of personalized design objects. For instance, using advanced manufacturing techniques provides a wide range of personalized experiences that can increase engagement for students traditionally underrepresented in STEM. Similarly, 3D printing has the capability of blending informal and formal environments. Students can work in afterschool makerspaces on projects that can contribute to learning in formal settings.

Barriers to 3D Printing in Learning Environments

Barriers to the proliferation of 3D printing in education include cost and training. Although the costs involved in 3D printing have come down significantly, they may still be prohibitive for many schools to allow even minimal deployment. Beside the capital costs for the equipment (the 3D printer) and software (CAD program, although there are free alternatives), there are recurring costs for materials consumed in the 3D printing process as well as maintenance for the 3D printer (and maintenance for commercial software). Knowledge of how to use 3D printing in schools requires training for teachers, students, school administrators, and the people who will maintain the system. Students need to learn how to use the technology without breaking the printer or wasting material (and time taken printing). School administrators need to learn how 3D printing fits within the overall academic mission and objectives of the school or school

system. Maintenance personnel need to learn how to maintain the equipment. Training for all of these stakeholders requires resources (time and money) that may pose barriers to deployment in schools.

Jennifer L. Chiu and Edward A. Pan

See also Constructivist Theory; Design and Development Research; Disruptive Technologies; Emerging Educational Technologies; Informal Learning Strategies; Learning by Modeling; Learning Objects

Further Readings

Berry, R. Q., Bull, G., Browning, C., Thomas, C. D., Starkweather, G., & Aylor, J. (2010). Use of digital fabrication to incorporate engineering design principles in elementary mathematics education. *Contemporary Issues in Technology and Teacher Education, 10*(2), 167–172.

Chiu, J. L., Bull, G., Berry, R. Q., & Kjellstrom, W. (2013). Teaching engineering design with digital fabrication: Imagining, creating, and refining ideas. In N. Levine & C. Mouza (Eds.), *Emerging technologies for the classroom: A learning sciences perspective* (pp. 47–62). New York, NY: Springer-Verlag.

Eisenberg, M. (2011). Educational fabrication, in and out of the classroom. In M. J. Koehler & P. Mishra (Eds.), *Proceedings of Society for Information Technology & Teacher Education International Conference 2011* (pp. 884–891). Chesapeake, VA: Association for the Advancement of Computing in Education.

Kroll, E., & Artzi, D. (2011). Enhancing aerospace engineering students' learning with 3D printing wind-tunnel models. *Rapid Prototyping Journal, 17*(5), 393–402.

Mellis, D., & Buechley, L. (2012). Case studies in the personal fabrication of electronic products. In *Proceedings of the Designing Interactive Systems Conference 2012* (pp. 268–277). New York, NY: Association for Computing Machinery. doi:10.1145/2317956.2317998

National Science Foundation. (2013). *Fabricating the future: 3-D printing molds new K-12 STEM model.* Retrieved from http://www.nsf.gov/discoveries/disc_summ.jsp?cntn_id=127769

Websites

Thingiverse: http://www.thingiverse.com

3G AND 4G NETWORKS

The world today proliferates with a huge range of mobile devices ranging from smartphones to tablets to laptops. This proliferation seems very likely to increase further to include wearable devices, sensors, and even smaller devices. These devices use radio communications to connect to the Internet, to communicate with each other, and to upload and download access to all kinds of data. Most of these radio interfaces are short range, for example, Bluetooth and Wi-Fi, operating in shared (i.e., unlicensed) spectrum; however, longer range communications (200 meters to 30 kilometers) always use licensed, dedicated spectrum, and as this is a scarce commodity, it is very much in demand by the various telecommunication cellular operators. The operators also need to provide backhaul connections—usually landline—from the various cell base stations to the Internet, corporate network, or other destination network. In most countries, the number of operators with the economic resources to acquire the needed radio spectrum and to backhaul the traffic through their access networks, is usually relatively small. In the United States, for example, four operators dominate—Verizon, AT&T, Sprint-Nextel, and T-Mobile.

The terms *3G* and *4G* generally refer to high-speed data services provided wirelessly to smartphones and other mobile devices by the cellular operators. The terms *3G* and *4G* refer respectively to third and fourth generation devices and communication technologies. Prior to this, first generation referred specifically to analog phones and communications, while the second generation marked the transition to digital devices and communications. Being digital, second generation phones were the first to provide data services, notably text messaging (aka SMS or short message service). However, we have come a long way in a very short time from low bit rate SMS to watching high definition videos on handheld devices. This entry first explains the distinction between 3G and 4G. It then discusses the high data rates made available by recent wireless technologies and the ability for multiple users to access cellular networks. Finally, it discusses some of the most recent advances involving 4G technologies.

The differences between second generation and later generations of mobile devices and communication technologies are not so clear cut. Third and fourth, and presumably even higher order, generations are, and probably will continue to be, defined by potential data rates that users can achieve on their mobile device. In other words, generations are defined by data rates as opposed to real technical advances in the underlying communications technologies.

For example, 3G—strictly speaking—requires a minimum data rate of 200 Kbps (kilobits per second). On the other hand, 4G demands a peak download rate of 100 Mbps (megabits per second) for highly mobile users and 1 Gbps (gigabits per second) for low mobility users. Because of the focus on potential data rates, rather than on technological advances, generations are now being

defined by something that most users can never experience. In the case of 4G, for example, the reality is that most users of 4G devices will not be able to get anything close to the claimed rates—in general, these optimal rates are really only possible if there are no other active users in that particular cell *and* the user has an extremely good wireless channel, that is, the user is probably just a short distance from the cell tower and with a very good line-of-sight path. A much more useful metric would be a typical peak data rate that a user could expect.

Notwithstanding the issues with the 3G/4G definitions, there have been many remarkable technological advances in mobile devices, wireless communication technologies, and indeed in the network infrastructure to support these high data rates and the wide range of applications enabled.

High Data Rates

The high data rates enabled by these new wireless technologies have been enabled by a number of major technological advances. Back in the late 1940s, Claude Shannon in a famous theorem showed that it is possible for an arbitrary communication channel to transmit error-free data up to some theoretical maximum. Of course, his theorem did not say how this maximum could be achieved and for a long time the Shannon limit remained little more than an esoteric concept. For a wireless channel, the Shannon limit is best expressed in units of bits per sec per unit of radio frequency bandwidth (i.e., bps/Hertz). In recent years, new transmission technologies such as OFDM (Orthogonal Frequency Division Multiplexing) and adaptive modulation and control techniques as well as new channel coding techniques have allowed spectral efficiencies to get closer and closer to the Shannon limit. What has enabled these advances in such a cost-effective manner on really small devices has been the huge advances in digital processing technologies over the past 20 years or so.

High data rates have also been enabled through the use of MIMO (multiple in, multiple out) antennas at both the transmitting and receiving ends of the radio transmission. To achieve high gains in the data rates, the antennas in these MIMO systems need to support completely independent transmission paths between individual transmitting and receiving antennas—this is of course a real technical challenge on small handheld devices where the antennas (usually hidden to the user) are very close together.

The term *LTE* (for Long Term Evolution) tends to be used interchangeably with 4G. LTE represents a set of technologies used across the radio interface, including OFDMA (Orthogonal Frequency Division Multiple Access), MIMO, adaptive modulation and coding, as well as technologies and procedures for channel estimation, resource allocation, among others.

Finally, high data rates have been enabled through the availability of more radio spectrum for cellular communications. In general, the transmission of analog signals requires more radio spectrum than digital signals. As, for example, digital television has replaced analog television, governments and telecommunication authorities have released now unneeded spectrum for other applications, notably cellular communications.

Multiple Users

With so many users transmitting and receiving all kinds of data, one might wonder how such limited radio spectrum can support all these devices. This is achieved through frequency reuse, that is, the same radio spectrum that's used in one radio cell is reused by other cells far enough away so that the interference is minimal. Initially all cells were the same size (i.e., same transmit power) so that interference management was quite well understood allowing the use of directional antennas to improve frequency reuse and, thereby, the total capacity of a cellular network.

One of the great challenges going forward is to meet the apparently insatiable demand for high-speed wireless access. One solution to this is for cellular operators to deploy more and more cells—especially really small cells—and to figure out how all these different types and sizes of cells (macro, pico, micro, femto) can work together cooperatively to maximize the reuse of radio spectrum; this cooperative activity is termed CoMP (coordinated multipoint).

LTE Advanced

The most recent version of LTE, called LTE-Advanced, supports the deployment of heterogeneous cells (i.e., a range of cells of different sizes including privately owned cells, called *home base stations*) along with CoMP techniques. This new standard also includes techniques on how to use disjoint radio spectrum for a single data transmission (termed *carrier aggregation*), the use of relays to extend the range of radio transmission, and enhancements to both uplink and downlink MIMO antennas using beamforming and other interference cancellation techniques. Theoretical maximum data rates for LTE-Advanced are 3 Gbps downlink and 1.5 Gbps uplink with 100 MHz of aggregated spectrum used for a single transmission and with eight MIMO antennas at the base station and four MIMO antennas at the mobile. Future advances are likely to include self-organizing networks, cognitive radio, and uplink/downlink interbase station coordinated MIMO.

Everything Over IP

One of the major changes in the 4G era is how, with 4G technologies such as LTE, the network that hitherto used a combination of traditional circuit-switched technology (supporting telephony) and packet-based data networking is converting to an Internet-based network. This technological convergence has huge ramifications not just for broadband wireless access but for telecommunications overall, especially landline telephony.

There is much more to a 4G network than a high-speed radio frequency connection between the mobile device and the cell base station. Since the network is now all IP, the operator's access network has to provide the same quality of service (QoS) to a voice call as traditional circuit-switched telephony. The *Evolved Packet Core* (EPC)—as the access network is called—requires a number of new IP-based protocols and architectures. Protocols include SCTP (Stream Control Transport Protocol), which supports multihoming and multistreaming; the Diameter protocol for authentication, authorization, and more; and the Session Initiation Protocol (SIP) for setting up and managing real-time voice and video sessions. Architectures include the IP Multimedia Subsystem (IMS) for continuity of media flows during handoff between different access technologies, use of EAP-based (Extensible Authentication Protocol) access control architectures for both trusted and untrusted access, and a novel Policy and Charging Control (PCC) Architecture to address QoS and usage-based charging.

Peter O'Reilly

See also Cloud Computing; Cyberinfrastructure Capabilities and Limitations; Data Streaming; Information and Communication Technologies: Competencies in the 21st-Century Workforce; Integrated and Networked Mobile Devices for Learning and Instruction; Internet of Things

Further Readings

Bhat, P., Nagata, S., Campoy, L., Berberana, I., Derham, T., Liu, G., . . . & Yang, J. (2012). LTE-advanced: An operator perspective. *IEEE Communications Magazine, 50*(2), 104–114.

Ergen, M. (2009). *Mobile broadband including WiMAX and LTE.* New York, NY: Springer-Verlag.

Ghosh, A., Andrews, J. G., Zhang, J., & Muhamed, R. (2011). *Fundamentals of LTE.* Upper Saddle River, NJ: Prentice Hall.

Olsson, M., Sultana, S., Rommer, S., Frid, L., & Mulligan, C. (2012). *EPC and 4G packet networks* (2nd. ed.). Oxford, UK: Academic Press.

Sauter, M. (2006). *Communication systems for the mobile information society.* Chichester, UK: Wiley.

TOOLS FOR MODELING AND SIMULATION

Modeling and simulation as an emerging discipline involves replication of systems through computational tools with the main goal to understand and predict phenomena represented by the systems. Through replication, these tools enable investigation of systems in settings that would otherwise be extremely difficult or even impossible to investigate, show what phenomena would look like if they took place at much faster or slower speeds than in real time, and avoid the risks and ethical constraints involved in real-world experiments; and they are usually far less expensive than conducting experiments with the real system at hand. Modeling and simulation tools not only are useful for scientists and engineers but also afford a unique learning platform for students of all ages. While a large array of tools are used by scientists and engineers for the actual creation of simulations (a few examples include MATLAB, Mathematica, and Ecolego), this entry surveys tools that utilize modeling and simulations for the purpose of learning and training. First, definitions of the terms *simulation* and *model* are considered. The entry then discusses tools that facilitate learning through the use of simulations, focusing on tools that provide dynamic models or microworlds. This use of existing simulation tools is contrasted with tools that enable learning through the actual creation of new models, with students engaged in the process of modeling in a way similar to that done by scientists.

Definitions

There are several ways to understand the distinction between models and simulations. Models simplify the way the world works by hiding information that is confounding, otherwise unimportant, or hard to see, while bringing to the foreground those elements that are central to the system. They help us visualize processes that could not otherwise be seen with the naked eye as a result of a very large or small scale, or speeds too fast or too slow to be noticed by the human eye. Allan Collins and John R. Ferguson classified theoretical models in science as structural, causal, and dynamic models. *Structural models* focus on the physical relationships between the model features (e.g., molecules and atoms model). *Causal models*, which are more conceptual, focus on the processes within a system that relate to the causal mechanism; for example, in an ecosystem food-web model, it is possible to see how an increase in a predator population might result in a decrease in its prey population. *Dynamic models* enable the users to see and test different assumption by changing the settings and observing the effects of these changes on how the model runs. Like dynamic models, simulations involve imitation of the behavior of a system or process over time; however, a simulation may also allow a person to play an active role within it.

What, then, is the relationship between modeling and simulations? While the main purpose of modeling is usually to expose and explicitly explain the underlying mechanism, the main purpose of simulations is to describe and reproduce the experience, often deliberately including the complexity presented in reality (e.g., a combat flight simulation), where the underlying mechanism is often only implicit. The act of modeling may result in a simulation, and the act of using a simulation may result in an understanding of the underlying model.

Uri Wilensky made the distinction between pedagogically using simulations and making them. While the discipline of modeling and simulations usually refer to the act of making models (*modeling*) and then executing these models (often dynamic models or *simulations*) over time, this entry also surveys tools that involve *using* simulations, although they do not include the act of modeling in the sense of generating a new simulation.

Learning by Using Simulations

As mentioned before, while models aim to simplify the way the world works, simulations deliberately include the complexity presented in reality. In fact, virtual reality simulations play an increasingly important role in different domains training including nursing, medical, pharmacy, business, and army simulations. For example, Second Life (a free online virtual-world environment developed by Linden Lab) has been used as a platform for generating nursing and medical simulations that are used widely in medical schools. As many of the virtual reality tools are not accessible (e.g., a flight simulator) in a typical classroom, we will survey tools that enable using dynamic models that simplify the way the world works, and in particular, microworlds.

Rooted in constructivist philosophy of learning and more specifically constructionist learning design philosophy that was initiated by Seymour Papert, microworlds are dynamic models of an environment mechanism, which enable learners to investigate the environment through manipulation of variables in a way similar to what would be done in conducting experiments in the real world. Unlike the virtual reality simulation described before, in a microworld the learner does not play a role within the simulation (e.g., a nurse, a pilot) but, rather, is an outside observer who is using the simulation to test how changes in the environment would affect the system behavior. Thus microworlds provide a platform for inquiry-based learning because they enable the cycle of defining a question followed by investigation, which in this case involves making observations of the microworld's behavior, leading to conclusions and reflection.

In addition, unlike simulations that opt to replicate the complexity of reality, according to Lloyd Rieber, a microworld is a purposeful simplification of reality to match the cognitive state of the learner and can get more complicated as the learner's mental model evolves. When interacting with a microworld, the learners should get no or little training to begin using the microworld. For example, in the charged and neutral atoms simulation, which is one of many simulations included in the Molecular Workbench open source developed by the Concord Consortium (see Figure 1), students can investigate how the intermolecular attractions and consequently the phase of the matter are affected by changes in temperature, changes in the van der Waals attraction, and whether the molecules are charged.

Many simulations tools are available and can be used as a tool to foster understanding of system phenomena through exploratory learning and through different forms of inquiry-based learning. Table 1 lists a small subset of key tools, each providing a large array of microworlds' simulations.

Learning by Making Models and Simulations

The simulations that were described so far involve learning by *using* simulations. Nevertheless, scientist and engineers learn about phenomena through the process of modeling—*making* new simulation and not by just using them. One way of modeling, which is referred to by Wilensky as "backward modeling," is done by starting at a phenomenon of interest and then replicating the phenomena on the computer. The set of computational rules that result in a successful replication could uncover the underlying mechanism of the phenomenon. Another way of modeling, which is referred to as "forward modeling," is done by starting with a set of rules to simulate a phenomenon that is yet to be seen. This kind of modeling is used when the goal is to make prediction about a particular situation that cannot be easily examined in the real world (e.g., What will be the effect of different levels of earthquakes on a given city?). Agent-based modeling is a bottom-up simulation modeling technique widely used for both forward

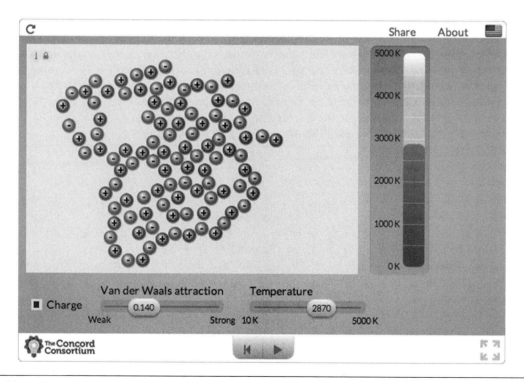

Figure 1   Next-generation Molecular Workbench

Source: Molecular Workbench, http://mw.concord.org. Copyright The Concord Consortium, http://concord.org; used by permission.

Table I Examples of tools that enable learning by *using* simulations and microworlds

Tool	Description	Content area include
The Physics Education Technology (PhET)	A large set of free online science simulations developed at the University of Colorado Boulder. The simulations are animated, interactive, and game-like environments in which students learn through exploration. Website: PhET: http://phet.colorado.edu	Physics, biology, chemistry, earth science, and math.
Molecular Workbench	Hundreds of freely available set of simulations developed by The Concord Consortium. In addition to the simulations, Molecular Workbench offers an authoring system for teachers for building activities and assessment around simulations and can also be used as a modeling tool for teachers and students for creating and sharing their own simulations. Website: Concord Consortium: http://concord.org, Molecular Workbench: http://mw.concord.org	Physics, chemistry, biology, biotechnology, and nanotechnology.
Web-based Inquiry Science Environment (Wise)	A free Web-based inquiry science environment developed at the University of California, Berkeley (in collaboration with the Concord Consortium) for students in Grades 5–12, where students observe and test micro and macro scientific concepts using interactive digital models. Website: Wise: http://wise.berkeley.edu	Life science, physical science, biology, chemistry, and physics.
Amplify Science*	A science and literacy integrated commercial curriculum for middle school that is being developed by the Learning Design Group at the Lawrence Hall of Science, UC Berkeley and Amplify. In this new Next Generation Science Standards (NGSS)–aligned curriculum, students acquire science concepts and inquiry skills using simulations and modeling tools.	Life science, physical science, and earth science.

*First release expected fall 2015.

and backward modeling. It models a system by defining the behavior of autonomous agents as a function of their environment and interaction with other agents.

Several tools (e.g., NetLogo, StarLogo) enable making these kinds of bottom-up agent-based models using basic programming skills. How can this practice be used for learning? A constructivist point of view might suggest that this type of activity, which puts the student in an active role that involves construction of science as opposed to receiving of science, may lead to deeper learning. For example, in NetLogo's wolf sheep model (see Figure 2), the modeler defined a set of rules for sheep, wolves, and their environment (e.g., a rule of a wolf could be

"Whenever there is a sheep nearby, if hungry, try to eat it with 40% probability of successful hunt."). When clicking on "go" the simulation starts to run resulting in population-size changes. In addition, it is possible for the modeler to input variables such as the initial population size of wolves and sheep and to specify the form of presenting the output (e.g., graph, text). With this type of activity, the students are engaged in the actual scientific practice of modeling as opposed to just using a simulation.

Other tools for creating dynamic models use a top-down technique, where the algorithm is not specified at the level of the individual agents but rather more globally. For example, Modellus (shown in Table 2) is

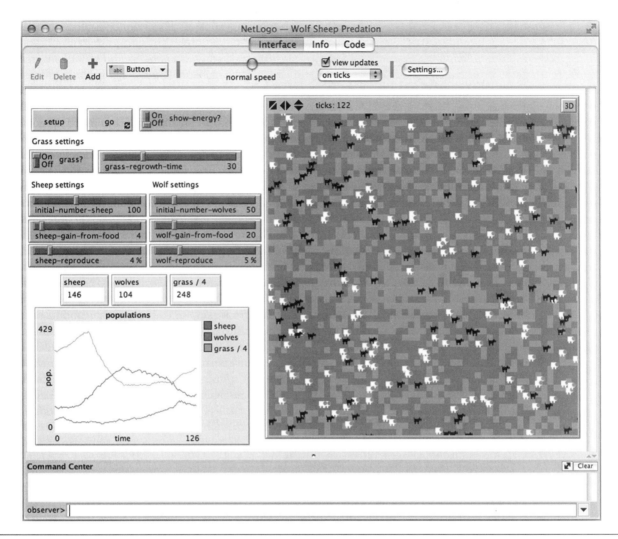

Figure 2   NetLogo Wolf Sheep Predation model

Source: NetLogo Wolf Sheep Predation model, by Uri Wilensky, 1997. Center for Connected Learning and Computer-Based Modeling, Northwestern University, Evanston, IL. Retrieved from http://ccl.northwestern.edu/netlogo/models/WolfSheepPredation. Copyright 1997 by Uri Wilensky. Used by permission.

Table 2   Examples of tools that enable learning by *making* simulations

Tool	Description	Content area include
Modellus	Modellus allows creation of interactive mathematical models using standard mathematical notation. Designed for high school and university students and teachers, this free application can be used to explore preexisting models and as an authoring system to create new models. Users enter mathematical expressions or equations and can then create an animation of the model (no programming is needed). Modellus: http://modellus.co/index.php/en/	Mathematics, physics, chemistry, geometry, and more

(Continued)

Table 2   (Continued)

Tool	Description	Content area include
STELLA	A commercial environment that is used by educators (K–12, colleges) and researchers to generate dynamic models and simulate systems over time. The environment enables students to simulate systems with input and output and the relationships between them. Outputs are displayed through graphs, tables, reports, and more. STELLA: http://www.iseesystems.com/softwares/Education/StellaSoftware.aspx	Economics, physics, literature, chemistry, calculus, and more
NetLogo	A free open-source programmable modeling environment for simulating natural and social phenomena developed by Uri Wilensky at Northwestern University. With NetLogo, the modeler can define the behavior of hundreds of agents (turtles) and environment units (patches) and run the model over time. The output can be displayed with graphs, bars, and scatter plots. Wilensky, U. (1999). NetLogo. http://ccl.northwestern.edu/netlogo/. Center for Connected Learning and Computer-Based Modeling, Northwestern University, Evanston, IL.	Natural sciences and social sciences including biology, medicine, physics, chemistry, mathematics, computer science, economics, and social psychology
StarLogo	A programmable agent-based modeling environment developed at MIT Media Lab and MIT Teacher Education Program that enables the creation of simulations of complex systems. StarLogoTNG is the next generation of StarLogo and enables in addition 3D graphics and sound, a blocks-based programming interface, and keyboard input making it an ideal tool for making educational games. StarLogo: http://education.mit.edu/starlogo/	Biology, physics, math, chemistry, programming, and more

a computational modeling tool where the teacher or students can model mathematical expressions behavior. STELLA, on the other hand, enables simulation with inputs and outputs and the relationships between them. All of the tools mentioned in this section also include a large set of existing models that can be used by students in similar ways to those described in the previous section; nevertheless, they are unique in that they also serve as an authoring tool for making new simulations.

Conclusion and Future Directions

According to the new National Research Council (2012) Framework for K–12 Science Education, the focus of learning should no longer be solely on the science content, or even on teaching practices in isolation, but rather on learning the content in the context of real-world practices. One of the eight practices mentioned in the framework is *developing and using models*. This entry surveyed both tools that enable using simulations and tools that enable making (developing) simulations. The benefits of *using* both virtual reality and micro-world simulations are very clear. Virtual reality simulations allow training experiences that are very close to reality without the risks involved, are usually much less expensive, and are very motivating. Microworlds allow exploration and inquiry-based learning in a very similar way to that done in reality. What about *making* models? On the one hand, from a constructivist point of view, when students are making a model, they take an active role that is likely to result in deeper learning. On the other hand, a concern is that asking students to program a model in biology will require spending a lot of class time teaching them to program. One way to scaffold this process is to start with an existing model that students can use and test, and then continue by modifying it. In addition to the cognitive value involved in both using and making simulations, getting into the shoes of a scientist by actually engaging in the same type of practices scientists engage with can be a powerful motivation with a big influence on learning.

What will tools for modeling and simulation look like in the future? While using simulations, users clearly recognize that their experience is in fact virtual and not the actual reality; a simulation is easily distinguishable from reality. The *simulated reality hypothesis* challenges this assumption by proposing that reality could be simulated in the future to a degree that it will be indistinguishable from the actual reality. Will such tools ever exist? Would students be able to learn about new cultures through actually experiencing the culture as a reality? Or perhaps have a firsthand experience of what it is like to be a germ inside the human body? The future will tell what kind of impact such learning experiences will have on our world.

Rinat Rosenberg-Kima

See also Learning by Modeling; Learning in the Manufacturing Sector With Simulated Systems; Learning With Simulations; Simulated Systems for Environmental Planning

Further Readings

Boulos, M. N. K., Hetherington, L., & Wheeler, S. (2007). Second Life: An overview of the potential of 3-D virtual worlds in medical and health education. *Health Information & Libraries Journal, 24*(4), 233–245.

Collins, A., & Ferguson, W. (1993). Epistemic forms and epistemic games: Structures and strategies for guiding inquiry. *Educational Psychologist, 28*(1), 25–42.

Gobert, J. D., & Buckley, B. C. (2000). Introduction to model-based teaching and learning in science education. *International Journal of Science Education, 22*(9), 891–894.

Khine, M. S., & Saleh, I. M. (Eds.). (2011). *Models and modelling, Cognitive tools for scientific inquiry.* Dordrecht, Netherlands: Springer-Verlag.

Papert, S. (1980). *Mindstorms: Children, computers, and powerful ideas.* New York, NY: Basic Books.

Rieber, L. P. (1996). Seriously considering play: Designing interactive learning environments based on the blending of microworlds, simulations, and games. *Educational Technology Research & Development, 44*(2), 43–58.

Shen, J., Lei, J., Chang, H.-Y., & Namdar, B. (2014). Technology-enhanced, modeling-based instruction (TMBI) in science education. In J. M. Spector, M. D. Merrill, J. Elen, & M. J. Bishop (Eds.), *Handbook of research on educational communications and technology* (4th ed., pp. 529–540). New York, NY: Springer-Verlag.

Wilensky, U. (1999). GasLab: An extensible modeling toolkit for connecting micro- and macro-properties of gases. In W. Feurzeig & N. Roberts (Eds.), *Modeling and simulation in science and mathematics education* (pp. 151–178). Berlin, Germany: Springer-Verlag.

Zyda, M. (2005). From visual simulation to virtual reality to games. *Computer, 38*(9), 25–32.

TOUCH-BASED AND GESTURE-BASED DEVICES

The term *touch screen* is generally used to describe any kind of display with a touch-sensitive surface that can be used for interaction by touching it with fingers or special devices such as styli or gloves. While touch screen development dates back to the 1960s, increased recent usage is due to mobile computing. This entry first explains the features of touch screens, their use in devices, and their interface and interaction design. It then discusses their relevance in education.

Touch screens have become the standard for interaction with mobile phones and tablet devices for many reasons. Touch screens allow for larger screen estate because less space is needed for physical buttons and controls. Touch screens can increase interaction speed by enabling users to directly select a target in a list instead of forcing users to scroll and click. Often, this kind of direct interaction is also considered more intuitive. Moreover, interface design is done in software and can be adapted for a specific application—for example, a full keyboard for text input, a purely numeric keyboard for making phone calls, and specific buttons such as play, pause, and stop for a video player, as shown in Figure 1. Finally, touch screens extend the scope of interaction by enabling users to perform gestures on the screen's surface that are interpreted differently based on shape, speed, context, and so on.

Devices and Technologies

The ubiquitous usage of touch screens in mobile computing has also resulted in a growing interest in touch screens in other devices. There is an increasing trend in exploring touch technologies for interaction with desktop computers and laptops, utilizing them on larger horizontal surfaces (e.g., to create interactive tables) and in large wall-mounted settings (e.g., to create a digital whiteboard). The success and broad user acceptance of touch interaction in mobile computing suggests that touch screens will play a bigger role in many other

Figure 1   Adaptive touch screen interface designs optimized for particular applications

contexts and devices. Broader acceptance will depend on such things as improvements of the technology, price, and ergonomic issues in everyday usage. For example, a common ergonomic problem encountered when using a vertically mounted touch device is the feeling of arm fatigue and heaviness when used over a long period of time.

The technologies used in common consumer touch screens are either capacitive or resistive. The latter contain electrically resistive layers placed on the screen's surface with a certain gap between them. When closing this gap by touching a point on the screen with a finger or any other object, voltage can flow between the layers, causing the system to register an input at that position. Aside from low cost, a major advantage of resistive touch screens is that they can be used with any kind of input device including gloves. This is not true for capacitive touch screens, which commonly can only be operated by plain fingers or special devices such as capacitive styli. The reason is that capacitive devices measure the distortion of the screen's electrostatic field when touched by a human finger, which serves as an electrical conductor. One of their major advantages of capacitive devices is that they enable the integration of multitouch technology, that is, the ability to simultaneously

recognize and track multiple input points at different positions accurately at the same time.

Interface and Interaction Design

Touch-screen interface design is not limited to a fixed set of physical buttons but is done in software. This enables designs that can be adapted to specific contexts such as data and use cases. This is beneficial for mobile devices and can have advantages for interaction in general because context-dependent visualization and adaptive, real-time feedback support intuitive ease of use.

Touch gestures made when moving fingers over the screen are often considered intuitive. It is, for example, assumed to be more natural to browse a list by dragging or flicking it across the screen instead of using a scrollbar, as shown in Figure 2. Multitouch gestures, where multiple input points are considered simultaneously, have the potential to create an even more engaging interaction experience. Probably the most common example to illustrate this are pinch gestures used for zooming, as shown in Figure 3, which are often considered very intuitive although there is actually no natural counterpart of such an interaction in the real world.

Figure 2   Drag and flick gestures versus scrollbar interaction

Figure 3   Pinch gestures versus dedicated zoom buttons

Relevance for Education

Mobile touch devices have several advantages for education, and their usage is beginning to transform teaching and learning. Advantages include the ability to easily carry them around, constant access to large repositories via wireless network connections, the possibility to easily update contents, and affordability. Content is not only restricted to static information but can be any kind of multimedia. Additionally, content can also be interactive with quizzes, animations, and movie clips.

While all these advantages are associated with touch screens, they are mostly rooted in the small form factor of mobile devices, network access, and support for interactive multimedia. Yet, touch technology adds usability and other advantages to these devices. They can be used by young children who are not able to operate keyboards. They offer access to learning material for students with learning disabilities. They are well suited to interactively explore and examine content and can foster curiosity and explorative learning by allowing users to zoom, rotate, or otherwise interact with content.

There are also drawbacks to the educational usage of touch interaction. The most obvious obstacle is the limitation of on-screen keyboards compared with physical keyboards. While entering text with a virtual touch-screen keyboard is often even considered acceptable, editing text is generally easier and faster to do with a keyboard and mouse. Likewise, handwriting on a touch screen is sometimes experienced as less natural and not as flexible as writing on a piece of paper. In general,

devices such as tablets are often considered to be more suited for media consumption and exploration rather than content creation. While features such as integrated cameras and microphones offer new possibilities for content creation by students, the lack of appropriate writing and accurate drawing functionality does provide a potential hindrance when adopting touch devices for classroom teaching.

Other touch devices that might be used beneficially in classrooms in the future include horizontally placed touch screens and large vertically mounted devices that can be used as interactive tables for group learning and as digital blackboards for interactive presentations. Many research projects have explored the benefits of touch-screen technologies, but improvements continue to occur and require additional research on usage and impact.

Wolfgang Hürst

See also Gesture-Based Learning and Instructional Systems; Human-Computer Interaction; Mobile Devices: Impact on Learning and Instruction; Mobile Tools and Technologies for Learning and Instruction; Tablet Devices in Education and Training

Further Readings

Berque, D., Johnson, D. K., & Jovanovic, L. (2001). Teaching theory of computation using pen-based computers and an electronic whiteboard. In *Proceedings of the 6th Annual Conference on Innovation and Technology in Computer Science Education* (pp. 169–172). New York, NY: Association for Computing Machinery.

Burd, B., Barros, J. P., Johnson, C., Kurkovsky, S., Rosenbloom, A., & Tillman, N. (2012). Educating for mobile computing: Addressing the new challenges. In *Proceedings of the final reports on innovation and technology in computer science education 2012 working groups* (pp. 51–63). New York, NY: Association for Computing Machinery.

McKnight, L., & Fitton, D. (2010). Touch-screen technology for children: Giving the right instructions and getting the right responses. In *Proceedings of the 9th International Conference on Interaction Design and Children* (pp. 238–241). New York, NY: Association for Computing Machinery.

Piper, A. M., & Hollan, J. D. (2009). Tabletop displays for small group study: Affordances of paper and digital materials. In *Proceedings of the SIGCHI Conference on Human Factors in Computing Systems* (pp. 1227–1236). New York, NY: Association for Computing Machinery.

Tse, E., Schöning, J., Rogers, Y., Shen, C., & Morrison, G. (2010). Next generation of HCI and education: Workshop on UI technologies and educational pedagogy. In *CHI '10 extended abstracts on human factors in computing systems* (pp. 4509–4512). New York, NY: Association for Computing Machinery.

TPACK (TECHNOLOGICAL PEDAGOGICAL CONTENT KNOWLEDGE)

Technological, pedagogical, and content knowledge—TPACK—refers to the framework developed by Punya Mishra and Matthew Koehler to describe the knowledge that teachers need in order to effectively teach with technology. The TPACK framework was developed to respond to two challenges confronting teacher educators. First, there was a systemic push for teachers to integrate technology in ways more consistent with the growth of technology outside of education. Second, there was limited treatment of technology for teachers, beyond generic uses. As Judith B. Harris and her colleagues reported, technology use in classrooms has historically been conceptualized and supported using a predominance of approaches that overemphasize technology and technology skills. These approaches typically include additional technology-focused teacher education courses; professional development workshops; and demonstration resources, lessons, and projects. Taken together, these approaches were labeled by Seymour Papert as *technocentric* because they begin with technology skills and only later aspire to help discern how these technologies can be used to teach content-based learning at different levels.

The TPACK framework, in contrast, characterizes what teachers need to know about technology by reconnecting technology to both subject-matter knowledge and teachers' pedagogical understanding. In this way, the TPACK framework builds upon the work of Lee Shulman and the construct of pedagogical content knowledge (PCK) that describes how and why teacher knowledge of pedagogy and content cannot be considered solely in isolation. PCK captured a unique type of knowledge that characterizes an interaction between pedagogy and content in order to implement strategies that help students to fully understand content. Similarly, the TPACK framework extends Shulman's notion of PCK by considering how technology, pedagogy, and content interrelate in order to create a form of knowledge greater than the sum of the three separate knowledge bases. This entry first describes the components of the TPACK framework and discusses the implications of the framework for teacher educators. It then discusses the different conceptual lenses the TPACK framework provides for researchers in the area of teaching with technology.

Components of the TPACK Framework

In order to characterize the knowledge needed to effectively teach with technology, three major knowledge components form the foundation of the TPACK framework. Four additional knowledge components characterize how these three bodies of knowledge interact, constrain, and afford each other. Together, these seven knowledge components—and attention to the context in which these knowledge components function—comprise the TPACK framework and are characterized as follows:

Content knowledge (CK): depth and breadth of understanding about the ideas, topics, or subject-matter knowledge that a teacher is planning to teach to students;

Pedagogical knowledge (PK): depth and breadth of understanding about a variety of instructional practices, strategies, and methods to promote students' learning;

Technology knowledge (TK): depth and breadth of understanding about technologies (new and old) for use in educational contexts;

Technological content knowledge (TCK): Understanding of the reciprocal relationship between technology and content; for example, what is being taught often defined and constrained by technologies and their representational and functional capabilities—accordingly, what is being taught affords or suggests some technologies over others;

Pedagogical content knowledge (PCK): Shulman's idea of the understanding needed to teach particular subject matter, including an understanding of assessment, common misconceptions, and adapting instruction to diverse learners in specific subject matter;

Technological pedagogical knowledge (TPK): an understanding of technology and pedagogical practices, which can, and should, constrain and afford one another;

Technological pedagogical content knowledge (TPACK): an understanding of the complex relations among technology, pedagogy, and content that enables teachers to develop appropriate and context-specific teaching strategies.

TPACK is grounded and situated in specific contexts, represented by the outer dotted circle in Figure 1. Teachers need an understanding of all of the knowledge components listed in this section in order to orchestrate and coordinate technology, pedagogy, and content into teaching. However, this understanding is tied to a specific context. What works in one classroom

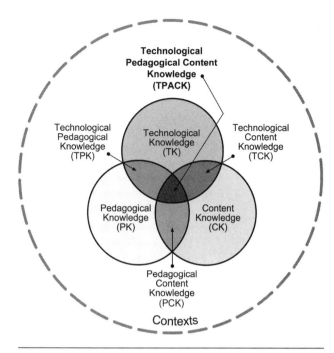

Figure 1   Components of the TPACK framework

Source: Reproduced by permission of the publisher, © 2012 by tpack.org.

context is not guaranteed to work in a different classroom with a different teacher, student, goals, or learning environment.

Implications for Teacher Educators

The TPACK framework characterizes the knowledge that teachers need in order to skillfully teach with technology. An important implication of the framework is that teacher educators must identify and utilize methods that best develop the complex and integrated forms of knowledge elucidated in the TPACK framework.

Researchers and teacher educators seeking to develop within the preservice teacher population must confront unique challenges, two of which are described here. First, preservice teacher candidates, for example, typically begin with minimal levels of all the TPACK constructs. Hence, there is not an existing knowledge base upon which to build knowledge of how to effectively integrate technology—TPACK. Second, as a new topic of research, there is not yet a corpus of evidence pointing to an agreed-upon approach, or route, to developing TPACK.

Despite these challenges, dozens of methods have been proposed for the development of the connected, contextualized knowledge described in the TPACK framework. Two approaches are described here:

(1) learning technology by design and (2) activity types. Learning technology by design is a method to develop TPACK by utilizing design teams that collaborate on the design of a piece of educational technology. In a group that may include content experts and technology experts, teachers work to solve authentic problems of practice over an extended period of time. Design teams have created online courses, educational websites, and technology-integrated lesson plans. In this approach, the assigned tasks require teachers to develop and integrate all of the knowledge components of the TPACK model at once. For example, in designing an online course, what is being taught (CK), what instructional strategies to use (PK), and the specific technologies (TK) are being developed and learned in an integrated way. In this manner, technology is used to teach specific content with specific pedagogy.

The use of activity types is a method to build on teachers' existing knowledge in subject-matter disciplines. Teachers build knowledge about technology upon already existing knowledge of pedagogy (PK), content (CK), and pedagogical content knowledge (PCK). In this approach, learning experiences are focused upon curricular goals. Each learning experience can be broken down into smaller components that specify what students do during each portion of the learning experience. For example, a learning experience in social studies might require students to do the following activity types in sequence: *read text, research, debate, create a timeline, design an exhibit,* and *deliver a presentation.* For each activity type, specific technologies that support learning are identified; PowerPoint, Photo Story, Movie Maker, iMovie, and Audacity are well suited to support the *deliver a presentation* activity type. Researchers have identified 44 activity types that commonly occur in social studies teaching, along with technologies in support of those activity types. Activity type taxonomies have also been developed for literacy, mathematics, music, physical education, science, secondary English language arts, visual arts, and world languages.

Learning technology by design and activity types are two examples that demonstrate the diversity of methods proposed for the development of TPACK. This diversity of method and approach to developing TPACK knowledge is also found in other approaches to developing TPACK.

Implications for Researchers

The TPACK framework provides different conceptual lenses for researchers to understand the phenomena of teaching with technology. Four of these lenses—descriptive, inferential, analytic, and applied—are briefly described here.

Descriptive Lens

Theories and frameworks help researchers to make sense of the world by providing concepts and terminologies with which to describe phenomena. Accordingly, the TPACK framework can provide the terminology and structure needed to describe the complex web of relationships that exist when teachers integrate technology into the teaching of subject matter. Separating technology, pedagogy, and content, and the complex relationships between and among these bodies of knowledge, may be difficult in practice. The TPACK framework can help researchers identify the important components of teacher knowledge that are relevant to the thoughtful integration of technology in education. The TPACK framework may help to provide the starting point for a conceptualization and discussion of complex relationships in a methodological and grounded manner. Accordingly, frameworks like TPACK are helpful not only for identifying phenomena of interest in the world worthy of study but also for providing the language to talk, conceptualize, and explore relationships.

Inferential Lens

Theories and frameworks allow researchers to make inferences about the world, the way it works, and the consequences of changes to elements in the system. The TPACK framework allows researchers not just to understand what effective teaching with technology is about but also to make predictions and inferences about contexts under which such good teaching will occur. As suggested in the TPACK framework, teacher education programs that focus on generic technology skills development independent of content are not sufficient; these programs only address knowledge of technology (TK) and ignore the connections with content (CK) and pedagogy (PK). In addition, the TPACK framework allows researchers to look more closely at successful programs of technology integration and suggest inferences about the causal mechanisms underlying their success.

Analytic Lens

Theories and frameworks can also guide the design and analysis of research. The TPACK framework provides a map of the constructs to be measured—the components of the TPACK framework. These measures provide data in support of research questions about the knowledge of individual teachers or groups of teachers, changes in knowledge over time, and the mastery of the knowledge components.

Quality measures of the constituent TPACK components are a prerequisite guiding much of the research in this area. How these components are measured as well as what these measurements represent raise important epistemological issues. However, what is evident is the close connection between the analytic frameworks guiding research in the area of technology integration and the conceptual framework provided by the TPACK framework.

Applied Lens

Theories and frameworks, particularly those in the arena of education, can help researchers to apply ideas to the real world. The TPACK framework offers two pragmatic insights into applied settings that help researchers build better learning contexts. First, by suggesting the types of knowledge individual approaches are likely to develop (or not develop) in teachers, the TPACK framework can scaffold an analysis of approaches to teachers' professional development. For example, the TPACK framework provides an applied approach for understanding why technocentric professional development approaches are unlikely to produce knowledge of technology that is connected to pedagogical and content knowledge—that is, knowledge that is truly needed by teachers. Second, the TPACK framework can guide the evaluation of teacher professional-development programs and learning contexts through the closely connected analytic lens that TPACK provides. By suggesting measures of teacher knowledge, the TPACK framework may prove helpful as a means of evaluation and communication about the components of teacher knowledge and the effectiveness of approaches aimed at developing teachers' knowledge.

Matthew J. Koehler and Punya Mishra

See also Measuring and Assessing TPACK (Technological Pedagogical Content Knowledge); Pedagogical Knowledge; Technology Integration; Technology Knowledge

Further Readings

Angeli, C., & Valanides, N. (2009). Epistemological and methodological issues for the conceptualization, development, and assessment of ICT–TPCK: Advances in technological pedagogical content knowledge (TPCK). *Computers & Education, 52*(1), 154–168. doi:10.1016/j.compedu.2008.07.006

Brush, T., & Saye, J. W. (2009). Strategies for preparing preservice social studies teachers to integrate technology effectively: Models and practices. *Contemporary Issues in Technology and Teacher Education, 9*(1), 46–59.

Graham, C. R. (2011). Theoretical considerations for understanding technological pedagogical content knowledge (TPACK). *Computers & Education, 57*(3), 1953–1960.

Harris, J. B., & Hofer, M. J. (2011). Technological pedagogical content knowledge (TPACK) in action: A descriptive study of secondary teachers' curriculum-based, technology-related instructional planning. *Journal of Research on Technology in Education, 43*(3), 211–229.

Harris, J. B., Mishra, P., & Koehler, M. J. (2009). Teachers' technological pedagogical content knowledge and learning activity types: Curriculum-based technology integration reframed. *Journal of Research on Technology in Education, 41*(4), 393–416. doi:10.1207/s15326985ep2803_7

Koehler, M. J., & Mishra, P. (2005). Teachers learning technology by design. *Journal of Computing in Teacher Education, 21*(3), 94–102.

Koehler, M. J., Shin, T. S., & Mishra, P. (2011). How do we measure TPACK? Let me count the ways. In R. N. Ronau, C. R. Rakes, & M. L. Niess (Eds.), *Educational technology, teacher knowledge, and classroom impact: A research handbook on frameworks and approaches* (pp. 16–31). Hershey, PA: IGI Global.

Mishra, P., & Koehler, M. J. (2006). Technological pedagogical content knowledge: A framework for teacher knowledge. *Teachers College Record, 108*(6), 1017–1054. doi:10.1111/j.1467-9620.2006.00684.x

Niess, M. L., van Zee, E. H., & Gillow-Wiles, H. (2011). Knowledge growth in teaching mathematics/science with spreadsheets: Moving PCK to TPACK through online professional development. *Journal of Digital Learning in Teacher Education, 27*(2), 42–52.

Papert, S. (1987). Computer criticism vs. technocentric thinking. *Educational Researcher, 16*(1), 22–30.

Shulman, L. S. (1986). Those who understand: Knowledge growth in teaching. *Educational Researcher, 15*(2), 4–14.

obligation to meet the expectations associated with integrating new technologies, content, and pedagogy. One solution is to blend the components of quality educational practice into a format that allows teacher candidates to gain the knowledge and skills necessary to become effective educators in 21st-century learning spaces. This entry discusses the format called the Technological Pedagogical Content Knowledge (TPACK) model, developed by Punya Mishra and Matthew Koehler. It first discusses the model and its development. It then discusses how changes in K–12 classrooms are consistent with the TPACK framework and how TPACK can be incorporated into the experience-based model of teacher education.

Mishra and Koehler present a view of how technology integration concepts can be encompassed into the work of teacher education. Their research led them to propose a new framework for technology integration that recognizes the complexity of merging a number of skills and expectations into a manageable approach for teacher educators. Their work extends Lee Shulman's earlier work that blends content and pedagogy knowledge and adds the complexity of integrating technology into content and pedagogy. They argue against the view that technology is an integral component in both content and pedagogy. They promote the view that there is an interrelationship of content, pedagogy, and technology. In their TPACK model, the three are interrelated and dependent upon each other (see Figure 1). While each area is a

TPACK (Technological Pedagogical Content Knowledge): Implications for 21st-Century Teacher Education

Teacher education programs have to adapt to ensure that teacher candidates are ready to teach in schools that are continually adding new technology. It is not enough for teacher candidates to know how to use technology for their personal use; it is essential that these future educators reexamine classroom practice to integrate technology into teaching. With the introduction of emerging technologies, the context of learning has changed dramatically, changing how best to prepare educators. This adds to the responsibilities of teacher educators to ensure that teacher candidates are prepared to integrate technology effectively into their teaching.

Margaret Niess argues that unless teacher preparation courses change dramatically, K–12 students will be robbed of a meaningful and productive education. Teacher education preparation programs have an

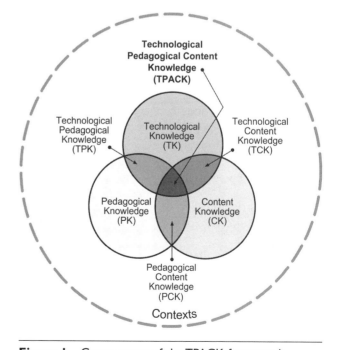

Figure 1   Components of the TPACK framework

Source: Reproduced by permission of the publisher, © 2012 by tpack.org.

stand-alone content area, they contended that the strength of the idea lies in the flow of emphasis within the instructional option or, to use their term, *contexts*.

Recognizing the merits of the individual areas of study, the emphasis of this model is how each component contributes to the others. The expectation is that when faculty members possess all the types of knowledge, for example, technological, pedagogical, and content, or combinations of the three, their means to addressing teacher education demands could become more dynamic and flexible.

Next Generation of Teacher Education

If one accepts that the classrooms of the 21st century are different from those traditionally found in school settings, then teacher education should change so as to prepare teachers for those classrooms and for dealing continually with emerging technology. Next-generation teachers need to become more agile and flexible in how to approach content and pedagogy while embracing technologies as a vehicle to augment and enhance educational practice.

Teachers need to learn to think differently about the context of the learning setting and how to bring the technology, the pedagogy, and the content together into meaningful learning opportunities for their students. They should be prepared to challenge their students to address learning in more meaningful ways that embrace creative and innovative learning. Through the use of technology-connected settings, they can create global contexts for learning. Mobile technologies offer many options that connect students to each other and to experts well beyond classroom walls. They also allow for formative checks of student understanding to assist in personalizing learning. Rather than only telling students facts, teachers should engage students in seeking answers to complex questions using the affordances of new technologies.

Technology allows teachers to redesign learning spaces. Jonathan Bergmann and Aaron Sams popularized the phrase *the flipped classroom* to describe a model of instruction wherein the teacher mixes direct instruction with experiential learning opportunities. Their suggestion is to assign students with technology-based instructional materials that students complete prior to coming to class. Then, in class, they are engaged in hands-on, integrated learning experiences that build upon that instruction. Learning becomes student centered, driven by new tools, new organizations, and new ideals. As the teacher creates these types of mixed learning experiences, technology resources become integrated into the content and the pedagogy, which is consistent with the TPACK framework.

Teacher education programs that are incorporating the TPACK model into the teacher education curriculum may also be making other changes in the curriculum, presenting multiple new demands on faculty members. Therefore, the important role of leadership in making such changes should be considered.

TPACK and the Experience-Based Model

Professional teacher education organizations are encouraging programs to provide more extensive and enhanced practice-based experiences within a teacher preparation curriculum. As a result, students enrolled in these programs have less time for work on college campuses and more time at K–12 school sites, where course work and practical experiences blend. This blending of theory and practice is an important opportunity, but it creates problems for teacher preparation programs, which are often constrained by policies with regard to the total number of required credit hours and other constraints. Some teacher educators support the move to including more time to practice in actual classrooms but are concerned about the sacrifice of content and pedagogy for classroom experience time. Technology rich environments may serve as demonstration sites for teacher preparation programs' next generation of instructional practices.

Preparing TPACK-ready teacher candidates is an integral part of redesigned teacher preparation programs. Such an effort may consist of shifting the orientation of the curriculum to the experience-based model. Faculty may need their own professional development prior to implementation of a new approach, which may mean leveraging funds to ensure successful implementation. It is important that educational leaders, such as deans, recognize their role in this process.

Conclusion

The adage, *we teach as we are taught* is especially apt when it comes to technology and teacher education programs. Teacher educators need to change their own practices, modeling TPACK-based practices that they expect teacher candidates will need in their classrooms. They need to prepare instructional opportunities for teacher candidates to become agile, thoughtful, creative, and innovative teachers who can use present and emerging technologies constructively in their own learning and with the learning of their future students. TPACK serves as an excellent model and point of reference for the next generation of educators, teacher preparation programs, and schools.

Mary C. Herring and Sharon E. Smaldino

See also Engaged Learning; Information and Communications Technologies for Formal Learning; Instructional Design Models; Pedagogical Knowledge; Technology Knowledge; TPACK (Technological Pedagogical Content Knowledge)

Further Readings

Bergmann, J., & Sams, A. (2012). *Flip your classroom: Reach every student in every class every day.* Washington, DC: International Society for Technology Education.

Koehler, M. J., & Mishra, P. (2008). Introducing TPACK. In AACTE committee on innovation & technology (Eds.), *Handbook of technological pedagogical content knowledge (TPCK) for educators* (pp. 3–30). New York, NY: Routledge.

Koehler, M. J., & Mishra, P. (2009). What is technological pedagogical content knowledge (TPACK)? *Contemporary Issues in Technology and Teacher Education, 9*(1), 60–70.

Mishra, P., & Koehler, M. J. (2006). Technological pedagogical content knowledge: A framework for teacher knowledge. *The Teachers College Record, 108*(6), 1017–1054.

Niess, M. L. (2008). Guiding preservice teachers in developing TPCK. In AACTE committee on innovation & technology (Eds.), *Handbook of technological pedagogical content knowledge (TPCK) for educators* (pp. 223–250). New York, NY: Routledge.

So, H. J., & Kim, B. (2009) Learning about problem based learning: Student teachers integrating technology, pedagogy and content knowledge. *Australasian Journal of Educational Technology, 25*(1), 101–116.

Socol, I. (2013, October). *Seven pathways to a new teacher professionalism.* Retrieved from http://speedchange.blogspot.com/2013/10/seven-pathways-to-new-teacher.html

Thomas, T., Herring, M., Redmond, P., & Smaldino, S. (2013). A blueprint for developing TPACK ready teacher candidates. *TechTrends, 57*(5), 55–63.

Zeichner, K. (2012). The turn once again toward practice-based teacher education. *Journal of Teacher Education, 63*(5), 376–382.

TRAINING USING VIRTUAL WORLDS

Using virtual environments to teach, learn, and practice the physical and mental skills required to perform given tasks is the area known as *training using virtual worlds*. A version of virtual training gained momentum in the later portion of the 20th century beginning with flight simulators; training using virtual worlds now encompasses several types of virtual environments, task-specific subcategories, and technologies. Desktop multiuser virtual worlds, which gained popularity several years later, gave easier access to virtual worlds to the general population and have created a strong following with educators and professional trainers. Virtual worlds provided a desirable vehicle to provide accessible training to their contingencies, capitalizing on the popularity of these environments for casual and gaming uses. Popular virtual worlds such as *The Sims* (Electronic Arts) and Second Life (Linden Lab) can be used to teach rather than used only for enjoyment. This entry first discusses the types of virtual worlds used for learning and the types of training possible using virtual worlds. It then discusses the benefits of training using virtual worlds and the potential for future growth in the use of virtual worlds for training.

Educational research has been focused on the kinds of virtual environments that best support learning and under what circumstances this learning occurs. Broadly, the research literature generally supports positive learning outcomes for educational activities within virtual worlds. The levels of success, however, are contingent upon several factors that mirror those of learning in real environments with the added burdens of hardware, software, and network issues faced by advanced technological applications. Some evidence has suggested that virtual worlds hold certain benefits that are not possible when learning in face-to-face situations in real environments. Even so, effective instructional design is a common key factor in successful virtual-world training, when the goals of the activity, game based or otherwise, and the desired learning outcomes should be aligned. The design of effective virtual environments, including desirable attributes and best practices, has also been an area of development given much consideration by scientists and scholars.

Types of Virtual Worlds for Learning

The term *virtual world* implies the interaction in an environment that is not real, but instead, created through and interacted with a computerized model and methodology. The word *virtual* often implies the use of 3D virtual spaces and objects as well. Computerized training environments can be described in terms of a large spectrum consisting of real-world and virtual-world components. The most common form of virtual worlds exists in desktop environments, in virtual and augmented reality environments, and in mobile devices.

Desktop virtual worlds are experienced though a traditional 2D computer screen or monitor, with the learner interacting through traditional peripheral devices like a keyboard and mouse. The virtual world consists of a 3D environment and the student is represented in the world by an avatar. Manipulation of a student's avatar can be through a first- or a third-person perspective. The environments may be single-user environments or networked environments in which numerous students

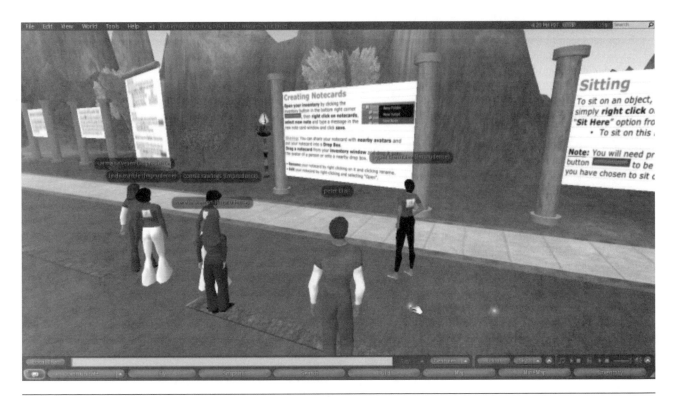

Figure 1   A training exercise for preservice educators in *Teacher Sim*
Source: Nancy Glomb.

can interact with each other and the instructor, as shown in Figure 1, which shows *Teacher Sim*, a virtual world developed by Peter Blair and Lee Mason using OpenSimulator.

Other categories of virtual worlds include mixed realities, in which some components of the environment are real and others are virtually represented using a digital technology. The emerging development of virtual components experienced through mobile devices fall into this category. In Figure 2, mixed reality is created using a mobile device and GPS location components for a geoscience training session. The device screen provides a question that must be answered correctly to move to the next location (inset A). In inset B, an image appears of a new location, and in inset C a base map shows locations passed (orange trilobites) and the new location that must be reached (green trilobite).

Types of Training Using Virtual Worlds

Training, the practicing of physical and mental skills required to perform given tasks, is of particular interest to educational professionals for its perceived benefits across a variety of tasks. The most common uses are for

- computer-based tools and programs, in domains such as art, design, foreign languages, and science;
- problem solving, in mathematics, science, and other domains involving higher order thinking;
- soft skills training, in areas such as leadership, decision making, management, diplomacy; and,
- medical training, in areas such as surgeries, injections, phobias, and mental illness.

Benefits of Training Using Virtual Worlds

Perceived benefits of training using virtual worlds often mirror those of simulation-based training and learning using social network technologies, depending on the configuration and design of the system. *Replication* is a benefit, in that students may practice over and over in virtual environments tasks that would otherwise be too costly or complicated to reproduce. Virtual surgeries and medical first-response training are examples of situations in which using real-world environments and objects may be too costly, too dangerous, or too difficult to arrange for skills repetition. *Reification* is the practice of making phenomena normally impossible to observe or manipulate into something perceivable by the senses. For example, in a virtual world spheres can

Figure 2   Mixed reality geoscience training exercise using a mobile device
Source: Brett E. Shelton.

represent atomic structures and arrows can represent evaporation and condensation.

Virtual worlds are better used for training in which virtual perceptual cues similar to actual cues are critical for optimal learning conditions. Technology that supports environmental and social presence may assist in engaging the learner in the desired educational activity, which relates to increases in time-on-task measures. It is theorized by several in the learning sciences community that experiencing phenomena through virtual experiences may change the way people come to understand certain complex phenomena as well. In other words, people may understand concepts and perform skills not only faster and more efficiently, but fundamentally with more complexity as well.

Higher motivation is often perceived as a benefit when training in virtual environments. Increased levels of motivation are often linked to better learning outcomes in virtual worlds. However, that motivational level often wears off after a period of time in the environment, and the activities within the environment become a more important motivational factor than the novelty of using a virtual world itself.

A common benefit of training in virtual worlds is that it may be used with individuals across geographical distances and can often be applied asynchronously for use across different times. The potential exists for scaling educational activities to wide audiences as well, through networked distribution of the environment and the wide accessibility of computerized Internet-based training. The benefits of training in virtual worlds translate into reduced costs in the time it takes to train, the expenses related to place, distribution, and assessment, and the perceptual benefits of virtual interaction.

Potential for Growth in Training Using Virtual Worlds

The amount of available resources (limited funds, expertise, etc.) for using virtual worlds in training and lack of attention in certain education and training areas without related entertainment applications have retarded the development of the mainstream virtual worlds training market. In the mid-1990s, it was thought that virtual-reality displays that were popular in labs would soon be available to the public and affordable for everyday users. However, these have yet to be developed at affordable costs for most consumers. Still, the potential for significant growth and impact in the area of virtual-world training environments exists and is likely to be realized in the future. Indicators of future growth in this area can be found, especially in the medical domain as well as in teaching training (e.g., *Teacher Sim*, *simSchool*, and Second Life environments for teaching training).

Brett E. Shelton

See also Alignment of Games and Learning Goals; Games in Business and Industry Settings; Games in Medical Training; Games in Military Training; Learning With Simulations; Mobile Tools and Technologies for Learning and Instruction; Simulation-Based Learning; 3D Immersive Environments

Further Readings

Dede, C. (1995). The evolution of constructivist learning environments: Immersion in distributed, virtual worlds. *Educational Technology, 35*(5), 46–52.

Dede, C., Salzman, M., Loftin, R. B., & Ash, K. (1997). Using virtual reality technology to convey abstract scientific concepts. In M. J. Jacobson & R. B. Kozma (Eds.), *Learning the sciences of the 21st century: Research, design, and implementing advanced technology learning environments* (pp. 361–413). Hillsdale, NJ: Lawrence Erlbaum.

Ptsotka, J. (1995). Immersive training systems: Virtual reality and education and training. *Instructional Science, 23*(5/6), 405–431.

Shelton, B. E. (2007). Designing educational games for activity-goal alignment. In B. E. Shelton & D. Wiley (Eds.), *The design and use of simulation computer games in education* (pp. 103–130). Rotterdam, Netherlands: Sense Publishers.

Whitelock, D., Brna, P., & Holland, S. (1996). What is the value of virtual reality for conceptual learning? Towards a theoretical framework. In P. Brna, A. Paiva, & J. A. Self (Eds.), *Proceedings of the European Conference on Artificial Intelligence in Education* (pp. 136–141). Lisbon, Portugal: Edições Colibri.

Winn, W. (1992). The assumptions of constructivism and instructional design. In T. M. Duffy & D. H. Jonassen (Eds.), *Constructivism and the technology of instruction: A conversation* (pp. 177–182). Hillsdale, NJ: Lawrence Erlbaum.

Winn, W. (2002). Learning in artificial environments: Embodiment, embeddedness and dynamic adaption. *Technology, Instruction, Cognition and Learning, 1*(1), 87–114.

TRANSMEDIA IN EDUCATION

Transmedia is a unique form of storytelling. The prefix *trans* means across, beyond, through, or changing quite thoroughly, so *transmedia* can be understood as across media, beyond media, or changing media quite thoroughly. Contrast this with *multimedia*, in which the use of more than one medium (book, video, music, pictures, etc.) is utilized. Transmedia, then, involves media applications that cut across, go beyond, or thoroughly change the underlying media.

While critical studies professor Marsha Kinder coined the term, media scholar Henry Jenkins is among the foremost leaders in the area of transmedia applications in storytelling. As a community, instructional technologists can help Jenkins to translate these ideas, which focus more on media products, directly into learning environment design. Transmedia, according to Jenkins, is essentially a way that the most important elements of a fiction are delivered across multiple channels to create a unified experience. Transmedia lends itself to complex narratives using multiple and interrelated characters and events.

For example, a transmedia learning experience is not simply the combination of three or four forms of a story. That is, the fact that a Harry Potter story can be read or watched does not make it an example of transmedia. Examples such as *Harry Potter* or *Hunger Games* present significant, complex narratives via more than one channel. These are examples of multimedia using several media to deliver a story; the entire story, however, is contained in *each* of the media channels. One can understand the narrative whether one has read the book, viewed a version of the story on video, or listened to an audio version. The essential parts of the story are contained within each media form, which is not transmedia. Transmedia is something more that is better understood as across media or beyond media in several ways, including active learner engagement.

While many are still unfamiliar with transmedia, this area shows great promise for significant engagement of learners in a wide variety of contexts, particularly those that lend themselves to rich storytelling. Understanding transmedia, for those who wish to deeply engage learners in units of learning, could be among the most powerful tools for literature and language arts available for use in schools now. However, there are significant drawbacks to this new approach to utilizing technology in learning environments, which this entry also explores.

Transmedia as Across Media

The notion of transmedia is the telling of a story with a narrative that involves several media channels. For example, part of the story may be contained within a video clip available online, another part may be present in a written book, another in a podcast, another in a full-length movie, another through a website, and yet another through a song available in a digital repository. Almost any medium can be used for the purposes of conveying a critical piece of a transmedia story. One of the important things to understand, however, is that the reader (viewer-participant) does not have the whole story by seeing only one channel. Generally, the story does not stand by itself through a single channel. Viewing a film will not tell the entire transmedia story; the reader must also engage other media to understand the total transmedia story.

Transmedia as Beyond Media

Transmedia also extends beyond what most think of as media. Transmedia can extend into a community or locale: Information may be shared as graffiti on the sides of local buildings, access to additional information may be given out via phone text messages or computer instant messaging, or specific landmarks may hold vital information to the story line through their historical landmark plaques or markers. A transmedia story can involve some or all of these additional information sources. In some ways, putting together the narrative in a transmedia story is like a digital road rally or scavenger hunt where one seeks parts of the story from multiple sources and various forms of information.

Transmedia stories share information across media as well as across episodes where a series of media representations (e.g., books, television shows, radio dramas) may be utilized. It usually is essential that the pieces of the series (the individual episodes, for example) stand on their own in terms of entertainment, information, interest, and story building, while, at the same moment, the pieces help readers build upon the story that is beginning to emerge in their minds, changing understanding as the story unfolds.

Transmedia Characteristics

Transmedia lends itself to engaging readers or viewer-participants in a networked society that is distributed, collective, collaborative, and inquisitive. Within such a society, the information age can be considered the enabling foundation; transmedia is both attractive and effective because it draws together the common interests among readers of the story. Because information in transmedia is disbursed across several sources, the consumers of transmedia must recognize that all information may not be available to one individual. A classic example of this is a transmedia product that requires

information from a building in San Francisco as well as information from others in New York City, Paris, and London. This requires a level of coordination and distribution of knowledge across collaborators, which is often useful for learning and emblematic of learning in the information age.

Transmedia Challenges

Learning within a transmedia genre is collaborative while utilizing distributed knowledge and collective intelligence. However, there are also significant problems with employing transmedia within classrooms. First, transmedia storytelling takes a great deal of time to create. With large budgets, or complete production houses full of production specialists, transmedia may still be a fairly complex matter. For a classroom teacher or a team of teachers, to consider creating materials across and beyond traditional media boundaries may be overwhelming. Nevertheless, it remains among the most powerful forms of storytelling available, in terms of serious engagement, collaboration, and collective knowledge building among learners. Transmedia can be more effective than other methods and means. Existing products, such as games, movies, and books, typically are not interdependent to the extent necessary to qualify as transmedia. Rather, a typical game, book, or movie stands on its own without the need to collaborate with others in an effort to construct a more complete and compelling story, which are the hallmarks of a transmedia product.

Examples of Transmedia

It is sometimes easier to understand transmedia by looking at specific examples. Most examples include two or three media forms such as a novel and animated series, or a trading card game and a video game, perhaps a television show and a novel connected through Web interactions. One of the original examples of transmedia was the 1996 production *Dreadnot*, an alternate reality game in which there is a story about a boy who has run away from home with an angel (for details, see an Internet version of *Dreadnot*). By comparison to newer transmedia examples, this early one feels like the black-and-white talkies in the dawn of film. In just a few short years, there has been a significant leap in terms of transmedia production, though the most important adage of transmedia still holds—good storytelling is good storytelling, and bad storytelling is bad storytelling. Many of the early transmedia attempts are typically limited to expansive linking more than actual use of several media and collaboration among distributed agents to convey, complete, or construct the story.

Two recent examples related to education and learning are *Hana's Suitcase* and *Love Letters to the Future*. *Hana's Suitcase* is a combination of movie, book, online news reports, website interaction, and physical artifacts. It tells the story of a suitcase that was taken from a little girl in Nazi Germany during her internment at a concentration camp and the effort years later to track down the girl's surviving brother. *Love Letters to the Future* is an interactive opportunity to write letters regarding our care of the planet (with an angle toward climate change) to future generations. As the reader is logging in a letter, or video postcard, the effort is interrupted by a message—a mysterious recording of a woman, Maya, transporting back from the future to tell about the horrible things happening because of not taking proper care of the planet. Real letters were collected and put into a time capsule, and the story of a dystopic future unfolds as clues are collected by the reader, videos are unlocked by collaborations among groups of readers, and individuals inform others of information available on their cell phones in certain cities. These two examples are particularly interesting from an educational perspective because they offer specific educational applications, which can be more clearly demonstrated as an educational or learning goal—to better understand Nazi concentration camps and to better understand the impacts of climate change and environmental negligence.

Even with these examples, it can remain difficult to understand transmedia without actually experiencing a transmedia example firsthand. Perhaps the best real-world example is the Boston marathon bombing on April 15, 2013. Before the advent of multiple media channels and 24-hour news coverage, the Boston Marathon bombing would have been first understood through a newspaper or perhaps a broadcast news report. That report would have shared basic information on the bombing and a lengthy, perhaps unsuccessful search for the bombers would have ensued. However, what the advent of the information age brought to an event such as the Boston Marathon bombing was the ability to involve huge numbers of sources in the deeper understanding of the story of the bombing. Crowdsourcing, as some would call it (crowdsourcing is a very common feature of transmedia as well), allowed the authorities to ask for every source of media recording of the event to be shared so that they could put together a more complete picture of what happened and who was where when. They took all the news and sports channel footage and also all the other security cameras, traffic light cameras, and *then* they asked for every person who was present and took photos or videos to share them. Millions of sources were given to the authorities. A National Public Radio report quoted an investigator as saying that they were certain that these sources contained images of the bombers, probably many times, and that the bombers would be found. All those spectators with smartphones, cameras, and video recorders were asked to submit their source materials. The distributed information was gathered in the same way that a story is gathered in transmedia examples, and in the real world, the authorities solved the mystery of who the bombers were by piecing together all the sources of information, collaborating with a huge number of experts and spectator-witnesses, and found a storyline that led them to the alleged bombers. This example, though not precisely the sort of *designed* transmedia product that is strictly defined as *transmedia*, is presented to help the reader to better understand the basic idea of transmedia along with its meaning and potential use to support learning and instruction.

Transmedia is a complex, expensive, project-based approach to storytelling that is likely to become more widely used in the future. Digital use among youth is such that multiple channels will likely be preferred and expected by consumers of stories. Within education, this kind of expectation may help to build a better understanding of distributed cognition. Learners who experience several transmedia units, projects, or stories in their educational careers may learn to access and understand information via multiple channels in real-world ways that may serve the needs of the information age in the future.

Transmedia has the potential to disrupt traditional classroom organization as it requires substantial time to develop, create, and consume as compared to brief units and predetermined curricula. Transmedia challenges traditional assumptions underlying standards and testing in that it allows learners to concentrate on a single topic for a longer period of time than is common in most classrooms today. It also moves the teacher from a position of power and information dispensation into a facilitator role as the learners have to rely on their own access to information across many media channels to piece together the story. This discovery, in itself, is a kind of learning that is powerful for future lifelong learning opportunities. Although transmedia can be expensive and overwhelming to consider for many teachers, it holds great potential for school change and engaging information age learning.

Alison A. Carr-Chellman

See also Augmented Reality; Disruptive Technologies; Emerging Educational Technologies; Simulation-Based Learning; Technology Integration; Ubiquitous Learning; Virtual Worlds

Further Readings

Bourdaa, M. (2013). "Following the Pattern": The creation of an encyclopaedic universe with transmedia storytelling. *Adaptation, 6*(2), 202–214.

Jenkins, H. (2006). *Convergence culture: Where old and new media collide.* New York: New York University Press.

Jenkins, H. (2006). *Fans, bloggers, and gamers: Exploring participatory culture.* New York: New York University Press.

Kidd, T. T., & Chen, I. (Eds.). (2011). *Ubiquitous learning: Strategies for pedagogy, course design and technology.* Charlotte, NC: Information Age Publishing.

Voigts, E., & Nicklas, P. (2013). Adaptation, transmedia storytelling and participatory culture. *Adaptation, 6*(2), 139–142.

Websites

Dreadnot: http://web.archive.org/web/20000308051149/http://sfgate.com/dreadnot/index1.html

Hana's Suitcase: http://www.hanassuitcase.ca/

Love Letters to the Future: http://www.youtube.com/watch?v=li4rYH2Wmlw

TWENTY-FIRST-CENTURY TECHNOLOGY SKILLS

Twenty-first-century technology skills are those abilities that enable students to access, analyze, manage, synthesize, evaluate, create, and share information in a variety of forms and media that incorporate a global perspective. Educators can leverage these technology skills to support 21st-century-learning outcomes that are associated with preparing students to meet the needs of an ever-evolving workforce. These skills are not directly associated with particular content areas but rather encompass skills that students need to be successful, lifelong learners in an increasingly interconnected world. Twenty-first-century skills usually refer to competencies in creativity, communication, collaboration, digital literacy, critical thinking, and problem solving.

Education experts, however, do not agree on a universal definition of 21st-century skills, and they disagree on whether technology skills should be taught and what learning environments should be developed to support their acquisition. Some say 21st-century learning is nothing more than 20th-century learning with better tools, and 21st-century technologies should be used to help students acquire more content knowledge. Some say basic skills such as reading and mathematics should be emphasized, and there is little evidence that classroom technologies have improved student learning. They urge society to focus on a broader, more liberal education, not one narrowly focused on preparing the workforce. Other experts say teachers should be entrepreneurs who use advanced technologies such as virtual reality and gaming to hold the interest of their students. Finally, others emphasize pervasive inequalities in technology access, use, and mastery that they propose perpetuate a racial and socioeconomic achievement gap. They argue that a list of skills is not enough to engage and prepare students for the challenges they face, and that schools need more dramatic, systemic reform.

This entry first discusses the reasons for schools to focus on new skills and ways of teaching. It then discusses various frameworks for 21st-century technology skills and the theoretical foundations of 21st-century technology skills. Finally, it discusses the assessment and implementation of 21st-century technology skills in schools.

Why Now? What Has Changed?

Many writers who focus on problems facing education have said that society is using machines and systems built in the last century to try to solve the problems of the 21st century. Even as early as the 1980s, researchers recognized that new communication and information technologies would dramatically alter educational structures. Authors such as Daniel Pink and Thomas Friedman write that society has entered the conceptual age where 21st-century skills like critical thinking and problem solving trump knowledge, and collaboration, innovation, and creativity play a major role in determining economic competitiveness. In addition, connectivity to information 24/7, constant social interaction, learning anytime and anywhere with any device, and the changing roles from consumer to creator have dramatically affected the way learning occurs.

The statistics for technological connectivity to information are overwhelming. The rapid adoption of mobile devices and the spread of Internet-connected smartphones and tablets have dramatically changed how users communicate with others and their relationships with the information. Researchers believe that a new culture of real-time information seekers who use their mobile devices to solve immediate problems is rapidly forming because of their ability to access data instantly through apps and Web browsers and through contact with members of their social networks. Students today spend countless hours online with others, blogging, social networking, and gaming, often doing these tasks simultaneously. Instead of being simply consumers of information, students create, remix, and share as easily as their teachers watch television. Learning does not necessarily take place within the walls of a classroom or from a textbook. Instead of depending on adults for information, students use free global communications tools to share ideas, collaborate, and learn new things.

The institutional structure of schooling has remained virtually the same for the past 200 years. Although most classrooms are connected to the Internet, the role of teachers continues to be one of information provider with textbooks serving as the primary structure and information source. Content is arbitrarily divided into subjects and grade levels and rarely linked to real-world contexts. Students are judged on their performance as individuals on tests. If anything, the structure of schools and the curriculum have become much more standardized over the past 20 years with the growth of state and federal mandates such as No Child Left Behind. *Teaching to the test* has become a common term, and researchers and educators alike say that this practice has encouraged teaching strategies that focus solely on how to improve test scores rather than learning.

In comparison, student characteristics have changed tremendously. The dramatic growth in, access to, and interaction with information is sometimes said to have created a student population that is bored with and disengaged from conventional teaching methods. Children enter schools as *digital natives* who have always interacted with a diverse array of technologies. Many educators are concerned that today's students have shorter attention spans and a reduced ability to concentrate because they read so much condensed content, have almost unlimited access to a variety of multimedia, and communicate primarily through a simplified texting language. Students expect instant answers because information is constantly at their fingertips. From apps that allow them to share their music to social networks where they post every minute of their lives, this is the *always on* generation.

But It's Not About the Technology

Education experts agree that it takes more than technology devices to transform classrooms into digital learning labs. When researchers investigated schools that exemplified creative uses of technology to determine what school leaders did, they found that their goal was not to teach students to use the technology. Exemplary schools focus on learning-centered goals that define the choice of technology tools. However, using technology can change the nature of content skills. For example, when information is available online as opposed to in a textbook, a student must make critical decisions about value, validity, and meaning. When a paper or project is shared online rather than only being seen by the teacher,

a student must be able to create content that is readable, engaging, and compelling for a diverse audience.

National and International Visions for 21st-Century Technology Skills

National Educational Technology Plan (USA)

The National Educational Technology Plan (NETP), developed by the U.S. Department of Education in 2010, outlines ways to improve teaching and learning through the use of technology. There are six themes in the NETP: learning, assessment, teaching, infrastructure, productivity, and research. The plan calls for education systems to use technology "to create engaging, relevant, and personalized learning experiences for all learners that mirror students' daily lives and the reality of their futures" (U.S. Department of Education, p. x). Assessment is a critical part of the NETP, and the plan calls for formative assessment as a student is learning in order to improve performance and provide data to make decisions to help students and improve the education system. In addition, the plan advocates for outcome assessments, citing practices used in industry to define outcomes and measure productivity.

The Partnership for 21st Century Skills

The Partnership for 21st Century Skills (P21) has developed "The Framework for 21st Century Learning," a multifaceted approach that includes both core subjects as well as skills that are required for lifelong learning. This holistic framework has two distinct elements: (1) student outcomes and (2) support systems designed to help students master these skills.

Student outcomes are divided into four parts: (1) life and career skills; (2) learning and innovation skills; (3) core subjects; and (4) information, media, and technology skills. Life and career skills emphasize skills that students need to function in a global world: flexibility, self-direction, personal accountability, goal setting, and leadership. Learning and innovation skills are structured around the 4 Cs of collaboration, creativity, communication, and critical thinking and problem solving. These are considered key skills that students should use to learn the content of the core subjects of reading, writing, and mathematics. The three literacy components of information, media, and technology skills entail being able to access and evaluate information, analyze media, apply technology effectively, use and manage information, and create media products.

In collaboration with content area organizations, the Partnership for 21st Century Skills developed a series of information and communications technology (ICT) literacy maps that illustrate sample outcomes for students in core academic subjects including English, mathematics, science, and social studies. The maps give educators concrete examples of how teachers can integrate these skills into core subjects, while making teaching and learning more relevant to the demands of the 21st century.

Supporters of the Common Core State Standards Initiative have criticized the P21 framework for overemphasizing skills that are rapidly changing in place of broadening student knowledge and understanding in core academic subjects such as history, science, and the arts. Many educational leaders dismiss the P21 initiative as a pedagogical fad and maintain that these skills have been in demand long before the 21st century.

International Society for Technology in Education

The International Society for Technology in Education (ISTE) developed the ISTE Standards (formerly the National Educational Technology Standards) a framework for learning, teaching, and leadership, for students, teachers, administrators, coaches, and computer science educators. The standards provide a way to evaluate the skills and knowledge needed to teach, learn, and support digital age learning. The standards emphasize higher order thinking skills such as problem solving, critical thinking, and creativity. ISTE provides resources such as an implementation wiki that includes lesson plans, videos, and scenarios to help educators use the standards to leverage technology for learning.

Assessment and Teaching of 21st Century Skills

The Assessment and Teaching of 21st Century Skills (ATC21S) project was headquartered at the University of Melbourne (Australia) and sponsored by Cisco, Intel, and Microsoft. ATC21S categorized 21st-century skills into four categories: ways of thinking, ways of working, tools for working, and skills for living in the real world, and selected two skills that encompass all of the skill areas—collaborative problem solving and ICT literacy. The goal of this project was to create an assessment framework with teaching and learning resources to help students develop 21st-century skills. ATC21s has developed tools to assess these skills and plans to share these teaching and assessment resources as well as professional development modules to help teachers understand and use the tools.

Theoretical Foundations for 21st-Century Technology Skills

Progressive Education

The idea of teaching students how to find and interpret information and apply critical thinking skills to real-world tasks is not a 21st-century idea. Most of the skills have been an integral part of the progressive education movement since the early years of the 20th century. In 1915, John Dewey and his daughter Evelyn wrote a book titled *Schools of To-Morrow*. In this book, they described the changes needed in education and emphasized that students did not need to add more information but rather needed to connect what they learned with their lives. Many education experts have argued that 21st-century skills are only an echo of progressive education ideas.

Technological Pedagogical Content Knowledge

Technological Pedagogical Content Knowledge (TPACK) is a conceptual framework developed by Matthew Koehler and Punya Mishra. It describes how technologies can be best employed in different pedagogies for facilitating the acquisition of content knowledge. TPACK identifies three primary forms of knowledge: content, pedagogy, and technology, and emphasizes the new kinds of knowledge that occur in the overlapping areas (see Figure 1).

The TPACK model emphasizes the need for all three areas—content knowledge, pedagogical knowledge, and technological knowledge—to be integrated in instruction.

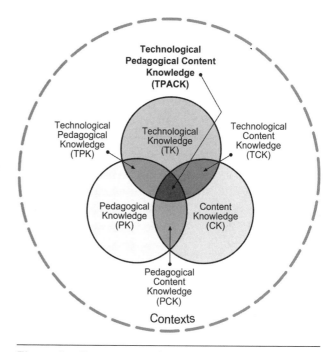

Figure 1   Components of the TPACK framework
Source: Reproduced by permission of the publisher, © 2012 by tpack.org.

Assessing 21st-Century Technology Skills

Assessment has become the educational buzzword of this century. Some education experts say the current emphasis on standardized tests is having negative effects on content areas that are not regularly tested, such as the arts, and that schools are devoting more and more classroom time to the subjects being tested. Many teachers are under enormous pressure to deliver the content needed to pass standardized tests, limiting how much time they have to explore the use of innovative techniques or digital media. Education experts argue that assessment needs to be more formative and incorporate more opportunities for authentic assessment that requires students to apply knowledge and skills to solve a problem or apply what they have learned.

The Coalition of Essential Schools (CES) describes ways to assess students through performances; performance-based assessments can be shared with the community outside of the school through *exhibitions*. In this model, assessment is part of daily work for every student. Although CES does not emphasize technology in its benchmarks, advocates describe many ways that teachers can use it as a tool to assess student progress in rich and concrete ways.

Digital media can be used to facilitate feedback for formative assessments about progress as learning occurs. Students receive feedback and have opportunities to improve performance on a cyclical basis as they reflect, form a hypothesis, test it, and either accept it and move on or rethink the hypothesis. When students use online learning, there are multiple opportunities to use technology for formative assessment since the learning management system can capture a rich array of data about their choices, knowledge, and strategy use that range from the number of hints needed, completion time, and sequential steps.

Implementation of 21st-Century Technology Skills in Schools

Most educators recognize the need to embrace technology to engage students and help develop 21st-century skills such as problem solving, creativity, and critical thinking. But roadblocks such as the focus on high-stakes testing, efforts to block websites such as YouTube, requiring cellphones to be turned off, and the lack of teacher knowledge about using these technologies has prevented many schools from following this path.

Many researchers argue that we need schools that embrace project-based curriculum and administrators should provide supportive leadership to turn classrooms into global communications centers that connect students to authentic audiences across the globe. To teach students 21st-century technology skills, teachers should be ready to adapt to any challenge and provide hands-on, technology-infused learning experiences that emphasize cognitive complexity and student empowerment. Students should learn how to sift through the enormous amounts of data made available by technology, find the information needed, and know how use it to solve a problem or answer a question.

Sara G. McNeil

See also Assessment of Problem Solving and Higher Order Thinking; Information and Communication Technologies: Competencies in the 21st-Century Workforce; Mobile Devices: Impact on Learning and Instruction; TPACK (Technological Pedagogical Content Knowledge)

Further Readings

Howland, J. L., Jonassen, D. H., & Marra, R. M. (2012). *Meaningful learning with technology.* Boston, MA: Allyn & Bacon.

International Society for Technology in Education. (2007). *ISTE Standards for Students.* Retrieved from http://www.iste.org/standards/standards-for-students

Levin, B. B., & Schrum, L. (2013). Technology-rich schools UP CLOSE. *Educational Leadership, 70*(6), 51–55.

Taylor, L. M., & Fratto, J. M. (2012). *Transforming learning through 21st century skills: The who took my chalk?™ model for engaging you and your students.* Upper Saddle River, NJ: Pearson.

U.S. Department of Education. (2010). *Transforming American education: Learning powered by technology.* Washington, DC: Office of Educational Technology, U.S. Department of Education. Retrieved from http://www.ed.gov/technology/netp-2010

Warschauer, M. (2011). *Learning in the cloud: How (and why) to transform schools with digital media.* New York, NY: Teachers College Press.

Websites

Partnership for 21st Century Skills: http://www.p21.org

Technological Pedagogical Content Knowledge: http://www.tpack.org

Ubiquitous Learning

Ubiquitous learning (aka *u-learning*) has its origins in ubiquitous computing. In a broad sense, *ubiquitous learning* is defined as "anywhere and anytime learning," encompassing any learning environment that enables learners to access learning content without any spatial and temporal constraints.

The exponential growth in handheld devices and wireless technology in recent years and increasing availability of high bandwidth network infrastructures have opened new accessibility opportunities for education. As a result, ubiquitous learning environments have started to emerge with potential to support lifelong learning and as a response to the traditional classroom-based learning that has been characterized as rigid, artificial, and out-of-context, making it very restricted in fulfilling the demands of real-life experiences and authentic learning needs of today's society. Ubiquitous learning environments break the boundaries of the classroom and enable learning to take place in the contexts where learners are able to relate with the learning scenarios in their own living and work environments, leading to a better learning experience.

The development of such ubiquitous learning environments is fueled even more by the surge of mobile and sensor technologies in recent mobile devices that have made it much easier to detect a learner's location, environment, proximity, and situation to contextualizing the learning process. It is now realistically possible to provide authentic learning by seamlessly integrating physical objects available in the learner's vicinity with virtual information in real time. Such ubiquitous environments widen the educational access to those who cannot come to a physical classroom and increase the richness of the instruction by integrating multiple sources of instruction, contextualization, and real-time location-aware learning—hence overcoming the limitations of classroom learning. Ubiquitous learning therefore provides opportunities for learners to learn in their own environments, in context, using the real-life artifacts that they can relate to their daily experiences.

Although ubiquitous learning strives for contextual and authentic learning in real-world environments, interactions between peers and between students and teachers to foster dialogue and reflection are also key components. Ongoing advances in real-time communication technologies through mobile devices support such interactions, making it possible to incorporate group collaboration, collaborative problem solving and other socially oriented learning activities in authentic real-world environments. This entry discusses several aspects of ubiquitous learning, including its focus on learners, analysis of learning in ubiquitous learning environments, support for teachers in such environments, and open questions regarding ubiquitous learning.

Learner Focus in Ubiquitous Learning Environments

Learners overcome the restrictions of classroom or workplace learning in ubiquitous learning by using their mobile devices and learning from real objects in their daily lives, true to the concept of anytime and anywhere learning. They access and interact with educational content whenever they need it, in different contexts, including formal, informal, and nonformal learning, just-in-time learning, and learning on demand.

Ubiquitous learning environments access data about learners and their surrounding context from different sensors and devices, such as active and passive radio frequency identifications (RFIDs), Bluetooth and Wi-Fi access points, and the learners' mobile devices. These data provide comprehensive information about learners' learning processes, including, for example, their current location and history of their movements, what technology is at their disposal right now, and their history of technology use, learning activities they have been engaged in, and where they performed those activities, their problem-solving history, and their interaction with peers, teachers, and both real-life and virtual learning objects. Data collected from such a learning environment can be updated in a dynamic learner model that opens opportunities for learner self-reflection as well as peer assessment.

With the huge amount of data available from various sources about the learners and their surroundings, ubiquitous learning environments are also capable of analyzing learners' learning processes as well as how learners interact with their environment. These data can be used to help teachers better understand their learners even when no face-to-face interaction between teachers and learners may be possible and help provide learners with appropriate hints and assistance as and when needed.

Analysis of Learning in Ubiquitous Learning Environments

To analyze the process of learning in ubiquitous learning environments, various attributes related to the learners and their surrounding environments are monitored and modeled in real time. These attributes are classified in four main categories: learner, location, technology, and context.

The attributes related to learner are further subclassified into four categories: competency-related, behavior-related, cognition-related, and affective states. Competency-related attributes include learners' current state of knowledge and skills in a subject matter, history of achieving competence, and efforts required in those achievements (such as the number of times a learner had to undertake assessment to demonstrate current level of competency, the last time the learner demonstrated competence in a particular topic, and associated possible knowledge decay). Behavior-related attributes include, for example, current learning styles, history of changes in learning styles, and other interaction-related preferences (such as choice of media for interaction and frequency of interaction). Cognition-related attributes contain information about learners' cognitive abilities (such as working memory capacity, associative learning skills, and inductive reasoning ability) and capacity to handle cognitive load. Finally, affective states include attributes such as motivation and emotions.

The location category gathers data about learners' current location, past history of learners' movement, and various learning activities conducted at those locations. Such data are received from multiple sources, such as various navigation sensors (Global Positioning Systems and cellular network base station identifiers), and the identification of real-life objects in those locations through technologies such as quick response (QR) code, Wi-Fi access points, and Bluetooth access points. Monitoring of various learners in ubiquitous learning also avails opportunities to create ad hoc study groups of learners within a particular geographic area, with particular needs and preferences, or those who could help each other with complementary expertise.

The technology category includes details of various technologies and devices available to learners as they progress in ubiquitous learning environments, and the capabilities of those technologies and devices, such as display capability, audio and video capability, available memory and bandwidth, and characteristics of the operating platform, such as available navigation mechanisms, supported media formats, and so forth.

Attributes in context category relate to the learners' immediate environment and the purpose of learning—for example, the type of location (such as laboratory, classroom, work, home, library, museum), the ambient attributes of the environment (such as noise level, lighting), learners' interactions with the peers and learning objects in the environment, and the goal of current learning.

Teacher Support in Ubiquitous Learning

Contemporary ubiquitous learning systems focus mostly on supporting learners and consider very little, if at all, on how to support teachers in such environments. Especially in ubiquitous learning environments, where learners are mobile at different locations and learn whenever and wherever they want, at a pace of their choice, it is difficult for teachers to keep track of learners' activities and determine when they encounter problems in learning. Technologies are under development to address this issue by explicitly catering to teachers in a ubiquitous learning environment by providing them with an infrastructure that presents them with detailed information about learners' learning process, provides intelligent support for detecting patterns in learners' activities and behavior, and assists teachers in intervening and helping learners to overcome learning difficulties.

Open Questions in Ubiquitous Learning

Ubiquitous learning is an emerging area and a number of research directions are evolving as research continues in this area. Some of the major open questions are as follows:

- What capabilities and competencies do learners possess relative to ubiquitous learning opportunities, and what are their preferences relative to the associated environment and learning process?

- What are the ways in which meaningful movement and interaction patterns of individual learners can be detected and analyzed? How do those movements and interactions relate to the interactions and learning activities at a particular location?
- What is the influence of the technologies that are accessible to the learners at a given point in time on the learning experiences? What influence do the technologies surrounding the individual learners have on learners' learning experiences?
- How do various components of context relate to the current situation of individual learners, and how do those components affect each other?

Kinshuk

See also Learning in Museums; Learning in Outdoor Settings; Mobile Tools and Technologies for Learning and Instruction; Radio Frequency Identification in Education; Tablet Devices in Education and Training

Further Readings

Graf, S., & Kinshuk (2008). Adaptivity and personalization in ubiquitous learning systems. *Lecture Notes in Computer Science, 5298,* 331–338.

Hwang, G.-J., Tsai, C.-C., & Yang, S. J. H. (2008). Criteria, strategies and research issues of context-aware ubiquitous learning. *Journal of Educational Technology & Society, 11*(2), 81–91.

Kinshuk, & Jesse, R. (2013). Reusable authentic learning scenario creation in ubiquitous learning environments. In Huang, R., Kinshuk, & Spector, J. M. (Eds.), *Reshaping learning—Frontiers of learning technology in a global context* (pp. 273–298). Heidelberg, Germany: Springer-Verlag.

Ogata, H., & Yano, Y. (2004). Context-aware support for computer-supported ubiquitous learning. In *Proceedings of the 2nd IEEE International Workshop on Wireless and Mobile Technologies in Education (WMTE'04)* (pp. 27–34). Washington, DC: IEEE Computer Society.

Yang, S. J. H. (2006). Context aware ubiquitous learning environments for peer-to-peer collaborative learning. *Journal of Educational Technology & Society, 9*(1), 188–201.

UNIVERSAL DESIGN

Universal design is a design philosophy and approach that allows equitable access to and usability of products and environments for all people regardless of abilities, age, and other human characteristics. In addition, this design approach is now being applied to equity and access to services for individuals as well. The early ideas and use of universal design were focused on the needs of people with disabilities and may have been driven by legislation about the rights of people with disabilities. However, a more current view is concerned that design should focus on the needs of all individuals whether they are old or young, with or without disabilities, and so on. Ronald Mace is credited as being the first to use the term *universal design* and founded the Center for Universal Design (CUD) at North Carolina State University. At the CUD, Mace and others compiled seven basic principles of universal design: (1) equitable use, (2) flexibility in use, (3) simple and intuitive use, (4) perceptible information, (5) tolerance for error, (6) low physical effort, and (7) size and space for approach and use.

Universal design was first used in various architectural fields to keep human needs and diversity in mind when designing buildings and other environments. In other words, with the application of universal design of various environments, the focus is that environments are esthetically pleasing in form and function and allow individuals to use and access them with minimal effort and with ease. For example, enlarging the size of doorways and removing thresholds between rooms allow individuals in wheelchairs to move through the entryways without being restricted. An example of product development is lift-off caps on bottles and cans for easy removal by people with limited dexterity or mobility.

Universal design has also been expanded into other fields where design or elements of creativity are emphasized. Universal design is relevant within the field of educational technology, which focuses on the design, development, and implementation of instruction and learning processes in various learning environments. Additionally, educational technology is not only for the process of design for instruction and learning, but also for development of instructional and learning products, which may incorporate technological tools but not always. This entry begins by describing legislation related to accessibility and then examines universal design in education.

Legislation Related to Disabilities and Accessibility

Universal design was also an outgrowth of the passage of national or regional legislation worldwide. In addition to the United States, countries such as Australia, China, France, Ireland, Sweden, and the United Kingdom, among others, enacted legislation for individuals with disabilities. With some variation, these legislative acts, or laws, protect people with disabilities against discrimination, provide them with certain rights, and enable them to pursue teaching or learning opportunities without being disadvantaged.

In the United States, parts of the Rehabilitation Act of 1973 focused on design and redesign of or adaptations to environments and products to accommodate individuals with various disabilities in their ability to use or access them with minimal effort. Later, U.S. legislation established the Individuals with Disabilities Education Act (IDEA) to further accommodate individuals with disabilities, but in educational settings. Later amended, IDEA also defined assistive technologies as a part of this legislation. Assistive technologies are various devices for individuals with disabilities so they can perform various tasks, functions, and activities that were extremely difficult or impossible for them to do without such devices. Within education, a variety of assistive technologies and methods for learners help them read and write, among other things. With a focus on e-learning, e-commerce, and other uses of the World Wide Web, the Americans with Disabilities Act (ADA) of 1990 as well as the Internet Web Accessibility Initiative by the World Wide Web Consortium (W3C) in 2001 required electronic accessibility for everyone. Other legislation in the United States further expanded such requirements and their implementation in colleges and universities.

Much of the focus of legislation has been about accommodations for disabilities, which may relate to physical and psychological disabilities such as various types of sensory impairments, limited mobility or dexterity, chronic illness, and learning disabilities. However, the Center for Universal Design in Education (CUDE) at the University of Washington maintains that disabilities are only one of the human characteristics to consider when designing a product, environment, or service for all. With this idea in mind, universal design has been extended to accommodate diversity among people—that is, providing accessibility and usability with minimum effort by people regardless of gender, age, nationality, ethnicity and language, abilities, and other human characteristics. Universal design then becomes more about all people rather than being focused on only those with disabilities; it has been known also as design for all and, sometimes, barrier-free design.

Universal Design Within Educational Realms

As previously stated, universal design was originally focused on meeting needs of people with disabilities; this was true in education realms with the provisions of special education programs and curricula to meet such needs of children in schools. Much of these early efforts were, and still are, focused on developing individual educational plans (IEPs) for each student who has special needs. However, U.S. school policies have also brought about the idea of inclusion related to individuals with disabilities, and this approach is gaining acceptance outside the United States. Inclusion means that children with special needs are taught alongside normally developing children rather than being placed in separate classrooms. IEPs are still used for students with special needs, but accommodations take place within the regular classroom as much as possible. This is also true for students in postsecondary education. Accommodations are made to the greatest extent possible to those students who have disabilities based on the policies and procedures within a given university.

Within educational settings, universal design has transitioned and become known as universal design for learning, universal design for instruction, or universal instructional design. Although defined somewhat differently, there are overlapping commonalities and principles among these terms.

Universal Design for Learning

Universal design for learning (UDL) was identified and defined in the 2004 version of IDEA passed by the U.S. government. Based on pedagogy and CUD's seven universal design principles, UDL is applied in educational settings to allow opportunities for every individual to learn. According to the CUDE, the nine UDL principles focus on individual student needs as related to (a) perception; (b) language, expressions, symbolism; (c) comprehension; (d) physical action; (e) expressive skills and fluency; (f) executive functions; (g) recruiting interest; (h) sustaining effort and persistence; and (i) self-regulations. The Center for Applied Special Technology (CAST) also focused on UDL and combined the nine UDL principles into three main guidelines to assist educators when developing curriculum, instruction, assessment, and support materials. These three guidelines consider flexibility when (1) allowing for a variety of ways to represent and present instruction (i.e., content and learning), (2) providing various means and opportunities for students to communicate and demonstrate their gained knowledge and skills while learning, and (3) promoting student engagement using various means to sustain learner motivation, effort, and self-regulation while learning. The overall purpose of UDL principles and guidelines is to assist teachers when addressing the individual needs and abilities of their students. Although UDL may incorporate technology, technology use is not a requirement in UDL practices.

Universal Design for Instruction

Universal design for instruction (UDI) is oriented toward the design, development, and implementation of instructional and learning environments, mainly within higher education settings. Instead of a focus on the needs of the individual, UDI considers the needs of all students to reduce any barriers within the instruction and learning processes without changing the instructional content or goals of a given course or curriculum or lowering the standards associated with the college or university. As with UDL, the original CUD's seven principles were the basis for UDI. The CUDE developed its UDI process to consider and use when developing instructional and learning materials as well as the corresponding environment. CUDE's UDI process is as follows: (1) identify the application to be considered for universal design; (2) define the universe by describing the intended users and their characteristics; (3) involve consumers in the application's design and implementation; (4) adopt specific guidelines or standards to the application design, production, and implementation; (5) apply these guidelines to maximize its use; (6) plan for accommodations of the application for individuals who do not have access to it; (7) train and support stakeholders on the institutional goals and practices related to diversity and inclusion; and (8) evaluate the application periodically with a diverse group of users and stakeholders and make modifications as necessary.

This UDI process can be used for developing courses in on-campus (face-to-face), online, or blended environments. Similarly, the Center on Postsecondary Education and Disability (CPED) at the University of Connecticut included the seven original universal design principles. These were combined with the principles of good teaching as identified by Arthur Chickering and Zelda Gamson. The CPED also included two additional principles of (8) a community of learners, and (9) instructional climate that is inclusive to the universal design principles in accordance with the visions and missions of higher education institutions.

Application of CPED principles consider that instruction and instructional environments should be (a) useful to and accessible by students; (b) accommodating to a variety of student abilities; (c) developed in an uncomplicated, obvious way; (d) communicated effectively to all students whether they have disabilities or not; (e) planned for accommodating learner pace and prior knowledge and skills; (f) planned to reduce any nonessential physical effort; (g) planned with consideration of appropriate size and space to accommodate students' physical characteristics and their communication needs; (h) within an environment that promotes interaction among participants (students and instructors); and (i) welcoming and inclusive for all students. CPED has also directed UDI principles and applications toward online and blended instructional situations in colleges and universities.

Universal Instructional Design

Of the three universal design approaches in education, universal instructional design (UID) is most closely aligned with the field of educational technology.

Universal instructional design is primarily an inclusive and innovative approach focused primarily on the design and delivery of instruction. UID is defined as the development of instruction that allows learning to occur for all students regardless of background, abilities, needs, or preferences. Although more often associated with UDI, the principles and processes of either UDI or UDL can be employed in UID during the development of methods and materials. The potential of UID is ultimately to provide any instructional or learning environment that allows equality of opportunity for every student to achieve the academic standards within any field or discipline. The Open Learning and Educational Support within the Teaching Support Services at the University of Guelph considers UID as a way of thinking about instructional design to increase opportunities for all students to learn while decreasing the need for special accommodations. Furthermore, UID is not about the development of individualized instruction. Instead, UID emphasizes that any instruction is to be presented or delivered in multiple ways and that, within the instruction, students be allowed alternatives for ways to respond, participate, and interact with the instruction, its environment, and other participants (i.e., students and instructors). In other words, for any given instructional or learning environment, there is a variety of, but equivalent, means for learners to access and engage in the essential learning experiences and to demonstrate their knowledge and skills.

Gayle V. Davidson-Shivers

See also Assistive Technology

Further Readings

Burgstahler, S. (2012). *Universal design: Process, principles, and applications: A goal and a process that can be applied to the design of any product or environment*. Seattle, WA: DO-IT at the Center for Universal Design in Education (CUDE), University of Washington. Retrieved from http://www.washington.edu/doit/Brochures/PDF/ud.pdf

Center for Applied Special Technology (CAST). (2011). *Universal design for learning guidelines* (version 2.0). Wakefield, MA: Author. Retrieved from http://www.cast.org

Center for Universal Design (CUD). (1997). *The principles of universal design* (version 2.0). Raleigh, NC: North Carolina State University. Retrieved from http://www.ncsu.edu/ncsu/design/cud/about_ud/udprinciplestext.htm

Center on Postsecondary Education and Disability (CPED). (2012). *Universal design for instruction in postsecondary education*. Storrs: University of Connecticut, CPED. Retrieved from http://www.udi.uconn.edu/index.php?q=content/universal-design-instruction-postsecondary-education

Davidson-Shivers, G. V., & Reese, R. M. (2012). Are your online assessments getting at learning or something else? In T. Amiel

& B. Wilson (Eds.), *Proceedings of World Conference on Educational Multimedia, Hypermedia and Telecommunications* (pp. 2611–2616). Chesapeake, VA: AACE. Retrieved from http://www.editlib.org/p/41131

Hackman, H. W., & Rauscher, L. (2004). A pathway to access for all: Exploring the connections between universal instructional design and social justice education. *Equity & Excellence in Education, 37*, 114–123.

Izzo, M. V., Murray, A., & Novak, J. (2008). The faculty perspective on universal design for learning. *Journal of Postsecondary Education and Disability, 21*(2), 60–72.

King-Sears, M. (2009). Universal design for learning: Technology and pedagogy. *Learning Disability Quarterly, 32*, 199–201.

Lieberman, L. J., Lytle, R. K., & Clarcq, J. A. (2008). Getting it right from the start: Employing universal design for learning approach to your curriculum. *Journal of Physical Education, Recreation and Dance, 79*(2), 32–39.

Scott, S. S., McGuire, J. M., & Foley, T. E. (2010). Universal design for instruction: A framework for anticipating and responding to disability and other diverse learning needs in the college classroom. *Equity & Excellence in Education, 31*(1), 40–49.

Teaching Support Services. (2012). *UID at the University of Guelph.* University of Guelph, Ontario, Canada: Author. Retrieved from http://www.tss.uoguelph.ca/uid

UNIVERSAL DESIGN FOR LEARNING

The term *universal design for learning* (UDL) is attributed to David Rose, Anne Meyer, and colleagues at the Center for Applied Special Technology (CAST) in Wakefield, Massachusetts. When the term was first used in the mid-1990s, it acknowledged the conceptual foundations of universal design in the field of architecture but sought to apply the benefits of accessible design to curriculum and instruction. A motivating factor for this philosophical approach was that students with disabilities were increasingly being educated in general education classrooms where they encountered barriers to learning. The promise of UDL suggested that, by understanding the special academic needs of individuals with disabilities, it would be possible to proactively design flexible learning materials and environments with embedded supports, thereby reducing or eliminating the need for curriculum accommodations. Despite the widespread support for the concept of UDL, the construct has proven difficult to define, measure, implement, scale, and evaluate.

The origins of universal design can be traced to Ron Mace, an architect, who understood the importance of appreciating human differences when designing environments and products. For example, since the 1930s, building codes in the United States have specified interior bedroom doors in a home should be 32 inches (81.28 cm) wide, whereas bathroom doors could be 28, 30, or 32 inches wide, based on the assumption the residents were ambulatory. This decision could later cause tens of thousands of dollars in remodeling costs to modify the doorway to make it accessible if a resident became impaired and needed to use a wheelchair. The keen insight about universal design is that there is relatively little cost involved when the architect designs all internal doorways to be 36 inches (91.44 cm) wide in consideration that a wheelchair user might potentially reside in the home. This design intervention proactively provides support for wheelchair users, but it also makes it easier to move furniture from room to room. Mace's advocacy about human differences sensitized the design community to issues of disability access and produced a legacy of fostering creativity to identify and eliminate barriers in the built environment.

Perhaps the best example of the success of universal design principles is the *curb cut.* Originally designed to improve mobility for people with disabilities within our communities, curb cuts accomplished that, but they also improved access for people navigating their communities with baby strollers, roller blades, bicycles, and so on. Another well-known example of accessible design is what is known as the *zero-entry swimming pool.* This type of pool design was created to provide access for individuals in wheelchairs but has proven to be excellent for anyone seeking to enjoy the water without becoming completely immersed. The historical lessons learned through the architectural application of universal design have led to a statement that serves as a mantra for universal design: Good design for people with disabilities can benefit everyone.

Rose, Meyer, and colleagues at CAST learned about universal design and began pondering its application in the field of education. Rather than wait for students to fail, it makes more sense to embed smart technologies that support all learners, including those with disabilities, into the classroom and learning materials before they fail. The goal of UDL is to proactively value academic diversity such that supports are embedded into instructional materials before a student needs them. The potential of UDL interventions is that they will facilitate the academic performance of students with disabilities, who may be considered the primary beneficiary of accessible design interventions, but also that UDL supports can affect secondary beneficiaries—that is, diverse learners who may benefit from scaffolds, but whom we may not be able to identify in advance. This entry presents the instructional design principles of UDL and discusses issues associated with putting UDL into practice.

Key Principles

CAST advanced the concept of UDL as a means of focusing research, development, and educational practice on understanding diversity and applying technology to facilitate learning. Challenging educators to think of the curriculum as disabled, rather than students, the CAST insights in translating principles of universal design from architecture to education are commensurate with advances characterized as a major paradigm shift.

CAST's philosophy of UDL is embodied in a series of principles that serve as the core components of UDL.

Multiple Means of Representation. Teachers today can provide their students with many choices on how to access instructional content: Watch a YouTube video, listen to a podcast, read text on a Web page, look up a topic using an Internet search engine, and more. The key notion is to break out of the one-size-fits-all model of relying solely on a printed textbook, which assumes that all students learn in the same way, and to encourage teachers to offer a wider palette of information containers to reach the diverse students they teach.

Multiple Means of Expression. This principle draws attention to the need to provide students with multiple methods of demonstrating what they know. Some teachers recognize the value of this principle as they allow students a choice of writing a paper, preparing a slideshow presentation, or recording a video, for example. The key notion is to provide students with choice in how they demonstrate what they have learned and the media they use to express themselves.

Multiple Means of Engagement. This principle encourages educators to design instructional materials and activities in ways that tap into learners' interests, challenge them appropriately, and motivate them to learn. This principle is firmly rooted in the research on learning that indicates deep learning is only accomplished through sustained engagement. Access to the curriculum is a prerequisite for engagement. However, sustained engagement is achieved by activities that are interesting, motivating, and at the right challenge level—what Lev Vygotsky calls the zone of proximal development and Mihaly Csikszentmihalyi calls flow.

CAST has elaborated these core principles through the development of *UDL Guidelines (2.0)*. Each of the three core principles has been expanded to include three guidelines that speak to the instructional design features that are needed to implement each principle. Whereas the guidelines were created for teachers and instructional designers to use as they create instructional materials, the guidelines have been criticized as being too abstract to inform specific instructional design interventions. Universal design organizations around the world are adopting similar guidelines, most notably in Europe (see, for example, the Design for All Europe and European Design for All e-Accessibility Network websites).

Future Directions: Translating UDL Theory Into Practice

Whereas universal design is often advocated as *design for all*, in practice this has been difficult to achieve. A more practical way to think about universal design is *design for more types*. This means that the goal is to understand the accessibility and usability barriers that individuals encounter and create new tools, products, and information resources that are inclusive to more individuals than would be the case with ordinary *design for the mean* approaches.

The promise of UDL suggests that instructional materials can be designed to provide adjustable instructional design controls. One way to think about these controls is to consider a volume control slider that is adjustable to be off or some level between low and high. Carol Ann Tomlinson speaks of this concept as *equalizers*. If designers conceptualize an equalizer as a volume control slider, such digital controls could be included in all instructional software and be accessed by students and teachers when an adjustment is needed. For example, an equalizer built into a digital reading passage would allow the student to adjust the text difficulty by moving the slider up (high) or down (low) until the student finds the *just right* level of text complexity to be able to understand the passage.

Dave L. Edyburn

See also Assistive Technology; Instructional Design Models; Instructional Design Practice; Instructional Design Research; Instructional Designer Preparation

Further Readings

Center for Applied Special Technology (CAST). (2011). *Universal design for learning guidelines* (version 2.0). Wakefield, MA: Author. Retrieved from http://www.udlcenter.org/aboutudl/udlguidelines

Csikszentmihalyi, M. (1990). *Flow: The psychology of optimal experience.* New York, NY: Harper & Row.

Edyburn, D. L. (2010). Would you recognize universal design for learning if you saw it? Ten propositions for new directions for the second decade of UDL. *Learning Disability Quarterly*, 33(1), 33–41.

Lazar, J. (2007). *Universal usability: Designing computer interfaces for diverse populations*. New York, NY: Wiley.

Lidwell, W., Holden, K., & Butler, J. (2010). *Universal principles of design: 125 ways to enhance usability, influence perception, increase appeal, make better design decisions, and teach through design* (2nd ed.). Gloucester, MA: Rockport.

McLeskey, J., & Waldron, N. (2007). Making differences ordinary in inclusive classrooms. *Intervention in School and Clinic, 42*(3), 162–168.

Preiser, W., & Ostroff, E. (2011). *Universal design handbook* (2nd ed.). New York, NY: McGraw-Hill.

Rose, D., & Meyer, A. (2002). *Teaching every student in the digital age*. Alexandria, VA: ASCD. Retrieved from http://www.cast.org/teachingeverystudent/ideas/tes

Task Force to Explore the Incorporation of the Principles of Universal Design for Learning into the Education Systems in Maryland. (2011). *A route for every learner*. Retrieved from http://marylandpublicschools.org/MSDE/newsroom/special_reports

Tomlinson, C. A. (1999). *The differentiated classroom: Responding to the needs of all learners*. Alexandria, VA: ASCD.

Vygotsky, L. (1962). *Thought and language*. Cambridge, MA: MIT Press.

Websites

EIDD Design for All Europe: http://www.designforalleurope.org

European Design for All e-Accessibility Network; http://www.edean.org

VERIFICATION AND VALIDATION OF DIGITAL RESOURCES

Verification and validation of digital resources are critical in determining the quality and utility of educational tools. As parts of the process of creating new digital resources or as methods for evaluation and selection of existing resources, effective verification and validation focus efforts and document results toward appropriate use of carefully vetted tools. The Institute of Electronic and Electronic Engineers (IEEE) Standard Glossary of Software Engineering Terminology defines *verification* as a process to evaluate a system (or system components) to determine whether it satisfies the conditions imposed at the start of the development phase. In other words, does the system or component meet the stipulated specifications of the original design or specifications set at the previous phase(s) of a process? *Validation* is defined as a process to evaluate whether a system or system component satisfies requirements at the end of the entire development process. Does the final product or process achieve the intended ends? Simply put, verification is aimed at determining whether a product was created according to plan, and validation determines whether the product serves the function(s) for which it is intended. Outside the educational context, the phrase "verification and validation of digital resources" can lead a researcher to a very technical perspective, addressing specific processes and techniques for use with digital hardware and software systems. A more holistic approach to digital resources in education is more useful.

Digital resources have become an integral element of education at all levels. They are the building blocks of much of current educational activity—in online courses, in the classroom, or in hybrid environments. The wealth of available resources can be overwhelming, and selecting and evaluating resources appropriate for each situation can be a daunting task. This breadth of variation makes it nearly impossible to prescribe *the* correct approach to the verification and validation of digital resources. Many factors affect the quality and utility of a resource; this entry outlines valuable approaches, techniques, and perspectives that can be helpful in judging quality and utility.

Sources and Context

Whether a resource is created for a project or is acquired through an Internet search, from a trusted educational institution, from a commercial publisher, or through online library research, a challenge is the verification and validation of a resource for use in specific educational contexts. The range of what can be labeled *digital resource* grows constantly. Jian Wang and Althea Pribyl list electronic serials/journals, databases, and websites. Digital resources also include learning objects, mobile applications, games, social media records, open educational resources (OER), and digital media artifacts of all kinds.

To verify and validate the resource in a process in line with the definitions, it is necessary to have at least two things:

- A reasonably complete description of the design for the item or of the design that resulted from the previous step in a process (verification)
- A clear description of the learning goals or objectives that the resource is intended to address (validation)

Obtaining these can be straightforward or challenging, depending on the origin and source of a digital resource. When a digital resource is created for a specific use and context, design documents and specifications are created as a natural part of the process and should be readily available, as should be clear descriptions of the learning objectives and goals of the item and of any larger project in which it will be used. If the verification and validation processes are aimed at selecting and determining the value of existing resources that are acquired in a more or less complete version, identifying or describing original design intentions and specifications is often challenging. Accompanying research and best-practices literature along with studies that use or address the resource(s) or descriptions made through investigation of the resources can permit the ex post facto creation of design descriptions and specifications for use in the verification process.

Parallel principles apply regarding validation. When using a resource that has been created for the specific context and purposes wherein it is being validated, the parameters for validation should be easily identified and set. They will be related to the design documents and choices and built on the overarching requirements of the educational intention. In the case of a found or acquired resource, the objectives and goals will be set in the plan to use the resource. It is imperative that the design of a learning experience include explicit objectives and goals if validation is to be performed; this is true for both the formative stages of evaluation and the summative evaluation.

Design specifications, created for a current project or extrapolated from existing evidence, and learning objectives and goals, usually explicitly stated for the project/system being validated, set the standards by which verification and validation of a digital resource can be thoughtfully and effectively executed. With this knowledge and an understanding of the context, validation and verification can proceed.

The Role of Literacies

Verification and validation of digital resources requires assessing and evaluating each resource, employing skill and experience in multiple literacies, including information literacy, media literacy, visual literacy, and digital literacy. Although it is difficult to master all of these literacies, they each have a place in the process.

Information literacy, the set of skills needed to recognize when information is needed and the ability to locate, evaluate, and make effective use of information, empowers an individual to make intelligent choices regarding information. (See the Association of College and Research Libraries website for links to a number of library standards and guidelines.) Information literacy enables learners to master content, extend investigations,

become more self-directed, and assume greater control over their learning. Note that this definition says nothing about the format or medium of the information and can apply to text, visuals, and audio resources. Information literacy constitutes an intellectual framework involving understanding, finding, evaluating, and using information; these are activities involving information technology, investigative methods, and critical discernment and reasoning. This requires careful investigation of the source of a resource, the perspective(s) of the provider(s) of the resource, and other elements such as timeliness.

Media literacy can be defined as the ability to access, analyze, evaluate, and communicate information in a variety of forms; media literacy often focuses on issues of control, including political aspects. (See the website of the National Association for Media Literacy Education for definitions, standards, and best practices related to media literacy.) The reference to a variety of forms hints at the importance, to this discipline, of the media in which information is presented. To verify and validate any digital resource, it is critical to assess who or what entity initiates or controls a particular resource. An obvious example is the difference between political parties' different approaches to information regarding contentious topics such as the Affordable Care Act/Obamacare or the right-to-choose/right-to-life controversy. The influence of a major corporation on stories from mainstream news providers may be less obvious or direct, but could still affect the tone and content of information. On the Internet, the various domain suffixes can indicate important differences among sources (e.g., .org, .edu, .com, .net, .tv, .gov, etc.), or may identify a specific country (e.g., .nl, .ca, .sg, .kr, etc.). These suffixes provide a first clue about the information and its likely veracity and reliability.

Visual literacy refers to a set of abilities that enable individuals to find, interpret, evaluate, use, and create images and other visual media (discussed on the Association of College and Research Libraries website). Because of the multimedia nature of many digital resources, any assessment of a resource's value should address the visual presentation. The quality of design can have powerful effects on any message, especially for a more sophisticated or experienced audience. The visual elements in a resource, their placement in a composition, and attributes such as size, color, value, line, and texture all contribute to the overall design and should be examined individually and collectively as part of any evaluation process.

Digital literacy refers to the interest, attitude, and ability of individuals to appropriately use digital technology and communication tools to access, manage, integrate, analyze, and evaluate information; construct new knowledge; create; and communicate with others to participate effectively in society (see the digital literacy standards presented on the website of the Ministry of Education, British Columbia). This definition parallels the definitions of other literacies previously noted. The use of the related verbs—access, find, retrieve, analyze, evaluate, interpret, use, create, and communicate—illustrates the commonalities among these literacies, and the addition of other verbs and modifiers points to the ways that they differ and complement one another. Because digital literacy focuses more on tools and systems, it is particularly valuable in verification and validation of digital resources. The phrase "appropriately use digital technology and communication tools" is integral to the verification and validation of digital resources because that is the central question in both processes.

Specific Applications of the Processes

Learning objects are an example of a class of resources for which verification and validation are necessary. Learning objects are a common digital resource for which there is a large body of research. David Williams outlines a model for evaluation of learning objects that can be easily extended to other types of resources. Evaluation requires a compilation of all the standards associated with objects, learners, and instructional theories, along with other stakeholder values; the evaluation of the learning object will involve an estimate of the quality of the instruction in terms of those standards, both formatively—to improve instruction for development purposes—and summatively—to assess its value for accountability purposes. In addition, the evaluation will determine degrees of compliance with technical standards. The potential and probable uses of a digital resource, especially relating to context, shape any criteria for evaluation, including verification and validation. For example, a digital resource used in a purely informational website requires different evaluative choices than does a similar object intended for use as part of an online course with specific learning objectives. The standards referred to in this process are shaped by external specifications and by the design specifications as originally stated or as extrapolated from post hoc research. For summative validation, the broader standards align with the experience and evidence of recent use of the resources.

It remains important to consider the disciplinary context of each digital resource throughout the processes. According to Bob Kemp and Chris Jones, different subjects and disciplines have divergent types of digital resources and use them for different purposes; nevertheless, academic progress requires digital resources, even as usages differ by discipline. When verifying or validating a given digital resource, its use within the target discipline or course of study necessarily influences each assessment.

Verification

The question with respect to verification is whether the technologies and tools were used appropriately in the creation of the resource to original specifications. If the technologies and tools were not effectively employed, it becomes difficult to determine whether other elements are correct. The choices made in regard to technology affect the delivery. If the tools were used well, it becomes possible to verify that a resource meets a given set of design specifications. Is the content in the final artifact the same as that described in the design? Are the depth and breadth of the content appropriate for the originally described audience(s)? Are the visual elements in keeping with their original description and intended use? Are the design choices correct, reflecting the specifications? If there are interactivity options, do they function according to the original plan? Do technical attributes meet specifications in keeping with the overall design? Other elements may require assessment, depending on the specific project, and answering questions such as these for all elements will form the basis for a holistic verification of a resource. Application of the principles and perspectives of the literacies outlined earlier will aid in forming and answering valuable questions. If the resource is being created specifically for a particular use, the verification process can be part of iterative design and development activities that ensure compliance with original specifications.

Validation

Validation asks whether the final version of the resource, once in use, fulfills the intended learning objectives and goals. Once the verification process confirms that the resource conforms to the original design, and the resource has been deployed, either in testing or piloting circumstances or directly into its intended use, the resource can be validated. The outcomes of the use(s) will inform the validation of the resource either formatively, if it is still in development, or summatively, perhaps as part of the assessment of some larger project or course of study. The first requirement, before deploying the resource, is a clear and complete listing of the objectives and goals of the use of the resource within the learning context. As with the original design documents, this listing should have been prepared before the resource was put into use, either as part of the design process (in the case of a newly created artifact) or as a result of examination and assessment of an existing resource leading to careful crafting of the objectives and goals for the target context. Multiple tools can be used in the validation process, including internal assessments such as quizzes, assignments, exams, and projects, or quantitative and qualitative reflective documentation by learners, instructors, or other users of the resource. Surveys, questionnaires, essays, interviews, and focus groups are some of the possible approaches. A systematic point-by-point examination of the results of the deployment of a digital resource using appropriate available tools, considering the perspectives of the literacies discussed earlier and using an instructional design and development lens, will provide robust and useful validation, either to determine adjustments at a formative stage or to make decisions regarding repeated subsequent use at a summative point.

Conclusion

The verification and validation of digital resources are invaluable in the design, deployment, and assessment of digital artifacts in educational settings. Because of the complex possibilities for creation, acquisition, and use of these resources, many perspectives and a broad range of tools must be employed to verify and validate resources. To verify, the assessment measures the existing resource against the original design specifications or specifications extrapolated from research on the item. Is the extant artifact the item that was described in design documentation? To validate, the results of use of the resource are measured against the proposed outcomes, either formatively or summatively, using available assessment tools and evidence. As used in the current context, are the target outcomes achieved by use of the resource? A digital resource, verified and validated, is available for effective use and re-use, and for extension into related contexts.

Thomas R. Hergert

See also Assessing Literacy Skills in the 21st Century; Design and Development Research; Digital Literacy: Overview and Definition; Formative Assessment; Information, Technology, and Media Literacies; Learning Objects; Multimedia and Image Design; Objectives-Based Assessments; Program Evaluation

Further Readings

IEEE Standards Board (1990). *Glossary of software engineering terminology* [IEEE Std 610.12–1990]. Retrieved from http://ieeexplore.ieee.org/stamp/stamp.jsp?tp=&arnumber=159342

Kemp, B., & Jones, C. (2007). Academic use of digital resources: Disciplinary differences and the issue of progression revisited. *Journal of Educational Technology & Society*,
10(1), 52–60. Retrieved from http://www.ifets.info/journals/10_1/6.pdf

Nikoi, S., & Armellini, A. (2012). The OER mix in higher education: Purpose, process, product, and policy. *Distance Education, 33*(2), 165–184. Retrieved from http://www.tandfonline.com/doi/abs/10.1080/.U4ZIyahdWSo

Wang, J., & Pribyl, A. (2007). The nature of the digital resource. *Collection Management, 32*(1–2), 141–153.

Williams, D. D. (2000). Evaluation of learning objects and instruction using learning objects. In D. A. Wiley (Ed.), *The instructional use of learning objects: Online version.* Retrieved from http://reusability.org/read/chapters/williams.doc

Websites

Association of College and Research Libraries, standards and guidelines: http://www.ala.org/acrl/standards

Ministry of Education, British Columbia, digital literacy standards: http://www.bced.gov.bc.ca/dist_learning/dig_lit_standards.htm

National Association for Media Literacy Education: http://namle.net/publications/media-literacy-definitions

VIDEO GAMES AND STUDENT ASSESSMENT

A *video game* is a game played by means of controlling images rendered on a television or computer screen. This entry discusses the use of video games as a means to assess students and collect student progress data related to the use of video games in the classroom.

Video games are a ubiquitous and significant part of children's and adults' lives, with estimates placing the number of video game players in the world at 4.9 billion players. These numbers increase even more when one considers the use of online discussions for sharing gaming strategies and skills. As use of mobile devices rises, more people are spending more time engaged in gaming.

This level of use points to the enormous potential of these games to engage students in academic pursuits, increasing their learning and performance. Video games also offer an innovative avenue for academic assessment. Video games have been used for several years in educational settings and content areas such as English, reading, and mathematics to engage students. Games offering continuous feedback affecting player choices have been used to develop and measure learning outcomes. Tracking student feedback and player choices provides a means for understanding student learning and targeting instruction using data-driven methods, though more research is needed on how best to harness the potential of video games, especially in the science, technology, engineering, and mathematics (STEM) fields.

As argued by Leonard Annetta, when a video game incorporates pedagogical approaches designed with specific learning outcomes in mind, the game can be used to measure learning and, ultimately, in assessment of student performance. An example of this approach is seen in video games called serious games or serious educational games.

Video games present the learner with complex representations of real-world problems within educational environments. These complex representations would not otherwise be possible for a student to interact with in the real world. For example, it is very unlikely that even undergraduate students in biological sciences would have access to, or engage in, learning within a Level 4 biosafety laboratory where professional scientists study dangerous microbes. Learners within video game environments are exposed to complex representations often requiring specific tasks to be completed to reach an objective and promote learning. Through task completion, knowledge construction takes place, with the game acting as a mediator.

Using video games as assessment tools allows educators to move from assessment based on content knowledge to knowledge application and authentic task-based analysis. During the past several years, education has moved from a traditional focus on foundation knowledge in reading, writing, and mathematics to standards that involve critical thinking and deeper skills necessary for burgeoning careers in STEM, for example. Students are increasingly confronted with the need to think systemically, critically, and laterally. Video games allow practice and analysis of these complex constructs.

Realms beyond education, including government and businesses, are developing game formats capable of assessing students' learning outcomes and monitoring students' skill levels. This embedded, unobtrusive assessment, or "stealth assessment," creates conditions for a more accurate examination of dynamic learning patterns in the classroom. In short, video games provide a way to develop solutions to problems that are less easily solved with traditional educational methods. Content-based educational assessments fail to address critical thinking approaches or control external factors such as sensory stimuli and degree of challenge relative to test-taker ability. Educators suggest that content assessments are not meaningful measures of student learning and do not account for key student gains outside of content retrieval capabilities. On the other side of the debate about assessments' role, policy makers demand educator accountability as the primary function of the test. This disconnect between educators and policy makers provides a stimulus for business and government to seek more appropriate and authentic measures

of student learning to drive decision-making processes for curriculum and learning.

The focus on accountability and assessment, coupled with the rise of inexpensive computing power, has increased the frequency and amount of data collected on students. Increased data collection has led to the development of data-driven decision-making (D3M) approaches, which are empirically based. The rise of D3M occurred in parallel with the rise of the accountability movement in education and refers to the use of data to inform educational decisions. Many educators lack the training in analysis and data mining to make use of the enormous amounts of data collected from assessments. Thus, vast data streams are underused. Recently, however, private organizations and universities have developed a new field that combines analysis of data with patterns-seeking analysis for large data streams, called educational analytics or educational informatics. These areas are on the forefront of assessment and D3M. The call by business, government, educators, and policy makers for more authentic and realistic assessment has driven much of the innovation in assessment in recent years. One potential way to reduce the gap between traditional content assessment and the modern assessment needs of educators such as D3M within this new paradigm of assessment is by using video games as assessments.

Initial forays into using video games in assessment arise from limited informative potential derived from multiple-choice items. At the same time that authentic assessment movement was gaining traction, computer processing power, three-dimensional rendering, memory, and computer speed became cost effective for general use. These advances in technology allow the rendering of lifelike virtual environments where students perform learning tasks and assessments, leading to the rise of the use of video games in education. Video games as assessment tools provide assessment opportunities not otherwise possible with traditional paper-and-pencil assessments. Video games allow immersive, complex problems requiring multiple modes of thinking. The complexity of problems presented within video game assessment arises from the ability of the game to mimic actual environments in which students provide answers and complete tasks. This, along with continuous feedback, creates the ideal mode for assessment of student learning. Continuous feedback also allows a conscientious student approach that includes persistence resulting from pleasurable frustration.

Along with task authenticity, properly designed video games and play create continuous, real-time data streams through data logging. Researchers have developed a method of student assessment and analysis of learning combining the modern measurement technique of cognitive diagnostics and data mining. These modern forms of assessment analysis form the backbone for the examination of student learning based in cognition and task completion. This allows students to apply multiple competencies to solve complex and ill-defined problems. Studies show that games built within this framework support learning across multiple fields, such as neuroscience, neuropsychology, educational psychology, and teaching and learning.

The future of video games as an educational tool depends on the successful integration of learning components, assessment, large data sets, and harnessing the power of these games to provide virtual environments and examine authentic tasks within the school environment. Games based on the key foundations in pedagogy and assessment provide the means to collect large amounts of data on student learning in authentic environments. They can also contribute to student engagement within the learning process and create opportunities for students to apply skills from the real world to better adapt to changing school standards and career requirements.

Richard L. Lamb

See also Assessing Learning in Simulation-Based Environments; Assessment in Game-Based Learning; Assessment of Problem Solving and Higher Order Thinking; Performance Assessment

Further Readings

Annetta, L. A. (2008). Video games in education: Why they should be used and how they are being used. *Theory Into Practice, 47*(3), 229–239.

Bourgonjon, J., Valcke, M., Soetaert, R., & Schellens, T. (2010). Students' perceptions about the use of video games in the classroom. *Computers & Education, 54*(4), 1145–1156.

Lamb, R. L., Annetta, L., Vallett, D. B., & Sadler, T. D. (2014). Cognitive diagnostic like approaches using neural network analysis of serious educational video games. *Computers & Education, 70*, 92–104.

Prensky, M. (2003). Digital game-based learning. *Computers in Entertainment (CIE), 1*(1), 21–21.

Squire, K. (2003). Video games in education. *International Journal of Intelligent Simulations and Gaming, 2*(1), 49–62.

VIRTUAL LEARNING ENVIRONMENTS

A *virtual learning environment* in the most general case refers to a learning situation that is supported by Internet-enabled technologies to provide tools for students to learn specific content, communicate and submit work, while providing components for an instructor to manage the learning process, collect input, and provide feedback to students. The concept is called *virtual* because students use computer programs and tools while working from remote locations to accomplish activities that would otherwise be done in real locations such as a school or training classroom. *Distance learning* is a term also commonly associated with virtual learning. In 1984, the New York Institute of Technology was among the first organizations to set up classes that could be accessed via students' computers to meet the needs of students who were unable to travel to campus. The viability of this learning format quickly spread and evolved in sophistication as personal computers and Internet connectivity became commonplace.

Virtual learning environments have advantages and disadvantages. Advantages include opportunities for students to learn while in locations other than classrooms using computers or mobile devices; these students might otherwise not have access to educational opportunities because of distance, time, economics, or other limitations. A virtual environment can also leverage technology, for example, to offer instruction from experts in content areas, via live video conferencing and other means. However, the lack of human face-to-face instructors can be a disadvantage for students who need traditional settings and who might be more comfortable working directly with teachers and peers. Students who may not have adequate computer skills to use the technology tools employed in virtual learning environments can feel isolated and be frustrated with the computer interfaces, which can result in diminished learning experiences and dissatisfaction. Virtual learning environments exist within two basic structures: learning management systems and virtual worlds.

Learning Management Systems

A learning management system (LMS) is a Web-based collection of software programs designed to support the management and delivery of learning resources and courses to students. An LMS has tools for registering students, delivering resources (text, audio, and video), tracking user logins, supporting online chatting, calculating grades, administering assessments, and uploading and storing user submissions. Additional components facilitate communication through e-mail, chat, discussion groups, and blogs. Content for individual courses is typically uploaded by an instructor who organizes information and media in modular or sequential form for student access. The LMS may be set up for student interaction either asynchronously or synchronously. Asynchronous designs allow students to access content at their own choosing, sometimes referred to as "anytime" or "in time" learning. An asynchronous design uses pre-loaded content such as text articles, e-books, graphics, and Internet links, as well as tools such as drop boxes and discussion forums. Synchronous LMS designs usually have most of the same tools found in synchronous designs, but a synchronous LMS enables students to meet online at specific arranged class times. Content is generally presented interactively by an instructor using a combination of tools that can project presentation slides and websites and allows students to interact and contribute during the class with microphones, chat screens, graphics tools, and video. Instructors provide feedback or grades using built-in LMS tools, which can compute averages or keep running totals of points as students proceed through the course.

LMSs are available as either commercial packages and as open source programs. Commercial examples used widely for education and corporate training include Blackboard and Desire2Learn. Open source LMS examples include Moodle and Sakai. A commercial LMS is a marketed, supported product usually with training and licensing options and is normally managed by the supplier with regular software updates and support. Open source learning management systems offer free source code and modules for building the environments without licensing fees, but the responsibility for installation and support lies with the agency or persons using the open source approach. On a larger scale, LMSs have been implemented to reach greater student numbers than are typically found in a course of study. These are generally known as massive open online courses, or MOOCs. A typical LMS course might serve 25 to 50 students, but a MOOC is designed to serve numbers of students in the thousands. The MOOC concept is offered in many universities in the United States and around the world.

Virtual Worlds Learning Environments

Another kind of virtual learning environment is created with sophisticated computer software and is known as a virtual world. While using many of the same basic functions as the learning management system, a virtual world provides an experience based on the idea of *learner immersion* or a simulated entry into a computer-created world for the purposes of learning. This is done by computer generation of three-dimensional places (or worlds) that replicate geographic surroundings; urban and rural locations; weather conditions; plant, animal, and human life forms; machines; and other common everyday structures of the real world. Virtual learning environments include educational situations as in schools and universities, as well as military and commercial training applications. Students may be potential firefighters, language learners, equipment or aircraft operators, emergency medical technicians, behavior management experts, industrial-mechanical technicians, sales executives, and other roles requiring experiential training.

A computer program interface, known as an avatar, provides the main vehicle for students to immerse themselves in and to interact with the learning context of the virtual world. The avatar is an animated object, usually human-like, which the student controls to walk in directions and to locations selected by the student. An avatar typically is enabled with a communication facility such that a student can type text that allows the avatar to *speak* to other avatars, or in some cases, the student can employ a microphone to talk to other students in the virtual world.

Learning in the virtual world is meant to be interactive, that is, by using the avatar, the student has the opportunity to interact with the environment and to experience the situation as though being physically present. A learning example in science could be using an avatar to learn about the water quality of a stream in a valley where local farmers are using pesticides on their crops. Rainfall is washing pesticides into the stream and killing fish and other life forms. The student, as an avatar, is provided a learning path to interview various virtual characters, to collect data and information on fish affected by the pesticide, write and submit an online summation, and then prepare a case to present to the town council on possible solutions to the pollution, while not harming the economics of the farming region.

Learning in a virtual-world environment is similar to the LMS, in that the content can be accessed by students participating from remote locations. Researchers such as Chris Dede and Sasha Barab have offered examples of students in highly engaging learning situations when working in virtual-world learning environments. The interactions with the content, the environment, and other students in the virtual world constitute a *situated learning* scenario in which students are able to use academic content in a real context as contrasted to reading information from a book for the purpose of testing knowledge of that content. Dede and Barab claim that deeper learning can result using this approach based on a student's enhanced experiences and connections with the content. An additional element of learning in a virtual-world environment is the concept of immediate feedback. Feedback in a virtual-world learning environment has similarities to an LMS in that an instructor can post comments to students or award points and grades. However, the feedback in a virtual world goes beyond what an instructor supplies—that is, the activity of the student, while functioning as an avatar, results in feedback from the environment itself. For example, when a student is successful at solving a problem, deciphering a code, or finding a correct path through a virtual landscape, the learning adventure will continue. However, when an answer is not complete or the student does not find the correct path toward the current goal, then the student must stop and rethink what has happened and try again until success is achieved. James Gee contends that this environmental feedback in itself results in a persistently engaged student and in a connected experience in which the student *lives* the content and therefore remembers it more deeply. Examples of virtual-world learning environments designed for use in public school settings include the River City and EcoMUVE projects from Harvard University, Quest Atlantis from Indiana University and Arizona State University, and Crystal Island from North Carolina State University.

Another virtual environment that has attracted thousands of users is called Second Life. This is a virtual world, but it contains all of the three-dimensional graphic elements described in a virtual learning environment. Second Life is not specifically designed for students and might be better described as a multiuser virtual environment available for a wide range of social networking activities. The presence of major universities and educational technology organizations in Second Life, however, illustrates that it is entirely suitable to be configured as a learning environment, but it is not dedicated and structured specifically for learning purposes. Second Life emulates the openness of the real world in that any user who creates an account may enter the virtual world and interact as he or she desires.

Virtual learning delivered via online LMSs, as well as in virtual-world systems, has transformed both the processes of education and the educators who plan and deliver learning to students. More students worldwide now have access to learning opportunities that were not previously possible because of distance, economics, and lack of technology. With continuing advances in technology and the increasing availability of sophisticated devices, many experts argue that the range and social impact of virtual learning environments is only in its early stages with many innovations yet to come.

Terry K. Smith

See also Avatars and Agents in Virtual Systems; Distance Learning for Professional Development; Games to Promote Inquiry Learning; Learning with Simulations; Virtual Worlds

Further Readings

Barab, S., Thomas, M., Dodge, T., Carteaux, R., & Tuzun, H. (2005). Making learning fun: Quest Atlantis, a game without guns. *Educational Technology Research & Development, 53*(1), 86–107.

Brown, J. S., Collins, A., & Duguid, P. (1989). Situated cognition and the culture of learning. *Educational Researcher, 18*(1), 32–42.

Dalsgaard, C. (2006). Social software: E-learning beyond learning management systems. *European Journal of Open, Distance and E-Learning, 2006*(2).

Gautreau, C. (2011). Motivational factors affecting the integration of a learning management system by faculty. *Journal of Educators Online, 8*(1). Retrieved from http://www.thejeo.com/Archives/Volume8Number1/GautreauPaper.pdf

Gee, J. P. (2003). *What video games have to teach us about learning and literacy.* New York, NY: Palgrave Macmillan.

Gerstein, J. (2009). Beyond the game: Quest Atlantis as an online learning experience for gifted elementary students. *Journal of Virtual Worlds Research, 2*(1), 2–18.

Ketelhut, D., Dede, C., Clarke, J., Nelson, B., & Bowman, C. (2007). Studying situated learning in a multi-user virtual environment. In E. Baker, J. Dickieson, W. Wulfeck, & H. O'Neil (Eds), *Assessment of problem solving using simulations* (pp. 37–58). Mahwah, NJ: Lawrence Erlbaum.

Rubin, B., Fernandes, R., Avgerinou, M. D., & Moore, J. (2010). The effect of learning management systems on student and faculty outcomes. *The Internet and Higher Education, 13*(1), 82–83.

Smith, T. K. (2011). Cultivating 21st century competencies in a virtual worlds learning environment (Doctoral dissertation). Pepperdine University. Retrieved from http://pqdtopen.proquest.com/pqdtopen/doc/902759479.html?FMT=ABS

Smith, T. K. (2013). Virtual worlds immersive learning: The Puebloans of Mesa Verde. In R. McBride & M. Searson (Eds.), *Proceedings of Society for Information Technology & Teacher Education International Conference 2013* (pp. 2965–2970). Chesapeake, VA: AACE.

Zhou, Z., Jin, X. L., Vogel, D. R., Fang, Y., & Chen, X. (2011). Individual motivations and demographic differences in social virtual world uses: An exploratory investigation in Second Life. *International Journal of Information Management, 31*(3), 261–271.

Virtual Schools and Programs

Virtual schools and programs offer courses that do not use face-to-face interactions with the teacher as the primary mode of instruction. Instead, the teacher and student interact with each other through the Internet. These interactions between can be synchronous through tools including webcams, microphones, and online meeting rooms. However, they may also be asynchronous with the use of tools such as e-mail, instant messaging, discussion boards, and feedback given on assignments. Regardless of the delivery model, educational technology must be integrated into all aspects of virtual instruction. A virtual school is able to grant credit for courses and award degrees. Conversely, a virtual program provides instruction but has course credit and diploma granted by the school the student is enrolled in full-time. Virtual schools are important partly because of their increasingly widespread use. Several states require students take online course to graduate from high school, and most colleges offer courses at least partially online. This entry begins with an overview of the development of virtual schools from mail-based correspondence courses. Next, the types of virtual schools are discussed, including K–12 and higher education institutions as well as the continuum from fully online to blended schools. Finally, the variety of content and technology options integrated in various schools is examined.

Development Overview

Virtual learning is a type of distance learning where the Internet is used to transmit lessons. The first distance learning in the United States used the postal service for submitting coursework, typically referred to as a *correspondence course*. This type of course has been in place since the early 1900s. In this model, students would typically review material in a textbook and complete some type of written assignment without aid from an instructor. That assignment would then be mailed to the teacher who would grade it, provide feedback, and mail it back to the student. This was a slow process because one had to wait for the postal service to deliver the assignment two ways. In the meantime, the student could either work ahead without having received feedback, or wait and slow down coursework even further. As radio, television, and VHS tapes were introduced, these new technologies were used to deliver content from teachers. Students would then submit assignments by mail much as they had previously. Fax machines did offer an opportunity to rapidly submit work and receive feedback from instructors but could be cost prohibitive depending on the long-distance phone charges and number of pages required. Because of the delays, the correspondence course method was used primarily as a last resort for those with geographical barriers preventing them from physically attending classes at an institution.

As computers and e-mail became more mainstream in the early 1990s, correspondence courses began to take advantage of the new technology. The pedagogical layout remained similar, but now the time to transmit assignments and receive feedback was drastically reduced. E-mail also offered a free and rapid way for the student and teacher to communicate. This meant that students could now more easily ask questions of their instructors before submitting assignments. Because K–12 instruction typically relies on more interaction between student and teacher, this e-mail format was used primarily in higher education.

With the advent of Web 2.0 in the early 2000s, Web-based applications began to appear. These innovations allowed online education that allowed students to interact with the content and each other directly on the course website. Tools began to emerge in the form of learning management systems. Previously, students visited a site to gather assignments and content to be completed offline. Discussion boards, drop boxes, online quizzing, and Web-based office applications allowed students to stay online for a majority of the course experience.

Many vendors provide learning management systems, but some of those prominent in market share include Blackboard, Desire2Learn, Moodle, and Sakai. Blackboard and Sakai were started in the United States; Desire2Learn is a Canadian company; and Moodle was founded in Australia. However, each of these platforms is used worldwide.

Types of Virtual Schools

Virtual schools and programs are typically divided into those serving K–12 students versus those serving higher education institutions and professional practice. In the K–12 arena, most of the early virtual schools in the United States were statewide initiatives or for-profit charter schools. In the last several years, district virtual schools have grown at a rapid pace and now make up a sizable portion of the market as well. State-run virtual schools typically depend on an appropriation from state legislators tied to serving a set number of students. This funding model has limited their ability to grow. In some states, the budgets for the state virtual schools are being reduced or eliminated. In their place, some states have privatized the virtual school by partnering with a non-profit organization, and others have decentralized and permitted the local districts to manage their own online learning needs. In turn, the districts may run their own schools or partner with a vendor.

An assumption of most K–12 virtual schools is that state-certified teachers provide the instruction. A different model that often does not have a teacher tied to it is credit recovery. In credit-recovery courses, students typically are going through online modules for a course previously failed. If successful, the student either gets a passing credit in addition to the previous failing grade or may even be able to replace the old failing grade with the new passing one. A local school that uses the credit-recovery program is the entity ultimately awarding credit, so the guidelines for eligibility are often left to each particular school or district. Many credit-recovery courses in the United States are not approved by the National Collegiate Athletic Association (NCAA) because of the lack of teacher interaction, so potential college athletes must retake courses in a traditional method. This situation is probably unique to the United States.

A continuum exists between fully online and fully face-to-face schools. When examining a specific virtual school or program, it is important to examine how much that particular school has instruction occur remotely. When a school has some instruction online and some face-to-face, it is using a blended model. However, the industry typically considers blended models to use at least 20% face-to-face and at least 20% online instruction. Therefore, a school that has 90% online instruction and 10% face-to-face instruction would still be considered a virtual school.

In higher education, the continuum between online and face-to-face schools also exists. In addition, the virtual school providers can be categorized based on institution type. Some virtual schools are based in traditional colleges whereas others are purely virtual. There are also a variety of both public and private institutions just as there has always been in higher education; however, the virtual setting allows the tuition at private virtual schools to be potentially more similar to public ones. The U.S. Department of Education has been investigating the performance of some for-profit private virtual schools in recent years relative to abnormally high federal student loan default rates. The default rates are related to lower graduation rates and job prospects for graduates. This federal pressure may ultimately lead to higher quality and more consistent experiences for online students across the variety of institutions.

Many higher education institutions provide online classrooms for all courses, even those taught face-to-face. For example, the Canadian province Newfoundland and Labrador provides access to a learning management system (LMS) for all secondary teachers. In higher education, the University System of Georgia provides LMS access for all courses taught at any of its institutions.

Trends in Online Education

The content used by virtual schools is generally either developed internally by staff or purchased from vendors. However, there is a trend in the field toward using free content called open educational resources (OER). These resources are free and typically have some type of Creative Commons license. As the cost for digital content is reduced and even eliminated for some schools, the focus is shifting toward the hosting, accessing, and distribution of digital resources. Learning object repositories (LORs) and content management systems (CMSs) house digital resources and allow tracking of usage and sharing across institutions.

Alongside the move toward OER, schools are also experimenting with giving students free access to some courses. These are called massive open online courses (MOOCs). A few examples of sites hosting these are Coursera, Udacity, and edX. The earliest examples were offered by prominent universities and had enrollments exceeding 100,000. In these courses, the teachers often post lecture videos with weekly assignments. Students complete the work and self-assess, peer assess, or take an online quiz that is computer graded. At the end of the course, students receive some type of certificate or badge. Colleges are experimenting with how to grant course credit for students who receive these certificates or badges from another institution. The MOOC model is expanding into other fields, including teacher training and K–12. The model itself is mutating into a number of variations including some without definite start and end dates as well as those with staff grading for a nominal fee.

The use of mobile devices has grown tremendously worldwide in recent years. This has led to a desire among students to be able to use mobile devices for online learning as well. Many online schools now have mobile optimized sites and their own mobile apps. These apps let students do many of the things the full sites do including view content, check e-mail and grades, and post discussions. The LMSs are also increasingly offering mobile apps that offer instructors their own set of tools to grade offline, post announcements, and send push notifications to students.

The trend in education is toward competency-based learning and away from seat-time requirements. The online classroom and capabilities of most LMSs are able to track student competencies. Therefore, the online class is currently a laboratory setting for a variety of experiments in competency learning. Instead of focusing on students completing all course assignments in order during the time the course is offered to receive a grade, students instead go through courses in personalized learning paths focusing on acquiring the skills mandated by content standards. The competencies may be tracked and managed through e-portfolios. A competency achieved through work in one course could be applied to needed competencies across other courses.

Predictive analytics in computer systems have changed the ways businesses manage websites and the overall efficiency of operations. Similarly, learning analytics is rapidly emerging as a disruptive force in online education. The LMS captures every click of every user. When this knowledge is combined with intelligent algorithms, it becomes possible to predict individual student success faster and more accurately than in the past. Instead of just identifying at-risk students and those behind in their studies, these systems will allow teachers and administrators to identify students likely to need additional help. This will allow intervention structures to be put in place faster than previously possible.

Joe Cozart

See also Asynchronous Tools and Technologies; Competency Models and Frameworks; Distance Learning for Degree Completion for Working Adults; Learning Analytics; Massive Open Online Courses; OpenCourseWare Movement; Synchronous Tools and Technologies; Web 2.0 and Beyond

Further Readings

Bailey, J., Myslinski, D., Lockett, E., & Alfonso, A. (2012). 2012 digital learning report card. *Digital Learning Now.* Retrieved from http://digitallearningnow.com/site/uploads/2014/01/2012ReportCard.pdf

Christensen, C. M., Horn, M. B., & Johnson, C. W. (2008). *Disrupting class: How disruptive innovation will change the way the world learns* (Vol. 98). New York, NY: McGraw-Hill.

Clark, T., & Berge, Z. (2012). Virtual schools: The American experience with international implications. In L. Visser, Y. Visser, R. Amirault, & M. Simonson (Eds.), *Trends and issues in distance education: International perspectives* (2nd ed., pp. 97–112). Charlotte, NC: Information Age Publishing.

Glowa, L., & Patrick, S. (2013). Re-engineering information technology: Design considerations for competency education. *International Association for Online K–12 Learning.* Retrieved from http://www.competencyworks.org/wp-content/uploads/2013/02/iNACOL_CW_IssueBrief_ReEngineeringCompEd_final.pdf

Lynde, H. (2013). *Trends in state-run virtual schools in the SREB region.* Retrieved from http://publications.sreb.org/2013/13T01_Trends_State-Run.pdf

Molnar, A. (Ed.), Miron, G., Huerta, L., Cuban, L., Horvitz, B., Gulosino, C., Rice, J. K., & Shafer, S. R. (2013). *Virtual schools in the U.S. 2013: Politics, performance, policy, and research evidence.* Boulder, CO: National Education Policy Center. Retrieved from http://nepc.colorado.edu/publication/virtual-schools-annual-2013

Watson, J., Murin, A., Vashaw, L., Gemin, B., & Rapp, C. (2010). *Keeping pace with K–12 online learning: An annual review of policy and practice.* Retrieved from www.kpk12.com/cms/wp-content/uploads/KeepingPaceK12_2010.pdf

VIRTUAL TEAMS

Virtual teams, whereby geographically dispersed individuals work together toward a common goal, developing and establishing effective work protocols and supportive relationships through technologies, have become a major component in today's organizations. Whether it is for work, learning, or problem solving in general, companies, nonprofit organizations, and schools must leverage collective resources and talents. When the nature of the problem goes beyond the scope of individual effort, educators and organizational leaders frequently form a team to resolve the issue. Although the literature on cooperative learning and collaborative problem solving is rich, extant literature on teams largely focuses on task and social dimensions of group work, paying less attention to managing the process of virtual group work and developing team members. To leverage what virtual teams truly offer, it is critical to understand what teams are, how virtual teams compare with traditional face-to-face teams, and most importantly, how learning, performance, and development should be managed in support of the team goal.

Teams and groups are two related concepts, and virtual teams are specific examples of small groups. Groups vary in size (community being the largest and dyad being the smallest), types (work group versus social group), membership requirements (voluntary versus externally imposed), and group history (previous experiences working together). Teams are often distinguished from groups in that they are largely formed by external individuals and emphasize greater shared responsibilities for accomplishments. Teams are generally considered a form of a work group. However, researchers who study groups working on tasks or work teams also use the term *group* as a unit of analysis. Here, the terms *teams* and *groups* are used interchangeably.

Teams have definable characteristics, sharing membership, goals, and responsibilities and acting as a unit of individuals as well as an individual. Teams are a social system belonging to a larger social system whose members' interdependence occurs because of the need for collaborative task-related performance. Virtual teams are not exceptions; virtual work or learning teams always operate within a larger system, such as a department, organization, or course community. Therefore, successful task completion is the primary importance of all teams, although the social dimension of member relationships and support cannot be ignored.

This entry begins with a description of virtual teams' core characteristics. Next, the entry focuses on research, including research into the tasks, technologies, learning performance, and development of virtual teams. This entry concludes with an examination of implications of such research for practice and future research.

Core Characteristics of Virtual Teams

Virtual teams can be distinguished from traditional teams in that they transcend distance, time, and organizational boundaries through technologies. In industry, virtual teams are formed to accomplish the organizational goal and tasks. Core elements of all virtual teams include shared understanding of the task, its goal, work procedures, member support, the quality of work or learning, and effective use of technologies. Although few definitive sources exist regarding optimal numbers of team members, virtual learning teams in school settings usually have three to six members, whereas in industry settings, the size of virtual teams tend to be larger (as many as 20 members) because they address highly complex problems. Groups larger than 20 members may be difficult to coordinate and manage.

Although there is a distinction between teams that are at the same location (co-located) and virtual teams, many co-located teams use the same or similar communication techniques as virtual teams use. It is important to (a) understand and leverage the growing dimension of virtual work in teams and (b) balance and leverage both sides of virtual and onsite (if strategically, pedagogically, and administrative supported) when members work or learn together as a team. These days, even in a co-located team, member interactions are becoming increasingly virtual, as onsite meetings may be expensive or difficult to schedule. As free or low-cost technologies that afford effective virtual group work continue to appear in the market, virtual teamwork will become more frequent and important henceforth. Understanding the scope of virtual group work relative to distance, geography, and culture is also important. Virtual teams whose members comprise individuals from different national, linguistic, or cultural backgrounds will require more efforts for member communications and coordination. Last but not least, the type of tasks and technologies used by virtual teams also can affect team processes and outcomes.

Importance of Typologies: Tasks and Technologies

Team learning or performance studies are difficult to compare because the research context varies greatly across studies. According to Joseph McGrath, most tasks performed by work groups can be captured by four quadrants. Each quadrant manifests two common task types: (1) generate (ideas or plans), (2) execute (performance tasks or contests/battles), (3) negotiate (resolving conflict of viewpoints or conflict of interests), and (4) choose (solving problems with correct answers or deciding issues with no right answer). According to McGrath, the degree of conflict versus cooperation varies depending on the type of task performed. To understand how teams are used to solve a problem through collective intelligence, David Jonassen

created an effective problem typology. From the easiest to the most difficult, problem categories include *algorithm*, *story*, *rule-using/rule induction*, *decision making*, *troubleshooting*, *diagnosis-solution*, *strategic performance*, *policy analysis*, *design*, and *dilemma*. The real insight of this task typology is that each problem type has archetype features and many examples, and problem difficulty has two core dimensions of *structuredness* (transparency, stability, and predictability of the problem space) and *complexity* (the breadth of knowledge and skill level, the difficulty of comprehending and applying the concepts involved, and the degree of nonlinearity among variables relationships). Given that most common complaints of virtual teamwork include the lack of shared understanding of what is expected as a team and by individuals, these task and problem typologies can be used to better communicate the purpose of the virtual team tasks.

Technologies—particularly the Internet and e-mail, with features such as low-cost message exchange and document sharing—have enabled global virtual work and learning teams to increase. Today, various options for technologies are available to virtual teams, including e-mail, online forums, Web blogging, collaborative writing software, messenger or texting tools, audio and video conferencing, knowledge management (KM), electronic performance support systems (EPSS), social network sites, and virtual worlds. One recent classification of technologies that captures the use of numerous Web and social media tools is from Derek Hansen, Ben Shneiderman, and Marc Smith. Their work shows that many tools can be positioned and used based on the pace of interaction (synchronous and asynchronous) and the granularity of content control—namely, *fine* (users control the smallest unit of content directly; a synchronous example is an electronic whiteboard, and asynchronous examples include collaborative writing documents, such as wikis and Google Drive), *medium* (users control medium-sized blocks of content that they can indirectly alter or that can be altered by others; synchronous examples include virtual worlds and multiplayer gaming, and asynchronous examples are online forums and contributing work to the KM system or online community or network), and *coarse* (users control large blocks of content and content is rarely edited or modified by others; synchronous examples include chat, texting, and Twitter, and asynchronous examples include e-mail and blog posting and commenting). Researchers Carmel Vaccare and Gregory Sherman point out that selecting technologies that are simple, stable, sustainable, scalable, and social is important for virtual teams. Virtual teams that are equipped with a clear understanding of tasks and effective technologies are ready to tackle team learning, performance, and development goals.

Learning, Performance, and Development of Virtual Teams

This section reviews topics of great importance as well as more research needs for leveraging virtual teams. Educators and business leaders must understand that teams are the primary driver of organizational as well as individual learning, innovation, and knowledge sharing. Work by notable scholars, such as Peter Senge, Ikujiro Nonaka, and Chris Argyris, support this view. In the past, learning and performance were conceptualized as two distinct elements: Individuals or teams learn first, and then, through application, performance improves. However, learning and performance improvement in virtual teams are possible only when team learning and performance are clearly defined and managed through virtual team development. When it comes to team performance, major indicators of team success include to what extent members of the team attained assigned performance goals, how the team produced high-quality work, and whether the team was productive. The *Balanced Scorecard* framework by David Kaplan and David Norton or Peter Drucker's *Five Most Important Questions* can help define the organizational and team's performance goals in support of the business strategies. Team learning is not a disconnected concept from team performance. Team learning includes the processes and outcomes of group interaction. If learning and performance should improve in virtual teams, established team learning approaches such as action learning, problem-based learning, and project-based learning can be applied to leverage what each framework offers regarding the selection of problems, problem-solving processes, resource use, outcomes, and the role of a facilitator. For instance, action learning emphasizes balancing individual and group learning while solving a problem and implementing actions; in that environment, action learning's core elements will be used, such as a coach who facilitates the process only and virtual team members' frequent actions of questioning, reflection, and feedback. In a similar vein, problem-based learning can help virtual team members pay more attention to the element of problem-solving reasoning and self-directed learning, whereas project-based learning can require teams to work with project sponsors and account for organizational impacts.

Virtual teams do not develop naturally. Instead, they develop directly through explicit communications. Seung Won Yoon's previous research has found that virtual teams develop through phases of orientation, scheduling and coordination, exploration, work and decision, progress check and evaluation, and refinement and submission of work. When inductive and deductive coding were combined to examine the semester-long interactions of seven intact virtual learning teams, task-related behaviors composed 59.3% of the interactions, followed by social (26.3%) and management-related behaviors (14.4%). Research on work or learning teams used to emphasize the task and the social dimension of members' behaviors only; however, Yoon's research found that many messages were not exchanged to address work tasks or member relationships, but rather to move the team forward (e.g., scheduling and facilitating virtual meetings, resolving or addressing technology issues, and exchanging conformity to manage virtual meetings), indicating that attention and support must be given to technologies, scheduling, and meeting facilitations. Another important finding was that, when teams experienced strong presence of negative forces, including frequent member absence, technical problems, ineffective work procedure, inability to access information, task avoidance, and topic digression during the progress check and evaluation phase, teams had to regress to one of the previous development phases to rectify work protocols (labeled as nonlinear progression teams); this inefficiency was not observed for teams (labeled as linear progression teams) with no or minimal experience in negative forces.

Last but not least, team dynamics challenge a simplistic view of functional focus on virtual teams. In virtual teamwork, member experiences and priorities can span multiple dimensions of social, psychological, relational, and team-functional issues beyond learning and performance. Marshall Scott Poole and his colleagues state that to examine related team research issues, researchers can adopt one of the following perspectives: psychodynamic, functional, temporal, conflict-power-status, symbolic-interpretive, social identity, social-evolutionary, social network, or feminist perspectives. For instance, focusing on concepts such as group norms, cohesiveness, and effectiveness can be supported by functional perspectives, which examines groups for input, process, and output, and patterns of relationships or changes in them within virtual teams can be approached from the social network perspectives.

Implications for Practice and Research

Virtual team facilitators and members need to keep in mind that virtual teams do not mature or develop automatically over time. Although virtual teams empowered by able individuals and powerful technologies can engage in collaborative problem solving, leaders and managers of virtual teams must articulate the project goal and tasks as well as provide access to effective technologies and necessary information/resources. As Chris Lema points out, virtual team members move forward in the direction of objectives, and members will resist the uninvited assignment of tasks, asking of efforts, and tilted emphasis on accountability. Virtual team leaders and facilitators must establish a mechanism that can unobtrusively capture the appearance and influence of development-negative forces (absence, task avoidance, technical problems, information access barriers, etc.); evaluate the workload fairness and the effectiveness of individual, subgroup, or team-level work procedures; and encourage clarification requests from the team when things are not certain. Yoon's previous research highlights that virtual team members should make explicit efforts to make their communications effective and efficient relative to work (task), member relations (social), and group management (development). As dispersed members rely on time-delayed and nonverbal computer-mediated communication and use various technologies, greater coordination and member commitment/participation are crucial for virtual team members to address the three important functions successfully.

As for researchers, advancements in technologies will continuously expand what virtual teams can do as the driver of and bridge for individual as well as organizational learning and performance. Also, analysis frameworks, such as network analyses, text mining, and analytics, enable researchers to examine member actions within or across virtual teams more efficiently and comprehensively to identify emergent patterns of team-level behaviors, and then correlate to numerous outcomes. Our understanding of what virtual teams do and contribute will greatly improve when research can explain and guide desirable member behaviors for learning and performance. The virtuous, reinforcing, and iterative cycle of connecting practice, research, and theory building must be actively applied to the study of virtual teams.

Seung Won Yoon

See also Collaborative Communication Tools and Technologies; Collaborative Learning With Technology; Distributed Cognitions in Computer-Supported Collaborative Learning; Information and Communication Technologies in Multinational and Multicultural Contexts

Further Readings

Guzzo, R. A., & Dickson M. W. (1996). Teams in organizations: Recent research on performance and effectiveness. *Annual Review of Psychology, 47*, 307–438.

Hansen, D. L., Shneiderman, B., & Smith, M. A. (2010). *Analyzing social media networks with NodeXL: Insights from a connected world.* San Francisco, CA: Morgan Kaufmann.

Lema, C. (2012). *Building and managing virtual teams: Five ways to create a high performance culture for remote workers* [Kindle version]. Retrieved from Amazon.com

Lepsinger, R., & DeRosa, D. (2010). *Virtual team success: A practical guide for working and leading from a distance.* San Francisco, CA: Jossey-Bass.

Levine, J. M., & Moreland, R. L. (1990). Progress in small group research. *Annual Review of Psychology, 41*, 585–634.

McGrath, J. E. (1984). *Groups: Interaction and performance.* Englewood Cliffs, NJ: Prentice Hall.

Poole, M. S., Hollingshead, A. B., McGrath, J. E., Moreland, R. L., & Rohrbaugh, J. (2004). Interdisciplinary perspectives on small groups. *Small Group Research, 25*(3), 3–16.

Yoon, S. W., & Johnson, S. (2008). Phases and patterns of group development in virtual learning teams. *Educational Technology Research & Development, 56*(5/6), 595–618.

VIRTUAL TOURS

A *virtual tour* is a vicarious travel experience. *Virtual* connotes computer-mediated, Internet-enabled, multimedia explorations, usually of real destinations. A comparable term in education contexts is *virtual field trip*. Virtual tours can extend to imaginary places, and the concept of a destination can be stretched, for example, to explore the inside of an atomic particle or a human body. Vicarious travel has a long history. Virtual tours in education contexts expand learning possibilities, though their use has both pros and cons.

History

Virtual tourists in earlier times sometimes were called *armchair travelers*. Armchair travel has always been viewed as broadly educational, whether informally for the general public or in schools. Travel descriptions are a starting point in the evolution of virtual tours. Travel literature dates at least to the second century, when the Greek geographer Pausanias wrote a 10-volume *Description of Greece*. Over the centuries, travel writing came to be supplemented with illustrations and, since the mid-19th century, with photographs. Sound and moving images were added in the 20th century.

With the advent of computers and the Internet, vicarious travel options further expanded through interactive multimedia. Unlike armchair travelers, today's virtual tourists influence their experiences by choosing which tour components to access and in what sequence. Virtual tours also may include collateral material, such as maps, study guides, quizzes, text references, and links to related websites.

Internet-enabled experiences allow virtual travelers to explore distant lands and historical sites, to tour museums and laboratories, and to visit other destinations. Persons who plan to relocate can view prospective homes, and travelers can choose hotel rooms through virtual tours. Various forms of the virtual tour serve users from the commercially minded to the culturally curious.

Educational Uses

Virtual tours can enhance teaching and learning, whether as part of the standard curriculum or to supplement or enrich instruction. In classrooms where tablet computers are used in place of textbooks, for example, virtual tours may be a primary component of the learning design. In other classrooms, they may expand the scope of the curriculum or provide enrichment similar to actual field trips.

Virtual tours require Internet connectivity. Most can be accessed through various devices—desktops, laptops, tablets, and smartphones. Individual students, small groups, or whole classes can access tours synchronously or asynchronously. With appropriate electronic interconnection, students in one place and counterparts elsewhere can tour together, whether they are within the same school, across town from each another, or on opposite sides of the globe. This capacity makes virtual tours a versatile instructional tool and may be especially helpful in classrooms where students bring their own devices. Teachers also can conduct tours for large-group engagement by using an interactive whiteboard. Additionally, computer-mediated accommodations for students with physical or mental challenges can be built into virtual tours using built-in device capabilities.

Virtual tours can be found online for students from elementary to university age. Many tours are constructed for general use but can be adapted to a variety of learning designs. Others are specifically made to supplement classroom instruction, often across multiple disciplines. Following are examples of four types of virtual tours.

Museums

The Louvre, a famous art museum in Paris, France, offers many virtual tours, including thematic "trails" that provide overviews of artworks. In-depth explorations of certain works, such as Leonardo da Vinci's *Mona Lisa*, include the physical structure of the work as well as the image, its creation, history, and other aspects. Animated "Tales of the Museum" are designed for younger students. Virtual tourists also can explore the museum's architecture and the place of the museum in the history of Paris. The website functions in French, English, and other languages, making virtual tours with a language-learning component another option.

Many major museums offer virtual tours with similar features, including the National Gallery of Art in Washington, D.C.; the Metropolitan Museum of Art in New York City; the Henry Ford Museum and Greenfield Village in Dearborn, Michigan; the Field Museum of Natural History in Chicago, Illinois; the Uffizi Gallery in Florence, Italy; and the Egyptian Museum in Berlin, Germany.

Libraries and Archives

The Library of Congress in Washington, D.C., offers online tours of its three buildings: the main Thomas Jefferson Building as well as the James Madison Memorial Building and the John Adams Building. Within the library reside resources for learning designers and teachers at all levels and across numerous disciplines. These resources include the American Memory collection, for example, which holds historical documents in fields from advertising to women's history. Collections of prints and photographs, historic newspapers, sound recordings, films, and maps also are freely available to be included in teacher- or student-created tours and learning projects.

Also in Washington, D.C., the National Archives offers a virtual tour experience titled Digital Vaults, a selection of 1,200 of its more than 10 billion records that can be explored by users of various ages. Topics range from Albert Einstein to civil rights.

Many public and university libraries offer virtual tours, including Columbia University Libraries in New York City; Seattle Public Library in Washington; Santa Monica Public Library in California; British Library in London, England; King's College Library at Cambridge University in England; and Vatican Library in Vatican City. Virtual libraries, which exist only online, provide another type of virtual tour. An example is the Jewish Virtual Library, a project of the American-Israeli Cooperative Enterprise. Virtual tours of archives offer experiences similar to those in libraries. Whitman College in Washington, for example, offers an Ancient Theatre Archive that provides virtual tours of Greek and Roman theatre architecture found throughout Europe, the Middle East, and northern Africa.

Historic Sites

Jamestown Settlement and Yorktown Victory Center is a re-creation of Colonial American sites in coastal Virginia. The popular tourist destination can be toured online through videos and podcasts, several specifically for use with students. A complementary Virtual

Jamestown website offers users access to digital research about the Jamestown settlement and "the Virginia experiment" in colonial America. This site is designed for educators and provides teaching materials, including interpretive essays, 3D re-creations, and historical documents such as newspapers, maps, and public records.

The historic sites category also encompasses (a) homes, such as those of abolitionist Frederick Douglass (Washington, D.C.), nurse and Red Cross founder Clara Barton (Glen Echo, Maryland), and German Renaissance artist Albrecht Dürer (Nuremberg, Germany); (b) significant buildings, such as the Cologne cathedral in Germany, the Roman Coliseum in Italy, and the White House in Washington, D.C.; and (c) various other sites, from the Civil War battlefield at Gettysburg, Pennsylvania, to Stonehenge in England.

Laboratories

The Thomas Jefferson National Accelerator Facility is one of 17 national laboratories funded by the U.S. Department of Energy. The actual lab is located in Newport, Virginia, but it has restricted visiting hours. Visitors under 18 years of age are allowed in only once a year. However, students of all ages can tour the lab online. Educators will find a "Student Zone" section for planning lessons, and users can subscribe to the Jefferson Lab's YouTube channel to see physics-related video programs, including images from the virtual tour.

Other laboratories with virtual tours include the Biodefense Laboratory of the National Institute of Allergy and Infectious Diseases (NIAID), part of the National Institutes of Health (NIH) within the U.S. Department of Health and Human Services (Washington, D.C.), and the Purdue University (West Lafayette, Indiana) Engineering Labs, including the Herrick Acoustical Laboratory. The range of available virtual tours continues to expand as more places enhance their Internet presence to include such activities.

Pros and Cons

Like any new use of technology, virtual tours have both supporters and detractors. Among the pros: Virtual tours expand learning opportunities and resources for educators and students, are cost-effective, and allow learners to experience places that they may not be able to visit in person. The cons include the risk of substituting vicarious for real experiences when the latter are available, adding more screen time to students' learning time when students could be more active, and isolating students from real-life experiences that could be deeper and more meaningful than virtual experiences.

Donovan R. Walling

See also Cultural Considerations in Technology-Enhanced Learning and Instruction; Design of Engaging Informal Learning Places and Spaces; Engaged Learning; Experiential Learning; Learning in Museums; Learning With Simulations; Virtual Learning Environments

Further Readings

Cooper, G., & Cooper, G. (2001). *New virtual field trips.* Westport, CT: Libraries Unlimited.

Keengwe, J., Onchwari, G., & Hucks, D. (2013). *Literacy enrichment and technology integration in pre-service teacher education.* Hershey, PA: IGI Global.

Kisielnicki, J. (2008). *Virtual technologies: Concepts, methodologies, tools, and applications* (3 vols.). Hershey, PA: IGI Global.

Maloy, R. W., Verock-O'Loughlin, R.-E., Edwards, S. A., & Park Woolf, B. (2010). *Transforming learning with new technologies.* Boston, MA: Pearson.

Nelson, K. J. (2007). *Teaching in the digital age: Using the Internet to increase student engagement and understanding* (2nd ed.). Thousand Oaks, CA: Corwin.

Ruffini, M. (2007). *Designing and creating virtual field trips: A systematic approach with Microsoft PowerPoint.* Boston, MA: Pearson.

Walling, D. R. (2014). *Designing learning for tablet classrooms: Innovations in instruction.* New York, NY: Springer.

VIRTUAL TUTEES

The term *virtual tutees* refers to computer characters that humans (the actual learners) teach in a virtual environment. As Robert P. Taylor noted 30 years ago, the benefits of using a computer as a tutee are that (a) the computer tutee is patient, and (b) human tutors must learn what they teach the tutee. Because learning is required before a student can teach, virtual tutees have been used to enhance student engagement in learning tasks. This entry reviews the emergence of computer-simulated teachable agents and the development of the Virtual Tutee System. The entry also examines the roots of the teachable agent approach in peer tutoring and its theoretical foundations in role theory and self-determination theory. The entry concludes with a look at directions for future research on virtual tutees.

Virtual Tutee Research and Development

Teachable Agents

Teachable agents, a new way of using pedagogical agents, were developed in 1990s by Gautam Biswas with the Teachable Agent Group at Vanderbilt University.

Teachable agents are computer-simulated tutees that K–12 students teach about an assigned content such as river ecology. Since its first development, numerous studies have used teachable agents. Reported benefits include students' increased responsibility for their own learning and improved reflection on acquired knowledge. The impact of teachable agents on student learning has been mostly positive, but there have also been limitations. For the most part, the use of teachable agents has been confined to K–12 educational settings. In addition, although research on teachable agents has indicated positive effects on student motivation and engagement, the theoretical foundations and relevant design principles that informed design were not explicitly discussed nor established empirically.

The Virtual Tutee System

More recently, Seung Won Park and ChanMin Kim developed the Virtual Tutee System (VTS) to engage college students in academic reading. The VTS is a Web-based environment in which students teach virtual tutees about required course readings. VTS design is grounded in role theory and self-determination theory. These theories give logical explanations for the effects of learning-by-teaching that are often found with the use of virtual tutees. The goal of the VTS is to promote students' active engagement and learning by nurturing their feelings of autonomy, competence, and relatedness through taking the role of tutor.

Theoretical Foundations

Learning by Teaching

The use of virtual tutees to facilitate the effects of learning by teaching emerged from peer tutoring, which has been used in education to enhance the learning and performance of both tutors and tutees. The benefits of being a tutor are often highlighted because they include improvements in academic achievement and in engagement, and attitudes. The student role of tutor has been applied to both teachable agents and the VTS, in which all students are tutors and all virtual characters are tutees; thus, the challenge of assigning students to tutor or tutee roles is avoided.

Computers Are Social Actors (CASA)

The human-computer interaction research referred to as computers are social actors (CASA) explains that people interact with computers as they do with other humans. That is, social expectations and behaviors used among people are applied in interactions with computers. Many pedagogical agent studies employed CASA in an attempt to create social presence. Users interacting with computer characters, avatars, and agents exhibit social behaviors and attitudes toward them. For example, when asked to evaluate pedagogical agents, participants comment on human characteristics such as politeness, friendliness, and trustworthiness. In research on and development of both teachable agents and the VTS, CASA was used to present virtual tutees as social beings so that student tutors would perceive their role of teaching as authentic and would interact with virtual tutees in social ways.

Role Theory

According to role theory as described by Theodore Sarbin and Vernon Allen, when people are assigned a specific role, they tend to exhibit the behaviors and attitudes associated with the role. Thus, when students are assigned the role of tutor, they are likely to behave like a teacher. In environments in which students teach virtual tutees, the students perceive themselves as having autonomy and responsibility. This perception in turn leads to a commitment to their own learning as well as their tutee's learning. In studies using teachable agents or the VTS, such a positive impact of the role of tutor has been observed.

Self-Determination Theory

Edward Deci and Richard Ryan proposed self-determination theory (SDT) to explain different types of motivation leading to different levels of engagement, learning, and performance. Mainly there are two basic motivations: One is intrinsic motivation, which is likely to yield behaviors for the sake of a person's inner interest and pleasure; the other is extrinsic motivation, which is likely to yield behaviors instrumental to certain outcomes that are independent of the behaviors. Intrinsic motivation tends to result in deep engagement and learning. In contrast, extrinsic motivation tends to result in shallow engagement and learning. However, not every learning task is interesting and enjoyable. Thus, SDT discusses four different types of extrinsic motivation (external, introjected, identified, and integrated motivation) and illustrates the possibility of a positive function of extrinsic motivation depending on perceived autonomy, competence, and relatedness. For example, when students perceive themselves as having greater autonomy, they tend to demonstrate more active engagement and learning even though intrinsic motivation is not present. As an application of SDT to the use of virtual tutees, the VTS was designed to create autonomous environments in which students have choices and flexibility in teaching foci and methods, even though they do not have inherent interest and enjoyment in the teaching content (i.e., required readings). The role of tutor grants students authority and control as well, which meets their need for competence. The social presence of virtual tutees and student tutors' interactions with the tutees foster the feeling of relatedness.

Implications for Research and Practice

Student engagement in learning activities is a concern of every educator. After all, without engagement, learning does not occur. However, as discussed earlier, not every learning task can elicit the student interest and intrinsic motivation that lead to active engagement. Especially in the VTS, the use of virtual tutees, grounded in SDT and with an explicit support for autonomy, competence, and relatedness, can be beneficial in a variety of learning environments in which student intrinsic motivation is lacking. For example, the VTS was used in teacher education courses to promote college student engagement in and learning from assigned readings. The VTS or other virtual tutoring environments using teachable agents can be implemented regardless of whether course formats are online, face-to-face, or hybrid. Such environments can be also used in the context of learning how to teach.

The positive impact of using virtual tutees has been reported in many empirical studies. However, further research needs to be done to find the ways in which virtual tutees can interact with student tutors more actively. Currently, virtual tutees tend to passively respond to student tutors' input rather than taking initiatives, whereas in real tutoring settings, tutees' input often guides the direction of tutoring. Also, the cost of developing virtual tutoring environments needs to decrease. Flexibility should be also embedded in the environments so that teachers (who teach student tutors) can customize the content and specific strategies easily for their students' individual needs. Lastly, the use of virtual tutees in teacher education needs to be further studied. In VTS studies with adult learners (i.e., college students in teacher education courses), some conversations in which student tutors engaged with their virtual tutees simulated more teacher-style talk than other conversations did. Further research is needed to identify the effects of virtual tutoring on the development of teaching capabilities to expand the benefits of systems using virtual tutees.

ChanMin Kim and Seung Won Park

See also Animated Agents in Learning Systems; Avatars and Agents in Virtual Systems; Pedagogical Agents

Further Readings

Biswas, G., Leelawong, K., Schwartz, D., Vye, N., & The Teachable Agent Group at Vanderbilt (TAG-V). (2005).
Learning by teaching: A new agent paradigm for educational software. *Applied Artificial Intelligence, 19*(3–4), 363–392. doi:10.1080/08839510590910200

Deci, E. L., & Ryan, R. M. (1985). *Intrinsic motivation and self-determination in human behavior.* New York, NY: Plenum Press.

Nass, C., Steuer, J., & Tauber, E. R. (1994). Computers are social actors. In B. Adelson, S. Dumais, & J. Olson (Eds.), *Proceedings from CHI '94: The SIGCHI Conference on Human Factors in Computing Systems* (pp. 72–78). New York, NY: ACM.

Park, S. W., & Kim, C. (2012). A design framework for a virtual tutee system to promote academic reading engagement in a college classroom. *Journal of Applied Instructional Design, 2*(1), 17–33.

Park, S. W., & Kim, C. (2014). Virtual Tutee System: A potential tool for enhancing academic reading engagement. *Educational Technology Research and Development, 62*(1), 71–97. doi:10.1007/s11423-013-9326-1

Robinson, D. R., Schofield, J. W., & Steers-Wentzell, K. L. (2005). Peer and cross-age tutoring in math: Outcomes and their design implications. *Educational Psychology Review, 17*(4), 327–362. doi:10.1007/s10648-005-8137-2

Roscoe, R. D., & Chi, M. T. H. (2008). Tutor learning: The role of explaining and responding to questions. *Instructional Science, 36*(4), 321–350. doi:10.1007/s11251-007-9034-5

Sarbin, T. R., & Allen, V. L. (1968). Role theory. In G. Lindzey & E. Aronson (Eds.), *The handbook of social psychology* (Vol. 2, pp. 488–567). Reading, MA: Addison-Wesley.

Taylor, R. P. (1980). Introduction. In R. P. Taylor (Ed.), *The computer in school: Tutor, tool, tutee* (pp. 1–10). New York, NY: Teachers College Press.

VIRTUAL WORLDS

Virtual worlds are computer-based immersive experiential environments. These worlds commonly manifest as video games or simulations, but neither game play elements nor simulations (as overt interactive experiences) are necessary for a virtual world. Virtual worlds can manifest in two dimensions (e.g., a text-based adventure such as *Legends of Zork*), but typically virtual worlds as defined more specifically for educational technology are three-dimensional: a multiuser virtual environment (MUVE) platform such as *Second Life*, or any number of video games experienced from a first-person perspective. A unique blend of these dimensional forms results in a third manifestation of virtual worlds: the isometric platform, such as the popular video game series *Civilization*, which is a three-dimensional environment rendered in two dimensions using an isometric tiling engine.

Regardless of dimensionality, these worlds offer a spectrum of immersion for the user, based on a mixture of engaging content and world realism (or engaging context). To achieve such immersion, users can interact with virtual worlds using a variety of interface types that take shape in two- or three-dimensional form. A common combination implemented in virtual-world platforms is a three-dimensional world controlled through direct manipulation of the world itself and by a set of two-dimensional dashboard controls displayed translucently on the display screen between the users and the world. Such an interface setup is commonly referred to as heads-up display, or HUD. Users and computer-controlled characters (often called nonplayer characters, or NPCs) are represented in three-dimensional virtual worlds with avatars that usually take humanoid (bipedal) form. Typically, a choice of two perspectives is offered to users as they navigate a three-dimensional virtual world: a first-person perspective as seen through the eyes of the avatar, and a third-person perspective in which the user can see the avatar as it moves through the space. In either case, the environmental perspective visualized for the user is generated in real time using one or more virtual cameras embodied within the space of the virtual world.

With increased sophistication of computer hardware, three-dimensional virtual worlds can now be experienced by one or more users (synchronously or asynchronously) across a wide range of device platforms, including desktop applications, Web-based applications, smartphones or handheld devices, and larger tablets. The maturation of touch- and gesture-based interaction (such as tablets and motion-capture systems) has afforded new ways to conceptualize the environments that can be presented in virtual worlds, especially in domains that lend themselves to sophisticated dynamics—such as physics and mechanical engineering.

The hardware and software technologies that drive virtual worlds are continuously advanced by a multibillion-dollar video game industry, as well as simulation training research such as that conducted by the defense industry. Further advancements for implementation of these virtual worlds for education and training are driven by research and development conducted by universities, corporations, and independent research institutions. This entry focuses on the use of virtual worlds in learning, including their use for measurement and assessment, and discusses implications of system dynamics for learning.

Learning and Virtual Worlds

As a platform for learning, the flexibility and extensibility of virtual-world technology afford support for many different models of learning and instruction, ranging from constructivist exploratory learning to modular, objective-driven instruction. The open-ended nature of the three-dimensional environments that can be delivered in virtual-world platforms lends itself to the exploratory nature of discovery-based learning, while the underlying software architecture that drives such worlds can also be manipulated to direct and support more structured instructional modules.

The increased sophistication (and realism) of content and context that can be delivered to learners via virtual-world platforms allows these worlds to serve as excellent arenas for realistic complex problem-solving scenarios. Such scenarios are beneficial for problem-based learning models as well as simulation-based performance training such as that conducted for firefighters and emergency medical professionals.

Learning within virtual worlds can occur individually or collaboratively—or as a well-designed blend of both settings. Although collaboration in virtual worlds can occur asynchronously, the immersive, interactive nature of virtual worlds lends itself to synchronous interaction, including options for simulated nonverbal interpersonal communication, such as hand signals and limited sets of facial expression graphics that can be dynamically applied to avatars as interactions occur in these worlds.

Virtual worlds are also an excellent platform for human performance improvement—especially physical performances that involve complex movements and interactions through space. Motion capture technology allows users to model and review human physical performance, creating the opportunity for iterative analysis of variations in a learner's motion as he or she acquires a physical skill. One example of such performance improvement is the refinement of motor skills for the precise handling of volatile materials; another example is the improvement of a golf swing. Similar performance improvement practices implementing virtual-world platforms are also used for rehabilitative applications of physical and occupational therapy.

The burgeoning field of interactive data visualization continues to manifest as a good fit for virtual worlds, especially concerning individual and collaborative exploration and understanding of complex multivariate data sets. With the addition of gesture-based touch screen interfaces to control and manipulate the visualizations of data that occur in these spaces, new forms of real-time data visualization to support complex decision making are possible.

Measurement and Assessment With Virtual Worlds

Opportunities for the evaluation of learning performances using virtual worlds as assessment systems employing a variety of types of measurement instrumentation are expanding broadly and deeply across many domains of learning because of the continually increasing technological sophistication of virtual-world platforms. Viewed through the lens of evidence-centered design (ECD), virtual worlds can be a platform for evaluation of demonstrated learning performance at speeds approaching real time, employing intelligent software systems for measurement and assessment that adhere to the four-process architecture of assessment delivery modeled as part of the ECD framework.

Specifically, the increased interactivity and open-endedness of environments learners can experience using virtual-world platforms—coupled with increasingly fast processing capabilities in the computer hardware supporting these platforms—holistic, real-time feedback can be provided to the learner based on increasingly granular opportunities for performance data (evidence) collection within and across channels of evidence that can be demonstrated by learners in such a space, such as location/movement, object interaction, and acts of communication. Many commercial video games employing virtual-world platforms provide such continuous performance feedback in the form of health meters, object inventories, timers, and complex scoring displays or dashboards such as one might see in a driving or flight simulation. Analyses of demonstrated performances—also known as learning analytics—can be integrated into the learning and assessment experiences supported by virtual-world platforms. Again, many commercial video games are excellent examples of such analytics through the provision of completion statistics as a user finishes each level of the game. These analytic experiences can serve the learner as an opportunity for self-assessment throughout his or her engagement with a virtual world, and such evidence can be delivered for review and evaluation by other stakeholders in the learning process such as teachers, administrators, and parents.

Another affordance of the continuously improving technologies supporting virtual-world platforms for learning is the increased level of unobtrusiveness that can be applied to measurement and assessment delivery during the learner's interactive experience. Such unobtrusive assessment, also known as stealth assessment, is assessment that doesn't feel like a test to the learner. In other words, evidence about the learner's performance in the virtual world can be gathered continuously (using previously described evidence channels) without the learner ever experiencing any disruption. For example, consider a virtual world designed to support training for emergency medical technicians, or EMTs. Essentially, the primary responsibility of an EMT is to keep a person alive between an incident site (such as an automobile wreck) and the nearest appropriate medical facility.

As the person is transported to the facility, EMTs must perform any number of tasks—such as cardiopulmonary resuscitation or body stabilization—to deal with any number of problems discovered as the EMT assesses the person's condition. The architecture of virtual-world platforms can support highly variable computer-controlled victim characters that provide realistic problematic conditions for an EMT-in-training to complete as part of the training scenario. As the learner performs the various tasks associated with this training session, his or her actions can be continuously captured as data and recorded in a database, with options for immediate automated performance measurement using scoring algorithms built into the system architecture or later assessment by human evaluators (or both). In short, if an experience can be fabricated in a virtual-world system, elements of performance associated with the experience can be tracked as observable (measurable) data for assessment of that learner's in-world performance.

Implications of System Dynamics for Learning

Systems thinking and system dynamics representations in the form of causal loop diagrams and stock and flow models can support learning in and about complex and dynamic systems and problematic situations. Although it is unlikely that most students, decision makers, and policy developers will become system dynamicists, there are effective ways to promote critical thinking about complex problems using the tools and techniques developed for system dynamics. Highly interactive simulations can be based on mathematically based stock and flow diagrams. Just-in-need feedback can be provided to students when representing their problem conceptualizations in a form consistent with a causal loop diagram. Holistic views of complex systems can also be promoted using causal loop diagrams. When the learning goal is to promote a deep understanding of the structure and behavior of complex and dynamic problem situations, then it is appropriate to consider integrating the tools and techniques of system dynamics.

Benjamin E. Erlandson

See also Adaptive Learning Software and Platforms; Assessing Learning in Simulation-Based Environments; Assessment in Game-Based Learning; Data Mining and Recommendation Engines; Games to Promote Inquiry Learning; Gesture-Based Learning and Instructional Systems; Information Visualization; Learning Analytics; Learning With Simulations; Performance Assessment; Serious Games; Stealth Assessment

Further Readings

Almond, R. G., Steinberg, L. S., & Mislevy, R. J. (2002). Enhancing the design and delivery of assessment systems: A four-process architecture. *Journal of Technology, Learning, and Assessment, 1*(5). Retrieved from http://ejournals.bc.edu/ojs/index.php/jtla/

Huang, R., Kinshuk, & Spector, J. M. (Eds.). (2013). *Reshaping learning: Frontiers of learning technology in a global context.* New York, NY: Springer.

Nelson, B., & Erlandson, B. (2012). *Design for learning in virtual worlds.* New York, NY: Routledge.

Nelson, B., Erlandson, B., & Denham, A. (2011). Global channels of evidence for learning and assessment in complex game environments. *British Journal of Educational Technology, 42*(1), 88–100.

Nitsche, M. (2008). *Video game spaces: Image, play, and structure in 3D game worlds.* Cambridge, MA: MIT Press.

O'Connell, J., & Groom, D. (2010). *Virtual worlds: Learning in a changing world.* Victoria, Australia: ACER Press.

Ward, M., Grinstein, G., & Keim, D. (2010). *Interactive data visualization: Foundations, techniques, and applications.* Natick, MA: A. K. Peters.

VISUAL LITERACY SKILLS IN SCIENCE, TECHNOLOGY, ENGINEERING, AND MATHEMATICS EDUCATION

Although civilizations have been using visual representations for thousands of years, the concept of visual literacy is relatively recent. John Debes introduced the concept in the late 1960s. Debes defined *visual literacy* as a collection of visual competencies that are developed through integrating different visual experiences. The focus on visual competencies and developmental skills in defining *visual literacy* drew increased attention of art educators and prompted the establishment of the International Visual Literacy Association (IVLA). Today, IVLA is one of the driving forces behind visual literacy research.

The contemporary understanding of visual literacy builds on Debes's definition and includes four aspects: (1) the developmental aspect—visual literacy competencies can be acquired and developed as other skills; (2) the social-constructivist aspect—the role of interactions of the learners with peers and the environment in the process of visual literacy acquisition; (3) the contextual aspect—visual literacy is not a universal collection of skills, but is context dependent; and (4) the cognitive aspect—visual literacy as a thinking tool, its role in developing and communicating ideas in different contexts.

This view of visual literacy emphasizes the ability to make sense and communicate visual information, as well as to use visual competencies as tools to generate deeper understanding and new ideas. The concept of visual information, often used in conjunction with visual literacy, is rather broad, so it might be perceived differently in different contexts. This makes visual literacy itself an eclectic and broadly defined field of research. Moreover, as rapid advances of modern technology open new venues for generating, manipulating, sharing, and making sense of visual images, the contemporary concept of visual literacy draws on visual and visual-spatial representations that could not have existed half a century earlier. The contemporary visual literacy research community had to expand the definition of visual artifacts to include visual media, computer-enhanced visualizations and manipulations of data, static and dynamic images, concepts, processes, heuristics, algorithms, trends, and relationships. These recent developments brought the concepts of visual and visual-spatial literacy (an ability to think in both 3D and 4D space; $4D = 3D + \text{time}$) much closer to the fields of science, technology, engineering, and mathematics (STEM) education. This should not come as a surprise, considering how often scientific breakthroughs of the 19th and 20th centuries relied on powerful visual representations (i.e., the discoveries of the electro-magnetic waves, the special and general theories of relativity, and the molecular structure of the genes). This entry describes key aspects of visualization in STEM education and provides several examples of pedagogical approaches for developing STEM visual literacy.

Key Aspects of Visual Literacy in STEM Education

A key aspect of low-tech and high-tech visualization in STEM fields is its functioning as a *thinking tool* that helps mathematicians, scientists, engineers, and students alike operate with abstract concepts, build visual models, illustrate known and uncover unknown relationships, and employ multiple representations (visual, algebraic, graphical, verbal, etc.) to solve problems. Today, visualization is an integral part of STEM fields, which explains why comprehending visual representations in STEM is crucial for constructing the meaning of abstract science and mathematics concepts and being able to manipulate them to solve problems.

Consequently, the cognition-perception dichotomy paradigm introduced by René Descartes in the 17th century that downplayed the role of visual skills has given way to a 21st-century paradigm that views visualization as an important cognitive skill critical in helping students develop higher order problem-solving abilities. The emphasis on a cognitive side of visualization in education is a paradigm shift that was fueled by the explosion of educational technologies in STEM fields. A quick look through contemporary secondary and post-secondary STEM textbooks, resources, pedagogies, and assessments illustrates the important role visualization plays in contemporary STEM education.

The Next Generation Science Standards (NGSS) is one of the most recent nationwide documents in the United States to place emphasis on visual literacy in STEM education. Among many other skills, the standards require students to be able to integrate qualitative scientific and technical information in written text with that contained in media and visual displays to clarify claims and findings; to understand the concepts of structure of function of complex and microscopic systems by modeling and visualizing them; by visualizing mathematics relationships between the variables and their implications on the behavior of these systems; and to be able to interpret the visualizations produced by others and to create their own visualizations to solve science and engineering problems and uncover different phenomena of nature.

Modern visual literacy researchers and educators reject the previously held assumption that visual literacy is subject-neutral. Instead of talking about a universal visual literacy, they embrace the concept of multiple visual literacies—a repertoire of context-embedded knowledge and skills of increasing complexity referring to a person's ability to make sense of and use visual artifacts relevant to a particular field of study to generate and communicate new understandings. Students might have a high level of visual literacy in the context of art education, yet a low level of visual literacy in the STEM context or vice versa. This is akin to being literate in an everyday life sense, yet not being able to understand a popular science article from the *Scientific American* magazine.

For example, Figure 1a displays a lifelike representation of a direct current (DC) electric circuit and Figure 1b shows a schematic representation of the same circuit. Although the lifelike visualization (Figure 1a) is relatively straightforward and might be interpreted correctly by students who had never encountered these topics in a formal physics study, the second image (Figure 1b) is much more specialized and difficult to interpret and use for circuit analysis without possessing the relevant background knowledge. Visual literacy in this context implies that a student is able to interpret the image and use it as a thinking tool to determine different parameters of the circuit (voltage across the light bulbs, current through them, etc.). Therefore, visual representations become an integral part of science knowledge, such that a person who can represent an electric circuit using the schematic diagram (Figure 1b) will more likely be able to succeed at solving relevant physics problems than will a person who uses a visual representation as an add-on feature of the problem.

Another important aspect of visual literacy in the STEM context is captured through the concepts of three- and four-dimensional (3D and 4D) visual-spatial literacy. These concepts are especially relevant in life sciences and engineering where students need to understand the evolution and development of 3D organisms and structures over time, thus making the visualization 3D and 4D. The importance of visualization in life sciences was illustrated recently by Alexander Tsiaras, the

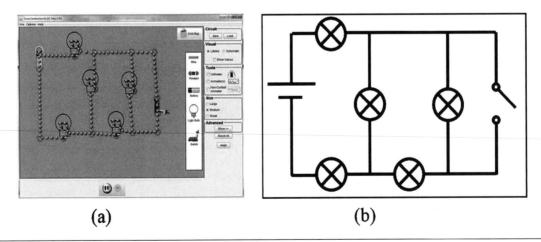

(a)   (b)

Figure I   Visual representations of a DC circuit consisting of a battery, a switch, wires, and five light bulbs; (a) is a lifelike representation of a DC circuit and (b) is a schematic representation of the same circuit

Source: For (a), see http://phet.colorado.edu/en/simulation/circuit-construction-kit-dc

founder, CEO, and editor-in-chief of TheVisualMD. com, who collaborates with researchers in medical fields, artists, and computer scientists to visualize biological phenomena. His award-winning movie *From Conception to Birth—Visualized* was watched by millions of people worldwide and prompted him to become one of the most successful TED speakers. The ability to think spatially is relevant to life science but also to many other disciplines, where multiple representations play a key role in helping students move along the novice-expert continuum or helping experts advance the frontiers of the unknown.

One important implication from the literature review discussed herein is that visual and visual-spatial literacies are cognitive developmental skills that can be fostered by specially designed pedagogical interventions. Therefore, the next part of this entry focuses on outlining a few successful pedagogical approaches that are currently used to help students develop visual and visual-spatial literacy in the context of STEM education.

Examples of Pedagogical Approaches to Develop STEM Visual Literacy

Using Computer Simulations to Help Students Visualize Abstract Phenomena

Lately, computer simulations have become common pedagogical tools in STEM education. However, not all of these simulations are based on the STEM education research. One example of a research-based family of STEM simulations is PhET resource. PhET resource uses computer simulations (i.e., virtual labs) to help students visualize abstract concepts such as forces, electric and magnetic fields, electric currents, chemical reactions, biological processes, the concepts of energy, algebraic functions, greenhouse effect, and so on. Unlike animations, these simulations allow the user to *manipulate* variables, change the configuration of the experiments and propose and test the results of virtual experiments (Figure 1a). In other words, visualization in PhET has become a *thinking tool* to enhance student problem-solving skills rather than just an additional illustration of the science phenomenon. Carl Wieman and his collaborators on the PhET research team have shown that the use of simulations in this way helps students construct a solid conceptual understanding and build bridges between the theoretical knowledge, its visual, mathematical, schematic and verbal representations, and its real-life applications. In the case of the simple DC circuit from PhET virtual laboratory (Figure 1a), Noah Finkelstein and his collaborators found that using simulations before the real-life labs helped students develop a much deeper conceptual

understanding of the phenomena and as a result be much more effective in the real-life lab. This result does not diminish the importance of using a real-life hands-on science laboratory, but shows the value of having students develop conceptual understanding through using virtual labs before experimenting with the real-life apparatus.

Using Data Collection and Analysis Technologies to Visualize Relationships

Another successful pedagogical approach that helps students develop visual literacy in the context of STEM education that combines visualization with other representations through data sensors was pioneered by researchers in late 1980s. This pedagogy is called *interactive lecture demonstrations* or *real live science*. It uses sensors that allow collecting live data and instantaneously displaying it in a graphical form for further analysis. As shown by Marina Milner-Bolotin and her collaborators, this pedagogy is especially useful for helping students visualize complex relationships and abstract science concepts that are difficult for many students to understand.

Although data can be collected using sensors directly, another popular pedagogy is called *video analysis*. This uses video recordings of various motion-related phenomena and then analyzes them frame by frame to collect detailed information and display it in graphical or analytical forms. This pedagogy is especially powerful in helping students develop scientific reasoning skills because visualization is often the first step in making scientific predictions about system's behavior. Combining this pedagogy with instantaneous feedback provided by electronic response systems (clickers) opens opportunities for using graphical representations for building deeper conceptual STEM understanding even in large undergraduate courses.

Using Graphing Software to Visualize Abstract Mathematical Relationships

Graphing calculators and graphing software are examples of visualization tools that have significant potential for engaging students in meaningful mathematics and science learning. Many of these tools are available for free (e.g., WoframAlpha, Desmos) and are accessible from students' mobile devices, thus becoming a part of their STEM toolbox. For example, dynamic mathematics software, such as GeoGebra, allows students to construct graphical representations of abstract mathematical relationships and operations and to visualize them, helping students make sense of abstract information through bridging multiple representations.

In addition, the ease with which students can produce these representations leaves time for exploring the effects of varying different variables on the resultant relationships. Some educators emphasize that students should first develop a skill in building these relationships without the technological aid, but a number of studies have shown that pedagogically sound use of technology allows developing higher order reasoning and critical-thinking skills that might be difficult to achieve in a technology-free classroom.

Using Geographic Information Systems to Develop 3D Visual Literacy

Whereas modern students have a wide exposure to Global Positioning Systems (GPS), our schools are just beginning to use the data from geographic information systems (GIS) to help students develop visual-spatial literacy. The GIS technology is very powerful, yet the development of pedagogical materials to help teachers design effective lessons using this visualization technology is still in its infancy. In one of its reports published in 2006, the National Research Council emphasized the lack of relevant curricula, educational materials, professional development, and vision for the use of modern technologies, such as GIS to help students develop visual literacy skills. Interestingly, often the pioneers in the field of using GIS for this purpose are rural schools, as reported by the National Center for Rural Science.

Using Visualization Software in Biological and Chemical Sciences

As mentioned earlier, visualization is a key tool in contemporary life science research. Thus, visual-spatial literacy plays an important role in biological sciences education. A number of biological software packages have been developed to help students and scientists visualize 3D and 4D processes. Static and dynamic visualizations are becoming a part of modern life science textbooks and laboratory activities. Moreover, although traditional visualization was mainly an animation that helped students see complex biochemical processes without an ability to interact with them directly, nowadays a focus is shifting to computer simulations that allow students to manipulate variables. The PhET simulations mentioned earlier have a number of very powerful simulations in biological and chemical sciences. Like the study on DC circuits, discussed previously, research evidence points out that the students who have an opportunity to engage with 3D biochemical structures through interactive visualizations have an advantage in learning the theoretical material. The purpose of these visualization activities is not just to illustrate the already known concepts, but to use them as thinking tools to help students build an understanding of new ideas and relationships, such as molecular structure of proteins and nucleic acids, its structural details, and organization. The educators who succeed in implementing this pedagogy emphasize that acquisition of visual-spatial skills in the context of their subject is an integral part of their subject content and problem-solving skills.

Another important life-science context where visual-spatial literacy is crucial is understanding the processing where the changes happen in space and over time, such as in developmental biology. The lack of visual-spatial 4D literacy, according to Jeff Hardin, is a big obstacle for student understanding of developmental processes. As modern 3D and 4D visualization technology used in video games becomes more powerful and students become more accustomed to manipulating 3D virtual objects in space and in time, it is important to investigate the impact of these developments on teaching complex biological and biochemical processes that can be significantly enhanced by 3D and 4D visualization.

Using Visualization Software in Engineering Science

Contemporary engineering relies heavily on the use of 3D and 4D visualization. Much of this visualization is done today using specialized software, such as AutoCAD, Mathcad, SketchUp, and various specialized software used in architectural design. At the same time, as fewer students take machine shop courses in high school, fewer undergraduates have real-life experiences dealing with 3D objects. This posts a significant challenge for engineering students because many engineering courses assume students have already developed visual-spatial literacy. This disconnect prompted Sheryl A. Sorby and her collaborators to implement special undergraduate engineering courses that focus specifically on developing visualization skills, such as sketching isometric pictorial representations from coded plans; producing multiview drawings; conducting 2D and 3D object transformations; visualizing cross-sections and surfaces of solids and solids of revolutions; and combining objects by cutting, joining, and intersecting. Sorby and her collaborators were able to show that this intervention helped students improve their visual-spatial literacy skills.

Conclusion

Modern technology provides unprecedented opportunities for helping students develop visualization skills in STEM contexts. To use these technologies successfully, however, educators have to develop pedagogies that use these technologies as thinking tools and not just as post-factum add-ons illustrating natural phenomena.

Visual-spatial skills are developmental skills, thus, students have to be provided with multiple opportunities to develop and practice them in the contexts where these skills are going to be used in the future. Modern visualization technologies and their educational applications have been developed to the level where we are ready to go beyond the initial attempts. Now educators must develop pedagogies that use available visualization technologies to their fullest to help students develop visual literacy.

Marina Milner-Bolotin

See also Learning by Modeling; Simulation-Based Learning

Further Readings

Committee on Conceptual Framework for the New K–12 Science Education Standards & National Research Council. (2013). *Next generation science standards: For states, by states*. Washington, DC: The National Academies Press.

Debes, J. L. (1969). The loom of visual literacy. *Audiovisual Instruction, 14*(8), 25–27.

Hardin, J. (2008). The missing dimension in developmental biology education. *Cell Biology Education—Life Science Education, 7*, 10–11.

Lowe, R. (2000). Visual literacy in science and technology education. *Connect: UNESCO International Science, Technology & Environmental Education Newsletter, 35*(2), 1–3.

Mathewson, J. H. (1999). Visual-spatial thinking: An aspect of science overlooked by educators. *Science Education, 83*(1), 33–54.

Milner-Bolotin, M., & Nashon, S. (2012). The essence of student visual-spatial literacy and higher order thinking skills in undergraduate biology. *Protoplasma, 249*(1), 25–30.

National Research Council (2006*). Learning to think spatially: GIS as a support system in the K–12 curriculum*. Washington, DC: The National Academies Press.

Richardson, D. C., & Richardson, J. S. (2002). Teaching molecular 3-D literacy. *Biochemistry and Molecular Biology Education, 30*(1), 21–26.

Sorby, S. A. (2009). Educational research in developing 3-D spatial thinking for engineering students. *International Journal of Science Education, 31*(3), 459–480.

Tsiaras, A. (2011). Conception to birth—Visualized. *TED Talks*. Retrieved from http://www.ted.com/talks/alexander_tsiaras_conception_to_birth_visualized.html

Websites

ComPADRE: http://www.compadre.org
Desmos: https://www.desmos.com
PhET: https://phet.colorado.edu
Vernier: http://www.vernier.com
Visual Literacy Association (IVLA): http://www.ivla.org
WoframAlpha: http://www.wolframalpha.com

VISUAL SEARCH ENGINES

A *visual search engine* is a search engine designed to visually display search results or to search for information in the World Wide Web through the input of an image. Visual search engines are a relatively new technology used to find desired materials in a visual form. Allan Paivio's dual coding theory and Howard Gardner's theory of multiple intelligences have indicated the importance of using visuals in teaching and learning. Visual search engines are highly related to information visualization along with information technologies and competencies in the 21st-century workplace, so it is necessary to understand visual search engines and their applications in educational technology. This entry presents an overview of search engines, considers the function and evaluation of visual search engines, and provides four examples of visual search engines.

An Overview of Search Engines

A brief overview of search engines in general will help people understand visual search engines. Search engines are programs used to search the World Wide Web for information based on specified keywords and return a list of search results where relevant keywords are found. The first search engine, Archie, started on September 11, 1990, by an MBA student named Alan Emtage at McGill University in Montreal, Canada. The popular search engine Google was started by Larry Page and Sergey Brin in a garage in Menlo Park, California, in 1996.

Common terms that help people better understand search engines include the following: (a) keyword, (b) search engine result pages (SERPs), (c) search engine optimization, and (d) spider. A *keyword* is a word used by a search engine in a search to find relevant documents, which can be webpages, PDF files, images, or other Internet-based resources. *SERP* refers to the webpage that a search engine returns with the results of its search. *Search engine optimization* refers to the accessibility of webpages to search engines and ways that boost their chances to be found in a search. A *spider*, also called a Web crawler, is a program that automatically fetches webpages and is used to feed pages to search engines.

Typically, search engines such as Google work in three major steps: (1) sending out a spider to fetch as many documents as possible; (2) creating an index based on words contained in each document through a program called an indexer; and (3) providing meaningful results by sifting through millions of pages recorded in the index and calculating relevancy to match each search through search engine software. Every search engine has its own algorithms or formula to determine its results and the ordering of the sites it lists in its results.

Visual Search Engines: Function and Evaluation

Visual search engines generally fall into two categories: (1) tools visually representing search results and (2) tools searching images based on visual characteristics. A visual search engine (especially those of the first category) is similar to a traditional text search engine and allows users to search via a keyword, returning results related to that keyword. The difference is that visual search engines return image links instead of text links as text search engines would. Visual search engines are mostly Web-based programs, and they are more interactive than text search engines. A multimedia plug-in is usually needed to operate interactive visual search engines, but the plug-in is generally free and easy to install. Those that do not need plug-ins are usually less interactive.

Visual search engines search images or patterns based on an algorithm recognizing and providing relative information based on pattern match techniques. There are two techniques currently used in image search: (1) search by metadata and (2) search by example. The metadata generation process, called *audiovisual indexing*, associates with each image the title of the image, its format, color, and other known characteristics, and then generates relevant data for the search. Search by example uses a different technique called *content-based image retrieval*. The search results are obtained by comparing images based on the content of the image such as color, shape, texture, or any other visual information extracted from the image. Some image search engines such as Google Images Search use both techniques. The visual display search is an alternative to the traditional results of text sequence links. Such visual search engines use a new way of presenting search results, but the search techniques used are the same as in other text search engines.

Sergi Minguez and Juan Dürsteler identified five important features of visual search engines:

1. Pre-visualization of the search results

2. Rich interaction in navigating and arranging the contents found

3. Use of filters to dynamically redefine the retrieved information

4. Use of tags or customized categories to add meaningfulness and intention to initial query

5. Use of maps to organize the results based on relevant attributes

Although visual search engines visualize the search results, they have some drawbacks. Visual search engines generally use more bandwidth, so they put a greater load on users' computer hardware. Many of the visual search engines may not translate well to the smaller screens of smartphones and other mobile devices. Accessibility issues for users with visual impairments also need to be considered when using visual search engines.

Visual search engines are not just about an appealing interface but also about the effectiveness of search. How to evaluate the effectiveness of a visual search engine? The currency, relevance, authority, accuracy, and purpose (CRAAP) criteria, created by the Meriam Library at California State University, Chico, evaluates visual search engines in a similar way to the text search engines. *Currency* refers to the timeliness of the information and is related to questions such as when the information was published or posted and whether the information has been updated. *Relevance* refers to the importance for the searcher's needs and answers questions such as whether the information is related to the desired topic or answers the searcher's initial question. *Authority* refers to the source of the information and answers questions related to the credentials of the author or organizations affiliated with the information. *Accuracy* refers to the reliability, truthfulness, and correctness of the content and answers questions about where the information is from and whether the information is supported by evidence. *Purpose* refers to the reason the information exists: What is the purpose of the information? Is it to inform, teach, sell, entertain, or persuade?

Visual Search Engines: Four Examples

Four visual search engines are introduced in this section: The first two are examples of visual display search, and the last two are examples of image search.

oSkope is a free search engine that visualizes search results in different styles such as grid, stack, pile, list, and graph. This search engine enables users to browse, search, and organize items from popular sites such as Amazon, eBay, Flickr, Fotolia, and YouTube. By clicking on the image icon, users can see a larger image with a brief description and a link to the original site. In addition to the capability of displaying the search results, users can also choose to graph the results of an oSkope search. A bar on the right side of the screen can be used to zoom in or zoom out the image icons on the search results page.

Visuwords is an online graphical dictionary that displays meanings of words and their associations with other words and concepts. It uses colors to represent parts of speech, such as blue for nouns and green for verbs. It also uses colors and links to indicate relationships among words. Users can drag the background to pan around and move the mouse over nodes to see the definition for each word. This user-friendly tool provides a unique way to show how words are related, linked, and derived.

TinEye, free for noncommercial searching, is the first image search engine on the Web using image identification technology rather than keywords or metadata. After a user uploads an image or enters the URL of an image, this search engine can find where an image came from, how it is being used, whether modified versions of the image exist, or whether there is a higher resolution version. TinEye, which regularly crawls the Web for new images, is an example of image search by example.

Google Image Search allows users to find an image by a keyword or an image uploaded to the search engine site or through entering the image URL. Using both image search by metadata and image search by example, this search engine pulls together highly effective results.

Hong Wang

See also Information and Communication Technologies: Competencies in the 21st-Century Workforce; Information Visualization; Verification and Validation of Digital Resources; Visual Literacy Skills in Science, Technology, Engineering, and Mathematics Education

Further Readings

Gardner, H. (1983). *Frames of mind: The theory of multiple intelligences.* New York, NY: Basic Books.

Minguez, S., & Dürsteler, J. C. (2009). Visual search engines. Inf@Vis!. Retrieved from http://infovis.net/printMag .php?num=198&lang=2

Paivio, A. (1986). *Mental representations.* New York, NY: Oxford University Press.

Websites

Google Image Search: http://images.google.com
OSkope: http://www.oskope.com
TinEye: http://www.tineye.com
Visuwords: http://www.visuwords.com

VULNERABILITY IN LEARNING

Vulnerability in learning refers to a learner's acceptance of the sense of dissonance, resistance, and fears associated with the effort to learn, as well as efforts revolving around self-efficacy. The concept of vulnerability within the learning process and the learning environment is relevant to the topic of educational technology. Vulnerability is directly affected by the social presence of the learner within a learning community, with social engagement being a vital component in more fully understanding the knowledge. Psychologist Lev Vygotsky argued that social presence was important for a sense of community and creativity. Philosopher Ludwig Wittgenstein argued that communicating with others was essential for developing understanding.

Social cognitive effort may be described as the impact of the social environment on the way a person understands information and thinks about it. As such, vulnerability in learning may be perceived as a social cognitive effort wherein the self-efficacy associated with a learner's confidence and conviction directly affects the "stay-with-it-ness" of a learner—the learner's capabilities and capacity to succeed within particular conditions, circumstances, and states of being. Educator Malcolm Knowles suggested that learners may find the process of learning to be frightening, so a supportive environment and accepting climate are necessary. As well, Knowles emphasizes the importance of learner accountability, which should also be a component of any supportive environment and accepting learning climate. In turn, psychologist Albert Bandura argued that vulnerability within the learning environment supports both self-efficacy and social cognitive effort and includes an individual's sense of safety and the ability to allow oneself to be vulnerable with the subject matter and with learning colleagues in a creative and inspirational manner.

In exploring the role of vulnerability in education, this entry discusses learning as a process of understanding, considers the role of motivation in learning, and explores learning as a social endeavor in which all members of the learning community contribute to the nature of an individual's learning experience. Vulnerability directly relates to educational technology in that learners must be open and willing to engage in an educational process that may engage them in thinking about knowledge in new and different ways. As such, vulnerability in learning may be suggested as a learner's underlying cognitive sense of safety within a community of learners, which supports the ability of learners to think "outside the box" and to accept different and new ways of thinking about knowledge without a fear of negative judgment and criticism. Just as educational technology frames knowledge acquisition and information in new ways, vulnerability in learning emphasizes a respect for the learner's progressive knowledge acquisition, analytic abilities, and understanding of information in fresh and novel ways. In an environment in which vulnerable learners are not negatively judged and criticized in a way that would deplete their sense of self-efficacy and engagement, they are better able to engage creatively in the educational process.

Learning as a Process of Understanding

The learning process is not merely one's ability to understand and engage information in new, different, and varied ways. A learner's sense of safety and freedom of expression within the learning environment affects his or her engagement with the learning environment as well as the learning community climate and the learner's sense of community morale. The instructional facilitator is important within the learning environment because the facilitator establishes the learning climate within the environment, while framing the learner's willingness to think, also perceived as a sense of acceptance of thinking, in original and creative ways about the information under study. It has been suggested that the process of learning is a social endeavor in which the learner's sense of belonging within the community, sense of self-efficacy, and comfortableness enable his or her sense of ease of thoughtful reflection about the subject matter.

The instructional facilitator guides the learner's understanding as a progressive endeavor, framing a working knowledge of the subject matter and modeling engagement with the subject matter so that the learner begins to conceptualize the subject matter in new ways, creating neural networks and engagement in thought processes. At the same time, the facilitator seeks to expand the learner's sense of ease with the subject matter and to encourage higher order thinking. Being part of a community of peers also contributes to the learner's ability to work with the subject matter in new ways; the community models the creativity necessary for thinking about and working with information in new ways as well as the freedom to represent oneself as vulnerable.

Motivation and Self-Determination Theory

Edward Deci's and Richard Ryan's self-determination theory, in which they discuss the difference between intrinsic and extrinsic motivation, is relevant to the discussion of vulnerability in learning. A learner's motivation, sense of self, and personality are intrinsically tied to the learning process. The learner's experiences within a learning environment can positively or negatively affect the way the learner approaches each learning community—whether he or she approaches the learning community with a sense of independence, self-sufficiency, proficiency, competency, empathy, sense of affinity, and a desire for connection with both the subject matter and the learning community colleagues, or whether the desire to engage subject matter and learner communities has been replaced by a sense of dependence, inability, and indifference. The learner's motivation to engage the learning community and the subject matter is integrally important in developing a safe environment in which the learner can engage at a deeper level of reflection and higher order thinking.

The instructional facilitator sets the climate of learning within the learning community through explicit statements of expectation, including the ability of the students to learn, and by modeling both vulnerability and a sense of cognitive safety and trust in other members of the learning community. Modeling is a significant component within a social cognitive environment, as others slowly develop a sense of exploration and test the acceptance of their vulnerability within the learning community. The resistance, dissonance, and fear associated with allowing oneself to share one's vulnerability within a social environment is replaced by inspiration, creativity, freedom, and a feeling of safety as the learner begins to think about the subject matter in new ways within the learning community.

Learning as a Humanistic Experience

Learning is a naturally social endeavor. The psychological needs of learners to communicate with others, to share their own ideas in safe environments, and to be supported in their own creativity and inspirations are vitally important to developing the learner's understanding of a subject matter and ability to engage in higher order thinking, as well as in enhancing the learner's sense of autonomy, self-worth, and competence with the subject matter. More explicitly, each learning community is a miniature social group with a sense of kinship and identity, wherein a learner can safely test his or her own cognitive understanding, develop a working knowledge and sense of informational competence, and expand his or her ability to work creatively in a safe environment before representing himself or herself as a person knowledgeable about the subject matter. Thus, each learning community is, in essence, an environment rich in vulnerability. The primary difference between a successful learning community and a potentially ailing learning community is that in a successful learning community, members can safely engage the subject matter in new ways, while being comfortable in expressing feelings of vulnerability, dissonance, resistance, and perhaps even a sense of fear of the subject matter.

Vulnerability Within the Instructional Process

The learning climate is developed through a combination of all personalities within the learning environment—instructional facilitator and learners—and directly affects the instructional process and associated successes. Vulnerability within the instructional process can further the achievement of learning objectives and cognitive efforts and can provide an opportunity for social support and for checking one's cognitive conceptual understanding amongst other learners. Vulnerability in learning may undergird a learner's ability to achieve self-efficacy and to engage the subject matter positively.

Caroline M. Crawford

See also Affective Factors in Learning, Instruction, and Technology; Distributed Cognitions in Computer-Supported Collaborative Learning; Knowledge and Skill Hierarchies; Measuring Contacts and Interactions in Social Networks; Measuring Learning in Informal Contexts; Motivation, Emotion Control, and Volition; Situated Learning

Further Readings

Atherton, J. S. (2013) *Learning and teaching; Knowles' andragogy: An angle on adult learning*. Retrieved from http://www .learningandteaching.info/learning/knowlesa.htm

Bandura, A. (1986). *Social foundations of thought and action: A social cognitive theory*. Englewood Cliffs, NJ: Prentice-Hall.

Bandura, A. (1997). *Self-efficacy: The exercise of control*. New York, NY: W. H. Freeman.

Deci, E. L., & Ryan, R. M. (2000). The "what" and "why" of goal pursuits: Human needs and the self-determination of behavior. *Psychological Inquiry, 11,* 227–268. Retrieved from http:// www.selfdeterminationtheory.org/SDT/documents/2000_ DeciRyan_PIWhatWhy.pdf

Knowles, M. (1990). *The adult learner: A neglected species* (4th ed.). Houston, TX: Gulf. Retrieved from http://www .umsl.edu/~henschkej/the_adult_learner_4th_edition.htm

Ryan, R. M., & Deci, E. L. (2000). Self-determination theory and the facilitation of intrinsic motivation, social development, and well-being. *American Psychologist, 55,* 68–78.

Vygotsky, L. S. (1933/1966). Play and its role in the mental development of the child. *Soviet psychology, 12*(6), 62–76.

Vygotsky, L. S. (1935). *Mental development of children during education*. Moscow-Leningrad, Russia: Uchpedzig.

Vygotsky, L. S. (1981). The genesis of higher mental functions. In J. V. Wertsch (Ed.), *The concept of activity in Soviet psychology*. Armonk, NY: Sharpe.

Wittgenstein, L. (1961). *Tractatus logico-philosophicus* (D. F. Pars & B. F. McGuiness, Trans.). New York, NY: Humanities Press.

WEARABLE LEARNING ENVIRONMENTS

Wearable learning environments include a variety of body-borne sensory, communication, and computational components that may be worn under, over, or within clothing. Steve Mann refers to these environments as smart clothing. Wearable learning environments have the potential to change the dynamics of how individuals acquire, store, and retrieve information. This rapidly evolving technology offers new frontiers for both researchers and users.

This entry begins with an overview of the evolution of wearable learning environments. Next, the use of wearable learning environments for performance support in the workplace and for cognitive and psychomotor learning in education is discussed. Finally, a brief glimpse into the future implications of these learning environments is presented.

Evolution of Wearable Learning Environments

The first wearable computer is attributed to Steve Mann in the early 1980s, with his experiments as a high school student involving wireless wearable computing. He also experimented with a backpack-mounted computer with smart glasses and a one-handed keying input device. One of Mann's applications provided photographically mediated reality, which was an early attempt at augmented reality in a wearable device. By 1989, the smart glasses concept evolved into the commercially available Private Eye providing the user with a 1-inch × 1-inch display worn close to the eye offering the equivalent of a 12-inch display seen from 18 inches away. Doug Platt

introduced a hip-mounted computer incorporating the Private Eye and a palmtop keyboard in 1991. The standard computer keyboard was replaced by a one-handed keyboard in future versions of the wearable computer. In 1993, Platt and Thad Starner combined the functionality of the Private Eye and the Twiddler, a commercially available one-handed keyboard, into the first context-aware system. This design became the basis on which the Massachusetts Institute of Technology (MIT) Lab's Lizzy, perhaps the first fully functional wearable system, was established.

Since the initial robust innovation in wearable computers at the MIT Media Lab, iterations have continued. A current implementation of a wearable computer is Google Glass. Over 20 years after his initial work at the MIT Media Lab, Starner was requested by Google Inc. to serve as technical lead for Google's Project Glass. While smartphones may currently offer many capabilities, these are only a part of the wearable equation. Current smartphones do not capture reality as it happens in the moment it happens. Reducing the time between intention and action is at the heart of wearable computing.

Innovation in technologies for learning continues to evolve in the context of wearable systems. Wearable computers as learning tools may have great potential for enhancing learning but research has yet to show this efficacy and positive impact in educational contexts. An analysis of the proceedings from the International Symposium on Wearable Computers spanning over 16 conferences beginning in 1997 through 2012 revealed that the number of published papers in the proceedings peaked at 47 in 2005 with 2012 being the lowest at 24 papers. The emphasis has shifted from wearable computers in earlier years to activity-sensing techniques more recently.

Wearable Learning Environments for Performance Support

Electronic performance support systems (EPSS) proved to be valuable in the workplace combining technology-enabled services with on-demand access. Advances in technology, reducing the hardware size and increasing computing speed and capability, spurred on advances in wearable learning environments as tools to support performance on the job. The MetaPark environment was designed to provide park employees with wearable context-aware devices capable of delivering necessary information in an appropriate format at the required level of detail. Synchronous and asynchronous communication, information recording and retrieval, and location and context awareness, including location-based messaging, offered wearers the ability to conference with other team members in an augmented reality environment. The wearable components available in MetaPark were similar to the factory automation support technology (FAST) system; the FAST architecture was more complex and included an advisor, training, and assessment components. With regard to performance support, FAST was able to provide workers with necessary information when and where it was needed anywhere within a factory. Access and use of interactive electronic technical manuals (IETMs) through wearables offers users necessary just-in-time information without referring to printed documentation that may consist of thousands of pages and hundreds of topics. The impact of wearable IETMs on learning and productivity has not yet been established, but users generally prefer the convenience of wearables over place-bound computers.

Wearable Learning Environments for Cognitive and Psychomotor Learning

The design and development of wearable computing is a challenging discipline. Technological advances have reduced the costs of wearable learning environment creation. Several researchers have developed a framework with the creation of a wearable learning environment as the foundation for middle school students learning concepts ranging from basic electricity and circuit theory to electronics and programming. The platform is a T-shirt breadboard made from a conductive fabric, Sheildit, where users can construct conductive paths and snap buttons are used for connections. Programming has been simplified through BrickLayer, a graphical-textual Web-based interface.

Researchers exploring wearable learning environments in science education created and tested a two-part learning environment comprised of a Web-based portal with activities for museum and park visits. The wearable consisted of a backpack-mounted laptop and a head-mounted display camera that combined virtual images with real-world vision. Both students with and without disabilities participated. While there were no significant differences in pre- and post-visit tests, the researchers suggested further research to determine how this type of technology could diminish barriers for those with disabilities.

Wearable learning environments have emerged across all types of psychomotor skill development settings including health care, sports, and military environments. The tactile interaction for kinesthetic learning (TIKL), while not a complete wearable learning environment, was used to analyze users' movements in a physical rehabilitation environment and provide real-time vibrotactile feedback for motor skill learning. In one study, real-time errors were reduced by 27%, learning rate increased by 23%, and correct performance increased by 27%. Running form may be improved through remote real-time training via a wearable learning environment worn by the runner comprised of a wireless data sensor, SunSPOT, and a headset in the field environment. At the remote environment, an advisor reviews the runner's form, providing feedback for improvements.

The effectiveness of a wearable computer integrated into soldiers' equipment on training has also been evaluated. Three studies were conducted, including a heuristic usability evaluation and two experiments regarding retention of declarative knowledge and transfer of procedural skills. The wearable system was found to be more difficult to use than a desktop interface simulation regarding the heuristic usability evaluation. No significant difference in the retention of declarative knowledge of 53 movement procedures was found among three instructional conditions, including the wearable system, the desktop interface simulation, and interactive multimedia instructional videos. Significant differences were found between the wearable system, the desktop interface simulation, and live condition regarding the transfer of procedural skills. Participants in the live condition completed a higher number of correct tasks and performed the procedural tasks faster than the participants in the wearable and desktop interface conditions.

Future Implications

While empirical research on wearable learning environments is limited, great potential exists. Proponents of these environments believe they will revolutionize computing. The positive impacts on performance support and both cognitive and psychomotor learning have been partially demonstrated. More research is necessary to understand the potential of wearable learning environments.

Byron Havard

See also Augmented Reality; Head-Mounted Displays in Learning and Instruction; Integrated and Networked Mobile Devices for Learning and Instruction; Mobile Tools and Technologies for Learning and Instruction; Touch-Based and Gesture-Based Devices; Ubiquitous Learning

Further Readings

Arvanitis, T. N., Petrou, A., Knight, J. F., Savas, S., Sotiriou, S., Gargalakos, M., & Gialouri, E. (2009). Human factors and qualitative pedagogical evaluation of a mobile augmented reality system for science education used by learners with physical disabilities. *Personal and Ubiquitous Computing, 13*(3), 243–250. doi: 10.1007/s00779-007-0187-7

Gotoda, N., Matsuura, K., Otsuka, S., Tanaka, T., & Yano, Y. (2012). Remote coaching system for runner's form with wearable wireless sensor. *International Journal of Mobile Learning and Organisation, 5*(3/4), 282–298. doi:10.1504/IJMLO.2011.045318

Lieberman, J., & Breazeal, C. (2007). TIKL: Development of a wearable vibrotactile feedback suit for improved human motor learning. *IEEE Transactions on Robotics, 23*(5), 919–926. doi:10.1109/TRO.2007.907481

Liu, D. (2004). Maintenance activities with wearable computers as training and performance aids. In *Proceedings of the 2004 Conference of the Computer-Human Interaction Special Interest Group of the Human Factors and Ergonomics Society of Australia* (OzCHI2004). Wollongong, NSW.

Mann, Steve. (2013). Wearable computing. In M. Soegaard & R. F. Dam (Eds.), *The encyclopedia of human-computer interaction* (2nd ed.). Aarhus, Denmark: The Interaction Design Foundation. Retrieved from http://www.interaction-design.org/encyclopedia/wearable_computing.html

Martin, T., Kim, K., Forsyth, J., McNair, L., Coupey, E., & Dorsa, E. (2013). Discipline-based instruction to promote interdisciplinary design of wearable and pervasive computing products. *Personal and Ubiquitous Computing, 17*(3), 465–478. doi:10.1007/s00779-011-0492-z

Najjar, L., Thompson, C., & Ockerman, J. J. (1999). Using a wearable computer for continuous learning and support. *Mobile Networks & Applications, 4*(1), 69–74. doi:10.1023/A:1019126226904

Ngai, G., Chan, S. C. F., Cheung, J. C. Y., & Lau, W. W. Y. (2010). Deploying a wearable computing platform for computing education. *IEEE Transactions on Learning Technologies, 3*(1), 45–55. doi:10.1109/TLT.2009.49

Taylor, G. S., & Barnett, J. S. (2013). Evaluation of wearable simulation interface for military training. *Human Factors: The Journal of the Human Factors and Ergonomics Society, 55*(3), 672–690. doi: 10.1177/0018720812466892

WEB ANALYTICS

Web analytics involves the collection and analysis of data generated by interaction with a website or a Web-based application. Web analytics can be used to enhance the performance of the site or application and to inform an organization of use and impact.

Web analytics have been used to investigate users' characteristics and interaction patterns. Web analytics can be used to predict which products might be of interest to specific customers. The analysis of page visits and site usage can help determine needs and focus. Web analytics can also be used in digital forensics to detect security threats and gather evidence for law enforcement. In the academic world, Web analytics can support organizational planning. For example, as more and more library resources and services are moving online, visits to an online catalogue system can aid in determining subscriptions and technical support for library services. The ubiquity of distributed information invites the integration of Web analytics in many sectors. Educational institutions can track traffic flow on websites, calibrate displays, and manage Web-based learning systems.

This entry begins with a discussion of the techniques and tools used for Web analytics. Next, it examines how Web analytics are used in online education. The final section of this entry focuses on the implications of Web analytics.

Techniques and Tools for Web Analytics

Clicks and page requests are the essential components of Web analytics. According to Bernard J. Jansen, Web analytics started in the 1960s with the analysis of Web logs. These Web logs can be categorized as transaction or search logs. Transaction log analysis (TLA) documents and measures direct interactions (e.g., clicks, page views, length of sessions); search log analysis (SLA) tracks searching behaviors (e.g., keywords used and recommendations followed).

Web analytics depends on quantitative data provided by host or third-party servers. Small packets of data called *cookies* are sent to a user. These cookies gather and send relevant information to a server system. This is known as server-side data collection. However, accurate data collection through this method becomes challenging. Internet service providers assign dynamic IP addresses to computers. User security options may block some or all cookies. Client-side data collection is an alternative. With this approach, the uniqueness, accuracy, and frequency of visits can be captured with snippets or tags written with various programming languages. These tags are usually embedded in the webpage requested by clients and can send relevant data such as length of page load to a server. A hybrid model of using both methods is often recommended, according to Brian Clifton.

As human-computer interactions on the Web have become predominantly omnipresent in daily life, Web analytics also uses qualitative techniques like surveys, interviews, and lab experiments to make more meaningful interpretation and reports. To determine quantitative or qualitative methods for Web analytics, key performance indicators (KPIs) need to be established. For example, a university that adopts a new learning management system (LMS) may experience unusually high demand for chat-based technical support. The objectives of an analysis might include evaluating the Web-based resources and services and assessing the need to adjust the personnel assigned to technical support. The KPIs can include paths used to reach the support page, clicks within the LMS, session length, readability of support materials, visibility of icons, and frequency of chat sessions. Each of these KPIs will then determine how the segmentation of Web data will be configured, collected, analyzed, and reported.

Learning Analytics and Online Education

In education, Web analytics can be used to generate data-driven reports for decision making about student services, organizational structures, and support for scholarships. They can also be used to measure student engagement, analyze interaction patterns, and inform teachers about student progress and instructional effectiveness. Academic analytics measure the performance of an educational institution or unit and provide information for decision making. Learning analytics involves collecting and analyzing data related to student learning behaviors. Depending on how much data can be culled in a Web-based environment or internal databases, there is overlap among Web analytics, academic analytics, and learning analytics.

Learning analytics collects, analyzes, and reports data related to learners and their learning contexts. Learning analytics can be used to document students' performance in technology-mediated learning and better understand Web-based learning environments. Learning analytics is rapidly evolving. Figure 1 illustrates data tracking of student interactions with an LMS, library resources, and other student services in a university. These interactions usually involve social media and other open Web resources.

With big data generated in these systems, learning analytics can contribute to many areas relevant to enhancing student learning success. These include and are not limited to (a) documenting student learning

process, (b) providing preventive interventions upon identifying nonparticipants, (c) evaluating teaching attributes in Web-based environments, and (d) applying advisory and other resources according to individual learner needs.

As a measure to predict success, learning analytics can document student presence in a networked environment with the data from the student information system (SIS) and LMS. In a fully online class, learning analytics can provide the basis for formative evaluation for teacher-student interaction patterns, course design, and content presentation. For instance, frequencies of student sign-ins to an LMS can be used as an attendance record. Tracking and analysis of clicks and length of a session in a content area, such as watching a video recording and taking a quiz or exam, can provide an estimate of a learner's behavior and learner-content interaction. Using analytics in an LMS, an instructor can timely detect students with inactivity, and then apply proper customized interventions, such as sending an individualized message to the student.

To optimize its potential, learning analytics can extend beyond quantitative data to include qualitative data analysis. For instance, discourse analysis of content in online discussion forums, blog posts, and revisions on collaborative wikis can generate meaningful information for teachers, designers, and students. The semantic patterns analyzed through qualitative content may also provide insight into student critical thinking development that is reflected in text and rich media created in online environments.

Depending on the goals set for learning analytics, KPIs can target student success or pedagogy improvement in the online environment, include both quantitative and qualitative data analysis, and provide the context for diagnosing technology support for students and instructors. These KPIs can be measured and reported with different types of techniques, including but not limited to, tracking individual learner behavior, analyzing learner characteristics based on aggregate profiles, recommending content or courses based on user history, and analyzing trends.

These applications can be achieved with analytics features built in the LMS and tools for general Web analytics. For instance, the University of Maryland-Baltimore County (UMBC) integrated Google Analytics in its LMS and enabled students to track and compare their learning activities within the LMS with a *Check My Activity* function. With the combination of Course Signal and PassNote, a professor at Purdue University can timely detect underperforming students and send personalized messages. For trend analysis, SNAPP (Social Networks Adapting Pedagogical Practice) can analyze and visualize the interaction patterns in online discussion forums. Degree Compass, developed at

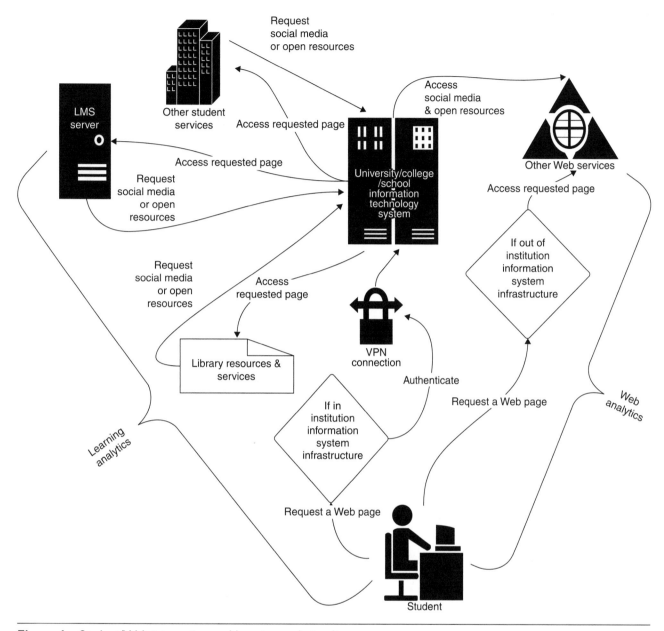

Figure 1   Student/Web interaction and learning analytics diagram

Austin Peay State University (APSU) and now owned by Desire2Learn, allows course recommendations at student, advisory, and institutional management levels. Recent developments (e.g., see wordnet.princeton.edu and netlytic.org) expand learning analytics to qualitative analysis, providing the potential for learning analytics to support writing and programming competencies.

Implications of Web Analytics for Learning

With increased integration of Web-based systems in the academic world, Web analytics is gaining visibility and prevalence at both macro- and microlevels. Young and interdisciplinary in nature, learning analytics is at its initial development and adoption stage. There are concerns about its use and adoption. For instance, to customize interventions to inactive students more effectively, data need to be assessed timely and accurately. With the complexity of blending technologies in both online and face-to-face modes, the disaggregation and interpretation of data can be convoluting. Collected expertise or consultation in data mining, statistics analysis, cyberinfrastructure, learning science, and instructional design may be needed for appropriate interpretation and application. Privacy concerns are also unavoidable as different systems are integrating and graduation cycles evolve. Using a variety of tools, applications, communication systems, and funding sources for development may also lead to questions about data ownership.

Despite these concerns and with big data constantly generated in higher education, according to the Horizon 2014 report, learning analytics will be soon adopted. In the meantime, with emerging mobile and wearable technologies, learning analytics will likely take on more exciting facets and contribute to continued morphing of teaching and learning.

Juhong Christie Liu

See also Data Mining and Recommendation Engines; Human-Computer Interaction; Learning Analytics for Programming Competencies; Learning Analytics for Writing Competencies

Further Readings

Clifton, B. (2008). Web traffic data sources & vendor comparison. *Omega Digital Media*. Retrieved from http://www.ga-experts.com/web-data-sources.pdf

Jansen, B. (2009). *Understanding user-web interactions via web analytics*. San Rafael, CA: Morgan & Claypool. Retrieved from http://www.morganclaypool.com/doi/pdf/10.2200/S00191ED1V01Y200904ICR006

Siemens, G. (2013). Learning analytics: The emergence of a discipline. *American Behavioral Scientist, 57*(10), 1380–1400.

Websites

Course Signal: http://www.itap.purdue.edu/studio/signals
PassNote: http://www.purdue.edu/passnote
SNAPP: http://www.snappvis.org

WEB 2.0 AND BEYOND

Children and teens live media-saturated lives, spending several hours per day engaged with cell phones, computers, and other multimedia. Frequently, their time is spent using Web 2.0 tools: highly interactive technologies and participatory spaces that are open, collaborative, and distributed. Examples of Web 2.0 tools include wikis, blogs, social networking sites, video or image sharing sites, multiplayer video games, and texting applications (apps). Contrary to stereotypical views of such technologies as nonacademic pastimes, these tools are full of possibilities for powerful, engaged learning that connects students' academic work to their everyday lives. A growing body of scholarship suggests that participatory

culture can help children and adolescents master core academic subjects as they develop proficiency with technology for communication, collaboration, research, and creation of new works. Because they are specifically designed for sharing information and ideas, Web 2.0 tools are ideal for building relationships that can sometimes extend beyond the school walls to include friends, peers, teachers, and subject matter experts. Through these interactions, students learn to analyze and evaluate evidence and alternative points of view, and to synthesize and make connections between information and arguments. They become part of a collective knowledge community where they assume shared responsibility for posing and solving problems in creative, collaborative ways. Participation in these interactive spaces encourages students to take risks and engage in friendly competition but also to collaborate with others and learn flexibility in decision making. This, in turn, advances academic goals by increasing student engagement, boosting comprehension, and facilitating inquiry-oriented learning. In the process, students learn how to be safe, ethical, responsible citizens in online environments.

Web 2.0 tools are usually *cloud-based*, allowing users to utilize resources on demand and to download, create, or remix content, and upload it to a shared resource pool for others to use. Web 2.0 applications are increasingly being designed for use with multifunction mobile devices (e.g., cell phones, tablets, iPads). Many of these tools are browser- and device-neutral, meaning that they allow users to access, edit, and share electronic content from any computer or device with an Internet connection. And because the infrastructure for these electronic tools is virtual, they typically do not require the hardware and other networking components such as stand-alone servers, connecting wires, cooling systems, and such, to operate.

In Web 2.0 settings, control of content is decentralized and nonhierarchical: All users are allowed to create, publish, and share information. Web 2.0 is sometimes referred to as the *read-and-write* Web because it facilitates interactions and interconnections between users and content using text, images, sound, video, and animation. The term *Web 2.0* is not tied to specific technologies, applications, or practices. Rather, the term broadly refers to a wide range of interactive communication tools and spaces. This entry explores the use of Web 2.0 in education, including accessibility, engagement, and achievement, and discusses benefits, challenges, and future directions.

Web 2.0 to Support 21st-Century Teaching and Learning

Interactive, participatory technologies have profound implications for education. Changes in the educational landscape, such as the increased emphasis on accountability and the adoption of Common Core State Standards (CCSS), require schools to retool to meet the needs of 21st-century students. Teachers must rise to the challenge of supporting and promoting appropriate uses of technology. Of course, students will still need to learn core academic skills and content, but their classroom experiences should also reflect the real world. School should be a place where students gain the knowledge and competencies they will need to effectively participate in a highly technological, information-based society. The Partnership for 21st Century Skills (P21) Framework provides a road map of sorts to help educators ensure that students have the knowledge, skills, understandings, and expertise they will need to live and work successfully in the digital age. In addition to basic competencies in core subjects, such as reading, writing, and computation, the P21 Framework calls for students to be proficient with *new literacies*, the technology-based tools that allow learners to build relationships and solve problems collaboratively; develop, implement, and communicate new ideas; elaborate, refine, and evaluate ideas; and engage in critical and creative thinking. Interactive Web 2.0 technologies can provide a pathway for combining 21st-century skills with core content knowledge using the framework of *technological pedagogical content knowledge* (TPACK). *Content knowledge* includes the essential academic subject matter that students must learn at school, while *pedagogical knowledge* includes the skills and knowledge that teachers need to know about teaching methods, instructional design, and curriculum development. *Technological knowledge* consists of knowing how to utilize multiple forms of technology in the classroom to combine content and pedagogical knowledge to meet the various instructional and social needs of students. In essence, TPACK emphasizes the formulation of knowledge and understanding by blending content, pedagogy, and technology to support instruction, learning, and assessment. Teachers seeking to enliven their day-to-day classroom teaching are increasingly turning to interactive Web applications and programs to expand students' educational experiences in ways that support TPACK-oriented, inquiry-based content learning.

With the growing acceptance of collaborative, constructivist theories of learning, the number of Web 2.0 applications aimed at teachers and students has exploded. Facebook, Twitter, Instagram, and Dropbox offer tools for sharing and distributing documents and content; sites such as Vimeo and YouTube support video sharing and provide spaces for comments and discussion. General purpose tools such as blogs and wikis offer a broad range of applications for sharing content, facilitating discussions, and collaborating in real time, while social networks and learning management systems designed specifically for educational use such as Schoology and Edmodo provide electronic spaces for groups—both students and teachers—to share files and digital resources. Increasingly, these sites are also being used for professional development purposes. Other popular examples of Web 2.0 for education include knowledge- and content-sharing sites such as and VoiceThread and Pinterest and content aggregators and Web curation tools such as MentorMob and Spigot.org.

Accessibility, Engagement, and Achievement

Today's classrooms are fast-moving, demanding environments. Individual students learn at their own rates and in their own ways, making it nearly impossible for teachers to create learning experiences tailored to each individual student. To aid in the design and creation of effective instruction that more closely matches the diverse learning needs of students, educators are turning to interactive Web tools. Teachers can utilize interactive technology to differentiate instruction by creating educational experiences that accommodate a broad spectrum of student readiness, levels of interest, and learning preferences. Web tools are well suited for instruction centered on the principles of universal design for learning (UDL), a framework for creating and adjusting instruction to address the needs of diverse students. Based on recent advances in how the brain processes information, UDL helps teachers accommodate a broad range of student needs by providing multiple ways for learners to acquire information and knowledge, multiple means for students to express and demonstrate what they know, and multiple means of engagement with content to tap into learners' interests and increase their motivation. The methods, materials, and teaching approaches for UDL can take a variety of forms. For example, students might learn about space and the solar system through photographs, digital animation, or simulations. They might travel back in time to experience another era such as ancient Rome or World War II, or step inside an organization like the United Nations in a role-playing game. They can actively investigate contemporary problems such as regional conflicts or climate change by working collaboratively on authentic projects that have real-world consequences. In each of these examples, Web 2.0 tools serve to enhance the teacher's repertoire of ways to represent content while tapping into learners' interests and providing flexible pathways for learners to engage with subject matter in ways that are meaningful to them.

On the assessment side, comprehension and achievement can be measured formatively or summatively through digital products ranging from slideshows to student-created videos, from interactive games to the creation of electronic portfolios. By widening the spectrum of ways to assess learning, it becomes easier to integrate instruction across subject areas. This is particularly important in schools where creative activities and artistic expression have been curtailed due to an increased focus on standardized testing. Photography, music, animation, Web authoring, and other projects that activate creativity and passion, while also connecting to performance standards, can arouse curiosity and trigger meaningful learning. Authentic assessments like these can in fact provide a more complete picture of what students know, understand, and can do with what they are learning. Indeed, interactive Web 2.0 tools can enhance any approach to teaching, learning, and assessment because they can serve as both a means (for instruction) and an end (for evaluation of learning).

Many interactive technologies serve an additional purpose: They facilitate student autonomy and competence while at the same time providing a mechanism for collective knowledge building and information sharing. These tools are sometimes termed *social software* because they facilitate group communication. The nature of these tools makes them ideal for designing educational environments that include the 4 C's of participatory culture: creation, circulation, collaboration, and connection. *Creation* refers to developing original content or modifying existing work; *circulation* means knowledge exchange and content dissemination; *collaboration* concerns collective efforts to foster knowledge building, problem solving, and creative expression; and *connection* pertains to connecting individuals and groups of people around shared interests. Participatory culture can support these richer ways of thinking and learning by weaving 21st-century interdisciplinary themes into core subjects.

Benefits and Challenges of Web 2.0

Interactive Web technologies are full of possibilities for children and youth to actively participate in their own academic development. But just as there are reasons to be excited about the accessibility of information in the online world, there are reasons, too, for concern. Although multimodal forms of teaching, learning, and communication can empower learners, educators must ensure that these tools are used in safe, ethical, and responsible ways. Two major concerns about online education are the issues of safety and electronic privacy. Although most school-based computer systems utilize firewalls, filtering software, and other network safeguards, all information on the Internet is potentially vulnerable to security breaches. Thus, a balance must be struck between the need to access information and

the need to protect the privacy of Internet users. As schools and society become more inundated with technology, a major responsibility for teachers is ensuring that guidelines for appropriate online behavior are clearly articulated and modeled. This might include requiring students to use aliases when creating online accounts, ensuring that students do not provide names or other identifying personal information on third-party sites, adhering to the school's acceptable use policy (AUP), and following the requirements of the Family Education Rights and Privacy Act (FERPA). Rather than describing the proper use of technology to students, most AUPs simply state what students can and cannot do by listing behaviors that are restricted in school settings. However, for students to become Web-responsible users, teachers need to explain what constitutes safe, responsible online behavior and why, and students need hands-on experience using Web 2.0 technologies in appropriate ways.

An important consideration when using Web-based tools is the issue of equal access to technology for all students. Care must be taken to ensure that students with physical, developmental, communication, or intellectual disabilities are not disenfranchised by well-meaning efforts to technologize mainstream classrooms. To address these concerns, teachers should utilize whatever formats, tools, and supports are available to maximize engagement and encourage active participation for all students. This might include using augmentative and alternate communication tools like adapted keyboards or touch screens, text-to-speech applications, voice recognition programs, word-prediction software, or audio and picture cues. It might require providing electronic feedback about progress (e.g., Screen Cast) from the teacher or facilitating collaborative work through digital forums where students can share documents, information, and ideas (e.g., Google groups). Increasingly, Web 2.0 applications are being designed specifically for use on multifunction devices such as cell phones and tablet computers to make learning more accessible and interactive.

Another technology-related equity issue is the current emphasis on raising scores on standardized tests. As teachers are forced to spend more time on reading, math, and test preparation, other subjects such as social studies, science, and the humanities are pushed aside. Minority and low-income children and teens are particularly affected by the current focus on strict accountability measures, and as a result, they are frequently the ones being shut out of the creative, interest-building multimedia learning experiences made possible by 21st-century technologies. These students are less likely to be in schools with access to the rich and growing set of digital applications that support inquiry-based, interactive learning. Their teachers, who are subject to sanctions if educational outcomes are not met, are often discouraged from using emerging technologies to improve learning or boost motivation. Instead, they are tied to a curriculum aimed primarily at ensuring students score well on high-stakes tests. Research indicates that students in these environments have fewer opportunities to develop an understanding of the relationships between ideas, concepts, and content areas than their peers who have grappled with the kinds of complex problems that are emphasized in classrooms where creative collaboration, active engagement, and student-centered learning are valued. Clearly, the digital divide is an issue that deserves more attention in technology discussions.

Future Directions

Not every lesson benefits from the use of technology. When used properly, however, Web 2.0 tools can promote higher levels of interaction and student engagement, making schools and education more relevant for everyone. Twenty-first-century teaching and learning require flexibility and adaptability, as well as leadership and collaborative skills—for teachers as well as for students. Emerging technologies that are implemented thoughtfully using the appropriate pedagogy and with specific instructional goals in mind will likely become indispensable tools for teachers seeking to anchor their instruction in deep comprehension and high-level thinking. By offering new possibilities for accessibility, shared resources, self-directed learning, and collaborative inquiry, Web 2.0 tools can help teachers reach all students—in every subject and at every grade level—in the classroom and beyond the school day.

Karla V. Kingsley

See also Emerging Educational Technologies; Information, Technology, and Media Literacies; Integrating Social Media Into Learning and Instruction; Social Media and Networking; Technology-Enhanced Inquiry Learning; TPACK (Technological Pedagogical Content Knowledge); TPACK (Technological Pedagogical Content Knowledge): Implications for 21st-Century Teacher Education; Twenty-First-Century Technology Skills; Universal Design

Further Readings

Gunn, T., & Hollingsworth, M. (2013). The implementation and assessment of a shared 21st century learning vision: A district-based approach. *Journal of Research on Technology in Education, 45*(3), 201–228.

Hofer, M., & Grandgenett, N. (2012). TPACK development in teacher education: A longitudinal study of preservice teachers

in a secondary M.A.Ed. Program. *Journal of Research on Technology in Education, 45*(1), 83–106.

Kingsley, K. V., & Brinkerhoff, J. (2011). Web 2.0 tools for authentic instruction, learning and assessment. *Social Studies and the Young Learner, 23*(3), 9–13.

Lankshear, C., & Knobel, M. (2006). *New literacies: Everyday practices & classroom learning* (2nd ed.). New York, NY: Open University Press.

Maloy, R., Verock-O'Loughlin, R.-E, Edwards, S. A., & Woolf, B. P. (2014). *Transforming learning with new technologies* (2nd ed.). Boston, MA: Pearson.

Schrum, L., & Levin, B. B. (2009). *Leading 21st century schools: Harnessing technology for engagement and achievement.* Thousand Oaks, CA: Corwin.

WEB 2.0/3.0 IN THE WORKPLACE

Web 2.0 is the term to describe a second generation of the World Wide Web that enables people to share information and collaborate online. Web 2.0 recognizes social media and social computing tools that have been widely used to support information sharing, social communication, and collaboration on the Web. The importance of Web 2.0 does not lie in the technology itself but more in the fundamental change in the way people access knowledge and communicate with others that it fosters. Web 2.0 significantly improves knowledge creation and sharing in the workplace by involving, engaging, and empowering people, and by creating a collaborative environment for social interaction between those who seek knowledge and those who hold the knowledge. As a result, Web 2.0 technologies have considerably reshaped communication processes and strategies in the workplace and promoted knowledge management and open innovation in organizations on a global scale. Thus, this entry focuses on these Web 2.0 technologies, including the changes they have wrought, and discusses future Web developments, such as Web 3.0.

Web 2.0 Technologies in the Workplace

Information technologies including Web 2.0 are of immense value in the world of an information explosion. Web 2.0 is a set of trends and tools that refers to the social use of the World Wide Web for cocreation and exchange of user-generated content. The main technologies and services of Web 2.0 include online forums, blogs, wikis, microblogs (e.g., Twitter), rich site summaries (RSSs), mashups, social networking (e.g., Facebook), social bookmarking, tag clouds, folksonomy, video sharing (e.g., YouTube), podcasts, and so on. Online forums have become more extensive and led to the proliferation of blogging. Wikis are used to enable communities to write documents on the Web collaboratively. The dissemination of news or other regularly changing Web content has evolved into RSSs. Mashup tools allow the combination of information or services from multiple sources on the Web to create new services. Social bookmarking enables users to annotate Web documents and share bookmarks such as comments, votes, and tags or keywords. Through social bookmarking or social tagging, users may have a tag cloud, which is a list of tags with the popular tags receiving a bigger or bolder font than less popular ones. Social tagging is also called *folksonomy*, the process by which a taxonomy or classification system is made by regular users of the Web, instead of by scientists or specialists.

Web 2.0 technologies have been widely used to support interaction among users for content cocreation and publishing, social networking and sharing, knowledge coconstruction and retention. They have largely extended learning opportunities in the workplace by fostering social interactions and learner-centered environment. In specific, technology has allowed more unstructured, self-governing approaches to the creation and transfer of knowledge, including the development of new forms of learning communities and networks. As a result, Web 2.0 is increasingly integrated with e-learning applications in the workplace for active learning and knowledge construction.

Web 2.0 Changes the Workplace

The social-technological innovations from Web 2.0 have considerably affected education and employment, restructured businesses, and driven economic change. When the idea of Web 2.0 emerged, many businesses and organizations found themselves facing new challenges and opportunities. Businesses increasingly rely on horizontal, collaborative relationships among employees, customers, and business partners on a global scale. The ability to communicate and collaborate with people inside and outside the business is becoming a key success factor in a fast-growing global business environment. The new landscape driven by Web 2.0 and its culture of networking, sharing, and collaboration is fundamentally altering people's relationships and activities with information and knowledge in the workplace.

Andrew McAfee coined the term *Enterprise 2.0* to describe how Web 2.0 technologies can be used in organizational settings, with a view to helping employees, customers, and partners to collaborate, share, and organize information via social media. Enterprise 2.0 is increasingly being integrated into the business world, changing the processes and culture in the workplace. Web 2.0 technologies become critical for many facets of

business operations: communication with customers and partners, streamlined business processes, analysis of data for forecasts and decision making, and use of digital media for marketing campaigns. Blogs, for example, facilitate reports on project status and, combined with RSS readers, provide an effective way for project sponsors to track the progress of the project. Wikis improve information sharing within and between teams while reducing document production and e-mail communication. With these Web 2.0 tools, people can collaborate more and travel less; self-managing teams can flatten organizations and reduce overhead; communities of practice can share best practices and reduce the number of costly mistakes.

However, Web 2.0 trends may lead to a plethora of promises by enthusiastic technologists. It is not enough simply to deploy the new technologies of interaction and collaboration and then sit back and wait for the benefits to accrue. Social media software integrated into existing business functions may lead to dramatic changes in business processes and challenges in internal communications. The first challenge is that busy employees may ignore or resist the new technologies despite training and prodding. The second challenge is that the use of the technologies may lead to unintended outcomes. Web 2.0 challenges the traditional top-down structure and command-and-control management approaches. It is usually unknown what outcomes will emerge as a result of opening up the interaction space. What will happen if the content on the new platform is uncomfortable for powerful people within a company? This poses a threat to traditional managers who see virtual participation as something that might potentially lead to chaos. Meanwhile, open communication via social media may also bring challenges to employees who expect to be directed instead of to be empowered.

To deal with the challenges, a new style of leadership is required to emphasize genuine listening, dialogue, and stimulation. Many employees are willing to participate when given signals and evidence that their input is being utilized. Moreover, making participation visible may stimulate new contributions and avoid unproductive discussions. In short, the implementation of Web 2.0 in the workplace requires not only the participation from employees at the grassroots level but also the involvement of senior management.

Moreover, there are other challenges caused by using Web 2.0 technologies. For many organizations, a common problem is the proliferation of information silos posed by the use of these new tools. Furthermore, security breaches are taking place as a result of increased Internet usage at work. Individual deployment of unauthorized stand-alone products is increasingly becoming a major security problem for many organizations. The problem is not about people from outside breaking in, but about people from inside breaking out. Internal and external unified communication systems promote the sharing of all resources within and across organizations in ways that were not previously possible; but without secure communications systems, it is impossible for organizations to share resources reliably and cost effectively. A model for organizing and securing information in a meaningful and effective way becomes an integral part for implementation of Web 2.0 in the workplace.

Web 3.0 and Beyond

The Internet development is accelerating at such a speed that Web 3.0 is arriving. *Web 3.0* is the term to describe the evolution of the Web as an extension of Web 2.0; there is much debate about what to call this new phase. Web 3.0 is also known as Semantic Web. The Semantic Web provides a common framework that allows data to be shared and reused across application, enterprise, and community boundaries. In a Semantic Web, contents are defined and linked using formalized representation technologies, enabling machines to interpret and process information on the Web. The Semantic Web has been described as the backbone for e-learning because it supports semantic annotation of content for reuse, the combination of learning resources, and personalized and context-sensitive learning.

Web 3.0 or Semantic Web is also called the *Intelligent Web* and enables automated agents to access the Web and perform tasks on behalf of users more intelligently by using Web content with semantic information. In short, Web 3.0, equipped with semantic Web technologies, distributed databases, natural language processing, machine learning, machine reasoning, and autonomous agents will be more connected, open, and intelligent.

The convergence of business, technical, and economic trends has driven the adoption of Web 2.0/3.0 technologies to make both the practice and outputs of knowledge work visible. Because of the challenges these technologies bring, there will likely be significant differences in learning and communication strategies. Because of the opportunities these technologies bring, these differences will matter a great deal.

Minhong Wang

See also Collaboration and Social Networking; Collaborative Learning With Technology; Diffusion of New Technologies in the Workplace; Education in Workplace Settings; Information and Communication Technologies: Knowledge Management; Social Media and Networking; Social Media in the Workplace; Web 2.0 and Beyond

Further Readings

Cheng, B., Wang, M., Mørch, A., Chen, N.-S., Kinshuk, & Spector, J. M. (2014). Research on e-learning in the workplace 2000–2012: A bibliometric analysis of the literature. *Educational Research Review, 11*, 56–72.

McAfee, A. (2009). *Enterprise 2.0: New collaborative tools for your organization's toughest challenges.* Boston, MA: Harvard Business Press.

Nonaka, I., & Takeuchi, H. (1995). *The knowledge-creating company: How Japanese companies create the dynamics of innovation.* New York, NY: Oxford University Press.

O'Reilly, T. (2005). *What is Web 2.0: Design patterns and business models for the next generation of software.* Retrieved from http://www.oreillynet.com/pub/a/oreilly/tim/news/2005/09/30/what-is-web-20.html

Wang, M. (2011). Integrating organizational, social, and individual perspectives in Web 2.0-based workplace e-learning. *Information Systems Frontiers, 13*(2), 191–205.

WIKIS AS A COLLABORATION TOOL

The term *wiki* comes from the Hawaiian phrase *wiki wiki*, which means "quick," "fast," "speedy," or "hurry." Wiki originated from the work of Ward Cunningham, who created the first wiki called *WikiWikiWeb* in 1995. The best-known example of a wiki is Wikipedia, the world's largest online encyclopedia constructed by users. Many other examples of wikis can be found in nearly every domain, including business, industry, and education. Wikis are a type of Web 2.0 technologies that enable people to share information, collaborate, and communicate with each other. Wikis are a type of social software that includes blogs, forums, podcasting, social networking, social bookmarking, Flickr, Facebook, and del.icio.us. More specifically, a wiki is a collection of webpages that are continuously edited collaboratively by multiple users. As such, wiki technology matches the evolution of the networked society that requires collaborative team skills. This entry discusses software for creating wikis, the use of wikis as a repository for shared information, the use of wikis in education, and the implications of wikis for teaching and learning.

Wiki Software Tools

There is a wide range of software tools for creating wikis. These are classified in two broad categories. The first one includes wiki services or wiki farms that are hosted by a service provider. The services may be free or fee-based. Examples of popular wiki farms are Wikispaces, Wikidot, and PBworks. The second category involves wiki tools that can be directly installed on one's own server, such as PmWiki, TWiki, Tiki Wiki, and MediaWiki, which is one of the best known tools, originally for use on Wikipedia, with thousands of applications. The content of MediaWiki consists of articles with a title and a body that may include text, images, figures, or other media. A community of users edits articles collaboratively. MediaWiki has a number of basic components, such as tool bars, navigation, and user options, that help users edit articles, as shown in Figure 1.

The key features of wiki software tools are ease of use, simplicity, flexibility, and speed of use. These features are implemented through a simple interface that enables multiple users to collaboratively create, edit, and publish content using a simplified HTML language, including text, paragraphs and headings, links, images, tables, lists, and files. Each edit is stored in a history log that records all changes being made, enabling users to "roll back" and recover previous content, and compare different versions of the wiki. Wikis also have a discussion page that enables asynchronous written communication, providing a space for negotiation and communication. In addition, wiki tools provide a number of technical functionalities that support the creation of wiki applications, such as technical support through

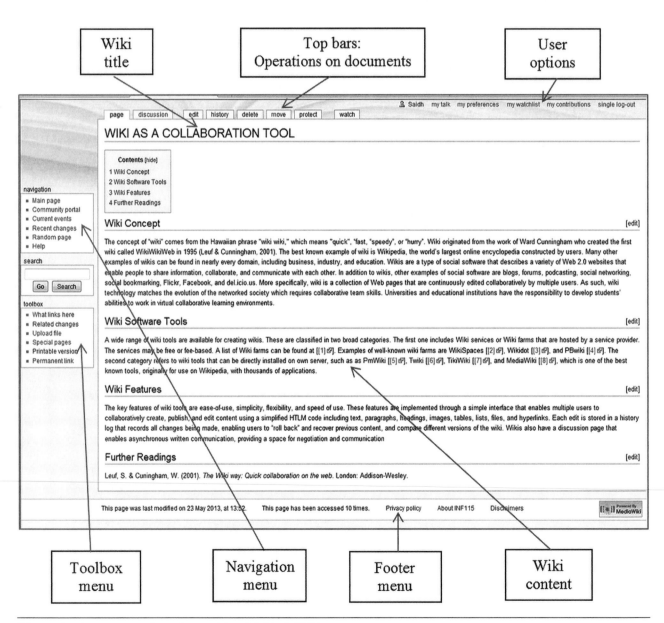

Figure 1 A representation of an article with MediaWiki components

developer and user documentation, user rights management and registration, tracking and restoring capabilities through the history log, browser and cross-platform compatibility, and installation procedures.

Wikis as Repository for Shared Information

Wikis as collaboration tools serve as a repository for shared information among online users in a variety of contexts. They provide an online space to create, edit, and store documents. Wikis include a wide range of applications from small-scale group projects with few pages to large applications with hundreds of pages. Well-known organizations such as IBM, Nokia, SUN Microsystems, Motorola Systems, and many other private companies and public institutions use wikis for project knowledge organization, document management, communication, and marketing. Wikis can be established as a private (or restricted) space, where individual users can participate, or public area, where anyone can be involved in information sharing. Wikis as collaboration tools facilitate collaborative writing and coauthoring. Alterations and changes are made directly in the text being written. Argumentations and critical reflections accompanying the revisions may be made in the discussion page. The main advantages of wikis as collaboration tools are as follows:

- Wikis can be accessed and edited from any location and any time, and by users with a computer, a Web browser, and an Internet connection.
- All participating users have access to the same version of the wiki.
- All previous versions of the wiki are available to users, allowing them to easily view the content and all previous modifications.
- Users can communicate and exchange information through the discussion page by posting comments and reflections.

Wikis in Education

Wikis used as collaboration tools can support teaching and learning processes in educational settings, in addition to supporting knowledge and information sharing in business, industry, commercial enterprises, and public institutions. Wikis have been used to support a variety of teaching and learning purposes in nearly all fields of education ranging from mathematics, sciences, arts, language, and engineering, to construction and health care. Examples of wiki uses in education are peer assessment, glossary, group project, course-content authoring, class project, course evaluation, teaching materials, knowledge repository, digital stories, and wiki books.

As such, wiki-based environments provide educators with opportunities for creating socially engaged tasks that require active student participation and knowledge construction. However, wiki use in education might not be easy and straightforward or intuitive for teachers and students for many reasons: insufficient training and familiarity with wiki technology, lack of group work and collaborative skills, lack of advanced functionality for written communication and discussion, insufficient customization of wikis, questions of accuracy and veracity of information being posted, and difficulties of negotiating content. In addition to using wikis for educational purposes, students can create new wiki applications. To produce a wiki of good quality, students need technical training to become familiar with wiki functionalities. Then, they should develop a sense of how collaboration can be achieved by coordinating their efforts. Finally, they need to be knowledgeable in the wiki content to be produced.

The utilization of wikis in education as a collaboration tool is in accord with constructivist and sociocultural learning theories that promote social engagement, collaboration, and group-based learning. *Collaborative learning* is an umbrella term for a variety of educational activities, including collaborative writing that aims at producing a joint written document by two or more students. Wiki-based collaborative writing encompasses knowledge about techniques used to produce a wiki content that is adapted to users' characteristics. It also involves writing strategies, roles mode (editor, writer, reviewer, etc.), document control, access modes, editing and viewing of the document, and discussion and communication modes.

Unlike blogs, which are organized chronologically with the most recent post on the top, wiki pages are structured around a specific content and purpose. The content of the wiki may be configured from multiple sources depending on the subject being studied. The study information may be found in textbooks and online course materials, retrieved from the Web, developed from the ground, or a combination. The writing development process may involve a number of structured steps such as information gathering, collaborative planning of the general structure of the wiki, development of the various parts of the wiki, and peer reviewing. Important for the content is the way it is transformed to a wiki-based form using basic HTML techniques to structure the document and adapt the material to users' characteristics.

Implications of Wikis for Teaching and Learning

Wikis in education are more than the addition of wiki technology, content, and collaborative learning. Rather, a wiki in education emerges from the interactions of these three components. It requires the acquisition of HTML basics to represent the wiki content, collaborative methods to create the content, and an understanding of the content and purpose of the wiki. The interweaving of these three components creates a new form of knowledge that students and teachers can bring into play any time they produce wikis for teaching and learning purposes. Wikis are not the only collaboration tools. Other tools such as knowledge management systems and electronic communication tools may be used to share information, but if the learning goal is to promote genuine collaboration, then it is appropriate to use wikis in education.

Said Hadjerrouit

See also Collaborative Communication Tools and Technologies; Collaborative Learning and 21st-Century Skills; Collaborative Learning With Technology; Web 2.0 and Beyond

Further Readings

Hadjerrouit, S. (2012). Wiki-based collaborative learning in higher education: A pedagogical evaluation. *International Journal of Innovation and Learning, 12*(1), 6–26.

Leuf, B., & Cunningham, W. (2001). *The wiki way: Quick collaboration on the Web.* Reading, MA: Addison-Wesley.

Meishar-Tal, H., & Gorsky, P. (2010). Wikis: What students do or not do when writing collaboratively. *Open Learning: The Journal of Open, Distance and e-Learning, 25*(1), 25–35.

Parker, K. R., & Chao, J. T. (2007). Wiki as a teaching tool. *Interdisciplinary Journal of Knowledge and Learning Objects, 3,* 57–72.

Thomas, P., King, D., & Minocha, S. (2009). The effective use of a simple wiki to support collaborative learning activities. *Computer Science Education, 19*(4), 293–313.

Trentin, G. (2009). Using a wiki to evaluate individual contribution to a collaborative learning project. *Journal of Computer Assisted Learning, 25,* 43–55.

Vygotsky, L. S. (1978). *Mind in society: The development of higher psychological processes.* Cambridge, MA: Cambridge University Press.

Websites

MediaWiki: http://www.mediawiki.org/wiki/MediaWiki

PBworks: http://pbworks.com

PmWiki: http://www.pmwiki.org/wiki/PmWiki/PmWiki

Tiki Wiki: http://info.tiki.org

TWiki: http://twiki.org

Wiki Farms list: http://c2.com/cgi/wiki?WikiFarms

Wikidot: http://www.wikidot.com

Wikispaces: http://wikispaces.com

WORKFLOW ANALYSIS

A universal way to describe any kind of work done by organizations is that inputs (I) are gathered, put through some kind of process (P), and result in outputs (O). This simple IPO model describes the machining and assembly of parts to make a jet engine, the treatment given to patients in a hospital, the education of students in a school, or any other kind of organizational work. The key to creating the outputs is the *workflow*, an organizational process that is designed to result in a specific kind of output. Workflow analysis is a technology for both describing an existing workflow and for evaluating it to allow change and improvement.

Workflow analysis is like building a jigsaw puzzle. Individuals may go about assembling a jigsaw puzzle in any way they choose, and in a group of people, different approaches will be observed. A designed workflow might specify that the first step is to find the four pieces with right angles—the four corners of the puzzle—then sort through the pieces to find ones with properties similar to the corners (color, pattern, etc.) before trying to fit them together, and repeat these steps and progressively build inward toward the middle. An organization needs to design its processes to ensure its outputs will meet all specifications, including cost, schedule, and quality.

It might seem that once a workflow is designed, it will remain that way indefinitely. That is almost never the case—workflows change and evolve over time. When a worker is hired, that person brings attributes that affect the way he works. For example, an accountant who is very proud of never making mistakes checks everything three times but seldom gets things done on time; a highly efficient nurse skips recording patient data until the end of a shift but, therefore, makes dangerous mistakes. Temporary changes to organization structure become permanent; a one-time project evolves into a new product line, for example. Workflow change is usually evolutionary, so change creeps into a workflow slowly and accumulates over time, bringing both positive and negative effects.

Workflow analysis can bring enormous benefits. One major hospital did a workflow analysis of processing a pneumonia patient through treatment and found that 17 of the 68 total steps were helpful while the other 51 steps were not. To obtain an International Organization for Standardization (ISO) 9002 process certification at a facility in England, a major chemical company found from its workflow analysis that only 1,100 of 3,000 process tests were needed, that cycle time fell from 15 to 1½ days at one plant, and that first-pass yields of product increased from 72% to 92% at another. A major analysis of avionics maintenance processes in the U.S. Navy during the Cold War resulted in a sixfold increase in productivity that saved hundreds of millions of dollars in terms of acquisition of new testers.

This entry focuses on technologies associated with workflow analysis, including a discussion of their strengths and weaknesses and whether such technologies compete or complement each other.

Workflow Analysis Technologies

There are two major approaches to workflow analysis, and both use technology in different ways. First, there is an eclectic set of approaches that may be described as graphic free style (GFS) that produces workflow maps for analysis. These GFS maps may be as simple as linked lines and circles, or applications of flowcharting and other information-technology diagramming methods, or video recordings of on-site work activities. The maps may serve many purposes, among them being process improvement, quality improvement and control, cost control, and job description. Much of the GFS approach grew from the need to *document what you do, and do what you document* as required for quality certifications from the ISO. The quality movement of the 1980s and 1990s added momentum to the use of these methods, and they have been institutionalized in Toyota's Lean Management practices.

The second major technology is the application of specialized software to both map the workflow and capture workflow data; this is commonly described as business process mapping, or BPM. BPM is based on a predefined model of a workflow, such that an organization must conform to the software model and use it to describe and measure events and outcomes in the workflow. BPM typically requires extensive training and preparation to install and deploy the software; version 9 of Oracle's PeopleSoft manual, for example, consists of 30 chapters and three appendices, and is over 500 pages long. Thus, specialized staff and equipment are necessary to install and maintain BPM software.

Relative Strengths and Weaknesses

Both GFS and BPM have strengths and weaknesses. GFS maps are relatively easy to create and thus permit faster application than BPM (the harder and longer job is to figure out what is really going on in a workflow). GFS is extremely flexible and can be applied to a process in a church organization equally as well as a tractor factory. Mapping software support can be as simple as the drawing tools in a word processor, and there are a number of effective freeware programs that can support GFS. Few or no specialized staff are required to

maintain it; in fact, GFS can be learned and applied by nearly anyone with a modest time investment. GFS is capable of capturing the tacit knowledge that individuals bring to a workflow or create within it, that is inevitably both a cause and a consequence of workflow evolution.

However, the format of GFS is difficult to control, and it is common for GFS applications to become a polyglot of different mapping symbols depending on the people doing the mapping. Where lines and circles are fine for one mapper, another may want to use every flowcharting symbol known to exist. There is no standard GFS system, and configuration control may be problematic. GFS does not automatically capture process data, and after a workflow map is completed, additional effort is required to measure workflow performance.

BPM methods, on the other hand, are good at both standardizing the method of mapping as well as capturing data on workflow processes; in fact, the capture of workflow data is one of the key objectives of most BPM tools so that organizations obtain process data as soon as the technology is deployed. The language of BPM is determined by the product selected and is almost entirely standard throughout the enterprise, a valuable characteristic for geographically dispersed organizations. Users have help with the BPM application through online tools as well as through the support staff and vendors eager to see their product perform.

But BPM has its drawbacks. It is far more expensive than GFS, both for initial acquisition and service-life support. The predesigned structure of most BPM systems limits its flexibility, and when a process that works cannot be accommodated by a BPM application, it is often necessary to change the process—a common complaint about BPM rigidity is that the BPM process is taking precedence of what is and should be occurring. In some cases, this rigidity has been a major contributor to outright abandonment of BPM applications. BPM is not effective at capturing tacit knowledge and thus has difficulty accommodating process characteristics other than those anticipated by the BPM model; this has sometimes lowered workforce morale in BPM implementations. As with GFS, there is no standard language for BPM.

Competitors or Complements?

Many view GFS and BPM as alternative, even competing, technologies for workflow analysis, but they may be better regarded as complements. A GFS workflow map, created prior to implementation of a BPM tool, can both yield the benefits of GFS and strengthen the BPM results. GFS information can be a basis for BPM roll-out decisions, where those processes most compatible with the BPM model can be inducted first, building BPM successes that improve the attractiveness of extended applications. Complex processes or those with significant embedded tacit knowledge will be discovered prior to BPM implementation, which may help avoid many of the rigidity issues that accompany BPM. These processes may be changed, but in some cases, they may simply be exempted from BPM, while inputs and outputs are still measured and recorded. Both GFS and BPM technologies are disruptive, and human beings generally resist change; in all cases, GFS provides opportunities for staff to participate in the workflow analysis, making the outcomes of workflow analysis less likely to be perceived as imposed.

GFS workflow analysis prepares a map that allows simulation software to be used to reflect the actual flow of work in a process. GFS methods allow the actual flow of work to emerge; this can be evaluated against other options, including potential changes from BPM. Using both tools together can thus be highly complementary.

John L. Kmetz

See also Causal Influence Diagrams; Cognitive Task Analysis; Knowledge and Skill Hierarchies; Learning by Modeling; Tools for Modeling and Simulation

Further Readings

Harmon, P. (2007). *Business process change: A guide for business managers and BPM and six sigma professionals* (2nd ed.). New York, NY: Morgan Kaufmann.

Kmetz, J. L. (2012). *Mapping workflows and managing knowledge: Capturing formal and tacit knowledge to improve performance*. New York, NY: Business Expert Press.

Appendix A: Chronology

The "History of Educational Technology" entry in this encyclopedia focuses on notable developments in the 20th century, with some discussion of earlier developments and those emerging in the 21st century. This chronology represents a view of educational technology developments from ancient times to the present. It is necessarily a partial view. Educational technology developments can be organized by associated developments in psychology (e.g., behaviorism, cognitivism, socio-constructivism, neuropsychology), by associated instructional approaches and strategies (e.g., apprenticeship, expository methods, programmed instruction, collaborative learning), or by other groupings, such as educational goal (e.g., productive worker, effective problem solver, critical thinker, responsible citizen). This chronology avoids such groupings because they tend to oversimplify trends, and they are easily used to suggest that there is only one good approach to supporting learning, instruction, and performance with technology—an unsupported and nonscientific view. The grouping here is by major period in history with selected technology developments that have had an impact on learning, instruction, and performance and include a few notes with regard to the perspectives, approaches, and goals associated with that development.

The intent is to convey the rapidly increasing rate of educational technologies that more or less parallels the rapid growth in technology in general. In addition, this chronology suggests a pattern that more or less parallels the growth of democracy and the democratization of education. Others can surely add additional notable developments, identify other important trends, and draw conclusions about the perspectives, approaches, and goals reflected in those developments. Many of the technologies in Table 1 were introduced for non-educational purposes and might be viewed as enabling technologies that later found use to support learning and instruction. This is a fact that permeates the history of educational technology—namely, a technology introduced in support of business, commerce, manufacturing, science, warfighting, or other enterprise often finds a use in support of education. Perhaps a new trend is developing that places initial emphasis on developing technologies for educational purposes. Perhaps. In any case, this chronology is also intended to suggest that emphasis should be placed on how developments evolve because typically, no single event or single person is or will be responsible for the design, development, and deployment of a technology that will improve learning, instruction, and performance.

Table 1 Overview of AES systems

Period	Dates	Technology/ Development	Notes
Ancient	~3000 BCE	Abacus	Early counting devices used to support commerce and productivity.
	~3000 BCE	Written language	Early text carved on stone tablets and later written on papyrus for record keeping in support of trade; charts and maps eventually added to text-based artifacts.
	~1500 BCE– ~400 BCE	Early schools and organized curricula	As early as ~1500 BCE in China; developed with the teachings of Confucius, Socrates, and Buddha (~550 to 350 BCE); emphasis on living well and ethics introduced in schools in this period.

(Continued)

Table 1   (Continued)

Period	Dates	Technology/ Development	Notes
Middle Ages	~1050–1450	Printing press	A movable type printing press was developed in China around 1050; an improved mechanical press developed by Johannes Gutenberg in 1450; mass production of books, especially religious and literary works; education for all made possible.
1500–1900	~1550	Slide rule	Developed by William Oughtred to support the work of engineers and mathematicians.
	~1550	Pencil	Graphite writing instruments encased in wood for personal use developed in Italy.
	~1608	Telescope	Refracting lens developed by Dutch scientists and then Galileo to explore the night sky and support astronomers.
	~1790–1810	Chalkboard	Chalkboards introduced for use by teachers to present information to all students at the same time.
	1810–1840	Punch card storage	Punch card storage supported the development of Charles Babbage's difference and analytical engines.
	1839	Camera	Louis Daguerre introduces the daguerreotype, making photography practical.
	1890s	Radio	Heinrich Hertz, Nicola Tesla, and others develop wireless transmission of electromagnetic waves, making synchronous mass communication and mass education possible.
	1890s	Moving pictures	Thomas Edison's kinetoscope introduced following the earlier development of the magic lantern and related devices.
20th century (1st half)	1915 and after	Instructional films	Instructional films have been used ever since to demonstrate procedures and present dramatic events.
	1915 and after	Audiovisual technologies	Technologies to create images and integrate them with text were commonplace in educational settings in the 1930s.
	1925	Television	John Logie Baird's demonstration of televised images in London using technologies developed in the previous century; television eventually supports mass communication and education along with radio.
	1945	ENIAC	Electronic Numerical Integrator and Computer (ENIAC) developed by John Mauchley and J. Presper Eckert at the University of Pennsylvania for the U.S. Army to solve complex numerical problems.
	1947	Transistor	Invented by William Schockley's team at Bell Labs; significant reduction in size by replacing vacuum tube technology.
	1948	Skinner box	Device invented by B. F. Skinner to demonstrate operant conditioning and the effects of reinforcement, following the puzzle boxes created by J. B. Watson and E. L. Thorndike.
	1949	Short code	An early high-level programming language created by John Mauchley that led to many subsequent high-level programming languages that eventually made educational computing possible.

Table 1   (Continued)

Period	Dates	Technology/ Development	Notes
20th century (2nd half)	1953	IBM 701 computer	Computers designed for business and industry become available and create the need for training on their use.
	1958	Integrated circuit	Invented by Jack Kilby at Texas Instruments and Robert Noyce at Fairchild Semiconductor; significant reduction in size with increased processing speeds.
	1967	PLATO	Programmed Logic for Automated Teaching Operations (PLATO), developed by Don Bitzer and colleagues at the University of Illinois.
	1968	TICCIT	Time-Shared, Interactive, Computer-Controlled Information Television (TICCIT), developed by Mitre Corporation with the University of Texas and Brigham Young University in the United States; used M. David Merrill's component display theory to structure and present lessons.
	1969	ARPANET	Advanced Research Project Agency's packet switching large-scale network of networks created to connect scientists and engineers working for the U.S. Department of Defense.
	1974	Alto	Xerox Palo Alto Research Center creates the first computer workstation with a mouse.
	1977	Commodore PET	The Personal Electronic Transactor (PET) was one of the first personal computers, quickly followed by the Apple II and many other personal computers with printed circuit boards using large-scale integrated circuits.
	1981	IBM PC	IBM enters the world of personal computing with an INTEL 8088 processor and MS-DOS operating system.
	1982	Internet	The Internet Protocol suite (TCP/IP) emerges along with consolidation of related efforts in the form of the global Internet with the support of the National Science Foundation in the United States.
	1991	Information superhighway	The High Performance Computing and Communication Act was crafted by U.S. senator Albert Gore and passed, leading to large-scale expansion of the Internet.
	1990s	An explosion of educational applications occurs	In the last decade of the 20th century, many course-authoring systems and learning management systems were introduced; intelligent tutoring systems were developed for a variety of educational applications, virtual learning environments, and virtual realities; and new approaches to learning, instruction, and performance proliferated.
21st century	2000	Augmented reality	Bruce H. Thomas launches ARQuake, an early augmented reality game building on a great deal of work in the area of virtual reality in the previous century.
	2002	Serious games	David Rejecsk and Ben Sawyer at the Woodrow Wilson International Center initiate the serious games initiative.
	2002	Social networking	The social networking site called Friendster is launched, followed quickly by many others, including Myspace, LinkedIn, and Facebook.

(Continued)

Table I   (Continued)

Period	Dates	Technology/ Development	Notes
	2006	Cloud computing	Amazon launches its Web Services bringing cloud computing to the forefront of distributing computer technologies.
	2008	MOOCs	Massive open online courses (MOOCs) are initiated with a course at Athabasca University in Canada.
	2012	Learning analytics	EDUCAUSE launches the learning analytics initiative to make practical the use of big data to improve learning.
	2014	Wearable technologies	Google Glass is available to the general public.
	???	Personalized learning	The application of technologies (e.g., learning analytics, dynamic student profiling, cognitive task analysis) to create just-in-time, just-on-task, and customized lessons and courses likely to be engaging and effective for individual learners with different backgrounds, interests, and learning histories.

Table 2   Links to other historical representations of educational technology

Resource Name/Description	Link
Educational Technology: A Definition with Commentary (AECT)	http://aectorg.yourwebhosting.com/publications/EducationalTechnology/
Educational Technology in Schools	http://elearninginfographics.com/timeline-of-educational-technology-in-schools-infographic/
Educational Technology Timeline (students at the University of Illinois)	http://people.lis.illinois.edu/~chip/projects/timeline.shtml
Edudemic's Quick Look at the History of Educational Technology	http://www.edudemic.com/a-quick-look-at-the-history-of-education-technology/
EduTech Wiki (Daniel K. Schneider)	http://edutechwiki.unige.ch/en/Educational_technology
History and Definition of Instructional Technology	http://arcmit01.uncw.edu/torkildsent/history_definition.htm; http://c.ymcdn.com/sites/aect.site-ym.com/resource/resmgr/AECT_Documents/AECTstandardsREV2005.pdf
History of Computers in Education	http://www.csulb.edu/~murdock/histofcs.html
History of Educational Technology (History of Education Media blog)	http://blitzlondon.blogspot.hk/2012/10/history-of-educational-technology.html
A History of Instructional Design and Technology (Robert A. Reiser) (behind a paywall)	http://link.springer.com/article/10.1007/BF02504506
Instructional Design Timeline	http://www.instructionaldesigncentral.com/htm/IDC_instructionaltechnology timeline.htm
Learning Machines (interactive NY Times website)	http://www.nytimes.com/interactive/2010/09/19/magazine/classroom-technology.html?src=tptw&_r=0

Table 2

Resource Name/Description	Link
Major Developments in Instructional Technology (20th Century)	http://www.indiana.edu/~idt/shortpapers/documents/ITduring20.html
Practice of instructional technology	http://www.personal.psu.edu/wxh139/IT_history.htm
UCSF Ed Tech History	https://wiki.library.ucsf.edu/display/EdTechStrategic/0.+UCSF+Ed+Tech+History
Wikipedia: Educational Technology	http://en.wikipedia.org/wiki/Educational_technology

In addition to these resources, one can also find additional resources on the Association for Educational Communications and Technology (AECT) website (see http://aect.site-ym.com) and many other locations on the Internet. For a view of 21st-century developments, one can consult the website of the New Media Consortium (see www.nmc.org) and view the *Horizon Reports*, which have been published each year since 2002 and identify and discuss emerging technologies likely to have an impact on learning, instruction, and performance.

J. Michael Spector, Dirk Ifenthaler,
Tristan E. Johnson, Wilhelmina C. Savenye,
and Minhong Wang

Appendix B: Glossary

accelerated learning A teaching and learning approach that involves the mental, emotional, and physical being of the learner to facilitate and expedite learning based on a better understanding of how the human brain functions, particularly in young adults.

activity theory A conceptual framework based on the activities humans perform on objects in the real world and the tools that are used to accomplish these activities.

adaptive and responsive websites Websites that continuously respond to changes in the context, that are optimized for a wide range of contexts, or that automatically make adjustments to layout and displays to fit a user's device.

anchored instruction An approach to designing learning environments that situates learning in a meaningful problem-solving or inquiry context.

assistive technology A product, device, or piece of equipment used to maintain, increase, or improve the functional capabilities of individuals with disabilities, impairments, or special needs.

augmented reality The addition of a computer-assisted contextual layer of information overlaid on a real-world context or situation, creating an enhanced or augmented reality.

biofeedback learning environment A holistic and systemic educational setting established through traditional biofeedback modalities coupled with other instructional and learning resources.

causal influence diagram A technique used by system dynamists to model the dynamic feedback relationships between the various components of a large and dynamic complex system.

change agency The process, role, or paradigm associated with introducing an innovation into a situation or its diffusion within a particular context.

cloud computing The use of a ubiquitous, easy-to-access, and readily available network of Internet servers to store files and provide services.

cognitive load theory An instructional/interface design theory based on the notion of identifying and minimizing extraneous and intrinsic cognitive load and maximizing germane load to optimize learning and performance.

competency-based approach An approach to learning and instruction that begins with specific sets of knowledge and skills (competencies) that a learner should master to be considered competent or certified in that particular domain.

component display theory The theory that specifies that instruction is more effective to the extent that it contains necessary primary (rules, examples, recall, and practice) and secondary (prerequisites, objectives, helps, mnemonics, and feedback) presentation forms.

computer adaptive assessment An assessment technique that adapts to a specific test-taker by identifying what the individual already knows and a likely range of subsequent questions to see the extent to which a learner has mastered the topic.

Creative Commons An intellectual property approach that grants various permissions to individuals to use copyrighted works; it involves a nonprofit organization that offers licenses, which copyright owners may use to allow different levels of use of their copyrighted works or waive all copyright interests in their works, putting them into the public domain.

criterion-based assessment A type of assessment that determines the extent to which a learner has mastered specific learning objectives; this approach is often found in competency-based approaches to learning.

cyberinfrastructure for learning and instruction Research and collaboration involving networked environments that provide (a) services including processing, data acquisition, storage, information integration, and visualization; (b) digital resources including text and media artifacts, software tools, and collections of scientific data; and (c) access to specialized tools including remote instrumentation, sensors and actuators, modeling tools, simulations, and interactive visualization tools.

cybersecurity The discipline of protecting information environments; it generally involves protecting and assuring the confidentiality, integrity, and availability of information and the information environments involved.

data streaming A method used to transfer data from a remote server to a user's computer or mobile device, allowing an application to run without having to wait until the file has downloaded completely.

diffusion In discussions of technology, *diffusion* refers to the spread of access to and usage of the technology; factors affecting diffusion include the availability of trial versions and levels, observed usage by colleagues, desirable attributes, and match with specific interests and needs.

digital archives Collections or repositories of materials that were originally in digital format (e.g., podcasts, videos, sound recordings, word-processing documents, wikis, and blogs) or nondigital formats, including paper-based or analog artifacts that have been digitized (e.g., books, official documents, tape recordings).

digital curation A set of interdisciplinary activities for collection, preservation, maintenance, and archiving of digital information and research data to preserve and add value to the information and data throughout their life cycles.

digital literacy Proficiency in the use and application of a wide range of digital tools, media, and resources, combined with a knowledge and understanding of the norms and practices of appropriate use of tools and resources.

digital repository A large database for the storage, retrieval, and reuse of digital artifacts and learning objects.

disruptive innovations New technologies and ways of learning and teaching that drastically change prior practice; examples include handheld mobile devices (e.g., smartphones, tablets), flipped classrooms, and personalized instruction.

distance education The use of Internet-supported instructional tools and learning environments to link teachers and students who are not together in a classroom.

embodied learning systems Systems designed to mimic the way the mind works; embodied learning systems create user transactions that pair and reinforce relationships between sensory manipulation and targeted knowledge development.

emotion control The ability of a learner to control or manage the many affective factors affecting his or her ability to act on goals (*see* motivation and volition).

engaged learning The formation of a deep connection between a student and academic material or a learning system.

epistemic beliefs The beliefs that a learner has about the subject domain and learning in general as well as a learner's self-assessment of his or her ability to master learning tasks in that domain.

e-portfolios A collection of work, objects, or documented processes selected by the portfolio author and put into an electronic or digital format; e-portfolios can contain text, images, video, or sound.

experiential learning An educational lesson or sequence that engages a learner in applying knowledge and skills previously introduced; experiential learning offers the learner opportunities to perform, share, analyze, connect, and apply new information.

flight simulator A simulated environment designed for pilot training to enable pilots to evaluate available information regarding the flight environment and experience the effects of their decisions in a highly realistic simulation setting; the use of a simulation allows pilots to practice in unusual situations that are too risky for live training and to develop strategies for handling a multitude of situations.

formative assessment Assessments provided to students during an instructional sequence with the goal of helping students master content and succeed in a course or program (also known as formative feedback).

four-component instructional design (4C/ID) An instructional design approach for complex learning tasks that distinguishes recurrent from nonrecurrent tasks and suggests heuristics to support nonrecurrent tasks and just-in-time information to support recurrent tasks; in both cases, the notion of increasing task classes is used to develop competency and whole-task training is emphasized.

game-based inquiry learning Games that promote seeking answers or solutions to a question; they typically begin with a question or problem situation that is likely to engage learners in efforts to seek answers or resolve the problem situation, and, as a consequence, develop understanding.

game-based transformational play Games that promote learning based on two basic notions: (a) intentionality, which requires that a learner be given the responsibility and power to make thoughtful choices (e.g., ask questions, explore, respond to prompts, solve problems) that influence various aspects of the narrative and its outcomes; and (b) legitimacy, which requires that the academic content within the game be meaningfully and believably connected to solving the dilemmas and achieving the goals of the narrative.

gamification The inclusion of aspects of a game in an instructional sequence, often to create motivation and focus to promote learning.

gesture-based learning Instructional systems and learning environments in which human gestures and bodily movement are included as forms of interaction.

haptic technologies Technologies involving kinesthetic movement and tactile sensation that engage the learner in making conscious decisions about what to move, how to move, and the types of manipulations that are made in a three-dimensional environment; haptic technologies are often found in simulators in which touching and feeling are an important aspect of learning.

head-mounted display A device that provides an enhanced view of surroundings; an example is a head-mounted display that allows a pilot to interact with a combination of real and virtual views of the outside world while flying the plane.

holographic imaging The capture of an actual object or scene from multiple perspectives resulting in a three-dimensional image that appears to adjust proportionally as a viewer shifts his or her perspective.

human performance technology The systematic and principled practice of improving the productivity of organizations and individuals through coordinated interventions that show measured results.

human-computer interaction A field formed by the intersection of human physiology, psychology, and behavior, especially regarding the use of and interaction with computer systems and digital devices.

identity in social media The blending of text and visual elements that in combination distinguish a particular social media user and allow each user to be individually identified and described.

informal learning Learning that occurs outside a school or training situation; it is a part of lifelong learning, typically open-ended and less organized and systematic than formal learning situations; examples include museum visits, ungraded online tutorials, and documentaries.

information visualization The conversion of data (numeric, textual, or multimedia) into visual representations; usually, data are converted into forms that differ from their original modality (e.g., musical notation is notational but it represents sounds).

instructional design Analysis, planning, design, development, implementation, management and evaluation of instructional systems, learning environments, and performance improvement interventions.

instructional transaction theory The extension of component display theory to include the notion of templates to support learning for activities (what people do), processes (how things work), and entities (concrete and abstract things) as the specific kinds of things to be learned.

intellectual property Human creations that can be protected by law; in the United States, there are three recognized types: (a) original works by authors (copyright law); (b) distinctive words, phrases, logos, or other graphic symbols (trademark law); and (c) inventions, discoveries, or procedures of a person or entity (patent law).

intelligent tutoring system (ITS) A computer system that can function as a human tutor partially or fully to help a student learn and master content, often making use of a database of common mistakes and misunderstandings to generate a unit of instruction to a learner who is faltering; generally includes a model of the domain to be learned, an instructional model, and a dynamic model of what a particular learner knows and has mastered.

interactive webinar A seminar that occurs via the Internet and that allows some form of interaction by participants; typical participant interactions include using a chat box or video conferencing facility to ask questions.

intersubjectivity   An approach to assess the quality of online discourse, with roots in philosophy, sociology, and psychology, involving a representation of knowledge constructed through a progression of contributions and sequences in an online discourse.

item response theory (IRT)   A theory useful for scoring of a test wherein a person's ability is estimated as a point on a continuum; statistical analysis is used to develop the continuum and to assess individual performance.

knowledge- and skill-based digital badges   A representation of a level or knowledge or skill achieved through an instructional or learning sequence offered and verified by a reputable organization.

learning analytics   Data-driven approaches that use large data sets and dynamic information about learners and learning environments for real-time modeling, prediction, and optimization of learning processes, learning environments, and educational decision making.

learning and instructional apps   Specialized programs or software applications designed to run on various types of mobile devices and computer systems and to provide support for learning.

learning games   Experiences that include (a) a form of play, (b) a narrative or conflict to drive play and create cognitive activity, (c) rules readily apparent to the learner, and (d) interactivity between the player and the game that includes feedback from the game system, and results in winning or losing, with reasons and scores provided.

management flight simulator   A computer-based simulation designed to imitate aspects of events, situations, or operations to forecast future effects, outcomes, or the cause of a past event; management flight simulators are useful tools to promote learning in and about complex and dynamic systems, and they provide an environment that is safe, cost effective, flexible, and conceptually and cognitively realistic.

massive open online courses (MOOCs)   Online (Internet-based and usually asynchronous) courses that are designed to accommodate massive enrollments; MOOCs typically offer open and free enrollment for anyone who wants to participate, limited feedback and assessment, and a certificate of completion without actual course credit.

media literacies   Knowledge about a variety of media types (e.g., print, broadcast, Internet) and their associated representation forms (e.g., newspapers, radio, television, blogs, social networks, animations, movies), along with the abilities to interpret, modify, create, analyze, and otherwise use media effectively.

metadata/metatags   Data and associated digital markers about an information resource that describe different characteristics and attributes of an information resource (e.g., title, author, date of creation, subject area, specific topic); metatags containing metadata facilitate search and retrieval and are widely used for learning objects, apps, and a variety of digital resources.

mindtools   Tools, resources, and environments designed to support and extend human reasoning and decision making, including critical thinking and higher order learning, and function as problem-solving and reasoning companions; examples include spreadsheets, pedagogical agents, and visualization tools.

mobile devices   Portable digital devices, including laptops, notebook computers, tablets, and smartphones, all of which may be used for learning and instruction.

model-based approaches   Learning and instructional approaches that integrate the concept of mental models and representations as critical for learning and the development of competence or that make use of models, especially interactive simulations, to promote and support learning; they typically emphasize the role of mental model development in a learning progression as well as the constructive role that modeling as a learning and assessment activity can play in developing understanding.

motivation   A person's desire to attain a goal. In education, *motivation* refers to a learner's desire to succeed and is often divided into intrinsic (internal to a learner) aspects or factors and extrinsic (external to the learner) aspects or factors; it is possible for a learner to have motivation but not act on that motivation (*see* volition).

natural language processing (NLP)   A field of artificial intelligence that provides a basis for computers to interpret input from a user that is expressed in a relatively unstructured and open natural language context; NLP works best when the range of likely responses is known or when several representative responses provide a basis to interpret an open-ended response.

neuroscience   The study of how the nervous system develops, its structure, and what it does; there is increasing emphasis on coupling neuroscience with instructional and learning science to develop a more comprehensive understanding of learning and instruction.

nine events of instruction   Robert Gagné's instructional approach that recognizes both internal factors (e.g., learner readiness and mental processing) and external factors (e.g., learning activities and feedback) that affect learning; specifically, the nine events prescribe the following: (1) gaining and maintaining attention, (2) informing learners of goals and objectives, (3) stimulating recall of prior learning, (4) presenting information, (5) providing learning guidance, (6) eliciting practice and performance, (7) providing timely and informative feedback, (8) assessing performance, and (9) enhancing retention and transfer.

norm-based assessment   A common type of assessment that involves the comparison of scores with those from a group of similar individuals; contrasted with criterion-based assessment.

objectives-based assessment   Measurement of how well students have learned with reference to (a) the performance (what the student should be able to do), (b) the conditions or circumstances under which this performance is to take place, and (c) the criteria for judging the quality of what the student does (also known as criterion-based assessment).

online mentoring   The use of distance technologies as the primary means of communication between mentors (knowledgeable and experienced persons) and learners (also called mentees or protégés) whereby mentors help learners develop knowledge; it is also referred to as telementoring, e-mentoring, virtual mentoring, cyber-based mentoring, Internet mentoring, and electronic mentoring.

open-access journal   An academic journal that readers can view online without a subscription and typically at no cost; such journals often make it possible to disseminate findings more quickly and more widely than is possible with traditional academic journals, although some lack the rigor of a traditional journal and in some cases authors are required to pay a fee to publish in an open-access journal.

OpenCourseWare movement (OCW)   An initiative to freely open graduate and undergraduate course materials such as lecture notes, syllabi, reading lists, exam questions, simulations, and video recordings of lectures to anyone who has an Internet connection; in 1964, the Education Resources Information Center (ERIC) effectively began this movement in the United States but when the 16 ERIC clearinghouses were closed in 2004, the services provided by the ERIC clearinghouses ended.

organizational learning   Application of learning (i.e., stable and persisting changes in knowledge and performance) to organizations with an emphasis on the organization's ability to continuously improve itself based on timely performance data relevant to its goals and objectives; organizational learning is linked to the continuous process improvement movement that has long existed in business and industry.

outdoor learning   Short field trips as well as longer learning expeditions associated with both formal and informal contexts; in addition to exploring traditional subjects and naturalism in general, participants often explore leadership, character development, and personal change by participating in hiking, climbing, skiing, mountaineering, white water rafting, boating, canyoneering, and other such activities.

pedagogical knowledge   A variety of approaches, strategies, and techniques to teach and support learning.

personal learning environments (PLE)   A learning technology that is designed around each student's goals or learning approach to help the student organize information and resources and assist in ongoing and progressive learning.

podcast   A type of digital media that allows recording and downloading audio or video files over the Internet.

problem- and task-centered approach   Learning and instructional approaches that emphasize experiential learning around meaningful problems and tasks.

radio frequency identification   (RFID) The wireless recognition of, and communication with, uniquely identified electronic devices; RFID is commonly used in smartphones, car keys, building access systems, passports, and identification cards.

recommendation engines   Specially designed systems that collect and store information (data) about people and activities that can be subjected to filtering and statistical analysis (analytics) to make recommendations about actions an individual could take or resources the individual might explore; these are now common in large online purchasing systems and are beginning to be developed to support online learning.

remote sensing technologies   The science and technology of obtaining reliable information about physical objects and the environment through the process of recoding, measuring, and interpreting imagery and digital representations.

repair theory Techniques developed for intelligent tutoring systems that can explain errors and misconceptions and can suggest appropriate remediation.

seamless learning The synergistic integration of learning experiences across a range of dimensions, such as spanning formal and informal learning contexts, individual and social learning, and across time, location, and learning media; it requires enabling and supporting learners to learn whenever they are curious and to seamlessly switch between the different contexts.

second self A study of culture, behavior, and perceptions of technology reported in the book *The Second Self* by Sherry Turkle in which computers are conceptualized as parts of social and psychological existence rather than simply as tools.

semantic web The World Wide Web Consortium's effort to make Internet information and resources more accessible, meaningful, and reusable through the use of a common resource description framework.

social media Various technologies, typically Internet-driven, that allow users to create, share, exchange, and review content and ideas through photo-hosting sites, online communities, multiplayer games and simulations, online shared courses, discussion forums, blogs, wikis, and social media networks.

social networking A personal learning network in which individuals use Internet-based tools to communicate with each other, sharing both text-based and multimedia-based information.

stealth assessment Assessment that is seamlessly woven into the fabric of the learning or gaming environment so that it is virtually invisible, blurring the distinction between learning and assessment; it is intended to be nonintrusive, invisible, and ongoing in support of learning while removing or reducing test anxiety without sacrificing validity and consistency.

student modeling The process of creating a dynamic representation of students' personal attributes (static and dynamic demographic, attitudinal, and personal traits) and knowledge to provide meaningful individualized support in the learning process.

student response systems Interactive wireless technologies that provide a means of communication between and among instructors and students; these systems allow instructors or students to post statements, questions, and responses online, and are sometimes associated with specific devices (also known as clickers) and smartphone apps.

summative assessment A summary analysis of what a student has learned at a particular point in time; typically, a summative assessment is given at the end of a course or grade level and is used for the purpose of determining to what extent a student has mastered the skills and learning necessary to proceed to the next level as well as for the purpose of assigning a final grade.

systemic change A concept that recognizes that learning and instruction typically occur within the context of a larger complex and dynamic system; to facilitate productive changes, a clear understanding of the interrelationships and interdependencies within the system and between the system and the external environment is required.

Technological Pedagogical and Content Knowledge (TPACK) An integrated mastery of Technological Knowledge (TK), Pedagogical Knowledge (PK), Content Knowledge (CK), and the overlapping domains of Pedagogical Content Knowledge (PCK), Technological Pedagogical Knowledge (TPK), and Technological Content Knowledge (TCK), which taken together are considered a unique and integrated body of knowledge.

technology-facilitated experiential learning An instructional strategy in which learners acquire knowledge through making meaning of their experiences in learning task engagements that occur in real-world settings.

3D immersive environments Technologies in which the user is immersed to explore or interact with an environment; an avatar is often used to interact with the environment, which may contain other animated agents and a variety of resources and artifacts.

3G and 4G networks Third- and 4th-generation devices and communication technologies and high-speed data services provided wirelessly to smartphones and other mobile devices by cellular operators; 3G devices have data transfer speeds generally between 144 kilobits and 2 megabits, and 4G devices have data transfer speeds that are 3.5 megabits and faster.

transformational play A design theory for learning experiences in which the learner is an agent in the learning process, making choices that shape the learner's understanding and in which the learner, content, and context are all dynamically transformed together through the learner's agency.

transmedia A unique form of storytelling that typically involves multiple media representations with interaction possibilities for readers; transmedia cut across media, go beyond a particular medium, and change the nature of storytelling through multiple representations and interactions.

21st-century technology skills The abilities that enable individuals to access, analyze, manage, synthesize, evaluate, create, and share information in a variety of forms and media that incorporate and integrate multiple perspectives.

ubiquitous learning Learning that can occur anywhere and at any time, encompassing learning environments that enable learner access to resources without spatial and temporal constraints.

universal design A design philosophy and approach that provides access to and use of products and environments for all persons regardless of ability, age, and other characteristics.

virtual schools/programs/courses The use of Internet-based technologies for presenting content and related resources, facilitating activities, and assessing outcomes in courses, programs, and entire schools.

virtual teams Geographically dispersed individuals who work together toward a common goal, developing and establishing effective work protocols and supportive relationships through technologies.

virtual tour A computer-mediated, Internet-enabled, multimedia exploration of a real or imagined destination.

virtual tutees Computer characters that humans (the actual learners) teach in a virtual learning environment; this approach involves the concept of learning by teaching.

virtual world A computer-based immersive experiential environment that involves learning activities and interactions with a variety of dynamically changing interaction possibilities.

visual literacy skills A collection of visual competencies that are developed through integrating different visual experiences; visual literacy is considered one component of digital literacy.

visual search engine A search engine designed to visually display search results or to search for information in the World Wide Web through the input of an image.

volition A person's ability to act on motivations or the ability of a learner to control and exert follow-through efforts to attain a goal; factors that may interfere with volition include emotions and epistemic beliefs.

wearable learning environments Environments that include a variety of body-borne sensory, communication, and computational components that may be worn under, over, or within clothing.

Web 2.0/3.0 Highly interactive technologies and participatory spaces that are open, collaborative, and distributed; examples include wikis, blogs, social networking sites, video- or image-sharing sites, multiplayer video games, and texting applications (apps).

wiki A type of Web 2.0 technology that enables people to codevelop and share information, collaborate, and communicate with each other or a collection of webpages that are continuously edited collaboratively by multiple users.

Note: This glossary of terms was compiled by Gloria Natividad from entries in this encyclopedia. It has been edited by J. Michael Spector to reflect the general notion found in various entries because many glossary terms occur in multiple entries.

Appendix C: Resource Guide

The following refereed journals and professional magazines are of particular relevance to the field of educational technology.

British Journal of Educational Technology:
http://onlinelibrary.wiley.com/journal/10.1111/%28I SSN%291467-8535

The British Journal of Educational Technology *covers the whole range of education and training, concentrating on the theory, applications, and development of learning technology and communications. There is a particular interest in the application of new information and communications technologies.*

Computers & Education:
http://www.journals.elsevier.com/computers-and-education

Computers & Education *is a technically based, interdisciplinary forum for communication in the use of all forms of computing in the area of educational applications.*

Computers in Human Behavior:
http://www.sciencedirect.com/science/journal/07475632

Computers in Human Behavior *is a scholarly journal dedicated to examining the use of computers from a psychological perspective. Original theoretical works, research reports, literature reviews, software reviews, book reviews, and announcements are published. The journal addresses the use of computers in psychology, psychiatry, and related disciplines as well as the psychological impact of computer use on individuals, groups, and society.*

Contemporary Issues in Technology and Teacher Education:
http://www.citejournal.org/vol14/iss3

Contemporary Issues in Technology and Teacher Education *is an online, peer-reviewed journal, established*

and jointly sponsored by five professional associations and has a unique commentary feature that allows readers to contribute short responses to articles.

Distance Education:
http://www.tandfonline.com/toc/cdie20/current

Distance Education *is a peer-reviewed journal of the Open and Distance Learning Association of Australia, Inc. The journal publishes research and scholarly material in the fields of open, distance, and flexible education.*

Educational Researcher:
http://www.aera.net/Publications/Journals/EducationalResearcher/tabid/12609/Default.aspx

Educational Researcher, *a journal of the American Educational Research Association, publishes scholarly articles that are of general significance to the education research community and that come from a wide range of areas of education research and related disciplines. The journal aims to make major programmatic research and new findings of broad importance widely accessible and includes feature articles, reviews/essays, and briefs.*

Educational Technology Magazine:
http://www.bookstoread.com/etp

Educational Technology Magazine *is a periodical covering the entire field of educational technology and is an influential journal for professionals and academics in the field.*

Educational Technology Research & Development:
http://www.aect.org/Intranet/Publications/index.asp

Educational Technology Research and Development, *a bimonthly publication of the Association for Educational Communications and Technology, is a leading journal in educational technology research. Its research section features articles on the practical aspects of research as well as applied theory in educational practice and is a comprehensive source of* current research information in instructional technology. The development section publishes articles concerned with the design and development of learning systems and educational technology applications. The journal's cultural and regional perspectives section (formerly International Review) contains articles on innovative research about how technologies are being used to enhance learning, instruction, and performance specific to a culture or region.

Evaluation and Program Planning:
http://www.sciencedirect.com/science/journal/01497189

Evaluation and Program Planning *publishes articles to help evaluators and planners improve the practice of their professions, develop their skills, and improve their knowledge base. The journal is based on the principle that the techniques and methods of evaluation and planning transcend the boundaries of specific fields and that relevant contributions to these areas come from people representing many different positions, intellectual traditions, and interests. The journal publishes articles from the private and public sectors in a wide range of areas: organizational development and behavior, training, planning, human resource development, health, social services, mental retardation, corrections, substance abuse, and education.*

Innovative Higher Education:
http://link.springer.com/journal/10755

Innovative Higher Education *is a journal featuring descriptions and evaluations of current innovations and provocative new ideas with relevance for action beyond the immediate context in higher education. The journal also focuses on the effect of such innovations on teaching and students and includes evaluation data, case studies, and more.*

Instructional Science:
http://link.springer.com/journal/11251

Instructional Science *is an interdisciplinary refereed scholarly journal aimed at promoting a deeper understanding of the nature, theory, and practice of the instructional process and of the learning to which it gives rise. The journal emphasizes reports of original empirical research, quantitative or qualitative, pertaining to learning and instruction broadly conceived.*

International Journal of Designs for Learning:
http://aect.site-ym.com/?page=international_journa

International Journal of Designs for Learning *provides a venue for designers to share their knowledge-in-practice through rich representations of their designs*

and detailed discussion of decision making. The aim of the journal is to support the production of high-quality precedent materials and to promote and demonstrate the value of doing so.

International Journal of Teaching and Learning in Higher Education:
http://www.isetl.org/ijtlhe

The International Journal of Teaching and Learning in Higher Education *(IJTLHE) provides broad coverage of higher education pedagogy and the scholarship of teaching and learning (SoTL) across diverse content areas, educational institutions, and levels of instructional expertise. The specific emphasis of IJTLHE is the dissemination of knowledge for improving higher education pedagogy. The journal is a publication of the International Society for Exploring Teaching and Learning and the Center for Instructional Development and Educational Research at Virginia Polytechnic and State University.*

International Journal on E-Learning:
http://www.aace.org/pubs/ijel

The International Journal on E-Learning, *a publication of the Association for the Advancement of Computing in Education, contains articles on advances in technology and the growth of e-learning to provide educators and trainers with opportunities to enhance learning and teaching in the corporate, government, health care, and higher education sectors.*

Interpersonal Computing and Technology Journal: An Electronic Journal for the 21st Century:
http://www.helsinki.fi/science/optek

Published by the Association for Educational Communications and Technology, the Interpersonal Computing and Technology Journal *is a scholarly, peer-reviewed journal focusing on computer-mediated communication and on the pedagogical issues surrounding the use of computers and technology in educational settings.*

Journal of Applied Instructional Design:
http://www.jaidpub.org

Published by the Association of Educational Communications and Technology, the Journal of Applied Instructional Design *is a scholarly journal intended to bridge the gap between theory and practice by providing reflective practitioners a means for publishing articles related to instructional design, and to encourage and nurture the development of the reflective practitioner in the field of instructional design.*

Journal of Computers in Mathematics and Science Teaching:

http://www.aace.org/pubs/jcmst/default.htm

The Journal of Computers in Mathematics and Science Teaching, *a publication of the Association for the Advancement of Computing in Education, offers an in-depth forum for the interchange of information in the fields of science, mathematics, and computer science. This is the only periodical devoted specifically to using information technology in the teaching of mathematics and science.*

Journal of Computing in Higher Education:

http://link.springer.com/journal/12528

The Journal of Computing in Higher Education *publishes original research, literature reviews, implementation and evaluation studies, and theoretical, conceptual, and policy papers that contribute to the understanding of the issues, problems, and research associated with instructional technologies and educational environments. The journal provides perspectives on the research and integration of instructional technology in higher education.*

Journal of Educational Computing Research:

http://www.baywood.com/Journals/PreviewJournals
.asp?Id=0735–6331

Designed to convey the latest in research reports and critical analyses to both theorists and practitioners, the journal addresses four primary areas of concern:

- *The outcome effects of educational computing applications, featuring findings from a variety of disciplinary perspectives that include the social, behavioral, and physical sciences*
- *The design and development of innovative computer hardware and software for use in educational environments*
- *The interpretation and implications of research in educational computing fields*
- *The theoretical and historical foundations of computer-based education*

Journal of Educational Multimedia and Hypermedia:

http://www.aace.org/pubs/jemh/default.htm

The Journal of Educational Multimedia and Hypermedia, *a publication of the Association for the Advancement of Computing in Education, is designed to provide a multidisciplinary forum to present and discuss research, development, and applications of multimedia and hypermedia in education. The journal's main goal is to contribute to the advancement of the theory and practice of learning and teaching using these powerful and promising technological tools that allow the integration of images, sound, text, and data.*

Journal of Educational Technology & Society:

http://www.ifets.info

Published by the International Forum of Educational Technology & Society, the Journal of Educational Technology & Society *is a refereed, online journal containing articles on the issues affecting the developers of educational systems and educators who implement and manage such systems. The journal aims to help these groups better understand each other's role in the overall process of education and how they may support each other. The journal includes discussions of case studies, empirical findings, conceptual frameworks, qualitative studies, and design and development research.*

Journal of Higher Education:

https://ohiostatepress.org/index.htm?journals/jhe/
jhemain.htm

The Journal of Higher Education *publishes original research reporting on the academic study of higher education as a broad enterprise.*

Journal of Interactive Learning Research:

http://www.aace.org/pubs/jilr/default.htm

The Journal of Interactive Learning Research, *a publication of the Association for the Advancement of Computing in Education, publishes papers related to the underlying theory, design, implementation, effectiveness, and impact on education and training of the following interactive learning environments:*

- *Authoring systems*
- *Cognitive tools for learning computer-assisted language*
- *Computer-based assessment systems and training*
- *Computer-mediated communications*
- *Computer-supported collaborative learning*
- *Distributed learning environments*
- *Electronic performance support systems*
- *Interactive learning environments, media systems, simulations, and games*
- *Intelligent agents on the Internet*
- *Intelligent tutoring systems*
- *Microworlds*
- *Virtual reality–based learning systems*

Journal of Research on Technology in Education:

http://www.iste.org/resources/product?id=25

The Journal of Research on Technology in Education *is a peer-reviewed publication of the International Society for Technology in Education. The journal publishes articles on educational technology research on topics ranging from original research to theoretical positions and systems analysis.*

Journal of the Learning Sciences:
http://www.tandfonline.com/toc/hlns20/current# .VCcBCRYhQ98

The Journal of the Learning Science *provides a multidisciplinary forum for the presentation of research on learning and education. The journal seeks to foster new ways of thinking about learning that will allow our understanding of cognition and social cognition to have impact in education. The journal publishes research articles that advance our understanding of learning in real-world situations and of promoting learning in such venues, including articles that report on the roles technology can play in promoting deep and lasting learning.*

Knowledge Management & E-Learning: An International Journal:
http://www.kmel-journal.org/ojs/index.php/online-publication

Knowledge Management & E-Learning: An International Journal *aims to publish recent, quality research articles in the multidisciplinary area of knowledge management and electronic learning. The journal seeks to foster a platform for leading research in the emerging new landscape of the knowledge-intensive economy, which requires the integration of knowledge and learning.*

Performance Improvement Quarterly:
http://www.ispi.org/content.aspx?id=152

Performance Improvement Quarterly *is a peer-reviewed, research-based publication of the International Society for Performance Improvement that aims to stimulate professional discussion and advance the interdisciplinary field of performance improvement and human performance technology through the publication of scholarly works including literature reviews, experimental studies, survey research, and case studies.*

Quarterly Review of Distance Education:
http://www.aect.org/intranet/publications/QRDE/subguides.html

The Quarterly Review of Distance Education *is a refereed journal publishing articles, research briefs, reviews, and editorials dealing with the theories, research, and practices of distance education. A publication of the Association for Educational Communications and Technology, the journal covers various methodologies that permit generalizable results to help guide the practice of the field of distance education in the public and private sectors.*

Review of Research in Education:
http://rre.sagepub.com

The Review of Research in Education *provides an overview and descriptive analysis of selected topics of relevant research literature through critical and synthesizing essays. The journal is an official publication of the* American Educational Research Association.

Simulation & Gaming: An Interdisciplinary Journal of Theory, Practice and Research:
http://www.unice.fr/sg

Simulation & Gaming *provides an international forum for the study and discussion of simulation and gaming methodology used in education, training, consultation, and research. This quarterly journal examines the methodologies and explores their application to real-world problems and situations.*

Smart Learning Environments:
http://www.springer.com/computer/journal/40561

Smart Learning Environments *is a pioneering journal focuses on modern technology's application in the education sector and explores technological involvement in the interaction between teachers and students. The journal collects articles on the reforms of teaching and learning through technologies in creating a digital education environment and to reflect and scrutinize the latest trends of technology use in education.*

Syllabus:
http://syllabusjournal.org

Aimed at teachers and professional practitioners, Syllabus *is a peer-reviewed publication of course syllabi and other teaching materials.*

Technology, Instruction, Cognition and Learning:
http://www.oldcitypublishing.com/journals/ticl-home

Technology, Instruction, Cognition and Learning *is an international, interdisciplinary journal of structural learning that promotes and disseminates interdisciplinary advances in theory and research at the intersection of four focus disciplines: technology, instruction, cognition, and learning. Its scope includes artificial intelligence, cognitive and development psychology, software engineering, cognitive science, structural and task analysis, knowledge engineering, distributed cognition, instructional systems and design, intelligent tutors, structural learning, problem solving, and system dynamics.*

Technology, Knowledge and Learning:

http://www.springer.com/education+%26+language/learning+%26+instruction/journal/10758

Technology, Knowledge and Learning *emphasizes the increased interest on context-aware adaptive and personalized digital learning environments. Manuscripts are welcome that account for how these new technologies and systems reconfigure learning experiences, assessment methodologies, as well as future educational practices.*

TechTrends:

http://link.springer.com/journal/11528

TechTrends *seeks to provide a vehicle for the exchange of information among professional practitioners concerning the management of media and programs, the application of educational technology principles and techniques to instructional programs, corporate and military training, and other information that can contribute to the advancement of knowledge of practice in the field. The journal also enables practitioners to stay current on the latest developments in the design, manufacture, and use of communications materials and devices. Very influential within the educational technology community,* TechTrends *is a publication of the Association for Educational Communications & Technology.*

THE Journal (Technological Horizons in Education):

http://thejournal.com/Home.aspx

THE Journal *aims to inform and educate K–12 senior-level district and school administrators, technologists, and tech-savvy educators within districts, schools, and classrooms on ways to improve and advance the learning process through technology.*

Turkish Online Journal of Educational Technology:

http://www.tojet.net

The Turkish Online Journal of Educational Technology *publishes academic articles on the issues of educational technology that address using educational technology in classrooms, how educational technology affects learning, and the perspectives of students, teachers, school administrators, and communities on educational technology.*

Index

Entry titles and their page numbers are in **bold**. Figures and tables are indicated by f or t following the page number, and volume number precedes the page number separated by a colon.

Internet literacy, **1**:213
Internet of Things (IoT), **1:422–424**, 423f, **2**:520
Internet Web Accessibility Initiative, **2**:800
Interpretation dimension of the visual world, **2**:542
Interpretive flexibility, **2**:673
Interrelationship fallacy, **1**:149
Interrogators (RFID), **2**:605
Interstate Teacher Assessment and Support
    Consortium (InTASC), **1**:96
Intersubjectivity and educational technology,
    1:425–426
Interval levels of measurement, **2**:494
Interviews, **2**:600–601, 763
Intrinsic legitimacy, **1**:261
Intrinsic motivation, **1**:110, 298, **2**:821
In-use TPACK, **2**:491
Invitational type of visual, **2**:543
IP Multimedia Subsystem (IMS), **2**:773
iPads, **2**:519, 703
iPhones, **2**:519, 606
IPISD. *See* **Instructional design models**
IPO model, **2**:848
IQ tests, **1**:11
IR (institutional repositories), **1**:201
IS (Innovativeness Scale), **1**:243, 245, 386
ISD. *See* **Instructional design models**
iSkills examination, **2**:751
ISO/IEC 19788 Metadata Learning Resource (MLR),
    2:505–506
ISPI (International Society for Performance
    Improvement), **1**:94–95, 348–349
ISTE (International Society for Technology in
    Education), **1**:96, 279–280, 370, **2**:751, 795
ISTE Standards, **1**:96, 279–280, **2**:795
ISTE Standards for Students (ISTE Standards·S), **1**:96
ISTE Standards for Teachers (ISTE Standards·T), **1**:96
ITEA (International Technology Education
    Association), **2**:751–752
Item analysis, **2**:687
Item banks, **1**:11–12
Item exposure, **1**:12
Item response theory (IRT), **1**:11, **427–428**
Items, **1**:427
iTunes U, **1**:379, **2**:583
IVLA (International Visual Literacy Association),
    2:825

Jacquard, Joseph-Marie, **1**:416
Jamestown Settlement and Yorktown Victory Center,
    2:819
Januszewski, Alan, **1**:126
The Jasper Project, **1**:28
Jasper series, **2**:588
Jenkins, Henry, **1**:300, **2**:790

Jennings, Nicholas, **1**:18
Jeung, J., **1**:59, 60t
jMAP, **2**:523
Job aids, **1**:367, 390
Job seeking, **2**:658, 662
Johnson, Larry, **1**:61
Joint Committee on Standards for Educational
    Evaluation, **1**:283
JollyMate, **2**:711
Jonassen, David, **2**:509, 747–748
Jones, Lynn, **2**:610
Jones International University, **2**:723
Joseph, Katherine, **1**:384, 386
Journey-based outdoor education, **2**:465
Joysticks, **2**:715
Just-in-time training, **1**:232–233

Kaptelinin, Victor, **1**:4
Kaufman, Roger, **1**:99, **2**:562
KBSs (knowledge-based systems), **1**:18, 365
Keller, Fred, **1**:76
Keller, John, **1**:38, 40. *See also* **ARCS model**
Key performance indicators (KPIs), **2**:563, 838
Keyboard options for people with physical disabilities,
    2:714–715
Keystroke-level model, **1**:353
Keywords, **2**:829
Khan Academy, **1**:36, **2**:516, 619
Kicklider, J. C. R., **1**:416
KIDS Project, **2**:625
Kilby, Jack, **1**:339, 416
Kim, ChanMin, **1**:14, **2**:821
Kinder, Marsha, **2**:790
Kindle, **2**:710t
Kinect, **1**:329–330
Kinetoscope, **1**:337
Kirkley, Jamie, **1**:62
Kirkley, Sonny, **1**:62
Kirkpatrick-Phillips framework, **1**:350
Klein, Gary, **1**:118, 154
Klein, James, **1**:183
Klein Associates, **1**:154
Kleinrock, Leonard, **1**:340
KLM-GOMS model, **1**:353
Klopfer, Eric, **1**:300
Knezek, Gerald A., **1**:280
Knight Commission on the Information
    Needs of Communities in a Democracy,
    2:488
Knoke, David, **2**:493
Knowledge, defined, **1**:105, 363
Knowledge, skills, and attitudes (KSAs), **1**:248–249,
    2:571t, 572
Knowledge and skill hierarchies, **1:431–433**